A HISTORY OF GERMANY
1715–1815

A
HISTORY OF GERMANY
1715-1815

BY

C. T. ATKINSON

FELLOW AND MODERN HISTORY LECTURER OF EXETER COLLEGE, OXFORD
FORMERLY DEMY OF MAGDALEN COLLEGE, OXFORD

WITH 35 MAPS AND PLANS

GREENWOOD PRESS, PUBLISHERS
WESTPORT, CONNECTICUT

Originally published in 1908
by Methuen & Company, London

First Greenwood Reprinting 1971

Library of Congress Catalogue Card Number 70-114456

SBN 8371-4807-3

Printed in the United States of America

PREFACE

THIS work is the outcome of an effort to produce within moderate compass some account of the affairs of Germany between the Peace of Utrecht and the final over-throw of Napoleon. In view of the dimensions to which the volume has attained I can hardly claim to have been success-ful in the task of compression, but I am more conscious of shortcomings in omitting things which ought to have been included than of having dwelt at excessive length on those aspects of German history with which I have endeavoured to deal. It may indeed be urged that the character of the subject must bear some share of the responsibility for the length to which the book has run. Germany between 1715 and 1815 was not a nation with a well-defined national life and history, but was merely a chaotic collection of states with conflicting aims and ideals, constantly engaged in struggles with one another; there can be no history of Germany as a whole, because, as this book endeavours to show, there was hardly anything that could be called "German"; particularism and localism were infinitely stronger than any unifying or centralising tendencies. But one has not merely to follow the fortunes of the principal portions of this infinitely subdivided "geographical expression," the struggles of these various members are so completely merged in the international history of Europe as a whole that the affairs of Germany only become intelligible, if at all, when narrated as part of the history of all Europe. It is no exaggeration to say that

Russia, Turkey, Great Britain and above all France play more prominent parts in German history in these years than do some German states of quite respectable size. Thus one cannot neglect battles fought outside Germany by the troops of German states; Marengo and Arcis sur Aube are quite as much part of German history as are Leuthen and Wagram, while the otherwise abortive victories of Prince Charles Edward in "the '45" helped to transfer Silesia from the Hapsburg to the Hohenzollern and thus profoundly affected the course of German affairs for over half a century. Thus, then, when one attempts to narrate the history of Germany from the death of Louis XIV to the overthrow of that other great enemy of Germany, Napoleon, one finds one's self committed to relating the course of European affairs so far as they took place in or immediately affected Germany, a very much more lengthy process than that of narrating the development of one country only. But it must also be remembered that while these affairs for the most part took the shape of wars or rumours of wars, military matters must be treated at some length if they are to be in the least intelligible. Indeed I am afraid that in the effort to compress my accounts of campaigns and battles I have failed not only to be succinct but even to be reasonably clear, and, still worse, that I have made statements which need more expansion and justification than they have been given, and have pronounced verdicts without a sufficient setting forth of the grounds on which I have formed my conclusions.

In deliberately choosing the military aspect of German affairs as the feature on which to lay most emphasis, I am aware that I have hardly touched upon the intellectual and literary life of the period. However, I have omitted this side advisedly, feeling convinced that it was in the main a thing apart, which affected the life of the country as a whole but little and certainly had hardly any effect on the politics of Germany. The "Potsdam Grenadiers" are more typical of eighteenth-century Germany than are Goethe and his fellows. It was only quite at the end of the period, in the days of the War of Liberation, that German literature can be really called " German," that it ceased to be merely cosmopolitan and became national. Considerations of space must be my apology for the inadequate treatment of the social state of the country ; when there is so much to be included something must be left out, and in preferring to dwell on the military history of the period I have taken the aspect of the subject which appeals to me most and with which I feel least incompetent to deal.

The appended lists of authorities do not of course make any pretensions to be exhaustive bibliographies : the first gives the names of the principal books from which I have taken my information, the second of some books to which I would refer any one who wants more information on particular points than is here given. Other references will be found from time to time throughout the book to other works which I have consulted less frequently or on special points. Some books (indicated by an asterisk) which appear in both lists have been published since the manuscript of the book was first completed, now some time ago, for unforeseen difficulties have caused considerable delay in the appearance of the book. I have thus not been able to utilise several volumes which might have been very helpful. Before leaving the subject of authorities I should like to make special acknowledgment of my indebtedness to two works, Dr. Ward's *England and Hanover* and Mr. Fisher's *Napoleonic Statesmanship : Germany*, the first of which I have found exceptionally useful when dealing with the attitude, not as a rule very rightly represented, of England towards Germany in the first half of the period, while Mr. Fisher's book I found peculiarly illuminating on a subject on which the German authorities I had utilised were copious rather than clear.

Further, I must plead guilty to what I believe to be generally looked upon as the perpetuation of a vulgar error,

my adherence to the incorrect form " Hapsburg " in preference
to " Habsburg," and my preference for such forms as Cologne,
Mayence and Ratisbon.   Strictly speaking they are no doubt
incorrect, but I prefer to use the forms to which I am accustomed.

Finally, I should have liked to have included a good many
more maps and plans, but of such things only a limited
number can be inserted, and when the requisite things are to
be found in the Clarendon Press *Atlas* and in M. Schrader's
Atlas de Geographie Historique it would be merely superfluous
to have given such maps as " the Development of Prussia ";
I have therefore preferred to increase the number of plans of
battles.

OXFORD, *June* 1908

CONTENTS

CHAPTER I

CHAPTER II

CHAPTER III

CONTENTS

CHAPTER IX

THE AUSTRIAN SUCCESSION WAR—TO THE PEACE OF AIX-LA-CHAPELLE

CHAPTER X

MARIA THERESA'S REFORMS AND THE DIPLOMATIC REVOLUTION

CHAPTER XI

THE SEVEN YEARS' WAR : CAMPAIGNS OF 1756 AND 1757

CHAPTER XVI

MARIA THERESA AND JOSEPH II—DOMESTIC AFFAIRS

CHAPTER XVII

LEOPOLD II AND THE EASTERN QUESTION

CHAPTER XVIII

GERMANY AND THE FRENCH REVOLUTION

CHAPTER XIX

THE FIRST COALITION

b

MAPS AND PLANS

AUTHORITIES

A

ARNETH, VON. Prinz Eugen, vol. iii.

,,   Maria Theresa.

,,   Maria Theresa und Joseph ii.

BROGLIE, DUC DE.

Frédéric ii et Marie Thérèse.

Frédéric ii et Louis xv.

Marie Thérèse Imperatrice.

Maurice de Saxe et le Marquis d'Argenson.

La Paix d'Aix la Chapelle.

L'Alliance Autrichienne.

CATHCART. War in Germany, 1812-1813.

CHUQUET, A. Les Guerres de la Révolution.

Dropmore Papers. (Historical Manuscripts Commission : MSS. of J. B. Fortescue, Esq., 4 vols. and 1 vol.*)

DROYSSEN. Friedrich der Grosse (Part v. of his Geschichte der Preussischen Politik).

ERDMANNSDORFFER. Deutsche Geschichte, 1648-1740, vol. ii.

FISHER, H. A. L. Napoleonic Statesmanship : Germany.

Geschichte der Befreiungskriege, 1813-1815, especially

VON HOLLEBEN, Geschichte des Frühjahrsfeldzuges, 1813.

FRIEDRICH, Geschichte des Herbstfeldzuges, 1813 (vols. i. and ii., also vol. iii.*).

HAUSSER, LUDWIG. Deutsche Geschichte vom Tode Friedrichs des Grossen bis zur Gründung des Deutschen Bundes.

HERMANN, ALFRED. Marengo.

HOUSSAYE, H. 1815 : Waterloo.

HÜFFER, HERMANN. Der Krieg vom 1799 und die Zweite Koalition (referred to as Hüffer, i. and ii.).

,,   Quellen zur Geschichte der Kriege, 1799-1800 (referred to as Hüffer).

Instructions aux Ambassadeurs de France. Autriche (edited by A. Sorel).

Bavière, Deux Ponts et Palatinate (edited by A. Sorel).

ONCKEN. Zeitalter Friedrichs des Grossen.

PFLUGK-HARTTUNG, J. VON. Vorgeschichte der Schlacht der Belle-Alliance.

PUTTER. The Political Constitution of the Germanic Empire.

RANKE, L. VON. Preussische Geschichte.

ROUSSET, C. La Grande Armée de 1813.

Royal Historical Society. The Third Coalition Against France (edited by J. Holland Rose).

Buckinghamshire Papers, vol. ii.

SCHWERTFEGER, B.   Geschichte der Königlich Deutschen Legion, 1803-1816.*
SEELEY, SIR J. R.   Life and Times of Stein.
SIBORNE, W.   Waterloo Letters.
,,   The Waterloo Campaign.
TURNER.   The Germanic Constitution.
USSEL, VICOMTE JEAN DE.   Études sur l'année 1813.   La Defection de la Prusse.
WADDINGTON.   Louis XV et le Renversement des Alliances.
,,   La Guerre de Sept Ans. (vols. i.-iii. going up to 1759; vol. iv.*).
WARD, A. W.   England and Hanover.
Wellington's Dispatches, vol. xii.   Supplementary Dispatches, vol. x.
WOLF.   Osterreich unter Maria Theresa, Joseph II and Leopold II.
YORCK VON WARTENBURG, COUNT.   Napoleon as a General (English translation).
ZWEIDINECK SÜDENHORST.   Deutsche Geschichte in Zeitraum der Gründung des
                Preussischen Königtum (referred to as Z. S.), vol. ii.
,,   Deutsche Geschichte von der Auflosung des alten bis
                zur Errichtung des neuen Kaiserreiches, 1806-
                1871, vol. i. (referred to as D. G. 1806-1871).

B

ARMSTRONG, E.   Elizabeth Farnese.
BEAMISH, MAJOR.   History of the King's German Legion.
BRACKENBURY, COLONEL C. B.   Frederick the Great (Military Biographies).
BRIGHT, DR. J. FRANCK.   Maria Theresa.
,,   Joseph II.
BRYCE, RT. HON. J.   The Holy Roman Empire.
Cambridge Modern History.   Vol. viii. The Revolution.
,,   Vol. ix. Napoleon.*
CHESNEY, COLONEL C. C.   Waterloo Lectures.
CLAPHAM, J. H.   The Causes of the War of 1792 (Cambridge Historical
Essays, xi.).
COQUELLE.   England and Napoleon (translated).
FORTESCUE, HON. J. W.   A History of the British Army (vol. ii. for Ferdinand of
Brunswick ; vol. iv. for 1793-1794).
GEORGE, H. B.   Napoleon's Invasion of Russia.
LORAINE-PETRE, F.   Napoleon's Conquest of Prussia.
,,   Napoleon's Campaign in Poland, 1806-1807.
MALLESON, COLONEL G.   Loudoun (Military Biographies).
REDDAWAY, W. F.   Frederick the Great (Heroes of the Nations).
ROSE, J. HOLLAND.   Life of Napoleon I.
,,   Napoleonic Studies.
SOREL, A.   La Question de l'Orient.
,,   L'Europe et la Revolution Française.
TUTTLE.   History of Prussia to 1740.
,,   Frederick the Great.

A HISTORY OF GERMANY
1715—1815

CHAPTER I

GERMANY IN 1715—THE EMPIRE AND ITS INSTITUTIONS

THE practice of dividing history into more or less conventional "periods" is always somewhat arbitrary and unsatisfactory, and at first sight there hardly seems much justification for treating the year 1715 as an important turning-point in the history of Germany. If one is seeking for an end, for a point at which some long struggle has been decided, some doubtful question settled, one would select 1648 rather than 1715, the Peace of Westphalia rather than those of Utrecht, Rastatt and Baden. If, on the other hand, a starting-point is sought, the unloosing of some hitherto unsuspected force, the appearance of a new set of actors, the opening of some great question, 1740 and the attack of Frederick II of Prussia on Silesia would seem to possess a far stronger claim. But the conditions which existed in 1740 and the forces which were then let loose did not spring into being in a moment; they were the fruit of years of development, and to appreciate them one must go back at any rate to the Peace of Utrecht. Similarly, great as were the changes summed up at the Peace of Westphalia, when one looks at it as a landmark in the history of the Holy Roman Empire and of that German Kingdom which, to its own undoing, was associated with the heritage of Charlemagne, it may be argued with some plausibility that the true failure of the Hapsburgs to make real their position as titular heads of Germany came with the premature death of Joseph I (1711). Germany from 1648 to 1815 was little more than a geographical expression, its history, such as

I

it is, is a history of disunion and disintegration; but between 1648 and 1715 it does possess a small degree of unity, and that is given it by the persistent attempts of France to profit by the weakness and divisions of her Eastern neighbour, and by the efforts of the Hapsburgs to unite the German Kingdom in opposition to the aggressions of Mazarin and Louis XIV. The Spanish Succession War, fought out largely on German soil and by German troops, had a very important bearing on the fortunes of Germany, and at one time it seemed that one result of it might be a great increase in the Imperial authority and prestige, and as if the practical independence of the territorial princes, established at the Peace of Westphalia, might be substantially reduced. But this was not to be, and as far as the constitutional condition of Germany was concerned, the Treaties of Utrecht, Rastatt and Baden, instead of undoing the work of 1648, confirmed it, and left the German Kingdom an empty form, a name with no real substance behind it.

Thus the condition in which the year 1715 found Germany differed in degree rather than in kind from that in which the Thirty Years' War had left her in 1648. The great movement of the Reformation had been fatal to the Holy Roman Empire: it had swept away the last relics of its pretensions to universal dominion by emphasising the national character of most of the states of Western Europe, and by introducing between them differences in religion which were of more than merely religious importance. The Thirty Years' War had done a like office for the German Kingdom: it had completed the ruin of the Emperor's authority over the lands which were still nominally subject to him. The forms of the old constitution, the Imperial title, the nominal existence of the Empire were to endure for another one hundred and fifty-eight years, but the settlement of 1648 amounted in all save the name to the substitution of a loosely-knit confederacy for the potential national state which had till then existed in the shape of the Empire. Not that the settlement of 1648 was the sole cause of this change, even the long and terrible war to which it put an end could not by itself have effected so great an alteration had it not been the last in a long chain of causes whose work was now recognised and admitted. At the Peace of Westphalia the Hapsburgs acknowledged principles which struck at the roots of the authority of the Emperor, they accepted because they had failed to prevent the results of the disintegrating tendencies which had been at work for so long. The practical independence of the Princes of the Empire was no new thing, but it now received formal recognition; the principle *cujus regio, ejus religio*, now reaffirmed, had been the basis of the Peace of Augsburg. It was all the more strongly re-established because, in the meantime, the Hapsburgs had led the crusade of the Counter-Reformation, and were now forced to leave in Protestant hands many secularised bishoprics as the token of the failure of their great endeavour.

Even before the Reformation the authority of the Emperor over the German Kingdom had been weak and uncertain, though Maximilian I had done much to assert it and had attempted more, while the possibility of converting the German feudal monarchy into a strong national sovereignty like those of England and France was still present. The process of disintegration had, it is true, gone much further in Germany than elsewhere, and localism was stronger and the central institutions were weaker than in France and England. What the Reformation did was that it introduced into Germany a new principle which served to complicate the contest between the spasmodic attempts of the Emperors at a centralising policy, and the disintegrating tendencies of which the Princes were the champions. The already existing aspirations to local independence received the powerful reinforcement of the new spirit of resistance which the revolt from Rome engendered. Seeing how strong the traditions of close relations between the Pope and the Emperor were, and how intimately the idea of the Empire was bound up with the idea of the Universal Church, it was only natural that resistance to the spiritual authority of the Pope should encourage resistance to the temporal authority of the Emperor. Moreover, when Germany was being divided into two antagonistic camps, the Catholic and the Protestant, it was impossible from the nature of the quarrel that the Emperor should be neutral. He could not be the impartial head of the whole nation, he must take one side or the other. It was with a crisis of the most momentous importance for Germany that Charles V was confronted in 1519 when he was required to make up his mind between Rome and Luther. Had he declared for Protestantism, and placed himself at the head of a national movement against the

Papacy, it is possible that the sixteenth century might have seen Germany really united.   If the Emperor could have obtained control of the vast territories of the Church, he would have acquired the revenues and resources so badly needed to make the forms of the central government an efficient reality. But such a course must have brought him into collision, not only with all those who clung to the old faith and the old connection, but also with those Princes who adopted Protestantism, partly because they found in it a principle by which to defend their resistance to the Imperial authority; they would not have been so enthusiastic in their support of Protestantism had the Emperor been of that persuasion.   Prelates and lay Princes alike would have struggled hard to hinder so great an increase in the Imperial resources and so great a change in the relative positions of the Emperor and his subjects, as that which would have been involved in his annexation of the ecclesiastical territories.   As things actually went, the Emperor's continued adhesion to Roman Catholicism gave the Protestant champions of local independence a permanent bond of union in their religion.   At the same time, even the Princes of the Emperor's own religion could not but be favourably disposed—as Princes —towards resistance to the Imperial authority and efforts to limit the Emperor's powers.

The Peace of Augsburg (1555) was of the nature of a truce rather than a settlement.   The evenly-balanced contending forces agreed to a compromise which actually secured to Germany over sixty years of religious peace of a kind, but it was absolutely lacking in the elements of finality.   The omission of any regulations for the position of the Calvinists, the failure to enforce any accepted rule as to new secularisations, were bound, sooner or later, to lead to a new conflict: it is only remarkable that the outbreak was so long delayed.   Meanwhile the acknowledgment of the principle *cujus regio, ejus religio* was a fatal blow to the Imperial authority and the first great breach in the outward unity of the Empire.

The circumstances under which the great struggle between the rival creeds finally broke out were such as to make it even more impossible for the Emperor to adopt a neutral attitude.   The local troubles in Bohemia which culminated in the famous "Defenestratio" of 1618 were only the match that fired the train, since for some time the Calvinists of Germany had been contemplating a war in defence of their religion. By adopting the Bohemian cause the Elector Palatine and his supporters brought themselves into a double collision with Ferdinand of Austria. By breaking the peace of the Empire they set at naught his authority as Emperor; but he was also King of Bohemia, and by assisting his revolted subjects the Calvinists assailed him as territorial ruler and as head of the Hapsburg house. Thus the Emperor could not interfere disinterestedly: he could not suppress the Calvinist disturbers of the peace without using the Imperial authority, such as it was, on behalf of his own dynastic territorial interests. Not merely was impartiality impossible, he was the leader of one of the contending parties. Much in the same way, by accepting the Bohemian Crown the Elector Palatine made it impossible for himself and his party to disassociate their defence of oppressed co-religionists from their own selfish interests and ambitions. Thus on the one side the cause of order and of unity became identified with intolerance and oppression, on the other anarchy and violence seemed to be the natural corollary to religious freedom. In this dilemma there were but two alternative possibilities. Either the Emperor would succeed in suppressing Protestantism both as a religious and as a political factor, and would thereby vindicate his authority, or by his failure in this attempt he would leave Germany divided between two hostile factions, one of which must always look upon the decadence of the Imperial constitution as the surest safeguard of its own existence.

In 1648 the Peace of Westphalia announced to the world that after thirty years of a most terrible and devastating war both combatants had failed, and had been obliged to assent to a compromise. That the Hapsburgs had failed, was proclaimed by their assenting to such a Peace. To their failure many causes had contributed; their want of material resources, Ferdinand II's incapacity and lack of states-manship, the lukewarmness of those Catholic Princes whose political aims would not have been served by the complete success of the Catholic cause if championed by the Emperor, but more especially the intervention of foreign powers who had good reasons of their own for dreading the establishment of Hapsburg supremacy over Germany. Yet such a result had at one time seemed probable, for Frederick's headlong folly had given the Emperor a chance a statesman would not have missed. But Ferdinand had misused his victory at Prague: he had endeavoured to do to Frederick what Frederick had failed to do to him, he had then driven the Lutherans into taking up arms by his efforts to reverse the compromise on which the territorial distribution of Germany rested: he had parted with Wallenstein at the bidding of the Catholic League when that general seemed to have Protestant Germany at his mercy. Had the Emperor believed in the honesty of Wallenstein, or in the wisdom and justice of the toleration advocated by that mysterious adventurer, sufficiently to stand by him, it is possible that his confidence might have been rewarded by success; but Wallenstein's record was not one to inspire confidence, and toleration was a policy not only in advance of the age but quite opposed to the traditions of the Empire and of the Hapsburg dynasty. Thus though the Peace left Bohemia and its dependencies in the Emperor's keeping, it left the Empire hopelessly and irretrievably disunited. As the next seventy years were to show, not even common dangers of the most formidable kind could weld Germany together effectively. The acknowledgment of the rights of the heretic minority in the Empire was in absolute conflict with the theory of Church and State on which the Empire was based; the concessions which the Princes had extorted reduced the Emperor's authority over them to a mere form, and made the name of Kingdom a complete anachronism when applied to Germany. But signally as the Hapsburgs had failed, their opponents could hardly claim to have been much more successful. The Imperial supremacy which Frederick v and the Calvinist Union had sought to destroy still existed, even if it was a mere shadow of what Ferdinand had hoped to make it. The Protestants, Calvinists and Lutherans alike, had succeeded in freeing themselves from the jurisdiction of the Pope, in wringing from the Catholic majority in the Diet a recognition of their right to freedom of worship in their own lands, and in defending their possession of those ecclesiastical territories which the Edict of Restitution had endeavoured to wrest from them. But they had not managed to obtain the rich and coveted abbeys and bishoprics of the South: indeed, on the whole they had lost ground. Bohemia and its dependencies had passed from them, and the skilful propagandism of the Jesuits was rapidly extirpating Protestantism from its former strongholds there. The adoption of January 1st, 1624, as the date by which the possession of disputed territories was to be determined on the whole favoured the Catholics, to whom it left a majority of the bishoprics. Moreover, the religious freedom thus won by the sword—and in no small measure by the swords of the Swede and the Frenchman—could only be retained by the sword. It was indissolubly connected with local independence and Imperial impotence; in other words, the disunion of Germany was its only guarantee. Identified as the Hapsburgs were with Rome, with intolerance, with the forcible promulgation of Catholicism, German Protestantism could not but look upon the Imperial institutions as hostile to its rights and could hardly do otherwise than seek to prevent anything which promised to restore their vitality. Loyalty to the Empire seemed to the majority of German Protestants incompatible with the safety of their religion.

The collapse of the old constitution not unnaturally occupied the minds of the pamphleteers and publicists of the day, and many were the schemes for reconstruction and reform put forward in the second half of the seventeenth century. Among the most important and interesting of these is the *Dissertatio de ratione status in Imperio nostro Romano Germanico*, written by Philip Boguslaw Chemnitz, a Pomeranian jurist of some repute, and published under the pseudonym of Hippolytus à Lapide. The treatise sets out an ideal which was never realised, and was based on a theory which was neither sound historically nor accurate as a statement of the existing facts, the assumption that neither the Emperor nor the Electors, but the whole Diet was the sovereign body. This may be accounted for by the fact that Chemnitz was actuated throughout by an intense hostility to the Hapsburgs. When he looks at them the sight of the sack of Magdeburg rises before his eyes, and the Edict of Restitution is for him the type of their acts and aims.

Chemnitz was not the first writer to find salvation for Germany in the decrease of the Imperial authority and in the increase of the powers of the Princes, but he may be taken as the best example of those who hold that view. He regarded the Emperor as the representative of an aristocratic republic, the sovereignty of which resided rather in the assembled Estates than in the Emperor. To him the Emperor was little more than the nominal head, the minister of the Estates, not their superior. Thus it is by the Diet, not by the Emperor, that the decision as to peace or war must be taken, to the *Kammergericht*[1] rather than to the *Reichshofrath*[2] that the final jurisdiction belongs. Throughout Chemnitz assails the Hapsburgs in unsparing terms; their pretensions are the principal danger to Germany, their power must be diminished, their Imperial authority curtailed and restricted in every possible way. "*Delenda est Austria*" is his panacea for the ills of Germany and the burden of every page of his pamphlet.

Rather different was the account given by Pufendorf, who, writing under the name of Severin de Monzambano, a fictitious Italian traveller who had made the tour of Germany, compared the Holy Roman Empire to the league of the Greeks against Troy, and pronounced it neither monarchy, aristocracy, nor democracy, but an anomalous blend of all three, "a half-way house between a kingdom and a confederation," which the Emperor was striving to make more like a kingdom, the Princes to make more of a confederation. The Princes, he pointed out, though nominally in vassalage to the Emperor from whom they held their fiefs, enjoyed a practical independence, having all sovereign rights in their own territories. Indeed one thing only prevented Germany from being as absolutely disunited as Italy: the possessions of the Austrian Hapsburgs formed a connected state which alone gave Germany some approach to unity by being able and willing to maintain the forms and institutions of the Empire.

Pufendorf's treatise provoked a reply from no less eminent a man than the philosopher Leibnitz, who in his *Contra Severinum de Monzambano* dealt mainly with the need for unity against the enemies of Germany. He dwelt on the defencelessness of the Empire, the utter absence of military organisation, the need for a standing army and of proper provision for its support. But he had also to point out how

[1] The Imperial Chamber of Justice; cf. p. 14.
[2] The Imperial High Court, the so-called "Aulic Council"; cf. p. 15.

slight were the chances that any permanent organisation would be established. To some Princes the present situation offered a good prospect of profiting by the troubles of their neighbours, others for religious reasons entertained suspicions of the use that might be made of a standing army, others again feared that it might be employed by the greater powers to suppress their petty neighbours, and thus Leibnitz's appeal to the Princes of the Empire to cultivate better relations with the Emperor fell on deaf ears.

The substantial accuracy of Pufendorf's description of the state of Germany will be realised when one examines more closely the Imperial constitution and the component portions of this anomalous mixture of a confederation and a kingdom. The Imperial office, nominally elective, had practically become hereditary in the Austrian branch of the Hapsburg family, which had provided the Holy Roman Empire and the German Kingdom with an uninterrupted series of rulers ever since the election of Albert II in 1438. But the elective element had not entirely disappeared : indeed, it might have been better for the Empire if it had. Its survival merely served to further the decadence of the Imperial institutions, for, from Charles V onward, each new " Emperor Elect " had had to purchase the suffrages of the Electors by means of " Election Capitulations " which circumscribed and curtailed yet further the meagre powers and rights still attached to his office.[1] Such influence and authority as the Emperor possessed was his on account of his hereditary possessions, not in virtue of his Imperial office.

Yet on paper his rights as Emperor were still considerable. In addition to the so-called *Comitial rechte*, those rights which he exercised on behalf of and by the authority of the Diet, he had certain " Reserved Rights " with which the Diet had nothing to do. He could veto measures submitted by the Diet, he could make promotions in rank, confer fiefs, titles of nobility and University degrees. Further, he represented Germany in all dealings with foreign powers, and it was from him that the Princes had to obtain the coveted privileges, *de non appellando* and *de non evocando*, which removed their law-courts from the superintendence of the Imperial tribunals and made their territories judicially independent. A certain amount of rather indefinite influence and prestige still, after all

[1] For those of Charles V, cf. Turner, p. 120.

deductions, attached to the Imperial office, and it need hardly be mentioned that the Emperor possessed in his hereditary dominions all the ordinary sovereign rights which the Princes enjoyed in their territories. Indeed, it was the great extent of the rights and powers of which the Princes had become possessed rather than any lack of powers theoretically his which made the Emperor so powerless and his office so anomalous.

The process by which this had come about has been admirably described by Sir John Seeley[1] as "the paralysis of the central government and, consequent upon that, the assumption by local authorities of powers properly Imperial." "A number of municipal corporations," he writes, "which in England would have only had the power of levying rates for local purposes and of appointing local officers with very insignificant powers, had in Germany become practically independent republics. Magnates who in England would have wielded a certain administrative and judicial power as members of Quarter Sessions, had risen in Germany to the rank of sovereigns." With all the Princes of the Empire practically independent in their domestic affairs and almost as completely their own masters in their dealings with foreign powers, not much scope was left for the intervention of the Emperor or of any of the machinery of the Empire. Only in regulating matters which concerned two or more German states was the Emperor likely to be called upon to act, and his intervention was rather that of the president of a federation of independent states than of the King of even a feudal monarchy. What he lacked was the force needed to compel obedience and secure the execution of his orders. The extent of his impotence may best be judged from the condition of the Imperial revenues and from the composition and organisation of the Army of the Empire.

To say outright that the Empire possessed neither revenues nor an army would strictly speaking be inaccurate, but it would be a great deal nearer to the real truth than to affirm that either of these effectively existed. Since 1521 there had been a unit of assessment, the so-called "Roman Month," which represented the amount voted by the Diet in that year for an expedition to Rome which Charles V was contemplating. The sum then voted, 120,000 florins, was calculated to provide

[1] *Life and Times of Stein*, i. 12.

4,000 horsemen at a rate of ten florins a month and 20,000 foot-soldiers at four florins.   Since 1521 fractions or multiples of this rate had been voted from time to time, for the convenience of utilising an existing assessment was enormous. Hard as it was to obtain payment of contributions even when the due proportions were assigned to those liable to pay, as was the case when the Imperial Roll of 1521 was utilised, the difficulty of collection and the friction arising out of it would have been multiplied many times had a fresh assessment been necessary whenever a vote was passed.   But even this was far from giving the Empire a standing army or even the machinery for raising one; it merely settled the proportions, and each new call for troops involved a fresh settlement by the Diet, which required almost as much diplomacy and negotiation as an international agreement for joint action. It was never certain whether the Diet would vote for sending men or money; though whichever form the contributions might take the Roman Month gave the proportion in which the individual states were liable.   It was, of course, to the advantage of the Emperor that the contribution should be in money, but the contributors preferred to send men: it gave them the appearance of allies rather than of tributaries, and, moreover, enabled them to exercise more control over the war: a contingent could always be recalled, it was less easy to recover a money contribution once it had entered the Imperial coffers.[1]   Nor was it certain whether the vote of the majority bound the minority, or whether only those who had voted in favour of a tax were liable to pay it.

Thus though many of its members possessed armies of considerable strength and efficiency, as a military power the Empire was an almost negligible quantity.   More than one attempt at reform was made in the second half of the seventeenth century.   In May 1681 the Diet issued a decree fixing the total force to be provided by the Circles at 12,000 horse and 28,000 foot, each Circle being given the choice between providing its own men or paying another " armed estate " (*Armirte Stande*) to supply its allotted contingent. But though a new unit of assessment was thus substituted for

---

[1] It is easy to see that this uncertainty very much increased the inefficiency of the defensive arrangements of the Empire: a noteworthy example was the delay over the despatch of troops to assist the Austrians in the Turkish War of 1663-1664.

the Roman Month not even now was a permanent force kept on foot, and in the War of the League of Augsburg there was continual friction between the "armed members" who provided troops and the "assigned" who contributed to their support. So inefficient was the protection afforded to the "assigned" states by the Army of the Empire that the Franconian and Swabian Circles finally resolved to reorganise their own resources, and by raising troops of their own to avoid being "assigned" any longer. With this object a scheme was drawn up by Margrave Louis of Baden-Baden, the colleague of Marlborough and Eugene in the Blenheim campaign, which was finally adopted (Jan. 1697) at a meeting held at Frankfort. These two Circles, with the Bavarian, Westphalian and the two Rhenish, formed the Association of Frankfort, undertaking to provide 40,000 men between them, and to draw up definite regulations for their equipment and organisation. This scheme would probably have provided a more efficient *Reichsarmee* than had hitherto existed, but the prompt conclusion of peace prevented it from being put into practice, and thus, never getting the chance of being tested in a campaign and put into working order, it remained a mere paper scheme. At the outbreak of the Spanish Succession War it was necessary to make entirely new arrangements, and that struggle found little improvement in the Army of the Empire. It was lacking in discipline, in homogeneity, in organisation, in equipment, in almost everything that goes to make an army efficient. The states which, like Hesse-Cassel and Brandenburg, possessed really efficient forces preferred to hire out their troops to fight the battles of the Maritime Powers rather than employ them in the less lucrative task of defending the "lazy and sleepy Empire,"[1] which was thus overrun again and again by French armies who levied in requisitions and in unofficial plunderings sums far larger than would have sufficed to provide troops enough to keep Villars at bay. Nowhere, indeed, was the disunion of Germany so evident as in its defensive arrangements, and the last appearances of the *Reichsarmee* during the Seven Years' War were a fitting finale to its career.

Not the least potent reason for the inefficiency of the defensive arrangements of the Empire was its poverty. Nearly

---

[1] *Portland Papers*, iv. 441 ; Hist. MSS. Commission.

all the lucrative sources of income had passed from the Emperor to the local rulers. The Imperial Chamber of Justice was supported by a special tax, first voted in 1500 and known as the Chamber Terms (*Kammerzieler*); a certain amount of revenue was derived through the exercise of the Emperor's "Reserved Rights" and the Imperial Cities paid a small tribute amounting to about 12,000 gulden;[1] but these sums were quite insufficient to defray the maintenance of the Imperial institutions, and the want of an Imperial revenue was one of the reasons why the Hapsburgs remained so long in unchallenged possession of the costly dignity they alone could afford to support.

Where there was hardly any Imperial income it is not surprising that there was no common Imperial treasury, still less any administrative machinery. Police was left to the Circles, an organisation the germs of which are to be found in the fifteenth century, but which had only been extended all over the Empire in 1512 by the Diet of Cologne;[2] but this attempt to provide for the execution of the judgments of the Imperial Chamber had never enjoyed more than a very partial success, and by the beginning of the eighteenth century the institution had fallen into abeyance in many parts of the country. In three of the Circles only, the Franconian, the Swabian, and the Westphalian, was the organisation sufficiently effective to demand serious consideration. This was because in these Circles there was no single Prince powerful enough to become predominant, as was, for example, the Elector of Bavaria in the Bavarian Circle; on the contrary, they included a very large number of Imperial Knights and of minor Princes, all so evenly balanced that the Princes chosen from time to time as Directors of the Circle had no chance of making themselves predominant. An even less effective piece of administrative machinery was the Imperial Deputation, created in 1555 to assist the Circles in the discharge of their duties. It was in effect a standing committee of the Diet, comprising the Electors and representatives of the other two Estates and

---

[1] In 1677 an edict fixed the gulden at 60 kreuzer, the thaler being 96: the equivalents in English money may be roughly estimated at half a crown and four shillings.

[2] Even then Bohemia and the lands of the Teutonic Order had been excluded from its operation.

of the Emperor-King, but it was no better able to make its authority effective than was the Diet. After the Peace of Westphalia efforts were made to reconstruct it; it was proposed by the Protestants that the Deputation should be drawn equally from the two religions; but as a majority of the Electors were Roman Catholics, this could only be done by permitting one Protestant to vote twice or by not counting one Catholic vote, both solutions being equally unacceptable. In the end nothing was done to increase the efficiency of the *Reichsdeputation*, and it was never of much influence or importance.

The judicial institutions of the Empire retained rather more vitality; but even they were in a moribund condition and had been hard hit by the anarchy and disorganisation produced by the Thirty Years' War. The most important of them, the Imperial Chamber (*Kammergericht*), had been established towards the end of the fifteenth century as a permanent court of justice in place of the feudal courts (*Hofgerichte*) which the Emperors had till then been wont to summon at irregular intervals whenever enough judicial business had accumulated. These had proved quite inadequate to meet the requirements of the Empire: indeed, the establishment of a permanent court of justice had been one of the measures most urgently advocated by the active reforming party of the day, led by the then Elector of Mayence, Berthold of Henneberg.[1] Maximilian I had given this court a permanent establishment of a President (*Kammerrichter*) and sixteen Assessors (*Urteiler*), and some additions had been subsequently made to its staff. It was a court of original jurisdiction for those holding immediately of the Emperor-King, of appellate jurisdiction from the courts of those members of the Empire who did not possess the liberally granted privilege *de non appellando*.[2] During the Thirty Years' War the Imperial Chamber had almost fallen into abeyance, but at the Peace of Westphalia and at the Diet of Ratisbon (1653) attempts were made to reform and reconstruct it. The number of Assessors was raised to fifty, and it was

---

[1] Cf. Turner, pp. 72, 104 ff. ; also *C.M.H.* i. 304 and 317.

[2] This privilege, granted to the Electors by one of the clauses of the Golden Bull, and since then extended to most of the chief Princes, prohibited appeals from the territorial courts to the Imperial Courts ; the corresponding privilege *de non evocando* forbade the Imperial Courts to call up cases from territorial courts.

provided that twenty-four of them together with two of the four Vice-Presidents should be Lutherans, and also that in all cases in which one of the parties was a Protestant and the other a Roman Catholic the Assessors chosen to decide the case should be equally divided between the two religions. Moreover, a commission was promised to expedite the procedure and improve the efficiency of the Chamber. But these reforms produced no real improvement. The revenues of the Chamber were quite insufficient for its expenses and it proved impossible to keep up the full staff. The decay of the Circles involved inefficiency in the execution of the decisions of the Chamber, since it was on the Circles that this depended.[1] And it is characteristic of the traditions of the Imperial constitution that the reforming commission, which was to have begun its labours in 1654, never really got to work till 1767. That under such circumstances efforts to wipe off arrears, to accelerate business, and to check factious appeals and undue litigation proved quite fruitless, will be readily understood. A disputed decision was practically adjourned *sine die* and the mass of arrears grew rather than diminished.

Soon after the establishment of the Imperial Chamber, Maximilian proceeded to set up (1492) a rival organisation which was far more closely identified with the Emperor than was the Imperial Chamber, whose members were jointly appointed by the Diet and by the Emperor. Originally this *Reichshofrath* or so-called "Aulic Council"[2] was intended to deal with all business from the Empire or the King's hereditary principalities; to it were also to be referred all cases in which he had to adjudicate as King. It was to be something more than a mere law court, it was also to exercise administrative functions in the hereditary possessions of the Hapsburgs. These objects, however, were not realised, and the Council had to be reconstructed in 1518, when it was put on a regular footing, with a President, Vice-President and sixteen Councillors. Its members were appointed by the Emperor, and with his death their commissions were to lapse. It was at this time also that the administration of the Austrian dominions, hitherto entrusted to it, ceased to form part of its functions.[3] In 1559 further changes occurred, Ferdinand I

[1] Cf. Turner, p. 114.   [2] Cf. *C.M.H.* i. 313.
[3] Pütter, *Germanic Constitution* (Eng. trans.), i. 358.

confining its sphere to Imperial business, and giving it jurisdiction as a high court of the Empire.   But it was not till the Peace of Westphalia that it received formal recognition as such from the Diet, which then for the first time took cognisance of it, regulating its procedure and applying to it the principle of equality between religions, which was the rule with the Imperial Chamber.   At the Diet of 1653 another attempt was made to reform it; but the Emperor, resenting the interference of the Diet and anxious to retain control over the Council, resisted the proposed changes and issued an Imperial edict (without allowing the Diet to intervene) introducing certain reforms.   On the whole, it was more efficient as a court of justice than was the Imperial Chamber, its decisions being reached more certainly and rapidly.   To a certain extent the spheres of the two courts coincided and collisions were not infrequent; but whereas the Imperial Chamber may be said to have dealt rather with cases between Princes or between subjects of different Princes, the Aulic Council's province included matters relating to fiefs of the Empire and cases in which the Emperor was personally concerned.   At the same time its position was somewhat complicated by its political aspect.   It had originally been an administrative rather than a judicial body and it had never wholly lost this character.   Indeed, as the Empire possessed neither a Privy Council nor a War Office, the Aulic Council may be said to have to a certain extent supplied their place.[1]

There was also another but even less important Imperial Court, the *Hofgericht*, which had its seat at Rottweil on the Neckar.   It represented the old royal courts of a period prior to the erection of the Imperial Chamber and the Aulic Council, and had been revived and re-established by Maximilian I in 1496, and again by Maximilian II in 1572.   Still it had always been disliked by the Diet, and the reforms of 1572 notwithstanding, its position was most insecure, so that one of the questions which the negotiators of the Peace of Westphalia had left over for the next Diet was that of its abolition.   It is perhaps unnecessary to add that the Diet came to no decision, and the Court protracted a useless and inconspicuous existence until the year 1802.[2]

Of all the institutions of Germany, however, the Diet

[1] Cf. *Z.S.* i. 26.   [2] Cf. Turner, p. 136.

(*Reichstag*) was the most important   Its origin may be traced back to the general councils annually summoned by Charles the Great.   During the Middle Ages it had occupied a position approximately corresponding to the *Etats Généraux* of France and to the feudal forerunners of the English Parliament.   A purely feudal body, in which tenants in chief alone might appear, it had undergone modifications parallel with the change in the position of the great feudal nobles.   As the Dukes of Bavaria and the Counts Palatine of the Rhine had developed into petty sovereigns, as their estates had become in all but name European states of the third and fourth rank, so the Diet also had changed.   It had really become a congress; those who attended it were, as a rule, mere representatives of the great feudatories who in former days had been wont to appear in person.   From a body which was practically an international conference measures tending to the efficient government of Germany were not to be expected.   Particularist ideals were bound to prevail over any feeble tendencies towards unity, the interests of Germany were sure to be sacrificed to local aims and objects, any proposal to strengthen the central institutions and to set the constitutional machinery in effective order could not but excite the opposition of vested interests, and was certain to be judged not on its merits but from the particularist point of view.   Yet even so, it was in the Diet that the nearest approach to German unity was to be found. The Netherlands, the Helvetic Confederation, Burgundy and other countries once part of the Empire had been lost to it, but not even the strongest and most separatist of the minor powers of Germany had obtained or even sought exemption from membership of the Diet.   No privileges corresponding to the right *de non appellando* marred the completeness of its sphere of influence.   Indeed, though the link it provided may have been more negative than positive, as long as it existed there could be no formal dissolution of the Empire.   It made no attempt to arrest the process of disintegration, it never considered or contemplated a constitutional reconstruction, but the fact of its existence did to some extent check disintegration and maintain the semblance of German unity.

Since the fifteenth century the Diet had been organised in three Chambers, the College of Electors; the College of the Princes, Counts and Barons; and the College of the Imperial

Free Cities. Of these that of the Electors was the most important, since to it fell the duty of electing a new Emperor when the Imperial throne became vacant. The privileges of the Electors were extensive: they not only enjoyed the rights *de non evocando* and *de non appellando*, but they received royal dues (*regalia*) from mines, tolls, coinage and the dues payable by their own territories and were to all intents and purposes independent sovereigns. The Golden Bull, which amongst other things had greatly exalted their status by declaring conspiracy against their lives to be high treason, had fixed their number at seven and defined the great court offices held by them. The three ecclesiastical Electors of Mayence, Cologne and Treves were respectively Arch Chancellors of Germany, Italy and Burgundy: among the lay Electors the King of Bohemia was Arch Butler, the Count Palatine of the Rhine was Arch Steward, the Duke of Saxony Arch Marshal, and the Margrave of Brandenburg Arch Chamberlain. Further, the Bull had attached the electoral votes to the electoral territories, which it declared to be inalienable and indivisible, while it made primogeniture the rule of succession to the lay Electorates. It was because of this declaration that the validity of Ferdinand II's action in depriving Frederick V of the Palatinate of his vote and transferring it with his territories to Maximilian of Bavaria was so hotly disputed, the partisans of the dispossessed family maintaining that the Emperor had exceeded his rights. They did not deny the Emperor's right to depose Frederick, but argued that as Frederick's offence had been personal, so his deposition was a purely personal matter and could not affect the right of his descendants to the Electorate. At the Peace of Westphalia the question was solved by a compromise, which altered the constitution as laid down in the Bull in several important respects. An eighth voter was added to the Electoral College; but while Charles Lewis, the eldest son of Frederick V, regained the Electoral dignity for his branch of the Wittelsbachs, he did not recover the office of Arch Steward, which his ancestors had held, but had to be content with the newly created office of Arch Treasurer and the Bavarian vote was recognised as the fifth, so that the compromise was decidedly in favour of Bavaria.[1] This solution left the balance of religions in the Electoral

[1] Cf. Erdmannsdörffer, i. 56.

College inclined to the Catholic side, which with Bavaria and the three ecclesiastical Electors had a clear majority over Saxony, Brandenburg and the Palatinate, even when the Bohemian vote, which had fallen into abeyance, is not reckoned to their credit.

Between the Peace of Westphalia and the end of the seventeenth century the balance was to some extent redressed by the creation of a new Electorate for the house of Guelph, (1692) when Ernest Augustus of Hanover obtained the coveted dignity for himself and his heirs ; [1] but any advantage the Protestants might have hoped to gain from this was lost through the conversion of Frederick Augustus of Saxony to Catholicism (1696) in order to improve his chances of obtaining the Crown of Poland, for which he was then a candidate, and by the accession of a Catholic branch of the Wittelsbachs to the Palatinate.[2] But by this time religious differences were beginning to lose some of their political importance, as may be gathered from the fact that, despite his conversion, the Elector of Saxony remained the recognised head of the *Corpus Evangelicorum*, in other words, the nominal leader of German Protestantism.

The connection which the success of the candidature of Frederick Augustus established between Saxony and Poland is also of interest as illustrating the increasing power and importance of the Electors. Saxony was not the only lay Electorate whose fortunes became closely linked with those of a non-German territory. The accession of George Lewis of Hanover to the throne of Great Britain (1714) started a connection which was destined to exercise a very important influence over the affairs of Germany during the next century, and the conclusion of the celebrated " Treaty of the Crown " (1701),[3] which recognised Frederick of Brandenburg as Frederick I, King *in* Prussia, may be said to mark the point at which the Hohenzollern became of European rather than of merely German importance. So, too, the close connection between Bavaria and France, the result of the policy followed by Maximilian Emanuel in the Spanish

[1] Cf. p. 45.
[2] In 1685 the Simmern line became extinct with the death of Charles, son of Charles Lewis, who was succeeded by Philip William of Neuburg. Cf. p. 44.
[3] Cf. p. 42.

Succession War, enabled yet another Elector to play the part of an almost independent sovereign with a policy of his own, and submitting to hardly any control from the nominal ruler of the country.

The College of Princes had in 1648 some seventy-six members with "individual votes" (*Virilstimmen*), forty-three of them laymen and thirty-three ecclesiastics, besides four bodies of voters who delivered a "collective vote" (*Curiatstimme*). Of these last there had only been three before 1640, one being given by the numerous prelates who were below princely rank, the other two by the Counts and Barons, divided for voting purposes into two so-called "benches," the Swabian and the Wetterabian. From this last body a new "bench" had been formed in 1640, under the title of the "Franconian Counts," while in 1653 the collective votes had been increased to five by the grant of a second vote to the Prelates. At the Diet of 1653–1654 a proposal had been put forward by the Counts that a fourth College should be erected for them and the Prelates; but the scheme found little support and nothing more was heard of it. The *Curiatstimme* ranked as equivalent to an individual vote, so that it would be fair to regard the voting strength of the College of Princes as about eighty in 1648, while by 1715 it had risen to over ninety. This increase was caused by the occasional exercise by the Emperor of his right to raise to the princely rank Counts and other nobles not hitherto in possession of a *Virilstimme*. This right, which gave the Emperor the power of rewarding his supporters and at the same time increasing his influence in the College of Princes, had been in dispute until the Diet of 1653–1654, at which it had been definitely recognised, with the limitation that those thus raised to the rank must possess as a qualification territories held immediately of the Emperor, a condition imposed to prevent the swamping of the College by lavish creations. At the same time there were never as many individual holders of *Virilstimmen* as there were *Virilstimmen*, for many Princes had come into possession of more than one qualifying piece of territory. Thus it was that the Electors were members of the College of Princes, Brandenburg having as many as five votes, while Austria possessed three, Burgundy, although actually in Spanish possession,

Styria and Tyrol providing her qualifications. The balance between the religions favoured the Catholics, who were in the proportion of five to four even after several of the votes attached to the secularised bishoprics of North Germany had passed into Protestant hands in 1648. Of these Halberstadt, Kammin and Minden had fallen to Brandenburg,[1] Magdeburg to Saxony,[2] Ratzeburg to Mecklenburg - Strelitz, Hersfeld to Hesse - Cassel, Schwerin to Mecklenburg-Schwerin, and Bremen and Verden to Sweden.[3] Another foreign ruler was also a member of the College of Princes as the possessor of Holstein. Glückstadt provided the King of Denmark with a qualification, but Savoy had allowed her vote to lapse into abeyance. Among the possessors of more than one vote may be mentioned the Palatine Wittelsbachs who had five,[4] the various branches of the Brunswick family who had also five between them,[5] while a like number were held by the Ernestine Saxons. Baden, Hesse and Mecklenburg had three apiece, and Würtemberg two, for Mömpelgard (Montbeliard) and Stuttgart.

Least in importance was the remaining College of the Diet, that of the Free Imperial Cities. It might have been thought that the constant quarrels between the two other Colleges would have been turned to good use by the third. The Princes were always bitterly jealous of the privileges of the Electors, and friction was frequent. But the Cities were in no position to profit by this. It was only at the Peace of Westphalia that the old dispute as to the value of their vote had been settled in their favour, and that it had been agreed that they should possess the *Votum decisivum* and not merely the *Votum Consultativum.* Even then the parallel questions, whether the Cities should be called upon to decide when the Electors and Princes disagreed and whether the Electors and Princes combined could carry a point against the Cities, had been left to the next meeting of the Diet, to be decided in 1653–1654 in a manner which made the recognition of their claim to the

[1] Her other votes were for Cüstrin and Eastern Pomerania.

[2] On the death of its Saxon administrator, Augustus, son of John George I, in 1680, Magdeburg reverted, as duly arranged, to Brandenburg.

[3] The cession of Bremen and Verden to Hanover (1720) added two votes to those possessed by the Guelphs.

[4] For Lautern, Neuburg, Simmern, Veldenz and Zweibrücken.

[5] For Calenberg, Celle, Grubenhagen, Saxe-Lauenberg and Wolfenbüttel.

Votum decisivum a mere farce, for it was settled that the Cities should only be called upon to vote when the other two Colleges were agreed. But the reasons for the unimportance of the Cities lay deeper than any mere uncertainty as to their constitutional position. Their position was uncertain because they had already fallen from their high estate. Some of the " Free Imperial Cities " were no longer free, some were no longer Imperial but had passed under other masters, and some were not worthy of the name of " city." Their decline had begun with the changes in the distribution of commerce caused by the great geographical discoveries of the fifteenth century. Even without the Reformation and the Thirty Years' War, the German cities would have been hard hit by the opening of the new route to the East round the Cape of Good Hope, and by the great advance in shipbuilding which had made commerce oceanic and had freed traders from the necessity of creeping cautiously along the coast. Moreover, the altered conditions of national life in England and France affected German trade adversely. Consolidated kingdoms quickly developed a very definite commercial policy. Protective measures fostered the growth of national commerce and industries to the detriment of the foreigner. The Merchant Adventurers of England disputed the Hanseatic monopoly of the Baltic, and the legislation of Edward VI and Elizabeth dealt the League a crippling blow by depriving it of its privileges in England. And while the old trade-routes of the Middle Ages were being deserted, while the spices of the East were finding their way to the North of Europe by other lines than the traditional route of the Adriatic, the Alpine passes and the Rhine valley, political as well as economic conditions were fighting against the cities of Germany. With the consolidation of the power of the territorial Princes their appetite for the acquisition of valuable sources of revenue increased in proportion, and more than one important city found it impossible to resist the pressure of a powerful neighbour. Of concerted action on the part of the cities or joint resistance to would-be annexers there was no trace. Not, as a rule, individually large enough or wealthy enough to be able to stand alone, the cities were not sufficiently in union among themselves to act together. Had they been ready to give up some part of their independent powers and to place themselves in the hands of the Emperor, they might have managed to escape having to submit to lesser potentates; but they took no steps in that direction and the Hapsburgs showed no inclination to meet them half-way.   But vigorous resistance was hardly to be expected in the unhealthy state into which municipal life had fallen.   In most cities a narrow oligarchy had usurped the local government and completely controlled the municipal institutions.   Add to all this the tremendous upheaval of the Thirty Years' War, the utter disorganisation of social, commercial and industrial life which it had involved, the lawlessness and violence which followed in the train of war, and it is not surprising that the Free Cities emerged from that struggle as political nullities, and that in the course of the next half-century their political importance decreased rather than recovered itself.   In 1715 they still numbered about fifty, though many of the largest and most flourishing of them had failed to retain the independence of which much smaller places were still able to boast.   Thus Leipzig had become subject to the Elector of Saxony, while Ulm was still independent.   It was not by size or by importance that the question of freedom or subjection was determined, it was by the accident of the strength of the would-be annexer. Sometimes, indeed, a city retained its independence through being the object of conflicting claims.   Thus Erfurt, though never technically a Free City, had managed to enjoy a considerable independence for some time by playing off against each other the rival claimants, the Electors of Mayence and Saxony, until in 1664 the former managed to arrange a compromise with his opponent and by the aid of the Rhine League forced the city to submit.   Bremen, more fortunate, though compelled in 1654 to admit the suzerainty of Sweden, contrived to regain her independence twelve years later by the assistance of Cologne, Denmark and the Brunswick Dukes.

Those cities which at the beginning of the eighteenth century remained independent were for the most part very conservative, unprogressive even to stagnation, being in the hands of narrow and unenterprising oligarchies and quite devoid of any real municipal or industrial life.   Nuremberg, despite her sufferings in the siege of 1632, and Frankfort on Main may be mentioned as exceptions to the general rule of stagnation, while the Italian trade enabled Augsburg to retain

some degree of prosperity and activity.   Hamburg and
Bremen had had the good fortune to be but little affected by
the Thirty Years' War, but the greatness of the Hanseatic
League was a thing of the past and in 1648 Lübeck was the
only other member of the League which retained its status as
a Free City, and even these three had lost much of their old
commercial importance.   Cologne also owed to her position on
the Rhine a certain amount of trade, but the control which the
Dutch exercised over the mouths of the Rhine proved a serious
obstacle to the development of the trade of Western Germany.
Another of the more flourishing cities of Germany had been
lost to the Empire when, in 1681, perhaps the most high-
handed of all the acts of Louis xiv deprived Germany of
Strassburg.   Outside the ranks of the Free Cities, Dresden,
Münich and Berlin were gradually rising in importance
with the consolidation of the powers of the territorial Princes,
and though Vienna had suffered severely in the great siege of
1683, the Austrian capital was in some ways the most flourishing
city in the Empire.   But Germany was primarily a rural not
an urban country; its cities were neither economically nor
politically to be compared with those of Italy and the Netherlands, and the unimportance of the College of Free Cities
accurately reflects the part which the towns played in German
history in the eighteenth century.

It would not be going too far to assert that in none of the
institutions of Germany was there anything which offered any
prospect of the attainment of unity or real national life.   Without a thorough reform of the constitution nothing could be
done and of such a reform there was little chance.   The Empire
as such was moribund, and in no direction was any source of
new life or strength to be found for it.   To a certain extent
the Hapsburgs had attempted in the years between the
Peace of Westphalia and those of Utrecht and Rastatt to
reassert the claims and pretensions which the Imperial title
carried with it, but their success had been of the slightest.   It
might have been thought that opposition to the encroachments
of Louis xiv would have served as a bond of union; that the
necessity for common defence against so powerful and aggressive a neighbour would have rallied the country round its nominal
head ; that the seizure of Strassburg and the other places claimed
by Louis in virtue of the verdicts of the *Chambres de Réunion*

would have called to life the dead or dormant national sentiment of Germany, would have brought home to the Princes
the need for co-operation and the dangers which they and
their neighbours were running through the pursuit of local and
particularist aims. If ever Germany was to be forced to
realise the need for unity, if ever a national movement was
to breathe fresh force into the old institutions and make the
German Kingdom something more than a mere name, one
might have expected this to have come about in the last
quarter of the seventeenth century. That something of the
sort was on foot is proved by the countless pamphlets, carica-
tures and squibs which flooded the country about that period,
among which the *Bedenken* of the great philosopher Leibnitz
are of more than mere ephemeral interest. In these he
pointed out with lucidity and force Germany's urgent need for
union and for proper preparation for war. But it was in vain
that he urged that the Emperor should put himself at the
head of the minor states, and that the Princes should join him
in securing that union of Germany which, according to the
writer, was the only security for the balance of power and for
the preservation of the peace of Europe. The Princes with
few exceptions showed no inclination to rally round the
Emperor, no disposition to make any sacrifices for the common
safety, or to abandon their purely particularist and selfish
policies. Louis XIV was fully aware of the merits of the
policy of *divide et impera*; he saw that localism was a force
which he might use to paralyse and render impotent his
neighbour on the East, and he rarely failed to find among the
Princes of Germany men whose assistance, or at any rate
whose neutrality, could be purchased for a reasonable price.
Thus in 1658 Mazarin had founded the League of the Rhine,
and though the action of Louis in attacking the Spanish
Netherlands in May 1667 under the doubtful pretext of the
Jus Devolutionis seems to have so frightened the members
of the League that they allowed their alliances with him to
expire in 1668 and declined to renew them, he was able
when attacking Holland in 1672 to secure the neutrality of
Bavaria, the Elector Palatine, Treves and Würtemberg, and to
obtain the actual support of Cologne, of the Bishops of
Münster and Strassburg and of Duke John Frederick of
Hanover. It was the lukewarm support he received from the

Princes, notably Bavaria, Saxony and Brandenburg, which caused the Emperor Leopold to assent to the inglorious Peace of Nimeguen in 1679. It was largely because Brandenburg had enrolled herself among the paid retainers of France that Louis was able to set his *Chambres de Réunion* at work to carry out his annexations unopposed, and his successful retention of Strassburg was not merely due to the almost simultaneous troubles in Hungary and the outbreak of a new war with the Turks. The Emperor had to agree to the Truce of Ratisbon in 1684, because Frederick William of Brandenburg saw in the necessities of the Empire a chance for pressing his very dubious claims on Silesia, demanding terms so extravagant that Austria refused to grant them, with the result that the projected coalition fell through, it being realised that unless all Germany were united behind him it would be useless for Leopold to throw down the gauntlet to Louis. The League of Augsburg in 1688 included the majority of the principal states of Germany, and the deliberate devastation of the Palatinate went far to exasperate popular feeling against Louis ; but the course of the war showed up not merely the utter inefficiency of the defensive arrangements of the Empire,[1] but also the lukewarm character of the support of many members of the Coalition. Those from whose territories the hostile armies were far distant exerted themselves but little on behalf of their compatriots on the frontier. From 1690 to February 1693 no contingent from Saxony took any part in the war, and only by bestowing on Hanover the largest bribe in his power, the coveted Electoral dignity, did the Emperor avert the formation of an alliance between the Brunswick Dukes, Brandenburg and Saxony, to bring the war to an end. Nor was Germany any more solid in its support of the Emperor in the War of the Spanish Succession. Duke Anthony Ulrich of Brunswick-Wolfenbüttel was only prevented from assisting the French by the prompt action of his cousins at Hanover and Celle, who occupied his territories and disarmed his troops, while the defection of the Wittelsbach Electors of Bavaria and Cologne threatened at one time to ruin the Grand Alliance by allowing the French to penetrate to Vienna and dictate terms to the Hapsburg in his capital.

Nor does the case appear any better when one turns to

---

[1] Cf. Erdmannsdörffer, ii. 25, and *Z.S.* ii. 41.

another important theatre and follows the course of the struggle with the still powerful and aggressive Moslem who was threatening Germany from the South-East. At no time was there a complete or a spontaneous rally for the defence of the Cross against the Crescent. Religious fervour and patriotism seemed equally extinct. Northern and Western Germany did little to beat back the tide of Turkish conquest in 1664, and the contingents of the Rhine League who shared in the victory at St. Gotthard on the Raab fought there at the bidding of their patron Louis XIV. In 1683, again, only two North German states were represented at the relief of Vienna, and the contingents of Hanover and Saxe-Weimar did not total two thousand men. Not a man from the Rhineland was there, and once again conditions which the Emperor could not accept were coupled with the protestations of zeal of which alone Brandenburg was lavish. Indeed, for any assistance the Emperor received in the task of ousting the Turk from Hungary a price, not a light one, had to be paid. The despatch of six thousand Hanoverians to the Danube in 1692, helped to earn the Guelphs the Electoral dignity ; and when, in 1686, eight thousand Brandenburgers appeared on the Danube, it was because the Emperor had consented to cede Schwiebus to the Great Elector.

It may be argued that the Princes of Germany were thus lukewarm, because they felt that the reconquest of Hungary would be of little benefit to Germany as a whole, and mainly concerned the Hapsburgs and their dynastic interests. This is perhaps to some extent true ; but no such plea can be advanced to exculpate those who not only failed to oppose the aggressions of Louis XIV, but were actually his accomplices and abettors. At the same time, it must be admitted that the Hapsburgs cannot escape the charge of having failed to do all they might have done. They were fatally hampered by the strong bias towards aggressive Roman Catholicism and the alliance with the Jesuits which made them objects of suspicion to the Protestant states, by the semi-Spanish traditions of the family, by their dynastic and non-German interests,—as, for example, the secret treaty of January 1668 with Louis XIV, providing for a partition in case the Spanish branch of the family should become extinct. Moreover, their autocratic traditions of government led them to repress rather than to encourage anything in the shape of a popular movement.   Indeed, if they had made more of an effort to reassert themselves and make good their nominal position in Germany, the more vigorous elements in the German polity would have been found opposed to them; for these elements, such as they were, took the shape of the efforts of the larger principalities at territorial independence and aggrandisement. The rise of Brandenburg-Prussia and Bavaria, their development from local divisions of Germany into minor European Powers, fatal though it was to anything like unity in Germany, certainly testified to the existence in those states of some degree of strength and activity.   Thus it is that when one attempts to trace the history of Germany during the eighteenth century, one is at once met at the outset by the fact that Germany as a whole hardly has any history; in its place one has the history of the various states of Germany, international not national affairs hardly to be distinguished from the history of Europe as a whole, since France and Russia and England were all more or less directly concerned with the rivalries of the different minor states.   At the most, the history of Germany can be said to deal with the complete decay of the constitutional life of the Holy Roman Empire and of the national life of the German Kingdom.   Even the modified national existence which had still existed at the end of the fifteenth century [1] had disappeared.   A distinguished authority on Romano-Germanic law, Michael Munchmayer, wrote in 1705 that it would have been about as possible to produce unity among Germans as to wash a blackamoor white.   Indeed, the disintegration had gone to such lengths that it is really rather remarkable that the forms of unity and of a constitution should still have been retained.

To have put an end to the nominal as well as to the practical existence of the Empire would doubtless have been logical, but politics are not ruled by logic; and while there was no special reason why the process of disintegration should have been carried to its logical conclusion, for no one in particular stood to profit greatly by that event, there were excellent reasons why it should have been left incomplete.   To the maintenance of the forms of the Empire as a hollow sham there were two possible alternatives, reconstruction and im-

[1] Cf. Professor Tout's chapter in vol. i. of the *Cambridge Modern History*.

mediate dissolution.   Reconstruction was out of the question ; even if there had been any real wish for it in Germany, of which there were even fewer indications in 1715 than in 1648, the other Powers of Europe would not have cared to see the Empire so remodelled as to become a reality.   Immediately after 1648 an attempt at reconstruction would have met with determined opposition from France and Sweden ; in 1715, if Sweden was no longer a force to be regarded, and France was temporarily incapable of active interference, disintegration had gone so far that the diplomatic support of France would have probably been sufficient to enable Brandenburg or Bavaria to wreck the scheme.   But, on the other hand, the dissolution of the Empire was about the last thing which anyone desired. The Hapsburgs were not the men to make great changes prematurely ; the formal dissolution of the Empire would probably have been the signal for the immediate outbreak of a struggle of the most fearful description, which could hardly have failed to surpass even the horrors of the Thirty Years' War ; a scramble among the stronger states for the possessions of the territories of those of their neighbours who lacked the power to defend their independence ; a carnival of greed, violence and aggression ; the universal application to the petty principalities of Germany of the rule that might is right.   This the continued existence of the Empire did at least avert : the semblance of law and order was maintained, private war and armed strife among its members were checked, if not altogether prevented.   The existence of the Empire protected the Principality of Anhalt against the danger of forcible annexation to Brandenburg ; it made it useless for the ruler of Hesse-Darmstadt to cast covetous eyes on the Counties of Isenburg or Solms ; it restrained Würtemberg from attempting to incorporate the Free City of Reutlingen and Bavaria from compelling the Franconian Knights to admit themselves her subjects as she was to try to do at the eleventh hour of the Empire's life.[1]   In a way, the very subdivision which made the Empire so weak and unity so unattainable prevented the Empire from being dissolved.   As Napoleon declared, " If the Germanic Body did not exist, we should have to create it."   Its existence was at least better than the anarchy which dissolution would have brought in its train.   The three

[1] Cf. pp. 467-468.

hundred and sixty-five states of one description and another which were included within it were, for the most part, too small and too insignificant to be capable of independent existence.   Not even the strongest of the minor states now rising into practically independent sovereign powers was ready as yet for the actual dissolution of the Empire.   The substance of independence was as much as Saxony and Würtemberg wanted, and it they certainly already enjoyed.   Having obtained ample freedom from the control of the Empire, they had no wish to complete its ruin ; and, ruin as it was, there was yet enough potential utility in the old fabric for Austria to find it worth the trouble of its maintenance.   The Imperial position, with its great, albeit shadowy, traditions, with its claims, disputed and obsolescent though they might be, might not be worth attaining at a heavy cost, but it was not to be lightly discarded.   If Louis XIV had found it worthy of his candidature, Ferdinand III had had good reason for keeping it if he could. Possibilities still lurked in it; it was not even yet beyond all chance of revival.   Joseph I had done not a little to reassert the Imperial claims and to raise the Imperial prestige and authority when he was suddenly cut off early in life: had he survived, there would have been a very different end to the Spanish Succession War and the Empire would have occupied a very different position in 1715.   And even then there was a chance that at a more favourable season the old machinery might be put into working order, the old constitution might again prove capable of being turned to good account.   So for nearly a century after the Peace of Baden the Empire survived, at once in the ideas it embodied the symbol of the German unity which had once existed, and in its actual condition the most striking example of that disintegration and disunion of Germany which is the main theme of these pages.

CHAPTER II

THE GERMAN STATES IN 1715

AMONG the three hundred and sixty-five states which together made up the German Kingdom the territories ruled by the Hapsburg family deserve the first place, even apart from their long standing connection with the Empire, since both in area and in population they exceeded all the others. "Austria," if by this convenient though somewhat anachronistic term one may describe the multifarious dominions of the Hapsburgs, was a conglomerate of provinces fortuitously brought together, differing greatly in race and language, in history and traditions, in social and political conditions, with little to connect them save the rule of a common dynasty, but for the most part geographically adjacent. Thus while no foreign territory intervened between Austria strictly so called and the group of provinces in which Bohemia was the chief and Moravia and Silesia the satellites, the territories attached to the Archduchy, Carniola, Carinthia, Styria and Tyrol, formed a connected group, and, to the South-Eastward, Hungary with Croatia and Transylvania continued the Hapsburg dominions in unbroken succession down the great highway of the Danube almost to the gates of Belgrade. Till 1715, Hungary and its dependencies had been the only non-German territories under the rule of the Austrian Hapsburgs, and from 1648 to 1683 Austrian Hungary had included but a small portion of the old Magyar kingdom, so that the non-German element in the Hapsburg polity, which was destined to be of such doubtful benefit during the eighteenth century, was as yet comparatively insignificant. Indeed, in 1648 the only detached portions of territory which Austria possessed were calculated to interest her in the defence of Germany rather than to distract her attention to other quarters, as was the case after 1715. At the Peace of Westphalia she did indeed surrender to France the Sundgau and other portions of Alsace, but she retained many scattered pieces of Swabia which may be comprehended under the title of "Further Austria" (*Vorder Ostreich*). Though separated from Austria by the Electorate of Bavaria and the Bishopric of Augsburg, these districts along the Upper Danube and in the Black Forest, among which the Breisgau and the Burgau were the most important, were within a very short distance of Austria's Alpine lands, Vorarlberg and Tyrol, and the Wittelsbach alliance with France may be understood when it is realised how these Austrian outposts in Swabia seemed to surround Bavaria with a cordon of Hapsburg territory, and to menace her with that annexation which she had been fortunate to escape during the Spanish Succession War. "Further Austria" might have served as stepping-stones to bring the Hapsburgs to the Middle Rhine, and enable them to assimilate the intervening territory just as Brandenburg's acquisitions in Westphalia[1] helped to plant her in secure possession of the Lower Rhine. The idea of acquiring Bavaria by annexation or exchange was one of the most constant factors in Austrian policy, the dream of Joseph II, the explanation and aim of many of Thugut's intrigues, not definitely abandoned till the need for obtaining Bavaria's help against Napoleon caused Metternich to agree to the Treaty of Ried in 1813.[2]

It would have been of the greatest benefit to Austria, whatever its effects on Germany as a whole, if, instead of conferring the Spanish Netherlands on the Hapsburgs the Treaties of Utrecht and Baden had carried out the project of giving them to the Wittelsbachs in exchange for Bavaria. Rich, fertile, thickly populated though they were, the Netherlands were a possession of little value to Austria. Lying far away from Vienna, they had not even Hungary's geographical connection with the "hereditary dominions." Hampered by the restrictions imposed by the Peace of Münster their trade and industries could not develop naturally, and though they had once been an integral part of the Empire, the folly of Charles VI in treating them as part of that Spanish inheritance he persisted in regarding as rightly his prevented the revival of the old connection. No real attempt was made to attach them either by interest or sentiment to their new rulers, and when the conquering armies of Revolutionary France threatened

[1] Cf. p. 21.   [2] Cf. p. 619.

to sever the connection between the Netherlands and the Hapsburgs Austria's defence of her provinces was so feeble and faint-hearted as to incur, almost to justify, suspicions that she desired to be rid of them.

Of the other acquisitions made by Austria in 1715, the Duchy of Milan also had once been subject to the Holy Roman Emperor, to whom it now returned; but here again the determination of Charles VI to regard it and his other Italian possessions, the island of Sardinia and the kingdom of Naples, as belonging to him as King of Spain, prevented any assimilation of these Italian dominions by Austria. In a way the connection with Italy influenced Austria but little in the eighteenth century; there was not much intercourse between Milan or Naples and the hereditary dominions, and it may be said that it was mainly because they excited the hostility of Spain and so helped to involve Austria in wars with the Bourbon powers, that these possessions affected her. It was only later on, when Austria had abandoned all efforts to reassert her position in Germany, that she turned to Italy to seek her compensation there.

Racial divisions and jealousies, the great problem which confronts the Hapsburgs at the present day, had not yet become a pressing question in 1715. The provinces were too loosely connected, too little in touch with one another, to trouble much about their relations with each other. The connection between them had to become effective before it could be felt to be oppressive. The sense of nationality was dormant, or, at any rate, inarticulate and without influence. The Government was everywhere in the hands of the nobles, who were but little affected by racial sentiment, except perhaps in Hungary. The nationalist movement in Bohemia in the nineteenth century has been largely a popular movement, the outcome in a sense of the great upheaval of the French Revolution. In 1715 there was not the least indication of anything of the sort. Hungary, it is true, clung resolutely to all its privileges and constitutional rights, and in the fifty years that followed the reconquest of Hungary from Turkish rule, the Hapsburgs found their relations with their Magyar subjects a frequent source of trouble. Hungarian disloyalty was a source of weakness to Austria which Louis XIV knew well how to turn to his advantage: in 1703, when Villars and·Elector Maximilian of Bavaria threatened Vienna from the Upper Danube, Hungarian insurgents were in the field lower down the river, and not until January 1711 was the insurrection finally suppressed and the authority of the Hapsburgs completely re-established in Hungary and Transylvania. One of the principal causes of this disloyalty was the mistaken religious policy of Leopold I, whose bigotry had prevented him from utilising the opportunity afforded by the reconquest from the Turks. Had wiser counsels prevailed when, after a century and a half (1541–1686), Buda-Pesth was delivered from Turkish rule, it might have been possible to attach the Hungarians to the Hapsburg dynasty. Religious concessions were all that were needed, for the so-called "Nationalist" party formerly headed by Tököli had been discredited by its alliance with the Turks and the townsfolk were very hostile to the nobles. But the influence of the Jesuits carried the day, and a fierce persecution of the Protestants was set going which caused the Hungarians to identify the Hapsburg dynasty with Roman Catholic intolerance. Not till Joseph I abandoned this impolitic persecution and granted toleration to the Protestant religion was the insurrection brought to an end, or the foundations laid for that reconciliation of the Magyars to their rulers which Maria Theresa was afterwards to complete.[1]   Thus in 1715, Hungary was hardly a great source of strength to Austria, and the almost complete autonomy which the country possessed helped to keep them apart. The constitutional relations between Hungary and the Hapsburgs had been put on a definite footing in 1687, when, at a Diet held at Pressburg, the succession to the Hungarian monarchy had been declared hereditary in the Hapsburg family. The Emperor had on this occasion shown a praiseworthy moderation: he had not insisted on his rights as conqueror, but had only introduced one other important modification of the Constitution, the abolition of Clause 31 in the Bull of Andrew II, which had established the right of armed resistance to unconstitutional government, a privilege similar to that of "confederation," which was to prove so potent a factor in the ruin of Poland. These concessions paved the way for the work Maria Theresa was to do, but the recognition of Hungary as a quite independent kingdom established that "dualism" which the twentieth

[1] Cf. p. 182.

century finds as a force more powerful than ever, and which has served as an effective barrier against the amalgamation of Hungary with Austria.

Regarding the dominions of the Hapsburgs as a whole, one might fairly say that the dynasty was almost the only bond between the groups of provinces subject to it. The germs of a common administration existed at Vienna in the Conference,[1] in the Aulic Chamber (*Hofkammer*), which was occupied with financial and commercial questions, and the War Council; but the existence of this machinery was hardly enough by itself to balance the all but complete autonomy of the provinces. Thus the War Council's task of organising an efficient standing army was made all but impossible by the excessive powers of the local authorities, each province having a separate budget and negotiating separately with the central authority as to its contribution towards the common defence. Bohemia had actually its own Chancery, which was at once judicial and administrative, being the supreme court of justice for Bohemia and its dependencies, and also the channel of communication between the local officials at Prague and the Emperor. The great need of the Hapsburg dominions was centralisation, and in dealing with the Austrian and Bohemian groups of territory, steady progress had been made by Ferdinand III and his sons. Joseph I was doing much when his sudden death deprived Austria of the ruler who seemed about to restore the authority of the Emperor and to weld together his disunited provinces. The change from local autonomy to centralised despotism was no doubt bitterly opposed by those who found themselves deprived of their cherished privileges, but in clipping the wings of the local Estates and wresting from the local nobles who filled those bodies their exclusive control over administrative and financial affairs, the Hapsburgs were following a policy which had every justification. The feudal aristocracies who controlled the provincial Estates administered local affairs with little regard either to the welfare of the whole state of which they formed a part, or to the interests of the mass of the population of the individual provinces. The general weal was sacrificed to a narrow particularism, the peasantry and burghers in each province were sacrificed to the selfish interests of the nobles.

[1] The Council of State had been reorganised under this name in 1709.

Provinces so disunited, feudal oligarchies so incapable of taking any but the narrowest local view, or of considering the interests of any class but their own, needed to be disciplined by the strong hand of a despotic government. Before patriotism could replace localism and selfishness the provinces must be knit together by a common administration.

Next to the Hapsburg dominions, the territories of the Electors deserve notice. The three ecclesiastical members of the College, the Archbishops of Cologne, Mayence and Treves, form a class apart. In the domestic affairs of the Empire these three tended, as Catholics, to take the side of Austria, except that the traditional connection of the see of Mayence with the office of Arch Chancellor, and consequently with the duty of presiding in the College of Electors, usually disposed its occupant to place himself at the head of that party which may be described as that of the "*Reich*,"[1] and which was usually opposed to the Hapsburgs. Thus Mayence is often found opposing the Hapsburgs, and making special efforts to thwart any measures with a centralising tendency lest constitutional liberties should be infringed. Yet it might have been expected that the exposed position of these ecclesiastical Electorates would have made their holders support any reforms which tended to bind Germany together and to make the Empire less defenceless against its aggressive Western neighbour. Mayence, it is true, had but little territory West of the Rhine, for the bulk of her lands lay in the valley of the Lower Main, the chief outlying districts being Erfurt and the Eichsfeld in Thuringia. Cologne, too, held the duchy of Westphalia in addition to the long strip along the left bank of the Rhine from Andernach to Rheinberg, but the Electorate of Treves lay almost wholly in the Moselle valley and was much exposed to France. The accident that the territory along the frontier between France and Germany was not only much split up but was also for the most part in the hands of ecclesiastical rulers, had contributed in no small

---

[1] The distinction between the body of the *Reich* and its head the *Kaiser* is one for which there is no satisfactory English equivalent. To translate *Reichs* by "Imperial" almost involves translating *Kaiserlich* by "Austrian," which somewhat unduly exaggerates the reputed indifference of the Hapsburgs to the *Reich*; but if one makes "Imperial" the equivalent to *Kaiserlich*, one is left without a word for *Reichs*: "national" would be misleading, "of the Empire" is a rather clumsy and not very clear way out of the difficulty.

degree to the weakness and disunion of Germany, and to make
her a ready prey to Bourbon aggression. Had Cologne or
Mayence been the seat of a hereditary Electorate in the hands
of an able and ambitious house like the Hohenzollern, the
history of the " Left Bank " would be very different reading.
But ecclesiastical rulers, if on the whole their territories were
not ill-governed, had not the urgent spur of the desire to found
an abiding dynasty as an incentive to the energetic development of their dominions or to the promotion of the welfare
of their subjects. Oppression by an ecclesiastical ruler was
infrequent, energetic government rather rarer, reforms and
progress almost unknown. Of the occupants of the ecclesiastical Electorates in 1715, Lothair Francis of Schönborn had
been Elector of Mayence since 1693, and had distinguished
himself by his patriotic conduct during the war of the Spanish
Succession. Realising that the Hapsburgs alone could afford
to maintain the institutions of the Empire, which he described
" as a handsome but portionless bride whose support involves
very heavy expenditure," he was, in defiance of the traditions
of his see, a firm adherent of the Hapsburg family, and had
played no small part in securing the election of Charles VI in
1711. As ruler of Mayence, he not only protected the city
with elaborate fortifications, but devoted himself to its interests,
and did much for its improvement and embellishment. His
colleague at Treves, Charles of Lorraine, had only just been
restored to his metropolitan city, which the French had
evacuated on the conclusion of the peace. Before the year
was out (Dec.) his sudden death at Vienna brought to a close
his brief four years' tenure of his see, his successor being a
member of the Neuburg branch of the Wittelsbach family,
Francis Louis, who had been Bishop of Worms since 1694.
The Elector of Cologne, Joseph Clement of Bavaria, had also
just regained his Electoral dominions with the Peace of Baden.
Though it had been his election to the see of Cologne which
had been the nominal *casus belli* between Louis XIV and the
Emperor in 1688, Joseph Clement had followed his brother,
Maximilian Emmanuel, into the French camp in the Spanish
Succession War, with the result that he had been driven from
his Electorate, forced to take refuge in France, and had finally
been put to the ban of the Empire in 1706. His reinstate-
ment had been one of the concessions which England's

desertion of the Coalition had enabled Louis XIV to exact; but it was not accomplished without some friction, for the Dutch, who were in possession of some of the fortresses of the Electorate, refused to quit Bonn unless the fortifications were destroyed, and finally had to be expelled by force. The incident, however, did not in the end prove serious, as an agreement was reached in August 1717 and the fortifications were duly destroyed, the same being done at Liège, of which, as well as of Hildesheim, Joseph Clement was the Bishop. In this plurality he was merely continuing a custom almost as traditional as that by which the Bavarian Wittelsbachs had supplied Cologne with an unbroken series of Archbishops ever since the election of Ernest of Bavaria to the see in 1583.

Among the lay Electorates, Bohemia was in the hands of the Hapsburgs, and the King of Bohemia had become so completely merged in the Emperor that it was a question whether the validity of the Bohemian vote were to be any longer admitted. Saxony was held by the house of Wettin, Brandenburg by that of Hohenzollern, the ambitions of the Guelphs had recently been gratified by the creation for them of a ninth Electorate, that of Hanover, while the Wittelsbach family supplied two Electors, separate branches of the house ruling Bavaria and the Palatinate respectively. Frederick Augustus of Saxony was one of the three Electors who, in addition to their territories within the Empire, were rulers of kingdoms outside its boundaries. The connection of Saxony with Poland was certainly one which had brought no benefits to the Electorate, whatever its influence on the distressful partner with which Saxony had been linked since July 1696. It had deprived the Empire of the assistance of Saxony in the great war against Louis XIV. It had involved the Electorate in the wars which had troubled the Baltic ever since Charles XII of Sweden had opened his chequered career by his attack on Denmark in 1700. It had brought the victorious armies of the Swedish king to Alt Ranstadt, and had seemed at one time likely to prove a link between the Western and the Eastern wars. Indeed, in 1715 Saxon troops were actively engaged in the expulsion of the Swedes from German soil, an enterprise in which Saxony's own interests were but remotely concerned. Moreover, in order that no impediment should be offered to his election to the

Polish throne by his Protestantism—which, it must be admitted, sat but lightly upon him—Frederick Augustus had " received instruction " and had been admitted into the Roman Catholic Church, by which means the Roman Catholic majority in the College of Electors was still further increased. Yet it is not out of keeping with the other anomalies of the Germanic Constitution that despite this conversion the Wettin family retained the nominal leadership of German Protestantism traditional in their line. It was not thought necessary to transfer to another dynasty the headship of the *Corpus Evangelicorum*, the organised union of the German Protestants which had been officially recognised at the Peace of Westphalia. Prussia and Hanover both laid claim to it when in 1717 the Crown Prince of Saxony married the eldest daughter of the late Emperor, Joseph I, and became a Roman Catholic, but no change was made: religious differences were no longer the potent factor in German politics they had once been and the headship of the German Protestants carried with it no real political advantages. But it is not to this that the comparative unimportance of Saxony after 1715 is to be mainly attributed. The Electorate, though fairly populous and including some of the richest districts of Germany, suffered much through the accidental connection with a foreign country to which no ties of interest, sentiment, race, or religion bound it. Moreover, it was involved in further troubles by its geographical position between the two powers whose conflict is the chief feature of German history in the eighteenth century, while its rulers during the period were men of little ability or importance. Frederick Augustus I did, indeed, achieve a European reputation by his unparalleled profligacy, but he was an indifferent soldier and an incompetent ruler, and his son and successor, Frederick Augustus II, cuts but a sorry figure in the Austro-Prussian conflict. It was also unfortunate for Saxony that John George II (*ob.* 1656) had done for the Albertine branch of the Wettin family what had been done for the Ernestine line a hundred years earlier on the death of John Frederick II (1554). By partitioning his territories in order to establish separate cadet branches at Merseburg, Weissenfels and Zeitz [1] for his younger sons Christian, Augustus and Maurice, John George weakened the resources at the disposal of the main

[1] Extinct respectively in 1738, 1725 and 1746.

branch of the Wettin family. This process had been begun with the partition of 1485 between the Albertine and Ernestine branches, from which one may date the decline of the Wettin family, or, at any rate, the disappearance of the chance of making Saxony a compact and powerful state, able to exercise a controlling influence over the fortunes of Central Germany, but the will of John George carried it another stage forward.

Unlike the Wettin family, the Hohenzollern were destined to play a far more important part in Germany after 1715 than had hitherto fallen to their lot. The reign (1640–1688) of the so-called " Great Elector," Frederick William, marks the beginning of the advance of Brandenburg. Not only did the territorial acquisitions which he made at the Peace of Westphalia increase considerably the resources at his disposal, but they helped to connect the central mass of his dominions with his outlying possessions on the Rhine and beyond the Vistula. But far more important were the reforms which he introduced into the constitutional and administrative economy of his dominions. Though "unable to introduce complete uniformity of system and practice into the affairs of his several dominions," Frederick William did "impose the principle of his own supremacy on every official, and made it felt as a positive force throughout the whole frame of local polity."[1] The credit of having laid the foundations on which the power of Brandenburg-Prussia has been built up is clearly his. The reorganisation of the army on a professional basis, the arrangement by which the sums devoted to its upkeep were separated from the rest of the revenue and placed under the Minister of War, the subjection of the local Estates to the power of the Elector, the overthrow of the constitutional liberties and privileges which impaired his absolute authority, the encouragement by the State of all measures by which the material resources and prosperity of the country might be fostered and increased, are all to be found in the days of Frederick William. Personal control, rigid economy and the unsparing exaction of efficiency from officers and civil officials, were the leading features of his system of government ; and though perhaps his work lacked the completeness and finish which his grandson, King Frederick William I, was to impart

[1] Tuttle, i. 224.

to it, it was well done, and did not fall to pieces when his guiding hand was removed.

In foreign policy also the "Great Elector" sketched the outlines of the policy which subsequent Hohenzollern rulers were to develope and complete. Of the patriotism and pan-Germanic ideals with which it has pleased some modern writers to credit him, it is hard to detect any traces among the shifts, the inconsistencies and the desertions which constitute his foreign policy: to him the aggrandisement at home and abroad of the House of Hohenzollern was the one and only end, and that end he pursued with an unflinching persistence and no small degree of success. Territorial acquisitions were what he above all desired, and he attained the great success of freeing East Prussia alike from Swedish and from Polish suzerainty. The Archbishopric of Magdeburg fell to him by reversion under the terms of the Peace of Westphalia (1680), he received Schwiebus in 1686 in return for the renunciation of a claim on Liegnitz, and 1666 saw a final division of the disputed Cleves-Jülich heritage. But despite the success of Fehrbellin (1675), Sweden still retained Western Pomerania and held the mouth of the Oder, and no territorial gain resulted from the policy of vassalage to France on which Frederick William embarked in 1679 after he had felt the weight of Louis XIV's hand in the Peace of St. Germain-en-Laye. His heir, Frederick III as Elector and I as King, has perhaps had less than justice done him by those who have done more than justice to the father. Less selfish and aggressive if less capable and energetic, he displayed a loyalty to the House of Hapsburg as head of the Empire which is in striking contrast to the shifting and tortuous policy of his predecessor. In the resistance of Germany to Louis XIV, the part played by Frederick I was certainly more consistent, more honourable, and, on the whole, more effective than that of the Great Elector. In domestic affairs he lacked his father's power of organising, his unsparing energy and his talent for rigid economy, but he did carry on the work which had been begun, and it would be foolish to dismiss as valueless that acquisition of the Prussian Crown with which his name will always be mainly associated. Personal vanity and pride, a love of titles and pomp, may have played their part in the acquisition, but it was an achievement of solid importance, which not only gave Frederick a better position in international affairs, but by enhancing the prestige and authority of the sovereign was of great use in assisting the consolidation of his scattered dominions. "The Crown" was no mere fad or whim, it was the logical conclusion to the "Great Elector's" work. Though based on Prussia, the Kingship extended over all the possessions of the Hohenzollern, and Frederick was "King in Prussia" not in Königsberg only, but in Cleves, in Minden and in Berlin.

One of the conditions upon which Austria had consented to recognise the new title was that Prussia should support the Emperor in his pretensions to the Spanish inheritance, and Prussian troops consequently played a prominent part in the campaigns of Marlborough and Eugene. Prussian contingents were to the fore at Blenheim, at Turin, at Oudenarde and at Malplaquet; but it has been well said that "Prussia had a policy but no army in the North, she had an army but no policy in the West." Her poverty compelled her to hire out to the Maritime Powers the troops she could not herself afford to support, and this it is which explains why at the Peace of Utrecht, Prussia's gains were insignificant. Guelders, on which the Prussian monarch possessed a claim in virtue of his position as Duke of Cleves, was handed over to him, and the Powers recognised Prussia's right to those portions of the Orange inheritance which had come into Frederick's possession since the death of his cousin William III. Mors and Lingen he had held since 1702, Neuchatel since 1707. But by the time the Peace was signed (April 11th, 1713) the first "King in Prussia" was no more, and his place had been taken by his son Frederick William I (Feb. 25th, 1713).

Some account has already been given[1] of the process by which the Wittelsbach family, which had begun the Thirty Years' War with one Electorate in the family, ended it with two. Of the two, the Bavarian line was incontestably the more important. Maximilian I, whose reign of fifty-three years (1598–1651) may not unfairly be described as the period in which the foundations of the modern kingdom of Bavaria were well and truly laid, not merely had won for Bavaria the coveted Electoral dignity and the rich lands of the Upper Palatinate, but he had been one of the first of the rulers of

[1] P. 18.

the minor states of Germany to establish his autocracy at the
expense of his Estates.   The Princes wanted to be absolute
in their dominions as well as independent of Imperial control,
for where lay the benefit of being free from external interference if they were to be hampered by constitutional
opposition at home?   Everywhere there were contests over
taxation between aggressive Princes and recalcitrant Estates,
and nearly everywhere it was not the Princes who had to
give way.   This was partly because the Estates were not, as a
rule, really representative and had no force behind them.   The
peasantry, unrepresented and inarticulate, accustomed to be
oppressed and to obey, heavily taxed and in a miserable
condition, were of no political importance; the towns had
been hit too hard by the wars and the complete disorganisation
of trade and industry to have any influence, and the nobles
alone were unable to prevent the establishment of more or less
absolute autocracies.   In this work Maximilian I had been
extremely successful; he had stamped out Protestantism in
his dominions, he had suppressed the opposition of the Estates,
and by his services to the Catholic cause in the early stages
of the Thirty Years' War he had made himself the leader
of the non-Austrian Catholics.   It was their position as the
only Catholic Princes capable of contesting the quasi-hereditary
claim of the Hapsburgs to the Empire that gave the Bavarian
house their special importance in international affairs, and
caused them to be looked upon with favour by the power
whose policy towards Germany was based on the maxim
Divide et impera.   The relations between France and Bavaria
were of slow growth: Ferdinand Maria (1651–1679) had
gone to the length of promising to support the candidature
of Louis for the Empire (1670), but Maximilian Emmanuel
(1679–1726) had at first rejected all the overtures of France,
had been an energetic member of the League of Augsburg, and
had only at length listened to the offers of Louis when the
death (1698) of his son, the Electoral Prince, had taken away
Bavaria's chief motive for alliance with Austria, the prospect
of Austrian support for the Electoral Prince's claims on Spain.
And there was always a reason for the Bavarian Wittelsbachs
to look with some suspicion on Austria; for, if the Hapsburgs
should ever succeed in obtaining a dominant position in
Germany, it would not be long before they would discover

adequate reasons for the incorporation in their own dominions of those Wittelsbach lands which intervened so inconveniently between Upper Austria and the Burgau.   Hence the alliance between Maximilian Emmanuel and Louis, and the chequered career of Bavaria in the Spanish Succession War, which afforded not less striking proofs of the advantages to France of possessing a client so favourably situated for forwarding her designs on Austria than of the utility to Bavaria of French protection against Hapsburg land-hunger.   It was to the good offices of France that Maximilian Emmanuel owed his restoration [1] to his hereditary dominions; and though the differences which kept France and Spain apart for the decade following the Peace of Utrecht tended to force Franco-Austrian hostility into the background for a time, the old policy was resumed by France when the Empire fell vacant in 1740.

The other branch of the Wittelsbach family was represented in 1715 by John William of Neuburg, the brother-in-law of the Emperor Leopold I and a constant adherent of the Hapsburgs.   He was the second of his line to rule in the Palatinate which had passed to his father, Philip William, in 1685 on the death of Charles, the last of the Simmern branch.   This branch had not long survived its restoration to the Electorate; [2] and though Charles Lewis (1648–1680), the eldest son of the "Winter King" by Elizabeth, daughter of James I, had done a good deal to restore prosperity to his diminished dominions, rebuilding the devastated Mannheim, refounding the University of Heidelberg, remitting taxation and giving all possible encouragement to commerce and agriculture, the celebrated devastation of the Palatinate by the French in 1674 and its repetition in 1689 had between them thrown back the work of restoration, besides contributing to embitter the relations between Germany and France.   The accession of the Neuburg line meant that another Electorate passed from Protestant into Roman Catholic hands, and Elector John William had been mainly instrumental in securing the inclusion in the Peace of Ryswick of the clause by which freedom of worship in the districts then restored by France was not to be allowed " where not expressly stated to the contrary." [3]

---

[1] It was not till 1717 that this restoration was finally completed.

[2] Cf. p. 18.

[3] This so-called "Ryswick clause" was used with effect against the Protestants

Moreover, despite the Compact of Schwabisch-Hall (May 1685), which had guaranteed freedom of worship to the Calvinist and Lutheran inhabitants of the Palatinate, Elector John William had inaugurated an era of rigorous persecution, which was only slightly mitigated by the intervention in 1705 of Frederick I of Prussia. In addition to the Lower Palatinate, the Neuburg line possessed the principality in the upper valley of the Danube from which they took their name, and the portion of the Cleves - Jülich inheritance which had fallen to their lot as representing one of the sisters of the last Duke of Cleves. This, as settled by the definite partition of 1666, included Jülich, Berg and Ravenstein, so that the rulers of the Palatinate possessed more territory in the Rhine valley than any other lay potentate. This exposed them to French hostility and may partly account for their loyal adherence to Austria; but the strained relations between the Neuburgs and their Bavarian cousins may also have tended to influence the attitude of the Palatinate in international affairs.

The balance of religions in the Electoral College, disturbed against the Protestants by the succession of the Neuburgs to the Palatinate and by the conversion of the Saxon Electors, had been to some extent redressed by the erection in 1692 of a new Electorate. The greater prominence of the Hohenzollern, and the misconceptions too often prevalent in England as to the true nature of the " beggarly Electorate " with which our country was so closely linked for over one hundred years, have contributed to somewhat obscure the real importance of the Brunswick family. Indeed, had it not been that the principle of indivisibility of territories was not adopted by the family till after the separation of the Dannenberg and Lüneburg lines (1569), and that the connection with Great Britain from time to time involved Hanover in quarrels with which she had little concern, it is hardly fanciful to imagine that Brandenburg might have found in Brunswick a rival quite capable of contesting with her the leading position among the North German states. But until just the end of the seventeenth century the lands of the Brunswick family were but little less divided than those of the Wittelsbachs or of the Ernestine Saxons, while partly

of some parts of Southern Germany in the early part of the eighteenth century. Cf. *Z.S.* ii. 134.

through this and partly through a premature disarmament the Brunswick Dukes had fared very badly at the Peace of 1648, when instead of sharing the Westphalian bishoprics with Brandenburg, they had had to content themselves with alternate nominations to Osnabrück.   However, by the year 1680 the various branches of the family had been reduced to four, the Dannenberg or "new Wolfenbüttel" line in the Duchy of Brunswick, the Lüneburg-Celle and Calenberg-Hanover branches of the "new Lüneburg" line, and the comparatively unimportant Dukes of Brunswick-Bevern, a cadet branch of the "new Wolfenbüttels." At this time George William of Lüneburg-Celle had only a daughter, the ill-fated Sophia Dorothea, while his brother Ernest Augustus of Calenberg-Hanover had only one son, George Lewis, afterwards George I of Great Britain.   A marriage between these two was therefore the natural method of giving effect to the principle of indivisibility adopted by the Lüneburg line in 1592, and in November 1682 the wedding took place, Ernest Augustus having been recognised two years previously by the Estates of Hanover as the destined successor of George William.   The will of Ernest Augustus, now "published by anticipation," laid down as the perpetual law of the family the principles of indivisibility and primogeniture. This arrangement was ratified by the Emperor in 1683 and duly came into force on the death (1705) of George William, undisturbed by the tragedy of the unlucky Sophia Dorothea (1694).[1]

But before this union of Lüneburg-Celle and Calenberg-Hanover, the dignity so ardently desired by the Guelphs as the consummation of their improved position had been acquired by Ernest Augustus.   In the necessities of the Emperor the Guelphs found a lever by which to lift themselves into the Electoral College.   Austria, occupied simultaneously with the recovery of Hungary from the Turks and the defence of Western Germany against Louis XIV, was in sore need of the considerable military force of which they could dispose; and when, in 1692, Leopold found that the Duke of Hanover

---

[1] In 1689 the Saxe-Lauenberg line, ruling the duchy of that name on the right bank of the Elbe above Hamburg, had become extinct; and, despite the opposition of several other claimants, among them John George III of Saxony, the Guelphs managed to secure possession of this valuable district, their right to which received Imperial recognition in 1716. Cf. Z.S. ii. 107.

was discussing with Sweden, with the Bishop of Münster, and with the malcontent Elector of Saxony[1] the formation of a "third party" within the Empire for the purpose of forcing the Emperor to come to terms with France, he had to give way. In March 1692 was signed the "Electoral Compact," by which the Emperor conferred the Electoral dignity on Ernest Augustus and his sons in return for considerable military assistance both on the Rhine and on the Danube.

The promotion of Ernest Augustus was received not with acclamations but with a chorus of protests, from the Electors jealous at the admission of an upstart into their ranks, from the Princes furious with the lost leader who had deserted them to gain the very privileges he had been foremost in attacking. However, by October 1692, Bavaria, Brandenburg, Mayence and Saxony had recognised the promotion, and most of the other states of Germany followed suit before very long. At the Congress of Ryswick the European Powers recognised Ernest Augustus as an Elector, and at length, in 1708, three years after the union of Celle and Hanover and ten years after the death of Ernest Augustus (1698), his son George obtained formal admission into the Electoral College. In 1714 he succeeded his cousin Anne as King of England, and from henceforward the fortunes of Hanover were destined to be affected by events on the Ganges and Mississippi, and by commercial quarrels in East and West Indies. To England also the connection was a doubtful advantage, though in many respects the Electorate compared less unfavourably with its ruler's new dominions than is usually assumed. If its population was only a little over a half a million as against the six millions of England and Wales, and its revenue only £300,000 as against £6,000,000, the Hanoverian army was but little smaller than the joint establishment of 31,000 men maintained in Great Britain, Ireland and the "plantations." Compared with the territories of their German neighbours, those of the Guelphs were fairly extensive, amounting to about 8500 square miles; but they were neither very populous nor very rich. Moorlands and sandy wastes formed a very large portion of the Electorate, which contained very few towns of any size, and was mainly agricultural, except for a few mining villages. Economically and socially alike the country was somewhat backward, its laws

[1] John George IV, *o.s.p.* 1694.

and system of government being mainly mediæval, local Estates retained enough vitality to prevent centralisation without being themselves efficient or energetic, while the peasantry were in a state of feudal subjugation and were extremely ignorant.

Outside the Electoral College the thirty-three ecclesiastical members of the College of Princes merit some attention. One of the Archbishoprics, Magdeburg, had passed into the possession of Brandenburg in 1680; the only other one, Salzburg, though nearly a fifth larger in area than any of the three Electorates,[1] consisted mainly of wild and unproductive mountainous country, and except in the river valleys its population was scanty.[2] Except that its holder presided in the College of Princes alternately with Austria one hears little of it. Of the Bishoprics, Trent (1650 square miles, 147,000 inhabitants) was chiefly important from its position between Austria and Italy; Bamberg (1400 and 180,000) and Würzburg (2100 and 250,000), which were situated in the fertile valley of the Main, were richer and more populous than the average; Liège (2300 and 220,000), also wealthy and populous, was still part of the Empire, and was generally held in common with Cologne, as was sometimes Münster also. This, the largest and most populous of all the ecclesiastical Principalities of Germany, its area being 4800 square miles and its population 380,000 persons, is less prominent in the eighteenth century than it had been in the last half of the previous century when ruled by that most unepiscopal but energetic prelate, Christopher Bernard von Galen, diplomatist, politician and warrior rather than ecclesiastic. Of the secularised Bishoprics of North Germany, Osnabrück (1200 square miles and 136,000 people), the largest of those so treated, was not wholly lost to the Roman Catholics, as it had been arranged at the Peace of Westphalia that it should be alternately in the hands of a Roman Catholic and of a Protestant "Administrator." For the rest, the College of Princes included the Grand Masters of the Teutonic Order and of the Knights of Malta, the Bishops of Augsburg, Basle, Brixen, Chur,

---

[1] It was over 3700 square miles, Cologne being 3100, Mayence and Treves both under 2700.

[2] The figures given in Z.S. (ii. 181) are Mayence 330,000 inhabitants, Treves 270,000, Cologne 240,000, Salzburg 190,000.

Constance, Eichstadt, Freisingen, Fulda, Passau, Ratisbon, Spires and Worms, and several Abbots.

Now that the Guelphs had attained to Electoral rank, the chief lay member of the College of Princes was perhaps the Duke of Würtemberg. This South German Protestant state is in some ways the most interesting of all the minor Principalities, since it possessed what most of its fellows lacked, a written constitution, established in 1514 when Duke Ulrich had concluded with his subjects the Treaty of Tübingen. In character it was somewhat democratic, for in Würtemberg there was hardly any aristocracy, most of the local nobles of Swabia being Imperial Knights, consequently the burgher element in the Estates was unusually powerful. The Estates owed their escape from suppression to the fact that the constitution gave them the power of the purse, and this they had managed to retain, so that the Duke found his authority much restricted by that of the Standing Committee of the Estates, and thus Würtemberg was a notable exception to the general rule of the establishment of princely absolutism on the ruins of local autonomy. Eberhard III (1623–1674) had lost his dominions in the Thirty Years' War but had regained them in 1648, when the little Principality of Montbeliard (Mömpelgard) passed to another branch of the family on the extinction of which (1723) it reverted to the senior line. Eberhard had made great and not unsuccessful efforts to heal the wounds which the ravages of the war had inflicted on his dominions, while the policy of supporting Austria which he had consistently followed was continued by his successors. In 1715, Würtemberg was under the rule of Duke Eberhard Louis (1677–1733), a man of considerable vigour and capacity, who had managed to obtain from the Estates the establishment of a small standing army, which enabled him to contest the authority of the Standing Committee and to be more tyrannical and extravagant than any of his predecessors. He had been able to do this because the Würtembergers had found that if the strict control the Standing Committee exercised over the Duke enabled his subjects to escape being sacrificed to the caprices of a ruling sovereign supported by military force, it also exposed them to injuries at the hands of their neighbours. *Das gute alte Recht* was no defence against the aggressions of Louis XIV, and Würtemberg suffered almost as heavily in the wars of

1688–1699 and 1702–1714 as in the Thirty Years' War itself. Hence the permanent army which the Duke was allowed to establish for the better defence of the 3500 square miles and the 660,000 inhabitants who owned his sway.

Between Würtemberg and the Rhine lay Baden, divided between the two branches of Baden-Baden and Baden-Durlach, ruled respectively in 1715 by Louis George (1707–1761), son and successor of that "Louis of Baden" who had played so prominent a part in the War of the Spanish Succession as the colleague of Marlborough and Eugene, and by Charles William of Durlach (1709–1738), chiefly noteworthy for having been, like his cousin, a warm supporter of Austria in the war of 1702–1714, but not over successful as a commander. Of the two, Baden-Baden was somewhat the larger, having an area of 770 square miles against 640 and 94,000 inhabitants against 73,000. Both branches of the family were Protestants, as were also the great majority of their subjects.

The territories of the House of Hesse resembled those of their Northern neighbours, the Guelphs, in being much sub-divided. The two main branches of the family sprang from the quadruple division which had followed the death of Landgrave Philip the Proud in 1567. Two of the lines then established had died out since then, Hesse-Rheinfels in 1583, Hesse-Marburg in 1604, the extinction of the last-named giving rise to a long contest for its territorities between the surviving branches, Hesse-Cassel and Hesse-Darmstadt. This had been decided at the Peace of Westphalia on the whole in favour of Hesse-Cassel, whose claims had been so warmly pressed by France and Sweden that the Emperor had been forced to cancel his original award in favour of his constant adherent Hesse-Darmstadt. Hesse-Cassel had also received the Abbey of Hersfeld and part of the County of Schaumburg, while its ruler, Landgrave William VI (1637–1677), had put a stop to all chance of further partitions by establishing the rule of primogeniture and indivisibility (1650). His son and successor, Landgrave Charles I, who was ruling Hesse-Cassel at the time of the Peace of Utrecht, merits certain attention as one of the first German Princes to turn his dominions into an establishment for the production and supply of mercenary troops. He had raised soldiers on a definitely and systemati-cally organised plan, which enabled him to dispose freely of a considerable force of excellent troops and thereby to earn large subsidies from Austria and the Maritime Powers, which subsidies, to his credit be it noted, he had spent on his country rather than on himself. One of the German Princes who profited by the expulsion of the Huguenots to welcome them to Cassel, to the great benefit of both sides to the bargain, Landgrave Charles had not adhered to the French alliance which had proved so useful to his family in 1648. Alarmed by the aggressions of Louis XIV, he had joined the so-called Magdeburg Concert of 1688 and had been one of the first German Princes to join the Grand Alliance, while Hessian troops had done excellent service under Marlborough and Eugene.

Considerably smaller and less populous than Hesse-Cassel it had 1750 square miles, mostly South of the Main, and 180,000 inhabitants as against an area of 2850 square miles and a population of 330,000—Hesse-Darmstadt followed a somewhat different policy. Like the Guelphs, it had been consistently Lutheran and consistently loyal to the Emperor; whereas Hesse-Cassel was strongly and aggressively Calvinist and, though loyal enough from 1688 to 1715, had at one time been closely allied with France and Sweden. Its ruler in 1715, Landgrave Ernest Louis (1678–1739), was no exception to the traditions of the family; the son of Louis VI, the founder of the University of Giessen, he had been a member of the Grand Alliance and had, like his cousin at Cassel, provided mercenaries for the Maritime Powers. Of the cadet branches of the House of Hesse those of Hesse-Rheinfels (new), Hesse-Rotenburg and Hesse-Eschwege sprang from Cassel; the Princes of Hesse-Homburg were an offshoot of the Darmstadt line dating from 1596.

But of all the families of Germany, perhaps the most subdivided was that of the Wittelsbachs; for in addition to the two Electors of that house, it possessed several members of the College of Princes, their territories lying for the most part in the Upper Rhenish and Bavarian Circles. Of these lines and of the Electoral branches the common ancestor was Stephen, third son of Robert III, Elector Palatine from 1398 to 1410. On Stephen's death in 1459 his dominions had been divided between his sons Frederick and Louis, ancestors respectively of the Simmern and Zweibrücken lines, the former of which had succeeded to the Electorate in 1559 and had held it till 1685.

A cadet branch of the Zweibrücken line had been established at Veldenz in 1514, and on the death of Wolfgang of Zweibrücken (1569) his lands were divided afresh, three lines being thus established, the Birkenfeld, the Neuburg and the Zweibrücken. Yet another branch was founded in 1614 when the lands of Philip William of Neuburg were divided between his sons Wolfgang William, who took Neuburg, and Augustus, who received Sulzbach.[1] In 1715 the Neuburg branch had succeeded to the Palatinate,[2] Sulzbach[3] was ruled by Theodore (1708–1732), Veldenz[4] had passed to the Elector Palatine on the death of Duke Leopold Louis in 1694, Birkenfeld[5] was under Christian II (1654–1717). Zweibrücken had been divided by John I (ob. 1604) between his three sons, but, of the three branches thus established, only the Kleeberg line survived in 1715. To this, therefore, the Zweibrücken lands belonged, it being represented by Charles XII of Sweden, the great-grandson of John Casimir of Kleeberg by Christina of Sweden, daughter of Charles IX. On his death in 1718 the Zweibrücken lands passed to a cousin, Gustavus Leopold, from whom they passed in turn to Christian III of Birkenfeld (1717–1735) in 1731. Thus the multiplication of the Wittelsbach branches was gradually tending to be somewhat simplified; but these infinitesimal subdivisions deprived the family of the political weight it might have enjoyed had all its lands been united under one ruler. But even then they were so much scattered that even a common ruler could hardly have given coherence and cohesion to little parcels of territory distributed about on the Lower Rhine (Jülich and Berg), the Moselle, and between the Danube and the Main.

No other family in South Germany is important enough to merit special mention; but as one passes Northward from the Bavarian and Swabian Circles to the Franconian and Upper Saxon, one meets at Anspach and Baireuth cadet branches of the Hohenzollern. These Margraviates had come into the hands of Elector Joachim Frederick in 1603, when the

---

[1] Neuburg and Sulzbach had belonged to the Landshut branch of the Bavarian Wittelsbachs which had become extinct in 1503, whereupon a struggle for their inheritance occurred between the Zweibrücken line and Duke Albert II of Münich: the matter was settled by a compromise, which left Neuburg and Sulzbach to the Zweibrücken.   [2] Cf. p. 44.

[3] In the Upper Palatinate, which it divided in half.

[4] On the Moselle just below Treves.   [5] Just to the East of Treves.

Culmbach line established in them by the *Dispositio Achillea* of Elector Albert Achilles (1473) had died out. Joachim Frederick had bestowed them on his younger brothers, whose descendants, William Frederick of Anspach (1702–1723, brother of Caroline, wife of George II of England) and George William of Baireuth (1712–1726), were ruling them in 1715. Their joint area amounted to about 2600 square miles and their population to over 360,000, rather above the average for the whole country, although no town of much size was included within their boundaries. The main importance of these Franconian Hohenzollerns lay in the fact that they provided their cousins at Brandenburg with a possible excuse for interfering in South Germany, and of obtaining a foothold South of the Main by the annexation of these Margraviates.

If the map of South-Western Germany may be described as a mosaic of petty states, that of Thuringia easily bears off the palm for bewildering intricacy of subdivision. What with the Princes of Reuss, of Schwarzburg, of the various branches of the Anhalt family, and the Counties of Mansfeld and Hohenstein, Thuringian geography would have been complicated enough, even if all the territories of the Ernestine Saxons had been united under one ruler. But the Ernestine Wettins surpassed even their Albertine cousins in the subdivision of their territories and in the number of their cadet branches; of these the most important were Saxe-Coburg, subdivided at the death of the famous Ernest the Pious (1605–1675) between his six sons, rulers respectively of Saxe-Gotha, Saxe-Coburg, Saxe-Hildburghausen, Saxe-Meinungen, Saxe-Saalfeld and Saxe-Eisenberg, and Saxe-Weimar, whose Dukes had been much more moderate in the creation of minor principalities, Saxe-Eisenach being the only offshoot enjoying a separate existence in 1715. Together the territories of the Ernestine Saxons amounted to nearly 2000 square miles, peopled by some 360,000 persons, the joint possessions of the Albertine line covering an area of 15,000 square miles and having a population of 1,700,000.

After the intricacies of Thuringia the affairs of Mecklenburg seem almost simple. A disputed succession to the territories of Gustavus of Mecklenburg-Güstrow, the last of the line (*ob.* 1695), had given rise to certain complications, but had been finally settled by the Treaty of Hamburg in 1701, which established the two lines of Mecklenburg-Schwerin, with which went Güstrow itself and the vote, and Mecklenburg-Strelitz, to which was given the secularised Bishopric of Ratzeburg. By one of the most remarkable provisions even in that country of constitutional anomalies and curiosities, when Mecklenburg had originally been divided between the Dukes of Schwerin and of Güstrow the Estates of the two divisions had remained united,[1] with the result that the Estates had been able to utilise the division for their own benefit and to defend their aristocratic privileges against their Dukes with no small success.[2] It might have been expected from the extensive seaboard which Mecklenburg possessed that she might have risen to influence and importance by means of commercial and maritime development, but the cession of Wismar to Sweden in 1648 and the admission of Sweden's claim to the tolls (*Licenten*) of the other ports of the country had spoilt this chance, and Mecklenburg remained a merely agrarian country, doomed to poverty and backwardness by the unfruitful character of her sandy soil, thinly populated, and of little weight in German affairs. In 1715 the 300,000 inhabitants of the 5000 square miles of Mecklenburg - Schwerin were ruled by Charles Leopold (1713–1747), soon to make himself important by the complications introduced into Baltic affairs by his attempt to establish a more autocratic administrative system in his dominions. Mecklenburg - Strelitz, not more than a fifth of the size or population of Schwerin, was under Adolphus Frederick II (1708–1749), a prince of no particular importance.

North-Westward of Mecklenburg lies a land whose story involves some of the very worst complications in all German history. To get a clear idea of the relations between Schleswig-Holstein, Denmark and the Holy Roman Empire, it is necessary to go back even beyond the extinction of the old line of the Kings of Denmark in 1448, when the Danish crown was offered to Adolphus VII of Schleswig-Holstein, a member of the Schauenburg family and a subject of the Emperor as Count of Holstein. The connection between Holstein, which admittedly formed part of the Holy

---

[1] Erdmannsdörffer, i. 73.

[2] The Estates were almost wholly composed of the local nobles, the peasantry being serfs, and the burghers devoid of any political power.

Roman Empire, and Schleswig, which no less certainly did not, had arisen through the cession of Schleswig to Count Gerhard of Holstein (1386) to be held as a fief of the Danish Crown. After various efforts by Denmark to recover immediate possession of Schleswig, it had been left in the hands of Adolphus of Schauenburg as a hereditary fief when Christopher of Bavaria had become King of Denmark (1439). When offered the Danish crown in 1448, Adolphus had declined it, but had suggested as a suitable choice his nephew, Christian of Oldenburg, who had then been offered the crown and had promptly accepted it. In 1459, Adolphus died childless, and Christian at once laid claim to Holstein as well as to Schleswig, claiming both as the nearest male heir of his uncle and Schleswig also as King of Denmark, the overlord to whom the fief should revert on the extinction of its holders. The Estates of the two provinces thereupon chose him as their ruler, but on the express conditions that they should be free for the future to select any of his descendants as their ruler, and should not have to take the King of Denmark.

The next landmark in the history of the Duchies was the division of Schleswig-Holstein made by Christian III of Denmark (1534 – 1558) in 1544, when the Duchies [1] were shared between Christian III and his brothers. This ultimately established two separate branches of the House of Oldenburg, the Glückstadt or royal line, and the Gottorp or ducal. Unfortunately for all concerned the division was not geographically symmetrical, but the possessions of the two branches were irretrievably intermingled, so that the Glückstadt line not merely ruled the Kingdom of Denmark, but also held portions of the Duchies, in virtue of which the King of Denmark enjoyed a seat in the College of Princes. As was only natural the relations between the two branches were not, as a rule, of the most friendly, for it was the constant endeavour of the Gottorp line to throw off altogether the ill-defined suzerainty which Denmark continued to assert and to attempt to make more definite and complete. To further their end the Dukes of Holstein-Gottorp are always to be found in alliance with Denmark's principal enemies, the Swedish Kings of the Vasa family, in whom they found willing protectors against

---

[1] Holstein had been erected into a Duchy in 1474, with a seat in the College of Princes.

Danish aggression. Thus in the Baltic wars of the seventeenth century this debatable land between Denmark and Germany was both the scene of hostilities and the prize of victory, and not till Sweden's day of greatness had come to an end at Pultowa and Friedrichshald [1] did Denmark achieve her principal object by the annexation of Schleswig (1721). Meanwhile the successful *coup d'état* of 1660 in Denmark had introduced a new complication by making that kingdom an absolute and hereditary monarchy with female succession, while in Schleswig-Holstein the Salic law still prevailed. In 1715 the Duke of Holstein-Gottorp was a minor, Charles Frederick, who had succeeded to the Duchies in 1703, his father Frederick IV having been killed when fighting for Charles XII at Klissow: the actual government of the Duchies was therefore in the hands of Christian Augustus of Holstein-Eutin, brother of the late Duke and head of the principal cadet branch of the family.

But in addition to the portions of Schleswig-Holstein which the Danish Kings had managed to keep, and which qualified them to rank as Princes of the Empire, they held other and larger territories in Northern Germany. The branch of the House of Oldenburg which had retained possession of the ancestral Duchy on the West of the Weser when Denmark came into the possession of the family, had become extinct in 1667, and Oldenburg, with its appanages of Delmenhorst and Jever, had passed to the King of Denmark, a connection being thus established which was to last over a hundred years. About half the size of Mecklenburg-Schwerin, Oldenburg was even more sparsely populated, having barely forty inhabitants to the square mile, and made practically no use of the possession of a seaboard to develop as a maritime state. Possibly its Danish rulers would not have cared to see the Duchy embarking on such a career, but it had no industries on which to base any attempt at commercial enterprise. Be that as it may, Danish rule, however, though mild and not oppressive, was never popular in Oldenburg and the termination of the connection was welcomed when it came by the inhabitants of the Duchy. [2]

Among his fellow-members of the College of Princes, the King of Denmark found his great rival in the Baltic, the King

[1] Cf. Chapter III.   [2] Cf. Chapter XVII.

of Sweden. In 1715 Sweden's hold on the possessions ceded
to her at the Peace of Westphalia was all but shaken off; the
Danes had occupied Bremen and Verden, Pomerania had been
overrun by the joint forces of Prussia, Saxony - Poland and
Hanover, and Stralsund was closely beset;[1] but technically
these portions of the Empire were Swedish still, and even after
the conclusion of that group of treaties of which the Peace of
Nystad is the most important, part of Western Pomerania
with Rügen and Wismar remained to the successors of
Charles XII, who must therefore be reckoned among the
Princes of Germany.

But while Sweden's constitutional relations with the
Empire were clear enough, the same can hardly be alleged
of the connection between the German *Reich* and the other
foreign power which had taken a leading part in the Thirty
Years' War. In 1648, France had received all the Imperial
rights over the three Bishoprics, Metz, Toul and Verdun, of
which she had been in actual possession since 1552, and also
over the Landgraviates of Upper and Lower Alsace, the
Sundgau and the town of Breisach, together with the provincial
prefecture (*Landvogtei*) over the ten Imperial cities of Alsace,
the so-called "Decapolis."   But while the three Bishoprics, the
Sundgau and Upper and Lower Alsace had been ceded in full
sovereignty, this had not been the case with the " Decapolis."
It would almost seem as if the uncertainty must have been
deliberate, that the clauses of the Treaty of Münster dealing
with the matter (Nos. 73, 74 and 87) were purposely worded
so vaguely that both parties could interpret them as they
wished.[2]   Moreover, Alsace, like other parts of the Empire,
was divided among many different rulers whose lands were
inextricably confused, the possessions of the Hapsburgs being
mixed up with territory belonging to the Bishoprics of Worms,
Spires, Strassburg and Basle, to temporal Princes like Zweibrücken, Baden and the Elector Palatine, to say no more of
Counts and Imperial Knights.   Formally these districts had
not been ceded to France.   Practically, however, they soon
came to be as good as French; for though the Princes of the
Empire who owned them were allowed to levy taxes from
them, to nominate officials to govern them and to collect
feudal dues and other items of revenue, they were not

[1] Cf. Chapter III.   [2] Cf. Erdmannsdörffer, i. pp. 39–47.

permitted to keep soldiers in these districts; any fortresses were occupied by French troops, only natives might be appointed to official posts, and the French taxed these districts just as they did those directly subject to the King of France. The towns of the Decapolis chose their own magistrates, and enjoyed local autonomy of a sort with exemption from some taxes; but a royal official was established in each of them to look after the interests of the King of France, and if the nominal connection with the Empire still existed, the events of Louis XIV's reign had left it hardly even a name.[1] The work of the *Chambres de Réunion* had been in part undone at Ryswick and Utrecht, but Strassburg, the prize of the most flagrant of all the "acts of power" committed by Louis, was not recovered for Germany.

Westward of Alsace lay yet another portion of the Empire which was rapidly ceasing to be German. Lorraine, long a debatable land between France and Germany, was in 1715 still in the hands of the descendants of Anthony the Good, the elder brother of the first Duke of Guise.[2] Situated as it was, Lorraine had inevitably been involved in the complicated relations of France, Spain and the malcontent French nobility. Seized by Richelieu in 1634, it had not been restored to its Duke, Charles III, till the Peace of the Pyrenees, and then France had reserved the right of free passage across the Duchy for her troops; and in subsequent wars Lorraine had been to all intents and purposes French. Leopold Joseph (1690–1729), its ruler in 1715, had regained the Duchy at the Peace of Ryswick, subject as before to the French right of passage, and during the Spanish Succession War a French garrison occupied Nancy, though the neutrality of the Duchy was on the whole maintained, and its Duke was thus able to apply himself energetically and with some success to the arduous task of restoring order and prosperity to his much harassed dominions.

Of the remaining members of the College of Princes but little need be said. Anthony Ulrich of Brunswick-Wolfen-büttel,[3] one of the few German Princes to join Louis XIV

---

[1] This information was derived from a course of lectures delivered by M. Rodolphe Reuss of the École des Hautes Études at Paris in 1898.

[2] Claude, *ob.* 1550.

[3] He had succeeded in adding the city of Brunswick to his dominions in 1671, and in 1679 acquired Thedinghausen from Sweden.

in 1702, when he had been promptly suppressed by the Hanoverian cousins he hated so bitterly, had died in 1714; his son and successor, Augustus William (1714–1731), was a man of little note. Anhalt, divided in 1603 between the Bernberg, Dessau, Kothen and Zerbst lines, and Aremberg had had *Virilstimmen* before 1648, but the Counts of Henneberg had been extinct since 1583, their lands had been partitioned between the various Saxon lines, Saxe - Weimar and the Electoral line giving the vote together. The vote formerly held by Savoy had lapsed through long disuse, that of Leuchtenberg had fallen to Bavaria, that of Saxe-Lauenberg to Hanover. But the College of Princes had from time to time been recruited by new creations, and seven new holders of *Virilstimmen* had appeared in 1653 and 1654, the Counts of Hohenzollern-Hechingen, Nassau-Dillenberg and Nassau-Hadamar, the Wildgrave of Salm, Barons Dietrichstein, Eggenberg and Lobkowitz, while subsequent additions had been the Counts of Auersberg (1664), East Friesland (1667), Fürstenberg (1667) and Schwarzenberg (1674).[1] Outside the ranks of these holders of individual votes were many other petty Princes, too numerous and too unimportant for individual mention, such as the Counts of Waldeck, Isenburg and Hohenlohe, who were only represented in the Diet through the *Curiatstimmen*.

Yet one numerous and important class requires description, the Imperial Knights, the rulers of the very pettiest states in all the mosaic of the infinite disunion of Germany. Lords of dominions which, as a rule, consisted of but a village or two, their position in the Empire approximated in some ways to the condition of subjects rather than of Princes. They had no footing in the Diet, not even a solitary *Curiatstimme* among the thousand members of their order. Indeed, in the greater part of the Empire, in Austria, in Bavaria and in North Germany, the lesser nobles, who roughly corresponded to the Knights in position and in the size of their holdings, had already been reduced to the footing of subjects. It was only in the Southern Circles in which there was no one predominant Prince that the Knights were numerous—in other words, that the lesser nobility had managed to become and remain sovereigns.

---

[1] These dates are those of the definite acquisition of the *Virilstimme*.

But they were sovereign only in that, holding immediately of the Emperor, they enjoyed rights of jurisdiction and taxation over their tenants, and were not subject to the Princes in whose territories their dominions were enclosed. If the majority of the petty states of Germany were much too small to be capable of developing that active political life which alone could justify their independent existence, much more was this the case with the Knights. Had the Princes been allowed to put a summary conclusion to the indefensible independence of this most anomalous class, it would have been a great boon to the unfortunate subjects of the Knights, and peace and order would have been much advanced. As it was, the territories of the Knights were as a rule Alsatias, to which robbers and broken men of every description commonly resorted. The robber Knights of the Middle Ages had disappeared, but things were still pretty bad, and no useful purpose was served by this independence. Indeed, it was most unfortunate that such a resident nobility, accustomed to local administration, a class which to some degree might have bridged the gap between Princes and subjects, should have been so completely ineffective for good. It was to the Emperor that the Knights owed their security against the Princes. To him they were of importance because the tax which they paid him, the *Charitätivsubsidien*, was one of the principal sources of his meagre income.[1] It was their affairs which provided the Imperial law courts with the bulk of their business, and the Knights were almost the only element in the Empire which, having no local or particularist interests, could be said to be members of the Empire, and to belong to it only. It might have been thought that on them and on the Cities the Emperor might have laid the foundations of a more national party by which to counteract the localism of the Princes; but the Knights were too weak and too scattered for united action, and in the eighteenth century the Hapsburgs had all but abandoned as hopeless the struggle against particularism. The Knights had, it is true, an organisation of their own, a Corpus composed of the "Knightly Circles" of Franconia,

---

[1] The Knights, being unrepresented in the Diet, always refused to pay the taxes voted by the Diet; nor did they contribute to the upkeep of the Imperial Chamber.

Swabia and the Rhine,[1] each of which was built up out of the "cantons" into which the Knights were divided; but for any practical political purpose this was of little value.

After this description of the political condition of Germany at the beginning of the eighteenth century, of the breakdown of the central institutions, of the want of union, of the utter absence of any national feeling, it will hardly be necessary to dwell at any great length on the social or the economic condition of the country. During the seventeenth century, Germany had been the theatre of more than one terrible and devastating conflict: for thirty years she had been the battle-ground of a war originally caused by bitter religious anta-gonisms and continued to satisfy the greed and ambition of foreign powers, a war waged mainly by mercenaries, soldiers of fortune whose main object was plunder and who were restrained neither by discipline nor by national sympathies from inflicting every variety of outrage and suffering on the wretched inhabitants of the countries they traversed. In the seventeenth century wars were not waged with kid gloves and neither commanders nor commanded were influenced for a moment by humanitarian scruples. And after thirty years of this there had come but a brief respite before the aggres-sions of Louis XIV had involved Germany in a new series of conflicts, which extended over forty-two years of which two-thirds were years of war. The double devastation of the unfortunate Palatinate and Marlborough's harrying of Bavaria were not calculated to heal the wounds left by the soldiers of Bernhard of Saxe-Weimar, of Tilly, of Pappenheim and of Condé. What wonder that Germany, which before the out-break of the Wars of Religion had been a rich and prosperous land, richer and more flourishing probably than any of its neighbours, had received injuries in these wars from which it is no exaggeration to say that it has taken her over two centuries to recover. From the Baltic to the Lake of Constance, from the Moselle to the Oder and the Moldau, the country had been fought over, plundered, ravaged and laid waste: in some places the population had fallen in 1649 to a tenth of what it had been in 1631, and there is probably no great exaggeration in the estimate which puts at a half the pro-portion of the population which perished in the savage and

[1] They stood quite outside the ordinary division into Circles.

devastating Thirty Years' War.[1] Since the Peace of West-phalia no doubt some progress had been made, but the wars of the second half of the seventeenth century, if less brutal and destructive than their predecessors, had retarded the recovery of Germany and greatly hampered the efforts of those of her rulers who had sought to encourage the revival of population and prosperity. In 1715 the country was in a much better condition than in 1648, but the recovery was a slow and chequered process.

The effect of all this on agriculture, on manufactures, on trade and commerce, can easily be understood. The Thirty Years' War had brought them all to a stand-still; and though, directly peace was concluded and order of a kind restored, agriculture had soon recovered some degree of its old prosperity, thanks to the magnificent natural qualities of the soil, the revival of trade and industry was a far slower process and the end of the century found Germany very backward. The skilled labourers had for the most part perished in the wars, or had betaken themselves to the far more lucrative and attractive callings of the soldier and the bandit. Mines and quarries had become unworkable through disuse. Means of communication had fallen into disrepair: bridges had been destroyed and not replaced. Moreover, the war had so disturbed the country that the little capital which was available for employment was but cautiously ventured. More settled political conditions must prevail before industry could revive, certainly before men could again take up the more difficult arts and crafts with any prospect of remunerative employment. And it had been when Germany, thus stricken by the Thirty Years' War, was just beginning to recover that there had come the great development of French industries and commerce under the fostering hand of Colbert. The scientific tariff which he erected against the Dutch did not spare Germany. England, too, was competing successfully with the Dutch for their carrying-trade and for a share in the commerce of the Baltic, so that in face of the strenuous rivalry of these great commercial powers there was little chance of a successful revival of the once mighty Hanseatic League. Moreover, the political subdivision of the country was a great barrier to its economic development. Different codes of law

[1] Cf. Z.S. i. pp. 41–45.

in different states, heavy taxation everywhere, internal tolls and taxes on commerce, a new customs-frontier every few miles, inefficient police arrangements, governmental and court establishments out of all proportion to the needs of the petty states, these were some of the many obstacles which the political complexity of Germany strewed in the path of industrial or economic progress.

Moreover, bad as were the political and economic conditions of the country, the state of moral and intellectual life was even worse. The horrors of the Thirty Years' War had produced a widespread demoralisation. Religious passions and animosities were temporarily exhausted but, as the next sixty years were too often to show, by no means extinct. Intolerance and persecution seemed the only means by which piety was displayed by the few rulers whom religious motives influenced in the least. Education had been thrown back centuries, schools were closed, the Universities flooded by the return of ex-students who had turned soldiers and now came back to an academical life for which their recent experiences had rendered them unfitted. The importation of the habits of the camp into the Universities was hardly calculated to make for intellectual progress, and the stagnation of German literature and thought during the greater part of the next century may be attributed in no small degree to the effects of the Thirty Years' War. Here and there some petty ruler, aping the *Grand Monarque*, might pose as a patron of the arts and letters, but usually it was in Paris or on French poets and painters that the taxes were spent which their lords and masters wrung from the miserable peasants of Germany. Yet even in this dead period a few great names are to be found, though not even Leibnitz can redeem the seventeenth century from the reproach which attaches to it in the intellectual history of Germany. The eighteenth century therefore opened with but faint hopes.

CHAPTER III

THE END OF THE NORTHERN WAR

NOT even when the conclusion of the Peace of Baden (Sept. 1714) finally closed the war which had arisen over the Spanish Succession was the whole of Germany at peace. The other great contest which had begun with the anti-Swedish coalition formed by Russia, Denmark and Saxony - Poland in 1699 had still several years to run. Charles XII, who had at one time threatened to interfere with decisive effect in the Western struggle, was no longer dominant in North-Eastern Europe. Within two years of the day when he set out Eastward from Alt Ranstadt his crushing defeat at Pultowa (June 26th, 1709) had sent him, a fugitive without an army, to seek the protection of the Turks, and marked the beginning of the end for Sweden's supremacy over the Baltic. The enemies Charles seemed to have crushed promptly had raised their heads again. Frederick Augustus of Saxony had denounced the Treaty of Alt Ranstadt directly he heard the news, and hastened to renew his alliance with Russia (Oct. 1709). Stanislaus Leczinski's tenure of the Polish throne had come to an abrupt conclusion, and the re-establishment of the Saxon dynasty at Warsaw had been effected without difficulty. Denmark, too, had repudiated the Treaty of Travendahl, unhindered by England and Holland, who were too well occupied elsewhere to be able to spare force to compel the Danes to respect their guarantee. Thus from all quarters the territories of the absent Swedish monarch had been attacked; the provinces East of the Baltic were assailed by overpowering forces of Russians backed up by the new fleet which Peter was creating; the Danes invaded Scania, and Sweden's one remaining field force, Krassau's, had to retire from Poland into Pomerania.

However, just as in the days of Charles' success the Western Powers had sought to prevent him from interfering

West of the Elbe, so after Pultowa it had been their object
to make certain that his overthrow should not lead to the
infringement of the neutrality of the Empire. Accordingly in
March 1710 the Emperor and the Maritime Powers had
signed a compact by which they agreed to guarantee the
neutrality of Sweden's German possessions if Krassau would
agree not to use them as a base for attacking Jutland or
Poland. Welcomed by the Swedish Senate though repudiated
by Charles, this " Neutrality Compact of the Hague " had on
the whole been observed, for Russia, intending to direct her
attacks on Finland and the Baltic provinces, was not disposed
to contest it ; and though Frederick I of Prussia would have been
glad to seize this chance of adding Pomerania to his dominions,
he could not afford to offend his Dutch and English pay-
masters. However, in August 1711, soon after the Peace of
July 1711 had extricated Peter from his critical position on
the Pruth, a force of 24,000 Russians, Poles and Saxons
crossed Prussian territory on their way to Stralsund and
Wismar, which they proceeded to besiege. Prussia's verbal
protests met with little attention, and as she had no idea of
embarking in the war on behalf of Sweden, she refrained from
enforcing her words by blows.

Thus the Baltic war had spread to Germany ; and though
Stralsund and Stettin successfully resisted their besiegers, a
Danish force invaded Bremen and forced that province to
swear allegiance to the King of Denmark (July to Sept. 1712),
though George Louis of Hanover anticipated them in getting
possession of Verden also by occupying it on the plea of
sanitary precautions against the plague. For a time, indeed,
matters went in favour of Sweden ; for Steenbock, landing in
Rügen with 10,000 men (Sept.), raised the siege of Stralsund
and then, taking the offensive against the Danes, won a
brilliant victory over them at Gadebusch (Dec.) and drove
them headlong into Holstein before their Russo-Saxon allies
could come to their help.[1] But his success was only temporary ;
pursuing his enemies into Holstein, he found himself surrounded
by vastly superior numbers, driven under the guns of the
neutral fortress of Tönningen and forced to capitulate (May

[1] The invaders of Scania had been defeated by Steenbock at Helsingborg
(Feb. 1710) and had evacuated the province, thus enabling Steenbock to cross
to Germany.

20th, 1713). Just before that, however, two important events had occurred. In February, Frederick I of Prussia had died, in April the Peace of Utrecht had been signed.

Neither the situation of his own kingdom nor that of Baltic affairs in general tempted Frederick William, the new "King in Prussia," to plunge at once into the Northern war. Anxious as he was to acquire the coveted Western Pomerania, it was difficult to see by what path the desired goal might be best reached. Prussia required a period of rest, time in which to restore order to the entangled finances, to prepare for an intervention which might easily prove disastrous if undertaken prematurely. Moreover, the relations of the Baltic Powers were in so complicated a condition that it was by no means clear what line of policy was best suited to the requirements of Prussia ; for little as the Hohenzollern liked the presence of Sweden at the mouth of the Oder, even Swedes were to be preferred to Russians or to Saxons.

The first opportunity of influencing the course of affairs which came to Frederick William was by means of a treaty with the Regent of Holstein-Gottorp. Christian Augustus of Holstein-Eutin, Administrator of the sequestrated see of Lübeck and guardian of the youthful Duke Charles Frederick, the heir presumptive of his childless uncle Charles XII of Sweden, was a person of no small importance ; and in his minister, Görtz, he had at his side an active, restless intriguer who hoped to suck no small advantage out of the position in which he found himself. Accordingly in June 1713 the Regent concluded a treaty with Frederick William by which Prussian and Holstein troops were to occupy Stettin, Wismar and the other Swedish possessions in order to secure their neutrality until the conclusion of peace, when they were to be restored to Sweden. Moreover, Prussia was to use her influence with Denmark to induce the Danes to evacuate Holstein-Gottorp and to agree to the succession of Charles Frederick to the Swedish throne. When he became King of Sweden, Charles Frederick was to hand over to Prussia Stettin and the Southern part of Swedish Pomerania. Thus Prussia hoped to obtain a hold on Swedish Pomerania which might prove exceedingly useful ; but the whole scheme broke down because General von Meyerfeldt, the Governor of Stettin, declined to accept it without the assent of Charles XII.

Unable to obtain Stettin by negotiation with Sweden, Prussia had to fall back on an agreement with Russia, whose troops proceeded to renew the siege of the town.   For some months it held out, but in September 1713 the garrison had to capitulate, receiving a free passage to Sweden, while the town was handed over to the Prussians by the Russian general Mentschikov, with whom Frederick William concluded the Convention of Schwedt (Oct. 6th, 1713).   This arranged for the occupation of Pomerania by the Prussians, who were to keep it neutral and prevent the Swedes using it as a base from which to attack the Allies.   This convention marked the point at which Prussia found herself forced to cultivate better relations with Russia, of whom she had hitherto been extremely jealous and suspicious : it was mainly due to the conclusion of the Peace of Utrecht, which set the Maritime Powers free to interfere in the Baltic, in which case it was to be feared they might seek to bring about peace on the basis of *uti possidetis* before Prussia had had time to make any acquisitions.   The next step in the Russo-Prussian alliance was a fresh convention, concluded in June 1714, by which Russia pledged herself to see Prussia secured in possession of Stettin and Pomerania to the Peene river, with the islands of Wollen and Usedom, Prussia undertaking a similar obligation towards Russia with regard to Carelia, Esthonia and Ingermannland.

But before this new alliance could lead to any definite result the situation was completely altered by the sudden reappearance of Charles XII, who arrived at Stralsund in November 1714 after an adventurous and circuitous journey from Turkey, while a few months earlier the death of Queen Anne had placed the British crown on the head of George Louis of Hanover and the British fleet at the disposal of the " Electoral " aims of the new King.   Hitherto England had been absolutely neutral in the Baltic struggle, though her commercial interests in those quarters caused her to watch events there with great care.   There had been a good deal of friction between England and Sweden over the capture by Swedish privateers of English merchantmen trading with Russia, and thereby infringing the " paper " blockade of the Russian coast which Sweden had declared.[1] England was therefore not merely serving an " Electoral "

---

[1] Cf. *England and Hanover* (A. W. Ward), p. 89.

policy when in 1715 she despatched a strong fleet to the Baltic. Indeed, but for the domestic complications of Anne's last few months, it is probable that ships would have been sent before the accession of George. The object upon which George I was most keenly set was the acquisition of Bremen and Verden, districts which would add enormously to the strength of his Hanoverian possessions. Jealousy of Russia and Prussia, however, made him disinclined to take part with them against Sweden, and he tried hard to persuade Charles to cede the coveted territory to him as the reward for Anglo-Hanoverian assistance against the Czar and the King of Prussia. But Charles with equal obstinacy and blindness refused this offer, which though certainly not dictated by generosity or by a wish to help Sweden, did hold out to him better prospects than he could hope to secure if he rejected it. This refusal drove George I into joining the Russo-Prussian alliance, to which Denmark also acceded. In June 1715 the forces of the Coalition began the attack on Sweden's last transmarine possessions; the Hanoverians and Danes laid siege to Wismar, a mixed army of Danes, Russians and Saxons accompanied by a Danish squadron undertook the reduction of Stralsund, freedom from interruption by sea being secured by the presence of Norris and the English fleet, which could be relied upon to exercise a restraining influence over the Swedish naval forces.

The undertaking was no mere military promenade. The Swedes resisted stoutly, and not till they had been driven from the island of Usedom (July 31st) could the siege-train be brought up along the coast from Stettin. On August 22nd they were driven from their lines at Peenemünde, on September 25th the Danish ships forced the passage into the Rügen Sound. Even then Stralsund held out, and it was found necessary to obtain complete possession of Rügen, a task successfully accomplished by Leopold of Anhalt-Dessau on November 15th and 16th. At last it became obvious even to Charles that further resistance was hopeless, and on December 21st he made his escape by sea; three days later Stralsund capitulated and received a Danish garrison. In April 1716 the fall of Wismar deprived Sweden of her last foothold in Germany.

Had the Allies been in anything approaching to union,

the end of the war could not have been long delayed, but their quarrels and cross-purposes gave Charles time to protract his resistance for some years yet.   Into the kaleidoscopic negotiations, schemes and intrigues of 1716–1718 it would be hopeless to enter: Görtz, Alberoni, the Scottish Jacobites, all conceivable alliances and arrangements fill the time.   One or two things, however, are clear.   Among the most important factors in the situation was the hostility of Hanover and Russia, which might even have brought about an alliance between Russia and Sweden when the death of the Swedish King, when attacking the Norwegian fortress of Frederickshald (Nov. 1718), ended his adventurous career and made the restoration of peace possible.   Charles XII, despite all his triumphs in the field, had done more harm to his own country than to his enemies.

This hostility between George I and Peter became acute over the affairs of Mecklenburg and Schleswig-Holstein. When George made the arrangement with Denmark by which he received Bremen (1715), he had assented to the annexation by Denmark of Schleswig, against which the Duke of Holstein-Gottorp protested, being supported in this by Peter, who now championed the cause of Duke Charles Frederick and gave him his daughter Anne in marriage in 1716. Secondly, the Russian corps which had passed through Mecklenburg in the spring of 1716 on its way to Zealand to take part in a proposed descent on Southern Sweden, had had some share in the capture of Wismar, and Peter had therefore laid claim to the port.   Much to his irritation his allies refused, not wishing to see him established so near the Elbe.   Now as his troops returned from Zealand in the autumn of 1716, the descent having been abandoned, they halted in Mecklenburg and took up their winter-quarters there.   In this way Peter was able to interfere in the constitutional quarrel then raging in Mecklenburg-Schwerin, where the Estates were resisting the efforts of their Duke, Charles Leopold, to alter the administrative system in the direction of absolutism.   The Duke seized the chance of securing Russian aid, married Catherine, daughter of Peter's brother Ivan, and confiscated the lands of the nobles who had appealed to the Emperor.   It was about this time that Peter was making overtures to France for an alliance in which Russia would have replaced Sweden as the Northern ally of the Bourbons.[1] England and France, however, were on the verge of concluding the alliance by which Stanhope and Dubois sought to maintain the situation established at Utrecht,[2] and Russia could obtain no more from France than a simple treaty of amity. Another result of the Anglo-French treaty was that Peter found it expedient to evacuate Mecklenburg, though some of his troops remained there in the service of Charles Leopold.[3]

In response to the appeal of the Mecklenburg Estates, an Imperial rescript committed the task of restoring the old constitution to Hanover and Brunswick-Wolfenbüttel, who in February 1719 poured 13,000 troops into the Duchy, and despite a check at Waldemühlen on the Sudo (March), occupied the territory and carried out the decree of the Empire, Charles Leopold being thus suppressed despite Peter's patronage.

The death of Charles XII had led to considerable changes in Sweden : the fall of Görtz was one of the earliest, for there was no party in favour of the Duke of Holstein-Gottorp. Ulrica Eleanora and her husband Frederick of Hesse-Cassel secured the throne without much difficulty, though the nobles succeeded in recovering much of the power of which they had been deprived by Charles XI. The new monarchs were not going to repeat Charles XII's folly in refusing any terms which involved the loss of territory. They soon came to terms with George I, and in November 1719 the Peace of Stockholm recognised him as possessor of Bremen and Verden in return for a sum of 1,000,000 Reichsthalers. George now exerted himself to secure good terms for Sweden from her other foes. By Carteret's mediation, Sweden recovered Stralsund, Rügen and Wismar from Denmark (July 1720), while Frederick William, though loath to make a peace in which Russia was not included, had already agreed to pay Sweden an indemnity of 2,000,000 dollars, but retained his conquests up to the Peene (Feb. 1720). With regard to Poland, Sweden had only to abandon her unfortunate protégé Leczinski, for whom she could do nothing.

George I had thus so far attained his ends that he had

---

[1] Cf. Martin, xiv. pp. 81 ff.
[2] Anglo-French alliance signed November 28th, 1716.
[3] Cf. *England and Hanover*, p. 96.

isolated Russia—the only Power still hostile to Sweden—
and England seemed on the high road to a war against
Russia on behalf of Sweden when the collapse of the South
Sea Company and the financial crisis which followed involved
the fall of the Stanhope-Sunderland section of the Whig
party. With the accession of Walpole and his followers to
office a new policy was introduced into the councils of
England; all idea of active intervention in the Baltic was
abandoned, and Sweden, left to her own resources, was not
able to get very favourable terms from Russia. The Peace
of Nystadt (Sept. 10th, 1721) marks the definite transfer
of supremacy in the Baltic from Sweden to Russia. With
the loss of Carelia, Esthonia, Ingermannland, Livonia and
the islands of Dago, Moen and Oesel, Sweden's day of
greatness came to an end, and Russia was firmly established
as the dominant power in the North-East of Europe.

The twenty years of war which this Peace brought to
an end afford in a way as striking an illustration of the
weakness of Germany as does the treatment which the
Empire received at Utrecht and Rastatt. Fought out though
it was largely by German troops and on German soil, German
interests played but little part in the struggle and received
but little attention in the Peace. Prussia had, indeed, won
the important city of Stettin and had gained control of the
mouth of the Oder; the German districts of Bremen and
Verden had passed from Sweden to one who was himself
a German, even if he owed his acquisition in no small
measure to non - German sources of strength, while the
definite cession of Schleswig to Denmark (1721) was not
without importance for the future. But the main result of
the war was that though the Baltic had changed masters it
was still under non-German control.

[Authorities for this chapter, besides Erdmannsdörffer and Zweidineck Südenhorst,
articles in *E.H.R.* on "The Foreign Policy of England under Walpole," 1900 and
1901 f. ; Ward, *England and Hanover*; Nisbet Bain, *Charles XII.*]

CHAPTER IV

PASSAROWITZ, SICILY AND THE PRAGMATIC SANCTION

A USTRIA had barely got rid of the great struggle for the Spanish inheritance when she found herself called upon to embark upon a new war against her hereditary foe in the South-East. Their success over the Russians in 1711 had much encouraged the Turks in their desire to retrieve the losses of Carlowitz, and they saw in the defenceless state of the Morea an opportunity for further gain. Both the Sultan Achmet and the new Grand Vizier, Damad Ali Pasha, were ambitious and aggressive, and they believed that the Venetian territories would prove an easy prey, and that the international situation would restrain the Great Powers from coming to the help of the Republic. They were both right and wrong. Right inasmuch as the Venetian hold on the Morea proved of the feeblest. Unprepared and unpopular, the Venetian garrisons were speedily swept out of the Peninsula, Cerigo followed suit, the Ionian Islands were in the gravest peril: only from Dalmatia were the Turks repulsed. Wrong because despite the critical condition of affairs in the North and despite the fear of possible complications in Italy—for Philip of Spain had never acquiesced in the arrangements of Utrecht, and would probably seize upon any embarrassment of Austria to interfere—the Emperor at the advice of Eugene decided to aid Venice.[1]

The first necessity was to send succour to Corfu, a point of great strategic importance, as its capture would enable the Turks to threaten Southern Italy and Sicily and would give their fleet a splendid base from which to operate in the Adriatic. Accordingly, by Eugene's advice an officer of great experience

---

[1] In April 1716 the Austro-Venetian treaty of 1684 was renewed, Venice promising her aid in case of a Spanish attack on the Italian possessions of Austria.

and capacity, John Matthias von Schulenburg, was sent to take command at Corfu (Dec. 1715), and his exertions were largely responsible for the fact that when the Turkish fleet threw 30,000 men into the island in July 1716, its defences and defenders were not found wanting.

Meanwhile Eugene, who was very anxious that the work which had been left unfinished at Carlowitz should be brought to completion, had been making great efforts to get ready an efficient army for the campaign on the Danube. As president of the War Council, Eugene was himself responsible for the readiness of the army; and though the chronic emptiness of the Treasury proved a serious hindrance to the mobilisation, he was able in July to collect 220 squadrons and 67 battalions, about 80,000 men in all, at Peterwardein. Meanwhile the Grand Vizier had assembled 200,000 men at Belgrade and advanced up the Danube. Eugene withdrew his men into the lines constructed at Peterwardein in the previous war by Caprara, and there gave battle (Aug. 5th). The fight was hotly contested; at one time the Austrian right became disordered owing to the difficulties of the ground, and the centre was also checked, but a dashing charge by Eugene and the heavy cavalry on the left restored the fortunes of the day and allowed the hard-pressed infantry to rally and recover their ground. Finally, after a most even struggle the Turks were overthrown with very heavy loss, the Grand Vizier being among the killed.

Eugene followed up his victory by laying siege to Temeswar, a strong and well-built fortress, which was so resolutely defended that there was time for a relieving army to be gathered together, though only to be beaten off on September 23rd. This sealed the fate of the town, which surrendered on October 13th after a bombardment, passing under Hapsburg rule after having been for a hundred and sixty-four years a Turkish possession. With it a large part of the Banat came into Austrian hands, including Pancsova and Mehadia. Another effect of the victory was that the besiegers of Corfu abandoned the attack on the hard-pressed fortress (Aug. 25th) on receiving the news of the battle, though no doubt the repulse of a grand assault they had delivered two days before contributed to induce them to retire.

With the Banat theirs, the next task for the Austrian

forces was to recover Belgrade, which they had lost in
1690 after a brief tenure. Early in June 1717 all was
ready for an advance. On the 14th, two corps from Peterwardein and from the Banat, including contingents from
Bavaria and Hesse-Darmstadt, united at Pancsova. Next
day the vanguard crossed the Danube by boats and constructed
bridges by which the main body crossed on the 19th
Belgrade was at once invested, but bad weather delayed the
siege operations, and it was not till July 22nd that the
bombardment could be begun. On that day the new Grand
Vizier, Chalil Pasha, had reached Semendria at the head
of a relieving army with which he proceeded to make a
raid into the Banat, and then, seeing that this would not
cause Eugene to relax his grip on the beleaguered city,
moved thither himself and took up a strong position with
his right on the Danube. Eugene, thus hemmed in, was
forced to hurl his troops directly against the Turkish camp,
strongly posted though it was (Aug. 16th). His scheme
for the attack[1] contemplated that his left should begin
the battle, but a heavy mist upset the plan. Some of
the troops went altogether astray and left a large gap
in the line, which had to be filled by bringing up part
of the second line. However, the attack proved a complete
success, the right outflanked the Turkish position, and after
two hours of fighting they were in complete flight, and
their camp in Austrian hands. At a cost of 1500 killed
and 3500 wounded, the victors had inflicted a loss of 20,000
on the Turks and decided the fate of Belgrade. Two
days after the battle the capitulation was signed, and on
the 22nd the Turks evacuated the town.

It might have been thought that two such campaigns would
have inspired the Emperor with a determination to push his
successes still further. The Turks had received two crushing
defeats from which it would be hard to rally. It seemed that
Austria had the ball at her feet, and that a vigorous prosecution of the war could hardly fail to give her secure possession
of the valley of the Lower Danube. But the opportunity
was allowed to pass and did not return again. For reasons
quite unconnected with the situation on the Danube, the
Emperor was ready to accept the proposals for peace

[1] Cf. *Z.S.* ii. 597.*

which the new Vizier, Ibrahim, laid before Eugene. The contingency contemplated in the Austro-Venetian treaty had arisen. In August 1717 a Spanish squadron arrived off Cagliari and landed a force which occupied the island of Sardinia almost without any opposition.

The reasons for this move are not far to seek. Philip V of Spain had never abandoned his claim on the former possessions of the Spanish crown in Italy, just as Charles VI had adhered to his pretensions to be King of Spain. Moreover, his marriage with the intriguing and active Princess of Parma, Elizabeth Farnese, by whom he was all but exclusively influenced, had given him additional motives for desiring to upset the Utrecht arrangements. Elizabeth's great aim was to obtain separate establishments for her sons, since Philip's children by his first marriage would naturally succeed to Spain, and she hoped to do this by preventing the Emperor from carrying out his design of obtaining the reversion of the Imperial fiefs of Parma, Piacenza,[1] Tuscany[2] and Guastalla. With this attempt the name of Alberoni will always be associated, though here it would hardly be appropriate to relate the measures by which that able and enterprising minister sought to bring the undertaking to a successful conclusion. But it may be mentioned that the refusal of Great Britain to accept the highly advantageous offers of commercial concessions which Alberoni made in hopes of securing her support must in part be attributed to the German policy of George I as Elector of Hanover. It was not only his general policy of loyalty to the Empire, but the particular desire to get the Imperial sanction for his acquisition of Bremen and Verden, which bound George to the Austrian alliance. At the same time it would be inaccurate to regard these as the only causes of the rejection of Alberoni's offers. As long as Gibraltar and Minorca remained in British hands an alliance between England and Spain was not very probable. Moreover, in May 1716 the breach which the events of 1712–1713 had caused between Austria and England had been smoothed over by the Treaty of Westminster, by which the Whigs sought to revive the old alliance which Bolingbroke had abandoned.

[1] In the hands of Alessandro Farnese, last Duke of Parma.
[2] Gaston de Medici, the Duke, was childless.

This Anglo-Austrian Treaty, however, did not involve Austria in any connection with the United Provinces, once again joined to England by the treaty of January 1716, nor did the Anglo-French alliance, concluded in November 1716, at first include Austria. However, when Spain, provoked by the arrest (May 1717) of the Spanish Grand Inquisitor on his way through Lombardy, hastened into war with Austria, although Alberoni had only had two of the five years he had asked for in which to make his preparations, the Emperor appealed for help to the Triple Alliance, and the negotiation of the Convention of London (April 1718) was followed by the conclusion in August of the Quadruple Alliance.[1] But before this took place, the peace had been negotiated by which Austria turned back from the path which lay open before her, and for the sake of a transitory rule over Sicily, sacrificed the best chance she was ever to have of securing predominance in South-Eastern Europe at the expense of the Turk. The Peace of Passarowitz (July 21st, 1718), which was brought about by the efforts of England and Holland, accepted as its basis the principle of *uti possidetis*. This left to the Emperor the Banat, Northern Servia, including, of course, Belgrade, Wallachia as far as the Aluta, and a small district in Bosnia, but confirmed Candia and the Morea to the Turks. Venice, however, retained enough places on the Albanian and Dalmatian coasts[2] to have good security for the safety of the Ionian Islands. The Peace of Passarowitz is, it is true, the high-water mark of the tide of Austrian reconquest, and to that extent it may be reckoned among Austria's days of greatness, but from the point of view of what might have been done, it must be regretted as a half measure, or rather as a fatal mistake. That the Crescent still floats at Constantinople may be attributed in part to Charles VI's fatal preference for the former possessions of the Spanish crown once so nearly his. Had Austria pushed on in 1718, when Russia was so fully occupied with the Baltic War that she could not have interfered, the "Balkan question" might have been solved before it ever arose. And, indeed, it was hardly

[1] This included one treaty between the Emperor and England, France and Holland, and another between the Emperor and Victor Amadeus of Sicily.
[2] *e.g.* Butrinto, Prevesa, Vonizza.

necessary to have stopped Eugene's victorious progress for the defence of Italy. True, that the Spaniards followed up their successful descent on Sardinia by an equally successful descent on Sicily in 1718, that Palermo capitulated almost at once (July), and that the ease with which the Spaniards conquered the island was good evidence of the unpopularity of the Savoyard rule. But this success was of little avail when Byng, by destroying the Spanish fleet off Cape Passaro (Aug. 11th), asserted the British control of the Mediterranean and severed the expeditionary forces from Spain. France and England combined were too much for the renascent power of Spain, and Austria was able, not without some hard fighting and one sharp check,[1] to recover Sicily. Philip found himself compelled to give way, to dismiss Alberoni and to agree to the terms proposed by the Quadruple Alliance. Austria obtained the coveted Sicily in exchange for the valueless Sardinia; Charles VI renounced his claims on Spain and the Indies, Philip V his on Italy and the Netherlands; the succession to Parma and Tuscany was promised to the children of Elizabeth Farnese.[2]

With the Treaties of Passarowitz, of London, of Stockholm and of Nystadt, one seems to have the questions which had been agitating Europe settled on a basis which offered a fair prospect of peace. But this settlement was not in any way final. It was only the prelude to a series of conventions, coalitions, alliances, leagues and treaties which fill the next decade. Elizabeth Farnese and Charles VI between them were to trouble the chanceries of Europe, not once but many times in the next ten years, and if there were to be few wars, that was not to be from want of "rumours of war."

Yet at this time, as in 1648, the chief concern of the states of Germany was with their internal affairs, and their chief need was peace and quiet, financial reform, the restoration of order, and reorganisation in general. Charles VI, however, failed to realise this, failed to pay proper attention to these urgent domestic needs, and unable to forget that he had once been King of Spain, devoted himself to futile efforts to reverse the arrangements of Utrecht, when the internal condition of the Hapsburg dominions and of the

---

[1] At Francoville, June 1719.   Treaty of London, January 1720.

Empire afforded ample scope for all the energies of the most active and ambitious of statesmen.

One of the measures most characteristic of the way in which, renunciations or no renunciations, Charles VI could not bring himself to accept the rule of Philip V in Spain, was the maintenance of a separate government for his Italian and Belgian possessions, which he looked upon as his in virtue of his rights as King of Spain and, consequently, as quite unconnected with the other dominions over which he ruled. Thus he established a separate "Spanish Council" to administer their affairs, and governed them through Spaniards of the party which had remained faithful to him, a circumstance which partly contributed to the ease with which his South Italian possessions slipped out of his grasp in 1733. Moreover, it was unfortunate that his Spanish tastes caused him to pay great attention to the views of these exiles in other matters of state with which they were hardly qualified to deal. The existence, therefore, of this dual system went far to increase the want of unity which was the great weakness of the Hapsburg dominions and which in another way Charles was striving hard to check.

Between the disconnected dominions of the Hapsburgs, which had indeed a central financial authority in the *Hofkammer* and a central military authority in the *Hofkriegsrath*, but were in all other matters quite independent of each other, the dynasty was the only real link. Yet the dynasty itself was threatened with a failure of male heirs. Not only had Joseph died without a son, but Charles had none surviving, and there were no male descendants of younger sons of previous Emperors to take up the burden. The heir of the Hapsburgs must be a female. It was on this account that Leopold I had in 1703 attempted to regulate the succession by making a formal arrangement (*pactum mutuæ successionis*) that, in default of a male heir, females should succeed by primogeniture, the special proviso being added that Joseph's daughters should precede those of Charles.[1] At that time, however, the existence of two separate branches of the family had been contemplated, Joseph's at Vienna, that of Charles at Madrid, whereas since then Charles had

---

[1] Cf. *Z.S.* ii. 559, etc. ; also A. Bachmann, *Die Pragmatische Sanction und die Erbfolgeordnung Leopold I's.*

succeeded to the whole Hapsburg heritage, and so might fairly claim that the case was altered and that the natural order of succession would place his own daughters before those of his brother. Accordingly in 1713 he issued a family law altering the order of succession,—which, after all, he had as good a right to do as had Leopold or any other head of the family—and putting his own daughters before those of Joseph. This done, he had to obtain the assent to this arrangement, known as the Pragmatic Sanction, of the daughters of Joseph and of the Estates of his various dominions, and also to induce the Powers of Europe to recognise it.

With the first two this was not hard. He was able to extract an acceptance of the Pragmatic Sanction from the Archduchess Maria Josepha when she married the Electoral Prince of Saxony in 1719; a similar formal renunciation was made by his other niece, Maria Amelia, on her marriage to the Electoral Prince Charles Albert of Bavaria. The assent to the arrangement of the Estates of Upper and Lower Austria, Bohemia, Carinthia, Moravia and Silesia was secured in 1720; Tyrol followed suit, but "saving its freedom and rights"; Croatia agreed in 1721, Hungary and Transylvania in 1722, the Netherlands in 1724.

To obtain its recognition by the Powers was, however, another matter, and was the guiding principle in all the foreign relations of the Emperor, determining his actions to the exclusion of other motives. The first step to which it led him was a somewhat remarkable change of front. An international congress was opened at Cambrai in 1722 to try to settle outstanding difficulties, but its negotiations broke down over the commercial quarrels of the Maritime Powers with the Emperor and with Spain. Elizabeth Farnese found that her Italian schemes would receive no support from England and France, the Spanish ministers, who set the prosperity of their country before the interests of the dynasty, found England unyielding on the question of the West Indian trade, and the Emperor, annoyed at the opposition of the Maritime Powers to his favourite commercial scheme, the Ostend East India Company, drew nearer his old enemy, Philip of Spain. Through the instrumentality of Ripperda, a Dutch adventurer in the Spanish service, the League of Vienna was concluded in May 1725. The keynote of this surprising arrangement was the proposal for a double marriage between the two daughters of the Emperor and the two sons of Elizabeth Farnese, the idea being that Don-Carlos as the husband of the elder sister should be elected King of the Romans, while Don Philip and the Archduchess Maria Anna should receive the Italian possessions of the family. Renunciations were exchanged by the Emperor and the King; and while Austria promised her good offices towards obtaining Minorca and Gibraltar for Spain, Philip v recognised the Pragmatic Sanction and promised his support to the Ostend Company, which was to be put on the same footing in West Indian waters as England and Holland.

This Ostend Company was the result of the adoption by Prince Eugene and the Emperor of a scheme, begun by private enterprise, to develope the trade of the Austrian Netherlands and to utilise the natural advantages of their geographical position, hitherto restrained and hampered by the artificial trammels of the Peace of Münster and the Barrier Treaty. So much success had attended the first efforts of the enterprise that Dutch hostility was greatly excited, and they proceeded to seize Belgian vessels and treat them as good prize. Upon this the Emperor took the enterprise under his protection, and the Ostend Company was formed in June 1722, to trade with the East and West Indies and with Africa. The Company established factories at Canton, in Bengal and on the Coromandel Coast; and its progress was soon such as to excite the jealousy of the Maritime Powers. It was not merely its commercial success which alarmed the eager traders of Amsterdam, for whose benefit Spain had been forbidden to trade to the Indies from Belgium in 1648.[1] It was not merely that Ostend promised to become a great trading centre, as Trieste was doing in the Adriatic; complete success would have made the Emperor much less dependent on the naval strength of Maritime Powers. Hence England supported the Dutch in their opposition to the Company; while France, though less concerned in the affairs of the Ostend Company

---

[1] The Emperor's contention was that the Netherlands had been thus restricted by the Treaty of Münster, because in Spanish hands they had ceased to be part of the Empire with which they were now reunited, so that the restrictions had ceased to apply to them. Cf. *Z.S.* ii. 622.

and anxious to avoid a war with Austria and Spain, followed —without enthusiasm—in the lead of England.

The result was that while Russia, Bavaria, Cologne,[1] Treves[2] and the new Elector Palatine, Charles Philip of Neuburg, who had succeeded his brother, John William, in 1716, adhered to the League of Vienna, a counter-coalition was formed by Townshend in the shape of the League of Herrnhaüsen (Sept. 1725), which included England, Holland, France and Prussia.[3] With Europe thus arrayed in two hostile camps, a great war seemed imminent. But except for Elizabeth Farnese, no one really desired war: the unnatural Austro-Spanish alliance was already showing signs of weakness, since neither partner displayed any intention of carrying out the pledges they had undertaken. Ripperda's unpopularity forced the Queen to discard him in favour of Patinol in May 1726. There was a strong party at Vienna, led by Eugene and Stahremberg, which was opposed to the idea of the Spanish match; and though the Spaniards undertook a fruitless siege of Gibraltar, while England blockaded Porto Bello and stopped the West Indian trade, the war did not spread to Germany or become general. In March 1728 the Convention of the Pardo brought the Anglo-Spanish war to an end, and in the summer a Congress was opened at Soissons.

The upshot of the Congress of Soissons was that in November 1729, Spain came to terms with England, France and Holland. The uncertainty as to the succession in France, the chief cause of the hostility which had, since 1715, prevailed between Spain and her natural ally France, and which had driven her into allying with her chief rival in Italy, was removed by the birth of the Dauphin (1729), and with the anti-Spanish party gaining the ascendant at Vienna and the Austro-Spanish marriage proposals obviously abandoned, Spain was ready enough to throw over the Emperor and the Ostend

---

[1] Clement Augustus, Archbishop-Elector and Bishop of Osnabrück, Paderborn, Münster and Hildesheim, a Bavarian Wittelsbach, elected in 1723.

[2] Archbishop-Elector Francis Louis, also a Wittelsbach, elected in 1716.

[3] Subsequent additions to this coalition were Hesse-Cassel (March 1726), Denmark (April 1727) and Sweden (1727), though in October 1726 Count Seckendorf detached Prussia from the League and bound her to the Emperor by the Treaty of Wüsterhausen, which promised Jülich and Berg to Prussia, Frederick William guaranteeing the Pragmatic Sanction.

Company, and to fulfil the commercial clauses of the Peace of Utrecht in return for a guarantee of the Italian Duchies to Don Carlos. To obtain the Emperor's assent to the Treaty of Seville was a more difficult task. Townshend had been successful in breaking up the League of Vienna without a war; he was anxious to avoid having to join France, Spain and Holland in forcing terms upon Charles VI, who had drawn closer his alliance with Russia in December 1728. And when ministerial changes in England resulted in Townshend's resigning his Secretaryship of State (May 1730), thereby giving place to William Stanhope, Lord Harrington, it was the pacific Walpole who was left at the head of the government. He was very anxious to maintain good relations with France and Spain, mainly for commercial reasons, but he saw in the Pragmatic Sanction a way of escape from the dilemma in which he was placed. George II guaranteed it both as King of England and as Elector of Hanover, and this induced the Emperor to give way on points on which he had hitherto resisted. By the Second Treaty of Vienna (March 16th, 1731) he abolished the Ostend Company, promised that Don Carlos should succeed to the Italian Duchies, and agreed to the occupation of several towns in Parma and Tuscany by Spanish troops.[1] This arrangement was, however, only secured at the cost of a rift within the lute of the Anglo-French alliance, for Fleury was very loath to guarantee the Pragmatic Sanction, and declined to follow England's lead, though Holland did do so. The truth was that the exceptional circumstances which had brought about the Anglo-French alliance were ceasing to exist: France and Spain were no longer necessary enemies, Chauvelin was using his influence against England, trade rivalries were forcing themselves to the front, and the question of Dunkirk was a fruitful source of disagreement.

The Second Treaty of Vienna marks the close of one distinct period of alliances and combinations. It did not give Europe the peace which Walpole desired, but the quarrel which was to bring about a renewal of war two years later may be more

---

[1] This took place, 6000 Spaniards being escorted to Leghorn by the English fleet and quartered in Parma and Tuscany, much to the disgust of Duke Gaston de Medici. In 1732, the Duke of Parma being dead, Don Carlos obtained possession of the territories of the Farnese, which the Emperor had actually occupied on the Duke's death.

justly regarded as the prelude to the War of the Austrian Succession than as part and parcel of the efforts to upset the Peace of Utrecht. The so-called War of the Polish Succession began, it is true, in that international storm-centre, but it owes its importance to having been the first attack of the Bourbon Powers, reunited by the first of the Family Compacts, upon the Hapsburg dominions.

It must certainly be admitted that in all these negotiations and coalitions, one has heard little of German powers and nothing of Germany. Charles was to some extent acting as head of the Empire in his attempts to give the trade of Germany an outlet to the ocean through his own dominions, but the real importance to Germany of all these diplomatic variations lies in the underlying attempt to get the Pragmatic Sanction recognised by the Powers. And in this Charles had been fairly successful. Spain had been the first to give her guarantee (in May 1725), Russia came next (August 1726), then (September 1st) the four Wittelsbach Electors, Bavaria, Cologne, the Palatinate and Treves, followed in October by Prussia at the Treaty of Wüsterhausen. The Elector of Mayence, the Duke of Brunswick, and various other minor Princes were also secured ; and though Charles Albert of Bavaria, who had succeeded Maximilian Emmanuel in February 1726, withdrew his recognition on the ground that the terms of the treaty of 1726 had never been fulfilled, and assisted by Saxony and the Palatinate obstructed the Emperor's efforts to obtain the assent of the Diet, this was secured in 1732, just after the concessions to Don Carlos and the abandonment of the Ostend Company had won the recognition of the Pragmatic Sanction by England, Hanover and the United Provinces. Still, as the event was to prove, these guarantees were little more than paper, and it would have been better if Charles VI had devoted his time to the constructive reforms which might have given his dominions the unity and coherence which they so badly needed and which would have been a far surer safeguard.

CHAPTER V

PRUSSIA UNDER FREDERICK WILLIAM I

IF the minor Powers of Germany play but unimportant parts in international affairs in the years following on the Peace of Utrecht, it must be admitted that, apart from the troubles to which the retention of the " Ryswick clause " in the Peace of Baden gave rise, their internal affairs equally fail to afford much material for history. One is not accustomed to attribute to religious motives a very important influence on international affairs after 1648, but what had happened in that year was that the religious differences had been slurred over rather than settled, and so the strife continued, though in a somewhat different form. In the latter half of the seventeenth century, Roman Catholicism had been stronger and more aggressive than Protestantism ; it had made marked progress among the upper classes, to whom it offered better social and financial prospects than did the rival creeds. Poverty and ambition had been effective missionaries in the leading Protestant families. Two[1] of the children of the " Winter-King " himself had been among the converts. Christian Louis of Mecklenburg-Schwerin had changed his faith in order to get a divorce which would let him marry one of the Montmorenci family; Ernest of Hesse-Rheinfels endeavoured by this means to gain the Imperial support in his disputes with his cousins at Hesse-Cassel. Of the conversion of Frederick Augustus of Saxony and of the change in the religion of the Elector Palatine with the accession of the Neuburgs, mention has already been made ;[2] but it is important to notice that some authorities go so far as to call these religious differences the principal cause of the weakness and disunion of Germany at this period.[3] Be that as it may,

---

[1] Edward, who married Anne of Gonzaga-Nevers, and Louise, a nun, *o.s.p.* 1709.

[2] Cf. pp. 39 and 44.

[3] *e.g.* de Broglie, *Frederic II et Marie Thérèse*, i. 250. Cf. Erdmannsdörffer, bk. iii. ch. 5.

religious dissensions did continue to give much trouble and to provide the Diet with the greater part of its occupation; such a question, for instance, as the objection raised by the Protestants to the reduction in the "matricular" contribution of Cologne on the score that the falling off in the trade and revenue of that city was due to the oppression of its Protestant inhabitants.

Among those on whom the "Ryswick clause" bore most heavily were the Protestant subjects of the Elector Palatine. John William had been largely responsible for the clause, and he put it into force with unsparing vigour. An era of persecution set in; the churches and estates of the Calvinists were confiscated on the most flimsy pretexts, their freedom of worship was seriously hindered; the Jesuits were greatly encouraged, and, despite all pledges to the contrary, were allowed to obtain control of the Faculty of Philosophy in the University of Heidelberg with disastrous results to the University. By way of bringing pressure to bear on John William, Frederick I of Prussia, a sturdy and consistent Evangelical, who had refused to make concessions to the Catholics even to gain the coveted "Crown,"[1] had threatened to levy reprisals on his Catholic subjects in Westphalia, and had thereby induced the Elector to withdraw some of his edicts; but John William's successor, Charles Philip (1716–1742), continued the policy of persecution. In 1719 he forbade the use of the Heidelberg Confession of 1563, and refused to let the Calvinists share any longer in the use of the chief church of Heidelberg, that of the Holy Ghost. At this point Hanover, Hesse-Cassel and Prussia intervened and by making reprisals on their Catholic subjects forced Charles Philip to give way sulkily (Feb. 1720), one manifestation of his discontent being his removal of his official residence from Heidelberg to Mannheim.

A rather better known episode in this persecution is the treatment of the Protestants who formed a majority among the inhabitants of the Archbishopric of Salzburg. Their Protestantism was of the staunchest, and nothing could induce them to forsake it. From 1668 to 1687 they had suffered grievously from Archbishop Maximilian Gandulph von Kuenburg, but since his time peace had prevailed until the election

---

[1] Cf. E. Berner, *Auf den Briefwechsel König Friedrichs von Preussen und seiner Familie.*

of Leopold von Firmian as Archbishop in 1727. He at once instituted a vigorous persecution only to meet with a stubborn resistance. The Archbishop declared his subjects rebels, and called in Austrian troops to " dragonnade " them into submission; and finally, in October 1731, he compelled them to leave their homes at the very shortest notice, not allowing the statutory three years' grace promised at Osnabrück. This proved Frederick William's opportunity, just as the Revocation of the Edict of Nantes had been his grandfather's. East Prussia had been depopulated and reduced almost to the condition of a desert by the ravages of cattle-disease and the plague, especially in 1709 and 1710, and Frederick William saw that the exiles would prove most desirable colonists. He therefore issued an edict (Feb. 1732) in which he offered a welcome to the Salzburgers, most of whom found their way to this haven of refuge; some stopped on the way in Franconia and Swabia, others pushed on to the Netherlands, a few wandered as far afield as North America. Though attended with great difficulties, the settlement in East Prussia was on the whole a great success, and Frederick William managed to extort from the Archbishop compensation for the confiscated property of the emigrants.

But the recolonising of East Prussia with the Salzburgers is but a small item in the work which Frederick William I did for the Hohenzollern monarchy. His is not an attractive or an edifying personality, but his place in the history of Prussia is one of the greatest importance. If the Great Elector had laid the foundations, it was not everyone who could have built upon them with such sureness and success, who could have so filled up the gaps in the original design and improved upon it. The twin pillars on which the success of Frederick II's foreign policy rested, the highly efficient army and the centralised bureaucracy under the exclusive direction of the autocratic head of the State, were the work of Frederick William. Intensely practical, hard-working, unsparing of himself or others, harsh, narrow-minded, in some points petty, but thoroughgoing in every respect, Frederick William preached the gospel of hard work and efficiency, and did not fail to practise what he preached. As in the Great Elector's, so in Frederick William's political creed, absolutism was the chief article. He had a great idea of the kingly office, of its duties no less than of its rights and privileges. Regarding his position as held from God, he accepted the fullest responsibility for all the acts of the administration, no detail being too petty to escape his supervision, while even when immersed in details he did not lose sight of the principles involved.

From the moment of his accession it became obvious that the Prussian state was on the verge of sweeping changes. The gorgeous funeral which Frederick William gave to his father may be regarded as emblematic of the obsequies of the ceremonious and extravagant order which had prevailed under the first King in Prussia. A complete reform of the Court establishment ushered in the new system. The household was cut down to a fifth of what it had been, the salaries of the few officials who escaped being dismissed were greatly reduced, luxury was banished, an almost Spartan simplicity and economy became the order of the day. Similarly, all branches of the administration were subjected to a relentless purging of sinecures and abuses. Peculation and corruption were severely punished, inefficiency was stamped out, a new spirit and a new discipline infused into the public service. Moreover, measures of organic reform were introduced with a promptitude which showed that they had for the most part been devised in advance.

Thus in August 1713 there appeared an edict regulating the affairs of the royal Domains. The King took them completely into his own control, only letting them out on short terms, raised the rents wherever it was possible, took every opportunity of increasing the Domains by purchase, invested any surplus in this way, and declared the whole Domain inalienable. The success of all these reforms may best be judged from the fact that the revenues of the Domains, which in 1713 amounted to 1,800,000 thalers, had risen to 3,300,000 thalers by 1740, a sum all but equal to the 3,600,000 thalers produced by the General War Fund. Together with this went reforms in the administration. Hitherto the Domains' revenues, with those of the Mint, Post Office and Customs, had been under one set of officials, the direct taxes—specially allotted to the Army—being under the Military Board.[1] Frederick William worked up this system further: a General Directory was organised to supervise the local officials responsible for the Domains

[1] Erdmannsdörffer, ii. 486 ff.

and indirect taxes, a Director of the War Commission (*Generalkriegscommissariat*) was put over the "war taxes" (*Kriegsgefälle*); but as this arrangement seemed to produce two Finance Ministers, the Finance Chamber (*Generalrechenkammer*) was established in 1714 to control both. However, this plan proved productive of much confusion and friction, and in 1723 Frederick William carried out a most radical change, abolishing the dual system, and substituting for it a central administrative body. Of this new General Directory, formed by the amalgamation of the two existing branches, and organised in five departments each under a Minister, the King was himself the head. To this central authority the local officials were completely subordinated, this arrangement practically doing away with the last shreds of local autonomy.

Corresponding to these changes in the financial administration was the supersession of the Privy Council, which had proved altogether too large for efficiency, as the chief engine of government. The King's personal activity was largely responsible for this, but the definite allotment of business to the separate Ministers had much to do with it. A leading feature in this whole scheme of reform was the delocalisation of the administration. Vacancies were never filled by a native of the district in which they occurred, for Frederick William meant the officials to be his servants, looking only to him as their master, indifferent to any interests but his, a hierarchy working automatically as his delegates. This, of course, involved the complete subordination of the local and municipal government to the central administration, the culmination of victory of the Prince (*Fürstenthum*) over the Estates (*Ständethum*). The *Landtag* (Diet) completely lost its powers, the nobles, who retained their great social privileges, being reconciled to the new order by being almost identified with the army, to whose interests all other considerations were postponed. On one occasion only was constitutional opposition offered. This was in 1717, when Frederick William introduced a scheme for doing away with tenure by military service, substituting a tax of fifty thalers per annum on each knight's fee (*Ritterpferd*) to be paid to the war chest. This aroused the nobles of East Prussia and Magdeburg, who objected greatly to being put on the same footing as the peasantry and townsfolk; but though the Magdeburg knights went so far as to appeal to the Emperor, who listened favourably to their complaints, Frederick William really triumphed. He granted the reduction of the tax from fifty to forty thalers as a concession to the Emperor, but this was a cheap price for the establishment of the principle. Equally successful was his attack on the municipal government. The towns were under petty oligarchies which kept the majority of the townsfolk out of any share in the government, so that the burghers benefited on the whole by being deprived of the relics of what had once been autonomy. The management of their finances was taken away from the towns and transferred to the central government, which also obtained control over justice and police, and in this way the old local oligarchies were really quite broken up, the royal tax-collector (*Steuer-rath*) in each town becoming the real head of the administration. If this government by the central authorities was oppressive and heavy, it was at least even-handed, economical and efficient.

The condition of judicial affairs afforded another field for the King's reforming activities. Almost immediately after his accession (June 1713), Frederick William adopted many of the reforms which Bartholdi, the Minister of Justice, had urged upon Frederick I in the previous year. He gave orders for the compilation of a code of Prussian law, of which an instalment was published by von Cocceji in 1721, though it was not till nearly the close of the century that the code was completed. Much was also done by von Cocceji at the head of the Court of Appeal in the way of clearing off arrears of work and accelerating the speed of judicial procedure so as to keep pace with new cases.

It was rather more difficult to obtain success when Frederick William turned his attention to the improvement of industrial conditions, as the fact that the old order continued to prevail over the border in Saxony and Hanover interfered considerably with his legislation as to the guilds, though an edict published in 1732 (*Handwerksgesetzgebung*) did subject them to State supervision and alter and adapt their bye-laws to new conditions. The object which Frederick William had before him in this branch of legislation was the development of the resources of the country. A system of rigid protection laid prohibitory duties on foreign competition and gave every encouragement to home manufactures. To aid the wool-weavers the export of wool and the import of English cloth were forbidden, while the whole army was clothed in local products. Recognising that he had plenty of other occupation without dabbling in colonial expansion, Frederick William abandoned the ill-fated African enterprise of the Great Elector, and not even the acquisition of Stettin tempted him to try to develop an oversea commerce. He sought to improve the social, and economic conditions of his subjects, but for a very definite purpose. His aim was to improve their condition "not by lightening their burdens, but by increasing their capacity for bearing burdens." For in all these reforms, in the centralising of the administration, in the increase and improvement of the Domains, in the accumulation of a great reserve war fund, in the bureaucratic organisation of the State under an autocratic ruler, Frederick William's great aim was to enable Prussia to support that large army, so out of all proportion to her territory and her population, which could alone give her weight in the councils of Europe. It was as a military state that Prussia was organised, to the Army that everything else was sacrificed, military power that was the object for which the Prussian kingdom existed. He is, perhaps, chiefly remembered on account of his favourite corps, the celebrated but not very serviceable " Potsdam Grenadiers " ; but it would be a grave error to let the solid merit of his military achievements be concealed behind their ranks. It is a remarkable fact that Frederick William, one of the most successful organisers of an army there has ever been, should have been one of the most pacific and least belligerent of rulers. His military fame must rest upon the army he built up and bequeathed to his son, not on what he himself did with it ; and yet that is a secure enough foundation for any reputation. If he cannot be reckoned more than "a very good peace general," it is because he did not attempt to test the weapon he had forged, not because he tried and failed.

The Prussian army at the accession of Frederick William I mustered some 38,000 men.[1] The new King's first step was to raise seven more regiments, and every political

---

[1] There was also a reserve in the shape of a Land Militia about 10,000 strong for home service or garrison duty, but it was before long disbanded as of little military value.

incident or complication was eagerly used as an excuse for fresh additions. By 1725 the army had been increased to 60 battalions of infantry and 100 squadrons of cavalry, a total, with garrison troops, of 64,000 men, of whom about 10,000 depôt and garrison troops were not available for field service. By 1740 its numbers had risen to 89,000, the field army comprising 66 battalions, 114 squadrons, including 9 of hussars, 6 companies of field and 4 of fortress artillery, and a Life Guard of 2500, the famous "Potsdam Grenadiers." But it was not merely its numbers which gave it importance. No effort was spared to increase its efficiency. A harsh and stern system of discipline was introduced and rigorously maintained. The utmost care was devoted to the exercising and training of the troops. Their drill was revolutionised by the introduction of a cadenced step and the reduction of the depth of formation from six ranks to three, both due to Leopold of Anhalt-Dessau. In all manœuvres a high standard was set up and reached, thus enabling the Prussian regiments to change from one formation to another with a rapidity and precision which was the wonder of the age. The movements of the parade-ground were accurately reproduced on the battlefield in a way which gave the Prussian generals a great advantage over less flexible and mobile opponents, who found it a matter of the greatest difficulty to change a position which they had once taken up, as their troops, being less carefully drilled, were apt to fall into confusion when they attempted to manœuvre in face of an enemy. Moreover, better discipline meant better fire-discipline, and the introduction of iron ramrods allowed a greater rapidity of fire. As a potent factor in producing a high state of efficiency the well-developed regimental system must not be forgotten. Of the value of *esprit de corps* Frederick William had a high opinion, and in his distribution of rewards and punishments he laid great stress upon it. Moreover, the partial territorialisation of the army encouraged a local feeling which helped to foster this regimental spirit.

To keep this great army up to its established strength was no very easy task, seeing that in population Prussia stood as low as twelfth among the countries of Europe, and that the army had to be raised by voluntary enlistment. It was found necessary, therefore, to supplement the local recruits by sending out recruiting-officers into the neighbouring countries, especially into the Imperial Cities. The Prussian recruiters made themselves notorious from Scandinavia to Transylvania, and from the Liffey to the Niemen; they were a constant source of friction with the authorities of other states, besides being a heavy expense.[1]

It was the difficulty and the great expense[2] of keeping up a voluntary army of the size which the King desired which at last decided Frederick William to adopt a system of modified conscription. In September 1733 he issued his famous "cantoning scheme," by which the country was divided into cantons, to which regiments were assigned for recruiting purposes, a regiment of infantry being allotted 6000 "hearths," one of cavalry 1800. Universal liability to service was recognised though with very liberal exemptions in favour of the nobles, the professional classes and certain trades which it was desired to specially encourage. This provided a fairly regular supply of recruits, but it was eked out by the enlistment of mercenaries on a large scale, so much so, indeed, that in 1768 only about half the army was composed of native Prussians, and at times during the Seven Years' War the proportion must have sunk even lower. One object in thus hiring foreigners was to let the native subjects of Frederick devote themselves to productive pursuits such as agriculture and manufactures, so that they might not be withdrawn from increasing the resources and tax-paying capacities of the kingdom. In time of peace, too, the native conscripts were only with the colours for a quarter of the year, being on unpaid furlough for the remaining nine months. The presence of the large proportion of foreigners of doubtful allegiance, together with the great harshness of the discipline and the many hardships of the soldier's lot, provides a sufficient explanation of the great prevalence of desertion in the Prussian army.

With the double purpose of bringing the nobles into closer touch with the Crown through the army, and of fostering

[1] A quarrel of this kind in 1729 nearly brought about a war between Prussia and Hanover, some Prussian recruiters having been arrested in Hanover, where the shelter given by the Prussian army to Hanoverian deserters was much resented.

[2] Out of the 7,000,000 thalers to which the total revenue amounted in 1740, no less than 5,000,000 were expended on the Army.

among them discipline and the military spirit, Frederick William drew his officers almost exclusively from the native nobility, who had hitherto held somewhat aloof from the service. The exaggerated militarism so characteristic of the Prussian "Junker" is due in large measure to this move on his part, while the great social gulf between officers and men made it easier to maintain that strict discipline and that rigid subordination of the lower ranks which were such marked features of the Prussian system. At the same time, it was made very clear that the army was the King's army, that the officers were the King's servants and their men the King's men rather than theirs. There was a struggle before the King could gain the complete control over the appointment of the officers and over the internal administrative economy of the regiments, but in the end he prevailed, and the completeness of his victory marked a great stride forwards towards absolutism.

With so strong a force at his disposal the unimportant part played by Frederick William in international affairs is a little surprising. This was partly due to his natural caution and self-control. Unless he saw the issues clearly, he would not let ambition or adventurousness plunge him into any hazardous or uncertain enterprise. Moreover, he was never presented with such an opportunity as that which Charles VI's death placed before Frederick II. Frederick William liked to know how far he was committing himself, and preferred to gain his ends by peaceful means, or, at any rate, with the minimum outlay of blood or money. It was most characteristic of him that in his one warlike enterprise, his share in the Northern War, he was fairly successful without acquiring thereby anything of a military reputation. With his other great object, the acquisition of Jülich and Berg, he was less fortunate than with his designs on Pomerania ; but it is nevertheless the key to his policy, more especially to his relations with the Emperor.

The truth of the matter was that Prussia was not on good terms with the majority of her neighbours, more especially with Saxony and Hanover, the other leading Protestant Powers of Germany with whom she might have been expected to be friendly. But Saxony through her connection with Poland was the possessor of the coveted West Prussia, while between Hanover and the Hohenzollern there were many causes of hostility. Hanover had utilised the Mecklenburg affair[1] to plant herself firmly in that territory, and did not evacuate it until some time after the Emperor had deposed Duke Charles Leopold and replaced him by Christian Louis, his brother (May 1728), and declared the Imperial edict (*Reichexecution*) void, her defence for the continued occupation being that the costs of the execution had not been paid.[2] East Frisia, where the Cirksena family was on the point of dying out, was another open question. Hanover claimed it under a "blood-brotherhood" made in 1693; Prussia's claims upon it had been admitted by the Emperor at the time of the restitution of Schwiebus in 1692. But beyond this there was personal ill-feeling between the two reigning families: George I had not been on good terms with Frederick William, and George II's feelings towards his brother-in-law were exceedingly hostile, though at the time of the League of Herrenhaüsen (1725), Townshend so far overcame the hostility between George I and Frederick William as to enlist Prussia on the same side as Hanover.[3]

But the adherence of Prussia to the Maritime Powers was not of long duration. In October 1726, Frederick William, finding that he could get nothing from England and France but vague promises of support in the matter of Jülich and Berg, and having no intention of being involved in a war with

---

[1] Cf. p. 69.

[2] Christian Louis obtained control of Mecklenburg, though not without difficulty, and finally succeeded his brother as Duke in 1747.

[3] It is important to notice that to the English Ministers Prussia seemed a natural ally. This may be traced all through the relations of Prussia with England and Hanover; those English Ministers who hoped to hold their enemies, whether Spain or France, in check by alliances with the German Powers, looked upon securing the alliance of Prussia as an essential step. Thus one finds Sir Thomas Robinson endeavouring to reconcile Maria Theresa to the robber of Silesia, while Walpole favoured an alliance with Prussia for political and commercial reasons, but found himself opposed by Hanoverian prejudices and hatred of Prussia. Horace Walpole (the elder) writes to point out the importance of gaining Prussia to the side of the Maritime Powers (*Trevor MSS.*, Hist. MSS. Commission, p. 50; cf. p. 51: "Europe, England, and Hanover want a political union and intimacy, and as the safety of England depends on the balance of Europe, I think I can demonstrate that the security of Hanover depends on both: here I fix my point of view, and shall date the duration of our apparent friendship with Berlin upon the measures pursued for this end"). But "His Majesty (George II) continues very averse to do anything that squints in the least towards favouring the King of Prussia" (*ibid.* p. 5). Again, Hanoverian hostility to Prussia plays a part, though it has to give way in the end, in the negotiations which culminated in the Treaty of Westminster of 1756; cf. pp. 186 ff.

Austria and Russia in defence of Hanover, allowed Count
Seckendorff to win him over to the side of Austria; and the
Emperor promised to try to induce the Sulzbach branch of
the Wittelsbachs to agree to the compromise which Frederick
William was ready to accept.[1] The matter stood in this state:
Charles Philip of Neuburg, the Elector Palatine, who held
Jülich and Berg in virtue of the 1666 compact, had no son,
his brother, Francis Louis, Elector of Treves, was, of course,
unmarried, so that the next heir was Theodore, Count Palatine
of Sulzbach (1708-1732).[2] The Hohenzollern therefore
claimed that Jülich and Berg should fall to them on the failure
of the males of the Neuburg line; but Joseph of Sulzbach,
eldest son of Theodore, put in a claim both on his own
behalf as descended from the Dukes of Cleves and in virtue
of his wife, Elizabeth, the eldest daughter of Charles Philip.[3]
The Emperor also had something of a claim, his mother having
been a sister of Charles Philip; but this he declared himself
ready to waive, resigning Jülich to the Sulzbachs, Berg and
Ravenstein to Prussia, if both would agree.[4] Upon this
the treaty of 1726 with Prussia was converted into a
definite alliance, Prussia guaranteeing the Pragmatic Sanction
and pledging her support to the Emperor, more particularly
to the husband of Maria Theresa, who would be the natural
Hapsburg candidate for the next vacancy in the Empire.
But the pledges which Austria gave to Prussia on this subject
were of a rather vague and indefinite character; the Hapsburgs
had no great wish to see the Hohenzollern in these Duchies
rather than the Sulzbachs who were Catholics, and it must
be admitted that Charles VI played fast and loose with
Prussia in the matter; for in the hope of obtaining the assent
of the Sulzbachs to the Pragmatic Sanction the Emperor
endeavoured to come to terms with them over Jülich and
Berg, and to mollify them by inducing Prussia to assent to
a compromise decidedly in their favour. Thus the matter
lingered on till, in February 1738, Austria, England, France
and Holland presented identical notes calling upon Prussia
and the Sulzbachs to submit the question to a conference.
To this Frederick William refused to agree, and conscious of
his isolation and of Austria's preference for the Sulzbachs, he

---

[1] Cf. *Z.S.* ii. 628.
[2] Cf. Wittelsbach Genealogy, p. 707.
[3] *Ibid.*
[4] Erdmannsdörffer, ii. 427.

decided to make overtures to France and so secure a means of putting pressure on the Emperor. Fleury, with the prospect of being involved in the impending Anglo-Spanish war, was glad of the chance of securing himself against Prussia's hostility, as he feared she might be subsidised to take part with England. In April 1739 a treaty was signed by which France promised to induce Charles Philip to agree to a partition which would leave most of Ravenstein and Berg to Prussia, while compensating the Sulzbachs with the remainder of the territory in dispute. A secret article further pledged Prussia to closer co-operation with France. But had it been the father and not the son who was on the Prussian throne at the moment when the death of Charles VI opened a question of the most momentous importance to Germany, it would hardly have been in accord with the whole tenor of Frederick William's policy to have allowed this treaty to commit him to anything like the action which Frederick II took. Not even the treatment he had received over Jülich and Berg would have quite induced the cautious Frederick William to bring French armies into the heart of Germany.

CHAPTER VI

THE LAST WARS OF CHARLES VI

IT is only from the study in disorganisation and misfortune presented by the Hapsburg monarchy in the last two wars in which the luckless Charles VI engaged, that one can fairly estimate the perilous nature of the crisis which his death precipitated. The Emperor's own shortcomings as a ruler had no doubt much to answer for, but they were aggravated by the persistent misfortune which followed him throughout his career.

At the moment when the death of Frederick Augustus of Saxony-Poland (Feb. 1733) opened the ever thorny question of the succession to that realm of troubles, the old system which had united Austria, the Maritime Powers and the minor states of Germany against France and Spain seemed about to be revived. The bonds of the Anglo-French alliance were slackening, and anyone with a less purely insular attitude than Walpole must have seen that the change in the relations of France and Spain brought about by the birth of the Dauphin must materially affect the footing on which England stood towards her old enemy but present ally. To some extent the old relations between England and Austria had been restored by Walpole's guarantee of the Pragmatic Sanction, and Hanoverian traditions made George II favour supporting the Emperor.

However, when through the old connection between France and Poland the succession question developed into a general European war, the Anglo-French alliance proved strong enough yet to keep England out of the strife. The new Elector of Saxony, Augustus III as Elector but Frederick Augustus II as King of Poland, came forward at once as a candidate for the Polish throne, and succeeded in securing Austria's support by guaranteeing the Pragmatic Sanction, and abandoning for himself and his wife, the eldest daughter of Joseph I, all claims on the Hapsburg dominions. Russia he won over by a promise to cede Courland to Count Biron, Catherine's favourite. Russia and Austria had not at first meant to support the Saxon, and had actually agreed with Prussia to adopt as their candidate Prince Emmanuel of Portugal.[1] But when the time came Emmanuel was found to be most unsuitable, and, moreover, Russia had never ratified the treaty. Thus, much to the disgust of Frederick William, to whom the presence of the Saxon line at Warsaw was most distasteful, the Löwenwolde arrangement was thrown over, and with it slipped away the chance that something might be done for Augustus William, Frederick William's second son. The opposition to Augustus of Saxony came from the elements which were opposed to Russian influence, the "National" party, which adopted with enthusiasm the cause of the ex-King Stanislaus Leczinski, who was put forward by his son-in-law, Louis XV. So large indeed was the party in Leczinski's favour that it carried the day at the election (Sept. 1733), but the intervention of a Russian army put the adherents of Stanislaus to flight, and enabled the Saxon party to proclaim Augustus as King (Oct. 5th). Stanislaus did indeed reach Dantzic, and stood a siege there; but France was unable to send him any effective aid, fearing to arouse English and Dutch jealousy by sending a squadron into the Baltic, and in July 1734 Dantzic had to surrender.

However, if Austria and Russia had carried the day in Poland, the entanglement of Austria in the Polish war gave France and Spain an opportunity too tempting to be allowed to pass. As a diversion in favour of Stanislaus, France had overrun Lorraine in the summer of 1733, and Marshal Berwick had laid siege to Kehl, taking it on October 28th; the defenceless state of Austrian Italy, denuded of troops for the war in Poland, proved an irresistible attraction to the covetous Elizabeth Farnese, and Charles Emmanuel III of Savoy eagerly grasped at so good a chance of further acquisitions in Lombardy at the expense of Austria. Chauvelin therefore found little difficulty about negotiating treaties between France and Savoy,[2] and between Spain and France;[3] but the jealousy which the Savoyards entertained towards Spain prevented these two alliances being combined in a

[1] Treaty of Löwenwolde (1732).
[2] Turin (Sept. 1733).
[3] The Escurial (Nov. 1733).

triple alliance. The Emperor thus found himself threatened in Italy and in Germany with a Franco-Spanish attack, but the Allies from whom he might have hoped to receive assistance failed him in his hour of need. Walpole allowed Fleury's promise that the neutrality of the Austrian Netherlands should be respected to lure him into leaving the Emperor in the lurch, a piece of short-sightedness which was to cost his country dear before ten years had passed. It would not be too much to say that if the Maritime Powers had come to the aid of Austria in 1733 the question of the Austrian Succession might have never led to a war. It was very largely the failure of Austria in this war, and in the disastrous Turkish war which she undertook partly in the hope of obtaining compensation for the loss of Naples, which encouraged her enemies to entertain the idea of partitioning her dominions in 1741. Nor did Walpole's pacific policy in 1733 achieve his object by ultimately averting the war with Spain over the West Indies. In the war of the Austrian Succession, England had to carry on a maritime and colonial war and at the same time to assist Maria Theresa to check a career of conquest on the part of the House of Bourbon, which might never have been begun had a revived Grand Alliance successfully withstood France and Spain in 1733–1734. Moreover, in 1733, Frederick William, and not, as in 1740, his more ambitious and grasping son, was on the Prussian throne, and it would not have been very difficult to obtain with English subsidies the assistance of that Prussian army which was to deal Austria more than one stab in the back between 1740 and 1745. Eugene, too, was still alive, and with proper support might still have done good service. And if Austria had not been humiliated and beaten between 1733 and 1738, if she had not suffered the losses of those years, and if her weakness had not been thereby exposed, Frederick II might well have hesitated before he dashed at Silesia in December 1740. It was because he saw that Austria was weaker than France that he seized upon Silesia, upon which he had no claim, rather than on Jülich and Berg, to which he certainly had some right. And that Austria was weak and a tempting prey to the spoilers was in large measure due to the fact that Walpole had preferred a temporary continuance of an insecure peace to opening his eyes to the true facts of the European situation.

One ally Charles might have secured : Frederick William of Prussia offered to lead his whole army to the Rhine, but only on condition of receiving an almost absolutely free hand, terms which even Eugene was somewhat unwilling to grant him. The Diet, it is true, did declare war (Jan. 1734) on France, but the utility of this declaration was diminished by the refusal of the three Wittelsbach Electors, Bavaria, Cologne and the Palatinate, to join in the resistance to the French.[1] That the campaign on the Rhine in 1734 should have gone altogether in favour of the French was therefore not surprising. A detached corps secured Treves and Trarbach, while the main army under Berwick besieged Philipsburg. Eugene was given the command of the force designed to relieve it, but neither the quantity nor the quality of his forces gave him any satisfaction; his auxiliaries were very slow to arrive, and when, Berwick having been killed in the trenches (June 12th), the Austrian commander did move up to attempt the relief of the fortress, the faint-hearted von Wutgenau surrendered (July 18th), almost under the eyes of the relievers. The new French commander, d'Asfeld, then moved on Mayence, but Eugene interposed so as to cover the city, and d'Asfeld relapsed into inactivity. Next year things went no better. The Elector of Bavaria mobilised his forces in rear of the Imperial army, and his hostile attitude prevented Eugene from doing anything beyond covering Mayence and the passes over the Black Forest. Even when 12,000 Russians reached Heidelberg (August), all that could be done was to force Charles Albert of Bavaria to dismiss his troops. Had the French been more energetic they might have repeated with every prospect of success the stroke which Marlborough had foiled in 1704, but their inactivity was partly due to a desire not to rouse the minor states of South-West Germany into active measures of defence. The operations on the Rhine were only important inasmuch as they diverted Austria's attention from Italy. There the success of the Allies had been even more pronounced; the French and Sardinians gradually drove the Austrians out of Lombardy, and, despite Mercy's stubborn resistance at Parma (June 29th, 1734) and Königsegg's victory on the Sesia (Sept. 15th, 1734),

---

[1] Good relations between the Bavarian and Palatine branches had been restored by the conclusion of a family compact in 1724.

forced them after a defeat at Guastalla (Sept. 19th, 1734) to fall back into the Tyrol and leave Mantua exposed: meanwhile the Spaniards overran the Two Sicilies with consummate ease. Almost without a blow they possessed themselves of Naples; by the end of 1733 only Capua remained in Austrian hands and nearly all Sicily had been lost, the rest following suit early in 1734. It was only the quarrels of the Allies that prevented them from ousting the Austrians altogether from Italy in 1735; but the rivalry of Sardinia and Spain proved the salvation of Mantua, and allowed Khevenhüller and Neipperg to maintain their positions on Lake Garda and the Adige.

By the autumn of 1735 even Charles VI had to confess himself worsted: deserted by his allies, slackly supported by the rest of Germany, at the end of his resources, and with a Turkish war impending, he had no option but to make peace. The Preliminaries of Vienna were signed with France in October 1735, and ratified in November,[1] though it was not till 1739 that the definite assent of Spain and of Sardinia was obtained. France abandoned Leczinski's candidature for Poland, but as a compensation he received the Duchy of Bar, with a promise of Lorraine; this he was to obtain as soon as the death of the last Medici should have set Tuscany free to be handed over to Francis Stephen of Lorraine as a compensation for the loss of his ancestral dominions. At Leczinski's death his possessions were to pass to France. It was a severe blow to the Empire, though severer to Francis Stephen, from whom a reluctant consent was purchased by his marriage to Maria Theresa (Feb. 1736), while Fleury had the satisfaction of having associated his name with one of the most important of the territorial acquisitions of France. The Emperor also had to cede the Two Sicilies to Don Carlos, and Novara and Tortona to Charles Emmanuel, but he recovered Parma and Piacenza. Naples was a serious loss, since its wealth had made it a very valuable and profitable possession; but the South Italian dominions had been isolated and very difficult to defend, and the territories left to Austria in the valley of the Po were much more compact. Finally, the Empire recovered Kehl, Philipsburg, Treves and Trarbach, and Charles VI obtained from France a recognition, though a recognition so conditioned and safeguarded as to be quite

---

[1] The definite peace between France and Austria was signed on Nov. 8th, 1738.

ambiguous, of the Pragmatic Sanction. It is also noteworthy that the "Ryswick clause," the abolition of which had been demanded by those Protestant members who voted for the war, was not mentioned in the 1738 treaty; and this was taken by the Protestants to be equivalent to cancellation, a view in which the Catholics practically acquiesced.

Shortly after the preliminaries had been ratified Eugene died (April 21st, 1736). Though not himself of German birth, he had been in peace almost as much as in war the mainstay of the Empire under the last three Emperors. He had just outlived the marriage of Maria Theresa to Francis Stephen; he must be considered fortunate in that he did not live to see the work of his last great victory undone in the unfortunate Turkish war of 1737–1739, in which Charles now became involved.

It was partly in fulfilment of his obligations to Russia, undertaken when Catherine guaranteed the Pragmatic Sanction in 1726, but also with the idea of recouping his losses in Italy at the expense of Turkey, that, at a time when peace, financial retrenchment and careful reorganisation were the crying needs of the Hapsburg monarchy, Charles VI embarked in a fresh war. Russia had declared war on Turkey in 1735 on the pretext that the Tartars, when attacking Persia, had violated the neutrality of Russian territory. Not being altogether successful in the campaigns of 1735–1736, she called upon Austria for the assistance which the Treaty of 1726 pledged the Hapsburgs to send. There were great debates as to the course which Austria should adopt; she might content herself with sending 30,000 men as auxiliaries and yet remain neutral as a whole, as Seckendorff and Palffy, the Palatine of Hungary, suggested; or she might embark upon the war as a full partner in the enterprise. Bartenstein, now coming to the front as Secretary to the Austrian Conference, was in favour of the latter plan; and it would appear that it was to this that Charles VI himself inclined. The position of a mere auxiliary was hardly consonant with his Imperial dignity, and therefore, though Poland and Venice held aloof, though his German vassals failed to support him, and in some cases absolutely refused to help, though hardly any part of the aid which the Diet voted ever reached the Emperor's coffers, though the condition of the Austrian army, administration and finances certainly did not warrant any such enterprise, he resolved to take part with his whole force in the campaign of 1737.

The military operations began with a fair measure of success. Seckendorff invaded Servia and took Nissa (July 23rd); but undue division of forces, failure to keep touch between the different corps, and the quarrels and jealousies of the commanders, produced the natural result, the Turks got the best of some minor affairs, and their successes spread to the main operations. Saxe-Hildburghausen was forced back from Banjaluka in Bosnia to Gradiska on the Save; Khevenhüller failed in an attempt on Widdin; and Nissa, the sole prize of the campaign, was lost within two months of its capture. Seckendorff, who as a Protestant and a foreigner was unpopular with the other generals and had little control over them, was rather unfairly made the scapegoat for the general failure: he was court-martialed and imprisoned; but his successor, Königsegg, did little better in 1738. He did defeat the Turks at Mehadia, and force them to evacuate Orsova, but he was unable to take Widdin; and far from following up a success he won at Cornia in July, by the end of the year he had been driven in under the walls of Belgrade, and, like Seckendorff, was removed from the command. However, the new general, Wallis, brought no change of fortune. Instructed to fight a decisive battle, he did so at Crozka, near Belgrade (July 23rd), with singular ill success, for his bad choice of ground more than nullified the good behaviour of the troops, with the result that after losing 20,000 men, he had to leave Belgrade to its fate and retire on Pancsova. All he could do was to begin negotiations with the Turks which his successor, Neipperg, completed. The Peace of Belgrade (signed Sept. 18th, 1739) was a sad contrast to Passarowitz and Carlowitz. Once again Western Wallachia and Servia, including Belgrade, passed under Turkish rule, and the boundary of Bosnia was restored to its position in 1699, the Danube and the Save forming the frontier. Thus Austria, which had embarked on the war in the hope that she might make gains to set off against her Italian losses, found herself involved in even greater humiliation. The war was in every way a failure. Its cost was great in men and in money alike. The reputation of the Austrian army received a severe blow; its unpreparedness, indiscipline and inefficiency were displayed to all the world, its most reputed and trusted generals were found wanting. Wallis and Neipperg shared the fate of Seckendorff; they were court-martialed both for their conduct of the military operations and still more for their precipitation in concluding peace. But such treatment was a little unfair to the generals, the fault lay rather with the government as a whole, and with the unsound condition of the Hapsburg dominions at that moment. Painstaking, anxious to do good, capable of seeing what it would be well to do, but quite incapable of the moral courage and hard work needed to carry the task through, Charles VI was persistently unfortunate throughout his reign, and in nothing so much as in its abrupt end. His death (Oct. 20th, 1740) was by no means expected. Only fifty-six years old, he might well have lived another fifteen or even twenty years; and it was confidently expected that he would survive his wife, Elizabeth Christina of Brunswick-Wolfenbüttel, who was very ill, in which case a second marriage might have produced the male heir of whom the Hapsburg dynasty stood in such great need.[1] He had, it is true, obtained the assent of nearly all the Powers to the Pragmatic Sanction, though Bavaria and the Elector Palatine had withdrawn that given in 1726; but, as Eugene had warned him, paper promises were to prove of far less value than a full treasury and an efficient army. He had also apparently solved the question of Jülich and Berg in favour of the Sulzbachs by a secret treaty with France in January 1739; but Fleury, feeling that the cards were in his hands, was just about to make a somewhat similar compact with Prussia.[2] No moment could have been more unfortunate than that at which Charles VI actually died. Austria was of all countries the least fitted for the troubles of a disputed succession; above all things she needed ten years of rest and recuperation, while, little though it was anticipated, the death of Frederick William of Prussia (May 31st, 1740) was destined to be of enormous importance to her. It was early in October when Charles was taken ill at his hunting-box at Schönborn and died in a few days, leaving to his successor a sea of troubles for many of which it is difficult not to hold him responsible.

---

[1] It was probably for some such reason as this that he neglected to secure the election of Francis Stephen of Lorraine as King of the Romans.

[2] Cf. p. 96.

CHAPTER VII

MARIA THERESA AND HER ENEMIES

IT was not merely the special circumstances of the moment at which Charles VI died, not merely the fact that his heir and successor was a young and inexperienced woman, which made the Hapsburg dominions in 1740 so tempting a prey to the would-be spoilers: the constitution of the disunited and incoherent realm and the relations between its different parts seemed to promise an easy success to the grasping claimants who were proposing to divide them. The accumulation of territories to which Maria Theresa succeeded was not a nation, it was not even organised as a federation. Under Charles VI little had been done towards binding together by administrative or judicial reforms the three main groups, the Austrian, the Bohemian and the Hungarian, which still remained in all essentials separate, while the outlying dependencies, in the Netherlands and Italy, tended rather to absorb the attention of their rulers and draw them away from the task, difficult enough already, of welding together the central dominions. The constitutional and administrative arrangements had undergone few changes since 1715. To a certain extent the Imperial authority had gained ground at the expense of local officials, but the progress of centralisation had been slow. The recognition of the Pragmatic Sanction, however, had done something to bind the provinces together; it had established a common principle of succession accepted and acknowledged all through the Hapsburg dominions, and though Charles VI had shrunk from attempting to push the process, further signs were not altogether wanting of a tendency towards the work Maria Theresa was to accomplish when she fused the separate Bohemian and Austrian Chancelleries and brought all the German dominions of the Hapsburgs under the same judicial and administrative system. But in 1740 these changes were still to come, and at that time, as far as constitution went, Austria

might still be said to have barely emerged from the Middle Ages; her government was still largely feudal in character, and in efficiency and organisation was far behind the other countries of Western Europe.[1]

In each province of the Hapsburg dominions the old constitutional forms lingered on, retaining enough vitality to hamper and impede the action of the central government, to diminish its authority and its control over the resources of the state, but devoid of the compensating advantages which might have been derived from a system of real and adequate representative government, since they had their roots in feudal privileges rather than in real and active constitutional life and liberties. In these assemblies (*Landtäge*) the power lay with the nobles; for while the burghers had few votes and less influence, it was only in the Tyrol that the peasantry were represented at all. And at this period, as they were soon to show, the Austrian nobility were sadly lacking in patriotism, in public spirit and in self-sacrifice. Charles VI had made great efforts to attach them to the Hapsburg dynasty, but his over-anxiety had defeated its own ends. Unduly lavish concessions and favours had only whetted their appetites and made them ask for more. Selfish and parochial, they looked to their own personal ends, or at the utmost to the interests of their provinces, rather than to those of the dynasty and the state. Still they were not merely an idle privileged caste, as was the case in France. If they enjoyed the benefits of their feudal position, they discharged its duties, officering the Army and controlling local government. Neither burghers nor peasantry were of much account. The cities differed in constitutions, in rights and privileges, and utterly lacked combination, either political or industrial. Those which stood on the lands of nobles paid them dues and performed services just as the peasants did. Inside the towns the power was usually in the hands of a narrow oligarchy, often a guild which had become obsolete and inefficient. Charles VI had made some praiseworthy efforts to sweep away the cramping relics of these mediæval institutions, but he had not had much success, and trade and industry were still subject to their blighting influence. To this must be attributed the comparative failure of the public works, of the encouragement to commerce, and of the

[1] Cf. Chapter II. pp. 35–36.

other efforts which Charles VI made to promote the material
prosperity of his subjects.   In the German districts there was
no serfdom, but in Bohemia the peasants were still unfree, the
chattels of their lords; and that all was not well with them
may be judged from the agrarian revolts which had broken
out in Bohemia in 1680, in Moravia as late as 1717.   A great
part of the land was in the hands of the clergy, who were
numerous and powerful, and not by any means a factor towards progress.   Though somewhat on the wane, the influence
of the Jesuits was still considerable enough to be deleterious.
The state of the judicial organisation and administration
urgently required reform, while even more complete chaos
prevailed in the finances.   The Court was wasteful, the taxes
were at once oppressive and unproductive, the revenue, which
stood at about 30 million thalers, was quite insufficient for the
Army and the administration.   All Charles VI's efforts to
reform the finances had broken down, and the two recent and
most disastrous wars seemed to have utterly exhausted the
resources of the country.   The Treasury was practically
empty, and the heaviness of the taxation had made the people
discontented and disaffected.   Nowhere were the effects of the
financial disorders and constitutional chaos more pernicious
than in their influence on the condition of the Army.   In
the first place, it suffered from the division of control between
the War Council, which attended to the levying of the troops,
and the local Estates, which provided the funds for their
maintenance.   A certain amount had been done of late years
to improve the Army, but its organisation left an enormous
amount to be desired.   Facilities for training the officers and
exercising the troops were lacking, and its whole tone and
prestige were suffering from the disastrous Turkish war.
Nominally fairly strong—the establishment for 1734 was
fixed at 150,000—the actual numbers bore little resemblance
to the paper strength; and of the 60,000 men to which the
Army actually amounted on a peace footing, the majority were
in Hungary, Lombardy, or the Netherlands, and only very few
were to be found in the central provinces.

   Nor had Maria Theresa much better cause for satisfaction
and confidence in the advisers on whom she had to rely.   The
Turkish war had left all her most famous generals under a
cloud, and not one of the ministers who composed the " Con-

ference" could be described as a pillar of strength. With
hardly any exceptions they were over seventy years of age,
and though they had once done good service, that day was
past. Age had brought irresolution; prejudices, timidity and
indolence had warped their judgment and diminished their
powers; the work was too much for them physically as well
as morally. The Chancellor, Philip Louis Sinzendorff, was
worn out, and quite unfit for his post; Alois Harrach, the
Land Marshal of Lower Austria, lacked vigour and capacity;
his brother Joseph, who was President of the War Council
from Königsegg's fall in 1738 till 1764, was younger than
the rest of the Conference, but not much more efficient, being
indolent and slow. Philip Kinsky, the Chancellor of Bohemia,
was dominàted by local and particularist ideas; he was devoid
of any wider patriotism, and his sole object seems to have
been to assist Bohemia to avoid bearing her proper burdens.
The Finance Minister, Gundacker Stahremberg, was perhaps
the most capable member of the Conference; he came of a
family eminent for its good services, and his own record was
honourable; but he was feeling the weight of his years, and he
was hardly fitted to cope with such a crisis as that of 1740.
Under these circumstances it was not unnatural that the
Secretary to the Conference, Bartenstein (1689–1757), an
energetic, rather opinionated man of considerable capacity in
some respects, but quite devoid of the higher qualities of a
statesman, should have enjoyed a rather greater share of
Maria Theresa's confidence in the early days of her reign than
he did later on, when experience enabled her to judge more
for herself, both of men and of policies.

That at this particular crisis Bartenstein's judgment was
much at fault cannot be denied. He relied blindly on the
gcod intentions of France, not seeing that the concessions
Charles VI had made in the hope of securing Fleury's good
offices had only brought the weakness and helplessness of
Austria before the notice of her enemies.

And when Maria Theresa looked round upon the Powers
of Europe, it must have been as probable enemies rather than
possible allies that the majority of them appeared to her.
True that they had almost all guaranteed the Pragmatic
Sanction,[1] but faithful observance of the most solemn treaty

[1] For list, see Erdmannsdörffer, bk. vii. ch. 5, and cf. p. 83.

engagements was hardly a characteristic feature of European statesmen in the eighteenth century.[1] Most of the Powers did return favourable replies to the circular which Maria Theresa addressed to them on her accession, announcing that she had succeeded under the terms of the Pragmatic Sanction, and claiming the fulfilment of their promises; but these replies also were mere paper securities of which the worthlessness was soon to be proved.

Of the claims which Maria Theresa had to fear, those of Bavaria and Saxony were undoubtedly the strongest. The Elector of Bavaria and the King of Saxony were in the first place the husbands of those daughters of the Emperor Joseph I who had been deprived of the succession to the Hapsburg dominions in favour of Maria Theresa.[2] Charles Albert of Bavaria had, moreover, a claim on his own behalf as a descendant of Anne, daughter of Ferdinand I of Austria. By the will of that Emperor, in case the descendants of his sons (Maximilian II and Charles of Styria) failed, those of Anne were to succeed. According to the Bavarian contention, Anne's heirs were to come in on the failure of the *male* line; but as the Austrians contended, and as was proved by the production of the authentic will from the archives at Vienna, it was on the failure of " legitimate " heirs that the contingency was to arise.[3] Still Charles Albert did not hesitate to claim the succession directly Charles VI died; and though his own resources were not sufficient to make him formidable, in the Polish Succession War the old relations between France and Bavaria had to some extent been renewed,[4] so that it was the support of France rather than the strength of Bavaria which made the Wittelsbach claim a danger. Moreover, there was in the Austrian dominions a faction which was decidedly favourable to the Bavarian claim, the party that had objected to the marriage of Maria Theresa to Francis Stephen of Lorraine; and this disaffection largely accounted for the feeble resistance of Upper Austria to the invaders in 1741, and for the discreditable readiness with which many of the nobles and officials of that province and of Bohemia submitted to the Bavarian and accepted office under him.

[1] Cf. Sorel, *Europe et la Révolution Française*, i. 24.   [2] Cf. pp. 78–79.
[3] Cf. von Arneth, *Maria Theresa*, vol. i. p. 97, and Wolf's *Austria*, bk. i. ch. I.
[4] Cf. p. 100 ; also *Instructions aux Ambassadeurs de France—Bavière*.

Augustus of Saxony-Poland ought, if gratitude had any influence over his policy, to have supported Austria, to whom he mainly owed his Polish crown. He did at first recognise the Pragmatic Sanction,[1] and place himself on Austria's side ; but before long the successes of Maria Theresa's enemies, the influence of Marshal Belleisle and of Montijo, the Spanish Ambassador at Dresden, and the rejection of the concessions he demanded as the price of his support,[2] caused Augustus to drift over to the other side and finally to participate in the attack on Bohemia.

Spain and Sardinia also made more or less formal claims on the Hapsburg territories, but their claims were of that class which would be amply met by a dividend of a shilling in the pound, and with a maritime war against England already engaging her resources, Spain would hardly have done anything unless France gave her a definite lead. And France procrastinated over her reply, making excuses of a formal nature, and waiting to see what was going to happen in the hope that she might direct events to her own advantage.

England, the United Provinces and Russia were thus about the only Powers from whom Maria Theresa had nothing to fear ; but unfortunately for her the course of affairs in Russia following on the death of the Empress Anne Ivanovna (Oct. 28th, 1740) resulted in the temporary supremacy of Münich and Ostermann, who were hostile to Austria, and thus deprived Maria Theresa of the assistance from that quarter which she might have hoped.

It seemed, therefore, that all depended on the action of France. Fleury is generally credited with a wish to preserve the peace of Europe, and is held to have been forced into a war he disliked by the importunities of a younger and more enterprising generation, just as Walpole was driven into the Spanish war. It would appear, however, that the acquisition of Lorraine by France under his auspices had whetted his appetite for further territorial gains, and that if he resisted Belleisle's proposals that France should seize this splendid opportunity of partitioning the Hapsburg dominions and so completing

---

[1] Von Arneth, i. 101.

[2] Namely, a strip of territory in Silesia giving military communication between Saxony and Poland, the royal title for Saxony, *i.e.* a kingdom within the Empire, together with those portions of Lower Lusatia which Prussia held as fiefs of the Bohemian Crown. Cf. von Arneth, i. 207.

the work of Mazarin and Louis XIV, it was rather from jealousy
of the proposer than from dislike of the proposal, and also
because France seemed at the moment on the verge of being
involved in the Anglo-Spanish war.   He had told the Elector
of Bavaria that the French guarantee of the Pragmatic Sanction
would not be observed if any third party should prove to have a
better right to the Hapsburg dominions than Maria Theresa had;
and, in the words of a contemporary,[1] to say that " the Queen of
Hungary has a right to her possessions not in prejudice to the
rights of others . . . is a door to evade the whole obligation."
    But it was by might, not by right, that the question was to
be decided.   While every one was watching France, the blow
fell from a very different quarter.   The young monarch who
had ascended the Prussian throne on the death of Frederick
William I a few months earlier was burning for an opportunity
to make a name for himself.   He would have no more of the
cautious policy of neutrality and inaction which had made men
sneer at the military monarch who never let his parade-ground
soldiers fire a shot in real earnest.   He was, moreover, a true
Hohenzollern in his desire for territorial gains, and in his
determination to seek them along the line of least resistance.
Energetic, ambitious, anxious to use the fine weapon his father
had left him and which he had at the very outset begun to
increase, adding no less than 16,000 men at once, he had
already given proof of his aggressive and imperious character
by his action in the Herstal affair.   Herstal was one of those
fragments of the Orange inheritance which had finally been
adjudged to Frederick William I when the quarrel between him
and Louis XV over that point was compromised in 1732.
The Bishop of Liége also laid claim to it, and had tried to
prevent the Prussian recruiters enlisting men there.   Frederick
William, when no friendly settlement could be arranged, had let
the matter alone.   Frederick II at once took forcible action,
marched troops into the district, exacted a contribution and
compelled the inhabitants to support the force in occupation,
disregarding absolutely the Emperor's orders to him to retire
from the territory.   It was a minor matter, but it was typical.
Regardless of forms or rights, Frederick II used force unsparingly to gain his ends, and paid heed to no commands that had
not force at their back.

[1] Robert Trevor to H. Walpole, *Trevor MSS.*, Hist. MSS. Com. p. 66.

Such a monarch was not likely to let slip the promising opportunity which the state of the Austrian dominions at Charles VI's death laid before him. Nor was it hard to find precedents for aggression. Included in the Austrian province of Silesia were the Duchies of Liegnitz, Wohlau and Brieg, which had passed into the direct rule of the Hapsburgs on the death in 1675 of George William, last Duke of Liegnitz. In that year the Great Elector had advanced a claim to these Duchies on the strength of an *Erbverbrüderung* or "heritage fraternity" entered into in 1537 by the then Elector of Brandenburg, Joachim II, and Duke Frederick of Liegnitz. However, not only had the arrangement never received the sanction of the Emperor, whose rights it undoubtedly infringed, but Charles V had protested against it at the time ; while in 1546 Ferdinand I, interfering as King of Bohemia and immediate overlord of Liegnitz, compelled the Duke to cancel the treaty. That technically Brandenburg had any case at all is difficult to believe,[1] though the Hohenzollern seem to have acted on the principle that a claim acquires validity from mere frequency of assertion. It was partly because the Emperor had taken possession of the Liegnitz inheritance in 1675, as being fiefs which naturally lapsed to their overlord on failure of heirs, and had flatly refused Frederick William any compensation, that the Great Elector had concluded in October 1679 a treaty which enrolled Brandenburg among the clients of France—a curious proceeding for a prince in whom some later historians have endeavoured to discover a champion of Germany against French aggression. In 1686 the matter had gone a stage further. Alarmed by the strongly anti-Protestant attitude of Louis XIV, and perhaps made uneasy by the Truce of Ratisbon (1684), which confirmed Louis in the possession of Strassburg, for which he must have felt himself in no small measure responsible, Frederick William began to seek opportunities of drawing nearer to Austria, offering his aid against the Turks and eventually against France—on conditions. These conditions, however, were more than the Emperor and most of his advisers were disposed to grant, for Frederick William suited his demands to the measure of the necessity of Austria. Ultimately, after much haggling, a treaty was signed in March 1686, by which in return for considerable subsidies and the

[1] Cf. von Arneth, *Maria Theresa*, i. 105.

cession of the little district of Schwiebus and a guarantee of the Lichtenstein claim on East Friesland, which had now passed to the Hohenzollern, the Great Elector despatched 8000 men to the seat of war in Hungary and abandoned all further claims on the Silesian Duchies.

But unfortunately this was not the end of the Silesian question. At the same time that this negotiation was concluded, the Emperor's envoy, Baron Fridag, concluded a secret treaty with the Electoral Prince, who pledged himself to restore Schwiebus to the Emperor on succeeding to the Electorate. The facts with regard to this negotiation are disputed, and the truth is not clear. The account given on the Prussian side[1] is that the Austrians represented to the Electoral Prince, who was one of the leaders of the anti-French party in Brandenburg, that the French party at the Court were insisting on the cession of Schwiebus to prevent an understanding between Austria and Brandenburg. The Austrian account, on the other hand, represents the proposal to surrender Schwiebus as coming from Frederick, who hoped thereby to secure the Emperor's good offices in the matter of his father's will. The Great Elector was at this time much under the influence of his second wife, Dorothea of Holstein-Glücksburg, who had induced him to bequeath to the four sons she had borne him, separate territorial appanages out of the lands he had acquired. Thus Minden was to go to Prince Philip William, Halberstadt and Reinstein to provide a territorial establishment for his brother Albert Frederick. That such an arrangement would have tended to weaken the power of the family seems certain, for there is little reason to suppose that its results would have differed from those which followed in Saxony from the very similar dispositions made by John George I.[2] Carefully as the Great Elector sought to reserve for his successor as Elector military and diplomatic control over the territories of the cadet-branches, even their partial independence must have proved a fatal obstacle to the completeness of King Frederick William I's administrative reforms. Under the terms of the will, the Emperor was appointed executor, and had he chosen to support the claims of the younger sons of the Great Elector, Frederick I might have found them difficult to resist. Thus, when the death of Frederick

[1] Cf. Droysen, *Geschichte der Preussischen Politick*, Part iv. vol. 4, pp. 154–204.
[2] Cf. pp. 39–40.

William brought the question forward, the surrender of Schwiebus was the price for the Emperor's consent to the setting aside of the will.   On making the restoration, Frederick declared that he resumed his claims on the Silesian Duchies; somewhat unjustifiably, for if it happened that the district received by Frederick William as compensation for the abandoned claim coincided with the price paid by his successor for the very definite service of quashing the Great Elector's will, one may fairly regard that service as the real compensation for the none too strong claim, a fairly ample *quid pro quo.*   Subsequent events, then, make it appear more probable that of the two versions the Austrian is nearer the truth.[1]

That the surrender of Schwiebus does not affect the Prussian claim on the Duchies may therefore be admitted, and at the same time it may be pointed out that the resumption of the claim by Frederick I cannot be regarded as in the least making up for its original invalidity.   The claim on Jaegerndorf was hardly any stronger when put to the test of facts.   This Duchy had once been in the possession of John George of Brandenburg, second son of the Elector Joachim Frederick (1598–1608), though the Hohenzollern title to it had never received Imperial recognition.   In 1622, John George of Jaegerndorf was put to the ban of the Empire for assisting Frederick V of the Palatinate in his attempt to deprive the Hapsburgs of Bohemia.   The Duchy was accordingly forfeited with all due formalities and annexed by Ferdinand II, and had remained in Hapsburg hands at the Peace of 1648.   Thus according to the laws and customs of the Empire the Hohenzollern title to Jaegerndorf was valueless, and indeed the only right which Frederick II possessed over Silesia was the right of the stronger.

When it is further remembered that in 1728 Prussia had formally guaranteed the Pragmatic Sanction, that Frederick II himself admitted that in his place Frederick William would have kept his word, the only thing that is surprising is that Frederick should ever have taken the trouble to produce any so-called " justification " for his action ; but it certainly is not a little striking to reflect that but for Charles VI there would have been no Frederick II in existence in 1740.   It was largely the Emperor's intervention, ill-timed indeed in the

[1] Cf. *Z.S.* ii. 21.

interests of his family, which had caused the irate Frederick William to refrain from executing the sentence of death pronounced against the then Crown Prince for his attempted desertion (1730). The return which Frederick II now made gives one some idea of the standards of international morality, public faith and private gratitude upon which he acted.

As a justification for the seizure of Silesia, it has been urged that if Prussia was to keep her position in Europe she must have more territory and population to support her disproportionate army, and that therefore she had to make what acquisitions she could;[1] an argument whose barefaced appeal to force is fully in keeping with the high-handed Prussian traditions, but which is not worth serious consideration. That Prussia had been ill-treated by Austria in the matter of Jülich and Berg[2] is undeniable, but that hardly gave Frederick a valid claim on Silesia; though if he had chosen to forcibly assert his claim to Jülich and Berg, and had marched troops into them in order to obtain security that they would fall to him on the death of their holder, his action would not have been liable to the censure which one cannot but pass on his utterly unjustifiable seizure of Silesia.   But the truth was that he was afraid of France—afraid that if he were to seize Jülich and Berg, Fleury might adopt the cause of the Catholic Sulzbachs and dispossess him, afraid that France might not like his presence at so important a point on the Rhine.   Moreover, Silesia was richer, larger, more populous, more conveniently situated with regard to Brandenburg, and the easier prey.   Frederick knew that he was not the only vulture gathered round the carcase of the apparently moribund Hapsburg monarchy; he knew that there were others as greedy as himself, and that he could rely on being imitated and probably supported, that Maria Theresa was beset by possible enemies, that France would probably view with approbation the humiliation of the Power which had struggled so hard to defend Germany against her, and he preferred plundering a woman in distress to incurring the displeasure of the Bourbon monarchy.   The pretext that Maria Theresa was threatened with an attack from Saxony— which had recognised its guarantee—and from Bavaria—which could not dispose of more than 20 to 30,000 men—was the merest subterfuge: even had it been true it would hardly

[1] Cf. *E.H.R.* 1889, p. 586.   [2] Cf. p. 95.

have justified a Power on friendly terms with its neighbour in taking forcible and uninvited possession of one of that neighbour's provinces because it has selected it as the reward for services not yet rendered. But there was about as much truth in the assertion as there was in the proclamation which Frederick published when he crossed the frontier, declaring that the step was taken in concert with Maria Theresa, with whom he was negotiating.

The invasion of Silesia was as successful as it was unexpected. The province was all but without a garrison; and even had it been at its full peace establishment of 13,000 men, that force would have been outnumbered by two to one by the 5000 cavalry and 22,000 infantry of whom Frederick took command at Crossen on December 14th, to say nothing of the 10,000 more troops who were a few days' march in rear. All that the Governor of the province, Count Wallis, could do was to throw the few troops he had into the fortresses of Brieg, Glogau and Neisse, which were hastily prepared for defence. Breslau, the capital of the province, refused to admit a garrison, and declared that it would be responsible for its own defence. Luckily for the Austrians, bad weather delayed the Prussian movements, and Frederick, as yet unaware of the value of promptitude, wasted six valuable days in an unnecessary delay at Herrendorf, five miles from Glogau (Dec. 22nd to 28th). This gave time for Brieg and Neisse to be put into such a condition that they could stand a siege. On December 28th the King's column resumed its march up the Oder on Breslau, leaving part of the reserve division to blockade Glogau, while Schwerin and the right wing, who had moved parallel up the Bober, occupied Liegnitz. The people of Breslau behaved with a culpable lack of patriotism and courage, tamely opening their gates on January 2nd on condition that they should not be forced to receive a Prussian garrison. Indeed, with the exception of the three fortresses of Brieg, Glogau and Neisse, and one or two minor places like Namslau and Ottmachau, the whole province submitted to the invader almost without firing a shot, nobles, townsfolk and peasantry displaying an apathy which did them little credit. By the end of January these three fortresses alone held out. The time which Frederick had wasted had been turned to good effect; and he was now learning the value of rapid movements, for his army was unable to go into winter-quarters but had to maintain the blockades of these towns. If the Austrians could gather a relieving army with anything like reasonable speed, the Prussian position might prove hazardous. And Maria Theresa was sparing no effort to avenge the injury which Frederick had done her, and to make him pay dearly for his insolent assumption of a victor's airs, his taking it for granted that she would not be able to regain Silesia. This attitude was an insult above all to the Austrian army, which looked upon the Prussians as mere soldiers of the parade-ground, and relied confidently on its own experience of real war to give it the victory over these troops who had never seen a shot fired in anger.[1] The Queen of Hungary therefore rejected with scorn the proposals made to her through Baron Götter, offering her Frederick's assistance against other enemies, and promising his vote at the Imperial election to Francis Stephen of Lorraine if she would cede the Silesian Duchies. The Chancellor, Sinzendorf, and one or two of the other ministers were for yielding; but Maria Theresa would not hear of concessions, and Bartenstein and Stahremberg were equally firm for " no surrender." Moreover, it looked as though she were going to find a friend in need in George II. In vain Walpole contended that what Great Britain required was the settlement of the differences between Austria and Prussia : in vain he opposed the action of George II in proceeding to Hanover in May 1741 to put himself at the head of the force he was collecting there ; the English nation was full of sympathy for Maria Theresa, and for once the King had the unusual experience of sharing the sentiments of his subjects. Walpole had to propose in Parliament a subsidy of £300,000 for the Queen of Hungary, and George II planned to take the field at the head of a considerable force, including, besides Dutch and British, 12,000 Danes and Hessians to be secured by a British subsidy, and 15,000 Hanoverians, 3000 at his expense as Elector, 12,000 in British pay. So threatening, indeed, was his attitude, that many of the Prussian reinforcements destined for Silesia had to be diverted to join the force which Frederick placed near Magdeburg under command of Leopold of Anhalt-Dessau to hold Hanover and Saxony in check, for Augustus III

[1] Cf. von Arneth, i. 219.

also, alarmed at the success of his Prussian neighbour, for whom he had no special love, was negotiating with Maria Theresa. It should also be mentioned that on March 2nd a treaty, amicably regulating various disputed points as to their boundaries, was signed between Austria and the Porte, the Turk thus displaying a very different spirit from the Christian neighbours who sought to profit by the embarrassments of Maria Theresa.

Meanwhile the army which Neipperg was bringing up through Moravia was drawing near the scene of action. Luckily for Frederick, the weakness of the Austrian army and the utter inefficiency of its administration combined with Neipperg's failure to appreciate the necessity for rapid action to make its movements as slow as Frederick's own had been in December. Thus the Prussians were able to storm Glogau (March 9th) and to bring up its besiegers to join the King at Schweidnitz long before Neipperg appeared on the Silesian side of the *Riesengebirge*.

Had Neipperg been a man of any real capacity, and had he made proper use of his excellent irregular cavalry to conceal his own movements and to acquaint him with the dispositions of the Prussians, he might have brought the military career of Frederick to an abrupt and inglorious conclusion. The Prussian troops were unduly scattered and out of supporting distance from each other, when Neipperg, moving from Olmütz by Freudenthal on Neisse, burst into the midst of their cantonments (April 2nd). Frederick happened to be at Jaegerndorf with some 4000 men, and might easily have been cut off and taken, but the Austrian was utterly unaware of the chance before him. He pushed straight on to Neisse, which he reached on April 4th, letting Frederick retire from Jaegerndorf by Steinau, where he rallied Kalkstein and 10,000 men, Friedland (April 6th), and Michelau, where he crossed to the left of the Neisse (April 8th), to Pogarell, where the detachment which had been blockading Brieg joined him (April 9th). Meanwhile Neipperg, having relieved Neisse, had moved on towards Brieg and Breslau, to which last place he was actually nearer than Frederick was; but once again his slowness and his total ignorance of his adversary's movements cast away the advantage on which he had stumbled. On the night of the 9th he reached Mollwitz, seven miles to the North-Westward of Pogarell, and here he was resting his troops when, about midday on the 10th, news was brought to him that the Prussian army was marching against him in full battle array.

The armies which were to fight the first battle of the war were of approximately equal strength, roughly 20,000 men each; but while the Prussians had but 4000 cavalry, Neipperg had 8600 of much better quality. On the other hand, Frederick had an overwhelming superiority in artillery, having sixty guns to eighteen.[1] Both armies were drawn up in the same style, in two lines with the infantry on the centre and the cavalry on the wings. Owing to a mistake of their commander, Schulenberg, the Prussian cavalry on the right did not extend outwards as far as they should have done. Crowding in unduly on the centre, they threw the infantry next to them into such confusion that three battalions had to fall back and take up their position at right angles to the rest, thus covering the space between the two lines of infantry. It was largely by this accident that the fate of the battle was decided; for when the Austrian left wing of cavalry, sweeping down upon the Prussian right, broke them at the first shock and drove them from the field, it was these three battalions which checked the victors when they turned against the Prussian centre. But for these battalions having been so posted as to cover the exposed flank of the infantry, the Austrian horsemen would have caught the Prussian infantry as they faced to the right to meet the charge at a great disadvantage, from which even their steadiness and excellent fire-discipline might have failed to extricate them. As it was, Römer and his cavalry could not break the steady lines of the Prussian foot, though they charged repeatedly, even attacking the second line in rear and forcing it to face right about to repulse the attack. Neipperg had meanwhile pushed his infantry forward to support the advantage gained by their cavalry, for the Austrian right had been no less successful than their comrades of the left, but the rapid fire of the Prussian infantry backed up by their superiority in artillery was more than the Austrian infantry could face, and they wavered, ceased to advance, and halted. For a time the fire-duel continued, then Schwerin—left in command when Frederick, thinking the battle lost by the defeat of his cavalry, had joined in their headlong

[1] Oncken (*Zeitalter Friedrichs der Grosse*, i. 323) gives the Prussian force as 35 squadrons and 31 battalions, the Austrian as 86 squadrons and 18 battalions.

flight—gave the order to advance. The Austrians at once gave way and fell back in some disorder towards Neisse, the Prussians making no attempt to pursue.

Such was the battle of Mollwitz, an action of far more importance than many in which much greater forces have been engaged. In military history it is remarkable as a display of the possibilities of really well-trained and disciplined infantry. Before Mollwitz and between armies of equal strength the better chance would have been held to be possessed by the side which had a two to one superiority in cavalry: Mollwitz showed the impotence of cavalry even when excellent against steady infantry whose fire-discipline was good. It was a victory for the army, not for its commander. Schwerin did much to encourage his men, but the victory was not due to superiority in generalship or in tactics. It was the lucky accident which placed the three battalions in the decisive position on the right flank of the centre which, combined with the years of hard work on the parade-grounds of Potsdam, won the battle. One might almost fancy that the spirit of Frederick William cannot have been far away when the army that he had trained was put to its first real test and came through it so victoriously. Frederick II's share in the success is not so easy to find.

As far as immediate military results went the victory was rather barren. Brieg was now bombarded, and on May 4th it fell; but Neipperg remained unmolested in his camp at Neisse, against which the Prussians made no advance. Thus if defeated at Mollwitz and unsuccessful in his endeavour to sweep the Prussians from Silesia, Neipperg had at least checked the conquest of the province and had recovered some lost ground; in August, indeed, he made a dash on Breslau which Schwerin just forestalled by occupying the town with 8000 men; and when at last the Austrians withdrew from Silesia and left Neisse to its fate, it was not because Frederick had forced them. In a sense it was his work, immediately it was the appearance of another enemy on the scene.

The political results of Mollwitz had been far more decisive than the military. Even before the end of March the "forward party" at Versailles had already so far carried the day that Marshal Belleisle set out to visit the minor Courts of Germany, and to win by persuasion and by bribery the support of the various Electors and Princes to the Bavarian candidature for the Empire; but it cannot be doubted that an Austrian victory at Mollwitz would have greatly altered the complexion of affairs. Mollwitz seemed to promise victories for the other claimants. Austria's incapacity to defend herself was published to the world, and Bavarian, Saxon and Spanish land-hunger received a powerful stimulant. Had Frederick been defeated, had Austria shown herself capable of defending her rights and of making good her title to her provinces at the point of the bayonet, these Powers might have found it advisable to reconsider their proposed policy. Fleury's conscientious scruples might have been awakened, he might have hailed it as an argument for combating Belleisle's policy, and have used this means of recovering the control of affairs now slipping away from him. As it was, France believed more than ever that the day had come for the final overthrow of the Hapsburgs and for the consummation of the work of the House of Bourbon. Belleisle did not, indeed, at once succeed in bringing about a definite agreement with the victor of Mollwitz. His first interview with Frederick, which took place before Brieg towards the end of April, left matters rather as they stood. Indeed Frederick, instead of welcoming the alliance which the French envoy proposed, rather sought to use the mediation of England to arrange an accommodation with Maria Theresa. Meanwhile Belleisle hastened to negotiate a treaty (May 28th) by which Spain and Bavaria, the principal claimants to the Hapsburg heritage, settled on their respective shares, while France by the Treaty of Nymphenburg (May 18th) pledged herself definitely to support the Bavarian on the understanding that she should keep her own gains.[1]

Spain was already stirring and preparing to forcibly assert Don Philip's claims on Lombardy. Charles Emmanuel of Sardinia and his ambitious minister, d'Ormea, were on the

---

[1] There is much difference of opinion as to what exactly was arranged: Droysen (*Friedrich der Grosse*, vol. i. pp. 273 ff.), with whom Oncken (*AG*, iii. 8, vol. i. p.355) agrees, would seem to believe that the treaty usually ascribed to May 18th is a fabrication, that the Franco-Bavarian alliance dated from the secret treaty of 1727, and that Belleisle merely negotiated the Spanish-Bavarian treaty: von Arneth (*Maria Theresa*, i. p. 193) and Ranke take the view adopted in the text: the essential point is that Bavaria accepted French aid in her attack upon Austria and in her candidature for the Empire, and that Belleisle arranged for a joint attack of Maria Theresa's enemies upon her. Cf. also Wolf, p. 31.

alert, balancing the inability of Austria to defend herself against the danger of undue acquisitions by the Spanish Bourbons. Augustus III of Saxony, anxious not to find himself on the weaker side, was negotiating with Belleisle, and in July a promise of Moravia and Upper Silesia secured his support for the Bavarian claims. The minor Powers followed this lead. The Elector Palatine, no longer at feud with his Bavarian cousins, and Clement Augustus o f Cologne,[1] brother of the "bold Bavarian" himself, were anxious to see the Imperial dignity in their family. Philip Charles of Eltz-Kempten, Elector of Mayence since 1734, was on the whole inclined to favour Austria, but let himself be guided by his nephew Count d'Eltz into accepting Belleisle's overtures, though without enthusiasm.[2] Francis George of Schönborn at Treves (1729–1756) followed the lead given him by his neighbours, while Würtemberg imitated the larger states around her by advancing claims upon parts of the Hapsburg dominions.

But even with these dangers impending, Maria Theresa resolutely resisted the efforts of the English envoys to induce her to come to terms with Frederick. All that the arguments and entreaties of Sir Thomas Robinson could win from her was an offer of Limburg; not an inch of Silesia would she yield. Her obstinacy may have been impolitic, it would perhaps have been wiser to swallow the insult to her pride involved in making up her mind to the loss of Silesia and accepting Frederick's assistance against her other enemies. A coalition such as the English ministers desired, of Austria, England and Hanover, Holland and Prussia, might have proved victorious over the Bourbons and Bavaria, but it is impossible not to sympathise with Maria Theresa's indignant rejection of the idea; and what she thus lost is to some extent compensated for by the moral advantage involved in her magnificent and courageous obstinacy. The appeal she was able to make to her subjects did awaken their slumbering patriotism and sense of what one may call "Austrian nationality": it would have been but a weak appeal that she could have made to any sentiment if she had stood forward as the ally of the man who had dealt with her so treacherously and insolently.

Frederick therefore, finding Maria Theresa obdurate, accepted

---

[1] Archbishop-Elector, 1723–1761.
[2] Cf. *Frédéric II and Marie Thérèse*, i. 295 ff.

the offered French alliance. By the Treaty of Breslau (June 5th, 1741), France guaranteed Breslau and Lower Silesia to Frederick; he in return gave up all claim on Jülich and Berg in favour of the Sulzbachs, and promised his vote and his help to the Elector of Bavaria. Such a treaty must effectually deny to Frederick any claim to have had the interests of Germany at heart. He placed himself at the disposal of the Power which had for over a hundred years been the greatest foe to Germany and German nationality. To argue that Austria drove him into the arms of France is ridiculous. There was another alternative : he might have held on to Silesia, rejecting the French alliance, and waiting till the advance of the Franco-Bavarians forced Maria Theresa to come to terms with him to save Vienna. The fact that he would have preferred to make terms with Maria Theresa is itself an indication that he realised that the intervention of France was contrary to the best interests of Germany, and it was only his own aggression and rapacity which made it impossible for the Queen of Hungary to seek the alliance of the rising North German Power to resist the insidious attempt of France to still further weaken and disunite her Eastern neighbour.

For a discussion of the wisdom of the policy of France this is hardly the place, yet it should be noticed that a different course of action might have suited France better. A statesman of keener perceptions than Fleury, a man of more political insight and broader ideas than Belleisle, might have seen that it was not from Austria that France had anything to fear. If it was to the interest of France that Germany should continue weak and disunited, there was much to be said for seeking to induce Austria to make slight concessions to Bavaria, Spain, Sardinia and Saxony, even perhaps to cede part of the Austrian Netherlands to France herself; but by assisting her against this new enemy France might have earned Maria Theresa's gratitude, and have separated her from England. It would be fatuous to urge that Fleury ought in 1740–1741 to have foreseen Sedan and the loss of Alsace-Lorraine, but the promptitude and decision of Frederick's action, the evidence of his strength afforded by Mollwitz, his obvious self-confidence and ambition, might well have made Fleury pause. If it was his object to prevent the rise in Germany of any Power capable of giving France trouble, he might well have asked himself whether it was good policy to assist a monarch so evidently capable of helping himself.

CHAPTER VIII

THE AUSTRIAN SUCCESSION WAR

TO THE TREATY OF WORMS

I T seems to have been at a meeting of the *Conseil du Roi* on July 11th that Louis XV and his Ministers decided what help they would send to their German allies. While one army under Belleisle himself was to join the Elector of Bavaria in yet another thrust down the Danube valley at Vienna, a second, to be commanded by Marshal Maillebois, was to cross the Rhine into Westphalia and so hold in check the "Pragmatic Army" which George II was collecting in Hanover. But for the present France abstained from a formal declaration of war against Austria, announcing that she was merely acting as an ally of the Elector of Bavaria, not as a principal, and that her troops were to be considered as mere "auxiliaries" of the Bavarians.[1]

When, on August 15th, the leading division of the French crossed the Rhine near Fort Louis, hostilities had already been begun with the Bavarians' seizure of Passau on the last day of July. However, it was not till September 11th that their combined forces, 50,000 strong of whom 34,000 were French, broke up from Scharding and advanced down the Danube. On September 14th they reached Linz which made no resistance, for the partisans of Bavaria were numerous in Upper Austria, and nobles and burghers flocked to take the oaths of allegiance to Charles Albert and to acknowledge him as their ruler. Had the Franco-Bavarians pushed on towards Vienna with any vigour, it is difficult to see how they could have failed to take the city. Its fortifications were not strong, its garrison was weak, and there was no quarter from which any help could

---

[1] A convention regulating the relations and status of these "auxiliaries" was signed at Versailles by d'Amelot and the Bavarian envoy Grimberghen on August 9th.

be obtained, for the only armies of Austria were that of
Neipperg, far away at Neisse, and the force with which Traun
was preparing to defend Lombardy against the threatened
Spanish attack. But not only did Charles Albert spend nearly
three weeks in useless inaction at Linz, not moving on till
October 5th, but when he had reached St. Polten on October
21st and was almost within sight of Vienna, he suddenly
changed his plan, retraced his steps up the Danube to Maut-
hausen, crossed to the left bank (Oct. 24th) and moved
thence by Freystadt upon Budweis in Bohemia. The reasons
for this remarkable move are hard to understand. That
Charles Albert was afraid that his communications with
Bavaria might be cut by Austrian troops recalled from Italy
seems unlikely, in any case it was not a serious danger; that
he had no siege-guns is not a sufficient explanation, for he was
in communication by river with the arsenals of Ingolstadt and
other fortresses ; more probably he did not trust either his
Saxon or his Prussian ally, and believed that only by moving
in person to Bohemia could he prevent one or other of those
two friends from forestalling him by annexing the province.
The responsibility for this fatal mistake, which Charles Albert
adopted at General Törring's advice, must be borne by the
Elector himself; but Belleisle, though absent at Frankfort at the
time, owing to the preparations for the Imperial election, approved of it, since he wished to draw nearer Frederick of whose
sincerity he had suspicions which were only too well grounded.

Maria Theresa had faced the Bavarian attack with fortitude
and resolution. Ten regiments were recalled from Italy, every
effort was made to raise recruits and bring together all available
soldiers, while her famous appeal to the loyalty and patriotism
of her Hungarian subjects really proved a remarkable success,
even though the "insurrection" was only decreed by the Diet
at Pressburg after the Queen had made considerable constitutional concessions and restored many political privileges. Her
courage in throwing overboard the traditional suspicion and
distrust with which the German ministers of the Hapsburgs had
always regarded the Hungarians, was justified by the altered
attitude of that people. But even though the "insurrectionary"
levy flocked to the Austrian standards, time must elapse before
it could be ready for battle, and meanwhile the danger was
pressing and the need great. From one quarter only could

Vienna be saved, for George II, Austria's only faithful ally, had been forced by the approach of Maillebois to conclude a treaty of neutrality (Sept. 27th), by which he pledged himself to abstain from assisting Maria Theresa or from giving his vote to Francis Stephen of Lorraine. Neipperg's army was the one force which could save Vienna, and Neipperg's army could only be set free by accepting Frederick's terms. It was a bitter humiliation for Maria Theresa, but there was no alternative. In vain she offered West Flanders to Louis XV, the Milanese and Tuscany to Bavaria, Lusatia to Saxony. England continually pressed her to come to terms with Frederick in order that she might devote all her energies to the only object about which the English cared, the defeat of France. Unable to fight both Frederick and the Franco-Bavarians, she was compelled to free herself of one enemy, and on October 9th the secret Convention of Klein-Schellendorf relieved her of the active hostility of Prussia at the sacrifice of Lower Silesia and of Neisse which was surrendered to the enemy after a mock siege. Frederick was glad to come to terms. His men had been in the field for ten months, and badly needed rest. To be spared the loss of life and the trouble of taking Neisse was no small gain. Moreover, he distrusted France, and had no wish to see her too successful.

Neipperg, who had been largely reinforced, accordingly broke up from Neisse on October 16th, his march being directed upon Prague, now threatened by 20,000 Saxons under Rutowski,[1] and by a division of French and Bavarians under Polastron from Amberg and Pilsen as well as by their main body from Budweis. Like Silesia, Bohemia was not in a good state to meet an attack; the province had been all but swept bare of troops, and even so important a point as Prague was weakly held. Once again a fatal slowness characterised Neipperg's movements. Not till November 7th did he reach Znaym, where Francis Stephen joined and took command. By November 17th the army reached Neuhaus, where it halted for four days, a mistake of the greatest importance, for a rapid advance would have brought them to Prague in time, the enemy being still widely separated. As it was, the delay allowed the Franco-Bavarians to concentrate under the walls

---

[1] A natural son of Augustus II, and half-brother of the more famous Maurice de Saxe.

of Prague on the 23rd, the Austrians being then at Tabor,
over fifty miles to the Southward.   At the advice of Rutowski,
whom Maurice de Saxe strongly supported, an assault was
at once attempted, and, brilliantly conducted by Maurice, it
proved a complete success (night of Nov. 24th to 25th).
Too late to save Prague, a failure for which he had only
his own slowness to blame, Francis Stephen and his 40,000
men fell back from Beneschau to a position in the rough country
between Neuhaus and Tabor, and there stood at bay.   For the
time both sides were inactive and operations at a standstill, the
only move, an Austrian attack on Pisek (Dec. 26th), being
easily repulsed by de Broglie, who had just (Dec. 20th) taken
over the command from Belleisle, the latter retaining his diplomatic functions for the election was now at hand.

So far both sides had shown up but ill.   Both had moved
with a culpable indifference to the value of time; but the
Elector's errors in strategy were not confined to slowness alone.
Instead of striking at Vienna, the great seat of his enemy's
power, when he had it almost in his grasp, he had concentrated
his whole strength upon taking a relatively unimportant town
in Bohemia, whose capture must have been involved in the fall
of the Hapsburg capital.   He had mistaken his objective; he
had struck at the branches not at the trunk of the tree, and in
so doing he had exposed Bavaria.

For while the campaign in Bohemia had resulted in a
deadlock, Maria Theresa had managed to collect at Vienna a
second army, the nucleus of which was formed by 4000 cavalry
and 8000 regular infantry from Italy, with 14,000 wild
irregulars from Hungary and the border countries, Croats,
Pandours, Tolpatches and all the other light cavalry, who had
no superiors in Europe in the arts of the raider and the
forager.   And luckily for Maria Theresa she had available in
Khevenhüller a general who possessed no small degree of that
promptitude, resolution and energy so lacking in Neipperg and
Francis Stephen.

It was on December 31st that Khevenhüller advanced up
the Danube with 16,000 men, Bärenklau with 10,000 more,
mainly irregulars, co-operating by moving on München through
Tyrol.   The move was an instant success: Upper Austria was
recovered, Bavaria overrun and laid waste by Bärenklau's moss-
troopers.   Ségur with the French troops left behind on the

Danube, some 10,000 strong, was driven in on Linz and cooped up there. Unable to escape, he was forced to capitulate on Jan. 24th, Törring, who tried in vain to save him, being beaten by Bärenklau at Scharding (Jan. 17th) and driven back to Ingolstadt. It was a remarkable coincidence that the very day that Ségur surrendered and that Passau also fell into Austrian hands, Charles Albert was being elected Emperor at Frankfurt as Charles VII.[1] Similarly, on the day of the new Emperor's coronation (Feb. 12th), his capital, Münich, was concluding a capitulation to save itself from being plundered by Menzel's hussars. With the exception of Ingolstadt and one or two other strong places, all Bavaria was in Austrian hands.

But Maria Theresa's successes had alarmed Frederick, and just as he had concluded the Convention of Klein-Schellendorf behind the backs of his allies, so now he proceeded to break it when it was no longer convenient to keep it. It had served his purpose: his men were refreshed by four months' rest, and he had obtained Neisse without fighting for it. His allegation that Austria had failed to keep the convention secret was a palpable untruth: Austria's interest was to keep it dark, and it does seem that Austria had tried to do so; whereas within three weeks of signing it Frederick had signed a treaty with France, Bavaria and Saxony for a partition of the Austrian dominions,[2] a fairly sufficient test of his sincerity. Frederick and his allies, however, found it harder to decide upon a plan of campaign than upon the terms of their proposed partition of Maria Theresa's dominions. Even before the news of the fall of Linz arrived there had been great debates. De Broglie, supported by Maurice de Saxe, was very anxious for a move due South to save Bavaria by a direct attack on the Austrian main army. This force was lying between Iglau, Neuhaus, Budweis and Tabor, itself inactive but materially assisting Khevenhüller's operations by protecting them from any interference by de Broglie. Frederick, on the other hand, favoured an invasion of Moravia, by which he would turn the right flank of the Austrians and threaten Vienna. But his allies objected to his proposals as

---

[1] The Elector Palatine managed to purchase with his vote the renunciation of the Hohenzollern claim on Jülich and Berg in favour of the Margrave of Sulzbach.

[2] Von Arneth, i. p. 335; cf. ii. p. 28.

they would have involved his using their troops to carry out his plan.[1]   Finally, they consented to let their left under Polastron assist Frederick's invasion of Moravia by attacking Iglau.   The Prussians had already crossed the frontier of Moravia before the end of December and had occupied Glatz and Olmutz, and when Frederick started from Wirchau on February 5th, he was almost unopposed.   However, when the news of Ségur's capitulation arrived, Polastron was at once recalled, though Frederick pushed on, furious at what he styled this " desertion."   His advanced guard got within forty miles of Vienna and Ziethen's cavalry penetrated even nearer, but Brünn, to which he had laid siege, resisted stoutly, de Broglie refused to move, the Saxons failed to bring up a promised siege-train, and with Hungarian irregular cavalry menacing his communications with Silesia Frederick had no alternative but to retreat.   By April 17th he was at Chrudim in Bohemia, very ill-content with de Broglie, though the latter after Klein-Schellendorf had no reason to trust Frederick too far, and might fairly plead that his original plan had been the better, since the enemy's army was the true objective, while his own corps was hardly in condition for much hard work.   Indeed, it was partly with the idea of securing his own retreat that about this time de Broglie occupied Eger and thereby opened communications with Harcourt, who had just reached the Upper Danube with some reinforcements from France.

Meanwhile the Austrians, now under Prince Charles of Lorraine, were about to take the offensive.   The Saxons had already been driven back into Bohemia, while three regiments of cavalry, four of infantry and 13,000 Croats, whom Khevenhüller had rather unwillingly detached (Feb. 19th) from his army, came up from Bavaria.   On May 10th, 30,000 Austrians[2] were at Saar on the Sasawa, moving on Prague with the double object of cutting in between Frederick and de Broglie, and of falling on the latter before his reinforcements could arrive.   But the move took them right across Frederick's front; and though the failure of his intelligence department and the unduly scattered positions of his troops caused him to miss his best chance, he did succeed in concentrating

---

[1] Cf. Maurice's letter to Frederick, comparing the latter's behaviour at Mollwitz with that of de Broglie at Pisek, *Frédéric II et Marie Thérèse*, ii. 196.

[2] 12 regiments of cavalry, 13 of infantry and the Croats.

28,000 men at Chrudim on the 13th. On the 15th he moved forward to Kuttenberg, which he reached next day, Leopold the younger of Anhalt-Dessau and his rear division arriving at Chotusitz.

Charles of Lorraine had planned to surprise the Prussian force near Chotusitz on the morning of May 17th, but the night march by which he attempted to carry out this scheme went wrong, and Leopold, learning his danger, was able to warn the King in time for him to bring back his division from Kuttenberg before 8 a.m. As at Mollwitz, both sides were drawn up in two lines with the cavalry on the wings. On the Prussian right Büddenbrock's cavalry overlapped their opponents, on their left Waldow's horsemen should have rested on a park wall, but to do this they were somewhat unduly extended, so that the Austrian cavalry here charged and routed them, while their infantry, outflanking the Prussian centre, attacked and captured part of Chotusitz. Büddenbrock, however, had overthrown Bathyanny's cavalry, only to be checked by von Thüngen's infantry, and routed and driven off by the cavalry of the second line. It was at this critical moment that Frederick, arriving from Kuttenberg with the reserve, restored the day. He seized the chance given him by the fact that the Austrian cavalry were chasing Büddenbrock off towards Kuttenberg and had thus left the flank of their infantry exposed, to shake their cohesion by a heavy cannonade and then to hurl his division upon the unprotected flank. His vigorous attack forced the Austrian left and centre to retire. This decided the day; for Chotusitz was still in dispute, and unfortunately for the Austrians the cavalry of their right were pillaging Leopold's camp to the neglect of their duties. Prince Charles was able to draw his men off in good order, for with the Prussian cavalry practically destroyed Frederick could not pursue. The stout fight made by the Austrians who, if their total losses were nearly 7000 had inflicted some 5000 casualties on the Prussians, including 2000 killed, and had practically annihilated the Prussian cavalry, made no small impression on Frederick. " It was a Prussian victory, but hardly an Austrian defeat," says von Arneth; and there is some truth in the judgment, for Frederick remained absolutely inactive and allowed Charles of Lorraine to reinforce Lobkowitz unmolested. Lobkowitz, moving down the Moldau on Prague as Charles of Lorraine moved forward to Chotusitz, had been attacked by de Broglie at Sahay (May 26th) and had retired again to Budweis; but Frederick's inaction enabled the Austrians, who outnumbered the French by two to one, to resume the advance and drive them in on Prague after some sharp fighting. Unable to hold Frauenberg, de Broglie retired to Pisek, thence to Pilsen, and finally to Prague, hard pressed by the Croats, and utterly unassisted by Frederick (June 4th to 13th); the garrisons he left behind were promptly cut off and taken, and the fall of Pilsen severed the communications between the French armies of Bohemia and Bavaria.

The explanation of Frederick's inaction is simple enough. Chotusitz had been fought for political reasons, as a move in the diplomatic game. Distrusting his allies, alarmed at the prospect of the active intervention of England on behalf of Maria Theresa, for in February Walpole had fallen and in the new ministry Carteret was in charge of foreign affairs, and discouraged by his failure in Moravia, Frederick was thinking of leaving France and the Emperor in the lurch. It was from him that the first overtures came; and if the Austrians had some difficulty in believing in his sincerity, they soon saw it was to their interest to close with him. On June 11th the Preliminaries of Breslau promised Frederick Glatz and Upper and Lower Silesia—with the exception of Troppau and Tetschen—and on July 28th a definite peace was signed at Berlin. Notwithstanding his protestations of devotion to the cause of his allies, Frederick had not hesitated to desert them when he found he could get what he wanted from Maria Theresa. His assertion that he only anticipated France in this treaty seems unsupported by the facts; so far from being about to come to terms with her, France was steadily refusing all Maria Theresa's offers.[1]

Frederick's desertion, coupled with that of Saxony, which under the influence of Great Britain definitely acceded to the Peace of Berlin on September 7th, left the French army of Bohemia in a perilous position. Not only was it weakened by a long campaign, by hard work and the privations due to the inefficient management of its supplies, but Belleisle, who had resumed the command, found himself exposed to greatly superior forces, absolutely isolated and "in the air." It helped

[1] *Frédéric II et Marie Thérèse*, ii. 340.

him but little that Harcourt with 10,000 men from France had reinforced the Bavarians and was holding Khevenhüller's diminished forces in check; for if Harcourt could " contain " Khevenhüller he could do no more, and had he attempted to move across the Böhmer Wald to the relief of Prague he would have given the enterprising Austrian an admirable opportunity for using his light troops to full advantage.

The interest of the situation was now centred at Prague, where the French garrison was holding out courageously. Maria Theresa was most anxious to secure them as prisoners; their unconditional surrender would be some compensation for the injury France had done her, and would be a valuable diplomatic asset. Her idea was to obtain an equivalent for Silesia, and for that purpose Bavaria seemed well adapted, in which case it would be left to France to compensate the Elector. France was equally set on rescuing Belleisle's army, and as the task was beyond Harcourt's means, it was decided to utilise the force on the Lower Rhine with which Maillebois had till now been overawing Hanover. By the end of August Maillebois was on the move, by September 12th he was at Amberg in the Upper Palatinate, whereupon the Austrians by orders from Vienna raised the siege and moved Westward to meet him, leaving 9000 light horse to continue the blockade.

As Maillebois approached the French division from Bavaria, now under Maurice de Saxe, moved up to join him, which it did at Bramahof in September. Khevenhüller, executing a parallel march, joined the Grand Duke of Tuscany, who was at Heyd barring the road to Prague, on September 27th. His departure from the Danube allowed Seckendorff to recover Bavaria. On October 7th the Bavarians reoccupied München. Bärenklau, too weak to hold his ground, fell back behind the Inn, leaving garrisons in Passau and Schärding.

Neither of the main armies was directed with much energy or skill, for Saxe alone among the commanders was anxious for battle. Not till October 6th did Maillebois advance from Bramahof to Eger (8th) and Karden (10th); he apparently hoped that this would allow the French from Prague to move out towards Leitmeritz and so join him; but though the garrison could easily have made their way out through the cordon of disorderly and inefficient irregulars, Broglie and Belleisle held on to Prague, hoping that Maillebois would come through to them, and that Bohemia would yet be theirs. But Maillebois was doing nothing of the sort. Bad roads, bad weather, tired and ill-fed troops, dismayed and disheartened him: beaten without a battle, he fell back to Eger, from there to Neustadt (Oct. 27th), and then moved slowly away to Bavaria, where he took up his winter-quarters (Nov.). Only a thoroughly inefficient and over-cautious commander like the Grand Duke of Tuscany could have let slip the chance afforded by this retreat; instead of falling on Maillebois as he retired, Francis Stephen let him get away unfought and unimpeded. Lobkowitz was sent back to take Leitmeritz, thereby isolating Prague of which he then resumed the siege, while the main army moved slowly South, parallel with Maillebois, like him crossing to the right bank of the Danube, at Braunau (Nov. 12th), and going into winter-quarters. It is difficult to say which commander showed least enterprise and least appreciation of the real needs of the situation and of those first principles of strategy, which concentrate attention on the importance of bringing one's enemy to action and rendering him incapable of doing damage rather than on out-manœuvring and evading.

At Prague Belleisle was now in sole command, for de Broglie had escaped just before communications were cut. The garrison might easily have held out some weeks longer; but Belleisle, seeing no hope of relief, decided to attempt to break out. To Chevert he entrusted the task of getting what terms he could for the 6000 invalids and details who were left behind, and on the night of December 16th/17th, 3000 horse and 11,000 infantry pierced Lobkowitz's lax blockade and after a trying march, which cost them 1500 men in ten days, reached Eger on the 27th. Lobkowitz, who ought never to have let them get through, also failed to pursue properly, but his culminating error was in allowing Chevert to capitulate with the honours of war (Jan. 3rd) and to retire to Eger. Chevert and his invalids could never have held the town against an assault; but Lobkowitz, a Bohemian nobleman who had much property in Prague, allowed Chevert's threats to burn the town to frighten him into granting such easy terms.

Still even if Belleisle and most of his shattered regiments

had managed to slip through Maria Theresa's hands, Prague was once more under the Austrian rule, Bohemia, with the exception of Eger and one or two other posts, was free from the French, and Belleisle's great scheme had failed completely. If it had benefited any one it was Frederick II, who had used Belleisle and the French as the catspaw with which he had secured Maria Theresa's reluctant consent to his possession of Silesia. But the French had not done with Germany yet: 1743 had more disasters in store for them and their luckless Bavarian client. The year opened with the death (Jan. 29th) of the aged Cardinal on whom so large a share of the responsibility for the war must rest; latterly Fleury had shown a desire to come to terms with Austria, even to anticipate 1756, and his death removed the chief influence in favour of peace; for though Belleisle was discredited, the man who now came to the front as the director of foreign affairs, the Duc de Noailles, urged a vigorous prosecution of the war. Cardinal Tencin, who came nearer than the other ministers to succeeding Fleury as First Minister, was more inclined towards throwing the strength of France into the scale on the side of Spain in the West Indian war then raging, but he did not oppose de Noailles' war policy in Germany.

During the winter there was much negotiating. England instigated Austria to offer terms to the Emperor, hoping so to detach him from the French alliance and to add him to a coalition against France. But as the Emperor held out for the complete restoration of Bavaria, and would not agree to the compensation elsewhere which Maria Theresa proposed, the negotiations were broken off. The only military event of the winter was the relief of Eger by du Chayla (April); the garrison ought to have been withdrawn, but was foolishly reinforced and replenished, though no military advantage could be hoped for from leaving it there.

It was at the beginning of May that the Austrians took the offensive on the Danube. The French and Bavarians were not on good terms: de Broglie's corps was in a thoroughly bad condition, its 67 infantry battalions mustered hardly 27,000 men, and 91 squadrons barely reached 10,000 sabres, there were many sick, and its equipment was deficient; moreover, he was opposed to the Emperor's proposal to take the offensive, and the result was that the Bavarians at Simbach and elsewhere found themselves exposed to the Austrian attack. Simultaneous attacks from North and East cut off the Simbach detachment; on May 9th it had to surrender, a few fugitives alone escaping to Braunau out of a force of over 6000. As the Austrians pushed on West the French recoiled across the Isar. A garrison which they left in Dingolfing was attacked and expelled by Daun (May 17th), and before the advance of the Austrians down the Isar Landau was evacuated. Crossing to the Northern bank of the Danube, Charles of Lorraine carried Deggendorf by storm, having first thrust three battalions in between the garrison and their bridge and so intercepted their retreat. Lobkowitz was now moving on the Danube from the Upper Palatinate, and to his attention Charles left the French, recrossing the river to deal with the Bavarians (June 6th). They proved unable to make a stand, but retired to Ingolstadt and thus exposed Münich which surrendered to Bärenklau, June 9th.

By this time de Broglie had abandoned all idea of defending Bavaria, and he now (June 7th) proposed an immediate retreat to join de Noailles, who was holding King George and the Pragmatic Army in check on the Main. It may fairly be surmised that this plan was not unconnected with Maurice de Saxe, for it certainly offered the best course of action under the circumstances; and despite despatches from France which ordered de Broglie to hold on to Ingolstadt, the Emperor's entreaties and the arrival of some 15,000 reinforcements, de Broglie steadily refused to resume the offensive, retiring on June 23rd to Donauwerth and declaring he would retreat to the Rhine. On the 26th a despatch of June 22nd arrived authorising a retreat but not a move to join de Noailles, nevertheless it was towards the Main that de Broglie moved. Had de Noailles waited for him, the extra numbers might have turned the scale at Dettingen and victory would have condoned disobedience, but the day after de Broglie left Donauwerth, Noailles gave battle and was beaten (June 16th to 27th). On hearing of this de Broglie moved straight to the Rhine; before the end of July he regained the left bank near Spires. His action was typical of the French disgust for the German campaign; the regiments ordered thither had nearly mutinied when they heard their destination, and as an English envoy wrote,[1] "the discourse among the French at Frankfort is,

[1] *Montagu House MSS.* (Hist. MSS. Com.) p. 404.

'What business have we here?'—they are very sick of Germany."

Left in the lurch by de Broglie, Charles Albert fled to Augsburg, while Seckendorff, who with the relics of the Bavarian army was at Rain, began negotiations with the Austrians, which resulted in the Convention of Niederschonfeld (end of June). This allowed him and his army to retire into Franconia and become neutral. Braunau, though defended by 4000 men, had already fallen. Ingolstadt held out stubbornly, but was at last forced to capitulate to Bärenklau on September 30th, Eger having surrendered three weeks earlier.

The force upon the Main, which de Broglie had proposed to join, was an army which had been collected on the Moselle earlier in the year to prevent the march of the so-called "Pragmatic Army" up the Rhine from intercepting de Broglie's retreat. One of the first-fruits of the fall of Walpole had been the more active part which England now prepared to play in the Continental War. In April 1742, British troops had begun to cross to Belgium, and by the middle of summer some 16,000 men[1] had been collected there under Lord Stair. This was not a very imposing force, but it was all that, thanks to Walpole's unwise economy, the country had at her disposal. Walpole had not merely neglected and starved the Army,[2] but he had not even attempted to remedy this weakness by hiring the mercenaries who formed the staple commercial product of so many of the minor states of Germany. Stair, a veteran of Marlborough's wars, united diplomatic with his military functions. The policy he favoured may be described as that of the "Grand Alliance." Maria Theresa must devote her whole resources to the expulsion of the French from Germany, and to following up their retreat by an invasion of France: in this Stair proposed to co-operate from the Netherlands. It is needless to add that this policy involved the abandonment of Silesia to Prussia, and when Maria Theresa at last gave way and signed the Preliminaries of Breslau, Stair's opportunity seemed to have come. The perilous position of the French in Bohemia called off Maillebois,

---

[1] 4 troops of Household Cavalry, 8 regiments of Horse and Dragoons, 3 battalions of the Guards, and 12 of the Line.

[2] Cf. J. W. Fortescue, *History of the British Army*, vol. ii. bk. vii., especially chs. i. and ii.

hitherto equally favourably placed for a blow at the Netherlands or at Hanover, into the interior of Germany and seemed
to lay the thinly guarded North-Eastern frontier of France
open for a blow down the Oise on Paris.   Had the Hanoverian
army at once hastened to join Stair, who had 14,000 Austrians
as well as his 16,000 British, there was practically nothing
between him and Paris but a corps of some 12,000 men at
Dunkirk.   The plan, if daring, was sound enough in idea;
for even if Stair had failed to take Paris, he might have fallen
back into Normandy and re-established communications with
England by sea.   But George II hung back: he developed
scruples, he was not at war with Louis XV, he was only the
ally of the Queen of Hungary and Louis the ally of the
Elector of Bavaria, and thus a fine chance was allowed to
escape.

For 1743 the Austrians were anxious to bring the
Pragmatic Army into Germany, hoping in this way to bring
pressure to bear on the minor Powers and influence them in
favour of Austria, even if France were not thereby induced to
come to terms.[1]   George II was well disposed to this plan,
and about the middle of February the British troops began
their move Eastward to the Rhine and then South up that
river.[2]   On the way 16,000 Hanoverians joined them; on
the Main, which Stair reached early in May, they were
overtaken by 12,000 Austrians from the Netherlands, whose
places in the fortresses had been taken by Hessians in British
pay.   The march had frightened Frederick of Prussia, he
protested vehemently against the English entering the
Empire; but his threats to intervene do not seem to have
received much attention or to have checked the advance for
a moment

On the Main, however, a halt was called, much to the
disgust of Stair, who was anxious to repeat 1704 by pushing
forward to the Upper Danube to make sure of intercepting
de Broglie's retreat.   But this move was too daring for
George II, and the halt gave France time to collect an army of
some 70,000 men under de Noailles, which crossed the Rhine

[1] Cf. *Trevor MSS.* p. 85.
[2] The march is described in great detail by Colonel Charles Russell of the
1st Guards in the *Checquers Court MSS.* (Hist. MSS. Com.), from which source
much information as to the whole campaign may be obtained.

near Worms unopposed (May 25th), for George would not let Stair cross to the South of the Main. Ségur was first pushed forward to reinforce de Broglie, and then de Noailles took post to oppose the further advance of the Pragmatic Army.[1]

The refusal of George II to allow Stair to retain any of the posts he had occupied South of the Main soon made its bad effects felt. It left the whole of the left bank free to the French foragers, and they also crossed to the right bank and drew supplies from that side. Straitened for supplies, the Pragmatic Army pushed up the Main to Aschaffenburg and just forestalled the French in the occupation of the passage there (June 7th to 18th). Two days later the King joined the army, which, through no fault of Stair's, began to find itself in great straits for food. The French barred the route to Bavaria higher up the river, and their foragers plundered the North bank freely between Aschaffenburg and Frankfurt. The only alternative to starvation was a retreat on the magazines at Hanau, where George hoped to be joined by 6000 Hessians in British pay and 6000 "Electoral" Hanoverians.[2]

The French commander saw his chance; five brigades crossed at Aschaffenburg to press on the rear of the Allies, Militia battalions and batteries of guns lined the Southern bank of the river, while 23,000 of his best troops under his nephew de Grammont took post on the Northern bank to bar the retreat. De Grammont's position was behind the little Beck which flows into the Main just East of Dettingen, while the wooded hills at whose foot the river runs seemed an effective obstacle to an escape Northward. Indeed the Allies were in a very perilous position. Raked by the batteries which inflicted heavy loss on their columns,[3] they had halted and front-faced to the South near Klein Ostheim, when de Grammont's corps was detected at Dettingen. Stair appears now to have intervened, and under cover of the cavalry

---

[1] De Noailles' army was of very mixed quality; it included the *Maison du Roi* and some regiments which had been in garrisons in the South and West, but the bulk of it consisted of the units which had escaped from Prague hastily reformed with Militia recruits of poor quality.

[2] *i.e.* in his pay as Elector.

[3] The bulk of the losses of the Austrians and Hanoverians were incurred in this way.

of the right wing (British and Austrian) a new front was formed facing de Grammont. On the right next the hills were four cavalry regiments, then an Austrian infantry brigade, then seven British battalions with another cavalry regiment next the river. A second line of five cavalry regiments and nine battalions, five British, four Hanoverian, was drawn up in rear. Farther away to the right rear the British Guards were posted on a height which covered a path over the wooded hills Northward. Probably because he saw this move of the Guards and concluded that the force in front of him was a rearguard seeking to cover a retreat, partly also because his men were being galled by Stair's guns, de Grammont suddenly anticipated attack by moving forward and crossing the Beck, a step which threw his troops into some disorder. The Allies also advanced, and a sharp fire-fight between the opposing infantries saw the French centre recoiling in disorder, when their cavalry, coming up on the right, fell upon the exposed flank of the British infantry near the river, where only a weak regiment of dragoons [1] covered it. For a time they were successful, but the steadiness and heavy volleys of the British infantry checked them, and the British and Austrian cavalry from the other wing came up to the rescue. The first few regiments behaved none too well and were routed, but the arrival of reinforcements turned the scale; the *Maison*, beaten off by the infantry, gave way before a charge by the 4th and 6th Dragoons and two Austrian regiments. This allowed the Allies' infantry to advance against the second line of French foot, " in high spirits at having repulsed the French cavalry." There was a sharp fight, but the murderous volleys of the British infantry—Marshal Neipperg " never saw such a firing " —were too much for the French. They were falling back in complete disorder, flocking down to the bridges, and Stair seemed on the point of annihilating de Grammont's broken corps when George II intervened to stop pursuit. His intervention was attributed by the British army to Hanoverian influence,[2] for Stair certainly seems to have strongly urged

---

[1] Bland's, now 3rd Hussars.

[2] "Nothing but a Hanoverian was listened to or regarded" (Colonel Russell). "The King halted, and the scene of action and military ardour was at once turned into a Court circle" (Colonel C. V. Townshend's *Memoirs of Marquess Townshend*,

a pursuit, and to have protested against the undue haste with which George pressed on to Hanau, leaving his wounded on the field to the care of de Noailles. Here he found the 12,000 Hessians and Hanoverians, but even so remained utterly inactive; and only when Charles of Lorraine came up to Cannstadt (July 9th) and Durlach (25th) did de Noailles retire behind the Rhine, crossing at Turckheim (July 17th) and occupying the Lauterburg lines.[1]

The failure to utilise the victory was almost as discreditable to George II as were the blunders which had made the Pragmatic Army fight at such a disadvantage. When at length Charles of Lorraine arrived much time was wasted over concerting a plan of operations, for Charles did not wish to be second in command, and therefore objected to George's proposals for a junction. Finally, the Pragmatic Army crossed the Rhine above Mayence (Aug. 24th) and moved to Worms (29th), de Noailles retiring to Landau. A little more vigour and a decisive success might have been gained: the French were intimidated, and reinforcements, including a Dutch contingent and four British regiments, had come up by way of Treves, but the Pragmatic Army remained inactive at Worms till September 24th, while the Austrians seeking to force a passage over the Rhine near New Breisach were beaten off (Sept. 3rd). Early in October the Allies dispersed, the Pragmatic Army returning to the Netherlands, the Dutch, the "Electoral" Hanoverians and the Hessians to their respective homes, the Austrians taking up winter-quarters in the Vorderland. If the campaign had not proved quite as brilliant a success as better handling of the Pragmatic Army might have made it, the Allies had reason to be fairly satisfied. The French had been expelled from Germany, and it seemed as though the next year might see the tables turned and Alsace and Lorraine invaded.

To some extent diplomatic considerations may account

p. 29); the Guards bitterly resented being put under the Hanoverian General von Ilten, whom they called "the confectioner of the Household Brigade—because he preserves them."

[1] The losses at Dettingen were heavy on both sides; the Allies had about 750 killed, 1600 wounded—800 being British, 550 Hanoverians, 1000 Austrians: the estimates of the French loss vary from 17,000 to 8000, of which the more moderate (cf. *Trevor* and *Montagu House MSS.*) seems more reasonable, though many were drowned in the Main.

for the sluggishness of the Pragmatic Army after Dettingen, though George II's want of strategic capacity and his failure to work harmoniously with Charles of Lorraine were more immediately important. The truth was that George II and Carteret did not see eye to eye with Maria Theresa. Looking to the humiliation of France rather than to the satisfaction of Maria Theresa as the principal object, they put pressure upon her to strengthen the Coalition by concessions to Bavaria and to Sardinia which she was ill-disposed to make. Thinking that France had been more completely beaten than was really the case, Maria Theresa was now determined to recover her husband's family land, Lorraine; and reluctant as she was to let Charles VII off so lightly, it is possible that she would have agreed to restore Bavaria to him and to recognise him as Emperor had Carteret been able to procure from the English Parliament the subsidies which he demanded as the price of his adhesion to the Coalition. But Carteret had little influence in Parliament and could not command sub-sidies: the old cry was raised that he was sacrificing England's maritime and colonial interests to Hanover, and Parliament was reluctant to support one so recently the client of France as Charles VII. Thus the "Project of Hanau" resulted in failure, and Carteret found himself compelled to give way. His policy was really one of using the King's Hanoverian predilections to assist his own European policy, a policy of "conquering America in Germany" which one of his bitterest assailants was one day to carry out triumphantly; but he had no party behind him, and could not combat the "Revolution Families" with success. In one quarter, however, he did succeed in gaining his ends, and the Treaty of Worms, signed September 13th, did bind the slippery Charles Emmanuel of Sardinia to the Allied cause.

If the course of events in Italy does not concern the history of Germany as closely as do the campaigns on the Elbe, the Oder, the Rhine and the Danube, it forms too important a part of the Austrian Succession War to be passed over hastily. The keynote to its varied fortunes is to be found in the double relations of Sardinia to Austria and to the House of Bourbon. Charles Emmanuel, the able and unscrupulous ruler of "the Prussia of Italy," and his minister, d'Ormea, while determined to reap all the advantage they could out of Maria Theresa's embarrassment, viewed with great hostility Elizabeth Farnese's schemes for her second son Don Philip. Lombardy, which she proposed to conquer for him, was the last place in which the Sardinians could with equanimity see Bourbons established. The instinct for holding the balance between the rivals drove Charles Emmanuel over to the side of Austria as being the weaker, and though he negotiated simultaneously with both parties, it was with Austria that he came to terms in February 1742. This treaty, arranged by English mediation, was of a provisional nature. Charles Emmanuel was to support Maria Theresa, while the thorny question of concessions was to be settled later.[1]

It was fortunate for Maria Theresa that she thus obtained the help of Sardinia, for she needed it badly. Escorted by the French Toulon fleet, whose superiority in force had deterred the English Mediterranean squadron under Haddock from attempting to dispute their passage, 15,000 Spaniards from Barcelona had landed at Orbitello in December 1741. Had the Neapolitans joined them at once Traun, who had had to detach most of his troops from Milan to save Vienna,[2] would have had a difficult task; as it was, their delays saved him. By the time that the Spaniards and Neapolitans united at Pesaro (Feb. 1742) the arrangement with Sardinia had been concluded and some reinforcements had returned from Austria. With 12,000 Austrians[3] and some 20,000 Sardinians, Traun took the offensive, invaded the territory of Modena, whose Duke (Francis III of Este) had just declared for the Bourbons, besieged and took (June 28th) that town, and generally displayed so bold a front that the Spanish commander Montemar fell back to Foligno. Here the Neapolitans left him, recalled home by the demonstration

---

[1] Charles Emmanuel demanded the Ticino as his Eastern boundary with Stradella and Finale: this last district had been sold to Genoa by Charles VI and Maria Theresa indignantly refused to rob Genoa by cancelling the sale. Its importance lay in giving the continental dominions of Sardinia direct access to the sea. It was Spain's refusal to let Charles Emmanuel have all Lombardy, a demand to which France was favourable, which caused the breaking off of the negotiations.

[2] Cf. p. 127.

[3] The Austrians relied entirely on German and Hungarian troops in Italy, they did not even hire Swiss mercenaries; and though their government was by no means unpopular and hatred of Sardinia would certainly have secured the fidelity of a Milanese militia, they had not raised any local troops.

of Commodore Martin's English squadron off Naples (Aug.
22nd), which had forced Don Carlos to retire from the
Coalition. Traun was, however, prevented from overthrowing
Montemar by the return home of the Sardinians. A Spanish
force under Don Philip passing overland through France, for
the English fleet under Matthews had severed communications
by sea between Spain and Italy, was threatening Piedmont. It
was repulsed (Sept.), but it brought Traun to a standstill.

Hoping to take advantage of this diversion, Elizabeth
Farnese now directed Gages, who had replaced Montemar,
to try a winter-campaign. Moving against Finale, however,
he was checked by Traun at Buonoporto, and fell back to
Campo Santo on the Panaro. Here on the afternoon of
February 8th, 1743, Traun attacked Gages, and by skilful
handling of his reserves at a critical moment won a handsome
victory. But various causes prevented him from making full
use of his success. He was in disfavour at Vienna, being
accused of maladministration of the Italian provinces and of
wasteful expenditure. Therefore, expecting to be recalled,
he took no steps towards pushing home his advantage.
Charles Emmanuel had come to the conclusion that it would
be well to come to a definite settlement as to the concessions
he was to receive before Austria gained any further success,
and the war languished, the only quarter in which much
activity was displayed being at sea.

The negotiations about the concessions were long and
complicated. Maria Theresa at last agreed to the demands
of Sardinia, but sought to make them conditional on her
recovering Silesia. Charles Emmanuel would not hear of
anything but an immediate cession, and England objected to
the reopening of the Silesian question, still hoping to bring
Frederick into line with herself and Austria against France.
In the end a threat that, if she did not yield, Charles
Emmanuel would come to terms with France, extorted from
Maria Theresa a reluctant consent to the Treaty of Worms
(September 13th, 1743). By this she ceded to Sardinia
Parma, Piacenza and the districts of Anghiara and Vigevano,
the last strips of Austrian territory West of the Ticino.
Charles Emmanuel abandoned all claims on the Milanese,
but received the reversion of Austria's rights over Finale. It
was agreed that the Bourbons should be expelled from Italy;

to this end Maria Theresa was to provide 30,000 men and to receive Naples and the Tuscan ports, Charles Emmanuel's 40,000 men were to win him back Sicily. England undertook to provide subsidies and the assistance of her fleet.

It is certainly open to question whether Maria Theresa was well advised in concluding this treaty. It was a direct challenge to France and Spain and, while France was heartily tired of the war in Germany, the threat of an Austrian invasion of Alsace, the danger of losing the acquisitions of 1738 and the wish to wipe out the humiliations of Belleisle's failure by victories in the Netherlands combined to arouse warlike enthusiasm and violent anti-Austrian feeling in France. To have taken the head of a German crusade to recover Alsace and Lorraine would have been a policy worthy of the best traditions of the Hapsburg House; but for such a policy England and Sardinia would have cared but little, and to organise a German league against France with the titular head of Germany a fugitive under French protection and the strong military power of Prussia indifferent if not actively hostile was impossible. It would certainly appear that Maria Theresa would have done well to have come to terms with France, to have acknowledged Charles VII as Emperor, and thus to have isolated Frederick. She could have counted on Hanoverian hostility to Prussia and the needs of the maritime and colonial war to keep England neutral, she might have even won the assistance of the Bourbons by some such concession as the cession of Tuscany to Louis XV's son-in-law Don Philip, she would have been better able to resist Sardinia's demands for concessions. France had no immediate object in continuing the war save the restoration of her military prestige. The attempt to partition the Hapsburg dominions had failed, and it is not a little difficult to see why the war should have gone on.

An explanation is perhaps to be found in the continued presence of Frederick II in Silesia. This was the real obstacle to peace on the Continent. Until she had recovered that province or obtained some territorial compensation for its loss, Maria Theresa would not rest content. But where was such compensation to be obtained? Bavaria seemed the most attractive alternative, but France could not look on and see her Imperial client deprived of his hereditary dominions, and such a solution would have aroused Prussia's fears and opposition. To win Lorraine or Naples and Sicily from the Bourbons and compensate the Elector of Bavaria by an exchange might have been more generally acceptable, but this scheme involved their conquest, which was sure to be no easy task. The deciding factor in the situation was Maria Theresa's poverty: she could do nothing without English subsidies, and she therefore had to fall in with the policy agreeable to England. And while England under Carteret's guidance was seeking to revive the Continental coalition against the Bourbons as the best means of combating their ascendency, the reaction had already begun in France, and the trend of feeling in favour of an active prosecution of the war was marked by the conclusion, on October 25th, 1743, of the Treaty of Fontainebleau, the Bourbon counterblast to the Treaty of Worms. By this famous treaty, the second of the so-called " Family Compacts," France recognised the rights of Don Philip to the Milanese, Parma and Piacenza. She also undertook to help Spain to recover Gibraltar and Minorca from England, and promised to definitely declare war on Austria and England.

CHAPTER IX

THE AUSTRIAN SUCCESSION WAR—*concluded*

TO THE TREATY OF AIX-LA-CHAPELLE

THE change in character which the war had undergone was marked by the first moves attempted by the French in 1744. The policy of intervening in Germany to assist the Emperor was discarded in favour of a direct attack on England by Saxe and 15,000 men from Dunkirk, who were to be escorted across the Channel by de Roquefeuil and the Brest fleet, and of a vigorous offensive in Italy, to allow of which it would be necessary to raise the blockade established by Matthews over Toulon when the Spanish fleet had taken refuge there in 1742. Both plans miscarried; de Roquefeuil was only saved by a lucky shift of the wind from destruction at the hands of Norris and the Channel Fleet;[1] while the famous "miscarriage off Toulon" on February (11th O.S.) 22nd, which threw so much discredit on the British Navy, showed that even a drawn battle was sufficient to foil de Tencin's schemes for gaining control of the Mediterranean as a preliminary to driving the Austrians out of Italy.

Far different was the case with their invasion of the Netherlands. When early in May 80,000 French troops, well equipped and accompanied by the King himself, crossed the frontier into the Austrian Netherlands, they found the Allies weak,[2] absolutely unready for war, at feud amongst themselves, with no recognised commander-in-chief. It was

---

[1] A French account in the *Gentleman's Magazine* for March 1744 makes it clear that had not the wind dropped, Norris would have brought on an action on the morning of February 24th; but the ebb tide forced him to anchor, and the violent gale which came on that evening proved the salvation of the French, who escaped under its cover to Brest.

[2] Only 55,000 of all nationalities.

hardly wonderful, therefore, if for a time the invaders were quite unchecked.   Courtrai (May 18th), Menin (June 5th), Ypres (June 25th) and Furnes (July 11th), in bad repair and indifferently held,[1] provided a series of facile triumphs.   The country between the Lys and the sea had passed into their hands, and they were about to attack Ostend, when they were suddenly forced to change their plans.   This was not due to their immediate opponents, though the Allies had at last collected a respectable force round Brussels,[2] but to the news of the Austrian invasion of Alsace.   To meet this danger a strong division of the army of Flanders was at once detached to the Upper Rhine, and Maurice de Saxe had to adopt a defensive attitude with the remainder.   That he succeeded in maintaining his position, and with it all the conquests of the early summer, is partly to be ascribed to his admirable defensive tactics, but even more to the quarrels, disunion and aimless proceedings of the Allies.   The Dutch had not yet declared war on France, and the party which favoured a French rather than an English alliance was strong.   As Colonel Russell wrote: "If we end by having a pacific campaign it will be owing to the Dutch, who will by all means avoid declaring war with France."   Still there was no little reason for their complaints that George II was not doing enough in his capacity as Elector of Hanover.[3]   The Hanoverian troops in the field ought to have been paid by Hanover and not by England, whose subsidies should have been used to hire Hessians and other neutrals; as it was, George II as King was hiring troops from himself as Elector, "one's right hand paying one's left," Robert Trevor calls it, and he put the matter succinctly when he wrote: ". . . nothing would so much contribute to save Europe, encourage the Empire and strengthen the Ministry's hands . . . as our Royal Master's drawing his Electoral sword and his Electoral pursestrings gallantly and unreservedly in support of our common cause."

Meanwhile the Austrians on the Upper Rhine under

---

[1] The Dutch had shamefully neglected these "Barrier Fortresses"; they failed to find the required garrisons and conducted the defence without zeal or endurance.

[2] By the end of May the Austrians had failed to produce more than 3000 men. The Dutch were equally backward, and loud complaints were heard at the absence of the "ungrateful Hessians."

[3] Cf. *Trevor MSS.* p. 106.

Prince Charles of Lorraine, though somewhat late in beginning operations, seemed in a fair way to possess themselves of Alsace. They had forced a passage at Germersheim on the last day of June, the Bavarian corps posted there, the relics of the army of the Emperor, being somewhat negligent, and Marshal Coigni, who lay to the North, having his attention diverted by a corps which crossed the river at Mayence, thanks to the Elector's connivance. Advancing to Lauterburg and Weissenburg, the Austrians took these posts and all but cut Coigni off from Alsace. He managed to retake Weissenburg and so push through to his province, but he was driven back to Haguenau and thence to Strassburg, and the route over the Vosges into Lorraine was left open. It was this critical situation which brought the King and de Noailles with 25,000 men from Flanders up to Metz at full speed. At Metz their progress was checked by the sudden illness of Louis, whose death was hourly expected (Aug.). Uncertain whether he would be in favour with the Dauphin, de Noailles betrayed a hesitation and indecision in his conduct of military affairs which might have proved serious had the Austrians displayed greater activity. Not till the King was out of danger did de Noailles advance, enter Alsace by way of Willer and join Coigni near Strassburg (Aug. 17th). A week later he had the pleasure of " assisting " at the repassage of the Rhine at Beinheim by the Austrians, an operation he altogether failed to hinder or harass, for the feeble attack which he did deliver upon their rearguard was easily beaten off and the difficult undertaking was accomplished in good order, a matter not a little creditable to Prince Charles and his chief adviser Marshal Traun.

But it was not the arrival of de Noailles on the scene which was primarily responsible for the Austrian evacuation of Alsace. The credit for having ruined the best chance the eighteenth century was to see of reuniting that province to the Empire is due to Frederick II. His fear that he might be disturbed in his possession of Silesia outweighed with him the natural satisfaction which every patriotic German should have felt at the prospect of seeing Alsace recovered from the Bourbons. Where Frederick William I or even the Great Elector would probably have welcomed the chance of wreaking the Empire's vengeance on its most formidable enemy,

Frederick II preferred to deal Austria yet one more stab in the back for the benefit of Louis XV.

That it would not be to his advantage if the Emperor were driven out of Germany and compelled to take refuge in France, Frederick was well aware. As early as the spring of 1743 he had been contemplating an alliance of the neutral Powers of Germany to bring about peace on terms favourable to the Emperor rather than to Maria Theresa, but he had preferred remaining in quiet possession of Silesia to risking anything for his nominal overlord. Since then many things had occurred which had awakened his suspicions. The Treaty of Berlin had not been in the list of treaties guaranteed at Worms; a treaty had been concluded between Austria and Saxony guaranteeing without specification *all* the possessions of Austria; it seemed possible that the hopelessness of his situation might induce Charles VII to come to terms with Maria Theresa and allow her to incorporate Bavaria in her dominions on giving him in exchange Alsace-Lorraine, Naples or the Netherlands. Frederick would have had no objection to seeing Austria take Naples for herself, but Maria Theresa, like Joseph II, aimed rather at re-establishing Hapsburg predominance in Germany than at fresh acquisitions elsewhere; there was even a prospect that the Electors—for not only Hanover, but Saxony and the Ecclesiastical Electors were now on her side—might be induced by Maria Theresa to set aside the election of Charles VII as invalid and to choose Francis Stephen as Emperor in his place. One may or may not believe in the genuineness of Frederick's alarm on behalf of the German constitution, but it cannot be denied that he had reason to tremble for Silesia; still one may fairly ask whether Maria Theresa would not have reconciled herself to the loss of Silesia and have acknowledged Charles VII as Emperor if the Union of Frankfurt had turned the scale against France and enabled her to wrest Alsace and Lorraine from the heir of Louis XIV?

The Union of Frankfurt was the league which Frederick with the assistance of Chavigny, the French envoy at Münich, organised in May 1744. It included, besides Charles VII, the new Elector Palatine, Charles Theodore of Sulzbach, who had succeeded to all the possessions of the Neuburg line, including Jülich and Berg, on Charles Philip's death in 1742, Landgrave

Frederick I of Hesse-Cassel and other Princes. Its objects were to restore the lawful constitution of the Empire, and to maintain the Emperor in his rights; to recover for Charles VII his hereditary dominions, and on this basis and with the guarantee of Silesia to Frederick to re-establish peace in Germany. By a secret article France guaranteed this compact, while some weeks later another secret treaty with the Emperor promised to Prussia large concessions in Bohemia, and to France fortresses in the Netherlands.

Good relations between France and Prussia had not been very easy to restore. With good cause each distrusted the other's sincerity. Voltaire's mission to Berlin in July 1743 had for this reason proved a fiasco, and not until Frederick saw France thoroughly committed to the war, both formally by having declared it and practically by having invaded Flanders, did he conclude an arrangement with Louis XV's government (June 5th, 1744). The possible hostility of Russia, where there was a strong anti-Prussian party led by Bestuchev, he had already to some extent neutralised by arranging for the marriage of Sophia of Anhalt-Zerbst (afterwards Catherine II) to Duke Peter, the heir of the Czarina Elizabeth.[1]

The first result of this alliance was that on August 15th, eight days after his ultimatum had been presented at Vienna, Frederick's troops streamed across the Saxon frontier on their way to Bohemia, and on September 2nd united before Prague with a column which had come from Silesia through Glatz. It was the presence of Frederick's 80,000 men in Bohemia which brought Charles of Lorraine back from the Rhine to repel this new attack. Prague, as in 1741, was weakly held; but it resisted for a fortnight, falling on September 16th, after which Frederick pushed up the Moldau with the intention of intercepting the Austrian retreat and catching them between his army and the Franco-Bavarians, whom he somewhat hastily concluded to be following hard upon their tracks.

This, however, was not the case. While the Austrians, marching with a celerity which was as commendable as it was unusual on their part, reached Donauwerth on September 10th and Waldmünchen on the border between Bavaria and

---

[1] He was grandson of Peter the Great, being the son of his daughter Anne and Duke Charles Frederick of Holstein-Gottorp.

Bohemia a fortnight later, de Noailles and the main body of the French had turned aside to besiege Freiburg in Breisgau. This was a move it is impossible to justify: they had given no specific pledge to Frederick, but common sense might have shown de Noailles that it would be well to co-operate with an ally so capable of lending useful help, while the obvious strategy was to press hard upon the Austrian retreat and bring them to action. The siege of Freiburg, which was begun on September 18th, had no definite strategical object, and served no really useful purpose. Probably the real reason why de Noailles forbore to send more than twenty battalions under Ségur forward into Bavaria with Seckendorff and the Imperial army, was that he did not wish to commit himself to a repetition of the fate that had befallen the last invasion of Germany; that lively recollections of their experiences in those quarters made his officers and men loath to revisit them, and that neither de Noailles nor the French government felt inclined to risk anything to the chance of Frederick's sincerity in co-operation.

Be that as it may, Frederick found that his move South-Westward had brought him into considerable danger. He had to recoil hastily from Budweis to Frauenberg, which he reached on the day (Oct. 2nd) that Prince Charles and Traun joined Bathyanny and 20,000 men recalled from Bavaria at Mirstitz. This compelled Frederick to retire precipitately behind the Sasawa, for his communications with Prague were threatened. Once more Maria Theresa had appealed to the Hungarians, and in reply clouds of their light horsemen were rallying to the Austrian standard and were making their presence felt by the Prussians, whose stragglers and foragers and outposts they harassed with great persistence and success.

Traun, though joined by a Saxon contingent on October 22nd, steadily declined to be brought to the pitched battle by which Frederick hoped to extricate himself from his troubles. Not even the most careful feints would tempt him. On November 4th, Frederick retired to Kolin, the Austrians moving up to Kuttenberg. Frederick next crossed to the North-East of the Elbe, intending to take up his winter-quarters behind that river; but the Austrians suddenly became active, pushed across the river at Teinetz, and so cut him off from Prague (Nov. 19th). The King had no alternative but to retire as best he could to Silesia: he was fortunate in that the Austrians did not move quickly enough to profit more by the scattered state of his troops, but his army suffered much and lost heavily on their retreat. The garrison of Prague evacuated the town and also made their way to Silesia after a disastrous march. Traun followed the Prussians into Upper Silesia early in the New Year, but the bitter weather made a winter campaign impossible, and he withdrew almost at once to Bohemia. He had the satisfaction of having—as Frederick himself quite admitted—altogether out-manœuvred the King of Prussia, but he had perhaps carried caution too far, and might have risked a battle when the Prussians had once begun to be demoralised by continually retreating. But a price had to be paid for the deliverance of Bohemia from the Prussians, and this was the expulsion of Bärenklau from Bavaria. With only 20,000 men to oppose the 32,000 of Seckendorff and Ségur, he had had to evacuate Münich (Oct. 15th) and retire behind the Inn, retaining possession, however, of Passau, Salzburg and Braunau. Freiburg meanwhile after a gallant defence had succumbed to the French on November 24th.

Two events of great importance marked the winter of 1744–1745. In November the Marquis d'Argenson became Foreign Minister of France. On January 20th the Emperor Charles VII died.

The foreign policy of d'Argenson presents a curious mixture of the obsolete and the premature. In his idea of establishing in Italy an independent federation under the hegemony of Sardinia, he was as much in advance of his times as he was behind them in thinking the humiliation of the Hapsburgs the chief object of French policy towards Germany. In his desire to accomplish this end, to put in practice the policy of *divide et impera*, he never seems to have stopped to consider whether the Prussian alliance might not prove a two-edged weapon. Opposed as he was to England and anxious to revive the French Marine, he failed to see that the hostility of Austria and Prussia might be relied upon to paralyse Germany and to keep her neutral in the Anglo-French contest for the seas which was of no immediate concern to Hapsburg or Hohenzollern.

The death of Charles VII involved the collapse of the

Union of Frankfurt, and opened up the question of the succession to the Empire. Even before the Emperor's death the Franco-Bavarian alliance had been showing signs of weakness. German feeling was anti-French; the Empress, an Austrian Archduchess, favoured a reconciliation with Austria; and the Emperor's best general, Seckendorff, distrusting the prospects of successfully holding Bavaria, was quite ready to come to terms. So averse was he to the war, that when in January an Austrian division attacked the French posts at Amberg, he refused to stir to its aid. Ségur attempted the relief, but was badly beaten, whereupon the town capitulated. Just about this time a refusal to comply with the Emperor's urgent appeal for reinforcements was received from Louis XV, and it is not too much to say that this was the final blow to Charles VII. "The Bold Bavarian," who must have found the Imperial dignity a very disappointing possession, was only forty-eight at his death (Jan. 1745). Led away by a not unnatural ambition and by the promises of French and Prussian assistance, he had embarked upon a course from which he had reaped no advantage, and which had exposed his unhappy subjects to great sufferings. It is hardly possible to keep pace with the number of times Bavaria changed hands. This ill-fortune was a warning to any who might aspire to the Empire. Charles Albert had tried to gain the headship of Germany by the aid of Germany's old enemy. It would be hard to condemn him for falseness to an all but non-existent German nationality and patriotism, but in letting himself be the puppet of France and his candidature be the cloak for French aggressions on Germany, he cannot be said to be free from responsibility for the misfortunes which befell him.

The death of Charles VII opened up to Maria Theresa an opportunity for attaining one of the principal objects of her ambition, her husband's election as Emperor. Nor was it easy to see where a candidate could be found to oppose Francis Stephen. Maximilian Joseph, the new Elector of Bavaria, was a mere youth and, even had he been willing to subject his country again to the perilous honour of having the Emperor for its ruler, his candidature could hardly have had any chance. As Protestants, if for no other reasons, George of Hanover and Frederick of Brandenburg were impossible. The Elector Palatine was on personal grounds quite out of the question, and there only remained Augustus III of Saxony, who had recently come to terms with Austria and Russia,[1] and therefore declined the offers of France and Prussia. Notwithstanding this, d'Argenson continued to hanker after the idea of inducing Augustus III to stand; and he urged that as a means to exercise influence over the Imperial election, France should once again assume the offensive on the Danube and join Frederick in Bohemia. This would entail standing on the defensive in the Netherlands, which he regarded as quite unimportant, and would prevent France lending much aid to the Spanish Bourbons in Italy, thereby withdrawing France from an alliance his feelings towards which are well expressed in his famous aphorism, " le destin de l'Espagne est toujours de nous ruiner."

But meanwhile Maria Theresa, acting with a remarkable decision and promptitude, had hurled a strong force under Bathyanny on the scattered Franco-Bavarian forces in Bavaria. He crossed the Inn on March 21st, took Landshut, Straubing and Dingolfing almost unopposed, drove Ségur in on Donauwerth, sent the Elector flying to Augsburg, and in a fortnight the unlucky Bavaria had once more suffered a change of masters.

The Elector had no alternative but to accept the offers Maria Theresa now made through her cousin the Empress Dowager. In vain Chavigny fought to keep Maximilian Joseph true to an ally who made no effort to succour him. On April 22nd, 1745, the Treaty of Füssen restored him to his dominions on his guaranteeing the Pragmatic Sanction, promising neutrality in the war,[2] and pledging his vote to Francis Stephen at the Imperial election.

This treaty, to which Hesse-Cassel and Würtemberg hastened to accede, was a great triumph for Maria Theresa and a corresponding blow to Frederick and France. Deprived of the moral support of her alliance with Bavaria, it is rather difficult to see what reasons France had for continuing the war. Probably the successes of 1744 in Flanders had whetted Louis XV's attitude for conquest: to make peace as matters then stood would be a somewhat humiliating confession of failure, and d'Argenson, who was a firm supporter

[1] The Treaty of Warsaw was arranged in January, but not ratified till May 18th.
[2] A secret article placed 12,000 troops at the disposal of the Maritime Powers on hire.

of the Prussian alliance, was possessed by the belief that he would be able to induce Augustus III to stand for the Empire. It was therefore resolved to adopt a vigorous offensive in Italy and the Netherlands as the means of extorting a good peace from Maria Theresa.

This decision was not palatable to Frederick. He had urged upon France an attack upon Hanover which should cut that country off from the ecclesiastical electorates and, as in 1741, intimidate the Electoral College, while another army should advance through Bavaria into Bohemia; but France had had enough of campaigning in Germany, and did not care enough about the choice of an Emperor to sacrifice to that object the chance of territorial aggrandisement in Italy and the Netherlands. The measure of Frederick's annoyance may be gathered from the fact that he offered to vote for Francis Stephen if Silesia were guaranteed to him. Short of money and other resources, he found himself threatened with the hostility of Saxony and of Saxony's patron Russia, the third party to the Treaty of Warsaw.[1]

Thus, while 50,000 Austrians under Bathyanny moved Westward after the conclusion of the Treaty of Füssen and establishing themselves near Frankfurt covered the meeting of the Electoral College, France instead of reinforcing Coigni, who had moved to the Middle Rhine after the fall of Freiburg, was devoting her principal efforts to the Netherlands. A magnificent army of 90,000 men under Marshal Saxe converged upon Tournay and laid siege to that important fortress (April 19th). To save it the Duke of Cumberland, who had been appointed commander-in-chief of the Allied Forces, collected some 50,000 men near Brussels and, moving up to its relief,[2] engaged Saxe at Fontenoy on May 11th (N.S.). Cumberland, whose daring blow at the most vulnerable point of the French line was hardly the mixture of stupid courage and ignorant incompetence described by some writers, was only baulked of success by the misconduct of the Dutch on

---

[1] This guaranteed the succession to Poland to the son of Augustus III, promised to reconquer Silesia for Maria Theresa and reduce Prussia to its original limits: Augustus III was to vote for Francis Stephen. As far as Russia was concerned it was the work of Bestuchev, who favoured Austria.

[2] Of this force, 53 battalions and 90 squadrons, the Dutch provided 26 and 40, the British 22 and 26, the Hanoverians 5 and 16, the Austrians only 8 squadrons, d'Aremberg having taken 24,000 men to the Main to join Bathyanny.

his left. They completely failed to second the efforts of the British and Hanoverian infantry, whose conduct on this day has probably never been surpassed and rarely equalled. Had the Dutch only engaged the attention of the French right and prevented Saxe bringing up troops from that quarter to hurl upon Cumberland's column, the French could not have averted defeat; as it was, Saxe was able to throw in all his reserves and win.[1]

Ten days after the battle the Dutch garrison of Tournay surrendered after a feeble defence, and Cumberland, unable to cover both Ghent and Brussels, had the mortification of seeing the former taken by the French on July 11th (N.S.). He had to retire to Vilvorde between Antwerp and Brussels, but he was unable to make any attempt to interfere with Saxe's operations against West Flanders, for he received orders to send back to England first ten battalions of infantry, and finally his whole army save five regiments of horse and one of foot. The reason for their recall was that on July 25th Prince Charles Edward Stuart had landed in Scotland. The connection between the " Forty-Five " and the course of affairs on the Continent, more especially in Germany, may perhaps seem remote, but it was the recall of Cumberland and his army quite as much as the slackness of the Dutch, the extreme efficiency of Saxe's engineers and artillerymen, or the absence of the Austrians, which was responsible for the ease with which the French in the latter half of 1745 overran West Flanders.

The absence of the Austrians from the Netherlands was due to their presence at Frankfurt for the Imperial election. From the moment the French crossed the frontier of Flanders, Francis Stephen's election was assured. Together, Frederick and France might have perhaps overcome the reluctance of Augustus III, but the futile negotiations which the untiring d'Argenson was conducting with Saxony merely prevented any chance of the French army on the Rhine taking the offensive, as d'Argenson supposed Augustus would not wish to push his candidature home with French bayonets.[2] When

---

[1] For Fontenoy, see the Hon. J. W. Fortescue's *History of the British Army*, ii. pp. 109-120; the *Trevor MSS.* p. 116; the *Gentleman's Magazine* for June and July 1745; the reports of Saxe and Ligonier, *E.H.R.*, 1897, pp. 524-527; pp. 51-70 of the *Life of Marquess Townshend*; and pp. 395-429 of de Broglie's *Marie Thérèse Impératrice*, vol. i.

[2] De Broglie, *Marie Thérèse Impératrice*, ii. 94.

d'Aremberg's corps arrived from the Netherlands and 20,000 Frenchmen were called up from the Rhine to fill the gaps which Fontenoy had made in Saxe's army, only forms remained to be gone through. On September 13th the Grand Duke of Tuscany was elected Emperor under the title of Francis I, the Empire returned to the Hapsburgs, and Marie Theresa had obtained one of her two main objects.[1]

From attaining the other, the recovery of Silesia, she was, however, as far removed as ever. After the abortive invasion of Upper Silesia in January, the Austrian main body had remained inactive on the Bohemian side of the mountains, their light cavalry scouring the country and pushing their raids over Silesia. Not till May was Frederick, who had to refit and rest his shattered army, able to deal effectively with them. Then Winterfeldt and Ziethen, now making his first appearance of any importance, routed and dispersed a large body of Austrian irregulars near Jaegerndorf. But it was the Austrians and not the Prussians who took the offensive in the campaign. On May 31st, Prince Charles of Lorraine left Landshut, intending to move upon Breslau down the Striegauwasser and cut the town off from Frederick and the main Prussian army, 70,000 strong, who were lying round Schweidnitz and Jauernik in the valley of the Schweidnitzwasser. Frederick made no attempt to defend the passes, and the Saxons, who formed the Austrian vanguard, were as far forward as Striegau before he moved Westward from Schweidnitz and, under cover of a sharp skirmish between his right and the Saxons, crossed to the left bank of the Striegauwasser on the evening of June 3rd. His object in thus delaying had been to make certain of a battle: had he defended the passes, the Austrians might not have pushed their attack home.

Had Prince Charles of Lorraine kept sufficiently close to the Saxons it is possible that the battle of June 4th might have had a very different ending, for the Prussian rearguard, which was to form their left, did not manage to arrive at the appointed time, having been delayed by the breakdown of a bridge over the Striegauwasser. Thus, when on the morning of June 4th Charles at length arrived on the field from Hohenfriedberg, the Saxons had already attacked Striegau,

[1] Frederick II abstained from voting, as did the Elector Palatine, but the validity of the Bohemian vote was acknowledged.

had been repulsed, and then thrown into confusion by a counter-attack of the Prussian cavalry, but Frederick's line was not yet formed. However, Charles hesitated, and hesitating gave Ziethen time to push his belated cavalry across a ford and throw himself into the gap in the Prussian line. At the same time the Prussian right advanced to turn the flank of the Austrian left, exposed by the rout of the Saxons, and the Austrians giving way all along the line fell back towards the passes. Had Frederick pursued vigorously he might have converted the Austrian defeat into a disaster; as it was, they straggled through the hills in some disorder, leaving 2500 prisoners behind, besides losing some 9000 killed and wounded. The Prussians, whose loss amounted to under 5000, were too much fatigued by their night march to profit by the enemy's discomfiture at once, but Frederick soon followed the retreating Austrians into Bohemia. Before his advance Prince Charles at first retired, but standing at bay at König-gratz brought Frederick to a standstill (July 20th). For about six weeks Frederick remained inactive on the Elbe: he could not drive the Austrians from their lines, and his own position was somewhat precarious. At the end of his resources, with no prospect of obtaining assistance from France either in men or money, he was really anxious to extract a peace which would leave him Silesia, and hoped by this bold offensive to lend weight to the representations George II was making to Maria Theresa. However, the country, as in 1744, was bitterly hostile to him: Austrian light troops swarmed upon his flanks and rear, cut off his convoys and foragers and so straitened him for supplies that when, on September 16th, the capture of Neustadt cut his line of retreat through that town to Glatz, he at once decided to retire on the other line, by Landshut and the Schatzlar Pass, while it was still open, and on September 18th he set out for Silesia.

So slow, however, was his retreat that Charles of Lorraine was able to get in between him and the Schatzlar Pass and to bar the retreat at Sohr. On the morning of September 29th, Frederick suddenly found the Austrians moving in battle array upon his unsuspecting camp. His cavalry outposts had served him badly, and it was only by his own extraordinary exertions and by the good drill and discipline of his men that he was able to form them up in time to meet the attack. The key to the

Prussian position was a hill upon their right which the Austrian left wing at once seized and, planting 28 guns on it, proceeded to enfilade their enemy.   Quick to see the importance of this point, Frederick concentrated all his efforts on its capture, and "refusing" his left, assailed the hill vigorously with the bulk of his infantry, while Büddenbrock and the cavalry of the right supported the attack by charging the Austrian cavalry opposite them and driving them back into some broken ground in their rear.   At the second attempt the Prussians mastered the hill and then turned to succour their left and centre, which were hard pressed, the village of Burghersdorf in the centre being in great danger of falling into the Austrian hands.   The intervention of the Prussian right proved decisive, the Austrians drew off, and Frederick found himself able to continue his march to Silesia unmolested.   If he had died before 1756 the battle of Sohr would be his chief claim to reputation as a tactician.   Surprised though he was, the promptitude with which he formed up his men, the quickness with which he realised the importance of the hill, the resolution and courage with which he concentrated all his efforts on this critical point, his good judgment in refusing his left, make Sohr as peculiarly his victory as Mollwitz had been his soldiers'.   The Austrians threw away the great advantage with which they began the battle by their fatal slowness and want of vigour.   An immediate and headlong attack before the Prussians could form up was all that was needed. Precision should have been sacrificed to promptitude, exactness to energy.   But Charles of Lorraine could not shake off the trammels of his pedantic training, and energy was a stranger to him.

Just before the battle, Frederick had concluded with George II a treaty of great importance.   Always anxious to bring the Silesian war to an end, and if possible to bring Prussia into line with Austria and the Maritime Powers against France, George II had at this moment an unusually urgent reason for wishing to achieve this end.   The same cause which had paralysed Cumberland's defence of the Netherlands, the Jacobite insurrection in Scotland, was filling George with alarms for the safety of his beloved Hanover, which he saw exposed to a French attack.   Accordingly he hastened to come to terms with Frederick, whom he found ready enough to listen to his overtures. On August 26th, 1745, by the Convention of Hanover the two Powers exchanged guarantees of each other's possessions, Silesia being definitely included among those of Prussia. Frederick further promised not to vote against Francis Stephen, and it was agreed that Maria Theresa should be allowed to accede to the treaty any time within the next six weeks.

But Maria Theresa did not require six minutes in which to decide. Indignantly refusing to accede to the Convention, she turned to France and, through the mediation of Saxony, made overtures which, in the light of the terms arranged at Aix-la-Chapelle, France was very ill-advised to refuse. Maria Theresa would have surrendered the greater part of the French conquests in the Netherlands—which after all concerned the Maritime Powers rather than Austria—in return for peace and the recognition of Francis as Emperor. But Louis xv's appetite for military glory and d'Argenson's equally infatuated adherence to the idea of the Prussian alliance caused the rejection of this chance of a substantial territorial gain. Maria Theresa fell back on the alternative of a joint attack upon Brandenburg in concert with her Saxon ally. Relying on Russia's intimation to Frederick that she would assist Saxony if the Elector were attacked by Prussia, Maria Theresa planned an advance down the Elbe by Rutowski's Saxons supported by an Austrian division, to be covered by an advance of the Austrian main body into Lusatia. This, if only it were executed with the necessary dash and secrecy, was by no means an unpromising scheme : it would have cut off Frederick in Silesia from his hereditary dominions. Secrecy, however, the indispensable condition of success, was not observed. Count Brühl indiscreetly let out the scheme to the Swedish Ambassador at Dresden, and by this means—for Sweden was on good terms with Frederick, whose sister Ulrica had married Adolphus Frederick of Holstein, the heir to Sweden—the Prussians were warned in time to make preparations. Accordingly, when Charles of Lorraine entered Lusatia on November 20th by the valley of the Lusatian Neisse, Frederick had already concentrated 35,000 men at Liegnitz, while the presence of 30,000 more at Halle under Leopold of Anhalt-Dessau checked the Western advance. On November 21st, Frederick moved West, thinking to fall upon the Austrian rear and cut

them off from Bohemia. But on this occasion their slowness
proved a positive advantage. It was on their van, not, as he had
expected, on their rear that Ziethen hurled himself at Hennersdorf on November 24th. The Saxons, a mere brigade of barely
3000 strong, were surprised and cut to pieces ; but the check,
slight as it was, sufficed to cause Charles to change his plan.
He fell back hastily to Zittau and thence by the pass of Gabel
to Aussig on the Elbe, moving from there down the Elbe to
the assistance of Rutowski and Grüne, against whom Leopold
of Anhalt-Dessau was advancing. It is possible that Charles
may have hoped to draw Frederick after him, and thereby
prevent him from assisting his general by involving the
Prussian main body in the hills ; but Frederick was not
tempted, and moved Westward by Bautzen on the bridge over
the Elbe at Meissen.

Meanwhile Leopold was moving on Dresden, somewhat
too slowly for Frederick's satisfaction, for his delays allowed
Rutowski to concentrate and Grüne to join the Saxons. The
campaign thus resolved itself into a race between Leopold, the
Austrians and Frederick. Would Leopold be able to defeat
Rutowski before Lorraine could arrive, or would Lorraine be
up in time for his army to unite with Rutowski and crush
Leopold before Frederick could succour him ? As usual,
Charles of Lorraine was very slow, and had not arrived when,
on December 15th, Leopold came up to the strong position
occupied by Rutowski and Grüne at Kesselsdorf, a few miles
North of Dresden. The position, however, had the grave
defect that the stream and ravine at the foot of the hill on
which the Austrians, who formed the right, were posted, while
making that wing all but impregnable, would hinder the delivering of a counter-attack. Accordingly the old general
massed his troops opposite Kesselsdorf, where the Saxons had
thirty guns well entrenched. Twice he hurled his men at the
battery, twice they were repulsed, but the imprudence of the
Saxon counter-attack gave Leopold the chance he wanted.
His cavalry fell upon the Saxons and overthrew them. The
infantry rallying under cover of this diversion came on again,
entered Kesselsdorf on the heels of the Saxons and carried
the great battery, whose fire the counter-attack had masked.
This decided the day ; the Saxons gave way in disorder, and
though the Austrians beat off an attack and got away safely

to rejoin Prince Charles, Dresden opened its gates at once and the Elector had to fly.

Leopold's victory proved really decisive. Even Maria Theresa could no longer resist. Not only did Saxony come to terms with Frederick and accept the Convention of Hanover, but England threatened to cease paying her subsidies unless she made peace with Prussia. In vain Harrach negotiated with Vaulgrenant, the French Minister at Dresden : Louis xv and d'Argenson were not prepared to effect a complete revolution in foreign policy at the moment when d'Argenson's schemes for detaching Sardinia from Maria Theresa's side seemed on the point of success and the expulsion of the Hapsburgs from the Italian peninsula appeared only a question of days.[1] Reluctantly she gave way, and on December 25th the Treaty of Dresden definitely gave up Silesia and Glatz to Frederick. In return he recognised Francis I as Emperor, and guaranteed the Pragmatic Sanction.

It must be admitted that Frederick was decidedly fortunate in being able to obtain from Maria Theresa all he desired when he was practically at the end of his resources. It was all very well for him to declare that Marshal Saxe's victory at Fontenoy was of no more use to him than a victory on the Scamander. There can be no doubt that the French successes in the Netherlands and Italy had great influence over Maria Theresa, for had Fontenoy been a victory for the Allies or the campaign in Italy different in its result, Frederick might have found her as unyielding as before. Indeed, he had good reason to be grateful to Charles Edward and the Scottish Jacobites, for that diversion was the principal cause of the Convention of Hanover, to say nothing of its influence on the campaign in the Netherlands. The Highlanders contributed in no small measure to the acquisition of Silesia by Prussia. Above all, it was fortunate for Frederick that the Czarina, on whose co-operation Austria and Saxony had confidently relied, should have so suddenly grown cool in the cause and have failed to do what was expected. It would not have been safe for Prussia to count on her continued neutrality, and her intervention in earnest would have turned the tables completely.

But if it was largely to the efforts of France and the other enemies of Austria that Frederick owed his success in capturing

[1] Cf. p. 164.

and keeping Silesia, his own share in this important acquisition was not small. The decision, the promptitude and the energy which he displayed form a striking contrast to the hesitation of Fleury, the helplessness of Charles VII, the tergiversations of Augustus III, and the dilatoriness of Neipperg and Charles of Lorraine. Frederick's policy was undoubtedly determined by an unscrupulous ambition and an unbridled selfishness; it was contrary to loyalty to the interests of Germany, it did not look beyond the aggrandisement of the Hohenzollern. But it had the merit of being consistent and resolute, and so far it deserved to be successful. Moreover, if Fortune threw many opportunities in Frederick's way, it was not every one who would have been able to turn these chances to such striking advantage.

With the Treaty of Dresden the purely German phase of the Austrian Succession War came to an end; the battles of the three years which the war had still to run were to be fought in other lands than Germany. In Italy Austria was undoubtedly fighting to obtain some compensation for the territorial loss she had undergone in Germany; in the Netherlands the French were seeking among other things to retrieve that military reputation which their performances on the Elbe and the Danube had tarnished; but though German troops were largely employed in both these theatres of war, and though Austrian territories were the scene of operations, it is the results rather than the events of these years which concern German history.

It has already been mentioned that the peril of her Italian possessions was one of the contributing causes of Maria Theresa's reluctant assent to the Treaty of Dresden. To be in danger of being expelled from Italy was indeed a striking contrast to the high hopes which she had entertained when she signed the Treaty of Worms; but things had not gone well for the Allies in 1744, and 1745 saw the Austrians apparently on the point of being ousted from the Milanese. Of all the losses which the Hapsburg monarchy had sustained in recent years, that of the rich lands of Naples was perhaps the most grievous, and the task allotted to Traun's successor, Lobkowitz, was to attempt to recover it. Spanish rule was most unpopular in Naples, and it was hoped that a popular rising against Don Carlos would certainly follow if the Austrian forces were once to appear on Neapolitan soil. But Lobkowitz had not penetrated beyond Monte Rotondo in the Campagna when the Spanish army of North Italy, aided by a French division under Conti, created a diversion by assailing Piedmont from Dauphiné (July 1744) and laying siege to the fortress of Coni. In great alarm Charles Emmanuel recalled his contingent with Lobkowitz's force, from which Maria Theresa also detached a regiment, that her slippery ally might have no cause to complain that he was being left in the lurch. Thus weakened, Lobkowitz had no alternative but to retire into winter-quarters behind the Metaurus (Nov.), and thence early in the next year to Modena. Meanwhile Leutrum's gallant defence of Coni had proved successful, the Franco-Spaniards raising the siege and retiring into Dauphiné, though they retained possession of both Savoy and Nice.

With the spring of 1745 matters took a turn even more unfavourable to the Allies. Genoa, annoyed by English interference with her commerce and indignant at the proposed cession of Finale to Sardinia, definitely threw in her lot with the Bourbons, and so opened the Riviera route for a junction between the Spaniards from Naples and the Franco-Spanish force under Don Philip, with whom was now associated Marshal Maillebois (April). Unable to dispute the passage of the Apennines against considerable numerical superiority, the Austro-Sardinians retired to Bassignano, whence the Austrians were before long called off by an advance of the Spaniards into the Milanese from Pavia. The Sardinians, left isolated at Bassignano, were attacked by the French and badly beaten (Sept. 27th), the whole country South of the Tanaro passing into the hands of the Franco-Spaniards, while the Austrians found themselves pressed back towards Tyrol by the Spaniards under Gages, who occupied Milan almost unopposed on December 19th. The only weak point in the military position of the victorious Bourbons was that in their eagerness to possess themselves of the Milanese the Spaniards allowed themselves to become somewhat widely separated from their allies.

It was now that the persevering but visionary d'Argenson threw himself into the task of concluding a separate peace with Charles Emmanuel, as the necessary preliminary to his favourite project of the federation of Italy. The negotiations of Turin proved abortive in the end, because the jealousy of Spain and Sardinia caused delays of the utmost importance which gave time for the conclusion of the Treaty of Dresden and the despatch of Austrian reinforcements to Italy. Charles Emmanuel was probably genuine enough in opening negotiations with d'Argenson: if Maria Theresa could not defend her own possessions, it was not his place or policy to risk his dominions for her sake. But the delays due to Spain's refusal to agree to the terms for which Sardinia held out gave the situation time to change so much that the shifty King, who feared the Bourbons more than he did the Hapsburgs, finally used the negotiations to lull Maillebois into a false security from which he was rudely awakened when, early in March, the Piedmontese troops were suddenly put in motion against the scattered Franco-Spaniards. Within a very short time Maillebois was driven back to Novi and the Austrians, returning, ousted Gages and Don Philip from the Milanese. Indeed, it was only by a brilliant counterstroke, a daring offensive return to the North of the Po, which drew the Austro-Sardinians after him, that Maillebois finally managed to save himself and his allies from being severed from France by a Sardinian attack on their communications. Even as it was the Franco-Spaniards had to retire behind the Var (Sept. 17th), leaving Genoa to be besieged and taken by the Austrians. The turn of fortune was complete; the more so because, on July 9th, Philip v of Spain had died, and with his death Elizabeth Farnese's influence had ceased to be predominant at Madrid. The new King, Ferdinand vi, was not prepared to sacrifice Spain to his stepmother's dynastic ambitions, and did not intend to risk much in Italy.

Masters of Italy, and with their ally Charles Emmanuel no longer in any danger, the Austrians would have moved against Naples had not the English insisted upon their undertaking an invasion of Provence. This enterprise resulted in failure, for a rising at Genoa forced the Austrian garrison to evacuate the town after several days of savage street-fighting (Dec. 5th to 10th), and the invaders had to fall back behind the Var (Feb. 2nd, 1747) in order to cover the siege of Genoa which was vigorously conducted by the Austrians with the aid of Admiral Medley and the English Mediterranean squadron. To relieve Genoa, Belleisle undertook as a diversion an invasion of Piedmont by the Col d'Assiette, which resulted, indeed, in a disastrous repulse from the strong position of Exilles (July 19th), but succeeded in drawing off the Piedmontese contingent from Genoa and so forcing the Austrians to raise the siege. With the repulse at Exilles the operations of the war in Italy were practically at an end, for, though the Austrians resumed the siege of Genoa in the next year, they were unable to take the town. As far as Italy was concerned, Maria Theresa had been successful: she had not only come through the war with undiminished territories, but was actually in possession of those of the Duke of Modena. That at the conclusion of peace she was unable to retain this conquest, but, on the contrary, had to sacrifice Parma and Piacenza, was due to the turn the war had taken in another theatre. Italy had to pay the debts of Flanders.

It was not so much the defeat at Fontenoy, but the Jacobite insurrection in Scotland which had left Flanders at the mercy of Maurice de Saxe. After the recall of Cumberland and his army Saxe found the Eastern Netherlands an easy prey. With England fully occupied at home and Austria comparatively indifferent to the fate of the Netherlands, the burden of defence was left mainly to the Dutch, whose adhesion to their allies was extremely faint-hearted. Indeed they went so far as to open negotiations for a separate peace; and, though these fell through, it would have been quite easy for France to detach the United Provinces from England and Austria had d'Argenson only listened to the advice of Saxe and permitted that general to make Holland the objective of his campaign. Had this been done there is little doubt that the Dutch would have hastened to make peace, in which case, with Ostend lost and Holland neutral, England would have had no landing-place near the scene of operations, and would have found co-operation with the Austrians exceedingly difficult. But d'Argenson was afraid of provoking an anti-French reaction in Holland, and therefore Saxe had to devote himself to the reduction of the Eastern Netherlands.

In this enterprise Saxe was able to avail himself of another French army, that of Conti, to which had been entrusted the task of demonstrating along the frontiers of the Empire in order to overawe the minor Princes of South and Western Germany and prevent Maria Theresa from recruiting the Coalition among them. But to do this there was no need of an army. The despatch of a French envoy to the Diet of Ratisbon to promise that France would respect the neutrality of the Empire was quite sufficient. Würtemberg and the Elector Palatine were decidedly favourable to France; and though Bavaria hired out 6000 troops to the Maritime Powers, the influence of Maurice de Saxe over his half-brother induced Augustus III to declare for the Empire remaining neutral, a policy which was cordially supported by the three ecclesiastical Electors whose principal desire was to keep the war out of their coasts. Thus Conti's army could be safely diverted from the Middle Rhine to the Netherlands, where it speedily reduced Mons (July 11th) and laid siege to Charleroi. Saxe had opened operations in January by a successful dash at Brussels, which had fallen after a three weeks' siege (Feb. 20th): he then dislodged the Allies from the Demer, forced them back into Holland and detached Clermont to form the siege of Antwerp, which he covered with his main body. Antwerp fell on May 31st, by which time a considerable force of Allies was beginning to collect at Breda to take the field; Culloden (April 16th) had set free a small English corps and the 6000 Hessians who had been sent across to Scotland in February, and Charles of Lorraine had come up from Austria with large reinforcements. Towards the end of July the Allies made an attempt to relieve Charleroi but were too late, its fall occurring (Aug. 1st) before they could get much beyond the Mehaigne. They then took post to cover Namur but were dislodged by the capture of Huy, which imperilled their communications and forced them to withdraw East of the Meuse. Namur was promptly besieged and fell before the end of September, while Lorraine was equally unsuccessful in an attempt to save Liége, being ousted by Saxe from his position at Roucoux after a sharply-contested action (Oct. 11th).

Thus 1746 closed with the Middle Meuse in the hands of Saxe, and only Maastricht left to cover Holland from attack. Nor was 1747 any more satisfactory to the Allies. Cumberland replaced Charles of Lorraine as commander-in-chief; but though he collected over 90,000 troops of all nationalities, he was unable to prevent the reduction of the mouth of the Scheldt by Saxe's trusted lieutenant Löwendahl, who took Sluys and Cadzand, and was only prevented from adding Zealand to his conquests by the timely arrival of a British squadron with reinforcements (April to May). Then, when Cumberland had succeeded in drawing Saxe from his lines between Malines and Louvain by moving up the Meuse to attack a detached corps under Clermont, he found himself anticipated by Saxe in an attempt to secure the Herdeeren heights just South-West of Maastricht (July 1st), and was defeated in the battle which was fought next day for that position. Lauffeldt was a repetition of Fontenoy, for the traditional immobility of the Austrians allowed Saxe to neglect them and concentrate his attack on the British and their German auxiliaries; and in this quarter of the field the misconduct of the Dutch at a very critical moment sacrificed the fruits of the splendid behaviour of the British, the Hessians and the Hanoverians. The Allies were able to save Maastricht, but Saxe could safely detach Löwendahl to besiege and take (Sept. 16th) the great fortress of Bergen-op-Zoom, with which most of Dutch Brabant fell into French hands.

Thus by the end of 1747 all but a very small part of the Austrian Netherlands had been conquered for Louis xv; and though, as d'Argenson had predicted, the French violation of Dutch territory had produced a reaction in Holland against the Francophil "Burgher party," the upshot of which was the practical restoration of the monarchical element with the election (May 1747) of William of Nassau-Dillenberg as Stadtholder and Captain-General of the Netherlands, this revolution was of more political than military importance, for the Dutch defence of their territories was extremely weak, not to say culpably negligent and indifferent.[1] But if the Maritime Powers had no reason to wish for another campaign on land, the pressure of England's supremacy at sea, now satisfactorily reasserted by the victories of Anson (May 3rd) and Hawke (October 14th) in the Bay of Biscay, was exerting an equally powerful influence over Louis xv in the direction of peace. Austria possibly would have liked to try another campaign in Italy, where she might have hoped to achieve something at the expense of Naples or Genoa, but England and France were both thoroughly weary of the war, and the negotiations of Aix-la-Chapelle, begun early in 1748, produced a definite

[1] Cf. *Checquers Court Papers*, Hist. MSS. Commission, pp. 376-391.

result on April 30th, when the representatives of England, France and Holland signed the preliminaries of peace. Maria Theresa's was almost the only voice to be raised in opposition to peace, for she had recently (May 1746) secured the promise of Russian assistance on a considerable scale, and she was afraid that the compensations which peace was bound to make necessary would have to be provided at her expense. In the hopes of getting better terms out of France by a separate negotiation, she instructed Kaunitz, her representative at Aix, to try to arrange a treaty with Louis XV; but France was simultaneously negotiating with the Maritime Powers, and as their naval supremacy made their hostility more formidable than was Maria Theresa's, it was with England and Holland that the preliminary treaty was signed.

Not till nearly six months later, however, was the definite treaty signed—six months of every kind of intrigue and bargaining. In the end, Maria Theresa found herself compelled to accede to the treaty by the fact that she could do nothing if deserted by England and Sardinia, while they were independent of her. At length, on October 16th, the plenipotentiaries of England, France and Holland affixed their signatures to the treaty; Spain followed suit on October 20th, Austria on November 8th, Sardinia on November 20th. From the point of view of German history the most important clauses were those which guaranteed Silesia and Glatz to Frederick II, which recognised Francis II as Emperor, and which guaranteed the Pragmatic Sanction except as regarded Silesia and Parma and Piacenza. To Maria Theresa and the Hapsburgs the evacuation by France of the Austrian Netherlands, the restoration of the Barrier-fortresses to the Dutch, who had done so little to defend them, the cession of Parma and Piacenza to Don Philip of Spain, and of the Ticino boundary in Lombardy to Charles Emmanuel,[1] and the restoration of Francis of Modena to his dominions, were also of great importance. The reciprocal restitution of conquests by England and France shows that the peace marks not an end but a pause in the great struggle for the sea, which affected Germany indirectly not a little and directly still more through the Anglo-Hanoverian connection.

If, then, it be asked what Power had gained most by the

[1] He had to give up Finale to Genoa, but recovered Nice and Savoy.

war, it would not be difficult to answer. By promptly taking advantage of the embarrassments of allies and enemies alike, Frederick of Prussia had gained territory and a reputation : he was still to have to fight for his share in the spoils, but of all the vultures which had gathered round the carcase of the Hapsburg monarchy he alone had succeeded in appeasing his appetite. It was not much consolation to France for all her efforts, her vast expenditure in men and money, her hard-won victories in the Netherlands, to have established Don Philip in Parma and to have materially assisted the rise of Prussia. As for Bavaria and Saxony, they had gained nothing, but they had been detached from the French alliance and were, for the immediate future at any rate, to be faithful allies of Austria. Sardinia had made another step forward. Spain, now that Elizabeth Farnese's power was no more, could follow under Ferdinand VI the dictates of national policy untrammelled by a dynastic attraction to Italy. Russia had made another appearance in the European area. England had retrieved a bad start at sea and, despite Fontenoy and Lauffeldt, had largely contributed to preventing France from retaining the Netherlands ; she might also claim to have helped the Hapsburg monarchy not a little to weather the storm which had threatened to engulf it, even if her actions had been prompted rather by her own interests than by the dictates of mere disinterestedness. Holland's part in the war had been but feeble and her power was obviously on the decline, while the bonds which bound her to the English alliance were as obviously becoming relaxed.

Finally, the question must be answered, how had Austria come through this time of trial ? Thanks largely to her own magnificent courage and resolution, to an endurance which had never failed, and to a determination which had been proof against all trials, Maria Theresa had brought her inheritance safely through a sea of formidable dangers, lessened, it is true, by the loss of Silesia and Parma, but strengthened in ways which amply compensated for those losses. Her dominions had been welded together by the war, which had done much to excite the loyalty and patriotism of the heroic Queen's subjects. It was not in Hungary only that Maria Theresa's appeals had touched an answering chord, though it was a great thing to have converted that source of weakness into a source of

Map to illustrate THE CAMPAIGN OF MOLLWITZ.

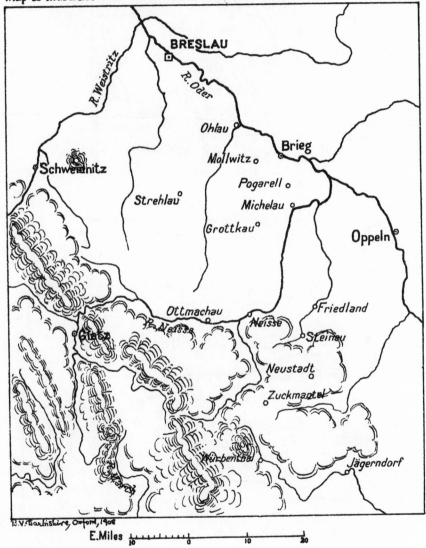

R. Weistritz

BRESLAU

R. Oder

Ohlau

Brieg

Mollwitz

Schweidnitz

Pogarell

Strehlau

Michelau

Grottkau

Oppeln

Ottmachau

Friedland

R. Neisse

Neisse

Glatz

Steinau

Neustadt

Zuckmantel

R. March

Würbenthal

Jägerndorf

B.V. Darbishire, Oxford, 1908

E. Miles   10   0   10   20

SOHR Sep. 30th 1745.

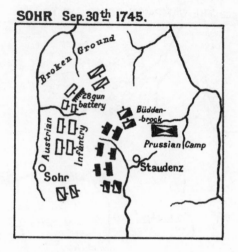

CHOTUSITZ or CZASLAU May 17th 1742.

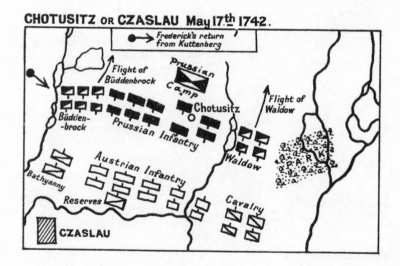

strength. The Imperial dignity had been won back and secured to the new line of the Hapsburgs. If clear signs were not wanting that the old Anglo-Austrian alliance had been strained almost to the breaking-point, Bavaria, hitherto an enemy and a client of France, and Saxony were now among Austria's allies; the Russian alliance of 1746, even if it be held to have been in itself undesirable, did strengthen her hands against Prussia, and the attitude of the Bourbon Powers was by no means uncompromisingly hostile. With one Power only were Maria Theresa's relations of an unfriendly nature. The guarantee of Silesia which she had at last given grudgingly and reluctantly was a pledge by which she could hardly be expected to abide. Other accidental circumstances had combined to prevent Austria doing herself justice in the struggle for Silesia : meanwhile the army had improved greatly during the war, and peace would permit of further increases and improvements, and a chance might come when the conditions would favour Austria more.

It was for these reasons, because Maria Theresa, far from being reconciled to the loss of Silesia, was still planning all possible means of recovering it, and also because the Anglo-French quarrel was undecided, that the Peace of Aix-la-Chapelle was a truce not a real peace, and that the settlement of the two great questions at issue was merely postponed until 1756–1763.

CHAPTER X

MARIA THERESA'S REFORMS AND THE DIPLOMATIC REVOLUTION

MARIA THERESA had agreed to the Peace of Aix-la-Chapelle with the less reluctance because even she had become convinced that peace was necessary, and that she had more to gain from it than from prolonging the war. She saw that the road to the recovery of Silesia lay rather through allowing her resources to recuperate and through reforms in her army and her administration than through a war which offered little prospect of a satisfactory issue. " Peace, retrenchment and reform " was therefore her programme on the morrow of Aix-la-Chapelle; and she was the better able to set about such a task because—as she herself put it—" Providence had relieved her by death of councillors too prejudiced to give useful advice, too respectable and too meritorious to be dismissed."

Of the septuagenarians of whom the Conference had consisted in October 1740, Sinzendorff had died in 1742, Gundacker Stahremberg in 1745, Philipp Kinsky in 1748. To Sinzendorff had succeeded Count Ulefeld, a well-meaning, honest but incapable man, unequal to the important position of Chancellor, which he owed in no small degree to the influence of Bartenstein. This latter, Secretary to the Conference since 1727, was virtually Minister of Foreign Affairs from 1740 to 1753. He had won Maria Theresa's confidence by supporting such favourite projects of hers as the proposal that Francis Stephen should be co-Regent, but his blind belief in Fleury's good intentions had somewhat shaken his credit. More of a lawyer than a statesman, narrow-minded and unprogressive, somewhat obstinate and self-satisfied, his influence declined as that of Kaunitz rose, and when the latter was summoned to office in 1753, Bartenstein practically retired from the administration. At the same time Ulefeld exchanged the Chancellorship for an office more adapted to his capacities, that of Grand Chamberlain (*Obersthofmeister*). The vacancy in the Chancellorship was filled by the man whose name must always be associated with that of Maria Theresa, whose chief minister he was and under whom he may be said to have almost ruled Austria. Wenceslaus Anthony von Kaunitz was in 1753 a man of forty-two years of age, who had served Austria as the Emperor's representative with the Diet at Ratisbon, as envoy at several Italian courts, as chief minister to the Archduchess Maria Anna in the Netherlands, as Ambassador at St. James', and as plenipotentiary at Aix-la-Chapelle. From 1750 to 1753 he was Ambassador to the Court of Versailles, and after laying the foundations for the Franco-Austrian reconciliation during this period he returned to Austria to become Chancellor in 1753. His principal contribution to the reforms which the Empress-Queen was now undertaking was the separation between the State Chancery (*Staatskanzlei*) and the purely Austrian Court Chancery (*Hofkanzlei*). Under him the State Chancery was transformed into a Ministry of Foreign Affairs to which was entrusted also the control of the affairs of Lombardy and the Netherlands. But while principally concerned with foreign policy, Kaunitz, whose authority completely surpassed that of his colleagues, exercised no small influence over domestic affairs. In the Moravian troubles of 1777 his voice was uplifted in favour of conciliation, and being a somewhat lukewarm adherent of the Catholic doctrine he was able to moderate the extreme measures to which a religious fervour verging on intolerance at times inclined Maria Theresa.

More immediately responsible for the domestic reforms were Count Frederick William Haugwitz (1700–1765), a Silesian nobleman who had adhered to the Austrian cause, Count Rudolf Chotek (1706–1771), a member of one of the oldest families in Bohemia, and Count Charles Hatzfeldt (1718–1793), another Bohemian noble. Of these three Haugwitz was probably the ablest, and it was in him that Maria Theresa found her most efficient assistant in the task of reform. When the Court Chancery was separated from the State Chancery in 1753 it was he who was placed at the head of what was henceforward to be virtually a Ministry of the Interior. In this capacity he was the founder of the centralised bureaucracy which Maria Theresa endeavoured to substitute for the semi-feudal system of government she had inherited. Haugwitz succeeded in abolishing the exemption of the nobility from taxation, brought the somewhat recalcitrant Estates under the control of the central government through the bureaucracy, introduced a new system of taxation, and centralised the administration. Chotek, first prominent as the negotiator of the Peace of Füssen,[1] reorganised the administration of Tyrol, Trieste and Further Austria between 1747 and 1748, became head of the Indirect Taxation Bureau (*Banco-Präsident*) in 1749 and President of the Treasury (*Hofkammer*) in 1759, thus obtaining complete control over the whole finances. In 1762 he succeeded Haugwitz at the Ministry of the Interior. His chief work was in connection with indirect taxation and the development of the resources of the country; its trade, manufactures, roads and bridges came under his control. More aristocratic in sentiments than Haugwitz, he was more in sympathy with the Estates, and not uncommonly there was friction between the two Ministers. Hatzfeldt, best known as President of the Council of State, succeeded in reconciling the nobles and clergy to the policy of centralisation in which he was a firm believer. Education was his principal care, but he did much during the Seven Years' War to obtain money. In 1765 he became President of the Treasury, on Chotek's death in 1771 Minister of the Interior, which post he resigned in the same year to Count Henry Blümegen in order to become head of the new Council of State (*Staatsrath*).

Another minister whose influence was considerable, though hardly so beneficial, was Count Joseph Harrach, who for twenty-four years (1739–1762), and to the disadvantage of the Austrian army, was President of the War Council. Incapable and quite past his work, he was an encumbrance on the efficiency of the Council and the army, and it would have been well for Maria Theresa had she made up her mind to dismiss him in 1756, when he was already seventy-eight years of age, instead of waiting till the end of the war, in which his incapacity cost Austria so dear.

The key to the reforms of Maria Theresa is to be found in her wish to free the authority of the central government

[1] Cf. p. 154.

from the trammels which the continued existence of what had once been a feudal constitution imposed upon it. She sought to make the State supreme over the Estates, to put the whole before the parts, the welfare of the Austrian monarchy and all the peoples subject to it before the local and provincial interests which had shown themselves so strong in Upper Austria and in Bohemia in 1741. Maria Theresa was not attacking real constitutional liberties when she endeavoured to sweep away the constitutional powers of the nobles and clergy and to take from them their immunity from taxation. The objects of her attack were mere relics of a past stage of development, now become obsolete and a danger to the higher interests of the State as a whole. "Despotic" though her actions may have been, in spirit she was far from Louis xv or even Frederick ii. She had a real wish for the welfare of her subjects, and her efforts to benefit the peasantry and improve their position show that it was not merely to increase the tax-paying capacity of her dominions so that they might support a vast army that she undertook these reforms.

The first and most important step was to deprive the provincial Estates of the authority they still possessed over the army. Before the army could be made a really efficient instrument for war, it was necessary to do away with the pernicious system of dual control by which the supply of funds for its maintenance depended on the fluctuating votes of the local Estates, which in each case strove continually to shift the burden of national defence on to the shoulders of the other provinces. Indeed the army was provincial rather than royal. Each province raised and maintained its own contingent mainly by taxes in kind. Uniformity of organisation was lacking, and the central government practically had to negotiate every year with each province for the support of the various contingents. Haugwitz's scheme, the so-called Ten Years' Recess, was intended to do away with this inefficient and cumbrous system. A fixed sum was demanded from each province, and to set the whole matter on a firm basis it was voted for a period of ten years, thus practically taking the army completely out of the control of the Estates. So new a departure could not fail to arouse considerable opposition from the nobility, more especially as their cherished privilege of immunity from taxation was at the same time taken away, all classes being liable to the new taxes which replaced the old payments in kind. In the Conference itself Count Frederick Harrach assumed the leadership of the opposition, but his colleagues did not support him, and Maria Theresa was able to carry her point, and with the aid of Haugwitz and Chotek to induce the Estates to pass the required vote. The reorganisation of the Austrian army which was thus made possible took for its model the Prussian system. The Army was brought completely under the control of the Sovereign, uniformity and system were introduced into its establishments, uniforms, pay, weapons and interior economy. A much more careful military training was introduced with a new drill and the iron ramrod of the Prussian infantry. Camps of exercise were started, manœuvres were held. Officers were given a chance of studying their profession though the restriction of commissions to men of noble birth was maintained. A modified conscription based on the lines of the Prussian cantoning system assured the means of keeping the regiments up to their establishment, and measures were adopted for the improvement of discipline, especially that of the Irregular troops. One important step was the regimentation of the Frontier Forces (*Grenzsoldaten*),[1] whose turbulence and excesses had done much to neutralise their efficiency as soldiers. In no department was so much improvement effected as in the artillery. In this branch Austria had no need to fear comparisons with other armies, though it may be questioned whether the very efficiency of their artillery did not somewhat defeat its own object by increasing their immobility and their love for strong positions and defensive tactics. It may be held, however, with as much plausibility that this preference for the defensive caused such great importance to be attached to the improvement of the artillery. One reform, however, which would have been of great service was not carried out. The War Council, of which the aged Count Joseph Harrach was the head, was organised as a civilian and not as a military board.[2] It was

---

[1] These *Grenzsoldaten* were a special institution: the whole population of the frontier districts from the Adriatic to Transylvania were organised on military lines, and were specially liable to service.

[2] It was in 1753 divided into three departments, dealing respectively with military organisation, discipline and supply.

not till the evils of this arrangement had exercised their pernicious influence in the Seven Years' War that Maria Theresa at
last (1762) dismissed Harrach, replaced him by Daun, and
substituted Generals for the civilians of whom the Council
had till then been mainly composed.   Khevenhüller and
Traun, the two commanders who had done most to distinguish
themselves in the War of the Austrian Succession, had not
survived till the peace;[1] but Neipperg did better at the War
Council than in the field, and to Wenceslaus Liechtenstein,
Director General of Ordnance since 1744, belongs most of
the credit for the great improvement of the artillery.

But the reorganisation of the Army was only one branch
of the reforms which were introduced.   Almost more important
was the amalgamation of the Court Chanceries (*Hofkanzleis*)
of Austria and Bohemia, whose separate existence had hitherto
been a great stumbling-block in the path of administrative
unity and efficiency.   While the Chanceries were relieved
of all judicial work, which was transferred to a High Court
of Justice erected at Vienna for Austria and Bohemia in 1749,
they were fused in a *Directorium* which was the chief instrument through which the central government exercised control
over local administration.   In each province there was a
subordinate court (*Representation*), which was the channel of
communication between the *Directorium* and the District
Councils (*Kreis-Ämter*) which were entrusted with the supervision of local affairs.   Their sphere of influence included the
control of municipal government and the enforcement of the
decrees of the central government; but Maria Theresa left the
actual work of local government very largely in the hands of
the local nobility, who, unlike the French noblesse, did identify
themselves with the country districts and did serve the State
in all its various departments.

Pressure of work upon the *Directorium* caused all
business connected with the finances to be altogether transferred in 1762 to the Treasury (*Hofkammer*), on which the
old name of "joint Chancery of Bohemia and Austria" was
restored to the *Directorium*,[2] and its head again became
Court Chancellor (*Obersthofkanzler*).   Subordinate to the
Treasury were the *Banko-Deputation*, an office which dealt
especially with the indirect taxes, the Ministry of Commerce,

---

[1] Khevenhüller died in 1744, Traun early in 1748.   [2] Wolf, p. 96.

the local financial chambers (*Landkammern*), and a special department for the management of the public debt and loans (*Hofrechenkammer*) not to mention Revenue and Customs officials.

In the management of the finances great improvements were effected, principally by Chotek, though the strain of the Seven Years' War completely upset the equilibrium between revenue and expenditure which he seemed to be reaching during the peace. Heavy taxes had to be imposed, and as the nobles were not taxed at the same rate as the peasants, even when their exemption had been abolished, the improvement in the financial administration added to the burdens on the taxpayers rather than reduced them. Much was done to increase the indirect revenue by giving encouragement to trade and manufactures. A rigidly protective tariff formed part of the system ; but internal tolls between province and province were much reduced and this hindrance to unity partly removed, though as Hungary remained outside this fiscal system, " dualism " was extended from the political to the economic sphere.

The reform of the judicial system was another task which engaged the attention of Maria Theresa and her councillors. A code of law was very much needed on account of the great differences between the various parts of the Hapsburg dominions, but it must be admitted that the Civil Code produced in 1767 was not one of the most successful efforts of the Theresian epoch. Long, unwieldy and somewhat unsystematic, under Joseph II it had to be replaced by a new codification. Better success attended the compilation of a Criminal Code. This " *Nemesis Theresiana* " of 1769, though it retained the rack and branding, and contained clauses dealing with sorcery and witchcraft, was yet a decided step in advance, and was improved by the abolition of torture in 1776. In 1788, Joseph's code superseded it.

In like manner, attempts were made to improve education. The Universities were subjected to sweeping reforms and taken over by the government as a State department, not perhaps with altogether the best results to education. Great attention was paid to the schools, both secondary and primary. Van Swieten, one of the most trusted advisers of the Empress, was principally responsible for this branch, and his reforms embraced technical as well as intellectual education, and must be regarded as a very remarkable contribution to the regeneration of Austria.

In the main, then, Maria Theresa's efforts to establish unity and a centralised system of government were successful. One hears little in her reign of the hostility between Slav and Teuton, between German and Czech. Her personal popularity was great, her courage and steadfastness in the time of danger had won the admiration and devotion of many of her subjects, and the strain and trials of the war served to show the different provinces that they had higher interests than merely seeking their own advantage, and that, after all, even their particular interests might be best served by union with their neighbours. Common perils surmounted safely helped to give unity. Indeed, after 1748 one may fairly look upon the epithet "Austrian" as implying more than merely "subject to Hapsburg rule," one may regard the phrase "Austrian nationality" as something more than a mere contradiction in terms when applied to Bohemians and Styrians. But there were still parts of the Hapsburg dominions which remained distinct and isolated. The "dualism" of Austria and Hungary was still a weak point in the Hapsburg monarchy, geographical even more than political and racial considerations prevented the Netherlands and Lombardy from ever becoming anything more than accidental additions to the central mass. Maria Theresa was too statesmanlike, too practical and too tactful to attempt to try to apply to these outlying provinces, devoid as they were of any connection with Austria and its immediate dependencies, the same reforms she was introducing elsewhere. She was able to see what escaped the notice of her doctrinaire son, that differences in circumstances necessitate differences in methods. She preferred to govern the Netherlands in the way best suited to their conditions, and her rule never provoked revolt in Belgium. They were left in the enjoyment of their federal Constitutions. The laws and privileges of the provinces, of which the *Joyeuse Entrée* of Brabant is typical, were left untouched. The Estates enjoyed local autonomy tempered only by the presence at Vienna of a Netherlands Council [1] and at Brussels of a Governor

---

[1] From 1757 on it was a department of the State Chancery.

of the Netherlands, usually a member of the dynasty with some capable nobleman as his chief minister. Thus Eugene had been Governor from 1714 to 1725; Archduchess Maria Elizabeth, sister of Charles VI, had succeeded him; Charles of Lorraine and his wife had held the post jointly, and after her death Charles retained it, though generally absent in Austria, till 1758. In his absence Königsegg, Kaunitz and others had acted as deputies, and from 1753 to 1770 Charles Cobenzl was virtual ruler of the provinces. All was not well, however, with the Netherlands. Though after 1748 their peace was untroubled, they were heavily taxed for the Seven Years' War, the government was corrupt and at once slack and oppressive; the Barrier-fortresses were allowed to fall into complete disrepair, and the natural development of the country was greatly hindered by the cramping fetters of the Peace of Münster. Still, if sluggish and unprogressive, the forty years during which Maria Theresa ruled the Netherlands were to be preferred to the stormy season which came in with Joseph II.

In Lombardy somewhat similar conditions prevailed. The Italian Council at Vienna [1] and the Governor-General at Milan administered a "paternal despotism" of an uneventful type, which smothered the original Spanish sympathies of the inhabitants without creating any strong loyalty for Austria. From 1754 till 1771 Duke Francis III of Modena, who had been reconciled to the Hapsburgs by the betrothal of his grand-daughter and heiress to one of Maria Theresa's sons, acted as Governor-General, with Beltrame Christiani and Charles Firmian as his ministers. These enlightened ministers carried out reforms of the same nature as those introduced by Turgot in France. Education was encouraged, the Inquisition abolished, and the right of the State to control the Church successfully asserted. Trade was relieved from restrictions, the possession of land made free, the numerous clergy compelled to bear a share of the public burdens. Thus even under the idle and wasteful Francis Lombardy prospered, and in 1771 the Archduke Ferdinand took over the government and continued to rule the country on the same lines.

With Hungary matters were rather different. It has been said that "Austria had an administration, but no constitution. Hungary a constitution, but no administration," and this is not

[1] Made a department of the State Chancery in 1757.

far from the truth. The Diet, composed of two houses, one of
the magnates and higher clergy, the other of lesser nobles and
deputies of the cities, controlled taxation, had an important
share in legislation and could veto the levying of troops.
National feeling was strong and by no means favourable to
Austria, so that any reform coming from that quarter was
likely to provoke opposition, whatever its merits. The control
of the country was in the hands of the nobles, for the burghers
had little influence and the peasantry and their goods were
practically the property of their lords. The nobles paid no
taxes, had great political, social and legal privileges, including
even freedom from arrest and imprisonment, and formed a
numerous, haughty and turbulent aristocratic caste.

Maria Theresa's appeal to Hungarian loyalty in 1741,
and the concessions by which she obtained very valuable
assistance, have already been mentioned. The Queen had
managed to evade the demands for the nationalising of
the administration and for complete Home Rule in financial
and military matters, but she had had to guarantee the
exemption of the nobility from taxation and to promise to
treat Transylvania as appertaining to Hungary. Even after
1741 the Hungarian army was weak [1] and its annual cost,
two and a half million florins, was only half of what
Bohemia, though much smaller, paid for the same purpose;
while of the annual revenue of 20 millions only four were
devoted to the general purposes of the whole State. In 1751,
therefore, Maria Theresa tried to induce the Diet to vote
an increase in the contribution. To this proposal the lesser
nobles offered a bitter resistance, though the magnates
supported the Crown. In the end (June 30th) a vote of three
and a half millions was carried. In the Seven Years' War,
Hungary put considerable forces into the field but contributed
little in money, while in 1764 a Diet refused to allow the
organisation of the " Insurrection " in regiments but did vote
an additional 600,000 florins. A third subject which Maria
Theresa broached at this meeting, a measure for the amelioration of the condition of the peasantry, met with unanimous resistance, but nevertheless she issued in 1766 an ordinance regulating their position, fixing their obligations, giving them a legal
status and means of redress. At the same time she gave up

[1] Only six regiments.

summoning the Diet, appointed Joseph co-Regent, and replaced the Palatine, a national quite as much as a royal official, by a Stattholder and Captain-General, a post conferred on Duke Albert of Saxe-Teschen. To this extent Maria Theresa managed to bring Hungary under her control, and she was successful on the whole in conciliating the principal families; but as the dualism was too strong to be overthrown, she, with her usual wisdom, refrained from directly attacking it. Local autonomy she found too flourishing to be brought under a centralised system, and so she left it alone. She did manage to curb and control the lesser nobles, but without diminishing their strength, as Joseph II was to find to his cost.

Meanwhile, changes no less important were taking place in the foreign policy of Austria. Not only was Maria Theresa doing all she could to build up her own military and financial resources in order to resume some day the struggle for Silesia, she was also seeking allies who would work with her for the abasement of the upstart Hohenzollern. Naturally she looked first to the other signatories of the Treaty of Warsaw which had been reaffirmed and re-enforced in 1746 by the addition of Russia; while England, still possessed by the old idea of holding France in check by utilising the traditional rivalry between Hapsburg and Bourbon, gave a general adhesion to the treaty in 1750, though not to the secret clauses which contemplated the dismemberment of Prussia. But this old Anglo-Austrian alliance was not quite the firm union it had been. The war had strained it almost to breaking point. England's steadfast refusal to help her against Frederick, England's share in wringing from her the Treaties of Berlin and Dresden, England's attempts to force her to unite with the robber of Silesia against the Bourbon from whom she had suffered so much less, and England's support to the demands of Sardinia, had made Maria Theresa feel that her English ally had done her as much harm as her French foe.

It was with this idea in her mind that shortly after the Peace of Aix-la-Chapelle, Maria Theresa requested the members of the Conference to submit in writing their views on the political situation, and their advice as to the policy most advantageous to Austria. The majority, including Marshal Königsegg, Colloredo, the Vice-Chancellor, and the Emperor himself, while admitting that the action of England had been selfish in the extreme, were not prepared to recommend any change in the old system of alliances. Very different, however, were the proposals of Kaunitz, the most recent addition to the Conference. Premising that under existing circumstances the Maritime Powers, Russia and Saxony were the natural allies of Austria and France, Prussia and Turkey the natural enemies, he pointed out that the traditional enemies, France and Turkey, were far less formidable than the new enemy within the Empire, especially as in the case of danger from France Austria could confidently rely on that English assistance which had not been and could not be reckoned upon against Prussia. But as Prussia was the chief danger, as, apart from all idea of regaining the lost Silesia, Austria must for the future be on her guard against another unprovoked attack, Kaunitz boldly proposed to try to win the alliance of France and to secure, if not indeed her assistance, at any rate her neutrality in the event of another Silesian war. The price which he proposed to pay was one which would be no real loss to Austria, cessions of territory in the Netherlands to Don Philip of Parma, son-in-law of Louis XV.

For a revolution so radical in her foreign relations, Maria Theresa was hardly prepared. It was true that the idea of coming to terms with France had already crossed her mind; more than once, notably towards the end of 1745, she had attempted to effect a reconciliation. It was true that the hostility between France and Austria no longer rested on any necessary basis. With a Bourbon on the throne of the Spanish Hapsburgs, with Germany so disunited that a pan-German crusade to recover the conquests of Louis XIV was quite out of the question, with France made secure on her North-Eastern and Eastern borders by the acquisition of a scientific frontier and occupied mainly with her colonial and maritime rivalry with England, the relations of Bourbon and Hapsburg were altogether different from what they had been when Henri IV and Richelieu had striven to free France from the " Hapsburg net " which then threatened her. That object had been long ago accomplished; France had nothing to fear from Austria, and in England and Prussia the two Powers had new rivals and new dangers to meet. However, the old traditions were still so strong that Maria Theresa and her husband, while regarding Kaunitz's project as a possible alternative, looked upon it mainly as a means of bringing pressure to bear on England in the adjustment of the differences which threatened to sever the old alliance. At the same time they thought it well to seek to promote more friendly relations with France, and with that object Kaunitz was sent to Paris as Ambassador in 1750. During his residence there (1750–1753) he laboured steadily at laying the foundations for the future alliance; and if the seed seemed at first to have fallen on barren ground, if he failed to prevent France supporting Prussia's opposition to the election of Joseph as King of the Romans in 1752, he made a beginning. Among others, Madame de Pompadour was won round to the new policy, and when Kaunitz returned to Vienna to take up the office of State Chancellor his successor Stahremberg continued his work.

Still Kaunitz himself would seem to have for the time abandoned his idea, and to have even urged that Maria Theresa should reconcile herself to the loss of Silesia and add Prussia to the Anglo-Austrian alliance. George II, however, hated Frederick and would not hear of it, while Maria Theresa was equally unyielding. It might perhaps have been the wiser policy in the end, but it would be unreasonable to blame Maria Theresa for her refusal to come to terms with the Power which had behaved so treacherously to her, and which in its dealings with Bavaria and France had shown itself no less fickle and untrustworthy as an ally than formidable as a foe. She could have no guarantee that at some crisis Frederick would not leave her in the lurch.

Thus between 1750 and 1755 only one real change in the diplomatic position of Europe occurred. This was the Treaty of Aranjuez in 1752, by which Austria and Spain came to terms with regard to Italy, guaranteeing the existing territorial conditions. Naples, Parma and Sardinia adhered to this treaty, and thus the tranquillity of Italy was secured for nearly forty years, and one obstacle in the way of Franco-Austrian reconciliation removed.[1] But the Anglo-Austrian

[1] Ferdinand VI, under the influence of his Queen, Barbara of Portugal, and his chief minister, Wall, an Irish refugee, was following a policy of peaceful commercial and industrial development and had more or less broken away from the French alliance. As long as he remained on the throne, Spain was neutral in the Anglo-French quarrel.

alliance was growing weaker. While Austria complained bitterly of England's action and policy in the late war, especially in the matter of Silesia, which had been guaranteed to Prussia by the Convention of Hanover, England could point with about equal justice to the way in which Austria had neglected the defence of the Netherlands. The suppression of the Ostend Company [1] was still a sore point with the Hapsburgs, and England's refusal in 1748 to have the Barrier Treaty abrogated had greatly irritated Maria Theresa: she now refused to pay the annual subsidy due to the Dutch or to repair the half-dismantled fortresses. Moreover, though England and Hanover had supported the candidature of the Archduke Joseph for King of the Romans, Hanover had backed up the claims advanced by the Elector Palatine for compensation from Austria for the losses he had suffered in the war.[2] Thus, altogether, Maria Theresa though still loyal to the old alliance, felt far from inclined to make any sacrifices and run any risks for the sake of England.

It was when matters were in this state that the great quarrel between England and France in North America over the valleys of the Ohio and Mississippi and all that their possession involved came to a head with the conflict between the French and Colonel Washington's Virginian militia on the Monongahela (July 1754). From that moment the two countries drifted steadily into war; for though it was not till nearly two years later that the formal declaration was issued (May 1756), hostilities on a considerable scale began with the despatch of Braddock's expedition in January 1755. That the declaration was so long postponed was due to the in-decision and irresolution which marked the proceedings of both home governments.

The struggle for the "hinterland" of the North American colonies of France and England does not seem at first sight to

---

[1] Cf. pp. 80–82.

[2] Conferences were held at Hanover in August 1750 to see how the Archduke's election could best be secured. The Electors of Bavaria and Cologne took the opportunity to demand certain financial concessions from Austria, while Charles Theodore of Sulzbach, Elector Palatine, claimed territorial indemnification. Of this Austria would not hear, since Charles Theodore had been a partisan of France. Prussia then refused to admit that a mere majority among the Electors was sufficient for the election of a King of the Romans. France, represented by Vergennes, was prepared to support Prussia and, after dragging on for two years, the whole negotiations came to an utterly inconclusive end.

have more than an indirect connection with the affairs of Germany. The issue of the conflict could not, of course, fail to alter the balance of maritime and colonial power, and to that extent must affect the political equilibrium of Europe, but that would hardly appear enough to have involved Austria and Prussia in the war. The connecting link between the Ohio and the Oder was supplied by the Personal Union between England and Hanover, and by the fact that in Hanover George II was particularly vulnerable. In Hanover he could be attacked by the French Army without the interposition of the guns of the British Navy or of the waves of the English Channel, and at this time the French Army was sufficiently influential at the Court of Versailles to override any arguments which the Marine Department might put forward through Machault in favour of making the war exclusively naval. Briefly stated, it was because the French Army would not agree to the neutralisation of Hanover, which Frederick urged upon them, that Frederick came to terms with England and agreed to defend Hanover, a step which left France no alternative but to come to terms with Austria, if not necessarily to commit herself to assisting Austria to recover Silesia. It was the French who tried to "conquer America in Germany," and so caused Pitt to meet them and beat them with their own weapons.

From the very first it was obvious that unless one side or the other would give way over the American quarrel—and if neither government seemed resolved on war, neither would bring itself to make the necessary concessions—France would attack England through Hanover. George II therefore set about providing for the defence of his Electorate in the old way; he sought to obtain the help of Austria, and through his alliance with her to hire soldiers from those minor Princes of Germany whose armies were always at the disposal of the highest bidder. He was ready to make an agreement with Russia for the purpose of keeping Prussia in check, but to join the anti-Prussian coalition was rather more than he was prepared to do.

George II therefore [1] called upon Austria to fulfil her obli-

---

[1] It is rather remarkable to notice how every one seems to have assumed that in case of an Anglo-French war the first step France would take would be an invasion of the Austrian Netherlands, and how one has England far more solicitous about their defence than is their own ruler, Maria Theresa.

gations for the defence of the Netherlands and in June 1755 the Hanoverian ministers Münchhaüsen and Steinberg drew up the famous " Project of Herrenhaüsen," whose failure may be taken as the parting of the ways between England and Austria. By this project George II was to unite with Austria and Saxony-Poland to maintain an army for the defence of Hanover, Saxony and the German dominions of Austria: this with the help of Russia would set free 30,000 Austrians to defend the Netherlands, in which task they were to be assisted by 6000 British and 14,000 Bavarians and Hessians in British pay. The project, however, was based on obtaining the requisite subsidies from the British Parliament, and it was here that it broke down. It represented George's policy as Elector of Hanover, and the refusal of Pitt to hear of so indefinite an extension of the system of subsidies caused its rejection ; a Hanoverian policy, in fact, was sacrificed to the wishes of England.

George had therefore to fall back on such definite subsidy-treaties as he could get Parliament to accept. He was able to arrange for 12,000 Hessians, and he also suggested that if Austria would increase her forces in the Netherlands he would make a treaty with her ally Russia. Kaunitz had already (June) offered to send some 12,000 men to the Netherlands if England would take her share in their defence ; but he now (August) flatly refused to send a man, alleging that the despatch of reinforcements at so critical a moment would merely precipitate war. Austria, indeed, no longer stood firm to the British alliance, she was ready to leave the Netherlands to their fate. She felt, and very rightly, as Holland did also, that the American question was not a matter of such concern to her as to justify her in involving herself in a war with France. With Russia, however, George was more successful, and in September a treaty was concluded by which Elizabeth promised to provide 55,000 men to defend Hanover against either the French or Frederick.

But if Frederick II had no great love for England or for George II he had no wish at so critical a moment in his fortunes to let his French alliance involve him in a war with England. As early as 1753 the treachery of one Mentzel, a clerk in the Saxon Chancery, had disclosed to him the secret articles of the Treaty of 1746, and he knew what he had to expect. If he were to attack Hanover on behalf of France, it would not only give Austria and her friends the opportunity they wanted, but it would cause England, which had hitherto refused to furnish Russia with the subsidies needed for the purposes of an attack on Prussia, to definitely array herself on the anti-Prussian side. Nor was the prospect of what might happen if he stood neutral while France attacked Hanover much more promising. His relations with Russia were not such as to make him welcome the introduction of 55,000 Muscovite troops into the heart of Germany to defend Hanover against a French attack. He therefore urged his French allies strongly to leave Hanover alone, to consent to its being neutralised. He was the more anxious to persuade the French not to attack Hanover because to reach it they must cross the Westphalian provinces of Prussia, and would probably want to use Wesel and the other Prussian fortresses on the Rhine as their base. Keenly awake to the possibilities of the situation, Frederick now began to cultivate better relations with his Hanoverian cousins, an object which was not a little advanced by a visit paid by his sister, the Duchess of Brunswick-Wolfenbüttel, to George II at Hanover.

His overtures were well received. When the Austrians refused to send troops to the Netherlands (Aug.), Münchhaüsen invited the good offices of the Duke of Brunswick towards obtaining a promise of Prussian neutrality in the case of a French attack on Hanover. Frederick, without actually rejecting these overtures, hastened to put himself in communication with the Court of Versailles, asking that the Duc de Nivernais, a friend of his and a warm partisan of the Franco-Prussian alliance, might be sent to Berlin to arrange matters. The French Government, however, with a most culpable negligence and indecision did nothing to make sure of Frederick's alliance. They still hoped that the American question might be settled without war and, while doing little or nothing to facilitate a peaceful solution by keeping their local representatives in America under control, they were still carrying on secret negotiations with England.

Unable to get any reply from France, Frederick did not neglect the other string to his bow. Through the Prussian Secretary of Legation in London, Frederick became aware of the definite terms of the Anglo-Russian treaty of September, which were hardly to his liking. At the same time he learnt that the proposed Anglo-Prussian treaty of neutrality would give him satisfaction in the case of some Prussian merchant-men which had been seized in the late war, would remove his fears as to Russia and renew England's guarantee of Silesia. Accordingly on December 7th he gave his assent to a convention which took the shape (Jan. 16th, 1756) of the Convention of Westminster. By this most important treaty England and Prussia expressed their desire to maintain peace in Germany and guaranteed its neutrality, though not that of the Netherlands; agreed to oppose the entrance into Germany or the passage through it of any foreign army; and guaranteed each other's possessions.

It has been said of this treaty that "the action of Frederick II stung the supine and pacifically disposed Government of Louis XV into taking the first step that made the second inevitable. . . . The anxiety of King George II to safeguard the Hanoverian frontier was the final cause of the Franco-Austrian agreement."[1] To describe as "pacifically disposed" a government which, like that of Louis XV, was pursuing "a policy of pin pricks" in North America, seems hardly accurate, "supine" it was; but surely the true "final cause" of the Franco-Austrian agreement, of the special character which it assumed and of the consequent course of the war, was the outvoting of those in France who were prepared to let Hanover be neutralised by those who sought to gain compensation for losses at sea and in the colonies by conquests on the Weser, in a word, of Machault and the Marine Department, by the more influential Army.

The true character of the Anglo-Prussian agreement may be seen from the fact that both England and Prussia regarded it as quite in keeping with their existing alliances. England explained it to Austria as a step towards an Austro-Prussian reconciliation.[2] Frederick continued to point out to France the advantages to her in her maritime war of the neutralisation of Germany. This was not the light in which France regarded the news, which arrived almost simultaneously with the English rejection of the French ultimatum. France was furious, some-

[1] *England and Hanover*, p. 181.

[2] The exclusion of the Netherlands from the guarantee of neutrality was intended to force Austria to join England and Prussia against France.

what unreasonably, for she only had herself to blame for it, at her ally's conclusion of a treaty with her enemy behind her back. Frederick's behaviour rather than the terms of the treaty infuriated Louis XV and his ministers, and caused them to regard with favour the proposals Austria was now putting forward again.

When the Anglo-Austrian negotiations broke down in August 1755, Kaunitz had revived his former project and had suggested through Stahremberg that France should join a great coalition to be formed against Frederick for the double purpose of recovering Silesia for Maria Theresa and of securing her and the other neighbours of Frederick against future unprovoked aggressions on his part. As a compensation, France might receive a rectification of her frontier towards the Netherlands, including the important fortress of Mons, the rest of the Netherlands might go to Don Philip of Parma in return for the reversion to Austria of his Italian duchy. Accordingly, in September 1755, Stahremberg and the Abbé Bernis met at La Babiole, but France, while quite ready for some form of alliance with Austria, was not prepared to do all Austria wanted. A counter-proposal from France for a guarantee of the possessions of Austria, France and Prussia, which was to leave France free to attack Hanover while Maria Theresa was to prevent Russia hiring out her troops for the defence of Hanover, was not at all what Austria desired. Matters were lingering on and a decision seemed distant, when the conclusion of the Convention of Westminster revolutionised the situation. Austria was still negotiating with Keith while France had recalled Nivernais from Berlin, so she had now the trump card in the alternative of an alliance with England and Prussia: the French ministry would have only had their own indecision to thank if England had united Austria and Prussia in a great continental coalition against France. It was therefore France which was the keener on concluding a treaty and from whom concessions must come.

The negotiations were long, intricate and delicate, neither quite liking to break with an old ally. At last Austria promised that if France would take active measures against Prussia, she would on obtaining Silesia and Glatz take similar steps against England. At a meeting of the French ministry a defensive treaty on these lines was agreed upon as a preliminary to a

closer union.   It is interesting to notice that Belleisle, the
Comte d'Argenson and the rest of the military party in France
were so far from regarding this decision as bellicose that they
opposed it steadily, fearing that it would secure peace and so
prevent the French army from seeing service on the Continent.[1]
    The first treaty of Versailles, which was concluded on May
1st, 1756, included three things : a Convention of Neutrality, a
Defensive Alliance and a Secret Convention.   The first pledged
Maria Theresa to neutrality in the Anglo-French war, Louis xv
binding himself to respect the Netherlands frontier in attacking Hanover.   The Defensive Alliance was the most important section of the treaty.   Both parties agreed to uphold
the Peace of Westphalia and other treaties since concluded
between them, guaranteed each other's actual possessions in
Europe against attack, except as regarded the Anglo-French
war already in progress, and promised to assist each
other, if attacked by a third party, with 24,000 men or
an equivalent in money.   Finally, the Secret Convention
promised Maria Theresa's aid to Louis should any Power
attack French territory as an ally of England, Louis undertaking a parallel obligation.   It also declared the Emperor
(for Tuscany), Naples, Parma, Spain, or any other Power whose
adhesion might be considered desirable, to be eligible for
admission to the alliance ; and both signatories agreed not to
make any fresh treaty without communication with the other
party.
    Such was the famous treaty of May 1st, 1756.   That it
was more to the advantage of Austria than of France is not to
be denied ; she was not involved in the war against England
which France pledged herself to continue as long as Austria and
Prussia were at war, and France was only to receive her compensation when Austria had regained Silesia and Glatz.[2]   It was
probably the ever-present fear that England might in the end
unite Austria, Prussia and Russia, an unlikely but not impossible
alliance for which Newcastle was still hoping, which induced
Bernis to recede in this way from his demand for reciprocity.
Shortly before the conclusion of the treaty, Maria Theresa had
the satisfaction of hearing from St. Petersburg that Elizabeth
would accede to the Franco-Austrian alliance, and would
contribute 80,000 troops to the attack on Prussia, promis-

[1] Waddington, i. 329.   [2] *E.H.R.* (1898), p. 793.

ing to continue the war until Maria Theresa had regained Silesia and Glatz. In the partition of the Prussian dominions, East Prussia was to go to Poland, which would in return cede Courland to Russia; Magdeburg was to fall to the lot of Saxony, Pomerania to Sweden.[1]

For France the treaty was the first step on a path which was to lead to humiliation and defeat, to loss of prestige and of position, which was to bring her appreciably nearer the Revolution; but it does not necessarily follow that the treaty was a mistake. In the first place, nothing can be clearer than the fact that the obiect of the French ministry in concluding this treaty was to secure the peace of Europe, to administer a snub to Frederick and show him plainly that he was by no means indispensable to France. That the French guarantee would prove insufficient to keep Prussia quiet never crossed the minds of Rouillé and his colleagues. In the meantime they hoped in the negotiations for a closer alliance which were now to be set on foot to obtain concessions in the Netherlands for France and for Don Philip as the price not of French aid to Maria Theresa's anti-Prussian schemes, but of French neutrality. To Frederick and to the other Courts of Europe who were un-aware of the impending developments of the treaty it appeared that all that France was doing was to secure herself against continental complications which could divert her attention from the colonial and naval war. Indeed, had not Frederick by his unexpected attack on Saxony provided the *casus fœderis* of the third clause of the Defensive Alliance and of the first of the Secret Convention, it is at least doubtful whether France would have been among his immediate opponents.

That France and Austria were throwing over their traditional policy is undeniable; but Austria had not found England so satisfactory an ally in the matter of Silesia that it was not to her advantage to discard the old alliance for a new and more promising combination. France also had more to fear from England and from Prussia than from Austria. There was no necessary hostility between Bourbon and Hapsburg: it was as a stronger Power whose strength threat-ened her independence that France had first fought Austria

---

[1] Cf. von Arneth, v. 46. The best account of these negotiations is that given in M. Waddington's *Louis XV et le Renversement des Alliances*, especially chs. v.–viii.

and no one could say now that France was in any danger from a Hapsburg preponderance.   Nor had the results of the policy of 1741 been such as to encourage France to adhere to her alliance with a monarch so regardless of anything but his own interests as was Frederick.   The real causes of the French disasters lay not in putting an end to an obsolete traditional policy, but in making the war continental by persisting in the attack on Hanover—but for which France need never have exceeded the limits of the assistance to which she pledged herself in 1756—in allowing Austrian interests to direct the war, and above all, in the utter inefficiency of Army, Navy and government which the war displayed, and of which neither it nor the treaty was the cause.

CHAPTER XI

THE SEVEN YEARS' WAR

TO THE END OF 1757

B UT it was not only Maria Theresa who had been turning to good use the years of peace since Aix-la-Chapelle. Frederick II had never deluded himself with the belief that he could count on the undisturbed enjoyment of Silesia; he knew that he must be prepared to make good his title to it by the means by which he had acquired it, and one of the chief reasons for his readiness to make peace in December 1745 was that he was then at the end of his resources, and imperatively needed a period of rest and recuperation. During the peace he had introduced many reforms, in the administration, in finance, in the domestic economy of the kingdom, in the judicial system.[1] The burden of taxation had hardly been lightened in the least; but while money had flowed freely into his depleted treasury, the strictest economy had been practised, and in 1756 he had a reserve fund of eighteen million thalers. Even more important were the measures which he had taken to increase and improve the army with which the very existence of the Prussian kingdom was so closely bound up. To increase it was his first object, and by 1756 it mustered 155,000 men. Garrison duty absorbed 27,000 of these; for the repairing and strengthening of many fortresses, especially in the newly-acquired Silesia, had made a considerable increase in the garrison-battalions necessary. The rest, 126 battalions and 210 squadrons, formed a highly efficient field army, which an iron discipline, a careful training on the parade-ground and in the manœuvres and camps of exercises which were held every year had made a force even more formidable than that which Frederick William had bequeathed to his son. In staff work, in organisation, in preparations for

[1] Cf. Chapter XIV.

194

mobilisation, great improvements had been made. No efforts
had been spared to collect vast reserves of clothing, weapons,
provisions and military stores of every kind. But it may be
doubted whether it was not even more to the King and
commander than to the soldiers that these years were so
useful. There was not the same room for improvement in
the Prussian army as there was in its commander. Frederick
had learnt a good deal about the art of war on the battlefields
of Bohemia and Silesia, and he devoted the peace to a careful
study of the profession of arms. It was now that he devised
and worked out the system of attacking in oblique order,
which was to win so conspicuous a triumph at Leuthen. Many
of the greatest qualities of a general he already possessed,
resolution, decision, a readiness to take risks, promptitude,
tenacity, unbounded self-confidence; but it was in handling
large masses of men in the manœuvres that he learnt to really
understand his weapon, on the drill-ground that he was able
to test and improve his system of tactics, in peace that he
prepared for war.

As has been already explained, Frederick did not regard
the Convention of Westminster as a complete breach with
France, and still expected her to agree to the neutralisation of
Germany. Even the negotiations between France and Austria
caused him no anxiety; for he, like his minister Knyphaüsen,
looked upon them as merely intended to secure the neutrality
of the Netherlands. The movements of the Austrian and
Russian troops, however, were of a character to arouse his suspicions, and when on June 22nd he received from his minister
at Dresden, Maltzahn, a copy obtained by Mentzel of a despatch
from Fleming, the Saxon representative at St. Petersburg, to
Count Brühl, speaking openly of Russia's hostile intentions
towards Prussia, he saw at once that war was inevitable.[1]
The mobilisation of the army began at once, and, in
opposition to the advice of Podewils and of Prince Henry,
Count Klinggraeffen, the Prussian envoy at Vienna, was
instructed to lay before Maria Theresa a request for an explanation of the movements of her armies (July 26th). Maria
Theresa's reply led Frederick to present an ultimatum
(Aug. 20th), pressing for more explicit explanations, and for
a definite statement that she did not mean to attack him

[1] Cf. Frederick's letter to Wilhelmina of Baireuth, June 22nd, 1756.

either that year or in the coming year. Maria Theresa answered that no offensive alliance against Prussia was in existence, and she threw upon Frederick all the responsibility for the armaments and for the military precautions she had been forced to take. On August 25th, Frederick received this answer; on the 26th he instructed Maltzahn to demand from the Elector of Saxony free passage through his dominions for the Prussian troops on their way to Bohemia; on the 28th he left Berlin, and on the 29th he crossed the Saxon frontier.

That in thus acting Frederick was only anticipating attack is true; there was a design on foot for a great coalition against Prussia, even if it was still in an inchoate condition; but it may be doubted whether he might not have gained more by waiting to be attacked; he threw away the moral advantage of being the defender and failed to achieve the military results he had hoped to win by adopting the offensive. And by attacking Bohemia through Saxony he enabled Maria Theresa to call upon France to fulfil her treaty obligations, and made it impossible for France to remain neutral. But for this he might not have had to reckon with more than the malevolent neutrality of France. Unless Frederick gained very striking military successes, unless he was able to destroy the coalition against him before it could really get to work, the moral and diplomatic advantage to Maria Theresa of being able to point once again to the unwarrantable aggressions of her ambitious neighbour would be enormous.

It would appear that in taking the offensive Frederick calculated—not without good reason—upon an easy success over the weak and not very efficient Saxon army.[1] After obtaining military possession of Saxony he would press on into Bohemia, and hoped to dictate a peace under the walls of Vienna which would leave Saxony in his possession and compensate Augustus III with Bohemia.[2] Nor were the prospects unpromising. He had for his main army some 70,000 men,[3] who converged upon the Saxon capital from Halle through Leipzig and Chemnitz, straight up the Elbe by Torgau and from Lusatia, while an independent corps under Schwerin, 27,000 strong, entered Bohemia by Glatz and

---

[1] Though 50,000 strong on paper, it was much below strength; and with some regiments absent in Poland, the available force was hardly 20,000.

[2] Cf. Waddington, i. 521–533.   [3] 101 squadrons and 67 battalions.

Nachod, moving on Königgratz. On paper Austria should have had in Bohemia and Moravia nearly 90,000 men to oppose to the invaders; but many corps had not yet arrived, and others were below strength, so that the force which General Browne collected at Kolin at the end of August only mustered 7000 horse and 25,000 foot, while Piccolomini in Moravia had no more than 22,000 men, 5000 being cavalry. The Austrian mobilisation was very far from complete, which may be taken as evidence that no immediate attack on Prussia had been intended, and at so late a season no help could be expected from France or Russia.

When Frederick crossed the Saxon frontier Augustus at first offered to be neutral and to hand over certain fortresses as a guarantee; but this did not satisfy Frederick who demanded also that the Saxon army should be incorporated in his own, or at least disarmed. Augustus would not agree to this, and it was decided to make a stand in the strong position of Pirna, where the Saxon army had been collected. The only alternative was a retreat into Bohemia for which Augustus was hardly prepared, as he feared Frederick would take the opportunity to annex the Electorate. By the middle of September, therefore, the Saxons were surrounded in the Pirna position, and Frederick, who had not expected anything of the sort, found his plans for the invasion of Bohemia suspended. He could not move on and leave the Saxons unmasked in his rear, while if he left behind a force sufficient to contain the Saxons, he would not be strong enough to besiege Prague or undertake any similar operation. The unexpected action of the Saxons therefore disarranged his whole plan; and had not Augustus and Brühl neglected to make an adequate provision of food and other supplies, so that the Saxons were unable to hold out till an Austrian army strong enough to effect their release could be collected, the invasion of Saxony might have ended disastrously for Frederick. The Saxon camp, protected by a brook and marsh in its front, resting on the Elbe and on the strong fortresses of Lilienstein and Königstein and well fortified, would have been almost impossible to storm. But that the inefficiency of the Saxon government displayed itself in the collection of supplies for four weeks only instead of four months, the sudden resolve of Augustus to stand at Pirna might have been attended by complete success.

As things were, General Browne, an able officer of Irish birth who commanded the Austrian forces in Bohemia, had only a very short time in which to effect the relief. Though inferior in force to the Prussians, and hardly prepared for instant action, he did not hesitate but pushed forward to Budin on the Eger to see if he could get into touch with the Saxons (Sept. 29th).

Frederick had already pushed Marshal Keith forward into Bohemia with a covering force, which had driven an Austrian detachment out of Aussig (Sept. 13th); and on hearing of Browne's advance he moved up and joined Keith (Sept. 29th), leaving some 40,000 men to blockade Pirna. On the 30th, Browne, who had had to wait for his guns and pontoons, moved from Budin to Lobositz, the Prussians also moving forward and occupying the hills of Lobosch and Homolka, just North of Lobositz, the same day. On the morning of October 1st the Croats, pushing out from Lobositz, found the Prussians in position.

The two forces were of nearly equal strength,[1] but in position the Prussians had an advantage, holding the hills on either side of the road from Lobositz to Welmina, while the Austrian right in and around Lobositz was cut off from the centre and left, which were behind the Morell Brook. The battle began with an advance of the Prussian cavalry in the centre; but though at first successful they were repulsed by the heavy fire of the Austrian infantry and of the guns behind the Morell Brook. Their supports then joined them, but were charged and routed by the Austrian cavalry. Browne now reinforced his right, and sent it forward against the hill of Lobosch; but Frederick parried this stroke by bringing up the second line of his right, which he could safely do as the Morell Brook covered that wing from a counter-attack by the Austrian left. There was a sharp struggle for the Lobosch-berg; but on the fall of their commander, Lacy, the Austrians gave way and retired through Lobositz, which the Prussians occupied. Beyond that they did not attempt to press their advantage, for Browne's centre and left were still intact, and his force drew off in excellent order, falling back next day to

---

[1] The Austrians had 34 battalions of infantry to 29, and were equal in cavalry, each side having 70 squadrons; but the Prussian establishments were rather higher.

Budin. Inasmuch as they had checked Browne's advance
on Pirna and had forced him to evacuate Lobositz, the
Prussians could claim the victory; but their losses, 3300 all
told, somewhat exceeded the Austrian, 2300 killed and
wounded and 700 prisoners, and they had had to fight very
hard for their success. Frederick could not but realise that
he had a different enemy to deal with than the comparatively
inefficient Austrian army of 1741–1745.

Browne's check had by no means been fatal to the relief
of Pirna. He had, on the contrary, drawn off Frederick and a
large part of his army and thereby reduced the pressure; and
on October 6th he started off with 8000 picked men, and
by forced marches by Kamnitz and Schluckenau reached
Mitteldorf, only three miles from Schandau, on the afternoon
of the 11th. Had the Saxons been ready to co-operate
promptly and to take advantage of the helping hand Browne
thus held out, the greater part of their army might have got
away; but the pontoons were in the wrong place, much time
was wasted, and when at last the crossing began (11.30 p.m.
Oct. 12th) every possible mistake was made. The utmost confusion prevailed, the camp was evacuated too soon, the crossing
was not properly covered against attacks in rear. Moreover,
the delay had allowed Winterfeldt to reinforce the division
facing Browne; and when, about 4 o'clock next afternoon,
(13th) the bridge broke down the Saxon army found itself
cooped up between Lilienstein and the Elbe in a position
commanded by Prussian cannon, and from which all the exits
were blocked by Prussian troops. To persist was hopeless,
surrender was inevitable, and very reluctantly Augustus had to
agree. He himself managed to get away to Warsaw, but
nearly 18,000 troops had to lay down their arms (Oct. 16th).
Browne, who had done his share, held on at Lichtenhayn till
late on the 14th, but then finding that the crossing had failed
had no alternative but to retire. By October 20th he was back
at Budin.

Thus Frederick obtained possession of Saxony, which
he proceeded to mulct in large sums of money, besides
forcing his Saxon prisoners to enlist in his army;[1] but the

---

[1] They took the first opportunity to desert, as the dislike for the Prussians in
Saxony was very strong. By February over 2500 had gone over to Austria, and
early in the next year three whole regiments deserted and made their way to Poland.

comparative success obtained at Pirna and Lobositz must not hide the fact that Frederick's plans as a whole had failed. The resistance of the Saxons had saved Bohemia by detaining Frederick until Browne had time to get his army together. By the time Pirna fell it was too late to attempt another move. The Prussians from Lobositz were back in Saxony by October 28th, and Schwerin, who had been held in check at Königgratz by Piccolomini's inferior force, retired to Silesia.

To trace in detail the complicated negotiations between Austria and her French and Russian allies which filled the winter of 1756–1757 would be an endless task. What is quite clear, however, is that Maria Theresa took a very different view of the aims of the treaty of May 1756 from that held at Versailles. While France was by no means pleased with the subordinate part which the strict fulfilment of that treaty would have assigned to her, and was anxious to put her whole force into the field against Hanover, Maria Theresa would have been quite content with the punctual execution of the obligations France had then assumed, with the despatch of an auxiliary corps by the Danube to Bohemia or Moravia. She was very anxious to avoid making the war general, lest she should give the appearance of truth to the accusations Frederick hurled at her, that she was introducing the French into the Empire and involving all Germany in war. She did not wish to do anything to alarm Holland or the Protestant Powers of North Germany, and would have been glad if it had been possible to neutralise Hanover; for, as she pointed out to the French ministers, she had no quarrel with England and was not concerned in the quarrel over America, which was altogether distinct from the treaty into which France and Austria had entered for the recovery of Silesia and the debasement of Prussia—an end, she hinted, quite as much to be desired by France as by Austria. France, she pointed out, was definitely pledged to assist Austria at the time that Frederick's attack on Saxony provided a *casus belli*; Austria had undertaken no such obligations towards the war which had previously broken out in America.

Thus, though at the outset France, irritated by Frederick's attack on Saxony in defiance of her guarantee, prepared to send the 24,000 men according to the treaty, and began collecting them at Metz, by October 2nd Stahremberg was writing to announce that the despatch of the auxiliary corps had been postponed for the present. France, indeed, had no wish to confine herself to the despatch of these auxiliaries so far afield as Moravia, where they would be out of her control, and would not be available for her designs on Hanover. She therefore prepared to take the field on a much larger scale, and d'Estrées was sent off to Vienna to arrange a scheme of operations.

It would appear that d'Argenson, Rouillé, Paris-Duverney, and their friends opposed the idea of playing a merely secondary rôle in the German war, because they feared that if they did this the war would be indefinitely protracted; their idea was to seize Hanover as a set-off against possible losses in the colonies, and then to operate on the Middle Elbe against Frederick in conjunction with the Austrians from Bohemia. As the first step, they proposed to assemble an army of observation on the Lower Rhine. However, they did consent that Austria should attempt to negotiate the neutrality of Hanover, an idea which had been mooted by the Hanoverian ministers as early as September 1756, and upon which Maria Theresa, anxious to prevent Frederick from identifying his cause with that of the North German Protestants, was keenly set. Hanover, indeed, was anti-Prussian, and would gladly have come to terms with the Empress; and England, though she did not intend to desert Frederick, would have liked to escape from the necessity of undertaking the defence of Hanover. But the proposal to extend the neutrality of Hanover to Brunswick and to Hesse-Cassel, practically to establish a line of demarcation which the French troops would have to respect, broke down when the French held out for *transitus innoxius*—in other words, freedom to use this neutral sphere for an attack on Prussia.

A great deal also turned on the question of " reciprocity "; when and on what conditions was Maria Theresa to hand over the Netherlands to France or to Don Philip? Austria was afraid of alarming England and the United Provinces, France wanted to force on a complete breach between Austria and her old ally. Despatch after despatch passed between Vienna and Versailles. On February 21st, Maria Theresa wrote to Stahremberg declaring her readiness to hand over the Netherlands on getting back Silesia and Glatz even if Frederick were no further reduced, while as the hopes of neutralising Hanover faded away, the idea of localising the war became more and more impossible of realisation. Finally, exactly a year after the conclusion of the First Treaty, the Second Treaty of Versailles was signed on May 1st, 1757. France promised to send to Maria Theresa's aid 24,000 French troops as auxiliaries, with 10,000 subsidised South Germans, also to put 105,000 men into the field on her own account. She also agreed to pay 12 million gulden a year, in monthly instalments, and not to make peace till Austria's possession of Silesia and Glatz had been admitted by Frederick and his allies. Austria's contingent was to be 80,000 men; she was to hand over Ostend and Nieuport to France as a security when the first instalment of the subsidy was paid, to hand over Mons, Ypres and several other towns on obtaining Silesia and Glatz, and to give the rest of the Netherlands to Don Philip when the proposed partition of Prussia should have taken place. By this Halberstadt, Halle and Magdeburg were to go to Saxony, Sweden was to recover the portion of Pomerania lost in 1720, Cleves and Guelders to be divided between the United Provinces and the Elector Palatine should they join the Coalition; Crossen was to be added to Maria Theresa's share. Louis XV promised to use his influence to get Joseph elected King of the Romans, while the treaty also included several less important clauses relating to Italy.

As finally arranged, the treaty was greatly in Maria Theresa's favour, for France had given way on several points, notably with regard to the payment of the subsidies. But it does not therefore follow that it represented a complete triumph for Austrian interests over French. Probably France would have been better advised had she confined herself to the despatch of the 24,000 auxiliaries; but it was rather in the practical execution of the policy than in the policy itself that she was to do herself so much damage. Maria Theresa must, of course, answer the charge of having so far sacrificed the Empire to her own ends that she was introducing French armies into the heart of Germany to compass the destruction of a leading German state. Yet it was not as much as Frederick had done when he accepted French aid in 1741; and there was no small difference between Maria Theresa's

action in invoking French help to enable her to recover a
province wrested from her by force, and Frederick's in calling
in France in support of a policy of pure aggression.   Maria
Theresa's action was retributive, if not indeed defensive—after
her experience in 1741 no one can blame her if she felt
insecure as long as Frederick was free to act as he pleased.

Simultaneously with the Franco-Austrian negotiations
similar negotiations were going on between Austria and
Russia.   Here Esterhazy, the Austrian Ambassador, found
himself opposed by the Chancellor Bestuchev who, if not fond
of Prussia, was now in the pay of England;[1] while Woronzov
the Vice-Chancellor inclined to favour Prussia, but was open
to conviction.   Olsuviev, the other influential minister, was
frankly for Austria.   In Russia as in France the news of the
attack on Saxony aroused great indignation : it quite decided
the attitude of Elizabeth, and with hers Woronzov's also.   A
difficulty was then caused by the question of territorial
readjustment.   Russia coveted Courland and Semigallia; but
the traditional policy of France had been to support Poland
against Russia and it might be difficult to get Louis xv to
agree.   A solution was found in the compensation of Poland
with East Prussia ; on November 13th, Maria Theresa agreed
to considerable modifications in the Convention of April, and
on January 11th, 1757, Russia notified her adhesion to the
Defensive Treaty of Versailles.   On February 2nd an Austro-
Russian Convention was drawn up, and on May 19th ratifications were exchanged.   But this was far from exhausting the
list of Austria's allies.   In January 1757 the Diet of the
Empire declared its adhesion to the anti-Prussian cause, its
aid being more valuable morally than materially, for it disproved
Frederick's assertions that the war was a quarrel between
religions, and it gave to the Coalition such constitutional
sanction as the obsolescent forms could convey.   Frederick, at
any rate, could hardly plead that he was the champion of the
Imperial constitution.   Hanover had done its best to keep the
Empire neutral, and it had been supported by Brunswick, by
Hesse - Cassel, by Saxe - Weimar and by Baireuth ; but the
majority of sixty to twenty-six by which the vote was carried
included many Protestant states, notably Zweibrücken,
Hesse - Darmstadt, Baden - Durlach and even the Anspach

[1] Cf. *Buckinghamshire Papers* (R.H.S.), and Waddington, i. 508.

Hohenzollern themselves. Maria Theresa received a promise of assistance from Wurzburg, which offered 6000 men, while Bavaria (4000), Cologne (1800), the Palatinate (6000), and Würtemberg (6000) hired considerable forces to France.[1] Sweden, another Protestant state, in which the Senate now in power was much under French influence and bitterly opposed to Prussia, to whom the monarchical party looked for support, was induced to join the Coalition by a promise of the restoration of Pomerania to the conditions of 1679.

Frederick was thus left with only England and Hanover and a few of the North German states on his side, for Denmark and Spain were resolved to keep out of the conflict, and the fact that the Orange faction favoured Prussia made the "Burgher party" in the United Provinces prefer neutrality. England, though taken by surprise by Frederick's sudden attack on Saxony, decided to support him steadily. To aid in the defence of Hanover, the corps of Hessians and Hanoverians, which had been brought over to defend England when the fears of an invasion were at their height, were sent back to Germany (Dec. 1756) to form the nucleus of an army to be concentrated on the Lippe, and Pitt obtained a vote of £200,000 from the House of Commons for the defence of the Electorate. This army, reinforced by 10,000 Prussians and by contingents from Brunswick, Hesse-Cassel and Saxe-Weimar, was also to defend the Prussian provinces on the Rhine, and hold in check the French "army of observation" should that force exchange a passive for an active policy.

For the campaign of 1757 both sides had made great preparations. Frederick by impressing unwilling recruits in Saxony had raised his forces to nearly 200,000 of whom depôts and garrisons absorbed about a quarter. Of the field army, he had only allotted 20,000 to East Prussia and 10,000 to the Rhenish provinces, so that including Schwerin's corps (12,000 horse and 32,000 foot) in Silesia he had over 120,000 available for an attack on Bohemia. His original intention would seem to have been to remain on the defensive and await attack, as he had done at the beginning of 1745; but this would have played into the hands of the Austrians,

---

[1] The attempts of Prussian officers to enlist recruits in the territory of Mecklenburg-Schwerin had resulted in a violent quarrel with its Duke, Frederick (1756–1785), and ranked the former among the supporters of Austria.

whose best policy obviously was to put off a decisive engagement until the advance of their French and Russian allies on either flank could make itself felt, and at length Frederick, yielding to Winterfeldt's representations, resolved to take the offensive. Four columns were accordingly directed upon Prague, the army of Silesia by Trautenau, Gitschin and Brandeis, Augustus William of Brunswick-Bevern with 5000 horse and 18,000 foot from Zittau by Reichenberg and Münchengratz, the main body under the King moving straight up the Elbe from Dresden and Maurice of Anhalt-Dessau from Chemnitz. The latter after being checked in a move on Eger joined the main column at Linay on April 24th, bringing it up to a strength of 15,000 horse and 45,000 foot.[1] This converging movement, of course, enabled the Prussians to move with much greater celerity than if they had all been concentrated upon one line of advance; but to plan the junction of these columns under the walls of a fortified town forty leagues from their base was, as Napoleon has pointed out, an exceedingly risky movement. Luckily for Frederick the situation of the Austrians was not such as to enable them to turn this chance to good advantage. General Browne had originally intended to take the offensive; he had collected large magazines near the frontier, and his dispositions, though not ill-adapted for an advance, proved most unsatisfactory when he was superseded by Prince Charles of Lorraine and that incarnation of indecision and undue caution resolved to assume a defensive attitude.

Thus when between April 18th and 20th the Prussian columns set out for Bohemia their enemies were too near the frontier and dangerously separated. On the right was Serbelloni (27,000) at Königgratz, Königsegg with 23,000 confronted Bevern, at and around Prague stood Browne with 39,000, on the left, at Eger, d'Aremberg had about 20,000. Frederick's plan was to keep Browne occupied upon the line of the Eger while Schwerin and Bevern fell on Königsegg, crushed him, captured his magazines, and came up on the right flank of Browne by Brandeis.

This scheme proved only partially successful. Königsegg checked Bevern at Reichenberg April 21st, and when Schwerin

---

[1] Waddington's figures are rather different; he gives Schwerin as 41,000, Bevern 18,000, Frederick 39,000, and Maurice 19,000; ii. 282.

endeavoured to intercept his retreat, slipped away across that general's front to Brandeis. Schwerin and Bevern united at Münchengratz on the 26th and moved rather slowly upon Prague, being delayed at Brandeis by the fact that Königsegg's rearguard had burnt the bridge over the Elbe. Meanwhile Charles of Lorraine, who had taken over command of the Austrians at Tuchomierschitz on April 30th, had withdrawn to Prague instead of adopting Browne's advice and giving battle on the line of the Eger at Budin. His action was characteristically over-cautious. A man of any dash or any real strategic insight would have seen that, with Schwerin and Frederick divided by the Elbe and several days apart, the true policy for the Austrians was to concentrate on one bank or the other, breaking down all bridges by which the Prussians could get across, and to fall either on Frederick or his lieutenant in force. This would have been fairly easy, for d'Aremberg had joined Browne and Königsegg was much nearer his main body than was Schwerin to Frederick.

The retreat of the Austrians allowed Frederick to move up to Prague unopposed, his van arriving on the White Mountain on May 2nd. Schwerin was still some marches away,—he did not cross the Elbe at Brandeis till the evening of May 5th, —and a more energetic commander than Prince Charles might have seized the chance of hastening Königsegg's movements and forcing an action on Frederick. But Charles was contemplating a further retreat to join Serbelloni, and was only dissuaded from doing so by Browne's urgent representations that such a move would be most disastrous to the prestige of the Austrians. Had Serbelloni shown moderate energy, had he used his cavalry to delay Schwerin, or pushed forward fast enough to reach Prague before Schwerin could reinforce his master, the stand would have been wise. As things turned out, by giving battle at Prague the Austrians had to fight Frederick and Schwerin combined with the nearest of Serbelloni's 27,000 no nearer than Aruval, eight and a half miles from the nearest point of the battlefield.

It was on the morning of May 6th that Frederick, leaving Keith with 30,000 men on the White Mountain, took 38 squadrons and 20 battalions across to the right of the Moldau and joined Schwerin. He did this un-molested by the Austrians, who were drawn up in position along the hills East of Prague, facing North, their left on the steep Ziscaberg, their centre and right on the rather more accessible Schanzenberg and Taborberg. In their front the marshy valley of the Roketnitz served to strengthen the position, the village of Hloupetin on the far side, which served as bridge-head to a road up a ravine giving access to the plateau near Hortlozes, having been occupied by a detachment. Had Frederick carried out his original intention of a direct attack, the Prussians would have had an extremely difficult task; but fortunately for his army he allowed Schwerin to prevail upon him to push the Prussian left wing round to the South, so that they could attack the easier Eastern slopes of the plateau by Sterbohol. This move outflanked the Austrian right and forced that division to alter its position hastily, its right moving from near Hostawitz to Sterbohol, its left coming up to the East of Maleschitz. Thus the Austrian line presented a salient angle somewhat insufficiently protected in the direction of Hostawitz. About 10 a.m. Schwerin having reached Potschernitz deployed his men into line, the cavalry on the left, the infantry in two columns under Winterfeldt and Bevern, and began climbing the slopes. He met with a stout resistance, and the swamps at the foot of the slopes proved difficult to cross. On the left his cavalry after being twice repulsed were reinforced by Ziethen and obtained the mastery over Lucchesi, whose horsemen they routed and chased from the field, thus neglecting their duty of succouring the hard-pressed Prussian infantry. Winterfeldt's men, checked by the artillery fire, were routed by a charge of some grenadiers whom Browne brought up, and Schwerin himself perished in the attempt to rally them. The Austrians pursuing too far got somewhat out of hand, for Browne had been badly wounded, and they had to retire when Schwerin's reserve gave Winterfeldt a point on which to rally. In falling back the Austrians were taken in flank by Bevern, whose men, separated by a spur of the hill from Winterfeldt's, had not shared in their comrades' disaster. Just at this moment the Prussian right, having carried Hloupetin, began to push up the ravine towards Hortlozes. This move was due to Mannstein, and was well seconded by Ferdinand of Brunswick, who planted a large battery on the hills by Hloupetin. Simultaneously Prince Henry of Prussia's division of the centre pushed across the

Roketnitz brook from Kyge and assailed the Taborberg, thus thrusting itself into the gap at the salient angle of the Austrian position, which had been left open by the advance of the left division of the right from Maleschitz to repulse Bevern. Prince Henry's appearance near Maleschitz decided the struggle on the right; Bevern, who had been checked, was able to carry Maleschitz, and the whole right and centre of the Austrian army was now in complete disorder. Their left, hitherto hardly engaged at all, now fell back in good order to Prague, its retirement being covered by some regiments of cuirassiers, who charged home with great effect against the Prussian infantry and prevented Frederick's cavalry from molesting their retreat.

The battle thus ended about 3 p.m. with the retreat of the Austrian army within the walls of Prague. Some 15,000 men, mainly the routed cavalry of Lucchesi's division, got away to the Southward, but 33 guns were left on the field and the killed, wounded, and prisoners amounted at least to 15,000. Frederick on his side lost 5 guns, captured from Winterfeldt by Browne's grenadiers, and the official return gave his losses as nearly 13,000. The move round the right of the Austrian position was the decisive stroke, as it forced the Austrians to alter their front in a great hurry, and to give battle in a position whose defects were shown when the counter-attack of their right exposed the salient angle of their line. At the same time the sudden illness of Prince Charles, who had been seized with a fit when trying to rally Lucchesi's cavalry, and the fall of Browne had contributed not a little to give the Prussians the victory by leaving the Austrians without a commander.

But though he had within a fortnight overrun Northern Bohemia, driven his enemies in on Prague, captured the valuable magazines they had collected, beaten them in a pitched battle, and cooped up nearly 50,000 of them within the walls of the Bohemian capital, Frederick had a heavy task still before him. Prague was now strongly fortified and well garrisoned, and was not likely to prove the easy prey it had been in 1741 and 1745. Unless the garrison showed unexpected faintheartedness or the Austrian government displayed a lack of energy in collecting a relieving force, Frederick might find himself in an awkward position. Nevertheless he set himself down to

the siege of the Bohemian capital, pushing out Bevern with
2000 cavalry and 5000 infantry in the direction of Kolin,
whither Daun and the corps formerly under Serbelloni had
withdrawn on hearing of the battle of May 6th.

Daun retired as Bevern approached, falling back towards
Czaslau. He was in no hurry for a battle, as the fugitives
from Prague, many of whom had joined him, were in no condition for immediate action, and considerable reinforcements
were coming up from Moravia and elsewhere. Moreover, it
would be to his advantage to draw Bevern away from the
Prussian main body.

The Prussians conducted the attack on Prague with no
little vigour, and by May 28th the batteries were ready for the
bombardment. Much damage was done to the town, but the
injury inflicted on its defences was but slight, and a violent
storm quenched the fires caused by the Prussian shells and,
causing the Moldau to rise rapidly, carried away Frederick's
bridges of boats. For forty-eight hours Keith's division on
the left bank was in great peril, but the Austrian commanders,
though they could have thrown 40,000 men upon his 15,000,
their bridge being intact, let this fine opportunity escape.
Luckily for Maria Theresa the general in command of the
relieving army was a man of more capacity and enterprise than
Charles of Lorraine, for had the fate of Prague depended on
that Prince its fall would have been only a question of time.
By the first week in June, Daun had collected a force of over
50,000 men, a third being cavalry, and on June 12th he
moved forward on Kuttenberg. Bevern had received various
reinforcements from time to time, but he was much weaker
than Daun and was driven in on Kolin (June 13th) after some
sharp fighting. The danger to his lieutenant forced Frederick
to come up himself and join Bevern at Kaurzim (June 13th)
with fresh reinforcements, which brought the covering army
up to 34,000, 16,000 being cavalry. Frederick entertained
but a poor opinion of Daun and his army, which he regarded
as a rabble of raw recruits, not exactly "stiffened" by the
runaways of May 6th, and he expected an easy victory, which
would enable him to press the siege to a successful issue.
He therefore resolved to attack at once despite his inferiority
in numbers and the strength of the Austrian position
(June 18th).

Daun had posted his army along the Kamhayek hills which slope up gradually to the South of the road from Planian to Kolin. His left at Radenin and Podborz was covered by a brook which served as the connection between a chain of large pools, and this with a swamp in rear secured him against a flanking movement. His right rested on the village of Kreczor at the opposite end of the heights, a corps of cavalry under Nadasky being thrown forward on the lower ground in front of Kreczor across the road to Kolin. The first reconnaissance showed Frederick that a frontal attack on the left or left centre would be most unwise but that a better chance offered on the right. Accordingly, repeating the manœuvre which had been so successful at Prague, he moved across the Austrian front to assail their right flank. This time, however, the manœuvre did not cause the Austrians to shift their position, and in moving across the enemy's front the Prussians were galled by the Austrian guns on the heights and the Croat sharpshooters lying in the cornfields at their foot.

Ziethen and the cavalry of the Prussian vanguard began well by driving Nadasky off to the South-East while the infantry, seven battalions under Hülsen, wheeling to the right when past Kudlirz, assaulted and carried Kreczor. Here, however, they were checked by a battery of twelve guns Daun had posted on the left of the village and by Wied's infantry and some Croats in an oak-grove to the South-West of it. This last obstacle also checked Ziethen's pursuit of Nadasky, and Hülsen, though reinforced by three battalions, could get no farther. According to the original plan he should have been supported by the infantry of the left under Maurice of Dessau, who were to have followed in his tracks, but this division found itself instead committed to a frontal attack on Brzisti just West of Kreczor. Frederick, anxious to get it forward, ordered it to face to the right long before it reached the proper turning-place, and losing his temper when Maurice expostulated, gave the order "forward" without adding the words "half left," which would have sent it to Hülsen's aid. Hülsen, indeed, used the diversion to push on and carry the battery behind Kreczor, but Daun brought up two infantry divisions from the second line to hold him and Maurice in check, four battalions of grenadiers recovered the oak-grove from Hülsen and pouring a flanking

fire into Ziethen's ranks forced him to retire before the rallied
squadrons of Nadasky. Meanwhile on the Prussian centre
things had gone altogether wrong. Mannstein, whose division
was following Maurice's along the road, was so much worried
by the Croat skirmishers that he wheeled a battalion to the
right to disperse them. The Croats stood their ground and
were reinforced, Mannstein also reinforced his men, and before
long his whole division was committed to a frontal attack on
Chotzemitz which made little progress. The arrival of the
reinforcement from the second line quickly restored the balance
on the Austrian right. Pennavaire's cavalry division attempting to assist Hülsen was foiled by a fine charge by two Saxon
cavalry regiments, more Austrian cavalry were thrown into the
fight, and at last the divisions of Hülsen and Maurice gave back
in disorder, their example being followed by Mannstein, whose
men lost heavily under artillery fire. On the Austrian left
Puebla's infantry came down from the heights above Breczsan
and, vigorously supported by Stampa's cavalry, assailed the
eight battalions under Bevern which formed the one intact
division of the Prussian army. Luckily for Frederick these
battalions made a gallant resistance, and at the cost of nearly
3000 men kept the road towards Planian clear for the fugitives
of the left and centre to stream past behind them.

Daun had won a great victory to which he had contributed largely himself. His excellent choice of the position,
his judicious handling of his well-served artillery, and his
promptitude and decision in reinforcing the threatened points,
had as much to do with the victory as the error in the
directions given to Maurice, or the blunder of marching the
Prussian army across the Austrian front within range of
their guns, which had led to Mannstein's becoming prematurely
engaged. Ziethen also must be held partly responsible, since
he failed to support Hülsen properly; but when all is said
and done the chief cause of the defeat was that Frederick
did not, after the victory outside Prague, at once push out
against Daun and destroy his detachment. On the morrow
of May 6th he would have had little to fear from the
demoralised army of Charles of Lorraine: 25,000 men
could have held them in check with ease. But Frederick,
underestimating Daun and the defensive capacities of Prague,
had tried to reduce in six weeks a fortress capable of holding

out much longer, and the defeat of Kolin was the result of his error of judgment.

Leaving Bevern and Maurice to withdraw the relics of the covering army over the Elbe at Nimburg, Frederick hastened back to Prague [1] to raise the siege. On the 20th of June the retreat began, the Austrians sallying out in time to fall on Keith, who was covering the movement, and inflict on him severe losses, including five guns and most of his baggage. More might perhaps have been done, but Charles of Lorraine was not the man to make the most of his chances. It was a great misfortune for Austria that Charles should have so far recovered his health as to be able to take command of the united armies which joined forces at Podschernitz on June 26th. A really vigorous pursuit ought to have clinched the success of Kolin by cutting off one of the two retreating columns, either the besiegers who moved by Budin to Leitmeritz, or the Kolin force, now under Prince Augustus William of Prussia, which had reached Bohm Leipa on July 7th. It was against this force that Daun and Lorraine turned, crossing the Elbe at Brandeis (July 1st) and moving by Münchengratz (July 7th) and Liebenau to threaten Augustus William's communications with Zittau and Gabel. On July 15th they took Gabel, which forced Augustus to retire to Zittau by the roundabout route through Raumburg. The Austrians had only twenty-five miles to cover against forty, and might have anticipated the Prussians at Zittau and cut them off completely. However, their ineradicable slowness once again let the Prussians be first at the critical spot, and Augustus William, whose men had suffered great privations and had deserted freely, finally reached a haven of refuge at Bautzen on July 27th. His failure to maintain his position had involved the retreat of Keith's corps from Leitmeritz to Bohemia, after which Frederick, leaving Maurice of Dessau on the Elbe, brought all available troops across to Bautzen to join the Kolin army and try to retrieve all by forcing a battle on Lorraine. But Lorraine stood firm in a strong position near Zittau, and Frederick had to retire in disappointment to Ostritz (Aug. 19th). Thus the invasion

[1] The Prussian loss was about 13,500, of which 12,000 were among the infantry, who were thus reduced to a third of their original strength; they left 45 guns and 5000 prisoners in Daun's hands. The Austrian losses slightly exceeded 8000.

of Bohemia, from which so much had been hoped and which had begun so well, ended in failure, and Frederick found himself at the end of August in the same position as he had occupied in April, only with his most trusted lieutenant dead and his army nearly ruined.

Nor was it very cheerful intelligence which reached him from the forces covering his flanks against the allies of Maria Theresa. Had not the Russian commanders, Apraxin and Fermor, been deterred by political considerations in addition to natural slowness and incapacity they could have done far more against the weak force opposed to them. As it was, their headquarters did not reach Kovno till June, and not till July 5th did the fall of Memel allow Fermor to rejoin the covering force under Apraxin. Even after this their movements were so slow and apparently meaningless that despite the great disparity of numbers the Prussian commander Lehwaldt ventured to attack them at Gross Jaegerndorf (Aug. 30th). A sharp fight resulted in a victory for the big battalions, Lehwaldt losing 4500 men and 28 guns; but if tactically a defeat, strategically it was a Prussian victory, for Apraxin made no effort to follow it up, but fell back to Tilsit and from there to Memel, pleading that he was too short of supplies to do anything further (Sept.). His retreat allowed Lehwaldt to move across into Pomerania, which the Swedes were overrunning, to drive them out of it, take Anclam and Demmin, and coop them up in Stralsund and Rügen. The true causes for Apraxin's strange conduct were not military but political: the Czarina was supposed to be at the point of death, and the admiration of the heir, Grand Duke Peter, for the Prussian King was notorious. Apraxin had no wish to make himself impossible by overthrowing his future master's hero.

Very different was the course of events in Western Germany. The Prussian corps on the Rhine had found it hopeless to attempt to hold Cleves and Mark against the vast army gathering to attack them. The French mustered 127 squadrons (at 160) and 107 battalions (at 720), a force imposing on paper, but overburdened with a vast staff of general officers, far larger than could be of any use, and accompanied by an enormous baggage-train. The troops were not in the best condition, the discipline and tone of the French army was bad, the administration defective and corruption rampant in the supply service. On April 8th d'Estrées occupied Wesel, but not till May 21st were the contractors, of whom Paris-Duverney was the chief, able to provide enough transport and supplies to permit a further advance. Against so large a force Cumberland, who at Frederick's request had taken command of the army which George II had collected for the defence of Hanover,[1] could do nothing but retire. He concentrated at Bielefeldt by June 12th and retired behind the Weser, the French moving slowly forward by Münster (June 1st) and Rheda (June 14th) to Bielefeldt (June 18th). Here they halted till July 8th, after which Contades with 20,000 men was detached against Cassel, which was duly occupied, the main body preparing to cross the Weser at Hoxter. This move at once threatened Cumberland's left, and covered the operations of a new corps it was proposed to put into the field between the Lahn and Main. The stroke roused Cumberland. To protect Hanover he broke up from Afferda and moved upstream to Hastenbeck, coming into contact with the French on July 24th. It was on July 26th that the French moved forward against Cumberland's position at Hastenbeck. It was fairly strong, a hill on the right, the Sintelberg, gave a good post for the 29 battalions and 30 squadrons of that wing. The centre, 22 battalions, was in rear of Hastenbeck, forming a connecting link with the 8 battalions of the left on the Scheckenberg. The only weak spot seemed to be a ravine in the left centre between Hastenbeck and the mountain, but this had been secured by the erection of three large batteries. However, it was against the left that d'Estrées directed his main attack, delivered by the gallant Chevert and 12 battalions. Despite a fog and the difficulties of the ground, Chevert accomplished his task, while d'Armentières in the right centre carried one of the three batteries but failed to keep Chevert and the centre in touch, so that Anlazy's division[2] had to be put in before another battery could be won or Hastenbeck carried by Contades. About 11.30 both these tasks had been accomplished. Cumberland's centre was pierced, his left seemed going to be cut off by

---

[1] Waddington, ii. 195.
[2] Partly composed of Austrians from the Netherlands.

Chevert, who was advancing to roll up the Hanoverian line, when the troops to his left were suddenly attacked and disordered by Breitenbach and the Hanoverian Guards. Two regiments under de Lorges gave way completely and the disorder spread to Anlazy's Austrians and Swiss. But the effort was too late; Cumberland had already given orders to retire, and Breitenbach's bold stroke only served to secure an unmolested retreat. Out of a force of 40,000, Cumberland had lost about 1500 of all ranks with 12 guns; but he had the satisfaction of inflicting on the enemy, who were superior by half his force, a loss of 1000 killed and 1300 wounded. He was a little precipitate in ordering the retreat, but Chevert's success had completely compromised his position. He made no attempt to stand before reaching Nienbourg on the Weser, where he rallied his men, moving thence to Verden (Aug. 8th), which he evacuated on August 23rd for Stade.

Meanwhile d'Estrées had been superseded by the Duc de Richelieu on August 3rd. This was the outcome of intrigues at Paris and had the effect of temporarily paralysing the activity of the French. However, the effects of the victory were considerable enough as it was. Hanover, Minden and Hameln capitulated without delay, the Duke of Brunswick came to terms with the victors and placed his duchy at their disposal (Aug. 10th). On August 20th, Richelieu, whose force had been considerably reinforced and included 4 Austrian battalions and 10 from the Palatinate, resumed his advance from Nienbourg on Stade. On August 21st he received from Cumberland a proposal for a suspension of hostilities, on the ground that there was no war between Hanover and France; but this he declined, although it seems to have suggested to him the notion of utilising the intervention of Denmark to make some arrangement of the sort. Before his appointment in place of d'Estrées it had been proposed to give him command of a new corps to operate between the Lahn and Main, and he was very anxious to be able to devote himself to his proper objective, Magdeburg. The retreat of Cumberland had drawn the French away from that point, and Richelieu found the prospect of sitting down before Stade most distasteful. The siege was likely to be difficult and unhealthy, the country was poor and ill-provided with roads, and if the defence was stubborn an English force which was believed to be at sea might arrive and raise the siege. Accordingly Richelieu availed himself of Danish mediation to conclude the famous Convention of Kloster Zeven (Sept. 8th). By this Cumberland agreed to send his auxiliaries to their homes, to canton the Hanoverians, who were not to be regarded as prisoners of war, on the farther bank of the Elbe, except for 4000 men who were to hold Stade under a Danish guarantee of its neutrality; while the French were to occupy Bremen and Verden. The motives which led the Duke of Cumberland to conclude this unfortunate arrangement and the tale of its reception by King George II belong properly to the biography of the ill-fated commander. If his tactics at Hastenbeck had not been of the most skilful, he cannot be held solely responsible for the Convention: it is quite clear that in concluding a convention of neutrality he was not exceeding his powers. He had orders to save the army at any price: on August 11th full powers to conclude a peace for Hanover had been sent to him, and it was not till September 16th, a week after the Convention had been signed, that new orders were sent, directing him to retire on Magdeburg.[1] This alteration was caused by George II discovering that his scheme for a separate peace for Hanover would not be acceptable at Vienna. The episode is really the last phase of that conflict between British and Hanoverian interests in which the Electorate was at last sacrificed to its partner.

As things turned out it was not only George II who was annoyed with the Convention. In France it was thought by no means satisfactory, as it did not secure the disbandment or disarmament of the Hanoverians; but the French were prepared to accept it. George II was unreasonably furious with Cumberland, and only refrained from denouncing the Convention because he assumed that the troops had been dispersed according to its terms and would be at the mercy of the French. On learning, therefore, that this had not been the case, and that a hitch over the details connected with the Hessians had caused delay in its execution, he decided to refuse to ratify it (Oct. 5th). The British

[1] Cf. Waddington, ii. ch. ix.

ministry had all along refused to be bound by it, and had declared that they would continue to support Frederick : they now (Oct. 7th) decided to take the Hanoverian army also into British pay.

George was able to tear up the Convention in this way because, directly it had been concluded, Richelieu had moved off from the mouth of the Elbe to Brunswick (Sept. 20th), and thence to Halberstadt (29th), Ferdinand of Brunswick's Prussian division retiring before him. Beyond Halberstadt, on which he had fixed as his winter-quarters, he refused to go, declaring, not without truth, that it would ruin the army, which, indeed, was in a bad condition, for Richelieu had been scandalously lax as to discipline. Austria urged that he should make one more effort, that something should be done in co-operation with Soubise and the Imperial army which had come up to the Saale. Had Richelieu been enough of an officer to keep his men in hand, and enough of a strategist to grasp the supreme importance of maintaining the advantage Soubise's advance had won, he would not have contented himself with the despatch of de Broglie with 17 squadrons and 20 battalions to reinforce Soubise but would have brought up every available man. Richelieu's inactivity at Halberstadt was largely responsible for the disastrous end of the campaign on the Saale.

The Franco-Imperial force on that river represented the junction of the original " auxiliary corps," [1] with the motley and half - organised army of the Empire which had been collected at Nüremberg by the Prince of Saxe - Hildburg-hausen. This force, a strange mosaic of detachments of half-trained and undisciplined militiamen, drawn from all the petty states of South-Western Germany, was without proper transport, commissariat and other administrative services. To take such a rabble into the field would be to court disaster, and it is not surprising if Soubise displayed considerable anxiety to avoid that contact with the Prussians for which Saxe-Hildburghausen was so zealous. His own corps should have included the 10,000 Bavarians and Würtembergers in French pay, but they had already been pushed forward to join the main Austrian army, and had been replaced by 8000 men drawn from Richelieu's army. With some 22,000 men (32

[1] Cf. p. 200.

squadrons and 31 battalions) Soubise set out from Strassburg at the beginning of August, and on the 25th joined at Erfurt the army of the Empire, which had left Nüremberg a fortnight earlier.

To settle the direction of their next move Soubise and his colleague found difficult, but the question was settled for them by Frederick, who, though everybody was expecting him to keep his force concentrated, suddenly broke up (Aug. 25th) from his position in Lusatia. Taking 12,000 men with him, and picking up Maurice of Dessau at Dresden on the way, he pushed across Saxony to Erfurt, which he reached on September 13th after a march of 170 miles. Before his approach Soubise recoiled into the hilly country round Eisenach, where he halted (Sept. 15th). Frederick made no attempt to force him to fight, but remained inactive at Erfurt until October 11th. This inactivity might have cost him dear against somewhat more enterprising opponents, but he was probably right not to push on against Soubise, who might have drawn him farther away from his other divisions by a continued retreat.

Frederick's move to the Saale had decided the problem of their next step, which had been troubling the Austrian generals. Not unnaturally, Maria Theresa was dissatisfied with the inaction into which the main army had relapsed after its success in Bohemia, and it had been decided to send a corps into Silesia to attempt the recovery of that province; but nothing had been settled as to its strength or objective, as no one could tell what Frederick would be likely to do. His move gave them two alternatives, either to follow him and try to catch him between themselves and the Franco-Imperial army, a policy which would in many ways have been the wisest, or to fall on Bevern and the corps left opposite them in Lusatia. It was on this second course that they decided, and accordingly Daun and Lorraine moved down the Neisse, but found Bevern in so strong a position at Ostritz that they hesitated to attack. One Prussian corps, however, offered more favourable chances to an assailant. This was Winterfeldt's division of 10,000 men, which stood at Moys on the right bank of the Lusatian Neisse, covering Bevern's left and protecting his communications with Silesia. Against this corps Lorraine detached Nadasky and d'Aremberg, and they falling upon Winterfeldt defeated him completely. He himself was killed, and his corps had 2000 casualties and lost

5 guns (Sept. 7th).   This reverse dislodged Bevern from
Ostritz (Sept. 9th).   He retired North-East to Bunzlau (Sept.
15th), and thence to Liegnitz (18th), covering Silesia, but
sacrificing his communications with Frederick.   He might
easily have been cut off from Silesia had Lorraine handled
his cavalry with any skill, or even succeeded in triumphing
over the difficulties of road and rain to the same extent as
Bevern did ; but it is hardly necessary to state that the cautious
and unenterprising Lorraine failed completely to anticipate
Bevern, and when a bombardment forced the Prussians from
their position at Liegnitz they were allowed to get away to
Breslau in comparative safety by a fine forced march, despite
the great numerical superiority of the Austrian cavalry.
Bevern was actually able to cross to the right of the Oder,
and gain Breslau along that bank (Oct. 1st) quite unmolested.

Slowly the Austrians followed to Breslau, where they
found Bevern, with the Lohe Brook and several fortified
villages in his front, sheltering almost under the guns of the
fortress.   An attack was proposed ; but Daun objected that,
even if successful, it would merely drive the Prussians back
into Breslau, which could not be taken without long-range siege
guns.   It was therefore decided that the main body should
take post near Breslau to cover the siege of Schweidnitz by
Nadasky and 20,000 men from any possible interruption by
Bevern.   It was a weak policy, for it kept the main Austrian
army uselessly inactive until the fall of Schweidnitz (Nov.
12th) set Nadasky free for further operations ; but it was not
so serious an error as the failure to intercept and defeat Bevern.
On November 19th Nadasky rejoined Lorraine, upon which it
was decided to try the attack on Bevern which had till then
been deemed inadvisable.   If they delayed much longer,
Frederick, who had won a great victory at Rossbach a fortnight before, would be back to help Bevern.   This was indeed
what he was attempting, hoping to be in time to save
Schweidnitz, and to catch the Austrians in flank and rear if
they fulfilled his expectations and retired on Bohemia before
Bevern's advance.

Bevern's position was one of considerable strength.   The
Oder and some marshy ground where the Lohe flowed into it
covered his right, and a row of fortified villages, Pilsnitz on
the right, Klein Mochber and Schmiedefeld in the centre,

Grabischen and Kleinburg on the left, with the Lohe as wet ditch in their front, made his line strong. It had, however, the defect of being over long for his numbers.[1] Under cover of a heavy cannonade the Austrians threw bridges across the Lohe and advanced to the attack (Nov. 22nd). Nadasky at first carried Kleinburg, but was driven out of it again and brought to a standstill. At the other end of the line there was a desperate and equal struggle for the village of Pilsnitz. In the centre, however, the battle was decided. A division under General Sprechor stormed the Prussian battery at Klein Mochber, pushed on to Grabischen and threatened the rear of the villages of Schmiedefeld and Hoefichen against the front of which d'Arberg was advancing. The combined attack rolled the Prussian centre back in disorder on Klein Gandau and this success forced Bevern's right to fall back to avoid being cut off, indeed the Austrian cavalry did catch and ride down several of the retiring battalions. Had Nadasky's attack proved as successful as that of the centre, the Prussians must have been cut off from Breslau, to which they now fell back, leaving 6000 killed and wounded, 3000 prisoners and 42 guns on the field. Next day the relics of the army crossed hastily to the Northern bank of the Oder and began retiring on Glogau. Bevern himself, reconnoitring the Austrian position, fell into the hands of the enemy and was taken (Nov. 21st). A garrison of 5000 men had been left in Breslau, but it was mainly composed of impressed Saxons and Silesians who had no inclination to fight for Prussia, and General Lestewitz had to surrender two days after the battle. His men almost without exception took service with the Austrians gladly; and if the Silesian population had shown indifference to the Austrian cause in 1741, there could be no doubt about their feelings now. Fifteen years of Prussian rule had been quite enough, and the re-establishment of the Austrian government was decidedly popular.

But if the victory of November 22nd had given the Austrians possession of most of Silesia their hold was not to pass unchallenged long. Frederick had secured himself against any further danger from Western Germany, and leaving Leipzig on November 13th, had reached Bautzen on the 21st. Three days later, at Naumburg on the Queiss, he

[1] 100 squadrons and 40 battalions, 35,000 men, as against nearly 80,000 Austrians.

heard of Bevern's defeat.   On the 28th he halted at Parchwitz, having covered 180 miles in fifteen days, a very fine march indeed in November.   The Austrians decided not to await Frederick's coming at Breslau but to move out against him, and accordingly they took post across the great road from Liegnitz to Breslau, their right at Nypern, their centre at Leuthen, their left resting on the Schweidnitzwasser, though the cautious Daun strongly urged that the right bank of this stream would prove a much better and stronger position.

The action on the Saale which had enabled Frederick to turn back to the help of Bevern had come about through a raid against Berlin by Hadik and 3000 men from the Austrian division in Lusatia.   The news of this raid, which resulted in the Austrians levying a contribution of 225,000 thalers on Frederick's capital and then retiring safely with their booty, brought Frederick back from Erfurt to Torgau (Oct. 14th to 19th).   With the enemy removed from their front, Saxe-Hildburghausen and Soubise were at liberty for an offensive movement, for which the Imperial commander was anxious, but the Frenchman, who had little confidence in the military qualities of his allies, disinclined.   Saxe - Hildburghausen, however, prevailed on Soubise to advance against the some-what exposed Prussian corps left to face them under Keith. Before their advance it fell back on Leipzig (Oct. 23rd); but Frederick at once turned back to its aid, calling up Ferdinand of Brunswick from Halle and recalling the divisions sent back to Berlin.   On October 28th, having concentrated some 45 squadrons and 27 battalions, between 20,000 and 25,000 men, at Leipzig, he moved out against the French and Imperialists, who had recoiled behind the Saale and picked up de Broglie and the reinforcements from Richelieu's army at Merseburg.

On October 31st the Prussian divisions reached the Saale to find the passages at Weissenfels, Halle and Merseburg held against them.   Had the Franco-Imperialists stood their ground, Frederick's task would have been difficult in the extreme, but they fell back in some haste to Mücheln and took post at the mouth of the defile through the hills by Merseburg (Nov. 2nd).   The Prussians, thus given an unopposed passage, reconnoitred the position on the 4th, but finding it too strong to make a direct attack advisable, remained halted opposite it, their right at Bedra, their left at Rossbach. Their inactivity encouraged Saxe-Hildburghausen to plan a bold move to the South-East, his idea being to circle round their left so as to get in their rear, cut their communications and drive them into the river.

A division under St. Germain was left at Mücheln to make a show and keep Frederick occupied while the turning movement was in progress. This started about 11 a.m., but the careful arrangements and rapid movement which might have earned success were conspicuous by their absence. Believing the Prussians to be retreating, they pushed on without sending out scouts, without adopting anything like a battle formation, without even leaving haversacks and kettles behind. Two regiments of Austrian cavalry and the cavalry of the Circles led, the infantry followed in three columns, supported by 10 French squadrons and covered on the left by 12 more.[1] Expecting nothing less than an attack, they were pushing on steadily Eastward when, about 3.30, the Prussians suddenly appeared on their flank. A low ridge which runs East and West from Leiha and culminates in the Janus Hill, the point for which the Allies were making, had completely concealed Frederick's movements and enabled him to surprise the over-confident Allies. The Prussian attack was led by Seydlitz, who, wheeling to the right on reaching the Polzen Hill and circling round, came sweeping down on the vanguard of cavalry. The cavalry of the Circles gave way at once, but the Austrian cuirassiers offered a gallant resistance which temporarily checked Seydlitz's charge and gave time for the five regiments of French cavalry which were in support to come up on the right near Reichartswerben. However, Seydlitz hurled his left against them, while his right engaged the Austrian cavalry, and his vigorous onslaught made them all give way : they rallied on four more regiments of French which Soubise brought up from the left, and even checked the Prussian front line, but a charge of Seydlitz's reserve sent them all to the right-about. Meanwhile a Prussian battery of 18 field and 4 heavy guns on the Janus Berg was pouring a heavy fire into the surprised columns, and Frederick's left wing of infantry, 12 battalions under his brother Henry, was coming on over the slopes to the right of the battery. Hastily the Allied infantry

---

[1] The total Franco-Imperialist force was 51 squadrons and 65 battalions, of which 16 and 10 formed St. Germain's division.

endeavoured to deploy and to advance against the Prussian positions, but the disorder in which they had marched produced hopeless confusion. The regiments of Piedmont and Mailly, the leaders of the two columns which now formed the right of the deployed lines, and those of Poitou and Rohan of the reserve, which had marched so fast as to get in between the two columns and so practically form a third line, behaved well and advanced steadily. However, they were met by a tremendous fire from infantry and artillery, and as they wavered Seydlitz's squadrons, which after putting the hostile cavalry to the rout had re-formed in a hollow near Tagewerben, came charging in on their right flank and rear. The second (actually the third) line gave way at once, and in a moment all was hopeless disorder. The troops of the Circles made no attempt to resist, and though one or two isolated French regiments stood their ground well, they were ridden down. By 4.30 all was over. Some cavalry from the French left intervened and their charge gave the fugitives some respite, but in the end St. Germain's division was the only body to leave the field in orderly formation : it acted as rearguard, and covered the retreat by Langensalza (Nov. 7th) to Hanau. Frederick made no attempt to pursue; he was well content with the advantage he had gained, and with good reason. With only 22,000 men against 36,000 French and 10 to 12,000 Imperialists, he had inflicted on his enemies a loss of about 3000 killed and wounded, 5000 prisoners and 67 guns. But the moral effects of the victory were even greater. It is difficult to say whether the blunders of the Allied commanders or the misbehaviour of the troops was the more discreditable. That of the Army of the Circles might have been anticipated by any one acquainted with its organisation and utter want of training and discipline. It is not necessary to attribute it to disaffection, or to pretend that the Darmstadters and Wurz-burgers found it impossible to fight against the " champion of German nationality." The Imperial army behaved as raw troops of indifferent quality are likely to do when taken by surprise. But that the bulk of the French should have behaved so ill is indeed remarkable, and speaks volumes for the demoralisation of their army. Maurice de Saxe's victories had temporarily restored its tone, but its state in 1757 was worse than it had ever been before. On the Prussian side

Frederick showed great coolness in letting the enemy commit themselves thoroughly to their turning movement before he launched his men at them; but the good discipline and efficiency of the Prussian army, as shown in the rapidity with which they broke up their camp and were ready for action almost directly they got their orders, the excellent fire-discipline of the infantry, the good work done by the Prussian artillery in combination with the other arms, and above all the splendid way in which Seydlitz handled his horsemen and utilised to the full the chances afforded by what was an ideal piece of ground for cavalry manœuvres, had even more to do with the result.

Thus freed from anxiety as to his right flank, Frederick could and did retrace his steps to Silesia. Too late to save Breslau, he halted at Parchwitz and there picked up the battered remnant of Bevern's corps, which the slackness of Charles of Lorraine had allowed to get away unmolested. Vigorous and stringent measures did something to restore the tone of the beaten army. Exhortations to do their duty, the example of the King's high spirit and determined courage, appeals to their *esprit de corps* and lost prestige raised in them the desire to do some deed to be named with Rossbach, and the army followed Frederick cheerfully when on December 4th he moved to Neumarkt and thence next morning against the Austrian position across the road to Breslau.

In thus bringing on a battle, Frederick was running great risks, for the Austrian position was fairly strong, and their force probably half as large again as his.[1] On the right, Lucchesi's corps stretched from Nypern to Leuthen, with an outpost at Börne in its front and its flank covered by peat-bogs and a wood. In the centre was the reserve under d'Aremberg, on the left Nadasky's corps, part of which from Sagschütz to the Schweidnitzwasser was drawn up *en potence*.[2] In front, South-West of Sagschütz, was the Kiefer Berg, a hill on which a large battery was posted under the protection of three Würtemberg battalions which were not altogether trustworthy.

Leaving Neumarkt about 5 a.m. Frederick fell on

---

[1] The Prussians had 128 squadrons, about 13,000 men, and 48 battalions, 24,000 bayonets, on the field. Lorraine's army mustered 144 squadrons and 84 battalions, and its units were rather stronger than Frederick's; but something must be deducted for the garrisons of Breslau and Liegnitz.

[2] *i.e.* wheeled back at an oblique angle to the main line so as to cover it.

Lucchesi's outpost at Börne just about daybreak and drove it out. This made Lorraine imagine that the Prussians intended to attack his right, which he too promptly reinforced from his reserves. The morning mists were still heavy, and the rolling ground in front also helped to conceal the movements of the Prussians, who, leaving a small force to feint against Nypern and so attract Lorraine's attention thither, were moving to their right in the famous "oblique order" which was Frederick's great contribution to the drill-book. They had been marching in four columns, the two outer ones composed of cavalry, the inner of infantry. The infantry now formed two lines, commanded by Maurice of Dessau and General Retzow, while Ziethen's horse (43 squadrons) took post on the right, Driesen's (40 squadrons) on the left, each having 10 squadrons of hussars in support, the rest of the cavalry forming a general reserve under Eugène of Würtemberg. A detachment of 6 battalions of infantry was in close support of Ziethen. The infantry of the first line after deploying formed half-right and advanced in that direction, the movement taking them obliquely across the front of the Austrian position so as to bring them into action against Nadasky's corps. When opposite Sagschütz (about 1 p.m.), Ziethen wheeled to the left and advanced against the refused part of Nadasky's line, but the Austrian commander was ready and hurled his cavalry upon Ziethen with success, the Prussian was driven back in disorder and only saved by his infantry supports, who checked Nadasky's charge. Meanwhile Wedel with the leading battalions of the Prussian main body had attacked the Würtembergers at the angle of the Austrian line. The mistake of confiding this important post to untrustworthy troops was now apparent. As Wedel came on, covered by a heavy cannonade, for the Prussians of Bevern's corps having lost their field-guns at Breslau had been furnished with heavy guns from the fortifications of Glogau,[1] the Würtembergers broke and fled, and Wedel pushing on stormed the 14-gun battery on the Kiefer Berg. Maurice of Dessau seconded Wedel's efforts, and as Nadasky's horse had fallen back on Gohlau when checked by the infantry, the whole Austrian left rolled back Northward. Lorraine now exerted himself to rally them, and the gallant resistance of the battalions in

---

[1] These were 12-pounders, the usual field-guns of the day being 6-pounders, or more often 3-pounders.

Leuthen village checked the Prussian advance long enough[1] for a new line to be formed behind the village, running from North of West to South of East at an angle of 75° to the old position. This charge was covered by the fire of a battery on some hillocks to the North of Leuthen which threw the left of the Prussian infantry (Retzow's division) into disorder, while Maurice of Dessau in the centre and Wedel, who with the six battalions attached to Ziethen now formed the right of the line, were held up by the Austrians in Leuthen, now reinforced from their original right. Lucchesi's cavalry also came up from the same quarter and were just charging in on the exposed flank of Retzow's infantry when Frederick delivered the decisive stroke by hurling Driesen's horse of the left wing from Radaxdorf on the flank and rear of Lucchesi. The Austrian cavalry were routed, and their flight exposed the flank of the new line, which Driesen promptly attacked. The whole Austrian army gave way in disorder, the defenders of Leuthen being cut off and taken, though their resistance checked the pursuit and gave time for the fugitives of the right and centre to get away. Similarly Nadasky's rallied cavalry covered to some extent the rout of the left, but the defeat was complete, and the Austrians had to thank the darkness that they were able to get away and rally next day behind the Lohe. They had lost too heavily to think of facing another battle, even if they had stood in Bevern's old position at Breslau where they could have utilised the heavy guns, which to their cost they had not taken to Leuthen. But one Leuthen had been enough; they had lost 27,000 in killed, wounded and prisoners; they had left 116 guns behind, and their fighting capacities were for the time annihilated. An additional 10,000 men were left to hold Breslau, in other words, to swell the numbers of the prisoners, for the garrison, quite demoralised, surrendered on the 21st after a very poor resistance, and Lorraine withdrew with the rest of his shaken army to Königgratz, which they reached after a terrible and exhausting march. Liegnitz copied Breslau's example at the interval of a week, and with its fall Schweidnitz became the only Silesian fortress still in Austrian hands.

Frederick, in whose military career Leuthen may fairly be regarded as the masterpiece, had lost some 6000 men, but

[1] 2.30 to 3.30 p.m.

Silesia was his.   His daring in attacking such superior numbers
had been amply justified by success.   The feint against
Nypern to divert attention from the true attack, the refusing
of Driesen's horse till the moment when they could be used
with telling effect, the skill with which the ground and the
mists were used to conceal the risky move to the right,
the able way in which the Prussian artillery was handled in
support of the infantry attack are much to his credit, even if it
be remembered that it was only with the most highly trained
and drilled troops that manœuvres demanding such exactitude
in execution could be successfully practised.   And once again
it may be remarked that the Austrian love for the defensive
and the want of enterprise betrayed by their commanders had
contributed to the Prussian success.   As Moltke has pointed
out,[1] they chose a position with a river behind them, extended
their lines unduly, were taken in by the feint on their right,
and let themselves be beaten in detail.   Proper scouting should
have warned them of the direction in which the Prussians were
moving, and the ineptitude which allowed Frederick to move
across their front without a counter-attack being made is only
paralleled by the unwisdom of their move out to Leuthen,
which forced them to leave behind a third of their guns,
including the heavier pieces of which such good use had been
made at Breslau.

But though this brilliant victory allowed Frederick to end
the campaign of 1757 in possession of practically as much
territory as he had held at the beginning of the year,[2] it must
be confessed that the outlook was not promising.   If his
tremendous exertions, his three victories, his heavy losses in
officers and men—that of Schwerin and Winterfeldt alone
meant much to him—had only sufficed to ward off dangers
and leave him where he had begun, what would happen in the
next year if Austria were to discover a general capable of
doing more than merely defend, if Russia were to take a
serious part in the campaign, if the French intervention were
to be directed with some approach to capacity?   Neither in
men nor in money were Prussia's resources very great; and
even with Saxony to draw upon another such year might
find Frederick near the limits of his endurance.

[1] Cf. Waddington, ii. 718.
[2] The Westphalian provinces were the only losses.

CHAPTER XII

THE SEVEN YEARS' WAR—*continued*

THE CAMPAIGNS OF 1758 AND 1759

DISMAYED only for a moment by the disaster of Leuthen,[1] Maria Theresa was soon busy with schemes for retrieving the failure of 1757. Vigorous measures were taken to increase and equip the broken army now rallying in Bohemia and to make it fit for service again, and the Empress proceeded to discuss with her allies a concerted plan of operations by which the isolated and disjointed efforts of the previous year might be combined with happier result.

In Russia there was greater keenness on the prosecution of the war than in the previous year. Elizabeth had been ill but had recovered, Duke Peter had been somewhat reconciled to Austria by the fact that Bestuchev, who had been intriguing against his succession, had been dismissed and replaced by Woronzov; and Apraxin's misconduct of the campaign had brought him before a well-deserved court-martial. After much correspondence it was agreed that the Russian main army should advance upon Posen, in which district it would threaten both Brandenburg and Silesia, and would cover the operations of a detached corps in Pomerania.

France was more inclined to repent of the war, and there seemed some chance that she might withdraw from it. Bernis was talking of peace; irresolution personified, he was quite overcome by the duties of a post altogether beyond his limited capacities. But Louis XV and Madame de Pompadour were set on a vigorous prosecution of the war in which the King felt his prestige to be involved. He might have been better advised to content himself with the mere furnishing of the auxiliary corps to Maria Theresa, but to tamely accept Rossbach and retire from the war would be too humiliating

[1] Cf. Waddington, ii. 734.

and Louis was resolved to go on. To decide on a plan of operations was more difficult, though both French and Austrians looked upon the destruction of the Hanoverian army as a necessary prelude to any attempt by the French and Imperial armies to move to the assistance of the Austrians either in Saxony or in Silesia. The idea of detaching Hanover from Frederick by a separate treaty had been put forward again by Kaunitz, but had met with a very decided rebuff from George II, who was now (Feb. 1758) growing extremely bellicose, and had quite abandoned the idea of following separate lines in his dual capacities as Elector and King. George's rejection of the suggested mediation of Denmark[1] went far to restore Frederick's confidence in his ally, a confidence which had been somewhat shaken by the refusal of the English ministry to employ their own troops in the continental war, or to send a squadron into the Baltic.[2] Suspicion of England's motives, a fear that this refusal to appear in the Baltic was prompted by a wish to keep on good terms with Russia, and a dislike of the appearance of subordination involved in the acceptance of a subsidy, at first caused Frederick to decline England's offers of financial assistance; but irksome though it was to him to admit it, he could not conceal from himself the fact that his own resources were by no means capable of meeting the demands upon them, and in March he announced his readiness to accept the proffered subsidy even though England remained obdurate against the despatch of a naval force to the Baltic.

So it was that on April 11th the lengthy and intricate negotiations between England and Prussia were brought to a satisfactory conclusion by the signature of a new treaty. Both parties pledged themselves to make no separate peace or truce without consulting their ally, and England placed an annual subsidy of £670,000 at the disposal of Frederick to be devoted to the maintenance and augmentation of the forces he was employing in the common cause.[3]   Simultaneously George II undertook to apply to Parliament for the supplies needed to maintain an army of 50,000 German troops for the defence of Hanover and Western Germany. The whole Hanoverian army had already been taken into British pay (Oct. 1757), and with the addition of contingents from Hesse

[1] Cf. Waddington, iii. 201 ff.   [2] *Ibid*. iii. 195.   [3] *Ibid*. iii. 208.

and Brunswick, and vigorous recruiting in Hanover, it was found possible to place 50,000 men at the disposal of Prince Ferdinand of Brunswick, the general whom Frederick, at the request of King George, had sent to take command of the army of Western Germany. Ferdinand combined in an unusual degree the qualities of daring and of prudence so indispensable to a general. His task as the commander of this army of Germans in British pay, which had to face the simultaneous attacks from West and South of greatly superior numbers of French, was one of enormous difficulty. Outnumbered always, he nevertheless frequently managed to be in superior force at the critical point, and his campaigns are brilliant examples of a defence carried on largely by means of the counter-offensive. Quick to take advantage of his adversaries' mistakes, he was not cast down by occasional reverses or over-boldened by success. He was patient, calm, a good administrator as well as a capable strategist and a skilful tactician, and England is to be accounted fortunate that she was able to borrow from her ally the services of one of the very few generals of the day capable of discharging with success the very difficult and important task she had undertaken as her contribution to the common cause, the defence of Western Germany against the French. Both to England and to Prussia Ferdinand's services were of almost incalculable value. One has only to consider how hopeless Frederick's plight would have been if at the time of Hochkirch or of Kunersdorf a French army had been in the same position as that in which Richelieu's found itself in October 1757, even after the none too skilfully conducted operations of that year, to be able to estimate what it meant to Frederick to be relieved of all further anxiety as to his right flank and rear. After the beginning of 1758, Frederick was quite secure in that quarter. To England, Ferdinand's work was not less useful. The army with which England was protecting her ally against French attacks was at the same time playing an indirect but still most important part in the struggle for America and India and maritime supremacy. It was preventing the French from " conquering America in Hanover," it was diverting their attention and their resources away from the sea and the colonies to the hills and rivers of Westphalia and Hesse; Montcalm and Lally were left almost unassisted in their gallant struggles in order that there might

be men and money for Soubise, Contades and Broglie, with
which they might acquire for themselves and for the French
arms a tarnished prestige and diminished reputation.   Nor
did Pitt fail to grasp the opportunity.   He had been so far
consistent in that opposition to England's embarking on a
large scale in continental warfare by which he had achieved
notoriety in his younger days that, much to Frederick's chagrin,
he steadily refused to employ British troops in Germany.   In
April 1758 he made the concession of occupying Embden,
which the French had just evacuated, with a British garrison ;
but this would seem[1] to have been mainly intended as a
concession to Newcastle.   Ferdinand's victories opened his
eyes and produced a complete change of attitude, none the
less commendable if it certainly was an inconsistency.   Crefeld
showed him that he had in Ferdinand a general in whose
hands British troops could be employed to the very great
advantage of the special interests of Britain as well as of the
common cause, and the result was the decision (June 27th) to
despatch 2000 British cavalry to the Continent, a force almost
immediately augmented to 9000 horse and foot.   In August
this contingent joined Prince Ferdinand at Coesfeld,[2] providing
his army with an element which, if it caused him occasional
uneasiness in camp and on outposts,[3] was perhaps its most
efficient and valuable portion in the day of battle.

Ferdinand's appearance on the scene was not slow to
produce important results.   Long even before the French and
Austrians could mature their plans for the coming campaign
the initiative had passed out of their hands.   The hitch in
the carrying out of the Convention of Kloster Zeven had
given rise to much correspondence between Richelieu and the
Hanoverian commander von Zastrow.   In consequence there
had been great delay.   The French general, who had retired
from Halberstadt upon Hanover, had actually given way
about the Hessians, and had agreed that they should be
allowed to go home without being disarmed.   This, however,
had not been done, and when the Brunswickers endeavoured
to depart (Nov. 19th) they were forcibly prevented by
the Hanoverians.   Five days later Ferdinand of Brunswick
reached Stade, took over the command of the Hanoverians
and their allies and announced to Richelieu (Nov. 28th)

---

[1] Cf. Waddington, iii. 207.   [2] Fortescue, ii. 341.   [3] *Ibid.* ii. 559.

the rupture of the armistice. Operations were promptly begun again by the bombardment of the French post at Harburg. Richelieu, whose disposable forces, 25 squadrons and 35 battalions, barely amounted to 17,000 men, was not only unable to move to its relief but even to hold on at Lüneburg. He fell back to Celle (Dec. 3rd) and drew in his outlying detachments, so that by December 13th, when the Hanoverians appeared, he had 28,000 men, 52 squadrons and 54 battalions, with him and was ready to accept battle if Ferdinand offered it Ferdinand's army, however, needed rest and refitting, and was hardly in a fit state for a winter-campaign, so he prudently decided to fall back to Lüneburg and there take up winter-quarters. This allowed Richelieu to remain on the Aller and Broglie to occupy Bremen, though Harburg fell on December 30th after a brave defence. On January 22nd Richelieu was recalled to France. He left his command in a thoroughly bad condition; discipline was practically non-existent, the equipment of the troops was most defective, their pay greatly in arrears, they plundered freely and committed every possible misdemeanour, resembling rather a horde of brigands than a regular and disciplined army. In numbers the army was still formidable, its 131 battalions gave over 60,000 men present, its 123 squadrons could horse nearly 14,000 sabres, but it was not concentrated or in any way posted with a view to resuming operations. Moreover, Clermont, who replaced Richelieu, though well-meaning and honest, had even less capacity than his predecessor, in whose military character negligence, greed and want of devotion to duty rather than want of strategic insight or resolution were the most important defects. Thus when, towards the end of February, Ferdinand of Brunswick, after giving his troops the rest and refitting they so much needed, broke up from his winter-quarters and advanced against Clermont's cantonments, it was with an unready and demoralised enemy that he had to deal. Taken completely by surprise, Clermont recoiled in such confusion over the Weser that Ferdinand resolved to push his successes further. By dislodging the French from Hoya (Feb. 23rd) he forced St. Germain to evacuate Bremen (Feb. 24th), and moving on against Clermont he caused that general to retire from Hanover (Feb. 28th) to Hameln. Minden, which was held by some 4000 men, delayed Ferdinand nearly a fortnight, but on March 14th it fell, and four days later the advance was resumed, Clermont, who had rallied about 30,000 men and contemplated an attempt to save Minden, abandoning the idea of a stand and retiring hastily towards Wesel. In the beginning of April the French army of Westphalia recrossed the Rhine at Wesel, having been ignominiously hustled out of Germany in less than six weeks. De Broglie also, who had replaced Soubise, was unable to maintain his position East of the Rhine and had to follow Clermont's example, quitting Cassel on March 21st and retiring to Düsseldorf, while the detachment till then in occupation of East Friesland regained the left bank of the, Rhine at Emmerich on March 27th.

Meanwhile in Bohemia the Austrians had been making great efforts to reinforce their main army, which, when Daun took command of it at Königgratz, March 12th, mustered 13,000 regular cavalry, 37,000 infantry, and 13,000 irregulars. The choice of Daun in place of Charles of Lorraine was a wise step. His military capacities were distinctly superior to those of his predecessor in command, and though he, too, was much hampered by the preference for the defensive and by the want of enterprise, which were the chief faults of the Austrian army, he was a tactician of resource and as yet commanded the confidence of his allies.

However, it was Frederick who was the first to move. During the winter he had achieved marvellous results in the difficult task of refitting his army, filling its depleted ranks and training his new recruits into efficient soldiers. Schweidnitz had been more or less blockaded all the winter, and on April 2nd the blockade was converted into a siege. General Thürheim made a gallant defence, and when on the 16th a successful assault on the all-important Gallows Fort forced the fortress to surrender, its garrison of 8000 men had been reduced to 5000. Daun had found it impossible to come to its relief; his preparations for a move were not complete, and Loudoun, who was in command of the advanced detachments near Branau, was driven in by superior forces on Potisch and prevented from attempting any diversion in favour of the garrison. With Silesia thus cleared of Austrians, Frederick resolved upon an invasion of Moravia, which, if successful, would allow him to threaten Vienna, which in any case would bring

him into fertile and unexhausted country and would draw the
Austrians away from the Oder, in which direction the Russians
were to be expected. Accordingly in the last week of April
the Prussians moved off to Neisse and entering Moravia in two
columns by Troppau and Jaegerndorf, united before Olmütz on
May 5th. The move created great alarm in Vienna, where it was
believed [1] that Frederick would merely mask Olmütz and push
on to the capital itself; and it was quite unlooked for by Daun,
who was expecting Frederick to invade Bohemia in co-operation
with Prince Henry and the 30,000 Prussians in Saxony. Thus
it was not till April 29th that the Austrian main body concentrated at Skalitz and moved into Moravia, 20,000 men
under General Harsch being left to guard Bohemia. On
May 5th Daun took post at Leutomischl near the Bohemio-
Moravian boundary, and there remained sometime, using the
light troops under von Jahnus and Loudoun to harass the
Prussian communications, in which they displayed untiring
energy and skill.

Urged on by orders from Vienna that Olmütz must be relieved, Daun at length moved up to Gewitsch, where he was
only two marches from the fortress (end of May). Now
began a somewhat intricate series of manœuvres; Daun kept
on shifting from one camp to another, hoping thus to occupy
the Prussian covering army and, if possible, induce it to attack
him in one of the strong positions he loved, or, at any
rate, to distract it and prevent the rapid advance of the siege-
works. These were not progressing very rapidly. Not till
May 20th did the siege artillery arrive, and the trenches were
not opened till eight days later. The Prussians did not shine
in siege-craft; their engineers were bad, and the activity of the
Austrian light troops on the lines of communication proved
a useful aid to the dash and energy with which Marshall and
his garrison made sorties. It was felt that much would depend
on the safe arrival of a vast convoy of 3000 waggons,
bringing ammunition and all kinds of military stores, which
set out from Neisse on June 21st escorted by 8000 men,
recruits, convalescents, drafts from Silesian garrisons and other
details.

To intercept this all-important train Loudoun, who had
some 4000 men, was ordered to take post on its line of route,

[1] Waddington, iii. 222

another 5000 men under Siskovitch being detached from
Daun's main body to join him.   On June 27th Loudoun was
at Sternberg, not far from the Domstadtl Pass, and next morning
the unwieldy convoy advancing from Bautsch found its passage
disputed near Guntersdorf.   There was a sharp fight.   At first
the Austrians had the upper hand, but Siskovitch had gone
astray and his failure to appear allowed Colonel Mosel to thrust
the Austrians aside, and that evening the convoy straggled
into Neudorffl, where it found Ziethen, who had been sent
out with 3000 men to bring it in.   But it had been so
much shaken by the rough handling it had received that it
needed rest and could not resume its march till the 30th; and
then as its leading waggons were reaching the Domstadtl Pass,
Siskovitch, whom the day's delay had allowed to retrace his
steps, assailed it on the left, Loudoun joining in from the right.
Some 200 waggons managed to get through, the rest were
forced to halt and laager, and ultimately fell into Loudoun's hands
after a stubborn fight, which cost the Austrians over 1000
men but made the relief of Olmütz a certainty.   Not only had
the Prussians lost over 4000 men killed, wounded and taken,
while Ziethen had had to fall back on Troppau to avoid being
taken and was thus severed from the King, but the stores the
convoy was bringing had been absolutely essential to the
success of the siege.

If Frederick must be held largely responsible for the loss
of the convoy, which he had done practically nothing to assist,
allowing Daun to occupy his attention, it was a bold move he
took in this extremity.   The road back to Silesia was beset by
the Austrians, but against a move into Bohemia they were not
so well prepared, and it would take him through their country
in which he could exist at their expense.   Accordingly on
July 2nd he moved away West, Keith leading one column by
Littau and Trubau, the King taking the road by Konitz to
Zittau.   The siege-train had for the most part to be left
behind, as to have taken it would have impeded the rate of progress and allowed Daun to intercept the march on Königgratz.
Daun's manœuvres to draw Frederick off from aiding the convoy had brought him to the South-East of Olmütz when the
siege was raised, and he failed to begin the pursuit till the 7th,
thus giving Frederick so much start that despite all the efforts
of Loudoun and Buccow and the light troops to check their

march, the Prussians reached Königgratz on July 14th, Daun being still several marches in rear.

At Königgratz the Prussians remained for ten days, Daun though decidedly superior in numbers[1] not feeling inclined to hurl his men against the strong entrenchments he had himself constructed earlier in the year. In this he was probably wise, but he certainly ought to have brought Frederick to action when the news that the Russians were nearing the Oder forced the King to evacuate Königgratz (July 25th). Daun had beset the three main roads to Silesia, but Frederick tricked him by taking instead the bad road by Skalitz, Nachod and Grüssau to Landshut (Aug. 9th). When he saw the Prussians in full retreat, Daun ought certainly to have risked something on a battle which might ruin the Prussian army, since even victory could only give them a free retreat.

But even when Frederick had left Landshut (Aug. 11th) with 15,000 men and was pushing across Lusatia to the assistance of his hard-pressed lieutenant on the Oder, Dohna, Daun's movements still left much to be desired. If it was useless to try to follow Frederick—and it probably was, for Daun was never a rapid marcher—he might at least have crushed the 40,000 Prussians left in Silesia under Keith. But this had been tried in 1757 and the result had been Leuthen; Daun therefore preferred to move to Saxony and see if, with the assistance of the Austrian corps in Northern Bohemia and of the reorganised but still somewhat indifferent Imperial army now, under the command of the Duke of Zweibrücken, which had come up to the frontier of Saxony, he could drive Prince Henry and his 30,000 Prussians out that country. This plan if carried out with energy and resolution promised well enough; but Daun not only moved at the rate of only nine miles a day,[2] but he left large detachments inactive in Silesia to watch Keith, from whom no forward movement was to be feared; and when he did gain touch with the Imperial army which had forced Prince Henry back on Gahmig near Dresden, he failed to attack but stood tamely on the defensive at Stolpen and Rädeburg, covering Bohemia against an attack with which it was not threatened. This extraordinary strategy

---

[1] Waddington (iii. 242) gives the Austrian force as 70,000, the Prussian as 40,000.
[2] Frederick did twenty-two miles a day when moving back to Saxony after Zorndorf.

was not the high road to the recovery of Silesia, but it
should not be laid at the door of the authorities at Vienna,
who urged in strong terms the need for prompt and vigorous
action.   If Daun had brought up every available man,
even if he still shrank from a direct assault on the strong
position at Gahmig, he ought to have been able to detach a
corps against Dresden, by which means he would have given
Prince Henry the choice between the equally distasteful
alternatives of losing Dresden and of fighting a battle to
save it against a very much stronger force.   But Daun as
little realised the importance of concentrating his forces to
secure any particular object as he did the value of promptitude
and decision in action.   He failed to concentrate all the troops
available, he equally failed to employ those he had with him
to turn his opportunities to account.

So far Fermor had shown himself but little improvement
     Very different was Frederick's conduct at this crisis.   If
in the Third Silesian War his strategy was not always above
criticism, if he owed much to the extraordinary blunders of his
opponents, in energy and in resolution at least he was never
deficient.   He never hesitated about striking a blow in season ;
he never allowed the prospect of losing men to deter him from
purchasing important advantages at the cost of a few hundred
lives.   And rarely did he show as brilliant an example of
determination and energy as in the critical month of August
1758.   Realising that Fermor's advance must not only
be promptly checked, but that a decisive victory over the
Russians was very essential to Prussia at that juncture, he
hastened by forced marches to Dohna's assistance.   Nine days
after leaving Landshut he reached Frankfort on the Oder
(Aug. 20th).   On the 21st he joined Dohna, who had fallen
back behind the river to Gorgast, just opposite Cüstrin, which
the Russians had been attacking since the 15th.

So far Fermor had shown himself but little improvement
on Apraxin.   After occupying East Prussia in January without
encountering any serious opposition, he had spent the next
five months in all but total inaction.   Not till the beginning
of July had the Russians at last advanced to Posen, ravaging
the country they passed through with equal thoroughness and
brutality.   Still, though they thus inflicted much injury on
their enemies, they made these districts quite useless to themselves as a possible source of supplies.   It is equally impossible

to perceive the object of Fermor in attacking Cüstrin. Observance of the elementary rules of strategy might have shown him that his proper objective was the army under Dohna, which had fallen back as he advanced, and was now on the left bank of the Oder. Similarly a move into Pomerania, which would have enabled him to co-operate more effectively with the Swedes, might have resulted in the reduction of Colberg and Stettin, and so obtained a base in Eastern Pomerania which would have given the Russians speedy communication by sea with their capital, and enabled them to escape the long overland journey across the miserable roads of Poland. By sitting down before Cüstrin, Fermor played into the hands of Frederick, especially as he at the same time detached 12,000 men under General Rumanjev to occupy Stargard and establish communications with the Swedes.

Frederick was not slow to act; directly his own division came up, although in ten days they had covered 150 miles, he at once set his whole army in motion and, after feinting against the Russians' bridge at Schaumburg, established a pontoon bridge at Gusteliese, 10 miles below Cüstrin, and there transferred his troops to the right bank of the Oder (Aug. 22nd to 23rd). The evening of the 23rd found him at Klossow, the Prussians having thus interposed themselves between Fermor and Rumanjev's detached division. Next day Frederick advanced to Neu Damm on the Mietzel and was successful in securing the passage of that river at that place, though the Cossacks managed to forestall him at Darmietzel and Kütsdorf and to destroy those bridges. Meanwhile Fermor had raised the siege of Cüstrin and moved up to Quartschen just South of the Mietzel (Aug. 23rd), apparently expecting a direct attack across that stream.

However, this was far from being Frederick's intention. A direct attack across the Mietzel would have in any case been a most difficult and risky operation; it would, moreover, have robbed him of the advantages he might hope to gain from his superiority in cavalry. In this arm he was very strong, his 83 squadrons giving him 12,000 horsemen, nearly double the numbers of the Russian cavalry, even when to Fermor's 3300 regulars are added the 3000 Cossacks. For cavalry operations the ground in rear of the Russian position, the wide and open plain to the South of Zorndorf and Wilkersdorf was far better adapted and it was there that Frederick meant to engage. But to gain access to this country it was necessary to embark on one of the wide turning movements which had succeeded so well at Leuthen and at Prague. Accordingly at dawn on August 25th the Prussian army, 12,000 cavalry and 25,000 infantry (38 battalions) crossed the Mietzel at Neu Damm, well to the East of the Russian position, and, covered from the Russian scouts by the forest of Massin, pushed Southward till they emerged in the open again at Balzlow. Thence they continued their move till past Wilkersdorf, when a turn to the right enabled them to deploy for battle in the position Frederick had selected, the open ground South of Zorndorf. With this lengthy movement the Russians made practically no attempt to interfere, although to an enterprising adversary it offered many promising opportunities for a brisk counter-stroke. But Fermor would appear to have been too much occupied with altering his own dispositions to venture on anything so spirited, and he thus tamely allowed Frederick to unopposed take up a position in which he was at once in touch with his own base, Cüstrin, and between the Russian main body and its baggage at Klein Cammin. It is possible that, as some authorities have argued, this success should have contented Frederick. Fermor, once his baggage had fallen into Prussian hands, could not have retained his position, but must have either attacked or retired at once. But Frederick above all wanted a victory in a pitched battle, and he attacked promptly, strong as the Russian position proved to be, because delay would have allowed Fermor to reinforce his 42,000 men by the 12,000 troops detached under Rumanjev.

The formation of the Russian army at Zorndorf has given rise to much controversy. They had certainly spent the night in one of those square formations in which they were accustomed to encounter Tartars and other mounted enemies whose mobility enabled them to change the point of attack with a celerity greater than that with which the indifferently trained Russians could face about to meet them. For such warfare it had great advantages, but against artillery it provided an ideal target, and it was, of course, most cumbrous and liable to become disordered, and it seems improbable that in the battle

it was really the formation adopted by Fermor.[1] Probably the
Russians had changed front from North to South but had left
a few battalions covering the ends of the two lines in which
the bulk of the infantry were formed. The cavalry were
posted behind the infantry, who were closely massed on a
narrow front on the sandy plateau North of Zorndorf, the
Western end of which is marked by the ravine of the
Zabergrund, the Eastern or left end by the village of Zicher
just beyond the similar ravine of the Langerbruck or Doppel-
grund. Yet a third of these ravines down which marshy
brooks flowed to the Mietzel, the Galgengrund, divided the
Russian right from their centre.

The Prussians opened the action with a brisk and effective
cannonade of about an hour's duration, after which the
infantry of their left advanced against the Russian right on
the Fuchsberg. The 8 battalions of the advance - guard,
East Prussians under Manteuffel, led the way, with the left
wing of the first line, 10 battalions under Kanitz, in support.
Unluckily for the Prussians, the flames and smoke from the
burning village of Zorndorf, to which the retreating Cossacks
had set fire, interposed between Manteuffel and Kanitz and
caused them to diverge, so that Kanitz instead of acting as a
support to Manteuffel came up on his right flank. Thus the
Prussian attack, which should have been delivered by a fairly
solid mass, developed into the advance of a long and thin
deployed line which was soon brought to a standstill by the
heavy fire poured into it by the Russians. A charge by the
cavalry of Fermor's right sent Manteuffel's wavering battalions
flying back in disorder behind Zorndorf, the greater part of
Kanitz's division becoming involved in their flight. Had it
not been for the Prussian cavalry, with which Seydlitz and
Maurice of Dessau hastened to the rescue, it would have gone
hard with Manteuffel, even with this prompt succour he
lost 26 guns. Still the success of the Russian right was
a double-edged triumph; as their infantry pressed forward
after the fugitives of Manteuffel and Kanitz, Seydlitz's heavy
cavalry came thundering in upon them, while Maurice and his
dragoons routed and drove off the Russian cavalry. Taken
at a great disadvantage and in considerable disorder, the
Russian infantry made a desperate but hopeless resistance.

[1] Waddington, iii 263.

After a horrible carnage they were all but exterminated, and only some broken remnants managed to escape.

But the battle was far from finished. Behind the Galgengrund the Russian centre stood firm, and their left held unshaken hold of the ground between the Langerbruck and Zicher. Against this last quarter of the enemy's position Frederick now prepared to advance, hoping to hurl the Russians back upon the unfordable Mietzel, now doubly impassable because the bridges had all been burnt. As before, he paved the way for his infantry attack by a cannonade, and between one and two o'clock his intact right, supported on the left by those of Kanitz's battalions which had managed to rally, moved forward to the attack. A counter-attack by the Russian cuirassiers, at first brilliantly successful, was checked by the Prussian dragoons; but the Russian infantry not merely offered a stubborn resistance but put to flight the greater part of the Prussian infantry, who fled back to Wilkersdorf and refused to be led forward again.[1] Fortunately for Frederick the battalions he had brought with him from Silesia stood firm when their comrades fled, and their desperate prowess aided by the repeated charges of the Prussian cavalry at last succeeded in shattering the Russian left and driving its fragments back upon the Mietzel, though even then the Russian centre remained firm in its position behind the Galgengrund and was still unshaken when night and exhaustion put an end to the stubborn conflict. Both armies had fought to a standstill, and the arrival of only a small reinforcement for either side would probably have turned the doubtful into a victorious issue.

However, no reinforcements appeared, and after the two armies had spent the next day (Aug. 26th) in watching each other without attempting to renew the engagement, Fermor slipped away during the night of August 26th to 27th, passing to the South of the Prussians, who made no effort to

---

[1] The majority of these men would seem to have belonged to East Prussia, which province, it should be mentioned, had passed into the hands of the Russians after a remarkably feeble resistance, greatly to Frederick's disgust (cf. Waddington, iii. 249). The troops who had accompanied Frederick from Silesia, whose conduct was so very different, seem to have included several battalions of the territorial regiments of the Oder valley, so that their steadfast resistance must be partly attributed to a desire for revenge on the Russian devastators of their homes, for evidence of the Russians' handiwork was only too prominent.

interrupt the movement. His retreat was a tacit admission of defeat, but it allowed him to rejoin his baggage at Klein Cammin, whence a few days later he retired to Landsberg. There Rumanjev rejoined him; but this reinforcement, whose presence on the 26th would have probably enabled Fermor to turn the tables on his conquerers, was too late to effect anything decisive. Frederick having gained his victory had gone off again to Lusatia, but he left Dohna with a force strong enough to hold Fermor in check; at least Zorndorf had deprived the Russian commander of all wish for another battle, even against Dohna, and he remained practically inactive until the beginning of November when the Russians set their faces homeward, having rather shown what they might do against Prussia, if only they were properly handled, than managed to obtain any very substantial gain for the cause of the Allies.

Thus Zorndorf, evenly contested as it had been and narrow as was the margin which had interposed between Frederick and failure, must be accounted a real victory for Prussia. Out of an army of 37,000, nearly a tenth were killed (3600) and the wounded and missing numbered almost 8000 more, so that it is not wonderful that the Prussians found themselves incapable of interfering with Fermor's move on Klein Cammin on the day after the battle. The Russian losses were even heavier, 5000 killed and prisoners, 13,000 wounded, with no less than 103 guns, though they had, it is true, captured 26 pieces from Manteuffel. The Prussian victory was mainly due to the cavalry and to the infantry which Frederick had brought with him; but the conduct of the infantry as a whole shows that the strain of the war was beginning to be felt, the gaps which Kolin and Breslau had made had been filled after a fashion, but the quality was not the same. Frederick could no longer rely quite so confidently on his troops to retrieve any errors he might make, and he had had an object-lesson in the endurance and determination of the Russians. Clumsy in manœuvring, lacking something of drill and discipline, their fighting power and tenacity made them formidable enemies.

It had not been part of Frederick's purpose to pursue the Russians. A more urgent task called him elsewhere. By forced marches he hastened back to the succour of Prince

Henry, and on September 12th he was again in touch with his brother. He had to thank Daun's undue caution that Prince Henry was there to welcome him, for the Austrian general, especially after his junction with the 40,000 men of the Army of the Empire, had been in ample force to have crushed the Prince. But he had delayed ; and though urgent orders from Vienna had at last brought him to the point of being about to deliver the belated blow, the arrival of Frederick caused him to relapse into a strict defensive from which Frederick was unable to lure him. Firmly posted at Stolpen, Daun had his left at Pirna covered by the Elbe, while on the other wing he had Loudoun at Bautzen. Meanwhile an Austrian corps under Harsch was pressing hard upon Neisse, and Frederick, growing anxious for that fortress, moved out to Bischofswerda, pushing Retzow on ahead to Hochkirch, which caused Loudoun to retire from Bautzen (Oct. 1st). Supposing the movement to be aimed at his own magazines at Zittau, Daun thereupon evacuated Stolpen (Oct. 5th) and retired by Neustadt to Kittlitz, hoping thereby to cut Frederick's communications with Silesia. It was a risky move to undertake in such close proximity to the Prussian army along whose front it was necessary to pass, but Lacy's staff work and arrangements were so admirable that the movement was practically complete before Frederick perceived it.

At Kittlitz, Daun covered both the road to Silesia by Görlitz and that to Bohemia by Zittau. Frederick came up to Bautzen on the 7th, and then, being increasingly anxious for Neisse, moved on to Hochkirch (Oct. 10th), meaning to push on across Daun's front, gain his flank, and so interpose between him and Silesia. However, he could not at once carry out this daring scheme, for he found it necessary to remain halted at Hochkirch for three days, probably in order to allow his provision trains to come up and rejoin him. This halt gave Daun an opportunity of which he for once did not fail to avail himself. The Hochkirch position was dominated by a hill to the North-East, the Stromberg, which Retzow had neglected to occupy and which was in possession of a strong Austrian detachment. Notwithstanding this Frederick proceeded to pitch his camp almost under its guns, despite the repulse by the Austrians of an attempt to gain possession of the hill (Oct. 11th). Further, with an access of over-confidence which was to cost him dear, he allowed Retzow and the vanguard (10,000 men) to push on beyond the Lobau-wasser to the Weissenberg, and thus to put a gap of fully four miles between them and the nearest support, Keith's division, which lay between Lauska and the King's headquarters at Rodewitz, while the rearguard, which in the battle formed the right, was at Hochkirch, some two miles to the South of Rodewitz.

Daun, it is true, was the very personification of caution, but for once Frederick had overestimated his enemy's lack of enterprise; and though warned by more than one of his lieutenants of the risk he was running, he refused to alter his position; his belief that Daun feared him far too much to ever contemplate taking the offensive against him was only increased by the elaborate fortification of the Austrian camp, which in reality served as the cover for preparations for an attack. During the night of October 13th/14th the Austrian measures were carried out with unusual secrecy and despatch: Loudoun led the left round to the South-West of Hochkirch, so that it outflanked the Prussian right, the Austrian centre stood ready to fall on Hochkirch from the South-East, while d'Aremberg and their right prepared to join in by attacking Lauska and Kotitz as soon as the battle was fairly begun. Thus even if Baden-Durlach and the Austrian reserve from Reichenberg should fail to keep Retzow and the Prussian van occupied, d'Aremberg would interpose between that division and Keith's. The woods which covered the hills on which the Austrians were posted hid their preparations from the Prussians, and the narrow space which separated the armies was all in favour of a surprise.

As the bells of the village clock-towers struck five o'clock the Austrian left advanced to the attack. Their success was immediate. The thin line of Prussian outposts was crushed in and the Austrians, falling on the enemy as they gathered hastily from their bivouacs, drove them back into Hochkirch in disorder, stormed a battery erected to cover the village, and, pressing on, hurled themselves against the houses and gardens among which the Prussians were endeavouring to rally. To a certain extent the fog and mist which had contributed to the surprise of the Prussians now proved of assistance to them by helping to disorder the Austrians and to conceal from them the full extent of their success. At any rate their first rush was stayed, and Frederick, warned by the thunder of the. Austrian guns that this was not the mere affair of outposts he had at first supposed it, hastened to bring up battalions from the centre and left to the succour of his endangered right. Thus when the Austrians resumed the assault of Hochkirch they met with a most resolute resistance, and for a couple of hours an even and desperate contest raged in and around the village. Keith perished in a gallant effort to recapture the lost 20 gun battery, and the Austrians following up his repulse made themselves masters of the greater part of Hochkirch. Maurice of Dessau brought forward his division only to be repulsed in his turn, and though a charge by Ziethen's cavalry saved his battalions from destruction, the rescuers were in turn thrown back in disorder by O'Donnell and some Austrian cavalry and Maurice himself went down in a desperate attempt to turn the fortunes of the day.

Meanwhile, on the extreme Austrian left, Loudoun's Croats routed the cavalry who were seeking to cover the right of Maurice's infantry and, supported by a detached brigade of the force which had assailed Hochkirch, they pressed on against Pomritz, engaging the Prussian reserves and even threatening their line of retreat. D'Aremberg also was beginning to push forward against Kotitz, although a little behind his appointed hour. Repulsed at the first attempt, he was more successful on renewing it, carrying a battery of 30 guns which had checked his first onset, forcing the defile of Kotitz and compelling the Prussians to recoil towards Rodewitz. By this time (about 9 a.m.) the long struggle for Hochkirch had gone definitely in favour of the Austrians, a last effort by the Prussian infantry having been worsted by Lacy charging at the head of some squadrons of heavy cavalry. However, thanks to their artillery, who sacrificed themselves to cover the retreat of the rest of the army, the Prussians were able to fall back to Pomritz, where the right and centre rallied on a couple of battalions brought up from the left, Bülow also checking Colloredo's attacks on Ziethen. The rallied infantry then began their retreat through the pass of Drehsa, a great battery collected by Frederick from all quarters of the field and established on the Drehsa heights managing to hold Loudoun at bay. In the end the guns were lost, a fate shared by those near Rodewitz, which had at first repulsed d'Aremberg only to be carried at his second attempt. Had Baden-Durlach not allowed Retzow to slip away from Weissenberg and come to the succour of his King, it might have been all over with the Prussian army. But Retzow was able to make his way to Drehsa and cover the retreat of the main body through the defile, the Austrians with an unnecessary prudence making hardly any effort to push home their success. They might well have renewed the attack. Their losses did not amount to more than 6000 all told; the greater part of Baden-Durlach's corps had not fired a shot; even in the left and centre 18 battalions out of 52 had hardly been engaged, and the captured guns might have been turned on their old owners. But Daun was just the man to be content with "having done very well":[1] satisfied with having won a great victory, with having punished Frederick's temerity and carelessness, with having captured his camp and most of his artillery and inflicted on him very heavy losses,[2] he let the Prussians draw off unimpeded to Doberschutz where they rallied in an excellent position behind the Lesser Spree. Not an attempt was made to follow up the great advantage which had been established, and thus Frederick was not only able to lie undisturbed in his new quarters until he had refitted and encouraged his beaten troops, supplied himself with fresh artillery, and called Prince Henry and 8 battalions from Dresden to his assistance but in the words of a French envoy in the Austrian camp, he was able "to behave as if he had forgotten the battle he had lost," to actually resume and carry out his original plan. Breaking up from Bautzen on the evening of the 24th he marched quite unobserved round Daun's position, for Daun supposed him to be retiring on Glogau, and pushing on to Görlitz he placed himself between Neisse and the Austrian main body.

Twenty-four hours late Daun started in pursuit of his daring adversary (Oct. 26th a.m.), but a reconnaissance of the Prussian position quite deprived him of any inclination to attack, and on October 29th he had recourse to the doubter's expedient, a council of war. It was obvious, he pointed

[1] Cf. Mahan's *Nelson*, i. 169.
[2] These probably amounted to 9000 all told, more than half being killed, taken or missing.

ZORNDORF Aug. 25th 1758.

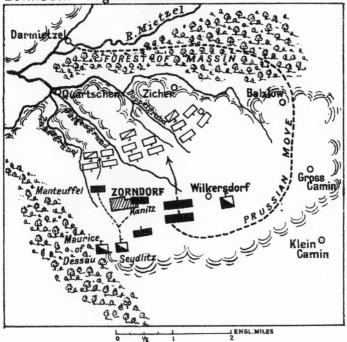

Darmietzel

R. Mietzel

FOREST OF MASSIN

Quartschen   Zicher   Balzlow

Manteuffel   ZORNDORF   Wilkersdorf   Gross Camin

Kanitz

Maurice of Dessau   Seydlitz

PRUSSIAN MOVE

Klein Camin

0   ½   1   2   ENGL. MILES

HOCHKIRCH Oct. 14th 1758

Drehsa   Kotitz

Guns covering retreat

Ziethen   Rodewitz   Keith   Lauska

Pomritz   Frederick   d'Aremberg

Maurice   Niethen

Meschwitz   HOCHKIRCH

Loudoun's move   20 Gun Battery

Croats   Colloredo

Daun

B.V.Darbishire Oxford, 1908.   0   ½   1   2   ENGLISH MILES

out to his officers, that if the King of Prussia moved to the
relief of Neisse he could not be stopped: it would be unreasonable to expect the Austrians to move with the same
celerity that Frederick always found possible, and it would be
equally impossible for Harsch to hold his own during the
three days which must elapse before the Austrian main body
could come to his aid. Daun therefore proposed that as soon
as Frederick started for Neisse, Loudoun, O'Kelly and Bela
with the light troops should follow hard upon his rear, so as
to give him the impression the whole army was after him,
whereas the Austrian main body should really take the opposite
direction, rejoin the Imperial army in Saxony and fall on
Finck and the small Prussian corps in that province, destroy
it and retake Dresden. But this plan, though put into force
when Frederick left Görlitz for Silesia (Oct. 30th), proved a
total failure. Daun did actually cover the distance from
Jauernik and Dresden between November 4th and 9th, but
he failed to cut off from Dresden the weak Prussian force in
Saxony, 18 battalions under Finck; a feeble attack upon
the city was checked by Schmettau's setting fire to the Pirna
suburb; whereupon Daun, not wishing to cause the destruction
of the capital of an ally of Austria, gave up the attack,
fell back to Rodewitz and there waited helplessly till Frederick
came back to Saxony. Frederick, though much harassed by
his pursuers, had relieved Neisse (Nov. 7th), Harsch sending
his guns safely over the mountains and then following himself
when the King drew near. Neisse safe, Frederick retraced his
steps. On the 18th he was back at Bautzen; on the 20th he
regained Dresden to find Daun in full retreat on Bohemia by
Pirna, and the Imperial army gone to Chemnitz after an
unsuccessful attempt on Torgau, foiled by the arrival of
Wedel and Dohna from Pomerania. Once again, therefore,
Frederick, despite a great defeat, was able to end the campaign
in no worse condition, save as regards his resources in men
and money, than he had begun it. His generalship was
often faulty: for the defeat of Hochkirch he had his own
incredible rashness to blame; at Olmütz he let Daun and
Loudoun out-manœuvre him, and he might have avoided the
carnage of Zorndorf, for he might have forced the Russians
to retire if he had seized their baggage and supply trains at
Klein Cammin on the 24th. But against these errors he can

point to the fine march into Bohemia after Olmütz, the decision and energy of the marches from Landshut to the Oder, from Zorndorf to Saxony, and from Silesia back to Saxony in November; above all, to the resolution unshaken by defeat and to the inexhaustible energy with which he retrieved the losses of Hochkirch. If there was one thing in which Frederick shone pre-eminent, it was his thorough appreciation of the cardinal rule of strategy, that "the advantage of time and place in all martial actions is half a victory, which being lost is irrecoverable." Daun, on the other hand, had failed to utilise his chances and had spoilt all by adopting Fabian tactics when they were least advisable. Austria's resources, when backed up by those of her allies, were much greater than those of Frederick; her troops were improving rapidly, those of her enemy had begun to deteriorate; it was to her interest to force the fighting, to pursue a policy of attrition; the waiting game was to Frederick's advantage, since it enabled him to save his soldiers and husband his resources. As for the Russians, they had once again neutralised by their utter want of strategy their good fighting capacities and the advantages of their position on Frederick's left flank. They had inflicted heavy losses on Prussia, both in men and in resources, but they had altogether failed to achieve results commensurate with their opportunities.

It was in no small measure due to Frederick's ally, England, and the army she was maintaining in Western Germany, that the issue of the campaign of 1758 had been as satisfactory as it had proved. Ferdinand of Brunswick had not failed to follow up his success in driving Clermont out of Germany. Resuming operations before his enemy had had time to finish refitting his troops or to make good his losses, Ferdinand crossed the Rhine at Emmerich (June 1st), boldly disregarding the neutrality of Dutch territory which Holland was quite unable to enforce. Clermont, his left thus turned, fell back to Rheinberg, but finding a stand there impossible, retired to Meurs (June 13th) and thence towards Neuss (June 16th), evacuating the province of Cleves and leaving the important fortress of Wesel quite isolated. Ferdinand could only spare men enough to blockade Wesel, not to attack it, but he pushed on against Clermont, whom he found on June 23rd strongly posted at Crefeld and ready to give battle. Ferdinand had only 33,000 men to oppose to 47,000; but nevertheless he attacked, demonstrating against Clermont's front and right in order to keep him occupied until the real attack, a turning movement round the French left to gain their rear, should have developed. With numbers so inferior the stroke was most venturesome, almost rash, but it proved a brilliant success. After a sharp action, in which the French lost 3 guns and had over 4000 casualties as against the 1700 of the Allies, Clermont was dislodged from his position and fell back precipitately to Cologne, which he reached on June 28th. His retreat exposed Düsseldorf which was promptly attacked. Its garrison, mainly troops in the service of the Elector Palatine, made but a feeble defence and on July 7th the town capitulated.

Indeed it seemed for a moment as if even Cologne would have to be evacuated; but this was to prove unnecessary. Contades replaced the unlucky Clermont, considerable reinforcements were hastily sent to his succour, and as a diversion the auxiliary corps under Soubise destined for Bohemia was called up from Hanau to the Rhine. Thus, thanks to the operations of Ferdinand, no help could be sent to Austria by France in this campaign.

These measures proved sufficient to stop Ferdinand. Soubise was successful in an action at Sondershausen near Cassel (July 23rd) against Isenburg and the Hessian corps on which Ferdinand was relying for the protection of his communications. The success was not followed up, since Soubise spent the next three weeks in inaction at Cassel, but it was enough to alarm Ferdinand, and with the enemy in his front growing rapidly stronger he saw that it was out of the question for him to maintain himself West of the Rhine. Accordingly, outwitting and outmarching Contades, he fell back to his bridge of boats at Rees. This had been attacked for a few days by a column under Chevert despatched from Cologne for the purpose of destroying the bridge and so cutting off Ferdinand's retreat, but in a sharp action at Meers (Aug. 5th) Imhoff and the division acting as bridge guard repulsed Chevert with loss. Even then Ferdinand's position was none too secure, for floods made the approaches to the bridge impracticable, and it had to be shifted down stream to Griethuysen and reconstructed there to enable the Allies to cross. However, this difficult operation was so quickly and successfully performed that by the evening of August 11th the Allied army found itself once more East of the Rhine, not a man nor a waggon having been lost in the passage. Contades followed Ferdinand across the river, crossing at Alpen a few days later; but the somewhat negative success of having forced the Allies to evacuate the left bank seemed for the time to quite content him, for after establishing his headquarters at Recklinghausen on August 21st and posting his troops along the left of the Lippe, he remained inactive for nearly seven weeks, unable to lure Ferdinand from his position behind that river and, though superior in numbers by three to two, unwilling to risk a direct attack. It was during this period that the British contingent of 6 cavalry regiments and 6 battalions of infantry joined Ferdinand (Aug. 21st); and thanks to this and to other reinforcements Ferdinand was able to maintain his position through the remainder of the campaigning season. Soubise alone gave him cause for anxiety by a not too energetic advance against Göttingen (Sept. 9th), which Ferdinand parried by thrusting Oberg and Isenburg forward against Cassel (Sept. 27th). A little more energy on Oberg's part, and Cassel might have been wrested from its feeble garrison, mainly composed of ill-disciplined and untrustworthy Würtembergers; but Soubise just got back in time and, reinforced by Chevert and a division lent by Contades (Oct. 8th), he brought Oberg to action on October 10th, successfully dislodging him from his position on the Lutterberg and driving him back in some disorder on Munden. But notwithstanding this victory Ferdinand's position remained unshaken; Lippstadt and Münster were secure, and with the arrival of November Contades fell back to the left bank of the Rhine to take up his winter-quarters, while Soubise broke up from Cassel and retired behind the Lahn. Thus Ferdinand could justly congratulate himself on having with inferior forces retained possession of the provinces he had wrested from Clermont earlier in the year. Of all the principal commanders engaged in the campaign of 1758 Ferdinand had most enhanced his reputation by its results.

In some ways the most important event of the winter months was the fall of Bernis. He had long ago come to favour a peace-policy and had been steadily losing ground at Court, so that his dismissal was no surprise. To him succeeded de Stainville, formerly French envoy at Vienna and now (Oct. 1758) Duc de Choiseul. He signalised his accession to power by negotiating a new treaty between France and Austria (Dec. 31st) by which the obligations of France were appreciably modified. She continued to pay large subsidies,[1] but she was no longer pledged to continue the war till Silesia should be recovered; she promised instead to do her best to win back the lost province. Similarly, France had to modify her demands; nothing more was heard of cessions in the Netherlands.

As usual, the winter was spent by both sides in arduous and energetic preparations for the coming campaign, while Frederick made desperate but unsuccessful efforts to embroil Turkey with Russia[2] and to intrigue with malcontents both in Sweden and Russia. The Allies also devoted much time and labour to preparing a plan for the operations of the summer, hoping to effect by a proper co-operation that complete overthrow of their adversary which 1758 might have seen had their efforts only been better arranged. One project which was for some time entertained, was that the Austrian forces should be divided into two quite independent armies, one to co-operate on the Elbe with the Imperial army and with the French auxiliary corps, the other to effect a junction in Upper Silesia with 40,000 Russians who were to reach that district by a march across Poland, the rest of the Russian army assisting the Swedes in Pomerania. However, two reasons prevented it from being adopted. In the first place, the French flatly declined to detach any auxiliary force to Saxony until they had crushed Ferdinand and his Anglo-Hanoverian army. Secondly, the Russians were most unwilling to divide their main body, but wished to act independently rather than as Austria's auxiliaries. Moreover, if they moved into friendly country like Poland they would not be able to provide for their troops by their usual fashion of making war support war, only in a hostile country could they indulge in wholesale requisitioning. Accordingly they proposed to wait till the grass had grown and then move against Stettin. But this proposal did not please the Austrians and a voluminous correspondence followed, the

---

[1] 288,000 gulden a month, together with 250,000 in lieu of the auxiliary corps of 24,000 men.

[2] Cf. Waddington, iv. 113.

final decision being that the Russian army should concentrate at Posen and move forward to the Middle Oder where it was to be joined by the Austrians, who were to devote themselves to keeping Frederick occupied on the frontiers of Saxony and Silesia until such time as the Russians were ready.

The result of the adoption of this plan was that the real opening of the campaign was very much delayed, and that a longer time than usual was available for the raising and training of recruits and for other preparations. But though both main armies remained long inactive, raids and forays were numerous, the Prussians being specially active and ubiquitous in gathering in supplies and in destroying those of their enemies. Once they ventured as far as Bamberg in Franconia (May), and a damaging blow was struck at the Army of the Circles which was forced to recoil with much disorder and loss to Nüremberg. Still for the first time since the beginning of the war Frederick adopted the defensive at the outset of a campaign. The days in which he could risk taking the offensive were past. His men were no longer the soldiers of 1756, or he would hardly have allowed Daun to lie inactive and undisturbed in his cantonments in Northern Bohemia while the slow-moving Russians were gradually concentrating at Posen.

The drain of war had made a very great difference in the quality of the Prussian army, while the fighting capacities of their enemies were rather improving. Zorndorf had taught Frederick not to despise the Russians, and Hochkirch would hardly have been possible to the Austrian army of the First or Second Silesian Wars. The fact that Frederick found himself compelled to increase the strength of his artillery until his guns reached the high proportion of $4\frac{1}{2}$ per 1000 men of the field army,[1] is an indication of the changing situation.

But if it was necessary for Frederick to remain strictly on the defensive, for Daun to adopt such a course was hardly sound strategy. Outnumbering the 130,000 men of whom Frederick could dispose by 30,000 Austrians alone, even when the 20,000 men of the Army of the Circles are omitted and the 25,000 whom Frederick had to detach against the Russians and Swedes are included in the King's total, Daun had no need to wait for the Russians. With numbers so superior the

---

[1] Compare Napoleon's action in 1813, when he stiffened his young conscripts with an exceptionally powerful artillery.

true strategy for him was to force an action, to compel
Frederick to fight and use up his resources. But after moving
up from Schurtz near Münchengratz, where he had lain so long
inactive, to Marklissa on the Upper Queiss (June 28th to July
6th), Daun once more relapsed into inaction, fearing to hurl his
90,000 men against the strong position near Landshut where
Frederick had entrenched the 50,000 who composed his main
body. Not till the end of July were serious operations begun,
and by that time the Russians had at last carried out their
share of the compact.

It cannot be alleged that the Russians had shown any
remarkable alertness in their movements. About the middle
of June they had begun to concentrate at Posen, but for some
time their force at that point was so weak that if Dohna, to
whom Frederick had again entrusted the defence of his Eastern
provinces, had known what a chance lay before him he might
have attacked Posen with a very fair prospect of success. However, Dohna though reinforced by 10,000 men under Hulsen
detached from Prince Henry's corps, failed to seize the opportunity and by the end of June the Russian army, over 50,000
strong, was duly concentrated at Posen. It was under the
command of the veteran Soltikov, who superseded Fermor
without thereby bringing to the direction of the Russian arms
the resolution and determination which had been so conspicuously lacking in the superseded commander.

Soltikov began his march to the Oder by quitting Posen
on July 7th and advancing by Tarnovo to Goltzen, where on
July 20th he entered the province of Brandenburg. His
opponent had sought to check the Russian advance by
threatening their communications with the Vistula, but, finding
his threat disregarded, fell back from Obornik to Zullichau.
There on July 22nd General Wedel joined the Prussian army,
having been sent by Frederick to replace Dohna with whose
conduct the King was most discontented. Wedel's orders
directed him to arrest the march of the enemy by bringing
them promptly to action; but he was not fortunate in the
manner in which he carried them into effect, and the battle
which he fought at Paltzig (July 23rd) resulted in a severe
defeat for the Prussians. Out of some 30,000 men they
lost over 8000, a quarter of whom with 13 guns were left
in the hands of the Russians, whose casualties did not exceed

5000. Even more serious was the demoralised condition in which the defeated army was left. Several regiments had behaved none too well in the action ; one battalion composed of recruits forcibly enlisted by the Prussians in the Austrian province of Upper Silesia revenged itself by deserting in a body to the Russians,[1] and, as its conduct on a more important battlefield a few weeks later was to show only too plainly, the army of East Prussia was no very solid bulwark for the Hohenzollern dominions. Quite unable to face his enemy again Wedel put the Oder between them and his broken corps (July 24th), and the Russians after occupying Crossen on the 25th pushed on to Frankfort and possessed themselves almost unopposed of that important town with its well-supplied magazines (July 31st).

The Russians had thus executed their share of the programme, and it was Daun's turn to perform his. He did not, indeed, propose to move his main body to the Oder ; it remained on the Queiss to hold Frederick in check, while some 18,000 men under Loudoun pushed across from Rothenburg past Priebus, where Hadik joined him (July 29th), and Sommerfeld (July 30th) to Zilchendorf on the Oder, where on August 2nd he established communications with the Russians. Much to Loudoun's annoyance, however, he found it impossible to induce Soltikov to cross to the left bank of the Oder, and he was in the end forced to transfer himself and his troops to the right bank in order to avoid being attacked and driven into the river by the Prussians who were now approaching.

Frederick had been prevented from intercepting Loudoun's march to the Oder by the celerity of his movements, a quality most unusual in the Austrian army, but he had lost no time in following him to that river, being well aware that the essential thing for him was to defeat the Russians.[2] Accordingly he called up Prince Henry to Schmottseifen to take command of the troops destined to defend Silesia and keep Daun in check (July 29th), he himself with some 35 squadrons and 20 battalions leaving Sagan on August 1st and pushing across to Müllrose on the Oder and Spree Canal, where on August 6th he effected a junction with Wedel and his broken troops. It was this move which forced Loudoun to

---

[1] Waddington, iv. 139.
[2] Cf. letter of July 25th to Prince Henry, *Correspondance Politique*, xviii. 449.

put the Oder between himself and the Prussians, and Frederick also had the satisfaction of forcing Hadik, who was following more slowly in Loudoun's track, to suspend his move and to fall back to join Daun in order to escape being cut off, a fate which did befall his rearguard at Spermberg (Aug. 3rd). Three days after the junction with Wedel, Frederick was reinforced by a division under Finck which he had summoned up from Torgau and which performed no inconsiderable feat in covering 160 miles in 9 days. The Prussian army was thus brought up to a strength of 106 squadrons and 63 battalions, well supplied with artillery. This concentration was made possible by exposing a dangerously weak force to Daun, and the Austrian commander was much at fault in not punishing his adversary's temerity, but Frederick knew the man he was dealing with, and risked a disaster in Silesia with impunity.

But it was not everywhere that this impunity was to attend Frederick. The enemies he had to face were not to be lightly estimated on the battlefield if their strategy was such as to justify him in calculating on their making mistakes. Determined to bring the Russians to battle, he proceeded to throw two bridges over the Oder at Goritz, 15 miles below Frankfort (Aug. 10th to 11th), and on the 12th he pushed up to Bischoffsee, ready to attack the formidable position which the Austro-Russians were fortifying on the heights of Kunersdorf just East of Frankfort. This step was exactly what Loudoun was hoping for. That energetic commander had been urging Soltikov to cross the river and force Frederick to fight, but he found the Russian most unwilling to commit himself to so venturesome a step, and it was with the utmost difficulty that Loudoun extracted from him a conditional promise to do so. Indeed, the Austrian was not a little afraid that the sole result of the Russian advance to the Oder would be their return to Posen as soon as they came to the end of their supplies and had collected all the plunder on which they could lay their hands. It was therefore a great relief to him when Frederick took the decision out of Soltikov's hands by crossing to the right bank and preparing to attack.

The position which the Russians and their allies had taken up on the heights which starting at Frankfort run North-Eastward from the Oder, was one of considerable strength in itself, and had been carefully fortified by them. Against attacks from the West it was protected by a wide extent of swampy ground, the Elsbusch, so that the Allies, whose line as a whole faced East, had no reason to be nervous for their rear.   The ridge was crossed at right angles by several narrow ravines, thus being divided into several quite independent heights, each capable of being separately defended.   Thus the Northernmost part of the ridge, the Mühlberg, which formed the left of the Allied position, was separated from the Kuhberg by one depression, the Kuhberg in turn was cut off from the central part of the ridge by the Kuhgrund and Tiefe Weg, and between the central mass and the Southern portion, the so-called Judenberg, intervened the rather wider ravine now known as Loudoun's Grund.   These three main divisions roughly corresponded to the left, the centre, and the right of the Russians' position, Fermor's division of 18 battalions being posted on the Judenberg with Loudoun's infantry (14 battalions) in support, the divisions of Villebois and Rumanjev (33 battalions) holding the central mass and the Spitzberg, a hill which projected from it so as to form a salient on which guns could be most advantageously placed, while Galitzin and the reserve (14 battalions) held the Mühlberg and Kuhberg, their left being thrown back at right angles so as to face North against a flanking attack.   The cavalry were for the most part in reserve, though some were extended beyond Fermor's right.   At the Eastern end of the Kuhgrund was the village of Kunersdorf, the greater part of which had been burnt to make it useless as cover, while from it a line of large ponds stretched Eastward to the forest which ran parallel with the ridge.   A deep ravine, down which the swampy brook of the Huhnerfleiss flowed into the marsh, served as a wet ditch to the Mühlberg, and separated it from the hills to the North which supplied the Prussians with good positions for their artillery.   Altogether it was a formidable position, as the forest hindered the march of an attacking army, and a general might well have hesitated before he launched his troops against it, even if the proportions had been reversed and the assailants had outnumbered the defenders by four to three. As it was, Frederick was attacking some 18,000 Austrians and 48,000 Russians with a force which certainly did not amount to 50,000.[1]   Both sides were well supplied with artillery, but here again the Allies had the advantage with 300 pieces to

[1] Cf. Waddington, iv. 157-159.

240, and as about half Frederick's infantry consisted of the East Prussian troops who had been beaten at Paltzig and who had behaved none too well at Zorndorf, he could hardly claim a superiority in quality. However, confident as usual of success, he did not hesitate to attack, since to desist would be a confession of inferiority.

From the first things failed to go right. Compelled by the ground to attack from the Eastward, the Prussians had to make a long march before they could get into position; and as Frederick intended to deliver his attack with his left wing against the centre of the Allied line, the troops had to be set in motion at 2 a.m. (Aug. 12th). The manœuvre was similar in character to that which had been adopted at Prague and at Zorndorf, and it was to be covered by the Prussian right, which had to demonstrate against the Mühlberg and to make a show of attacking that point in order to draw the enemy's attention. However, the march through the forest proved more difficult than had been expected; the passage of the Hühnerfleiss caused great delays, the artillery stuck and floundered among the swamps, and the whole operation was so much retarded that Frederick altered his plan, ordered his columns to swerve to their right and to direct their march against the Mühlberg, instead of pushing on past the pools which run East from Kunersdorf in order to attack the Spitzberg. This change of plan caused more confusion, but about mid-day the advance-guard debouched from the woods and prepared to attack. An hour or so earlier the action had been begun by the Prussian artillery, which was cannonading Galitzin's position from the hills now known as the Fincksberg and Kleistberg.

The first rush of the Prussian infantry was completely successful: undeterred by the salvoes of grape poured into them at short range, they scaled the slopes, closed with the Russian infantry and after a savage struggle drove them off the Mühlberg into the ravine at its foot, capturing 40 guns and many prisoners. But there were no cavalry at hand to take advantage of this success, to charge the flying Russians as they streamed across the low ground between the Mühlberg and the next part of the ridge, so that they were able to rally and form up across the ridge ready to withstand the next attack. Moreover, it proved impossible to turn the captured guns on their late owners, and only 4 pieces could be got into position on the Mühlberg which were heavy enough to reach the opposite slope, where Soltikov had plenty of heavy guns and used them with effect. Meanwhile the infantry of the Prussian left and the majority of the cavalry were still struggling through the forest on their way to Kunersdorf; and though Finck and his 8 battalions managed to push across the Hühnerfleiss and come up on the right of the advance-guard, a brigade of the right wing went astray and was out of action for over an hour.

About 2 p.m. the Prussians advanced again, and once more with success. Though reinforced by Austrian grenadiers whom Loudoun brought up, the Russians were ousted from the Kuhberg and driven behind the Kuhgrund. Here another sharp fight took place, till after the missing brigade of the Prussian right had arrived and after the capture of the cemetery of Kunersdorf had allowed the defenders of the Kuhgrund to be taken in flank, the Allies were forced back to their next line of defence, the Tiefe Weg. But by this time the gallant regiments of the Prussian advance-guard and right wing were almost exhausted. They had been marching and fighting for thirteen hours and more, without food, in exceedingly hot weather, and their losses had been enormous. They had accomplished wonders, but the Russian hold on the ridge was hardly shaken; they replaced their broken units with fresh battalions from their centre and right, a numerous and powerful artillery posted on the Spitzberg swept the narrow space between Kunersdorf and the Tiefe Weg, where alone the Prussians could hope to gain access to the plateau. But Frederick would not listen to those who urged him to be content with the partial success he had achieved; to have wrested half the field of battle from the enemy was not enough for him, they must be driven into the Oder.

By this time his left, mainly composed of Wedel's troops, had at last come up, and while the cavalry pushed through the intervals in the line of ponds under a heavy fire from the hostile artillery in order to hurl themselves against the Spitzberg, the infantry of this division made their way up the steep and narrow slope from Kunersdorf. Their efforts were not less valiant than those of their comrades of the right, but they were equally unsuccessful. Brigade after

brigade was pushed up the slope in close formations through
which the hostile cannon ploughed lanes of dead and wounded :
one and all were unable to gain their end. The cavalry
suffered the same fate and, as they were reeling in confusion,
a well-timed counter-charge by Loudoun's cavalry completed
their overthrow and drove their shattered remnants into the
shelter of the woods, after which the Austrians falling on
the infantry thus exposed cut them to pieces. All hope of
victory was now gone, but Frederick attempted to exact from
the relics of his right yet one last charge of which they
were quite incapable. Then at last the Allies took the
offensive and swept the Prussians back all along the line,
back past the Kuhgrund, back past the Kuhberg, back till they
made a sort of rally on the Mühlberg. They even repulsed
the first assault of the Russians on this refuge ; but when
Soltikov brought up some of his still intact right, the
Mühlberg, with the guns and most of the prisoners Galitzin
had lost earlier in the day, passed again into Russian hands.
With this the murderous struggle ended ; the Prussian army,
scattered in headlong flight through the forest, was only saved
from complete destruction by the failure of the victors to
pursue. All order was lost, the bonds of discipline were
relaxed, nearly every gun was left behind and the whole
army was a helpless mob. Luckily for the fugitives night
soon fell, the exhaustion of the Austrian and Russian cavalry
prevented a pursuit, while the Cossacks who had played but
little part in the battle devoted themselves to plunder. Had
they attended to their proper task it must have gone hard
with Prussia ; indeed Frederick, believing all was lost, prepared
to commit suicide. He had known defeat before but not
such a disaster. Even from Kolin his army had got away
in some semblance of order, but this seemed irreparable.
Nearly 8000 had fallen, 5000 prisoners were left in the victors'
hands, as many more wounded filled the hospitals of Goritz
and Cüstrin, while at least 2000 deserters failed to rejoin the
Prussian standards. The Russian losses were far from slight,
amounting in all to some 15,000, while the Austrian casualties
came to over 2000 ; but heavy as these were, the inactivity of
the victors was inexcusable. Had Soltikov realised how far
worse was the condition of the Prussians, he would not have
allowed the fatigue of his troops to prevent him from falling

on their rallied relics as they recrossed the Oder by the bridge of boats at Reitwein next day. But he remained inactive and the exhausted Prussians carried out the passage un-impeded. Not till the 16th did Soltikov cross the river and with that he declared the Austrians must be content; he and his army had done their share, it was now for Daun to play his part.

The respite afforded him by the delays of the victors gave Frederick's courage time to revive. Within a few days all thought of suicide was past and he was making every effort to retrieve the disaster. Hardly ever were his great powers of organisation, his resolution and his tenacity more strikingly displayed. He fell back towards Berlin, called to his aid the division under Kleist from Pomerania, trusting to the normal inefficiency of the Swedes for the safety of that province, scraped together from depôts and fortresses every man and every gun that could possibly be spared, and before very long had again collected quite a respectable force. But remarkable as his exertions were, it was really to his adversaries that he owed his escape. Had they pressed their advantage the Prussian monarchy, reeling under the shock it had received, could hardly have survived. But the ineptitude of Daun and Soltikov passes comprehension. A finer chance they could not have hoped for, a feebler use of it Frederick could not have desired.

Under the circumstances it did not perhaps matter very much what Daun did as that he should act promptly and vigorously. Had he marched direct on Berlin, had he fallen on Prince Henry and the comparatively weak force opposite him at Schmottseifen, had he directed his blow against Fouqué and the still weaker force in Upper Silesia, or had he adopted the really sound strategy of attacking Frederick and endeavour-ing to repeat Kunersdorf at Fürstenwalde whither the King had now retired, he could hardly have failed to be successful, and his superior numbers would have secured him against a reverse. But as usual his lack of energy was fatal. Even a Kunersdorf could not rouse him from the caution and in-decision which had become habitual with him. Though Maria Theresa saw clearly that Frederick was the trunk whose fall would bring all the branches down with it,[1] she could not

---

[1] Cf. Waddington, iv. 189.

induce Daun to realise that a blow at the Prussian army would do far more to recover Silesia than all the skilful manœuvrings proper to the warfare of positions to which he clung so tenaciously. It is easy to imagine what Frederick or Ferdinand of Brunswick would have done in Daun's place, and one can picture the energetic Loudoun chafing as he saw the fruits of the victory he had done so much to win slipping through the nerveless grip of his over-cautious superior.

While Daun and Soltikov were wasting time in futile discussion the favourable moments slipped by. Frederick's forces were gradually regaining respectable dimensions, and when at last, after many delays, Daun moved to Spermberg (Sept. 9th) in order to co-operate with Soltikov in the attack on Frederick which should have been made three weeks earlier, he allowed himself to be diverted from this object by 30,000 men. Prince Henry had been lying at Schmottseifen since the end of July, successfully braving the risks of being attacked by Daun and his 50,000, and had moved up to Sagan (Aug. 28th) in the hope of effecting a junction with his brother. Finding that the Austrian and Russian main bodies were so posted as to render this all but impossible, he changed his plan. Leaving Sagan on September 5th he marched up the Bober to Kunzendorf, destroyed the Austrian magazines at Friedland and caused de Ville to retire hastily from Görlitz to Bautzen, thereby exposing Bohemia to Prince Henry. This had the desired effect of drawing Daun off from Frederick's neighbourhood. The news of Prince Henry's move reached Daun at Spermberg just as the tardy blow against Frederick seemed at last about to be delivered. He was alarmed not only for his magazines but for the safety of Dresden, which had capitulated to the Army of the Circles on September 4th. This force had bestirred itself when at the end of July the departure first of Prince Henry's corps for Sagan and then of Finck's for the Oder had left Saxony denuded of Prussian troops, and the Duke of Zweibrücken had without much difficulty possessed himself of Leipzig, Torgau and Wittenberg before moving against Dresden in conjunction with an Austrian force under Brentano and Maguire. But these successes had not been longlived. Frederick had been able, thanks to Daun's inactivity, to detach Wunsch and Finck to the Elbe, and these officers had defeated St. André and

10,000 of the Imperial army and had recovered Torgau and Leipzig. Daun therefore, being most anxious not to lose Dresden again, hastened after Henry when he heard of the latter's move Westwards, even though this involved abandoning the proposed co-operation with Soltikov. On September 13th Daun joined de Ville at Bautzen, Prince Henry taking post at Görlitz till the 23rd, when he set out for the Elbe, drawing after him Daun in some fear for Dresden. By forced marches the Austrians reached Kesselsdorf on the 29th and got into touch with the Army of the Circles. Meanwhile Henry, content with having drawn Daun still farther away from the Russians, fell back towards Strehla, at which place he on October 4th effected a junction with Finck, so that he now had 40,000 men under his orders.[1] Daun, whose 75 squadrons and 64 battalions made him superior to his adversary by 10,000 men, endeavoured to bring him to battle; but Henry had little difficulty in avoiding the snares laid for him, and even inflicted a sharp check on a division under d'Aremberg which was seeking to cut his communications (Oct. 29th). However, Daun was pressing somewhat closely on Prince Henry when the news that Frederick, now free from all fear of the Russians, was on his way to the Elbe caused the Austrian to recoil to Wilsdruf (Nov. 14th) where he took post in the hope of being able to cover Dresden.

Frederick had been set free to devote his attention to Saxony by the departure of Soltikov for the Vistula. When Daun had turned back from Spermberg to follow Henry to Bautzen the Russians, now reinforced by some 10,000 more Austrians, moved into Silesia to form the siege of Glogau. But Frederick, though his available force only mustered 24,000, mostly survivors of Paltzig and Kunersdorf, hastened to its succour, outmarched Soltikov, and barred his path at Neustadtl (Sept. 24th). The Russian refused to attack, fell back across the Oder (Sept. 30th) and announced his intention of withdrawing to his winter-quarters with the middle of October, a measure he actually carried out at the end of the month. Loudoun's Austrians, thus cut off from their friends, had to regain Moravia by a long and painful detour by Czenstochov and Cracow. Thus by the middle of November the situation had undergone a complete change,

---

[1] 103 squadrons and 53 battalions.

and Frederick, passing from deepest depression to the opposite extreme, was contemplating taking the offensive against Daun just though Kunersdorf had never been fought and lost. Much encouraged by the remissness of his enemies, which had allowed him time to rally and retrieve his position, he had returned to his old faults of over-confidence in himself and undervaluing his enemy. Before the end of October he had detached some 30 squadrons and 18 battalions to reinforce Prince Henry, and on November 14th he himself took command of the Prussian forces in Saxony and at once embarked on an elaborate movement by which he expected to drive Daun out of the Electorate.

The measure by which he proposed to effect this was not a frontal attack on the strong position at Plauen to which Daun had now recoiled, but a turning movement round the left flank of the Austrian position directed against their communications with Bohemia. This task Frederick entrusted to one of his most capable lieutenants, Finck, to whom he gave some 35 squadrons of cavalry and 18 battalions of infantry, in all about 14,000 men. Finck's instructions were to move from Nossen by Dippoldiswalde to Maxen, where he would be on Daun's line of communications with Bohemia and could thrust out flying columns against the Austrian magazines. But this position in rear of the Austrian camp was one of peril, and it was essential that Finck should be supported by an advance of the Prussian main body against Daun's front. This was not forthcoming, for Frederick would seem to have expected that the mere appearance of Finck in Daun's rear would be enough to send the Austrian army back in confusion to Bohemia. He was to be grievously disappointed. Daun had already detached Brentano's division to oppose Finck and he now moved on Dippoldiswalde with that of Sincere, over 19,000 strong (Nov. 19), and occupying that point placed himself across the line by which Finck had advanced and by which he would have to retreat if checked by the forces ahead of him. These included Brentano's division to the Northward, a brigade under Palffy across his line of advance Eastward at Dohna, and 7000 men of the Army of the Circles to the South-East. Trapped between these vastly superior forces, Finck's position was hopeless. Early on November 20th the triple attack began, from North, from East, and from South-

West. It was from this last quarter that the principal attack came, and before the advance of Sincere's troops, directed by Daun himself, the Prussians soon had to give way, they were driven in disorder from the heights near Maxen to Schmorsdorf. Here they rallied, but Daun and Brentano got into touch and pushing on expelled the Prussians from their refuge. Flying headlong to Bloschwitz they found their way barred by the Imperial Army and by Palffy's brigade. An attempt of the cavalry to escape under cover of night proved unsuccessful, and with the morning surrender came. The entire force had to lay down its arms as prisoners of war, a success purchased by the Austrians at the cost of some 1000 casualties. Finck must not be blamed for the disaster, he had done all he could, and the responsibility must rest with Frederick, who despatched so weak a force on so difficult an errand and then failed to give his unfortunate lieutenant timely or adequate support.

It might have been expected that a blow like that of Maxen would have been turned to good use by the victorious general, but Daun once again failed to profit by his success or to act against Frederick with the same energy and promptitude with which he had utilised Finck's isolation. He did fall on another Prussian detachment, Diericke's at Meissen, and drove it over the Elbe with a loss of 1500 men and 8 guns (Dec. 3rd), but he made no move against Frederick, who was reduced to making a despairing appeal to Ferdinand of Brunswick for the help he could expect from no other source. But though Ferdinand promptly sent off 12,000 men, who arrived at Freyberg on December 28th, they could not have reached Frederick in time if Daun had been prepared to risk anything. No doubt the weather made operations difficult and a failure might have involved the loss of Dresden; but, important as was the safe retention of that city by the Allies, it was but a sorry result for a campaign which had seen Frederick brought to the brink of ruin at Kunersdorf. The three critical weeks of August which Soltikov and Daun had so failed to use must be reckoned as one of the greatest dangers the Prussian monarchy has ever encountered; and, seeing how near he had been to total disaster, Frederick had more cause to congratulate himself on the outcome of the campaign than the Allies had. Still, when in January the enemies retired into their winter-quarters the outlook for the Prussian King was unpromising. He had for the first time in the war lost territory, and despite the marvellous way in which he had recovered from the staggering blow of Kunersdorf his military reputation had not been enhanced by the events of the year. For Maxen, as has been said, the responsibility was mainly his, and at Kunersdorf he had attempted a task beyond the capacities of his army and had sacrificed the solid if partial advantage of the capture of the Mühlberg in the desperate endeavour to carry the whole position.

Once again he had good reason to congratulate himself on the skill and success with which his right flank had been protected during this critical year. Once again the French had been prevented from lending a helping hand to their ally by the interposition of the Anglo-German army of Western Germany so efficiently commanded by Ferdinand of Brunswick. Though always opposed by greatly superior forces, Ferdinand handled his troops so skilfully and judiciously that he was able to hold his own and the campaign saw him successful in the principal battle of his career.

Much to the annoyance of the French, who had no intention of beginning their operations till June, Ferdinand was in the field before March was out. Collecting some 30,000 men at Cassel he opened the campaign by falling on the cantonments of the Army of the Circles in Franconia, inflicting considerable losses upon it and practically putting it out of action for some months. Then returning to Fulda (April 7th), he made a rapid march Southward, hoping to recover Frankfort-on-Main of which Soubise had possessed himself somewhat treacherously soon after the New Year. But he did not succeed in catching Soubise's successor, de Broglie, napping and on April 13th he found his way barred by a slightly superior force at Bergen, a few miles north of Frankfort. A sharply contested action followed, turning mainly on the village of Bergen, which formed the key to the French position and was bravely held by 8 battalions of Swiss and Germans in the French service, while on the French left was posted the Saxon contingent attached to de Broglie's army. Repeated attacks somewhat insufficiently supported by Ferdinand's artillery failed to wrest Bergen from the possession of the French, and after these had been repulsed the action developed into a cannonade which lasted till nightfall. Ferdinand's stroke had failed, he had lost between 2000 and 3000 men with 5 guns, and there was nothing for him but a retreat into Hesse. By April 23rd he had established himself at Ziegenhayn near Cassel, the French having made hardly any effort to pursue. At Ziegenhayn he remained till May 15th, when he moved to Lippstadt, leaving a division under Imhoff to cover Hesse.

Ferdinand had moved to Lippstadt because he expected the attack of Contades and the Army of the Rhine to be delivered against either that fortress or Münster; but in this he was mistaken. When Contades took the field it was on Giessen that he moved from Düsseldorf, and near Giessen that he was joined by the available portions of the Army of the Main (June 1st). With 100 battalions and 80 squadrons at his disposal, Contades advanced northwards into Hesse-Cassel; on June 10th de Broglie occupied the town of Cassel. Too weak to risk a battle to save Hesse, Ferdinand had to call Imhoff to him and take post at Büren, leaving Wangenheim and a Hanoverian division to protect Westphalia, which was menaced by the 20,000 Frenchmen left on the Lower Rhine under d'Armentières. Ferdinand had by this time been joined by Lord George Sackville and the British contingent who had not taken part in the dash against Frankfort. However, the position proved untenable and Ferdinand fell back to Lippstadt, while on June 29th Contades resumed his advance and once more Ferdinand had to retreat as the French general kept on pushing his right wing on ahead so as to turn Ferdinand's left. Unable to get a chance of dealing a blow at the outflanking wing, for Contades and the main body were never out of supporting distance, Ferdinand had to keep on retreating.

One of the principal objects of the French movement was to isolate Ferdinand from the Prussians, and it was for this reason that it was his left which was always turned. On July 9th, by the surprise of Minden, Contades secured a passage over the Weser, a success of great importance, for it placed it in his power to secure possession of other passages lower down the river, and by thus preventing Ferdinand from crossing to the right bank, to cut him off from all chance of communicating with Frederick. The only means of avoiding this open to Ferdinand, who at that moment was at Osnabrück, was to retire down the Weser and so secure the passages. This, however, involved risking the all-important fortress of Münster on which largely depended Ferdinand's communications with England through Embden.   It had just been left exposed to d'Armentières and the Army of the Lower Rhine by the calling up of Wangenheim's division to the main army, which even when thus reinforced was inferior to that of Contades. However, there was no help for it, and Ferdinand fell back to Stolzenau on the Lower Weser, where he took post (July 14th).   Meanwhile Contades had halted at Minden waiting till d'Armentières, who had formed the siege of Münster, should have also reduced Lippstadt.   Only by forcing on a battle could Ferdinand hope to save the fortresses, and with this object in view he detached a small force of men under the Hereditary Prince of Brunswick to seize Gohfeld, and so threaten the French communications with Cassel (July 31st).

However, Contades did not now need to be forced to fight.   Much encouraged by the news that Münster had fallen (July 25th), and that d'Armentières was about to attack Lippstadt, he had resolved to profit by the apparent dispersion of his enemies ; for while the division at Gohfeld seemed too far away to take part in any action, another portion of Ferdinand's army had been pushed forward to Todtenhausen so as to protect convoys coming up from the Lower Weser, and seemed dangerously exposed.   Accordingly he resolved to quit the strong position behind the Bastau brook, in which he might have awaited an attack with the greatest confidence, to advance against Ferdinand and drive him off.   Very early on the morning of August 1st, therefore, he put his troops in motion, crossing the Bastau and deploying in front of Minden.

The ground on which the battle was to be fought was a more or less triangular piece of open country, very suitable for the movements of cavalry.   On the East ran the Weser, on which the French right under de Broglie was to rest, to the South-West the Minden Marsh covered the French left, while to the North-West an affluent of the Bastau and the forest of Heisterholz served to cover the movements of Ferdinand. That general's force was divided into two ; he himself with 31 battalions and 42 squadrons, which in the battle formed his right and centre, lay between the villages of Hille and

Fredewald, Wangenheim with the 19 squadrons and 15 battalions of the left wing holding the villages of Todtenhausen and Kutenhausen on the edge of the forest and somewhat in advance of the rest. Contades' scheme was that his right, de Broglie's corps supported by the infantry divisions of Nicolai and St. Germain, should advance against Todtenhausen and capture it: under cover of this the rest of the army should deploy on a semicircular front, its left, composed of infantry, resting on the marsh, more infantry on the right keeping touch with de Broglie's corps, while the bulk of the cavalry, drawn up in three lines, formed the centre. Had these movements been carried out promptly they might well have proved successful, but de Broglie hesitated, not wishing to attack till Nicolai's arrival should secure his flank, and the delay was turned to good account by Ferdinand. He hastened the deploying of his troops to such purpose that by 8 a.m. it had been completed without any intervention on the part of the French, while on his extreme right he was able to secure the village of Hahlen and so establish in an excellent position several batteries of artillery who played with much effect on the French. Moreover, by the time that de Broglie began to press his attack on Todtenhausen, touch had been established between Wangenheim and the left of the main body.

The artillery of both sides had been busily employed for some time, when suddenly to the general surprise the 6 British and 3 Hanoverian battalions which formed the right of Ferdinand's infantry began to advance straight to their front against the cavalry who formed the French centre. The reason for this unexpected move was that an order of Ferdinand's that the advance, when made, should be with drums beating, was misinterpreted as a direction to the division to advance immediately "on sound of drum." It certainly took the French completely by surprise, and had the most astonishing results. The French cavalry promptly charged, but were thrown back in disorder: the second line fared little better, it shook the infantry for a moment but was itself routed. In vain the French batteries poured in a heavy fire: they could not stop "that astonishing infantry." In vain the third line of French cavalry hurled itself upon them. Though it broke through some of the battalions in the front line, it failed to shake the second, which Ferdinand, quick to utilise the advantage accident had given him, had promptly reinforced with 6 battalions. As the third line of squadrons reeled back a splendid opportunity was presented to the Allied cavalry of turning the French defeat into an overwhelming disaster. But in an evil hour for his reputation, Lord George Sackville, who commanded the 24 squadrons, 15 of them British, of the Allied right, failed to obey the repeated orders of his commander-in-chief: it is only too probable that his disobedience was deliberate, and that he sacrificed the public service to his own personal spite against Ferdinand.

Still even without Sackville's cavalry the plight of the French was pitiable. Their centre was completely broken, the efforts of Beaupreau's infantry to succour the cavalry by storming Maulbergen had failed, and the division was cut to pieces by some Hessian squadrons. Before the advance of Imhoff and the Prince of Holstein's cavalry, Nicolai had to give way: his guns were taken. On the French left the infantry, more than half of whom were Saxons, recoiled in disorder when attacked by the English infantry and by the Hanoverians of Scheele and Wutgenau. The Anglo-German artillery, admirably served, wrought havoc among the flying masses, and had not de Broglie's intact corps intervened to cover the retreat a complete disaster could hardly have been avoided. As it was, Sackville's inaction and the steadiness of de Broglie's wing allowed the French to recross the Bastau and the Allies, content with their success, halted outside the fortifications of Minden.

Indeed they had achieved a remarkable success. Though inferior by at least 12,000 to the 81 squadrons and 80 battalions of Contades, the Anglo-German army had at a cost of less than 3000 inflicted on their enemies one of 8000 at the lowest estimate, while 10,000 would probably be nearer the mark. Of their own casualties, one-half occurred among the 6 British battalions who had played so conspicuous and important a part in the action, the 3 Hanoverian battalions who had shared in the charge getting off more lightly with 300. Forty-three guns were among the prizes of victory, and as the division at Gohfeld had simultaneously fallen on the French at Hervorden, beaten them and cut their communications with Paderborn, Contades had to recoil promptly up the Weser upon Cassel.

Ferdinand certainly owed his victory mainly to the 9 battalions whose advance almost unsupported against the French cavalry was certainly the most brilliant and remarkable feat accomplished by any infantry in the war. The high proportion of their losses shows how large a share of the fighting fell on them. But Ferdinand's own contribution to the success of the day was not inconsiderable. The clever manœuvres by which he induced Contades to leave his formidable position and give battle on ground which was far more favourable to his adversaries, was only less meritorious than the promptitude with which he seized the unexpected chance given him by the advance of the 9 battalions. Instead of being disconcerted by so surprising a turn of events, Ferdinand at once supported the advancing infantry with great skill, handling his artillery so as to materially assist the advance, and sending up fresh battalions to their help. Had Sackville only done his duty, Minden would probably have been a more complete rout than Rossbach.

Ferdinand cannot, however, escape criticism for his conduct immediately after the battle. A prompt pursuit could hardly have failed to be successful, and it ought to have been possible to anticipate the French at Cassel, for the line by which they retired was not of the most direct, and their march, hampered by a great quantity of baggage, was very slow, ten days being spent in covering 110 miles. But Ferdinand hardly attempted to pursue, and on the 12th, when the French main body crawled into Cassel after a tedious and painful march through a difficult and unfriendly country, during which a good many of the Saxons took the opportunity to desert, his headquarters had not got beyond Stadtberg. At Cassel, Contades regained touch with d'Armentières, who had raised the siege of Lippstadt. However, his stay at Cassel was not to be long. Extremely afraid of being cut off from the Rhine, he fell back to Marburg directly the appearance of part of Ferdinand's army at Corbach (Aug. 18th) seemed to indicate a turning movement against the French left. Nor did Marburg afford more than a temporary resting-place. On September 4th it also was evacuated and a retreat made to Giessen, where a halt was called behind the Lahn. Ferdinand, whose move on Wetzlar had caused this retreat, followed to the Lahn, and took post on the north bank, having first taken Marburg (Sept.

11th). He made no attempt to force the French position, for his army had been considerably reduced by the detachments he had had to make, notably for the siege of Münster. This was a slow affair ; but when the Prince of Lippe Bückeburg [1] replaced General Imhoff in command of the besiegers (Nov.) matters progressed more rapidly till, on November 21st, the garrison found themselves forced to capitulate. However, it was then too late for Ferdinand to undertake any serious operations, especially as in response to Frederick's urgent appeals he had detached (Dec. 9th) a strong division to Saxony to the succour of the hard-pressed King of Prussia. Indeed the chief breach in the inaction of the two armies which faced each other across the Lahn from September to the beginning of December came from the French. In November the command of the army was transferred from Contades to de Broglie, and the new commander, having at his disposal a corps of some 10,000 Würtembergers whose Duke had just concluded a new convention with France, employed this reinforcement to threaten Ferdinand's left flank by pushing them forward to Fulda (Nov. 20th). But this exposed them to a counter-stroke, and on November 30th the Hereditary Prince of Brunswick surprised the Würtembergers, who had scattered to pillage, inflicted on them over 1500 casualties and drove them back in great disorder. This reverse, combined with the news of the fall of Münster, induced de Broglie to withdraw from Giessen to Friedberg (Dec. 5th), though on the retreat of Ferdinand to his winter-quarters the French reoccupied their old cantonments on the Lahn (Jan. 1760), the Saxons and Würtembergers being between Hanau and Würzburg, and the Army of the Lower Rhine, now under de Muy, to the West of that river. Ferdinand's men were distributed between Westphalia and Hesse, some being posted from the Lahn to the Werra so as to cover Hesse from the South, the rest extending from Münster to the Upper Weser. Thus closed a campaign in which, despite their superior numbers, the French had completely failed to maintain the ground they had gained in the opening stages : Ferdinand's tenacity, resolution and skilful manœuvring and the excellent fighting qualities of his English and Hanoverians had brought him safely out of a very awkward situation, and

[1] Cf. p. 372.

he could congratulate himself on having driven the invaders out of the territories it was his task to guard, and inflicted on the French the severest defeat their principal army suffered during the war. Moreover, he had been able to detach to the aid of the King of Prussia a really considerable reinforcement. It is easy to picture the plight in which Frederick would have found himself had Minden been a French victory. He could hardly have survived Kunersdorf.

The months of inaction which followed the long-drawn-out campaign of 1759 were as usual spent by Austria and her allies in recriminations over the disasters of the past year, and in planning schemes for accomplishing in the coming campaign all that had not been achieved in the last. France, not without reason, was much discouraged, and would have been glad to come to terms with England, for Minden was not the only blow which the Bourbon monarchy had suffered at the hands of King George. Lagos, Quebec and Quiberon were quite enough for one year, and the only ray of hope in the situation was the accession of the inveterate enemy of England, Don Carlos of the Two Sicilies, to the Spanish throne left vacant by the death (Aug. 1759) of Ferdinand VI. But in the end, after much correspondence and negotiating, France remained true to her alliances, and the only important change was a modification of the Austro-Russian treaty by which it was agreed that East Prussia was to fall to the share of Russia and not to be given to Poland.

CHAPTER XIII

THE SEVEN YEARS' WAR—*concluded*

FOR the campaign of 1760 two alternative schemes were proposed. Daun was in favour of that of Lacy, which contemplated a defensive attitude until the Russians should arrive; Loudoun, on the contrary, pleaded for a vigorous offensive which would not give Frederick time to recover the heavy losses of the previous year, a proposal with which Kaunitz on the whole concurred. Finally, though Soltikov induced the Czarina to refuse the request that an auxiliary Russian corps should be detached to join Loudoun, it was decided to adopt a modification of the latter's scheme. While the main Austrian army in Saxony was to watch Frederick, Loudoun was to assemble a second army, 40,000 strong, in Bohemia and attempt Silesia, the Russians co-operating by crossing the Oder at Frankfurt and besieging Breslau.

At the end of May, Loudoun moved forward from Königgratz to Frankenstein, where he took post (May 31st). Opposed to him was General Fouqué at Landshut, with some 12,000 men, Prince Henry having moved up from Sagan to the Wartha to check the Russian advance from Posen. Loudoun's real objective was the fortress of Glatz, but he had first to dispose of Fouqué. By feinting at Breslau he induced Fouqué to leave Landshut, to which place he promptly pushed forward his advanced guard, himself taking post at Pischwitz and forming the blockade of Glatz. Frederick thereupon (June 14th) ordered Fouqué to reoccupy Landshut. It was a disastrous order: the Prussian's advance was checked on the ridge behind Landshut and Loudoun came up with large reinforcements. On the early morning of June 23rd a converging attack was delivered on Fouqué's unfortunate force. The two principal redoubts were carried after nearly two hours' fighting, and by 9 a.m. the survivors of the division had laid down their arms. Some few escaped, but 1500 were killed and 8300 taken, mostly wounded, the Austrians having some 3000 casualties in a force of 30,000.

To retrieve this disaster, Frederick set off for Silesia himself; but Daun moved by Bautzen and Görlitz over the Queiss at Naumburg and united with Loudoun, whom he had called up to the Katzbach, on July 7th, Lacy being with a separate corps at Bischofswerda, Frederick in an interior position at Bautzen. Finding his road to Silesia barred by the junction of Daun and Loudoun, the King fell back on his other alternative. Turning round he dashed at Lacy (July 8th) but missed him, for that general slipped away back across the Elbe and joined the Army of the Empire at Gross-Sedlitz. Frederick thereupon assailed Dresden only to meet with a stubborn resistance from the valiant Maguire, the commander of the garrison. It was in vain that a siege-train specially brought up from Magdeburg bombarded the city (July 18th); Maguire held out most stubbornly until Daun returned to his assistance. Daun had waited to let Frederick really commit himself to the attack on Dresden before he started (July 15th) to its relief. On the evening of the 18th he fell on a Prussian post near Weissig with complete success and was thus able to get into communication with Maguire. Frederick had to raise the siege and draw off (July 29th) to Zehren below Meissen, and there cross to the East of the Elbe. Daun, who was considerably superior in numbers, once again neglected a good chance by not forcing on a battle.

Meanwhile Loudoun had returned from the Katzbach to Glatz, and pushed on the siege with such vigour that on the 21st the trenches were ready and on July 26th, after a redoubt and the covered way had been stormed, the fortress surrendered. Loudoun promptly pushed on to Breslau, arriving there July 31st, and at once began preparing to bombard it. Luckily for Prussia, General Tauenzien, the officer in command of the 7 weak battalions which with numerous convalescents formed the 4000 men of the garrison, was a soldier of great resolution, who held out stoutly although Loudoun bombarded the city with great effect. In making this dash at Breslau the Austrian general had counted on the assistance of Soltikov who had promised to leave Posen on July 23rd and to be at Breslau in ten days. Loudoun quite reasonably expected that his Russian colleague would give occupation to Prince Henry and prevent him interfering with the siege, and it was much to his disgust that he learnt on August 2nd that whereas Prince Henry, who had made a rapid march from Landsberg on the Wartha, was pressing on his outposts, Soltikov was still East of the Oder and would not reach Breslau for another week. Compelled to raise the siege, Loudoun fell back to Striegau (August 7th) to avoid losing his communications with Daun. Meanwhile Frederick had started for Silesia on August 3rd, and on the 7th he reached Bunzlau, having covered 100 miles in five days. Daun, moving parallel more slowly, though far faster than his usual pace, was at Bautzen on the 3rd, at Schmottseifen on the Queiss on the 7th. Frederick's object was now to effect a junction with his brother before the Russians, who were now quite close to Breslau, could fall on Henry and overwhelm him. Accordingly he moved on (August 9th) to the Katzbach, and on the 10th reached Liegnitz by the left bank of the river, Daun moving along the right. At Liegnitz, Frederick found himself beset by enemies; a move across the Katzbach proved unavailing, and on the 13th he returned to Liegnitz. To the South lay Daun at Jauer, to the South-West, at Goldberg, Lacy, forming Daun's rearguard, to the East, Loudoun at Koischwitz. To cover the despatch of his transport trains to Glogau to replenish his supplies from that ample magazine, Frederick evacuated Liegnitz, leaving all his fires burning (p.m. Aug. 14th), and advanced to the Pfaffendorf Heights, where he meant to encamp and there to await the return of his convoy before pushing through by Parchwitz to join Prince Henry. His men had barely reached the position when about 3 a.m. (August 15th) they were suddenly attacked from the Eastward. The assailants were Loudoun's corps, which in accordance with a scheme already arranged was moving up to seize the same heights and so bar the way to Glogau; at the same time Daun was to fall on the Prussians from the Southward and Lacy to assail them in flank from Goldberg. Frederick's change of position had upset this scheme, but Loudoun was not the man to draw back. Though taken by surprise, he boldly attacked Frederick's position, which rested on the right on the Katzbach at Panten and was covered on the left by the Hummel Wood. His men had hardly been prepared for the case shot with which they were greeted as they came up in close order, but Loudoun rose to the emergency. He extended his lines to the right and gradually forced the Prussian left back, though they managed to prevent him from turning their flank. Had Daun come up on the Prussian rear at this time and fallen on Ziethen and Wedel, who lay behind the Schwarzwasser, Frederick's position would have been precarious; but neither Daun nor Lacy put in an appearance. Repeated attacks by Loudoun could thus be met by fresh troops from the Prussian reserves. At last about 6 a.m., seeing no signs of his colleagues, Loudoun drew off in excellent order, having lost 10,000 all told out of some 30,000. It was not his fault that the scheme for the annihilation of the Prussians had miscarried. Indeed, Daun and Lacy were very much to blame. Deceived by Frederick's stratagem of leaving the fires burning in his old camp, they had not discovered his departure till about 2 a.m. They then moved very slowly, never heard the sound of Loudoun's guns as the wind was blowing from the West, and came up to the Schwarzwasser about 5 a.m. to find Ziethen drawn up to receive them. A mild attack by Daun's vanguard was so warmly received by Ziethen, that when Frederick's columns appeared in his support Daun drew off, while Lacy, who had been detached to cross the river higher up, failed to do so. Superior in numbers as he was, Daun ought to have brought Frederick to action. He had been somewhat remiss in letting Frederick get away unobserved; but his failure to succour Loudoun need not be ascribed to jealousy of his more capable subordinate, his conduct was too much of a piece with his habitual deliberation and want of enterprise to justify that suspicion, but it was a serious error not to have forced on a battle.

Frederick utilised his success with the utmost promptitude. Within four hours of the end of the battle he was moving off towards Parchwitz, having sent a peasant with a message to Prince Henry which he was instructed to let fall into Russian hands. The Russian vanguard under Czernitchev, already across the Oder, alarmed at the prospect of being attacked simultaneously by Henry and Frederick, fell back at once to the safety of the right bank, while Frederick pushed on to Breslau, encamping near that city on the evening of the 19th. Liegnitz had, however, been an escape rather than a victory;

and, as before, if the Austrians and the Russians had combined vigorously they might have gained a decisive advantage. But after Loudoun's experience of Daun's co-operation on August 15th, the Russians were very chary of trusting overmuch to the Austrian commander, and he, preferring to out-manœuvre his enemy rather than force him to fight, wasted time on manœuvres which were useless because their object was not the only object which could have been of any real benefit, a decisive pitched battle. The inactivity of the Russians allowed Frederick to leave 12,000 men under General von Göltz to observe them and to call up the rest of Prince Henry's corps to join him (August 29th), and with his force thus increased to 50,000 men, he was able to foil all Daun's efforts to form the siege of Schweidnitz. But this was all he could achieve and meanwhile in other quarters the Prussian arms were not over successful. In Saxony, von Hülsen had been beaten by the much improved Imperial army which had taken Torgau and Wittenberg and practically driven him out of the country. In Pomerania, Colberg was sore beset by sea and land by a joint force of Swedes and Russians, though towards the end of September a detachment from the corps of von Göltz managed to raise the siege.

It was not much to the credit of Soltikov that von Göltz should have been able to make this detachment in safety, but the Russian general was busy planning a raid on Berlin by 5000 men under Tottleben, supported by Czernitchev's corps. In this Daun decided to co-operate, and Lacy from near Bunzlau was pushed up by Cottbus to Berlin (Sept. 28th to Oct. 7th). He found that after a futile bombardment Tottleben had fallen back on the arrival of a corps under Eugene of Würtemberg. Next day, however, Czernitchev arrived, and despite Hülsen's reinforcing Eugene with his corps from Saxony, the Prussian troops had to evacuate Berlin, which capitulated (Oct. 9th), and to retire to Spandau. Heavy contributions were exacted from the city, but the raid proved for all practical purposes as barren as that of Hadik in 1757; for on a rumour of Frederick's approach the Allies took their departure, Lacy for Torgau, the Russians for the Oder.

Frederick had indeed broken up from Bunzelwitz on October 7th, and had moved on Berlin, his movements being, as usual, quite unimpeded by the over-cautious Daun; but at Güben he heard that Berlin had been evacuated. He then left von Göltz, reinforced to 20,000 men, in Silesia and moved rapidly into Saxony. He reached the Elbe near Wittenberg (Oct. 26th), crossed and picked up the divisions of Hülsen and Eugene (14,000) next day. Before his approach the Army of the Empire had fallen back from Wittenberg on Leipzig, while Daun had left his old positions (Oct. 7th) and moved to the Elbe by Naumburg (10th) and Ullersdorf. On the 22nd Daun joined Lacy near Torgau and then crossed to the left bank so as to get nearer the Army of the Empire. On the 27th he was at Eilenburg, Frederick moving to Düben (Oct. 29th) and pushing Hülsen out to Leipzig (Oct. 31st), from which the Imperial army retired. Daun thereupon fell back upon his magazines at Torgau (Nov. 1st). Here Frederick resolved to attack him. The Austrian army was ranged between the Suptitz heights, where their right and right-centre lay, and the town of Torgau, which was on their left. In front of the left, formed by Lacy's corps, was a large pond, connected with the Suptitz heights by a stream, the so-called Rohrgraben. For defence against a frontal attack from the South the position was extremely strong, so Frederick, despite the fact that he had under 50,000 men to oppose to Daun's 63,000 with 360 guns, decided on a double attack. Ziethen (18,000) was to advance up the great road from Schilda to Suptitz and attack the heights in front, timing his movements so as to coincide with the appearance on the right rear of the Austrians of the Prussian centre and left, as the result of a wide sweeping movement through the woods to the West by Weidenhayn and Elsnig. Ziethen, having a far shorter distance to go than the turning columns, should have delayed until Frederick was ready; but Frederick was behind time, and the Prussian right coming into touch with Lacy's outposts swerved to the right towards Torgau and became prematurely engaged, only to be beaten off with heavy loss. Meanwhile Daun, whose light troops had informed him of Frederick's flanking movement, had altered his dispositions to meet the attack, forming a new front facing North-West and well provided with guns from the reserve artillery park at Grosswig. Frederick's own division, the innermost of the

three columns engaged in the turning movement, was the
first to come up, and though alone it advanced to the attack
about 2 p.m.; but the heavy fire of the Austrian guns played
havoc with the Prussian grenadiers and the attack failed.
Hülsen coming up about 3 p.m. was put in with no better
success, his men failing to face the guns.   Meanwhile nothing
had been heard of Frederick's extreme left, which was
blundering about in the woods.   It arrived about 4.30, just
in time to check the Austrians who were following up the
repulse of Hülsen's foot, but this success was only temporary.
Daun rallied his men, brought up new regiments from his
reserve, and when about 7 p.m. he was wounded and had to
leave the field, it was with the full assurance of victory.   But
at last Ziethen came up against the Suptitz heights, on which
he should have directed his attack much earlier, and renewed
the fight.   The Austrians, disordered by their victory and
surprised by this unexpected attack, repulsed Ziethen once
but he came on again: an undefended causeway over the
Rohrgraben was found, and about 8 p.m. the Prussians were
in possession of the Weinberg behind Suptitz village and the
Austrians were in retreat on Torgau.   Both sides had lost
heavily, the Prussians somewhat the most, as the failure of
their early attacks had cost them in addition some 3000
prisoners.   It was a curious action.   Frederick's original plan
failed because he had not allowed enough time, and because
Ziethen did not obey orders.   His own attack was premature
and disastrous, and, finally, it was only Ziethen's renewed
attack in the dusk which turned an imminent defeat into a
victory.   The Austrians allowed victory to be wrested from
them through unsteadiness in the hour of success.   Torgau,
however, failed to shake the Austrian hold on Saxony.
They did retire across the Elbe, but Frederick was in no
position to follow up his success, and the end of the campaign
saw them in their old positions round Dresden, Frederick
wintering at Meissen.   In his absence from Silesia nothing
had been achieved; the departure of the Russians, the badness
of the weather, and his inability to bring von Göltz's corps to
action had prevented Loudoun from taking Cosel.   Farther
North, Werner after relieving Colberg had had a slight
success over the Swedes at Pasewalk, which was quite enough
to paralyse any Swedish attack on Berlin.

In this year Ferdinand of Brunswick had for once not been able to hold the ground he had won in the previous campaign. Reinforced before the campaign opened by 5 regiments of cavalry and 8 infantry battalions from England, he took the field in May, taking post at Fritzlar with his main body, a detached corps being at Kirchhain on the Ohm and the troops guarding Westphalia between Coesfeld and Hamm. Not till the middle of June did the French, who had a great superiority in numbers, move up from the Main by Giessen. Ferdinand moved South to meet them, but the failure of General Imhoff to hold the pass of Homberg in front of Kirchhain allowed de Broglie to force this barrier and reach Neustadt (June 24th). The French commander now endeavoured to hold Ferdinand in check while St. Germain and the Army of the Rhine were coming up to Corbach to join the Army of the Main. On July 7th de Broglie also marched off towards Corbach, upon which Ferdinand endeavoured to get in between him and his colleague, seize the Sachsenhausen Pass, and so prevent their junction : St. Germain was too swift for him, and Ferdinand's attack was beaten off with considerable loss (July 10th). He fell back to Sachsenhausen, called up Spörcke from Westphalia to Volksmarsen on the Diemel and remained facing the French, who lay to the Westward of him at Corbach. A move against his left he foiled at Emsdorff, where a British dragoon regiment[1] greatly distinguished itself (July 16th); but more serious threats against his communications forced him back to Kalle, on which de Broglie pushed out a corps under de Muy, St. Germain's successor, to Warburg on the Diemel to cut Ferdinand off from Westphalia. This was Ferdinand's chance: he fell on de Muy's corps at Warburg (July 31st) and routed it completely, with a loss of 8000 men, a charge by Lord Granby and the British cavalry deciding the day. He had, however, to evacuate Cassel and take post North of the Diemel covering Westphalia. Here he held de Broglie in check; but that marshal's superior numbers allowed him to detach strong corps to threaten Brunswick and Hanover along the right bank of the Weser, while Ferdinand could not move against him without exposing the important fortress of Lippstadt. Accordingly as a diversion, Ferdinand detached

[1] 15th Light Dragoons.

his nephew, the Hereditary Prince of Brunswick, Prince
Charles William Ferdinand, the "Brunswick" of Valmy and
Auerstadt, with 47 battalions, 10 of them British, and 30
squadrons, 8 of which were British, to attack the French
base, Wesel (Sept. 23rd). The investment of Wesel
(Sept. 30th) had the desired effect, for de Broglie
detached 32 squadrons and 31 battalions under de Castries to
its relief. Crossing at Cologne, October 12th, after a very
fine forced march, de Castries came up to Rheinberg (Oct.
15th), and thus forced the Prince, who had only 22
squadrons and 21 battalions available, to move out against
him with. A rash attempt to surprise the French at
Klostercampen miscarried, and after a sharp fight (Oct.
16th) the Prince found himself compelled to recross the
Rhine, raise the siege of Wesel and take post in Westphalia
to cover Lippstadt and Münster. Ferdinand thus found
himself unable to shake de Broglie's hold on Hesse, and the
campaign closed with the Anglo-German army lying North
of the Diemel, with Göttingen in French hands and Hanover
and Brunswick exposed to their attacks through their possession of the passage of the Weser at Münden.

After a winter which had been spent in the usual abortive
discussions about making peace, Daun was once again, much
to the annoyance of the Allies, placed in command of the
Austrian forces for the campaign of 1761. There was indeed
no alternative, for the senior officers of the army would have
all refused to serve under one as much their junior as Loudoun
or even Lacy, so that these two were both impossible. As
before, Daun's plan of campaign was purely defensive; the main
army, 100,000 strong, was to gather in Saxony and to confine
itself to observing Frederick, while the subsidiary corps under
Loudoun in Silesia, reduced to 30,000 men, was to protect
Glatz against recapture and to cover Bohemia and Moravia
from attack. Loudoun protested vigorously against so preposterous a plan. He saw clearly that it was not "masterly
inactivity" but a vigorous offensive which was the true line,
that Frederick could be beaten by attrition even if he could
not be beaten in the field. His views were warmly supported
by Kaunitz; and as Buturlin, the new Russian commander,
seemed most anxious for an energetic prosecution of the war,
it was arranged that Daun and the main army should "contain"

Frederick in Saxony, while Loudoun with a second army was to operate in Silesia with the assistance of the Russian main body. Colberg was, as before, to be attacked by the Russian fleet and by a detached corps by land. Hardly had this plan been adopted when Frederick, leaving 30,000 men in Saxony under Prince Henry, hurried to Silesia with the rest of his available forces to join von Göltz, whom he thus saved from Loudoun. It seems probable that one of Peter's adherents in the Russian Council had betrayed the plan of campaign to the Grand Duke's favourite hero. Loudoun, however, contrary to expectation, was not compelled to leave Glatz to its fate but maintained his post. With some difficulty he obtained re-inforcements from Daun, until by July 19th he had nearly 60,000 men. With these he set out by Frankenstein and Münsterberg, intending to join the Russians, who were creeping up slowly to the Oder along the Polish frontier. Frederick by a rapid march planted himself across Loudoun's path at Neisse (July 23rd), but the Austrian induced his Russian colleague to push on down the Oder and to cross below Breslau, which he did on August 12th. A rapid march brought Loudoun to Liegnitz, and on the 19th a junction was effected near that town. Out-manoeuvred in the attempt to prevent the junction, Frederick was reduced to a purely defensive attitude, and took post at Bunzelwitz near Schweidnitz (Aug. 20th). Loudoun urged Buturlin to attack at once before the Prussians could fortify their position ; and as the Austrians and Russians had more than double Frederick's force,[1] a prompt attack would have had excellent chances of success. But while Buturlin hesitated, Frederick entrenched himself with feverish haste and the favourable moment passed. Buturlin's hesitation was not unconnected with political considerations. Elizabeth was in a most precarious state of health, at any moment the news might arrive from St. Petersburg that she was dead, and it would not be exactly a passport to the new Czar's favour to have just assisted to destroy the last army of Prussia. Accordingly, Loudoun had the mortification of seeing the favourable opportunity escape ; and he must have been heartily relieved when, on September 9th, Buturlin departed home-wards but left a corps under Czernitchev 16,000 strong behind

---

[1] Oncken, ii. 326, gives Austrians 83,000, Russians 42,000, Prussians 50,000 : von Arneth, vol. vi., does not put Loudoun above 60,000.

him.   Loudoun's enemies had profited by his failure to achieve
success even when he had 60,000 men under him to complain
bitterly and intrigue against him, and orders had been sent
to him to detach 40,000 men to Saxony to enable Daun
to take up winter-quarters in Lusatia, when he was able to
confront his critics with the capture of Schweidnitz.   Want of
provisions had forced Frederick to leave Bunzelwitz about
September 23rd.   He had moved as though to invade Moravia,
but he could not draw Loudoun off from Schweidnitz.
Detaching light troops to follow and harass Frederick, Loudoun
moved on Schweidnitz with 15,000 men and assaulting its
somewhat dilapidated works at five places (p.m. Sept.
30th), carried it by storm.   By 7 a.m. October 1st, Schweidnitz
was for the second time in the war in Austrian hands.[1]   This
blow checked Frederick's stroke at Moravia, he fell back to
Strehlen to cover Breslau, Brieg and Neisse.   Loudoun should
now have been reinforced by every available man from Daun's
army ; but instead of this the former plan was carried out on
a modified scale, and Loudoun had to detach over 10,000 men
to Saxony.   Here it is hardly necessary to say Prince Henry
had found little difficulty in " containing " the much superior
forces of Daun and the Imperial army under Serbelloni.   Not
even when Loudoun's men came up was he as much as
expelled from Saxony.   His manœuvres were skilful and did
him great credit, but it was to Daun's want of strategic insight
that he really owed his escape.   One success only the Allies
did gain.   Colberg, closely blockaded by the Russian fleet,
and hard pressed by Rumanjev with 35,000 men, was forced
to surrender (Dec. 16th) after Eugene of Würtemberg had
failed in a gallant attempt to relieve it.   With Colberg much
of Pomerania passed into Russian hands.

From the Western theatre of war came news which must
have cheered Frederick.   An advance into Hesse in February

---

[1] In connection with this episode von Arneth points out how unfair it is to attribute
all the non-success of the Austrian arms to the interference of the *Hofkriegsrath* at
Vienna with the operations of the generals.   That body was concerned with raising
recruits and providing supplies for the army, with its administration not with its
operations.   It was the generals, especially Daun, who continually referred important
points to the decision of Maria Theresa and Kaunitz, though they begged the
commanders not to do so but to act on their own initiative.   Loudoun in this instance
acted on his own initiative ; and though he thus interfered with a plan arranged at
Vienna was not reprimanded in any way.

by which Ferdinand attempted to surprise the French in their winter-quarters, met with great success for a time; but in pressing on to reach a district in which he could feed his troops as he went, he was forced to leave large detachments behind to besiege Cassel and Marburg, and de Broglie concentrating a considerable force at Giessen defeated the Hereditary Prince of Brunswick at Grünberg (March 21) and forced Ferdinand back behind the Diemel. Here he had to await reinforcements and to refresh his exhausted men, while Soubise collected 100,000 men at Wesel and prepared to advance Eastward through Westphalia, de Broglie with 60,000 coming up from Hesse. Not till June 13th did Soubise cross the Rhine, whereon Ferdinand, his army refreshed by ten weeks' rest, moved boldly West to Dortmund to threaten the French communications. This move, indeed, left open the road by which the two French armies could unite; but it startled Soubise, who made no attempt to turn on his enemy, but hastened to Soest to unite with his colleague (July 10th). Their joint force mustered over 100,000; Ferdinand, even after Spörcke's Hanoverians, who had been forcing de Broglie, joined him, had only 60,000; but he stood firm on the Southern bank of the Lippe at Vellinghausen, and the French, finding that before they could take Lippstadt they must beat Ferdinand, attacked him (July 15th to 16th) there, only to be defeated with heavy loss. The brunt of the battle fell on the Allied left, where Granby's corps, mainly British, was posted; but the failure of Soubise to support de Broglie was the chief cause of the defeat. Discontented with each other, the French generals then separated, Soubise returning to Wesel, followed by the Hereditary Prince, de Broglie moving East to threaten Hanover, with Ferdinand after him. As soon as the two marshals were well apart, Ferdinand struck at de Broglie's communications with Frankfort (Aug. 10th), a blow which brought him back from Hameln and Göttingen to Cassel; a second move across the Weser against Hanover was frustrated in the same way (Sept.), while later on again a corps which de Broglie detached to Brunswick (Oct.) was headed back, though he did retain Göttingen. Meanwhile Soubise moved into East Friesland, took Embden and threatened Bremen, but was forced to retire by the Hereditary Prince. Thus for all their twofold superiority in numbers the French achieved nothing in yet another campaign.

But if Frederick had once again reached the end of a campaign without being destroyed, his plight was of the worst. His resources were strained to the utmost, and he had nothing to which he could point as a set-off against Colberg and Schweidnitz. On the other hand, Choiseul's bellicose views were things of the past and he was seeking to bring about peace by means of separate negotiations between England and France. Indeed, he had gone to the length of drawing up a draft treaty with John Stanley, the English agent at Paris, when Stahremberg reminded him that such a treaty, if it left England free to prosecute the war on behalf of Prussia, would be contrary to the most recent Franco-Austrian agreement, that of 1758. This produced a warm conflict between the Allies, Kaunitz having little difficulty in showing that Choiseul's conduct, whether the right policy for France or not, was a breach of her obligations. He would, however, have raised no objection if the peace had debarred both France and England from assisting their old allies, but the negotiations never reached this point. For some time past the relations between England and Spain had been of a strained character, and Choiseul's fertile brain saw in this a chance of throwing the weight of Spain into the colonial and maritime struggle which had gone so badly for France. Pitt, fully aware of the Franco-Spanish negotiations,[1] was anxious to bring matters to a crisis, and placed before his colleagues the definite issue of peace or war. They seized the opportunity of getting rid of him, though it is probable that they were for the most part genuinely convinced of Spain's good intentions. They were undeceived, however, when Spain, the Plate Fleet once safely in, adopted so uncompromising a tone that England had no option but to declare war (Jan. 5th, 1762), whereupon the Anglo-French negotiations were broken off. Choiseul, hoping that the aid of Spain would enable France to retrieve the losses she had sustained, was once more as bellicose as ever, and when Austria made tentative inquiries as to the attitude of France towards a peace, she found her ally inclined to go on with the war. Austria herself was not disinclined to peace. Her resources had been strained to their limits. Every possible financial expedient had been tried, an income-tax, a 10 per cent.

[1] The secret treaty was signed August 16th, 1761, but the Spanish declaration of war was deferred until the treasure-ships from Spanish America should be in.

succession-duty, heavy poll-taxes on a graduated scale.[1] But even so the expenditure far exceeded the revenue, and, much against Lacy's wishes, before the campaign of 1762 every regiment had to be cut down by two companies.

Pitt's fall (Oct. 5th, 1761) was in itself something of an encouragement to Austria. The new King, George III, had boasted that he was no Hanoverian but "gloried in the name of Briton," and his new minister, Bute, wished to take advantage of the national dislike for paying heavy subsidies to German Princes by getting rid of the continental war. But any advantage that Austria might have gained in this way was more than balanced by the death, on January 5th, 1762, of the Czarina Elizabeth. Nothing could have been more timely for Frederick. The failure of the Russian armies to accomplish all that might have been hoped from them was in no degree due to lack of goodwill or keenness on the part of Elizabeth. It is partly to be attributed to the inefficient state of the Russian army, especially. of its administration, but still more to the fact that the Russian generals were well acquainted with the Grand Duke Peter's enthusiastic admiration for Frederick.[2] To this admiration Peter proceeded to give practical expression, first by concluding an armistice with Prussia and recalling Czernitchev's corps from Loudoun's army (March), then by making a definite peace (May), evacuating East Prussia altogether without any demand for compensation —which caused much discontent in Russia,—and guaranteeing Silesia to Frederick. He in return guaranteed Holstein to Peter. Sweden, whose part in the war had been neither prominent nor very satisfactory to herself, followed her neighbour's example and concluded (May) the Treaty of Hamburg, which restored the *status quo ante bellum*. The only compensating feature of the situation—from an Austrian point of view—was that all the arguments of the Prussian agents failed to induce Lord Bute to obtain from Parliament a renewal of the subsidy for the King of Prussia.

For the campaign of 1762, Austria gathered two armies, that in Silesia being once again entrusted to Daun, that in Saxony, which was to co-operate with the Army of the Empire,

---

[1] Cf. von Arneth, vi. pp. 255 ff.

[2] Peter III was the son of Anna, daughter of Peter the Great and Charles Frederick of Holstein-Gottorp.

to Serbelloni. But neither the latter nor his Imperialist colleague, Stolberg, proved a match for Prince Henry, who managed to separate them and drive the Imperial army back upon Franconia. Meanwhile Daun was confining his efforts to covering Schweidnitz and Glatz against Frederick, now reinforced by the release, by Peter's orders, of all the Prussian prisoners in Russian hands, and by the return of Czernitchev's corps which Peter declared it was his duty as a Lieutenant-General in the Prussian service to place at Frederick's disposal. When Czernitchev joined him at the end of June, Frederick took the offensive, feinting at Daun's left as though about to invade Bohemia. An attempt by Wied to seize the Adelsdorf position (July 2nd) was parried by Daun, and after some more futile manœuvres Frederick resolved to assault the Austrian positions South of Schweidnitz, between Burkersdorf and Dittmannsdorf. A corps under Wied moved round to the East to attack the Austrian right at Burkersdorf in rear, Möllendorf attacking in front (July 20th). Daun was somewhat remiss in looking after his rear and Brentano, sent up to save Leuthmannsdorf, arrived too late and failed to retake it, the result of which was that Daun fell back towards the Bohemian frontier and left Schweidnitz to its fate. In the action of July 21st, Czernitchev had played a passive but important part : his corps had manœuvred with the rest of Frederick's force, and its conduct had not given any reason to suppose that it was going to move away homewards next day. But yet another change had taken place in Russia. Peter's Germanising tendencies had offended the army and the clergy, his surrender of East Prussia had aroused Russian patriotism and, above all, his treatment of Catherine had offended her so bitterly that she placed herself at the head of a conspiracy which resulted in the deposition (July 9th) and murder (July 19th) of the unfortunate Czar. Catherine, though on the whole favourable to Austria, went no farther than to recall Czernitchev, otherwise she accepted the treaty of May; but short as Peter's reign had been he had managed to do a great deal for Frederick, and among the causes which enabled Prussia to surmount the dangers which threatened her Peter's assistance must take a high place. Entrusting the siege of Schweidnitz, which was begun on August 4th, to General Tauenzien, Frederick took post between Peterswaldau and Seitendorf to cover it. Daun made one attempt to raise the siege, but the failure of Lacy and Brentano to adequately support Beck's headlong onslaught on Bevern's corps at Peilau (Aug. 16th) convinced him that the task was impossible, and he fell back to the Bohemian frontier. Schweidnitz made a resolute defence, and the Prussians lacking skill in siege-craft it was not till October 9th that it surrendered. Daun was much to blame for his inactivity during this period. Exhausted as Austria was, Prussia was equally far spent; and had Daun pushed against Berlin and burnt it, or joined Serbelloni in Saxony and forced a battle on Henry, he might have even at that late hour turned the fortunes of the war, or at the least relieved Schweidnitz. In Saxony there had been a last flicker of military activity. At the end of August the Imperial army which had retired to Baireuth came back to Dresden through Eger and Chemnitz and joined the Austrians. Their advance forced Henry to leave his camp at Pretzchendorf and retire to Rossen (West of Dresden) on October 22nd, but Henry, catching the Army of the Empire isolated at Freiberg (October 29th), inflicted a severe defeat upon it which drove it back to Dippoldiswalde. It was perhaps appropriate that the last battle of the war should have been so typical of the utter collapse of the Imperial fabric, which the Silesian wars had reduced to a condition of all but complete decay.

One set of operations remains to be mentioned. The campaign of 1762 was not the least creditable of those fought by Ferdinand of Brunswick and his able English lieutenant, Granby. As usual, the French had two armies in the field, that of the Main under Soubise (80,000) posted from Altenkirchen by Cassel to Langensalza, that of the Rhine under Condé (30,000) between Cleves and Cologne. Ferdinand was first in the field, moving up to the Diemel early in June; and when Soubise came up to Wilhelmsthal and pushed de Castries forward in front of his right to Carlsdorff, Ferdinand moved against him. The French were already retiring when Granby, coming up from Warburg, fell on the corps of de Stainville, which sacrificed itself to cover the retreat of the main body, and cut it to pieces (June 24th). Soubise retired across the Fulda and took post between Cassel and Lutternberg, but Ferdinand again attacked him (July 24th) with success, and by pressing against his communications drove him out of Hesse before the end of August. Condé now coming up from the Rhine, joined Soubise (Aug. 30th) after beating off the Hereditary Prince, who had followed his movements.   The French then moved on Cassel to cut Ferdinand off from that town ; but he was too quick for them and, hastening up the Lahn, headed them off at Wetter (Sept. 15th).   They fell back and took post along the Ohm, their left at Marburg, their right at Homberg, Ferdinand taking post opposite them.   They made one attempt to force a passage by the bridge of Amöneburg (Sept. 21st); but though the attack was pushed home bravely, Granby's division (2 cavalry regiments and 8 infantry battalions) came up to the succour of Zastrow's Hanoverians and beat off every attack.   It was the last offensive movement of the French in the war.   Cassel, blockaded by Ferdinand as he moved South, was now (Oct. 16th) regularly invested.   On November 1st it fell, and in a fortnight came the news that an armistice had been concluded.

When it became obvious that not only was no more help to be expected from Russia, but that France was going to conclude a peace with England upon terms which would leave Maria Theresa isolated, even the Empress Queen resigned herself to relinquishing the attempt to recover the province filched from her in 1741.   Glatz, it is true, was still in her hands ; but she recognised that its retention was not worth the expense of another campaign, and while much of Saxony was still in Frederick's hands, the French had thrown away the trump-card in the diplomatic struggle by evacuating Prussia's Rhenish provinces without handing them over to Austria.   It was a step of which Maria Theresa had good right to complain, for the advantages which the Allies had won were thus sacrificed without any equivalent.   About the same time that preliminaries were signed at Fontainebleau between England and the Bourbon Powers, negotiations were opened between Austria and Prussia through the channel of Augustus III, the King of Poland being empowered to take advantage of Austria's pacific dispositions to get such terms as he could for his distressed Electorate.   Under this cloak, Austrian dignity was to some extent spared the humiliation involved in the evacuation of Glatz, on which Frederick absolutely insisted. Finally, after long negotiations the Peace of Hubertsberg (Feb. 15th, 1763) restored the arrangements of the

Berlin Treaty of 1745. Saxony recovered her lost territories, but Maria Theresa's efforts to regain Silesia had proved altogether unsuccessful. The only concession that could be extorted from Frederick was a promise of the Brandenburg vote at the election of a King of the Romans to Maria Theresa's eldest son, Joseph.

Thus in the end Prussia emerged without any territorial loss from a war in which with better management the Austrian schemes against her might have easily been brought to a successful conclusion, a war in which the star of the Hohenzollern monarchy had seemed on several occasions to be about to be permanently eclipsed; the great struggle left her exhausted and heavily burdened indeed, but with the prestige of having beaten off the attacks of an apparently invincible coalition. The credit for this result belongs very largely to Frederick himself. His only right to the possession of Silesia lay in his power to take and to keep it; but in enforcing the doctrine that might is right he had displayed a vigour, a tenacity, a courage in the most desperate extremities, which go far towards redeeming his case. If he could not plead, as Maria Theresa had been able to plead in 1741, that he was being attacked without just cause, he could at least claim the sympathy that naturally attaches to the weaker side, even though had he succumbed in the struggle he would have only had himself to thank for having originally provoked the contest. If his strategy and tactics were by no means free from serious error, and if he owed his escape very largely to the deficiencies of his enemies; their errors, their slowness, their hesitation, their failure to bring on the pitched battles by which alone the contest could be decided, only serve to show up in favourable light the opposite qualities of resolution, promptitude and vigour which marked the operations of Frederick. One man alone upon the Austrian side can be put upon a level with the Prussian King, and Loudoun never had the opportunity to give full scope to the talents which he was able to show that he possessed. He almost alone among the opponents of Frederick seems to have realised that a vigorous offensive would reduce the Prussian monarch to his last gasp far sooner than all the out-manœuvring in the world; that a policy of attrition by pitched battles was the true strategy; that the Allies could better afford to lose men or battles than Frederick could. Time after time Frederick was allowed to recover from blows which if promptly followed up must have been fatal. Moreover, Frederick was better served by his allies than was Maria Theresa by hers. If Daun deserves to be called slow and unenterprising, what is to be said of Apraxin and Fermor? Soltikov too, if an improvement on his predecessors, was quite as much to blame as Daun for the failure of the Allies' plans. Nevertheless, despite the inefficiency of her generals, Russia did actually play the deciding part in the war. Elizabeth's death was without question the decisive event of the long struggle: had she lived Frederick, if deprived of England's subsidy, could hardly have survived the campaign of 1762. As it was, Peter's short reign was just long enough for him to save Frederick, if in so doing he brought about his own fall. The part of France in the continental war was inglorious and ineffectual. Her armies received check after check from the altogether inferior forces of Ferdinand of Brunswick, whose reputation was as much enhanced by the war as that of Loudoun himself. Not one of her generals rose above mediocrity, most fell much below that level. Richelieu failed to pursue the advantages won in the only pitched battle of the war which resulted in a French success, but he did just enough to show the vast importance to Frederick of the work of the Anglo-Hanoverian army of Western Germany. In bringing that force together, maintaining it in the field, paying and supplying it, England, though at the same time achieving ends of her own, did Frederick a service of incalculable value. The rancour with which Frederick regarded his former ally and paymaster may be taken as some measure of the importance to him of Bute's departure from the policy of Pitt.[1] Indeed, paradoxical and somewhat exaggerated as the statement may sound, it may almost be said that it was France which saved Frederick by

---

[1] The question of Bute's policy towards Frederick belongs rather to the English side of the Seven Years' War. For refusing to continue the subsidy Bute had a fair case, especially in view of the intervention of Spain, and after the death of the Czarina Frederick was no longer in danger. But Frederick had some reason for his belief that Bute had meant to leave him in the lurch, and in the course of the Anglo-French negotiations the relations between England and Prussia became greatly strained. In the end, however, it was England which secured the restoration to Frederick of his Westphalian territories, and such cause for complaint as Frederick had was rather against the manner in which Bute had conducted his measures than against his actual actions.

taking an active part in the coalition against him. It was because France was attacking Hanover that England had to take active steps on behalf of Frederick. Had Hanover been neutralised and the French share in the war confined to the fulfilment of the obligations contracted in 1756, it is not likely that a single English soldier would have set foot on German soil, or that English money would have found its way into Frederick's coffers.

But if Frederick must be considered fortunate in having weathered the storms of the Third Silesian War, his prestige and the whole position of Prussia not only in Germany but in Europe were enormously enhanced by the result. If Prussia was still second to Austria in Germany, her position far more nearly approached to that of Austria than it did to that of Bavaria, or Hanover, or Saxony. She was not only a practically independent state, for so were they to all intents and purposes, but she was a factor of principal importance in the affairs of Europe, while they were only subordinates, accessories, minor members of alliances. Austria's position in Germany had not indeed been directly assailed by Prussia. Frederick had not sought to substitute the Hohenzollern for the Hapsburgs as the leading power in Germany. It can hardly be said that there was any " German " side to his policy. He aimed at independent political existence. In his relations with the minor states of Germany he sought at the most to prevent Austria reviving the old Imperial forms with which she was still invested. It may be argued that in a way he was fighting the battle of the German Princes, inasmuch as success in the humiliation and partition of Prussia would have altogether altered the footing on which Austria stood in relation to the other members of the Empire; but even so to fight for the independence of the German Princes was not to fight for Germany or for German nationality. On the contrary, it still further increased, if possible, the disunion of Germany and the decay of the Empire. To a certain extent, no doubt, German sentiment rejoiced in the defeat of the French at Rossbach. That rejoicing, however, was mainly due to the misconduct of the French, whose indiscipline, exemplified in rapacity and marauding, made them hateful to the inhabitants of the countries they visited. There were no such rejoicings over Leuthen or Torgau. The re-establishment of

Austrian rule in Silesia was not unpopular, nor did the Silesian peasantry indulge in guerilla warfare against the Austrians. The Prussian plundering incursions into Thuringia and other parts of the Empire roused the bitterest resentment and dislike, and if the army of the Empire failed to do any damage to the Prussian cause, it is not necessary to attribute that to goodwill towards Frederick. The Würtemberg contingent in the Austrian army in 1757 was notorious for the desertions from its ranks, but they deserted to avoid taking part in a war about which they did not care, not because they saw in Frederick the champion of oppressed German nationality. Desertion was rife in both armies, and was hardly ever, except in the case of the Saxons forcibly drafted into the Prussian ranks,[1] sentimental or political. It was always practical, due to want of food, to want of pay, to hardships of one sort or other. The only real effect of the war on Germany was to complete the utter disintegration of the German kingdom which had suffered so much through its association with the Holy Roman Empire. Germany was yet to drain the cup of humiliation to the dregs; but that Germany was trampled under foot by the Corsican upstart until at last her sufferings aroused the slumbering sense of German nationality and German unity, was in no small measure due to the fact that the Silesian wars had destroyed all possibility of the Hapsburg House reuniting Germany under its leadership or breathing new life into the moribund fabric of the Empire, and that the Revolution found her a mere geographical expression, no less devoid of unity than Italy itself.

[1] Cf. p. 199, footnote.

CHAPTER XIV

AUSTRIA AND PRUSSIA AFTER THE WAR AND THE PARTITION OF POLAND

ON the restoration of peace the first object to which Frederick turned was the repairing of the ravages of the war. It was no light task. Not only had the provinces which had been the theatre of war been plundered and swept bare by the contending armies, but even the districts which had escaped the presence of the belligerents had been drained dry of men and money to enable the King to prosecute the struggle. Frederick promptly dismissed some 30,000 of his troops, sending them back to till the fields; he disposed of his cavalry and artillery horses to the farmers; the war-chest which had been replenished by great efforts for the campaign he had not had to fight disgorged its contents, which were sparingly and prudently distributed to relieve the most pressing needs. The war had, of course, been paid for in large part by the contributions exacted from countries he had overrun, above all from the luckless Saxony, by the large subsidies from England, by depreciating the coinage, which was now redeemed at only one-fifth of its face value, and by withholding their salaries from the civil servants of the state. They had been paid in promissory notes, which Frederick now proceeded to pay off in the depreciated currency at its nominal not its real value. It was a characteristic act, a gross piece of injustice which meant ruin to a good many overworked and underpaid officials, but a successful stroke, for it materially reduced the claims upon the Prussian exchequer.

The measures which Frederick took at this time to promote agriculture and industry, to attract colonists to the depopulated provinces, to increase home products and make Prussia independent of foreign countries, especially of Polish corn, do not differ in kind from the similar steps taken by his father.[1]

Cf. Chapter V.

Roads, bridges, canals and other public works were undertaken. Extensive reclamations of waste and swampy lands
added nearly 1500 square miles to the cultivatable area of
the kingdom. A rigid policy of protection unsparingly enforced did much to establish in Prussia industries hitherto
unknown. The production and manufacture of silk and
cotton goods, the promotion of the woollen industry by
prohibiting the export of the raw material, while sheep
farming was encouraged by the introduction of Spanish
sheep, the offer of bounties to attract the skilled workmen
of other countries to Prussia, were all part of an economic
policy based on the principles of the Mercantile System and
enforced with a thoroughness few other monarchs could rival.
Commerce it was not Frederick II's policy to foster. In his
eyes the future of Prussia was not on the sea; and although
Embden, acquired in 1744, was made a free port and the
tolls on the Oder were lowered for the benefit of Stettin,
he looked rather to the creation of a self-centred, self-sufficing
State, producing a large revenue and capable of supporting
a large army. The effect of his economic policy on the
social conditions of the kingdom served to accentuate the
spirit of militarism he did so much to foster. Apart from
the *Ritterpferd* which he maintained[1] the nobles were as a
class exempt from taxation ; and this distinction did much
to perpetuate class barriers, to keep down the townsfolk and
the peasantry, whom Frederick looked upon merely as tax
and recruit producers, and to prevent them from uniting.
Moreover, the political condition of Prussia assisted to repress
the tax-paying classes. Absolutism had been made the guiding
principle by Frederick William I; Frederick II did not in the
least diminish his hold on power. Not even the nobles
shared to any extent in the administration of the country.
It was in the hands of a well-organised, centralised bureaucracy,
efficient but unsympathetic. Throughout the country, from the
bailiffs who administered the Domains through the *Landräthe*,
who, like the Sheriffs in mediæval England, kept the peace,
attended to the levy of contributions and acted as the King's
agent in their district, and the tax commissioners who were
responsible for the excise and the police, to the members of
the General Directory itself, all the officials were the King's

---

[1] In 1745 he allowed it to be capitalised and redeemed.

servants, owing their appointments to him, responsible to him alone. The defects of the system were not, of course, apparent, whilst the man on whom the supreme direction of affairs devolved was as resolute, as vigorous and as efficient as Frederick, but the burden he could bear was too much for a less capable successor. His ministers, depending entirely on him and accustomed to look to him for orders rather than decide even minor points on their own responsibility, were clerks and subordinates rather than administrators, and the removal of his guiding hand was followed by the breakdown of the system he had inherited from his father and had handed on unchanged in the main though improved in details. He had been vigilant and strong enough to check corruption and peculation, but those inherent defects of an over-centralised and underpaid bureaucracy proved too much for an inefficient wielder of the central power.

In the organisation established in 1723 Frederick II did not make many changes. The Directory, originally organised in four departments on a territorial basis, was increased by separate departments for trade and manufactures and for military affairs. The Provincial Chambers formed the links between the Directory and the local *Landräthe* and tax commissioners. Foreign affairs were entrusted to an altogether separate department, including usually two or three ministers, one of whom was of special importance, and may be looked upon as the chief. Similarly the War Council (*Geheime Kriegs Rath*) was quite a distinct body. In the reform of justice and the judicial system, Frederick did rather more. Aided by von Cocceji, head of the Department of Justice since 1738, he sought to grapple with the expenses and delays of litigation, the collusion and corruption of solicitors and assessors, and the overcrowded state of the judicial bench. In 1746 the control over justice, hitherto exercised by the Directory, was transferred to the special legal Department. Procedure was abridged to expedite litigation. The number of the judges was reduced, and good jurists appointed at adequate salaries. Arrears of work were systematically tackled by Cocceji, province by province, and were cleared off. The Common Law was codified, and the confusion arising from the mixture of Roman, Teutonic, and barbarian laws materially reduced, the new code being based on Roman law, but modified to suit the social system of Prussia. Subordinated to the Department of Justice was the *Consistorium*, a body which looked after education and religious affairs; but Frederick, himself practically a Free Thinker, was not the kind of man to pay overmuch attention to the latter subject. The only important step he took in this respect was the establishment of religious toleration for practically all creeds, the Jews alone being still subjected to very considerable restrictions.

Frederick's system was one which bore heavily on most classes of his subjects. Taxation was heavy, and the partial exemption enjoyed by the nobles therefore all the more emphasised their position as a separate caste marked off from the rest of the nation by social and fiscal privileges. The lot of the peasantry was far from easy. If not exactly slaves, they were certainly not free, being *ascripti glebæ* and as such liable to change masters with the estates to which they belonged. Not only had they to pay a quite disproportionate share of the taxes, but it was from them that the recruits were drawn under the cantonment system. They had to spend much of their time working for their lords, to hand over to them a large part of the produce of their labour, and to perform personal and menial services. Nor was it, as a rule, possible for a peasant to better his station in life. Frederick, while realising to some extent the evils of the situation, refrained from making any attempt to alter them, for fear apparently of in any way subverting the rigid discipline on which the Prussian state was based.

This rigid discipline was felt as much by civilian officials as by soldiers. The Civil Service was so harshly and vigorously treated that it was not wonderful that it was not popular. The absolutism of the King and the cramping fetters of official routine left no scope for the development of individual initiative and efficiency. The machine of the Prussian administration happened to be efficient under Frederick II, but the efficiency was due to external impulses and not to any inherent quality. Lacking in organic vitality, it derived its efficiency from the King's vigilant and inspiring personality; left to itself it was bound to perish under the weight of its own routine. It has been well described as "an organised bureaucracy with a numerous personnel, with roots and branches shooting in every direction, with a code of procedure that provided for nearly every problem that might arise and a system of discipline that kept all the parts in a state of harmonious subjection." Yet with all these good qualities it was a mere machine, it needed a master hand to guide it.

Not dissimilar were the conditions which prevailed in the Army. Here again there was a rigidly enforced uniformity, a highly organised administration, a system which, in the thirty years of peace that intervened before it was again engaged in any serious war, was allowed to become the end in itself and not the means. The parade-ground was allowed to obscure the battlefield, and when Lord Cornwallis visited the Prussian manœuvres in 1785 he found that the practical had been sacrificed to a precision carried to the verge of pedantry.[1] The deep gulf fixed between officers and men might help to make the maintenance of due subordination more easy, but it was detrimental to true cohesion, and the savage discipline needed to keep in proper subjection an army mainly composed of foreign mercenaries to a certain extent defeated its own ends. Worst of all was the fact that so large a proportion of the men were not subjects of the King they served. This made the Army non-national; and though Frederick II, who had the gift of leadership and of getting the last ounce of work out of all his subordinates, Ministers of State and privates of foot alike, did manage to keep his men together by a belief in him and by the glamour of his reputation, his successors had no such qualities. But after 1763 the Prussian army was resting on its well-earned laurels. There was no other army on the Continent which could compare with it, and the defects which were to prove fatal to it in 1792 and 1806 had yet to develope to their full extent.

Like her enemy Frederick, Maria Theresa was also engaged on the task of reconstruction. She had failed in the purpose she had set before her, she had been forced to leave Silesia in Prussian hands and to acquiesce in the failure of the plans so carefully laid and matured. Yet in some respects Austria's position in 1763 was not as bad

[1] Cf. his letter to Colonel Ross, *Cornwallis Correspondence*, i. 212.

as might have been expected.   The war had cost her dear
in men and in money, but a large part of the expense had
been defrayed by the French subsidies, and since the abortive
invasion of Moravia in 1758 the Austrian territories had
escaped being the theatre of war.   Her provinces were therefore, at any rate when compared with the miserable condition
of Saxony, East Prussia, Silesia and Westphalia, in a fairly
flourishing state, and when once the excessive burdens
imposed during the war were removed their condition
improved rapidly.

But the war had been a severe trial to the civil and
military organisation of Austria, and in several directions
further changes in the system remodelled by Haugwitz were
shown to be necessary.   Of these the most important was
the establishment (1758), at the suggestion of Kaunitz, of a
Council of State to advise the sovereign, and so secure a
more efficient supervision of the whole administration than
the Directory had so far provided.   This Council was to
be composed of leading men of great experience and influence
in the state rather than merely of the heads of the various
departments of the government, though the Chancellor was
to be a member *ex officio*.   It was to advise and supervise,
not to execute, and foreign and military affairs did not come
within its province, while the non-German provinces were not
subjected to it.[1]   Haugwitz, whom Chotek succeeded as Court
Chancellor (*Obersthofkanzler*), and Count Henry Blümegen,
afterwards to be one of Joseph II's principal subordinates,
were the chief members of the new Council, and the young
Archduke Joseph was constantly present at its discussions.

Soon after the Peace of Hubertsburg the election of
Joseph as King of the Romans, defeated on a former occasion
by Prussian opposition, was brought to a successful conclusion.   Frederick was pledged to vote for Joseph by the
terms of the Peace, Hanover had all along favoured his
election, the ecclesiastical Electors could easily be secured
by a small outlay, and Saxony was the close ally of Austria.
Any opposition that Bavaria or the Palatinate felt inclined
to offer was removed by various promises and slight concessions, and the election was unanimous.

Despite the disappointment of the high hopes Maria

[1] Wolf, p. 96.

Theresa had based upon the new alliance with the House
of Bourbon, it was now one of her principal objects to
maintain that alliance, and if possible to draw it closer by
a series of marriages between members of the Bourbon and
the Hapsburg families. Thus Joseph had married Isabella
of Parma, and on her death at the early age of twenty-one,
in November 1763, it was suggested that he should marry
another Princess of the same family, while three of the
Archduchesses were married to Bourbon Princes, Caroline to
Ferdinand of Naples in April 1768, Amelia to Ferdinand
of Parma in 1769, Marie Antoinette to the Dauphin, afterwards Louis XVI of France, in 1770. Even more political
importance attached to the marriage of the Archduke
Leopold, the second surviving son of the Empress, to the
Infanta Louise, daughter of Charles III of Spain, as it was
agreed that the Emperor should hand over to Leopold the
Duchy of Tuscany, all claims on which Joseph resigned.
The wedding had only just been celebrated at Innsbruck
when, on August 18th, 1765, the Emperor was suddenly
smitten by an apoplectic seizure and died. Francis Stephen
of Lorraine is a man who plays a prominent part in history
through the accident of his marriage to Maria Theresa rather
than by reason of his own very mediocre capacities. Neither
as a statesman nor as a general did he distinguish himself,
and Maria Theresa's excessive grief and extravagant praise
of his virtues cannot hide the fact that he had never been
in himself a person of much weight. The Empress seems
for a time to have contemplated retiring into a convent and
handing all power over to her son, who styled himself
Emperor from the moment of his father's death, and whom
she now took into partnership with her as joint ruler
(Dec. 1765). But this idea did not last long, and Maria
Theresa soon again assumed the reins of government,
though sharing her power with her son and to a great extent
with Kaunitz. Seeing how completely Joseph's views on
most questions of importance differed from his mother's, she
conservative, religious to the verge of bigotry, aristocratic in
sentiment, well versed in affairs and well acquainted with
men, he an ardent reformer, tolerant and broad-minded,
almost indifferent in religious matters, a tactless doctrinaire
unable to distinguish the practical from the unwise, it is

much to his credit that they should have worked together as smoothly as they did and should have got on so well. Causes of friction were frequent, several big differences occurred, but Joseph always preferred to give way to his mother's opinion rather than cause a deadlock by persisting in his own, even when thoroughly convinced of its justice. Kaunitz, too, had a difficult task. The strongest ties of regard, affection and gratitude bound him to the mistress he had served so faithfully and by whom he had always been implicitly trusted. To have to intervene as a third party between the Empress and her son, especially as on many matters he agreed with Joseph, was no pleasant task, but on the whole he came out of the ordeal with great success.

Joseph was not slow about setting out on a career of reforms. He cut down the establishment, the ceremonial and the expenses of the Court, gave up the vast hunting establishment left by his father, turned the Prater into a public park, devoted the private fortune bequeathed to him by his father to assist in the conversion of the debt and the reduction of the interest from five to four per cent. Such were the economies he effected that by 1775 the revenue not only balanced the expenses, but there was actually a surplus of five and a half million gulden, a condition of affairs almost unprecedented in Austria.

In the ranks of the Ministers several changes occurred about this time. Haugwitz had died in 1765, Chotek, his successor as *Hofkanzler*, in 1771, on which Hatzfeldt became the minister next in importance to Kaunitz. Kolowrat succeeded Hatzfeldt at the Treasury; and when, in the hope of securing unity in the administration, Hatzfeldt was made President of the Council of State, the post of *Hofkanzler* was given to Henry Blümegen. In the reform of the army, Joseph was keenly interested. Daun had already in 1762 replaced Joseph Harrach at the head of the War Council, and did good service till his death in 1765. Joseph thereupon appointed Lacy to the vacant post, thereby passing over some thirty other officers, among them Loudoun, certainly Lacy's superior on the field of battle. But administration was Lacy's province, and he did excellent work in improving the organisation, drill and equipment of the army, establishing a definite General Staff, attending to fortifications and bringing the Supply Department properly under the control of the War Council. These reforms were of the greatest benefit to the army, but they led to collisions with the civil authorities and even with the Emperor, and in 1774 Lacy retired, being replaced by Andreas Hadik.

But while doing all this as head of the Hapsburg dominions, Joseph was at heart even more anxious to revive the Empire and to galvanise it into fresh life. The task was an all but hopeless one, but it does seem that there is no small truth in the remark that " Joseph was a Lorrainer, not a Hapsburg." If that saying implies that Joseph's great desire was to be able to restore the Empire to a really active and working condition, it is probably right. A study of his foreign policy [1] does seem to show that it was on the Upper rather than on the Lower Danube that his hopes centred. Bavaria meant more to him than the Balkans. But the Aulic Council (*Reichshofrath*) was a poor weapon with which to effect great reforms, and the Imperial Court (*Hofgericht*) was dilatory and negligent and treated its office as a mere source of profit. The condition of the *Reichskammergericht* at Wetzlar was no better. Hopelessly corrupt and inefficient, it had let cases accumulate till in 1772 over 60,000 were waiting to be decided: one case in particular had been going on for a hundred and eighty-eight years. Joseph ordered a Visitation (May 1767), the first since 1588, but it could do little good. It was not of much use to dismiss indolent and corrupt officials when the root of the matter lay in the complete collapse of the Empire. It had practically ceased to exist, and in its stead were numerous small states more or less independent, too small for any real national life of their own, too independent to allow of any united national life, while the more powerful among them devoted all their energies towards self-aggrandisement in every possible way. It may be argued that under Joseph II Austria was just as ready to grasp at any scrap of territory on which she could lay her hands as was any other Power. The accusation is in large measure true ; but in seeking to increase his dominions in Germany, Joseph was acting as Emperor, as representative of the unity—such as it was—of Germany, not merely as the head of his family, or even as one among the " great

[1] Cf. Chapter XV.

Powers" of Europe. He was striving to restore reality to the historic position which he held.

The first country whose affairs claimed the attention of Germany after the close of the Silesian Wars was its unhappy neighbour on the East, Poland. In October 1763, Augustus II of Saxony-Poland had died. Neither as the enemy nor as the ally of Austria had he had much success. His Electorate, the buffer state between the contending forces of the Hapsburgs and the Hohenzollern, had suffered enormously in the wars: his Kingdom had served as the base for the operations of the Russians, and its condition was but little better. His death was probably accelerated by the disasters and disappointments he had gone through, and it was followed in December by that of his successor, Frederick Christian. Thus, not only was the Polish throne vacant, but the Saxon House was unable to put forward a candidate for the vacancy, since the heir to Saxony, Augustus, son of Elector Frederick Christian, was only twelve years old. Austria now found herself in an awkward situation. She strongly approved of the presence of the Saxon dynasty at Warsaw, since her interests were best served when the Polish throne was occupied by a Prince independent of Russia and not over friendly with Prussia. Despite the alliance with France, she rather distrusted the extraordinary intrigues by which Louis XV sought to obtain the Polish throne for the Prince de Conti. Still she was unable to find a suitable candidate to oppose to Stanislaus Poniatowski, the Polish nobleman whom Russia with the support of Prussia now put forward. Poniatowski's candidature was not altogether popular in Poland. The Czartoriski family with which he was connected was the main strength of the Russophil faction, and the opponents of this faction would probably have been prepared to resist his election had Austria and France shown themselves ready to support such resistance. But Maria Theresa had had enough of war: she did not mean to appeal to arms again if she could help it, and her diplomacy was henceforward greatly hampered by this unwillingness to fight. Austria and France accordingly had to content themselves with the empty protest of withdrawing their representatives from Warsaw, and in September 1764, Poniatowski was duly elected. His election was really a triumph for Russia, for Frederick had played a somewhat

subordinate part, and the overtures he before long made to
Austria may be interpreted as a recognition of the dangers
with which Germany was threatened by the undue aggrandisement of her formidable Eastern neighbour. It was clearly
Russia's policy to absorb Poland if she could, failing that
to subject the Republic completely to her influence. Neither
of these courses would have been to Frederick's liking, since
both would put barriers in the way of his acquisition of the
coveted district of West Prussia. But apart from this, it was
certainly not to his advantage or to Austria's that Russia
should become predominant in Poland. Had Austria and
Prussia combined to set the Polish constitution on a rational
basis and to help Poniatowski, who showed himself less
amenable to Russian authority than had been expected, to
assert and maintain his independence, Poland might have been
made an efficient " buffer state " against the Russian advance;
but Silesia barred the way to a reconciliation and Frederick's
aims were to be attained by the disintegration of Poland
rather than by its revival. Moreover, Maria Theresa's religious
bigotry caused her to look with disfavour on the proposal to
remove the disabilities of the Dissidents, one of the main
causes of Polish disunion. She would have been glad to unite
with France to guarantee the integrity of Poland, but she distrusted Frederick too much to co-operate with him in anything
and she was specially anxious to prevent him gaining any
influence over Joseph, who was already somewhat inclined tc
hold sceptical and cynical views of political and religious affairs.

Meanwhile the troubles of Poland culminated in conflicts
between the adherents of the Greek Church and of the
Catholic religion. The attempt of Stanislaus to abrogate
the *Liberum Veto* was foiled by Russian opposition (Nov.
1766), and in the following year the Russophil party formed
the Confederation of Radom, terrified the Diet into accepting
certain modifications of the constitution and appointed
Catherine its guardian. In reply, the Catholics, led by
Marshall Krasinski, formed the Confederation of Bar. Religious riots on a large scale followed, and practically the
whole country was plunged into civil war. Russian troops
intervened on behalf of their partisans and, in pursuing some
Polish fugitives, violated the frontier of Turkey. France had
already been urging the Porte to send assistance to the Poles,

and the Turks were not slow to declare war (Oct. 1768). One important result was that Austria, wishing to observe strict neutrality, guarded her frontier with a strong military cordon, while to prevent disputes the frontier was marked out by a line of posts bearing the Austrian eagles. The opportunity was taken to include inside these limits the district of Zips, formerly part of Hungary which had been pledged to Lladislaus Jagellon by the Emperor Sigismund. The reoccupation of this district, geographically part of Hungary since it took Poland over the Carpathians, was carried out with Stanislaus Poniatowski's full agreement; but at Joseph's orders the line of demarcation included Sandez, Neumarkt and Csorsztyn, which were also claimed as part of Hungary.

The situation called forth from Kaunitz a characteristically ingenious plan for the recovery of Silesia. An alliance was to be formed between Austria, Prussia and Turkey to save Poland and check the Russian advance. Poland was to provide the "satisfaction" for Prussia, which in return for her good offices was to receive Courland and West Prussia but to surrender Silesia to Austria, while Turkey would find her share of the benefits of the alliance in getting safely through a war which from the very start had gone ill with her. This plan, however, was too revolutionary and too chimerical to commend itself; Maria Theresa and even Joseph hated the notion of any alliance with Prussia. Still, Kaunitz saw that if Austria did not mean to give actual support to Turkey, and of this there was no intention, the only possible course was joint action with Prussia; and as the result of his persistent advocacy of this course there occurred the celebrated interviews between Joseph and Frederick at Neisse in August 1769 and at Neustadt in the following year. Frederick used all the arts of which he was master to flatter and cajole the young Emperor, whose admiration for the renowned Prussian King was far from being to the liking of Maria Theresa. No immediate results followed, however, except that Frederick saw he need not fear Austrian opposition.

Meanwhile the danger of war was increasing. The Russian successes against the Turks continued, and Austria collected a large force in Hungary ready to fall on the communications of the Russians should they advance across the Danube. In July 1771, Thugut, Austria's representative at Constantinople, con-

cluded a convention with Turkey by which Austria undertook
to save Turkey from a peace on humiliating terms. In return
she was to receive Little Wallachia and a large subsidy.
Maria Theresa objected strongly to the transaction, for which
Joseph and Kaunitz were really responsible. She refused to
ratify it, feeling that it compromised Austria's dignity, took
an unfair advantage of a Power which had acted most
honourably in Austria's hour of need in 1741, and also fearing
that it would lead to war. It was to this prospect that
Frederick also objected. He did not wish to be involved in a
war against Austria and Turkey on behalf of Russia, nor was
he anxious to see Austria and Russia arrive at an understanding. It was quite a possibility that Austria might induce
Russia to content herself with moderate gains, and might
obtain these concessions from Turkey, and that then Russia
and Austria might firmly oppose any partition of Poland,
thereby preventing Frederick from acquiring the much-coveted
West Prussia. For a partition was the expedient by which
Frederick sought to extricate the three Powers from their
dilemma. It would hardly be profitable to follow the complicated intrigues, proposals and counter-projects in detail.
The idea of a partition was not, of course, new. Maximilian II
in 1573, Charles X of Sweden in 1657, Alberoni, even
Augustus II of Saxony in 1733, had suggested schemes for it;
but Frederick and his brother Prince Henry [1] were responsible
for bringing it forward now. Catherine disliked it as preventing her from absorbing all Poland; it was only with real and
sincere reluctance that Maria Theresa at last listened to the
urgent advocacy of it by Kaunitz and Joseph. Russia had
forborne to push her successes across the Danube for fear of
Austrian intervention; she was ready to relinquish Moldavia
and Wallachia if compensation could be found in Poland.
But when Austria proposed that the Czarina should, in consideration of Austria's mediation of a peace between her and
Turkey, support Austria in resisting any division of Poland,
Catherine declined to accept the proposal, and Kaunitz found
that the Czarina and Frederick were already in practical
agreement, and that they had no intention of letting go those
portions of Poland which they had resolved to annex. It would
appear that this had been settled as early as February 1771

---

[1] Cf. Mirabeau, *Secret History of the Court of Berlin*, i. 312.

when Prince Henry visited Catherine. In November, Frederick
informed van Swieten, the Austrian envoy to Berlin, that
Russia intended to take compensation for the Danubian
Principalities at the expense of Poland. In December, Austria
learnt definitely that Frederick meant to annex West Prussia
as his share. The only problem, since it was out of the
question for Austria to prevent the Partition, as Choiseul had
fallen and England was fully occupied across the Atlantic, was
whether she should join the spoilers or mark her disapproval of
their action by protests. There was no question in the minds
of Joseph and Kaunitz. Their "land hunger" was almost
worthy of a Hohenzollern. The balance of power must be
maintained; Austria could not afford to stand aside when her
neighbours were making territorial gains. The doctrine of
compensation by equivalents was a specious cloak for greed.
Even Maria Theresa would have raised no objection to the
annexation of West Prussia if Frederick would have resigned
Glatz and part of Silesia, a concession he refused to contemplate. To sharing in the Partition she was strongly opposed,
and indignantly repudiated the charge that Austria had begun
the spoliation of Poland by the occupation of Zips. Super-
ficially, of course, this would seem to be the case, but there was
a great difference between the reoccupation of a small piece
of territory, Poland's right to which was certainly disputable,
and wholesale annexations amounting to a third of the whole
country. At the same time it was unfortunate that the pretext
should have been given to people who knew how to use it as
well as Frederick and Catherine did.

In February 1772 the Russian Ambassador definitely
invited Austria's co-operation in the treaty of partition arranged
by Frederick and Catherine, intimating that Austria's action
would in no case affect the resolve of these two contracting
parties. At this Maria Theresa yielded with the greatest
reluctance and unwillingness, whereupon it was discovered
that Galicia had formerly been part of Hungary, and a formal
claim was produced. Kaunitz as usual claimed more than he
dreamt of getting in order not to get less than he hoped; but
Joseph, taking over the direction of the affair, marched troops
into the districts he meant to have, and thus secured what he
wanted. On August 2nd, 1772, the treaty of partition was
signed at St. Petersburg, and on September 26th Austria

published a proclamation annexing Galicia. Poland was powerless to resist, and in September 1773 bribery coupled with threats of violence wrung from the reluctant Diet its consent to the scheme. Kaunitz would have been glad to take the opportunity to make certain reforms in the Polish constitution, notably the abolition of the *Liberum Veto*, and to add to the Royal revenues by secularising certain bishoprics; but these suggested improvements of the condition of the Republic were not at all to the liking of Russia and Prussia, and though in the next fifteen years a certain number of minor reforms were effected, to maintain the weakness of Poland was a cardinal point in the designs of Catherine and of Frederick.

Of the three participators in this high-handed action, Russia took the largest share, advancing her Western frontier to the Dwina and Druck. To Austria there fell Lemberg, Belz and parts of Cracow and Sandomir, a district which contained valuable salt mines. Prussia, which contented herself with Pomerelia, Marienburg and Ermeland, with the larger portions of the Palatinates of Kulm, Posen and Gniezno, obtained the territorial connection with East Prussia which had so long been coveted by the Hohenzollern; and her share, if the smallest in area, was of far more advantage to her than was Austria's to Austria, even if the all-important Dantzic still remained unabsorbed.

The Partition of Poland is an action which it is much easier to condemn in the strongest terms than to extenuate in the least. It is the typical example of the "land hunger," which so dominated the rulers of Europe in the 18th Century as to make them quite impervious to the dictates of common fairness. It is an action quite in keeping with Frederick's previous career; and the only reason why Catherine's share in it excites surprise is that Russia would so obviously have preferred to keep Poland undivided in the hope of wholesale annexation; but one is not prepared to find Maria Theresa in such company or sharing in so discreditable an action. The truth would seem to be that Joseph and Kaunitz between them were too much for her.

That the dismembered provinces, those at least which fell into the hands of Austria and Prussia, profited materially by the exchange, hardly affords in itself a sufficient justification for their annexation. Indeed, it rather lends force to the argument that by stopping short of a complete partition the three Powers had deprived themselves of their only defence. Had they pleaded, as they might reasonably have pleaded, that the condition of Poland was so bad that partition was the only remedy, that reform was out of the question, the plea might be admitted, but the admission only makes the partial partition the more inexcusable. A complete partition would have involved conflicts that might have ended in war, and the partners preferred to avoid that.

Joseph proceeded to carry his point as to the administration of his new province. Galicia was treated like one of the regular Austrian provinces, and a Chancery was established for it at Vienna instead of its being placed directly under the control of the State Chancery as were Lombardy and the Netherlands, or, as the Hungarians desired, incorporated as Zips had been in Hungary. In 1775 it was given Estates after the pattern of the German provinces; but their functions were to advise rather than to decide, and the question they had to settle was not " whether " but " how " taxes should be raised. On the whole, Austrian rule soon became fairly popular, though the nobles regretted the exemption from taxation and the greater licence to please themselves which they had enjoyed under Polish rule.

Meanwhile one result of Austria and Russia agreeing upon joint action in Poland had been to avert all danger of a collision between them on the Danube. Russia agreed to restore Moldavia and Wallachia to Turkey, and this she did when, after an abortive congress at Fokschau, brought together under the auspices of the ministers of Austria and Prussia (August 1772), had failed to bring about peace, repeated defeats caused Turkey to conclude the disastrous Peace of Kainardji in July 1774. It is not exactly to Joseph's credit, nor to that of Kaunitz either, that Austria, pretending that she had fulfilled her share of the 1771 compact in inducing Russia to relinquish the Danubian Principalities, retained possession of the Bukovina district [1] which her troops had occupied at the time of the Austro-Turkish convention. The district was maintained under military rule till 1786, being under the General commanding at Lemberg subject to the supervision of the War Council; it was then united to the adjacent province of Galicia.

[1] Northern Moldavia, formerly part of Transylvania but lost to the Turks in the 15th Century.

CHAPTER XV

THE FOREIGN POLICY OF JOSEPH II

THE share of Austria in the Partition of Poland is not least interesting as affording evidence that the direction of the foreign policy of the Hapsburgs was passing from the hands of Maria Theresa to those of her ambitious and energetic son. It was Joseph whose desire for territorial acquisitions had brought Austria into line with the holder of Silesia, Joseph who must be held responsible for the unworthy subterfuges by which a cloak of right was given to the retention of Bukovina, an action which was a poor return for Turkey's conduct in 1741. And in the next international incident in which Austria was involved it was again Joseph who was the principal mover: Maria Theresa's part was limited to that of a commentator.

If there was any district in Germany upon which a Hapsburg was likely to look with covetous eyes it was the country to the West of him, not very much farther up the Danube. The importance of Bavaria to Austria is one of the commonplaces of strategical geography: the years 1703–1704 and 1741–1744 tell their own tale. Moreover, to acquire even a part of Bavaria would enormously strengthen Austria's political prestige in the Empire, enable her to exercise a far greater influence in Southern Germany, and afford some compensation for the diminution which the German element in the Hapsburg dominions had suffered in the loss of Silesia. For these reasons, if for no others, Joseph took no small interest in the succession to Maximilian Joseph, the childless Elector of Bavaria. As to the immediate heir, indeed, there was no doubt. Charles Theodore of Sulzbach, Elector Palatine since 1742, was the next representative of the common ancestor of the Bavarian and

Palatinate branches of the House of Wittelsbach.[1] But Charles Theodore was also without legitimate heirs; he cared very little for Bavaria; took no account of the wishes of the Bavarians or of his heir presumptive, Charles II of Zweibrücken-Birkenfeld,[2] in whose hands the scattered possessions of the Landsberg, Kleeberg, Zweibrücken and Bischweiler branches[3] had become united. So far as he cared for anything except the gratification of his own pleasures, Charles Theodore was interested in the dominions he already possessed on the Rhine, and was especially anxious to preserve Jülich and Berg from falling into the hands of Frederick II of Prussia, whom he suspected of designs upon them. It was not very difficult, therefore, for Joseph to come to an agreement with him. Negotiations for an Austrian guarantee of Jülich and Berg in return for the Elector's recognition of the claims on Bavaria which Austria had no difficulty in finding when a pretext was wanted, had begun in 1776 and were in progress when, in December 1777, Maximilian Joseph died.

Maria Theresa was opposed to the line of action upon which Joseph and Kaunitz had resolved. It rather too much resembled the treatment she had herself received in 1741 to find favour in her eyes. To bring up an old 15th Century arrangement by which the Emperor Sigismund had granted Lower Bavaria to Albert V of Austria as a female fief[4] and to claim Lower Bavaria on the extinction of the main Wittelsbach line in virtue of this former ownership, was only veiling mere greed for territory under a transparent covering of legality. For the claim on parts of the Upper Palatinate as fiefs of the Bohemian Crown there was perhaps a rather better case, and the Emperor had the right to sequester a vacant fief of the Empire, though to annex it to his hereditary dominions would exceed his powers. However, despite the Empress-Queen's disapproval, Joseph and Kaunitz proceeded to conclude a convention with Charles Theodore (January 2nd, 1778) by which the Elector recognised Austria's right to

---

[1] This was Lewis II, Duke of Bavaria (1253–1294) and Elector Palatine; at his death (1294) his territories had been divided, Bavaria going to Lewis III, Emperor 1314–1347, the Palatinate to the latter's brother Rudolf.

[2] A distant cousin, descended from Wolfgang of Zweibrücken (1532–1569), the common ancestor of the Neuburg, Sulzbach, Birkenfeld and Zweibrücken lines.

[3] Cf. genealogy (p. 707) and p. 52.

[4] Albert had sold it to the Duke of Bavaria.

Lower Bavaria, to Mindelheim in Swabia, and to certain Bohemian fiefs with which last alone he was to be invested. The prospect of arranging an exchange for the whole country was also held out, for Austria was already contemplating getting rid of a distant province which was a burden rather than a benefit to her, the Netherlands. On the ratification of this convention, Austrian troops promptly occupied the Upper Palatinate (Jan. 16th, 1778).

However, this merely served to provoke an agitation in Bavaria against the project of division, and the Duchess Marianne, widow of Duke Clement of Bavaria,[1] put herself at the head of the party which desired to preserve the integrity of the Electorate. Charles of Zweibrücken had expressed in general terms his acquiescence in the scheme; but when he found Frederick II inclined to support him, he issued a protest against the violation of his rights as heir-apparent. Frederick, fearing the aggrandisement of Austria, at once refused to recognise Austria's claims. Saxony had a claim on the allodial property in Bavaria, and was anything but friendly to Austria; while Hanover, though on the whole favouring the Austrian claim, did not go beyond benevolent neutrality.[2]

Now was the time when the Franco-Austrian alliance on which Kaunitz and Maria Theresa set so much store, and which they had spared no pains to maintain, was to be put to the test. But it was Joseph's distrust of the alliance, not Maria Theresa's confidence in it which was to be justified. Vergennes was now in power in France and from him no support to the aggrandisement of Austria was to be expected; even if France, inspired by the news of Saratoga, had not been on the point of renewing the struggle with England for the dominion of the seas, Vergennes would never have consented to take any steps on behalf of the Hapsburgs. Nor did Russia's attitude correspond to Joseph's hopes; on the contrary, she inclined to support Frederick.[3]

Negotiations continued through the early part of 1778. Charles Theodore would have gladly exchanged Bavaria against the Netherlands; but the "Old Bavarian" party was opposed to this, and though Frederick did propose conditions

[1] The younger brother of Maximilian Joseph, who had predeceased the Elector.
[2] Cf. Ward, *England and Hanover*, p. 200.   [3] Wolf, p. 176.

upon which he would have agreed to the annexation of Eastern Bavaria by Austria, they were so exorbitant[1] that Joseph refused them. Accordingly, on July 3rd Frederick issued an ultimatum, declaring that Austria had no just claims upon Bavaria, and two days later he crossed the Bohemian frontier near Nachod.

The chief feature of the War of the Bavarian Succession is its utter absence of military interest. Practically there was no fighting, beyond a certain amount of skirmishing, and but little manœuvring. Both armies were numerous rather than efficient. In both the administration and equipment were somewhat deficient; and while the Austrians for political motives adopted the defensive Frederick was not prepared to attack. Indeed, both sides displayed not a little nervousness and a decided wish not to risk anything on the chances of a general action, the more so because negotiations were still proceeding. Maria Theresa, thinking Joseph was prepared to give way, had despatched Thugut to Berlin to renew them (July). However, nothing came of this attempt to avert hostilities. Both sides regarded the pretensions of the other as exorbitant, and neither was ready to abate its own. In August, Frederick advanced somewhat farther into Bohemia, Loudoun recoiling before him; but the difficulty of getting supplies and the ravages of disease effectually checked the Prussian advance. The Austrian position at Königgratz was too strong to be attacked, and in September Frederick retreated. He had not done anything to add to his military reputation in this, his last, campaign.

Maria Theresa was now using all her influence in favour of peace, and with Russia, guided by Panin whom Potemkin, the Czarina's favourite, had won over to Prussia's side, threatening to support Frederick unless peace were made directly, and no prospect of any help from France, even Kaunitz and Joseph realised the hopelessness of securing Bavaria. An armistice put an end to the minor warfare which had continued with but little result through the winter; in March a congress met at Tetschen, and the upshot of its deliberations was a peace signed on May 13th, 1779. By this Austria agreed to

---

[1] Mindelheim, Swabia, and part of the Upper Palatinate to go to Saxony, which should hand Lusatia over to Prussia, while Charles Theodore was to receive Guelders or Limburg in return for the cessions made to Austria.

cancel the Convention of January 1778, but received the strip of territory between the Danube on the North, the Inn on the West, and the Salza on the South and East, a district some 850 square miles in size and containing 60,000 inhabitants. As a settlement of its claim on the allodial property Saxony received 6,000,000 gulden and the little district of Schönberg, while Prussia's right to absorb the Franconian margraviates of Anspach and Baireuth[1] was to pass unopposed. The Duke of Mecklenburg-Schwerin, who had also advanced a claim on the Bavarian inheritance, was bought off with the privilege " de non appellando." This peace was guaranteed by France and Russia, and in the following February it was accepted by the Empire.

Of the Powers concerned in the Peace of Tetschen, Russia had undoubtedly gained most in influence. She rather than France had held the balance in her hands: her decision as to the exchange of the Franconian margraviates against Lusatia and as to the amount of compensation for Saxony had been accepted: it was really the very decided line she had taken which had foiled Austria's attempt on Bavaria. Had she supported Austria's claims, as Joseph seems to have expected she would, there would have been a very different story to tell. Prussia also had gained, but rather indirectly than materially. The war had cost her 29 million thalers and 20,000 men, but Frederick was able to represent his action as a disinterested intervention on behalf of the Princes of the Empire against an Emperor bent on turning to his own advantage such relics of a constitution as survived. Such a description of Joseph's policy is not altogether fair. It would not have been to the disadvantage of Germany if the tide of French conquest, so soon to overwhelm her, had found her a little less weak and disunited, had found an Empire which was not practically extinct, and an Emperor whose authority did mean something; but Joseph does appear in the light of one prepared to seize every opportunity of profiting by his neighbours' necessities to increase his territories. Rather different was the action of Maria Theresa. That peace

---

[1] The Baireuth Hohenzollern had become extinct in 1769 with Frederick, 6th Margrave: his territories passed to the Anspach line. In 1792, by arrangement between Frederick William II and Christian Frederick, 9th Margrave of Anspach, the Franconian margraviates were incorporated with Prussia.

was so soon restored was largely due to her influence. Had her advice been followed throughout, Austria would have been spared the humiliation of a check for which 850 square miles were hardly an adequate compensation. It was almost the last episode in the career of the great Empress, for her health was beginning to fail. One last collision, however, was to take place between her and her lifelong enemy Frederick, and one is glad to be able to relate that in this last encounter Maria Theresa triumphed. The contest was over the election of a Coadjutor to the Elector of Cologne.[1] This office Maria Theresa succeeded in obtaining for her youngest son, Maximilian, Frederick's efforts on behalf of Joseph Hohenlohe being frustrated (August 1780).

But her failing strength would not much longer enable her to continue the daily round of duties in which she still persisted. In November she became rapidly worse, and on the 29th she died. What she did for Austria it is hard to overestimate. Her indomitable courage and perseverance carried her dominions through an almost unexampled danger and made the surmounting of that very danger a source of union and strength. She did much to reconcile Hungary to the Hapsburg dynasty, to reform the administration and the social, financial and political conditions of the countries over which she ruled. A woman of the highest character, a true mother of her people, a " benevolent despot " in the very best sense of the words, she had the tact and sympathy to see what was possible and suitable, and to avoid the errors into which her more impetuous, more theoretical and more self-centred son fell. In all the annals of the House of Hapsburg, there is hardly any name which can be put on the same level as that of Maria Theresa.

The importance of the part played by Russia in the affair of the Bavarian Succession is best attested by the eagerness with which Joseph now sought to secure the friendship of the Czarina. Even before the death of Maria Theresa, Joseph had made a journey to Russia, had had an interview with Catherine at Mohilev in Lithuania (August 1780), and had subsequently visited Moscow and St. Petersburg. Maria Theresa, who was not unnaturally prejudiced against Catherine

---

[1] This was Maximilian of Rottenfels, Dean of Cologne 1756–1761, elected Archbishop in succession to Clement Augustus of Bavaria, April 1761.

as a person, had disliked this journey very much, but Joseph found the Czarina most anxious for better relations with Austria. The alliance between Russia and Prussia, first concluded in 1764 and renewed in 1772, had expired in 1780 and had not been renewed, for Frederick did not by any means desire to see Russia's power further increased, and Catherine had not found Prussia a very satisfactory or cordial ally. She was now occupied with schemes for ousting the Turks from Europe and establishing a Christian kingdom under Russian protection on the Bosphorus; and in carrying out such aims it was far more important to secure the alliance, or at least the neutrality, of Austria than that of Prussia. Accordingly, after much correspondence an arrangement was made between Austria and Russia in May 1781 by which both Powers guaranteed each other's possessions, while Joseph promised to join Russia within three months should she go to war with the Porte, and also guaranteed Oldenburg to the younger branch of the House of Holstein. Catherine for her part promised to assist Austria in case of a Prussian attack, while in the course of the year Joseph announced his adhesion to the "Armed Neutrality" in the war between England and her Bourbon enemies, an alliance of which Catherine was the chief bulwark. It was not to be long before the Czarina was to have an opportunity of making use of the Austrian alliance. Disturbances among the Tartars of the Crimea in the course of 1782 threatened to lead to serious trouble with the Porte; but though Joseph was not prepared to join the Czarina in using this *casus belli* to begin the crusade for the dismemberment of the Ottoman Empire on which her wishes were set, he was able to help her to force Turkey to give way. A large force was collected on the frontiers of Hungary to lend weight to the diplomatic representations of Joseph on behalf of the Russian claims to suzerainty over the Tartars, and it was very largely the prospect of having to face Austria as well as Russia which caused the Turks in January 1784 to accept a convention [1] which secured the Crimea and the Kuban to Russia. Austria's only gain from this treaty was the opening of the Danube to commerce; but Joseph now reckoned confidently on the support of Russia for the various projects which he was hoping to realise.

[1] That of Ainali Karak.

Mention has already been made of the anomalous relations in which the Netherlands stood to their Austrian rulers, and also of the great obstacles to the development of the Netherlands, the Barrier Treaty of 1715 and the closing of the Scheldt in accordance with the Peace of Münster. Maria Theresa had succeeded in reducing the annual subsidy paid to the Dutch garrisons from a million gulden to half a million, but she had been unable to get rid of the Dutch, whose presence was a constant source of friction. It was after a journey in Belgium in 1781 that Joseph, realising the full extent of these encumbrances, decided to seize the favourable opportunity of the war between England and the United Provinces to get rid of them. He confined himself at first to announcing to the Dutch that they could withdraw their garrisons, as he intended to " slight " the majority of the towns in question. The more important question of the Scheldt he did not at this time raise, herein giving way to Kaunitz, who believed that it would almost certainly provoke a war with France. The Dutch found that they had no alternative but to withdraw their troops, and with the exception of Luxemburg, Ostend and the citadel of Antwerp, the fortifications were demolished. The Barrier Treaty had also contained certain agreements as to territorial cessions which had never been properly carried out, and Joseph, taking advantage of a technical infraction of the Belgian frontier by Dutch troops, denounced the treaty as null and void, and demanded a readjustment of the frontier. At the same time he raised the question of the opening of the Scheldt to commerce.[1] A Belgian vessel had been fired upon while in Belgian waters (Oct. 1783), and this served as the occasion for Joseph to demand the slighting of the Dutch forts on the Scheldt, the removal of the guardships and the surrender of Maastricht and its dependencies. These demands were based on the terms of a convention made in 1673 between Holland and Spain. To enforce his claim, Joseph collected some 20,000 troops; but they were ill-supplied with artillery, and were without the pontoon-train so urgently needed in a country so much intersected by watercourses as Holland, and the Dutch, by opening the sluices and inundating the frontier districts, made military operations impossible. However, it was not military difficulties but the attitude of France which made

---

[1] Cf. Oncken's *Frederick*, vol. ii. p. 824.

Joseph draw back. Had Holland stood alone, Joseph might have obtained his demands, but the Anglo-Dutch war had led to a renewal of the old alliance between France and the democratic party in Holland. This, the so-called " Burgher party," had been revived by the influence of de Vauguyon, French envoy at The Hague since 1776, and Vergennes was not prepared to allow Holland to fall away from the new connection, as would probably happen if France by failing to support her forced her to fall back on England's aid. Accordingly, when negotiations were broken off after Fort Säftingen had fired upon a brigantine flying the Emperor's colours and had forced it to strike (Oct. 1784), Joseph found the influence of France thrown into the scale against him. Russia, it is true, favoured Joseph's action, and neither England nor Prussia seemed prepared to intervene in favour of Holland; but the resolute language of Vergennes convinced Joseph that the risks were too great. The question seems to have been with him to a large extent one of dignity. He did not greatly care for the welfare of his Belgic provinces, but he resented the restrictions imposed upon them as a slight on his prestige.[1] Therefore, when he found that to persevere with his plans would involve the ruin of the Franco-Austrian alliance, he fell back upon another and more promising project.

If the Netherlands could not be freed from the encumbrances which prevented the development of their natural resources and made them so unsatisfactory a possession, it might be possible to exchange them for a country of far greater value to Austria, the Electorate of Bavaria. The idea of the exchange was not altogether new, but Joseph thought the moment favourable for realising it. By making concessions to France in the matter of the Scheldt he might induce her to sacrifice Bavaria for the sake of Holland, for to Vergennes at least it seemed better for France to have a Wittelsbach than a Hapsburg as her neighbour in Belgium. The support of the Czarina, Joseph hoped he had won by pointing out to her how much the acquisition of Bavaria and the consequent improvement of Austria's resources and military position would increase her ability to assist Russia's schemes in the East. The Elector, Charles Theodore, cared very little for his Bavarian subjects, to whom no real ties bound him; if the exchange could be

[1] Cf. F. Magnette, *Joseph II et la liberté de l'Escant.*

arranged on terms which would gratify his personal interests he was quite prepared to sacrifice the wishes of the Bavarians and the interests of his Zweibrücken cousin. All that seemed really necessary was to secure the consent of Charles of Zweibücken to the agreement. But, somewhat unexpectedly, when the Russian Ambassador to Bavaria approached the Duke on this matter, he was met by the most uncompromising reply : rather, Charles declared, would he be buried under the ruins of Bavaria. Such an answer could mean one thing only ; it was dictated from Potsdam, and the Duke had received trustworthy assurances that he could count upon the assistance of Frederick II. This was indeed the case. As jealous as ever of Austria, alarmed by her alliance with Russia, whose power he had had such good cause to appreciate, determined to thwart her wherever possible and to prevent her from recovering influence or authority over the minor Princes of Germany, Frederick had been playing skilfully on the distrust which Joseph's attempts to assert his rights as Emperor and his efforts to increase his hereditary dominions had caused among the petty sovereigns of Southern and Western Germany. Quite without any general patriotism, oblivious of anything but their own personal and dynastic interests, even the more enlightened and unselfish among them were bitterly hostile to the Imperial pretensions, and the decay of the Imperial institutions had already proceeded so far that they were practically past reviving. Had Joseph been able to come forward with a definitely Imperial programme it is just possible that he might have done something, but as things stood it was impossible to prevent the suspicion that under the cloak of the interests of the Empire he was seeking to aggrandise the Hapsburg-Lorraine dynasty : the "Imperial" could not be distinguished from the "Austrian." But while Joseph had not the power to do what Ferdinand II, though with much better chances and with Wallenstein behind him, had failed to accomplish, or to enforce unity on Germany, nothing could have been more alien to his principles or his practice than an appeal to the people, to the spirit of German nationalism which was not yet awake ; he would have been glad to regain the powers his predecessors had lost, but he had no idea of replacing the moribund Empire by something new.

It was therefore easy for Frederick to form a confederation

of German Princes for the defence of their rights against the Emperor's encroachments. In effect much the same as the Union of Frankfort of 1744, since both were aimed against Austria, in theory the *Fürstenbund* was somewhat different, since its avowed objects were anti-Imperial, while the earlier league had been formed to defend the then Emperor. But Frederick was only inconsistent on the surface: he sought in both cases to extend Prussian influence over Southern and Western Germany at the expense of the Hapsburgs. The project of the formation of such a confederation was set forth in a memorandum addressed to the Prussian ministers von Finckenstein and Hertzberg in October 1784. In this the King of Prussia spoke of resisting the Emperor's attempts to bestow all vacant sees on his nephews from Tuscany and Modena, and by then secularising the sees to gain a permanent Hapsburg majority in the College of Princes—a danger about as chimerical as the other peril against which this protector of the German constitution was ready to invoke foreign aid, namely, that the Emperor should convert the Diet at Ratisbon and the Imperial Chamber at Wetzlar into the instruments of a tyrannical despotism.[1]

Joseph was, it is true, making somewhat futile efforts to restore the Aulic Council and the Imperial Chamber to some measure of efficiency, but these were hardly enough to justify Frederick's extravagant fears. In the matter of the *Panis-briefe*, a claim that the Emperor should appoint a lay canon in every ecclesiastical corporation, he was seeking to revive a right which had not been exercised since the 14th Century, and he was undoubtedly anxious to get his candidate elected whenever any sees fell vacant, as, for example, the choice of the Archduke Maximilian as Coadjutor in Cologne and Münster. That he also entertained designs upon the Cities, the ecclesiastical dominions and the minor states of South Germany in general is probable enough; it is also probable that incorporation in Austria would have brought to the peasants and artisans in these petty principalities considerable material benefits, which might perhaps have been set off against the infringement of the rights of the rulers and upper classes. If the attainment of German unity was desirable in any way, there is no reason to blame Joseph for having wished to reassert

[1] Oncken's *Frederick*, vol. ii, p. 834.

the claims of the Empire as against those local lords whose disregard of the Imperial authority had received the sanction of prescription bestowed upon them by many centuries.

No such league had actually been formed, when in January 1785 Charles of Zweibrücken appealed to Frederick for assistance in the matter of the Bavarian exchange. This was the opportunity Frederick wanted, and in March Hertzberg and von Finckenstein laid before the King projected articles of association of a Union of Princes of the Empire to guarantee and maintain the existing constitution and territorial arrangements of Germany. Its members were to act together in the election of a new King of the Romans or in the creation of a new Electorate. No distinction was to be made between religions, and it was definitely stated that armed resistance could be offered to the proposed exchange of Bavaria. July 23rd, 1785, may be taken as the date of the definite formation of the Union, as it was then that the terms of association were signed by the Electors of Brandenburg, Hanover and Saxony. In October the Elector of Mayence, the Dukes of Saxe-Weimar, Saxe-Gotha, Zweibrücken and Brunswick declared their adhesion to it ; their example was followed in November by the Margrave of Baden and the Landgrave of Hesse-Cassel, and gradually by most of the other members of the Empire, the only dissentients being Cologne, Treves, Hesse-Darmstadt, Oldenburg and Würtemberg.[1] This body thus commanded a majority in the Electoral College, and as the Elector of Bavaria had hastened to withdraw his consent to the exchange as soon as he found how matters were going—in February 1785 he denied that any such scheme was in existence—Joseph's plan was again foiled.

Moreover, his failure was not confined to Bavaria alone. To obtain French assent to the exchange he had withdrawn most of the claims he had made upon Holland. He had accepted French mediation and this practically implied the abandonment of his designs upon the Scheldt. To the great disgust of his Belgian subjects, who saw the high hopes of commercial prosperity they had based on Joseph's demands thus irretrievably disappointed, he gradually abandoned claim after claim. Finally, in November 1785 the Treaty of

[1] These last two were connected with Russia ; Hesse-Darmstadt was consistently on the Austrian side.

Fontainebleau reaffirmed the Peace of Münster and maintained the closing of the Scheldt, though some of the forts were handed over to the Emperor, others "slighted," and the frontier restored to its condition in 1664. Maastricht remained in Dutch hands, but ten million gulden, of which France paid four and a half, were handed over to the Emperor as a pecuniary compensation. Thus Joseph received a decided rebuff, and at the hands of France. The support of Russia had not passed much beyond words, and the discontent of the Belgian population at the way in which their interests had been sacrificed was destined to lead to further trouble. So complete a surrender after such protestations smacked of insincerity and gave good grounds for complaints that Belgian interests were altogether disregarded by the Emperor. The internal troubles so soon to convulse the Austrian Netherlands,[1] may be traced in part to the failure of Joseph's designs on Bavaria.

After these disappointments it was not unnatural that Joseph should have asked himself whether the Russian alliance had proved as beneficial as he had hoped. It was not to Austria's interests to assist Russia's advance upon Constantinople unless Russian influence were going to obtain for her corresponding advantages in Germany. But with France decidedly unfriendly, and with the minor Princes of Germany leagued together under Prussian influence, it seemed that the only alternative to the Russian alliance was complete isolation, and for this Joseph was not altogether prepared.

However, in the year following the formation of the *Fürstenbund*, the death of Frederick II[2] seemed to make a new policy possible. The generation which had known Silesia as part of the Hapsburg dominions had passed or was passing away. Joseph for his part had never entertained that intense and personal feeling of hostility to the Hohenzollern which had animated his mother, and he seems to have contemplated a reconciliation with Frederick William II. The new King, the son of the unfortunate Augustus William whose conduct of the retreat from Bohemia had so annoyed Frederick II in 1757, was of a very different calibre to his famous uncle. He had none of the calm self-command, of the cold-blooded calculation, of the clear-sightedness, of the acute judgment, of the initiative,

---

[1] *Vide infra*, pp. 340 ff.   [2] August 17th, 1786.

energy and resource, of the capacity for sustained efforts, of the power to work himself and to exact work from others, which had made Frederick II so successful a ruler. Frederick William's talents were mediocre ; he had neither the will nor the capacity to be a really efficient ruler, or to effectively control and supervise the elaborate governmental machine of which as King he was the pivot, and the decay of Prussia under his rule must be in large measure attributed to his utter failure to fill his uncle's place. Personally he was the slave of his passions, extremely self-indulgent, yet mingling superstition with sensuality and a kind of morbid religious devotion with his debaucheries, a strange mixture which recalls Louis XV but has nothing in common with the Atheistic cynicism and deliberate selfishness of Frederick II.

It was not unnatural that Joseph should have entertained the project of a Prussian alliance. As he explained to Kaunitz, Austria and Prussia if united would have nothing to fear from any other Power, and might be able to secure a lasting peace. A common nationality and a common language would provide a bond of union which ought to be able to obliterate old prejudices and hostility, and, if Austria could forget the past and forgive Silesia, it should have been possible to present to the growing influence of Russia that barrier which the Silesian question had hitherto prevented the two leading Powers of Germany from forming. But it was not to be. Joseph's doubts of the value of the Russian alliance were not shared by Kaunitz, who could not be expected to get rid of his distrust of the Power he had sought so hard to humble, and he pleaded strongly against the proposed overtures to Prussia. Moreover, Frederick William retained as his Foreign Minister the man who represented the traditions of hostility to Austria which had been the foundation of his uncle's policy, and as long as Hertzberg was in power at Berlin a reconciliation between Austria and Prussia was out of the question. Accordingly Joseph, not without misgivings, accepted Catherine's invitation to visit her and in May 1787 undertook a visit to Russia. With the Russian Court he journeyed through the newly-acquired provinces on the Black Sea, and it would seem that in the course of this progress he pledged himself to support the schemes of aggrandisement at the expense of Turkey which Catherine entertained. However that may have been, in August 1787 the Sultan, alarmed by the unconcealed preparations of Russia, startled the world by suddenly arresting the Russian Ambassador and issuing a declaration of war. By the Treaty of 1781, Joseph's obligations were limited to an auxiliary corps of 30,000 men; but he was ambitious of military fame and anxious to obtain a share in the direction of the war by taking a principal's part in it, and accordingly he collected in Southern Hungary an army of 130,000, and in February 1788 declared war.

The results of this step fell very far short of Joseph's anticipations. The failure owing to fog of the attempt to surprise Belgrade, which Joseph had made even before the declaration of war, was typical of the Austrian performances. For the campaign of 1788 the principal force under Joseph himself was to attempt the invasion of Servia, while a subsidiary force on the right under Loudoun assailed Bosnia, and another on the left under Coburg co-operated with the Russians in Moldavia. Loudoun was fairly successful, capturing Dubitza, Novi and Schabatz, while despite the late arrival of the Russians, Coburg did take Choczim on the Dniester (September) and so pave the way for an advance into Wallachia. But the main army not only was unable to attempt the siege of Belgrade, it failed to prevent the Turks invading and ravaging the Banat; and though Joseph, hurrying thither, forced them to retire, this was at best a negative success. The truth was that Joseph had not the qualities needed by a successful general. Though a keen soldier, he was deficient in strategical insight; and as he never knew where to draw the line between a commander-in-chief's due supervision of his subordinates and meddlesome interference, his lieutenants altogether lacked confidence in him. Moreover, the army suffered terribly from disease, and in November Joseph himself had to return to Vienna very much out of health.

It was not only the ill-success of the campaign which caused Joseph anxiety. Prussia, as usual finding her opportunity in the embarrassments of her neighbours, was on the alert, eager to utilise the Austro-Turkish war to make good her own designs on the much-coveted Polish towns of Dantzic and Thorn. Hertzberg and Frederick William II had just secured no slight advantages by their intervention in Holland on behalf of the House of Orange. The old struggle between the Stadtholder and the burgher aristocracy of Amsterdam had come to a head in 1786. An armed rebellion had forced William V and his wife Wilhelmina, Frederick William's sister, to fly from The Hague and appeal to England and Prussia for assistance. This the two Powers were very ready to grant, Prussia largely for dynastic reasons, England in order to detach Holland from her new connection with France, on whose support the Burgher party were relying. But at the critical moment (Feb. 1787) Vergennes died, and France, without a minister capable of controlling her or following a consistent foreign policy, looked on feebly while England and Prussia interfered to suppress the insurrection, restored the Stadtholderate and concluded an alliance in which Holland was included. This successful episode greatly increased the prestige of Prussia, though no doubt the ease with which it was accomplished may have contributed to the utterly false estimate which Frederick William formed of the possibilities of intervening in a not dissimilar situation in France five years later. The formation of the Triple Alliance (June 1788) seemed to provide Hertzberg with a powerful influence which he could bring to bear upon the situation in the East of Europe. His idea was to offer to mediate between Turkey and her enemies, and so manipulate the terms of peace as to induce or compel Austria to resign Galicia to Poland, which would then reward Prussia's good offices by the cession of Dantzic and Thorn, now as ever the key to all Prussia's intrigues. There was at least no uncertainty about Prussia's objects. As a compensation, Austria was to keep Moldavia and Wallachia, while Russia might bring her boundary up to the Dniester. Should Prussia's mediation be refused, a threat of armed interference would, Hertzberg hoped, prove efficacious, especially if he had the Maritime Powers at his back. They also were ready for intervention, but their objects were not quite the same as Hertzberg's. Trade interests, both in the Baltic and in the Levant, made Pitt anxious for the restoration of peace ; beyond that he was not prepared to go.

Joseph was so far alarmed by the attitude of Prussia, which besides encouraging the Porte was in communication with the Hungarian malcontents[1] and was fostering the growing trouble in Belgium, that he at first thought to

[1] Cf. p. 345.

checkmate Prussia by a prompt peace with Turkey, with or without Russia. Kaunitz, however, dissuaded him strongly from this, and neither Russia nor Turkey seemed inclined to peace. The only result of the negotiations, therefore, was that the opening of the campaign of 1789 was much delayed. During the winter, Suvorov had stormed the great fortress of Oczakov on the Black Sea (Dec. 7th, 1788), while the death of the Sultan, Abdul Hamid (April 27th), had placed on the Turkish throne Selim III, a keen and energetic ruler, bent on the active prosecution of the war. His first step was to disgrace the Grand Vizier and replace him at the head of the army by the Pasha of Widdin. However, the new commander received two severe defeats at the hands of Coburg and Suvorov ;[1] while Loudoun, who replaced the worn-out Hadik in command of the main Austrian army (August), also took the offensive with success. Breaking up from Semlin he crossed to the south of the Save and laid siege to Belgrade (Sept. 18th). The suburb was stormed on September 30th, and eight days later the town capitulated. Its fall was followed by the surrender of the fortresses between the Drina and the Timok, Semendria, Kladowa and others. Bosnia, Moldavia, half Servia and the greater part of Wallachia were in Austrian hands, and Austria seemed on the verge of great successes when the news of the outbreak of trouble in Belgium (August) and the threatening attitude of Prussia paralysed her advance. The greater part of the Austrian troops had to be transferred to Bohemia, leaving on the Danube forces hardly adequate to maintain the ground already won, while little help was to be expected from Russia, whose attention had been diverted to the Baltic to meet the vigorous attacks of Gustavus III of Sweden.

For this intervention, Hertzberg was mainly responsible. It was not to Austria only that he was hostile, his attitude towards Russia was equally antagonistic. Thus he fostered and abetted the Swedish King's hostility to Russia, and by addressing himself to the anti-Russian faction in Poland seemed to have secured control of that country. It appeared certain that the spring of 1790 would see the sword of Prussia thrown into the scales on the side of Turkey, when in February 1790

---

[1] On July 31st at Foksani and in September at Martinestyi on the Rymnik, both places just West of Galatz.

the situation was completely altered by the death of Joseph II and the accession of a more practical and competent statesman in Leopold II.

Ever since the campaign of 1788 Joseph had been in very bad health, and the constitutional troubles in Hungary and the outbreak of rebellion in Belgium, where he had hoped all was settled, had naturally aggravated the physical and mental strain.   In great bodily pain, he had the misfortune to see his cherished schemes leading to failure and disaster everywhere, his reforms misunderstood, his efforts to increase his dominions frustrated, Belgium in open rebellion, Hungary seething with discontent, similar troubles impending in Tyrol, a powerful coalition apparently about to intervene to take advantage of his domestic and foreign embarrassments.   So black was the outlook, so formidable the crisis which he seemed to be going to leave to his successor, that Joseph could not persevere on his chosen course.   In January 1790 he gave way to the constitutional opposition of Hungary, cancelled all his edicts save only those in favour of the serfs, and restored the administrative system to the footing on which it had stood at Maria Theresa's death.   It was with the greatest reluctance that he did this, but there seemed no alternative.   One other step which he took just before his death was to re-establish a special Conference to deal with foreign affairs, which included Kaunitz and Lacy and the Treasurer, Count Rosenberg, while Count Hatzfeldt was put in charge of domestic affairs.   On February 20th Joseph died at the early age of forty-eight (born March 1741).

CHAPTER XVI

MARIA THERESA AND JOSEPH II

(Domestic Affairs)

IF from the time of the Partition of Poland, Joseph II had begun to exercise the predominant influence in the direction of the foreign affairs of Austria, this was as much the case in domestic policy; for though Joseph treated his mother with great deference and paid much attention and respect to the ideas and suggestions of Kaunitz, he had made up his own mind on many important points and was determined to push through without delay the reforms which he desired. Both Maria Theresa and Kaunitz found the pace which Joseph set too hot for their liking. Well-intentioned, energetic, a very hard worker, keenly and genuinely anxious to benefit his subjects, Joseph was too much of a doctrinaire, too little of a practical man to distinguish between the possible and the ideal and to be able to adapt to his extraordinary complicated collection of dominions measures better suited to a Utopia. The problem of Austria was one which Joseph failed to look at from an Austrian point of view : he was too detached, too little acquainted with the feelings of his subjects, too little touched by the local patriotism and provincial *esprit de corps* which animated them. He could not see the parts for the whole, they could not see the whole for the parts. Thus wise and salutary as many of his schemes were in themselves, they were applied to situations and circumstances so unsuitable that the good often became evil. Want of tact, want of patience, want of knowledge of men, want of sympathy with other men's views, all these played a large part in the comparative failure of the reforms of Joseph II.

Among the institutions which needed reform, the Church stood out prominently. It was rich, powerful, numerous, but backward, negligent and superstitious. It was still in the

16th Century, and as there was little chance that it would be reformed from within, the State had to undertake the task. Joseph I had done something in this way, Charles VI had also dabbled with the question, while the second decade of Maria Theresa's reign had seen the Church courts regulated, the increase of clerical estates checked and the condition of those already in Church hands improved by their administration being put under the supervision of the Chancery (1750). It was between 1770 and 1780, however, that more radical measures were taken, and for these Joseph was mainly responsible. Austria was strongly Catholic, but the reforming movement of the period enjoyed the support of public opinion, since it did not touch the teaching or dogma of the Church, but only affected it as a social and political institution. It is true that the number of fast- and feast-days was curtailed, but that was done for an economic reason, to diminish the interference of such religious ceremonies with labour and industry. In the same way the efforts to combat the many superstitious and semi-pagan rites and practices which still prevailed hardly affected the real tenets of the Church. The more important reforms related to the jurisdiction of the clergy over the laity, into which a commission inquired between 1765 and 1780, with the result that the laity were only subjected to ecclesiastical courts in matrimonial affairs, to the property of the Church, which was made liable for a fair share of the ordinary taxes on landed property, and to the monasteries, whose powers and privileges were much reduced, while the abuses with regard to their acquisition of property were checked by monks being forbidden to witness wills, and so exercise undue influence over dying testators. The amount of property a novice might bring in on being admitted was also regulated, and the purchase of lands by monastic bodies was subjected to State control. Other useful measures were the limitation of the right of asylum (1775) and the redistribution of the Bishoprics, as the mediæval scheme was now quite obsolete. Maria Theresa founded new sees at Görz, Leitmeritz, Königgratz and Brünn, and erected Olmütz into an Archbishopric. Joseph II created six more sees, transferred three others to new places, and managed to detach those districts which while politically part of Austria belonged to non-Austrian sees from the dioceses to which they belonged. Thus Linz, one of his own foundations, and Vienna, a see created by Charles VI, shared the portions of Upper Austria hitherto subject to Passau.[1] These arrangements were completed by 1783, and, though only after some demur, were duly accepted and ratified by the Pope.

That reforms so extensive should have led to a conflict with the Papacy was only natural, for they certainly infringed the privileges and pretensions of the Pope. It would seem that Joseph had studied the famous pamphlet, *De statu Ecclesiæ et legitima potestate Romani pontificis*, by means of which Febronius had exercised so much influence over Catholic Germany in the 18th Century, expressing views which were widely held. Something had already been done in this direction, for in 1755 an order had been published directing that all excommunications should be made known to the government, and in 1767 old ordinances were revived which forbade the promulgation of Papal Bulls without the leave of the State. Joseph himself would probably have gladly gone a good deal further than this in the direction indicated by Febronius. His views were, to say the least, Erastian in the extreme, and there were those who accused him of being a freethinker and could make out a plausible case in support of their charge. However, though he may have contemplated emulating Henry VIII in breaking the bonds of Rome, that was a step for which Austria was certainly not prepared. Public opinion had been mainly on Joseph's side in his quarrel with the Papacy over his reforms; and the famous " Ems Punktuation " of 1786, by which the four German Archbishops reduced the Papal authority over Germany to quite narrow limits,[2] shows that the anti-Papal feeling in Germany was not confined to the laity; but a complete breach between the Papacy and the Holy Roman Empire was out of the question. Moreover, the wisdom of the Popes in making timely concessions assisted to disarm hostility. The relations between Austria and Clement XIII (1758-1769) had at times been very much strained, but Clement XIV (1769-1774) gave way on most of the points at issue, and Pius VI (1774-1799) yielded to the unimpeachable orthodoxy of Maria Theresa what he would never have conceded to Joseph, whom he regarded as little better than an Atheist.

In some ways, however, the most important feature in the

relations between Church and State during this period was the part played by Austria in a movement common to almost all Europe, the attack on the Jesuits. This was of special importance in Austria, since it involved the liberation of education from the hands of the Jesuits who had till then enjoyed an almost complete control of it. In Austria the Jesuit Order was wealthy and powerful and most unpopular, and it was not only the lay officials, but the Bishops who disliked them and were anxious for their overthrow. Maria Theresa had at first held back from the general attack, regarding the abolition of the Order as a purely ecclesiastical affair, which ought therefore to be left solely to the Pope. However, on the publication of the Bull abolishing the Society of Jesus, she did not hesitate to put it into execution. A commission was appointed to look after their affairs, which issued its report in January 1774. The property of the Order was confiscated, but it was appropriated to the objects to which it had been, theoretically at least, devoted, pious works and education.

The fall of the Jesuits opened the way to really consider-able reforms in education.[1]   Over 200 *Gymnasia* were in their hands, and they practically controlled the Universities through being supreme in the Philosophical and Theological Faculties. The education they gave was still the education of the 16th Century.   Nothing had been done to keep in touch with modern developments; all modern studies were neglected, and their scholars could hardly write their own language. The leader of the attacks on the educational system of the Jesuits was the celebrated Viennese physician, Gerhard van Swieten, a man who enjoyed a considerable share of Maria Theresa's confidence.   Under his leadership the great Medical School of Vienna was founded, while Philosophy and Theology, released from Jesuitical trammels, made great strides.   The Legal Faculty had already (1753–1754) been reformed, and it was kept up to date; while the University was brought under State control, not, perhaps, the ideal chance for its development, but still an improvement on its complete subjugation to the Church.   The *Gymnasia* were also reformed, Professor von Gaspari being mainly responsible for the new measures.   Modern subjects like History and Geography

[1] Cf. Wolf, Bk. ii. ch. 2.

were introduced into the curriculum; and though it was impossible to establish complete uniformity, or from want of qualified teachers to dispense altogether with ex-Jesuits as instructors, a great deal was done to reduce confusion to order and to establish State control. The reform of the elementary schools (*Volkschülen*) presented fewer difficulties. Here again what was actually accomplished fell short of what was aimed at, but primary education on a fairly liberal scale was provided under the ordinances of 1774. Finally, in 1778 the educational Commission which had been established in 1760 was put under the direction of the Chancery.

After the death (Nov. 29th, 1780) of Maria Theresa, Joseph carried his Church reforms still further, and between 1781 and 1784 many very important measures were added. He was bitterly opposed by the Papal Nuntios and by the Archbishops of Gran, Olmütz and Vienna; but he had at his back a strong reforming party, including Kaunitz, the younger van Swieten, Vice-Chancellor Greiner, and the Bishops of Laibach and Königgratz. The first point of attack was the relations of the Austrian clergy with Rome. Joseph began (March 1781) by renewing the *Placitum Regium* of Maria Theresa, by forbidding any communication between monastic Orders in Austria and their headquarters at Rome or their branches in other countries and by cutting out of the Service-book the Bulls *Unigenitus* and *In Cœna Domini* (claiming dispensing power for the Pope). He followed up these steps by attacking the monasteries. Austria teemed with monastic establishments,[1] many of them in a bad condition, some on the verge of bankruptcy. All that Maria Theresa had done was to impose on them a share in taxation and regulate their liability to ecclesiastical law. Joseph went further, he sought to diminish their number. In 1781 the monasteries devoted to the speculative[2] life were closed, and the funds thus obtained were devoted to the local clergy, whose numbers and position Joseph sought to improve. In 1782 the assault fell on the Carthusians, Augustinians, Carmelites, Capuchins and Franciscans: their convents and monasteries were shut, the inmates being pensioned off. It was in vain that Pius VI came to Vienna (March 22nd to

---

[1] In 1781 there were 2163 in Austria with 65,000 inmates.   [2] *Beschaulich.*

April 24th, 1782) to expostulate; his visit had little effect beyond lowering his own prestige. He could not go very far, for he was much afraid of a schism; and if the Pope adopted an unconciliatory attitude, Joseph would have had a good excuse for trying to nationalise the Roman Catholic Church in Austria and to assert its independence of Rome. He always supported the Bishops whenever they were in opposition to the Pope, and he exacted from them an oath to the Emperor which bound them not to do anything contrary to the interests of the State.

Such being Joseph's attitude towards the Church, it is hardly remarkable to find that under his rule Austria was well ahead of the rest of Europe in the matter of religious toleration. This had not been so under Maria Theresa. Her devotion and her real piety included not a little of the spirit of bigotry and intolerance. Her hand had fallen very heavily upon the Protestants. They were excluded from all offices, not allowed to have freedom of worship, except in Hungary where they were very numerous, over three millions, and they had to have their marriages blessed by a Roman Catholic priest; and Joseph had great difficulty in checking a fierce persecution of the Moravian converts to Protestantism in 1777. The condition of the Jews was even worse: they were not allowed to own houses in Vienna, and the Ordinance of the Jews of 1753 imposed upon them a series of restrictions of a similarly galling nature.

But under Joseph things were very different. Lutherans, Calvinists and the Greek Church enjoyed freedom to worship, might build prayer-houses and schools, own land and houses, enter the professions and hold municipal, civil and military offices. Thus it was hardly wonderful that the Protestants in Austria, who had only numbered 74,000 in 1782, had reached 157,000 in 1787, many who had conformed outwardly to Roman Catholicism now professing their real beliefs. The Jews also shared in the benefit of Joseph's reforms. To make them more useful citizens he removed some restrictions, allowing them to attend schools and universities, and giving them some measure of freedom. This toleration was not shared by all Joseph's Ministers. It was most distasteful to Hatzfeldt, the President of the Council of State, and Blümegen (Court Chancellor), while a good many more officials, notably in Bohemia, were dismissed on account of their persistent opposition to the policy. But while Joseph thus did much which provoked the opposition of the Church, it would be most unjust to regard him as its enemy. He was a Catholic and not an Atheist, he was not even a Free-mason or a " Voltairian." If he freed education from Church control and made it secular, if he made the State altogether independent of the Church, it was because he sought the good of the State, that wider whole of which the Church formed a part.

In other directions Joseph took up and extended the reforms initiated by Maria Theresa. In codifying the civil and criminal law, in introducing greater simplicity into the laws relating to marriages (published 1783) and to suc-cession and inheritance (1786), he did good work. The property law of 1786 and the penal code of 1787 show a distinct advance and are quite modern. Much that was barbarous was removed from the penal code; the property of a person under a charge but as yet unconvicted was respected; duelling was treated as murder.

In another sphere Joseph had pushed on further even in Maria Theresa's lifetime than she was herself prepared to go. This was the agrarian question. Maria Theresa was sincerely anxious for the well-being of the peasantry, to protect them against oppression and undue exactions on the part of their lords, but she herself was at heart one of the old aristocracy of Austria. With her, good treatment of the lower orders was a matter of the heart, not, as with Joseph, of the head, an obligation which the ruler must observe, not a right which the subjects could demand. She was utterly untouched by the theories and principles which dominated him. However, she made no opposition to his schemes for the regulation of the " Robot."[1] The condition of the peasantry differed considerably with the provinces. In the Sclavonic lands they were much worse off than in the German districts; in Hungary they were unfree, and weighed down by heavy burdens which the lesser nobility among the Magyars stoutly defended against Joseph's efforts to remove them. In Austria itself and in Tyrol the peasantry were best off, though the Bohemian nobles were the best farmers and landowners in the

[1] Services due from the peasants to the landowners.

Hapsburg dominions, and did much to improve their estates and the conditions under which their tenantry existed, rebuilding villages, draining swamps and looking after the forests. In the lands along the Drave the peasantry were attached to the soil, but enjoyed a fair amount of personal freedom. They could acquire personal property and dispose of it by will, and were not fettered by restrictions as to marriage. In Carinthia and Styria only Catholics were allowed to own houses and the population was as a whole backward, though cases occurred of peasants leaving as large a fortune as 30,000 gulden.

The chief aims of Joseph's reforms were the abolition of serfdom, or, where he could not actually effect this, to render fixed and definite the uncertain claims of the lords. His first efforts in these directions provoked strenuous opposition on the part of the Estates, and even to some extent from the administration, which in composition and in sympathies was very largely aristocratic. In 1770 an Ordinance was published for Bohemia, which forbade the lords to forestall or to press labour or exact dues on marriages or on the purchase of land by their tenants. After much opposition and trouble it was decided that the matter should be left to be settled by arrangement between the lords and their subjects; but though this was done on the Royal domains, elsewhere it remained for the most part a dead letter, with the result that in 1775 the peasants, losing all hope of getting relief by any other way, endeavoured to extort it by an insurrection. The troops, however, were quite untouched by popular sympathies and the revolt was suppressed without difficulty.

In no way deterred by this revolt, Joseph pushed on with his schemes of agrarian reform. He regarded those who had opposed his measures as responsible for the rising, and in August 1775 he induced Maria Theresa to grant a " Robot patent " by which the services due were fixed so as not to exceed three days' work a week, while it was possible to commute this for money or produce on a settled system. The relative contributions of the vassal and the lord to the land-tax were also fixed, and in 1778 a supplementary edict defined the normal " Robot " as two days. Altogether this was a marked advance on previous conditions, but Joseph was not content. Soon after he became sole ruler, he published an edict abolishing personal serfdom (Jan. 15th, 1781). The sixth article of this document promised the peasants freedom to marry as they would, freedom to move their residence, the right to the products of their labour, and abolished several other of the more oppressive "incidents" of their vassalage. However, the peasant was not even now withdrawn from all dependence on the lord. He was still responsible to him, attended at his court, and had to perform the services due according to the " Robot," unless he had already commuted them. But these services were now fixed, and the peasantry could obtain legal redress in cases of infringement of the arrangements. In September 1781 another edict greatly reduced the criminal jurisdiction of the lords, and took the peasantry under the protection of the State, which appointed public advocates in all the provinces to act as counsel for the peasants. The result of these reforms is well summed up by Wolf.[1] " Before the time of Joseph II, the peasantry formed a class of the people : after Joseph they were again an estate (*Stand*), with public rights and duties."

Closely connected with all this was the reassessment of the land-tax, for Joseph was most anxious to reduce the burden on the peasants, declaring that unless the peasantry were prosperous the kingdom could not be. It was a work of great difficulty, for when a reassessment was ordered in April 1785 nobles, clergy, Estates and even many of the ministers themselves protested and offered all the opposition they could. In September 1789, however, the new rates were published. Houses were to pay 10 per cent. of their rent, agricultural land 12¼ per cent. of its gross produce, the communities being made responsible for the tax. The peasantry had in addition to pay 17¾ per cent. to their landlords. But this system proved a failure. The work had been done rather too hastily and had been somewhat scamped, the rate being fixed a good deal too high; and as the whole plan was most unpopular Leopold I rescinded it on his accession.

It was not merely over these matters of the position of the peasantry and over the land-tax that Joseph came into collision with the nobility, who still held a most important

[1] P. 287.

and influential position in the Hapsburg dominions. They still retained under their control, minor justice, police and the supervision of the schools, they had great power and influence locally, they had never been detached from the land and made mere satellites of the Court as their contemporaries in France had been. Moreover, they had in the Estates of the various provinces a constitutional means of making their views known, so that the efforts which Joseph made at every favourable opportunity to restrict the sphere of activity of the Estates were really attacks on the aristocratic element in the government and constitution. His great idea was to promote the happiness of the many by diminishing the powers of the few, and it was with this object that he attacked social and fiscal privileges, as in the matter of the "robot" and land-tax or the political powers of the nobles, as in forbidding in 1782 all payments by the Estates which the government had not authorised. But this policy was far from being popular, even with those most closely associated with the Emperor and holding the principal offices under him. Zinzendorf, then President of the Debt Commission (*Hofrechenkammer*), declared in February 1787 that neither the ministers nor the Council of State were competent to decide upon a new system of taxation, and that it should be referred to an assembly of " Notables." Joseph accordingly sought to recruit his bureaucracy independently of class distinctions; but while the bureaucrats too often displayed a want of the zeal, single-mindedness and self-sacrifice which Joseph somewhat over-confidently expected, the Emperor was much at fault in seeking to impose on Austria a system she was not fitted to receive. Conscious of his own sincerity and of his zeal for the welfare of his subjects, Joseph could not understand that the old distinctions of provinces and classes which he yearned to sweep away, the old constitutional forms and rights which marred the completeness of his bureaucratic absolutism and in which he could only see the obsolete relics of an unenlightened past, did not appear in the same light to other people, that it was possible to differ from him and his policy honestly and without bad motives. Thus it was that he failed to appreciate the opposition he aroused, sought to override rather than to conciliate it, outstripped even those of his ministers and subjects who on the whole approved of his policy, never gave his measures time to live down opposition by successful working, and was always "taking the second step before the first."

Joseph, indeed, was by no means as absolute and autocratic as was, for example, his neighbour Frederick II. In Austria the personality of the ministers still was of great importance, especially when there was among them such a man as Kaunitz. President of the Council of State, Chancellor, Minister of the Interior,[1] he exercised an enormous influence over domestic and foreign affairs alike. Methodical, precise, a trifle slow, he was quite the reverse of the more erratic and impetuous Joseph; and on many points, notably the treatment of Hungary and the Netherlands, they were at variance, while Kaunitz clung with the utmost tenacity to the system of foreign policy he had introduced in 1756; and not until the French Revolution had developed into a danger to all Europe, and Frederick II was dead, did he so far overcome his habitual distrust of Prussia as to advocate an alliance with the Court of Berlin.

No one else among the Austrian ministers could compare in authority with Kaunitz. Henry Blumegen, Court Chancellor from 1771 to 1781; Leopold Kolowrat, his successor in that office; Count Seilern, the Minister of Justice; Rudolf Chotek, nephew of Maria Theresa's Minister and assistant to Kolowrat till 1789, were all thoroughly competent as subordinates, but not capable of doing much independently. Trained for the most part in the Theresian school, they tended to be conservative: Blumegen resigned when, in 1781, Joseph united the financial and political administration; Chotek, though a strong advocate of the supremacy of the Crown, was too much of an aristocrat to accept the abolition of serfdom: he resigned in 1789 as a protest against the new system of taxation. Zinzendorf, a man of great financial and commercial knowledge, and a keen supporter of Joseph's Church policy, disliked the agrarian reforms and was much opposed to the suppression of all constitutional forms. Kolowrat, Zinzendorf's predecessor as President of the Debt Commission (1771 to 1782) and subsequently Director of the united financial and political administration, had strong aristocratic and constitutional sympathies which made him a half-hearted agent for Joseph.

[1] Wolf, p. 224.

Moreover, Joseph was not able to allay the rising discontent by the most effective of all palliatives, reduction of taxation. His reforms were for the most part expensive: a bureaucracy, especially if it is to be honest and efficient, must be adequately paid; it was impossible to cut down the sums devoted to the army, and with hospitals, sanitation and charitable institutions all making great demands Joseph had rather to increase than to diminish taxation. He also sought to readjust the burden, as, for example, by reassessing the land-tax, and so make it easier to be borne, and to increase the tax-producing capacities of his dominions by public works, by fostering industries and manufactures, and by encouraging trade. Under Zinzendorf as Governor Trieste made great progress: in 1782 it had an import trade of 8½ million gulden and exported 13 millions' worth. In 1790 the number of vessels visiting the port had risen from the 4300 of 1782 to 6750 6 per cent. being Austrian. However, on the whole Joseph's efforts to make income and expenditure balance were not very successful. Whenever careful economy had produced a surplus, some shift of foreign policy was sure to swallow it up and leave a considerable deficit. Thus in 1783 the revenue reached 78,000,000 gulden and exceeded the expenses by nearly four millions; but the question of the Scheldt sent up the outgoings to 84 millions, 87 millions and 85¾ millions in the next three years. In 1787 there was again a surplus, the revenue reaching 92 millions, the expenditure 85⅓; but the Turkish War proved most costly, and at Joseph's death there was a deficit of nearly 28 millions and a debt of no less than 370. Still he did effect great reforms in the financial administration, swept away a great many obsolete and unnecessary posts, allowed several unproductive old taxes to expire, and found new sources of revenue in stamps, newspapers and the tobacco monopoly. Tariff reform was another important sphere in which Joseph did good work, although he failed to get rid of the customs-boundary between Austria and Hungary. He was a strong Protectionist, and the tariff of 1784 was mainly designed to keep out foreign competition, though subsequently it underwent considerable modifications.

Joseph's difficulties, great enough when confined to the problems arising out of Austria, Bohemia and their dependencies, were multiplied enormously by Hungarian autonomy, and by the resistance of the Netherlands to the reforms he sought to introduce into that isolated portion of his dominions. In both these countries, reforms were urgently needed, but in both the old constitutional forms were strong enough to serve as the nucleus for the resistance of all those vested interests which Joseph had attacked and offended.

The Netherlands were, as a rule, governed by some member of the Imperial family, assisted by a Minister Plenipotentiary. Up till 1780 Charles of Lorraine acted as Stadtholder, and on his death Albert of Saxe-Teschen and his wife, the Archduchess Marie Christina, youngest daughter of Maria Theresa, succeeded to the office; but Joseph treated them more as representatives of the dynasty than as responsible for the government, which was mainly in the hands of Count George Adam Stahremberg. The latter, however, resigned in 1783 as he found his advice neglected by the Emperor, and Count Belgiojoso succeeded him.

The reforms which Joseph proposed to introduce into the Netherlands were of much the same kind as those attempted in Austria. Trade was in a bad condition, owing largely to the closing of the Scheldt,[1] the administration was neither very efficient nor very honest, justice was proverbially tedious, the economic and social condition of the country unsatisfactory, the defences inefficient, and the Church wealthy and influential. It was the Church, therefore, that Joseph first attacked. He applied to the monks in the Netherlands the same measures as he had applied in Austria (1782), and with fair success; for while the clergy offered bitter opposition, the mass of the people acquiesced. In 1786 further trouble was caused by the foundation of a Seminary at Louvain to give the clergy a rather more liberal education than that which they were receiving in the Episcopal schools. This measure the Papal Nuntio, Zondaderi, and the Archbishop of Malines, Count Frankenberg, resisted so stoutly that the latter had to be recalled to Vienna and the former sent back to Rome. Thus Joseph alienated the clergy completely, while the provinces as a whole, disappointed at the failure of his efforts to free the Scheldt, had not appreciated the proposed exchange against Bavaria, and not unreasonably cared but little about a ruler who admittedly wanted to get rid of them. Accordingly, when

[1] Cf. p. 322.

in January 1787 Joseph published edicts abolishing the Council of State, the Privy Council, the Secretariat and the Financial Council, which were all to be replaced by a Council of the Governor-General of the Netherlands, remodelling the judicial arrangements completely, taking away the privileges and special jurisdictions of the nobility, dissolving the old provincial boundaries and constitutions and dividing the land into nine " Circles " each under an Intendant, it was the clergy who fanned the flame of discontent into resistance.

Joseph's proposals aimed at unity, coherence and centralisation of administration; but the Belgians adhered to their cherished autonomy and regarded the establishment of absolutism as a tyrannical outrage. They preferred their feudal and federal arrangements, even if they were in Joseph's eyes quite indefensible. Moreover, equality before the law was a breach of each man's rights to the privileges of his class ; the burghers hated the conscription and the Austrian criminal procedure, and the nobles were especially hostile to the scheme. When the Estates of Brabant met (April 1787) the opposition soon found its voice and gave vent in no measured terms to its disapproval of the new measures. Belgiojoso was vigorously denounced ; and the Viceroys, after vainly trying to quell the discontent, were compelled to withdraw the obnoxious edicts and cancel the new arrangements in order to avert an actual outbreak (May 30th). Joseph, however, determined to persist, and to overcome opposition by force if necessary. Convinced as he was of the excellence of his reforms, and that they could not fail to prove beneficial, he could not conceive that honest opposition could be offered to them and totally failed to comprehend the feelings of his Belgian subjects. Much against the advice of Kaunitz he refused to make any concessions, replaced Belgiojoso by Trautmansdorf, and gave the command in the Netherlands to d'Alton, superseding General Murray, who had hitherto averted a conflict by concessions, notably by withdrawing the troops from Brussels.

With Trautmansdorf really in the place of the Viceroys and the rough and stern d'Alton at Trautmansdorf's elbow, the reign of coercion was not far off. Nevertheless, 1788 on the whole passed off quietly enough, though arbitrary arrests, the suppression of the Press, and the prevention of public meetings served rather to muzzle than to stamp out the spreading disaffection. When the taxes for 1789 had to be voted, the first two orders of the Estates of Brabant consented to vote them, but the Third Estate refused, and its example was followed in Hainault. Joseph determined to use force. In June a new ordinance was published, suppressing the *Joyeuse Entrée*, the principal charter of Belgian liberties, abolishing the Council of Brabant,[1] doing away with the Estates, and establishing an entirely new system of local administration and a new High Court of Justice. To force the Belgians replied with force. A Revolutionary Committee assembled at Breda to direct the insurrection, which spread like wildfire. The troops, few in number and somewhat disaffected, were unable to hold their own. All Flanders had to be evacuated. Brabant rose, and the troops had to be concentrated at Brussels, and to confine their efforts to holding out there and maintaining the line of communications by Namur and Luxembourg. Two distinct parties were now taking shape in the insurgent ranks. One, aristocratic and conservative, led by Van der Noot, was contemplating appealing to the Triple Alliance to which the recent (1787) intervention of England and Prussia in Holland[2] had given birth. The other, guided by the able but uncompromising Vonck, was frankly democratic, and looked for help to France, where revolutionary principles were gaining ground rapidly; and it was this party which took the lead in the attack on the troops. The insurrection had occurred at a time most unfavourable to Joseph. He was deeply implicated in the perennial Eastern Question, and his relations with the other Powers, notably with Prussia, were somewhat strained. He was therefore in no position to continue his coercive policy, especially as he feared that Prussia might take the part of the insurgents and intervene in Belgium. Accordingly he revoked his ordinances, promised to dissolve the Louvain Seminary, restored the *Joyeuse Entrée*, issued a general amnesty, and sent the Vice-Chancellor, Philip Cobenzl, to the Netherlands (Nov. 26th). But these concessions were interpreted as merely signs of weakness, and the insurgents, much encouraged, attacked Brussels and forced

---

[1] The High Court of Justice, which had important political functions as guardian of the constitution.

[2] Cf. p. 325.

d'Alton to evacuate it (Dec. 12th) and fall back to Luxembourg. Flushed with success, they declared that the Emperor had forfeited his sovereign rights, and in January 1790 deputies from the revolted provinces met at Brussels and proclaimed their independence as the United States of Belgium. It might have been predicted, however, that unless one of the Great Powers recognised this new State its independent existence would be shortlived. France was not unwilling, but the Belgian constitution was too aristocratic for her, and early in 1790 France was not in a position to take a very active line in foreign affairs, while Prussia could not act alone; and though the threat to recognise the Belgian Republic was an effective card in the diplomatic game, it was not very seriously intended. Thus, though Joseph did not live to see it, as soon as Austria's hands had been more or less freed by the Convention of Reichenbach and the subsequent Peace of Sistova, the Belgian Republic was called upon to defend itself and failed to answer to the challenge.

Belgium, however, was not the only part of the Hapsburg dominions in which the discontent aroused by Joseph's reforms became a really serious matter. Hungary, despite the reforms of Maria Theresa, who had exercised a practically absolute power over it from 1765 to 1780, was still a feudal state, almost untouched by modern changes. Since 1764 no Diet had been summoned. The office of Palatine had been replaced by those of Stadtholder and Captain-General, posts conferred on Albert of Saxe-Teschen; but Hungary retained a great deal of autonomy, the local officials being for the most part elective, and the strength of the lower nobility was still very great. Moreover, the various abuses on which Joseph was waging war everywhere flourished with special vigour in Hungary. The judicial system was obsolete, education in the hands of a wealthy but rather ignorant clergy, the nobles controlled the government and did nothing, the peasants were unfree and weighed down with heavy burdens. Here as elsewhere the Church was the first institution to experience Joseph's attacks; but though the granting of toleration to Jews and Protestants, the suppression of the monasteries and the exaction of a new oath from the Bishops were all declared to be breaches of the constitution, they were as a whole accepted quietly enough, and it was not till after Joseph's visit to Hungary in 1784 that trouble really began.

To a proud and sensitive race like the Magyars it was an insult that German should have been proclaimed to be the official language, as was done in 1784, another decree announcing that in future only German-speaking persons would be appointed to official posts. An even more serious grievance was Joseph's interference in the social and economic arrangements of the country. In August 1785 an edict was published abolishing serfdom. It met with bitter opposition from the serf-owning territorial magnates, and as a matter of fact remained a dead letter. In Transylvania the disappointment of the peasants resulted in a social rising which developed into a "Jacquerie." Many landowners were murdered, many castles and houses pillaged and burnt before the insurrection was ruthlessly and sternly repressed. Both sides put the blame on Joseph. The peasants felt that he had deserted them and had not fulfilled his promises: the nobles looked on his reforms as the cause of the trouble and were indignant with his leniency towards the insurgents. But further measures were to come, amounting to a widespreading alteration of the constitution, including the re-division of the land into ten Circles, each under a Commissary, a royal official who was to be responsible for public order, for raising taxes, levying recruits and similar work. This was an interference with local government, hitherto the province of the nobles, higher and lower, and caused much dissatisfaction. But Joseph paid no heed to the rising opposition, nor attempted in the least to conciliate it or to give his reforms time to make themselves more acceptable in practice. He hurried on from one reform to another. The conscription, introduced in 1785, was bitterly resented as an attempt to supersede the national "Insurrection." A census was taken in 1785 as the preliminary to a reform of the land-tax, from which by the rescript of February 10th, 1786, nobles and clergy were to be no longer exempt. In December 1786 an Imperial rescript announced a complete change in the administration which would have the effect of subjecting it completely to the Emperor's control.

However, foreign complications made it impossible to put all these new arrangements into force. The outbreak of the Turkish War, actually begun in December 1787, though not formally declared till February 1788, made it necessary to demand a vote of men and money, and in Hungary the principle that "redress of grievances should precede supply" was well understood. The nobles and the other bodies to which the Emperor applied demanded that the Diet should be summoned. Joseph steadily refused, fearing that the Diet would be more than he could control. Opposition accordingly grew stronger, and so did the pressure of the financial needs. Moreover, as in old days, there was a small party in Hungary which was ready to appeal to external assistance against the sovereign. The quarter to which this section looked was no longer Constantinople but Berlin. Frederick William II when invited to guarantee the freedom of Hungary did not show himself prepared to go quite to that length. He and his influential minister, Hertzberg, were glad to use the threat of supporting discontent in Hungary to forward their objects on the Vistula, but they had no intention of going any further. Moreover, Hungary as a whole was quite loyal to the dynasty ; the cause of discontent was the reforms which might be withdrawn, there was no real wish for independence. However, the danger of Prussian intervention added yet another anxiety to the load of troubles under which Joseph was fast giving way. Bitterly disappointed as he was at the results of his well-meant reforms, at the ingratitude with which his efforts for the good of his subjects had been met, at the failure of his schemes for the revival of the Empire and of his ambitious foreign policy in general, his health, never of the best, was breaking down completely. It was a final blow that in January 1790 he found himself obliged to concede almost all that Hungary demanded. He cancelled his reforms and restored the old arrangements, but even now he refused to call a Diet. Whether he would have had to do so in the end is a question which his death (Feb. 20th) left unanswered.

Many different verdicts have been pronounced on Joseph II. If he was deficient in judgment and in the power of suiting his policy to his circumstances, if he failed to appreciate the ideas of his subjects or to make allowances for their prejudices, there are few monarchs of whom it can so confidently be asserted that their chief care was the public good, and fewer still who have been so consistently unfortunate.

He set up a high ideal of duty, and practically killed himself in trying to carry out a policy which was dictated by the best motives. Shortlived as were many of his reforms, unsuccessful as were many of his schemes, he yet did accomplish much. He got rid of much that was effete and obsolete, aroused a new spirit in Austria, and enunciated principles on which others were to base their work.

CHAPTER XVII

LEOPOLD II AND THE EASTERN QUESTION

L EOPOLD, the third son of Maria Theresa, was forty-three years of age when Joseph's death called him from Florence to Vienna. In 1765 he had been given his father's Grand Duchy of Tuscany of which he had taken over the direct rule in 1770, it having till then been in the hands of the Marquis Botta d'Adorno and, since 1776, of Count Orsini-Rosenberg. Under Leopold's rule, Tuscany had been orderly, peaceful and prosperous; and he had carried out, though on a smaller scale and with rather more success, much the same measures of domestic reform that Joseph II had attempted in Austria. Where, however, Leopold differed from Joseph was in possessing strong constitutionalist sympathies, which enabled him to appreciate far more fairly the opposition which Joseph could not understand. Though admirably loyal to Joseph, he felt that his brother had gone too far in the matter of Hungary, and he was inclined to make really considerable concessions to the Belgian insurgents. To coercion and arbitrary action he was on principle opposed, for he looked upon monarchs as delegates and representatives of their subjects; indeed, he had gone so far as to contemplate the introduction into Tuscany of some form of representative government, but had abandoned the project on account of the lukewarmness of the nobility and the obstructionist attitude of the clergy.

Leopold came to the Austrian throne with the fixed determination to make peace as soon as possible, since he saw that it was badly wanted and was an essential preliminary to putting the internal affairs of his dominions on a sound basis. Moreover, it was clear that the Turkish war was not by any means the "walk over" for which Joseph II had hoped, and that, in view of Prussia's evident hostility, Austria would do well to make peace before she suffered any serious disaster on the Danube. Already Austria had been forced to mass nearly

150,000 men on the frontiers of Poland and Prussia, and on March 29th, 1790, Hertzberg completed the negotiation of a treaty with Poland by which Prussia promised in return for Dantzic and Thorn to obtain Galicia from Austria for Poland, guaranteed the Polish constitution and pledged herself to assist Poland, if she were attacked, with 18,000 men. This treaty was certainly a breach of Prussia's engagements to Austria and Russia, but its provisions were never carried into effect. In the first place, financial considerations made it impossible for Prussia to act without the support of the Maritime Powers, and they were anxious for peace, more especially as Leopold had hinted to England that unless he got help somewhere he would have to surrender Belgium to France. Pitt had no liking for the ambitious and aggressive policy of Frederick William, and the maintenance of Austrian authority in Belgium was one of the cardinal points of his policy, so that Leopold's overtures were well received, and when two Austrian envoys arrived at the Prussian headquarters at Reichenbach (June 26th, 1790) the ministers of the Maritime Powers insisted on being present at the conference and pronounced decisively in favour of the maintenance of existing arrangements. Hertzberg's schemes were thus completely upset. Moreover, Frederick William, who was so determined not to be the tool of his responsible ministers that he was absolutely controlled by irresponsible favourites like Lucchesini, rather distrusted Hertzberg and was already feeling a little nervous about the spread of democratic principles in France. Poland also would not give up Dantzic and Thorn unless she got adequate compensation, and nothing short of an overwhelming defeat would induce Austria to give up Galicia. In so unpromising a state of affairs Frederick William decided to come to terms with Leopold, in whose political creed hostility to Prussia was not, as it was with Kaunitz, the principal tenet. Indeed, Leopold had fathomed the true condition of things in Prussia, and realising the divergence of opinion between Hertzberg and his master, with great adroitness addressed himself directly to Frederick William and his confidants, Bischoffswerder and Lucchesini. The result was that an agreement was soon reached, both monarchs being ready to facilitate the restoration of peace by renouncing all idea of territorial gain. Austria was somewhat loath to give up all her recent acquisitions, especially as Alexinez and Orsova had been taken (April), and Clerfayt had gained a considerable victory over the Turks at Kolafat (June 26th). However, Loudoun's death (July 14th) damped the ardour of the bellicose, and so on July 27th, the same day that Clerfayt gained another victory on the Danube, at Florentin, the Treaty of Reichenbach was signed. It was really a triumph for Leopold, who by clever diplomacy escaped from a rather awkward position. The Triple Alliance guaranteed the restoration of Austrian authority in Belgium, and promised to bring about peace with Turkey. As to the cession of Galicia to Poland not a word was said, and Prussia had, for the time being at any rate, to forego the coveted Dantzic. Frederick William also pledged his support to Leopold's candidature for the Empire. Six weeks later the armistice of Giurgevo (Sept. 19th) put an end to the hostilities between the Austrians and Turks, and in December a congress was opened at Sistova to settle the terms of peace.

Leopold was thus able to devote his energies to the resettlement of Hungary and to the reassertion of Austrian authority in Belgium. In Hungary he had a far from easy task. The whole country was in a turbulent and disorderly condition. Conciliatory measures were interpreted as confessions of impotence, and when the Diet was opened at Ofen on June 8th the most extravagant claims were advanced and a strenuous opposition offered to Leopold's proposals. The Diet actually went to the length of proposing that the constitution should be guaranteed by Prussia; upon which Leopold, who had already carried conciliation to the extreme limit of reasonableness, prepared to use force. It was this domestic difficulty, however, which caused him to modify his tone at Reichenbach, as Prussia held a strong card in the diplomatic game in the threat to acknowledge the Belgian Republic or to assist the Hungarians. Fortunately Leopold's firmness produced the desired result. The clergy and the burghers were now on his side, and the Diet, deprived of the hope of Prussian intervention by the conclusion of the Treaty of Reichenbach, gave way. On November 15th, Leopold was crowned at Pressburg. This did not end all troubles, for the Diet went in detail into the land question, the organisation of the administration and of justice, and the question of the position of the Protestants. Not a jot of their privileges and rights could the nobles be induced to give up, and the result was that Hungary, to which Joseph's reforms would have opened the door to progress, relapsed into and remained in a condition of stagnation. Though no longer serfs, the peasantry were still unfree. The townsfolk were without power or influence. The nobles, free from taxation and from military service, retained their position as a privileged and dominant aristocracy. But at this price Leopold had succeeded in restoring peace and order to the most troublous portion of his dominions. Had he lived it is quite likely he might have attempted, in some form or other, the much-needed reforms which for the time being he had had to sacrifice.

About the same time a Diet was held in Transylvania. Here the problems were much simpler. Things had been at once restored (March 1790) to the condition which had existed before Joseph's innovations, and the Emperor now (Feb. 1791) decided upon the separation of the Transylvanian from the Hungarian Chancery. He also succeeded despite the opposition of the local nobility in securing the abolition of serfdom.

In the case of the Netherlands, the chief danger was that of foreign intervention, but the idea that England would take the side of the rebels was always a mere chimera. France was too well occupied at home to do anything, and the Treaty of Reichenbach removed all anxiety as to Prussia, although a Prussian officer, von Schönfeld, had been given the post of commander-in-chief by the Clerical section among the insurgents. This party, led by Van der Noot, had gained the upper hand in a fierce struggle with the democratic section, the Vonckists, who were more inclined to approve of the reforms in general and were therefore prepared to listen to the pacific overtures of Leopold. The Emperor was most anxious to avoid bloodshed, but the Clericals would not hear of a compromise. The Bishops preached a crusade against him, and were ready to throw themselves into the arms of France, though no help was forthcoming from that quarter, partly because Pitt had let it be understood that in case of a French intervention he would assist Austria. Finally, in November, no surrender having been made by the appointed time (Nov. 21st), an Austrian corps of 33,000 men was put in motion. On the 26th Namur fell, on the 30th Brussels was reached, on

December 2nd it opened its gates. Practically no resistance was made and the country as a whole welcomed the Emperor's troops. This success was used with the utmost mildness. Leopold declined to exercise the rights of a conqueror. He issued a general amnesty, dissolved the hated Seminary, restored the University of Louvain, allowed the Church free disposal of its revenues and made no attempt to get hold of the ringleaders. Indeed, the Vonckists were the only people who had any cause to grumble. They had hoped to see something in the way of democratic reforms, and in their disappointment they began to plan a new rising, in which they hoped for the support of France, now rapidly passing under the control of the democratic party.

But though the discontent excited by Joseph's well-meant reforms had nowhere else reached so high a pitch as in Hungary and the Netherlands, it was by no means non-existent in the "hereditary dominions." Leopold had begun by repealing Joseph's land-tax and new laws as to land-tenure (March 1790). He then summoned assemblies in the various provinces to discuss further measures. It is interesting to notice that while the demands of the various assemblies included a share in legislation for the Estates, their general tenor was retrograde rather than Radical. They did not attack the absolutist régime as such, and where they did desire modifications of the existing state of things, it was rather in the direction of feudalism than of democratic representative government. In Moravia 1628 was taken as the golden time to which the Estates wished to return: Joseph's land-tenure system was denounced as "derogatory to the nobles and the State." In Styria the nobles bitterly opposed a proposed increase in the representation of the cities. In Bohemia local autonomy was demanded. In Carinthia the upper classes condemned the encouragement of education as dangerous and subversive of order. In Tyrol alone it was the peasants and burghers who offered opposition; but Tyrol was constitutionally quite different from the other provinces, and even there the demand was for freedom from the conscription and restriction of official posts to local men.

The truth was that in all these districts feudalism was making a last effort to assert itself against the enlightened absolutism which Maria Theresa and Joseph had planted so strongly that it could not be completely overthrown. There was no feeling in favour of any really constitutional movement, and Leopold· was able to restore order and reassert his authority without abandoning any very valuable rights. What was done in the way of alteration or reform was done by the authority of the head of the State through the bureaucracy, which Leopold strove hard to keep up to a high standard of efficiency.

The best means of judging fairly the work of Maria Theresa and her sons is to compare the Austria of 1792 with the Austria of Leopold I. In population and material prosperity there had been an enormous advance. Bohemia alone had 2,700,000 inhabitants as against 800,000 in 1648. Manufactures and industry were if anything too carefully fostered by the State. If Joseph had not done all he desired for the peasantry, they and the burghers had received considerable encouragement from the efforts of their rulers on their behalf. They had been taught self-respect; more enterprise, ambition and industry had been instilled into them. The Jesuit monopoly of education had been broken down, and thought freed from the trammels hitherto imposed on it. One effect of this was the great intellectual activity of the period, in literature, in the theatrical and musical worlds.[1] In music the period was of special importance, for Vienna served as a half-way house between Italy and Northern Germany. Mozart was prominent at the Court of Maria Theresa, Haydn was a native of Lower Austria, and Beethoven took up his residence at Vienna in 1792, and gave a new impetus to musical life there. It was during this period that Vienna developed its character of a gay and lively capital, much frequented by the German nobility and even by the leading Magyar nobles, who maintained great state and spent money freely. A good deal was done for the improvement of the capital by Leopold I and succeeding rulers, especially for sanitation, which needed reform very badly, for between 1770 and 1782 the death-rate was as heavy as 40 in the 1000.[2] It may have been partly owing to the social amenities of Vienna that its inhabitants concerned themselves but little with politics. They might protest, as in

[1] Cf. Wolf, pp. 415 ff.
[2] The population was about 250,000, Paris at the time having 700,000 people, London, 900,000.

1789, against the heaviness of the taxation, but they did not trouble about Joseph's ecclesiastical reforms ; and even the storm and stress of the Napoleonic wars did not affect them to anything like the same extent as it did the North Germans. They neither suffered as much nor felt the degradation of Napoleon's domination as keenly, so that even the enthusiasm of the War of Liberation left them comparatively untouched.

Even the Treaty of Reichenbach had not got rid of the Eastern Question. It had only made a provisional arrangement by which the war was prevented from spreading further ; peace had yet to be made, and it was by no means certain that it would be possible to arrange it on terms satisfactory to all concerned. However, one result of the treaty was that no opposition was offered to Leopold's candidature for the Empire. It was felt desirable in view of the state of affairs in France that the interregnum should be brought to an end as soon as possible, and on September 30th, 1790, Leopold was unanimously elected. His first important act as Emperor was to issue a protest (Dec. 14th) against the decrees of the French Assembly of August 4th, 1789, abolishing feudalism and its appendages, on the ground that they violated the treaty rights of those members of the Empire who held lands in Alsace. But this protest was a mere paper form, and was only important as an indication of future trouble; for the time being Leopold's most pressing task was to bring about peace with Turkey, and to put his relations with Prussia and Russia on a satisfactory footing.

Though disposed to establish good relations with Prussia, Leopold had no intention of throwing Russia over altogether ; and Russia, if relieved by the Peace of Verela (Aug. 1790) from the hostility of the still respectable naval power of Sweden, was yet afraid of a coalition between the Triple Alliance, Poland and Turkey, and therefore desired to retain the Austrian alliance, although negotiations for peace between Austria and the Porte had begun at Sistova in December 1790. These at first failed to produce any satisfactory result. The Turks demanded that Austria should not merely give up her recent conquests but Bukovina also, a proposal Austria absolutely refused to entertain, so that the negotiations were broken off (Feb. 10th). It seemed as if Leopold's efforts to avert a general European war would be unsuccessful, for Pitt had committed himself to forcing Russia to relax her grip on Oczakow, and in conjunction with Prussia he was preparing to present an ultimatum to Catherine. Leopold had no wish to embark in a war against England and Prussia in order that Russia should keep Oczakow, but the failure to arrange terms with Turkey made his position very awkward. It might have been difficult for him to avoid supporting Russia against the Triple Alliance had not relief come from England (March). Public opinion proved absolutely hostile to the proposed intervention on behalf of Turkey, and Pitt found himself compelled to abandon the idea. Prussia showed no disposition to take up arms alone on behalf of Turkey, Russia's position was enormously improved and the Turks found themselves compelled to modify their attitude towards Austria. Negotiations were accordingly resumed (May), and after several hitches, were finally brought to an end by the Peace of Sistova (Aug. 4th, 1791). This renewed the Peace of Belgrade and the subsequent Austro-Turkish commercial treaties. Austria restored the conquests she had made since February 1788, but a separate treaty ceded to her Old Orsova and a small strip of territory in Croatia.[1] The Russo-Turkish War was brought to a close about the same time by a preliminary treaty at Galatz, which was completed by the definite Peace of Jassy in January 1792.

The real importance of the cessation of the Turkish War was that it removed one of the principal obstacles to those better relations between Austria and Prussia for which, mainly on account of the state of affairs in France, both Leopold and Frederick William were anxious. Kaunitz, of course, was still opposed to anything in the way of an alliance, but the Vice-Chancellor, Philip Cobenzl, received Bischoffswerder when he visited Vienna early in 1791 to convey Frederick William's overtures to Leopold. The truth was that both in Austria and in Prussia the monarchs were taking the direction of affairs from the ministers who had till then guided them; and while despite the prejudices of Kaunitz, who could never forget Silesia and 1740, Leopold was coming to favour a reconciliation with Prussia, Frederick William, without actually dismissing Hertzberg, was abandoning the traditions of the system of Frederick II which Hertzberg represented.

[1] Cf. Wolf, p. 383.

In June 1791, Bischoffswerder revisited Leopold, then at Milan, and acquainted him with Frederick William's desire for a personal interview.   Leopold was not long about deciding. On June 18th he informed Bischoffswerder that he approved of the project of an alliance and would be glad to have an interview with Frederick William.   It was arranged that this should be held in Saxon territory at Pillnitz, and in the course of the summer ; and with this Bischoffswerder departed (June 24th).   The foundation of the First Coalition had been laid.

CHAPTER XVIII

GERMANY AND THE FRENCH REVOLUTION

AMONG the causes of Leopold's anxiety for peace with Turkey, even on terms hardly in keeping with the military successes Austria had gained in the war, was his wish to have his hands free to deal with France. Few things are more remarkable than the way in which the earlier stages of the movement which was to exercise so enormous an influence over every branch of German life were overshadowed by the Eastern Question. | Far from engaging the attention of Germany or of Europe as a whole, the French Revolution was, until the year 1791, regarded as a purely French concern, important to the rest of Europe only because it prevented France from taking her usual part in international politics. It was looked upon as likely to paralyse the power of France, to weaken her, to engage her in civil and domestic strife, and to make her a negligible quantity in the calculations of the Foreign Ministries of Europe. Leopold had, of course, to take into consideration the chances of the complication of the situation in Belgium by the intervention of French revolutionaries; but when the Belgian insurrection had been suppressed, and the Bishop of Liége, in virtue of a decree of the Imperial Chamber of April 1790, had been restored to his dominions and to his ancient rights, there seemed no immediate likelihood of trouble.[1]

The causes to which the intervention of the Powers of Europe in the affairs of France is most commonly assigned, the support of monarchical principles against a militant and subversive democracy and Leopold's anxiety to succour his sister and his brother-in-law, were not perhaps the most important

---

[1] An insurrection had broken out in Liége in the autumn of 1789, the Bishop, a Count von Hoensbrook, had been forced to fly to Treves, upon which Prussia marched troops into the Bishopric to restore order. This intervention was mainly designed to give Prussia a foothold in the Netherlands, but on the restoration of better relations between her and Austria she abandoned the Liègois and withdrew her troops.

factors in embroiling France with Europe in 1791–1792. These motives did exist, and did influence Leopold and Frederick William II, though neither of these monarchs was animated merely, as was the Swedish knight-errant King, Gustavus III, by a chivalrous desire to come to the assistance of the imperilled Bourbons; nor did their notions of propriety and orderliness receive the same shock that the excesses of the Revolutionists inflicted upon the order-loving mind of George III. Leopold can have known but little of his sister; and the Franco-Austrian alliance, which he is supposed to have wished to preserve, had been practically non-existent ever since Vergennes had first obtained the direction of the affairs of France. Frederick William II interfered rather more as the champion of absolutist and monarchical principles; but he was a true Hohenzollern and in his eyes the strongest argument in favour of intervention was the prospect of obtaining territorial acquisitions at the expense of the weakened France, torn by internal dissensions, with which he expected to have to deal. Quite apart from these questions, however, there were two points over which a collision between France and the Empire was inevitable, the rights of those Princes of the Empire who held land in Alsace, and the support and shelter given by the Princes of Western Germany to the bands of French *emigrés* who were collecting along the Eastern frontier of France and breathing vengeance on the enemies from whom they had fled.

Of the many anomalies in the constitution of Germany in the 18th Century, the relations which existed between Alsace and the Empire were about the most remarkable.[1] Alsace had been ceded in full sovereignty to France in 1648, but "saving the rights of the Empire." What this exactly meant was never clear—probably it was never meant to be clear. In any case the important fact was that many Princes of the Empire, including among others the Elector Palatine, the Electors of Treves and Mayence and the Bishop of Worms, held lands in Alsace by feudal tenure and had thus been affected by the decrees of August 4th, 1789, abolishing feudalism altogether. They had protested vigorously against this infringement of the rights secured to them by the Peace of Westphalia, but they had not been able to get the National Assembly to see eye to eye with them in the matter. Just before Joseph's death the

[1] Cf. pp. 57–58.

deputies of the Upper Rhenish Circle had petitioned him to protect their rights in Alsace, and Leopold's election capitulations had pledged him to see justice done. In December 1790 the Emperor took the matter up, addressing to the French Assembly a request for the restoration of the old conditions, to which that body returned no answer. The question was then referred to the Diet; but no further steps were taken beyond the publication of a decree (*Reichsschluss*) upon the subject. Meanwhile the emigration had begun, and French nobles were beginning to cross the frontier and to collect in the cities along the Rhine, where they were for the most part welcomed by the local authorities, who looked with great disfavour on the Revolutionary principles now beginning to make themselves felt beyond the French frontiers.

As a whole, Germany was so very different from France, socially, politically and intellectually, that the ideas of the Revolution gained but little ground even in the more advanced parts of the country, and the influence which the Revolution exercised was one of reaction rather than of attraction. Split up into petty principalities, Germany lacked the homogeneity and uniformity which made France strong, compact, and concrete in thought, which enabled the Revolution to identify itself with the country, to overthrow the Bourbons by accusing them of being dynastic rather than national, and to make *incivisme* the worst of crimes. It was not merely political unity that Germany lacked. Socially and economically there were far greater differences between districts only a very small distance apart than there were between provinces at one end of France and those at the other. This was partly due to the want of homogeneity in administration; but other causes affected it also. Differences in religion were reflected by marked differences in condition between Catholic and Protestant states. On the whole, the former were backward, poor and ignorant; the latter, more wealthy, enlightened and prosperous.[1] Even in the intellectual sphere the same effects were to be traced. It was want of unity in Germany which tended to make thought abstract, to build up separate literary schools which gloried in their independence and isolation. Where the unity of France made it possible to establish a so-called "equality," the localism and particularism

---

[1] Cf. Mirabeau, *Royaume de Prusse.*

of Germany kept classes apart and prevented fusion not merely between the higher and the lower, but also between corresponding strata in different states. If the French Revolution gave birth to German nationalism, it did it by first strengthening local patriotism. The subjects of an Imperial Knight had to become Würtembergers or Bavarians before they could become Germans. The substitution of states of moderate size for the multitude of petty principalities whose existence was so strong a barrier to unity of interests or of ideas, seemed a stopping short on the road to the unification of Germany, but it was an essential preliminary to the attainment of any approach to that end. The process was one of degrees. Good government and the abolition of the abuses of the *ancien régime* were more desired by the peoples of Germany than self-government was. For that they were not prepared—they were in too backward a stage of political development. They looked to their rulers to play the part of the enlightened despot and to effect for them the reforms they needed. Thus, where the dynasty rose to the occasion and identified itself, as in Prussia, with the adaptation of the French Revolution to local needs and aspirations, it gained enormously in prestige and influence from a movement which had overthrown the ancient monarchy of France.

It was a curious circumstance that the first impulse given by the clearing away of the old system through French influence was in the direction of getting rid of French influences, especially over language and thought. The first of the "rights of man" was the right to be a German, and this made itself apparent in poetry, in philosophy and in art. The French tastes, education and ideas which had ruled the courts of Germany were gradually ousted. No German Prince had been more under French influence than Frederick II. The Louis XIV of Prussia, French in language and utterly without national feeling, though alive to the advantage of posing as the defender of Germany and the champion of German interests, it was a little curious that he should have done something to revive German feelings by his victory at Rossbach over an army mainly composed of Germans, and representing the only bond between the various parts of Germany, the Empire. The truth was that great as was the power and influence of France over Germany, so far as the elements of a national feeling existed hostility and opposition to France were its principal ingredients. The formidable

Western neighbour was a constant menace to Germany. If the generations had long since passed away which had seen the Palatinate devastated, Heidelberg laid in ruins, Mannheim given to the flames, there must have been many Hessians and Westphalians who retained vivid recollections in 1792 of the performances of the soldiery of " Père la Maraude "[1] and his successors in the Seven Years' War. The loss of Lorraine was only half a century old, and the centenary of the seizure of Strassburg must have recalled the bitter memory of Germany's helplessness in the face of the *Chambres de Reunion* to every patriotic German, if indeed any German living in 1792 had a claim to that description. The German Princes might outrage their patriotic sentiments by assisting in the aggrandisement of France at the expense of Germany, but their insulted national pride could only be healed by a corresponding increase in the compensation they must receive. Frederick II might stoop to accept the help of France in robbing another German Power of one of its provinces, Charles of Bavaria might condescend to owe his precarious tenure of the Imperial throne to the heir of Louis XIV, but one and all professed to look upon France as a foreigner even when receiving benefits at her hands, one and all were ready, if it suited the momentary exigencies of their policy, to invoke the name of Germany, to allege German national interests and to pose as the watchful defenders of Germany against France.

But although the condition of Germany in 1792 was such that there was but little likelihood of resistance to French aggression, Germany was not as accessible to the influence of the new French propaganda as were Belgium and Holland and Italy. It would not, of course, be true to represent Germany as quite untouched by sympathy with the Revolution. The high ideals of some of the men of 1789 were fully in keeping with the doctrines of the *Illuminati*; the notion of Liberty, Fraternity and Equality, the appeal to the "rights of man," the tendency to regard all humanity as one, all these were eagerly welcomed by the cosmopolitan " intellectuals" to whom patriotism was at best only a heroic weakness. Schiller and Goethe raised no protest against the advance of the French frontier to the banks of the Rhine; Kant and Fichte welcomed the overthrow of privilege, of class distinctions, of feudal restrictions as steps

[1] The Duc de Richelieu.

towards the millennium of liberty and the rule of the intellect, they did not stop to reflect that reforms effected by a foreign conqueror have but an uncertain guarantee. Yet the men who welcomed the Revolution were politically of little weight. Trees of liberty were planted at Hamburg, in several places the taking of the Bastille was celebrated; but this was of scarcely any political significance. The governments of Germany saw in the new movement a danger to be closely watched and suppressed; and even if men like Thugut had not been on the alert to prevent the Republican propaganda from taking hold, the country offered an unfruitful soil to the seed. The inhabitants of Southern and Western Germany had but little in common with the French, they received laws and constitutions from France without being in any way assimilated.

The reasons for this are not hard to discover. In Germany there was nothing to correspond to the French *bourgeoisie*, no class capable of throwing off the yoke of the nobles. Feudalism had still so strong a hold upon German society that the idea of achieving political independence hardly seems to have entered into the minds of the peasantry: they were still too much under the authority of their lords, and the lords, on their part, were identified with their estates and with the local administration in a way which France with her idle and absentee *noblesse* could not parallel. Thus, except where the mediæval state of things had begun to pass away, the Revolution in Germany was not a root and branch affair, for in most places the mediæval system retained sufficient vitality to stand being reformed. In a few places only was it already so far advanced towards decadence that it could be swept completely away. Among these the territories on the left bank of the Upper Rhine had advanced about the furthest. Here the inhabitants were for the most part vine-growers, more alert, more excitable and more vigorous than the sluggish and submissive agricultural population lower down the river. Round Mayence there really existed the nucleus of a German Republican party, a *Tiers-État* in embryo. The peasantry in this part were proprietors, and having much more civil liberty than was the case elsewhere in Germany, were sufficiently advanced to desire still more.

It was a district without political traditions, very much split up, largely in the hands of ecclesiastical rulers who, expecting that before long the threatened secularisation of the ecclesiastical territories would deprive them of the duty of governing, were therefore preparing themselves for the loss of their administrative functions by neglecting them. Nor were the lay rulers much more formidable barriers to French influence. The Palatinate branch of the Wittelsbach family governed indifferently, the Zweibrücken branch distinctly ill. The Imperial Cities had no real municipal life or patriotism : the oligarchies which ruled them were weak and discredited. Any movement towards democracy among the lower classes was bound to tell in favour of France, and there was nothing whatever to check French aggression or even annexation. Förster and the rest of the Republican party at Mayence would probably have preferred a Cisrhenane Republic under French protection to direct incorporation, but civil and social liberty, good government and the abolition of feudal abuses were quite enough to reconcile the districts West of the Rhine to annexation. To a modified degree this was true of most of South and Western Germany. The application of the Napoleonic system brought great material benefits, received through the local dynasties which had accepted French protection. It was only when this came to involve the rigid enforcement of the Continental System and a heavy drain of conscripts to fight in a quarrel which did not concern the states from which they were drawn, that French protection was found to be a yoke too heavy to be borne and that Napoleon's arbitrary rearrangement of the map of Germany excited opposition. Nothing so clearly illustrates the weakness of the resistance of Germany to the French in the war against the First Coalition as the very gradual way in which South and Western Germany deserted the failing fortunes of the Emperor in 1813. The difference between the attitude of Prussia, which had received no material benefits, but only insults and injuries from Napoleon, and that of Baden or Würtemberg, which would not join the Allies until Austria and Prussia had promised to respect the reorganisation effected under French influence, is typical of the state of Germany between 1792 and 1814. The "national" movement of 1813-1814 was made possible by France and by France alone. It was not merely that she neutralised the material benefits of her rule by the even greater material injuries of the conscription and the Continental System, it was not merely that Napoleon's actions betrayed his selfishness and his lack of consideration for German interests, and that his arbitrary and oppressive rule brought home to the client-states the fact that their "protector" was in truth a tyrant and an oppressor. By suppressing the material obstacles which had till then prevented the union of the German peoples, by concentrating the petty states and uniting them in medium-sized states, France opened avenues to that national life which her propaganda, no less than the example of the national resistance of England, Spain and Russia, had fomented/ The overthrow of the relics of the Empire left the ground clear for the construction of something not intimately associated as the Empire was with disunion, localism and *Kleinstaaterei*.

But as things stood in 1792 the action of Germany was bound to be determined rather by the relations of the various members of the Empire to one another, than by any national feeling. Disunited, without an army, almost without a constitution, for the Diet, which was the sole bond of union between the states of Germany, had fallen into such disrepute that only 14 Princes out of 100 eligible to send representatives and only 8 cities out of 51 troubled to be represented at Ratisbon in 1788, Germany cannot be said to have adopted any attitude towards the French Revolution, because no "Germany" capable of adopting an attitude really existed. In place of Germany stood Austria and Prussia, whose opposition was to soon reassert itself despite the temporary reconciliation between their rulers, and the whole host of minor states, lay and ecclesiastical, each following its own local and dynastic policy without any glimpse of a wider patriotism. Yet disunited, distracted and divided as Germany was, there still existed a German idea, a confused notion of Germany as a whole, a sense of unity and nationality which the neighbours and enemies of Germany had always sought to suppress, and which not even the Germans themselves had done anything to arouse. The intellectual revival which was making itself felt throughout Germany in the latter half of the 18th century had not taken a national line, even where it had touched political or social grievances. It had done much to arouse intellectual activity, to make people think, to pave the way for the reception of new ideas, but the idea of German nationality was not one to which the leaders of German thought had as yet paid any attention. If the German idea existed it was in a state of suspended animation.

Of the domestic situation of Austria and of Prussia enough

has already been said; but seeing that the war which was about to break out affords the classical example of the utter disintegration of Germany, it may be well to make a brief survey of the principal minor states and their rulers, and trace the chief changes which had taken place among them since' 1715. To follow their history in detail is impossible: in those where there is any history to be followed it is but little connected with the general course of affairs outside of which it lies. Too small for the most part to develope very marked differences either socially, economically, or intellectually, the minor states of Germany tend to lack individuality, and it is only by means of their rulers that one can distinguish between them. When it has been said that the 18th Century was the age of the "benevolent despots," and that in some of the minor Princes of Germany the benevolent predominated and in others the despotic, one has said almost all that is to be said. ·

Next to the Hapsburgs and the Hohenzollerns, the family which in 1792 held most land in Germany was that of the Wittelsbachs. The extinction of the Neuburgs in 1742 had brought the Lower Palatinate[1] into the possession of the Sulzbach branch, who already held the principality of that name in the Upper Palatinate together with the part of the Cleves-Jülich inheritance assigned to them in 1666.[2] On the extinction in 1777 of the Bavarian line the Elector Palatine had succeeded to the 14,000 square miles and the 1,100,000 subjects of his cousins at Münich, while his heir, the Duke of Zweibrücken, ruled some 70,000 people inhabiting a district of under 900 square miles. On the accession of Maximilian Joseph of Zweibrücken to Bavaria and the Palatinate in 1799, the representative of all these Wittelsbach lines was the ruler of the third largest accumulation of territories in Germany, in all 21,000 square miles with about 2½ million inhabitants, which had an additional importance from their strategical position on the Upper Danube, which gave Bavaria the power of being either Austria's stoutest bulwark or the most useful ally of her enemies. Charles Theodore, the reigning Elector in 1792, was on the whole a good administrator, though by no means popular. He was a somewhat bigoted Roman Catholic, and his readiness to acquiesce in Joseph II's designs on Bavaria did

---

[1] 5300 square miles, with about a million inhabitants.
[2] Some 660 square miles and 50,000 people.

not much recommend him to his Bavarian subjects. In the Palatinate he was far better liked. There he felt at home: there he did a good deal for education and for the encouragement of art and literature. Heidelberg and Mannheim were both embellished and improved under his direction, Mannheim becoming the best and most famous theatrical centre in Germany.

In inhabitants the territories of the Wettin dynasty in Saxony exceeded the Wittelsbach lands; but in the valleys of the Saale and the Middle Elbe population was far denser than on the Upper Danube and along the foothills of the Alps, despite even the ravages in which the Silesian struggle had involved the unhappy Saxons. Frederick Augustus III had been a minor under the regency of his uncle Xavier for the first five years of his rule (1763-1768), and it was just as well for Saxony that he therefore did not come forward as a candidate for that Polish crown which had brought so little advantage either to Saxony or to its rulers. Under his wise and enlightened rule Saxony had enjoyed peace which had permitted the return of some degree of prosperity, education, agriculture and forestry all coming in for much encouragement and protection.

Of the other territories of the Wettin family the Electoral line had recovered Merseburg, Weissenfels and Zeitz on the extinction of the three cadet branches established by the partition of 1656, but there still existed in 1792 several small principalities belonging to the Ernestine line of which Saxe-Weimar alone merits special notice.

Under the beneficent and wise rule of Duke Charles Augustus (succeeded 1758, a minor till 1775) it was the intellectual centre of Germany. Goethe had settled at Weimar in response to a special invitation from the Duke, and the University of Jena was one of the most flourishing and vigorous in the whole country. Schiller was one of its most popular teachers, Wieland and Herder completed the quartette whose presence made Weimar famous. But Charles Augustus was not so much addicted to the intellectual as to be unmindful of the material side of life. The finances of the little state were in good order; agriculture, mining and industries flourished; public works of importance and benefit were undertaken. Politically the Duke was an adherent of Prussia: he had been active in negotiating the formation of the League of Princes in

1785, and he was to take part in the campaigns of 1792 and 1806 as a Prussian General.

After the close of the Seven Years' War one hears but little of the Electorate of Hanover.[1] If under George I and George II the British partner in the "Personal Union" had had some cause to complain that its interests were sacrificed to those of Hanover, under George III, who prided himself on his freedom from the Hanoverian prejudices of his predecessors, the tables were completely turned. Hanoverian battalions had shared in Elliott's successful defence of Gibraltar (1779-1783), and in Murray's scarcely less honourable capitulation at Minorca (1782). At this very moment (1792) the 14th and 15th Hanoverian regiments formed part of the British forces in India,[2] a quarter in which by no stretch of the imagination could Hanover be said to be much concerned. But if no longer given the first place in the affections of its ruler, Hanover was not badly governed, though the administration was altogether in the hands of an unprogressive aristocracy, which not only filled the Privy Council, the body by which the government was administered, but also controlled the local Estates. These were of more importance than they would otherwise have been owing to the absence of any general assembly for the whole Electorate. Thus every new tax had to be agreed to by all these Estates, which caused constant delays and hindrances. This absence of centralisation was not overcome by any special energy or activity on the part of the Privy Council, whose authority was restricted by the existence of a separate department for the domains, mines and forests, and of an equally independent War-Chancery. Still the government if unenterprising was mild and unoppressive; and if in some parts the peasantry were still serfs, they were on the whole fairly prosperous. Politically, Hanover tended to act with Brunswick-Wolfenbüttel and with Prussia, though the old hostility to the Hohenzollern was by no means extinct. It still lingered among some of the leading men; but at the time of Joseph's attempt to exchange the Netherlands for Bavaria, Hanover adhered to the League of Princes.

---

[1] Hanover had during the 18th century acquired the County of Bentheim, pawned to it in 1753, and the little districts of Blumenthal (1741) and Seyn Altenkirchen (1782).

[2] Cf. Cornwallis Correspondence.

The Duchy of Brunswick-Wolfenbüttel, though little more than a sixth of the size of the Electorate, its area being not much over 1500 square miles, was in proportion more populous and wealthy; but along with the rest of North-Western Germany it had suffered a good deal during the Seven Years' War. On the extinction of the "new" Dannenberg line with Duke Louis Rudolf in 1735, the Duchy had passed to Ferdinand Albert of Brunswick-Bevern, the head of a cadet branch established in 1666. He died in the same year, and was succeeded by his eldest son Charles, who ruled the Duchy for forty-five years and did it great service. The great Ferdinand of Brunswick, who died in 1792, was the second son of Duke Ferdinand Albert, while other members of the family were also closely identified with the Prussian service. Duke Charles was another of those Princes who did a good deal for education and for literature. The celebrated Lessing was given the post of Ducal Librarian in 1770, the *Collegium Carolinum* was founded at Brunswick, a Museum was established, and the schools were thoroughly reformed. But the Duke was an extravagant ruler, and contracted debts which the limited revenues of his territories[1] did not suffice to discharge. Thus he was very glad of the opportunity which England's American troubles afforded to him as to the other needy owners of Germany's principal article of export, mercenaries, for filling his coffers and finding occupation for his men. In January 1776 he concluded a subsidy treaty by which in return for 110,000 thalers a year and a lump sum of 50 thalers a head, 4300 Brunswickers were taken into British pay.[2]

Duke Charles was succeeded by his eldest son Charles William Ferdinand, "the Hereditary Prince" of Crefeld and Minden, the "Brunswick" of Valmy and Auerstadt, who proved no less benevolent and careful as a ruler than gallant as a soldier. Under him the Duchy made considerable advances: the burden of taxation was reduced, the poor-laws were improved, and the country well-governed. Following his father's policy, he adhered firmly to the Prussian alliance, and

---

[1] They amounted to about 1,500,000 thalers per annum: Oncken, *Zeitalter Friedrich der Grosse*, ii. 709.

[2] This force was sent to Canada, and shared in Burgoyne's gallant but ill-fated expedition.

commanded the Prussian force which made the unopposed promenade to Amsterdam in 1787.

But as a provider of mercenaries, Brunswick was quite eclipsed by Hesse-Cassel. Of the 29,000 Germans whose services England hired in 1776–1777, Hesse-Cassel provided nearly 17,000. From the days of Landgrave Charles I (1676–1730), Hesse-Cassel had been pre-eminently a military State. His sons Frederick I (1730–1751)[1] and William VII (1751–1760) had followed in his steps, the latter supplying a large contingent to the army in English pay with which Ferdinand of Brunswick disputed Western Germany with the French. Of this war Hesse-Cassel was so unfortunate as to be one of the principal theatres: it endured great hardships and was much thrown back, so that the chief task of Landgrave Frederick II (1760–1785), an energetic and careful ruler, was to foster in every possible way the restoration of his dominions to a prosperous condition. He introduced the cultivation of the potato, reformed the land-laws and the system of weights and measures. He established a cantoning system after the Prussian model, and maintained his forces at a high level of efficiency. At the same time, he was not behind the other Princes of the day in encouraging the arts and education. His son William IX, the builder of the famous castle of Wilhelmshöhe, followed the same policy. While Hesse-Cassel had continued throughout the 18th Century to adhere to the Prussian alliance, which was one of the family traditions, Hesse-Darmstadt had been no less loyal to her traditional policy of fidelity to the Emperor. Its rulers during the period, Ernest Louis (1678–1739), Louis VIII (1739–1768), Louis IX (1768–1790), and Louis X (1790–1830), were always on the side of Austria, and in the Seven Years' War Hesse-Darmstadt was distinguished by its antagonism to Prussia, the patron and ally of Hesse-Cassel.[2] Louis IX is best known in connection with his military establishment at Pirmasens, held by a special regiment of grenadiers to whose training he had devoted much time. In contrast to the other Princes of the day, he steadily refused to hire out his men to foreign Powers, and it was not his

---

[1] King of Sweden (from 1720–1751) in virtue of his marriage with Ulrica Eleanore, sister of Charles XII.

[2] It may perhaps be worth mentioning that in 1866 it was Hesse-Cassel which was annexed to Prussia ; Hesse-Darmstadt has retained its separate existence.

subjects who acquired for the name of " Hessian " so unfavourable a reputation in the American War.[1]

In extent the possessions of the House of Mecklenburg were more considerable than those of families of greater importance in German history; but one does not hear much of either Mecklenburg-Strelitz or Mecklenburg-Schwerin except for the quarrel between Duke Charles Leopold and his Estates, which had so nearly involved England and Hanover in a war with Russia.[2] Both duchies had been so fortunate as to lie outside the theatre affected by the Seven Years' War, in which they had remained somewhat apathetically neutral, failing to profit economically by the sufferings of their neighbours. The most noticeable feature with regard to Mecklenburg was the definite constitutional acknowledgment in 1755 of the free condition of the peasants, whose condition had been steadily growing worse since the Thirty Years' War. They were not merely bound to the soil, but were actually serfs. The whole district was one of the poorest and most backward in all Germany, and neither Frederick Francis I of Schwerin (1785–1837) nor Charles of Strelitz (1794–1816) played at all a prominent part in the Revolutionary epoch.

Not long after the end of the Seven Years' War an important change had taken place in one of the states of North-Western Germany. The Duchy of Oldenburg had, as has been already stated, been under Danish rule since 1666, but the Holstein-Gottorp family had never admitted Denmark's right to hold it, and in 1773 Paul of Russia,[3] now the representative of the main line of the Holstein-Gottorp family, managed to arrange a compromise. He renounced his claims on Holstein in favour of Denmark, which thereupon ceded Oldenburg to the Czar's cousin, Duke Frederick Augustus of Holstein-Eutin, Prince-Bishop of Lübeck, a grandson of Christian Albert of Gottorp, the great-great-grandfather of Paul.[4] This change was much appreciated by the Oldenburgers, who found in Frederick Augustus a mild and beneficent ruler, while on his death (1785) his nephew Peter Frederick Louis, who acted as Regent for the imbecile heir, Peter Frederick William, governed on very similar lines.

---

[1] Cf. Trevelyan, *American Revolution*, Part II.   [2] Cf. pp. 69–70, 84, 94.

[3] Peter III of Russia was a Holsteiner on his father's side, Charles Frederick of Holstein having married Anna, daughter of Peter the Great.

[4] Cf. p. 56.

Baden, divided since 1536 between the Baden-Baden and the Baden-Durlach lines, had been reunited twenty years before the outbreak of the Revolution on the extinction, in 1771, of the Baden-Baden line. Augustus George, who had succeeded to his brother Louis George in 1761, was, like his brother, childless, and in January 1765 he concluded with his cousin of Baden-Durlach the compact which came into operation in 1771. Charles Frederick of Baden-Durlach, who thus reunited the old territories of the House of Zahringen, had succeeded his grandfather Charles William (1709–1738), chiefly noticeable as a warm supporter of Austria in the Spanish Succession War, when only ten years of age, and in the eighty-three years (1738–1821) in which he ruled he saw great changes in the fortunes of Baden. As the ruler of territories coterminous with France, he was naturally much concerned by the events taking place over the border, and was most anxious to prevent Baden having again, as in 1688–1697 and 1702–1714, to bear the brunt of the war and to be once more reduced to a condition of devastation and ruin. He saw a prospect that all the good work he had done would be undone in one campaign, and his conduct in the coming wars was directed largely by this fear.

Of all the minor states of Germany there are few which have so individual a character as Würtemberg. Even into the 18th Century it retained enough of a constitution[1] to distinguish it from the other states. But, as has been explained,[2] the necessities of a more effective defence against the French than the enjoyment of constitutional liberties had altered the position of affairs, and forced the Würtembergers to allow the Duke to strengthen his position greatly by raising a standing army. Thus Eberhard Louis was far more autocratic than any Duke since 1514. Under him Würtemberg experienced the evils of French influence in peace as well as of French hostility in war. The extravagance of his Court, his efforts to ape the " Grande Monarque," to make the Ludwigsburg vie with Versailles, his subjection to the notorious Countess Christina von Gravenitz, brought much harm on his subjects. His successor Charles Alexander, a cousin, who had till then ruled over the territory of Winnenden, acquired by Eberhard III in 1668, was not much of an improvement. He had gone over to Roman Catholicism in 1712 partly from pique at the

[1] Cf. pp. 245–246. [2] Chapter II.

refusal of the Committee to increase his appanage, and had not his rule (1733–1737) been abruptly closed by his sudden death he would have attempted to overthrow the constitution by a *coup d'état* in which he hoped for Austrian aid. His eldest son, Charles Eugene, was a minor, and did not take over the government till 1744, having been educated in the meantime at the Court of Berlin. He was at first a faithful adherent of Prussia, but his extravagant ways and his love for the theatre, for indulging his architectural fancies, for keeping up a considerable state and a luxurious mode of living, involved him in financial necessities. To extricate himself he concluded a subsidy-treaty with Louis XV in 1752 by which he placed 6000 men at the disposal of France. In the Seven Years' War he fulfilled his obligations by forcibly impressing five regiments of 1000 men each in deliberate disregard of the constitution; a most unpopular measure, as the indifferent behaviour of the Würtemberg regiments at Leuthen[1] proved. The Committee protested against this action and appealed in July 1764 to the Aulic Council, accusing the Duke of levying heavy poll-taxes without the consent of the authorised representatives of the taxpayers, of ill-treating the Church, and generally of denying justice. The Aulic Council, acting with a most unusual precipitation, declared in favour of the Estates within two months of receiving the appeal, and in 1766 the Duke had to dismiss his minister Montmartin. In 1770 a compromise was arranged, and till the Duke's death in 1793[2] Würtemberg enjoyed a period of peace and comparative prosperity, his encouragement of culture and intellectual life generally, his foundation of a large library and of the so-called "Carlsacademie" going hand in hand with the usual measures by which a "benevolent despot" sought to improve the manufactures, agriculture, trade and revenues of his dominions.

Of the other minor states there are not many which call for special remark. The Franconian branch of the Hohenzollern had ceded its territories to its cousins at Berlin just before the outbreak of war in 1792. The Anhalt-Zerbst line became extinct in 1793, and its territories were divided between the other branches of the family at Bernberg, Dessau and Köthen.

---

[1] Cf. p. 226, and Oncken, *Friedrich der Grosse*, ii. 162.

[2] Charles Eugene was succeeded by his son, Louis Eugene, who died in May 1795, S.P.M.

Count William of Lippe-Schaumburg deserves mention as the founder of the famous military school at Wilhelmstein, at which Scharnhorst was educated. A typical soldier-prince, he did with his peasants in Lippe-Bückeburg on a small scale what the Landgrave of Hesse-Cassel did on a larger, and he is also notable for his reorganisation of the Portuguese army after his campaign in Portugal in 1762.[1] The two lines of the House of Reuss, raised to the rank of Princes in 1778 and 1790 respectively, the Schwarzburg family, divided between Schwarzburg-Sondershausen and Schwarzburg-Rudolstadt in 1681, Waldeck and Hohenlohe were among the larger of those infinitesimal principalities which complicate the map of Germany in 1792 and whose pretensions to independence and to sovereign rights contributed so much to the disunion and defencelessness of Germany. One family also deserves mention, more because of its connection with the United Provinces than on account of its part in the affairs of Germany, that of Nassau. After a variety of changes[2] the position of head of the family had passed to the Nassau-Dietz branch, which had recovered the Stadtholderate of the United Provinces in 1747.[3] Of the ecclesiastical states, the Free Cities, and the Imperial Knights, it might be enough to say that they were in 1792 fully ripe in the annexations they were shortly to undergo. Only the jealousy and rivalry of the larger states had prevented a general scramble for these tempting morsels

[1] Cf. Oman, *Peninsular War*, ii. p. 208.

[2] The House of Nassau had split up into two branches in 1255, Walram II and Otto I, the sons of Henry II, obtaining respectively the territories South and North of the Lahn. In 1627, on the death of Louis II, his three sons divided the lands of Walram's branch into the Idstein, Saarbrück-Usingen and Weilburg lines. Between 1718 and 1775, Charles of Nassau-Usingen reunited the Idstein territories with Saarbrück and Usingen, and his sons Charles William (1775–1803) and Frederick Augustus (1803–1816) obtained acquisitions of territory at Lunéville and ruled their lands in common with those of their cousin Frederick William of Nassau-Weilburg (1788–1816), the Duchy of Nassau being formed by the union of the two lines in 1816. Meanwhile Otto's line, of which the Orange-Nassau line in the Netherlands was an offshoot, had similarly split up into three branches on the death of John VI (1606), the Hadamar (extinct 1711), Dillenburg (extinct 1789), and Dietz lines. This last branch had by 1792 reunited all the possessions of the line, so that William V of Holland (1751–1806) was also a member of the Empire as Prince of Nassau.

[3] On the death of William III of England (1702), John William Friso of Nassau-Dietz had inherited his Netherlandish possessions, and it was his son William IV (1711–1751) who was chosen as Hereditary Stadtholder in 1747.

taking place long ago. Directly the French Revolution produced the necessary disturbance in the political equilibrium of Germany, the secularisation of the Bishoprics, the "mediatisation" of the Knights and the annexation of the Cities were bound to come. In 1792 four Archbishops (the three Ecclesiastical Electors and Salzburg), sixteen Bishops and about thirty other prelates were represented in the Diet, not to mention secularised Bishoprics such as Paderborn and Osnabrück.

The three Ecclesiastical Electors in this year were Frederick Charles Joseph of Erthal at Mayence (elected 1774), Clement Wenceslaus of Saxony (son of Augustus II, elected 1768) at Treves, and the Archduke Maximilian Joseph of Austria (elected 1785) at Cologne. The Elector of Mayence was also Bishop of Worms; the Elector of Treves held Freising, Ratisbon and Augsburg in addition to his Electorate; Maximilian of Cologne had been Bishop of Münster since 1780. More important in some ways than any of these Electors was Charles Dalberg, Coadjutor to the Elector of Mayence, who managed, thanks to the Elector's official position as Chancellor of the Empire, to exercise a considerable influence over German politics. For the rest, the Bishops and Abbots were for the most part scions of noble houses, often good and honest rulers, but as a rule too much hampered by their Chapters to do much even when zealous for reform, so that the ecclesiastical states were on the whole very backward.

Fifty-one[1] Free Cities maintained an independent existence in 1789, but many of them, especially among the thirty-one in the Swabian Circle, were of no importance whatever. Of the once-powerful Hanseatic League, Bremen, Lübeck and Hamburg still maintained a commercial union; but of the others which had been represented at the last Hansetag at Lübeck in 1669 only Cologne remained a Free City. Brunswick had been forced to submit to the Duke of Brunswick. Minden was in Prussian, Dantzic in Polish hands. Osnabrück had succumbed to its Prince-Bishop, Rostock to the Duke of Mecklenburg-Schwerin. Frankfurt on Main with 60,000 inhabitants, Nüremberg with 80,000, Augsburg and Ulm with

[1] The matricular list of 1521 gives a total of eighty-four cities, since when several (e.g. Basel and Metz) had been annexed by foreign Powers and others (e.g. Donauwörth) incorporated by neighbouring states.

between 30,000 and 40,000 were still of comparative importance; but even in them there was little real municipal life, still less any political union between one and another. Had the Emperor been able to bind the Free Cities to him, had they and the Imperial Knights been willing to sacrifice the shadow of a useless independence for a real union under the head of the Empire, it might have been possible to make "Germany" something more than a geographical expression; but not only was the jealousy of the other states certain to thwart any move from one side or the other, the narrow and obstinate localism of the Cities caused them to cling to their privileges and their separate existence and condemned them to decadence and impotence.

Indeed it was with edged tools that the Emperor and Frederick William II were playing in 1792 when by associating themselves with the cause of the Bourbons they gave an excuse for an attack on Germany to the rising tide of French national feeling with which the Revolution was soon to become identified. Disunited, worse than disunited, distracted by jealousy and localism, Germany could ill afford to give a foothold within her borders to the compact force which the Republic for all its internal commotions wielded as a factor in the European situation.

CHAPTER XIX

THE FIRST COALITION

A S has been already mentioned, it was over the questions of Alsace and of the *emigrés* rather than through the connection between the Hapsburgs and the Bourbons that the Revolution actually came into conflict with the European Powers, though the hostility of the Revolutionary party in France towards Austria was largely due to their fear of intervention. It is quite true that the first steps towards interference taken by Leopold were of the nature of an intervention in the cause of monarchy. The Note issued to the monarchs of Europe in May 1791 did not do more than call attention to the fact that the situation of the King of France was a matter of concern to the other Powers, and at the time Leopold was honestly trying to keep the Comte d'Artois and the rest of the *emigrés* in check. He was by no means anxious to intervene and, although ready to do what he could by diplomatic means, dreaded having to use force. The flight to Varennes (June 1791) was undertaken against his advice, and its failure forced his hand. While negotiations with Prussia were carried on in hopes of arriving at an alliance on definite terms, Leopold issued the " Declaration of Padua " (July 6th), explaining to the other monarchs the steps he proposed to take. These included the recall of his Ambassador, the collection of troops on the frontiers, and the summoning of a conference. This circular excited great indignation in France and made popular feeling, already aroused by shelter and support given to the *emigrés* by the Rhenish Princes, very hostile towards Austria. In August 1791 Leopold and Frederick William met at Pillnitz on the Elbe, a few miles above Dresden, and the Declaration which they issued (Aug. 27th), inviting the co-operation of Europe in helping the King of France to "lay the bases of a monarchical government in liberty," served to still further fan the flame of resentment and hostility to Austria. " It is difficult and dangerous," wrote Lord Auckland to Mr. Pitt,[1] "for sovereigns possessing an absolute authority to become the armed mediators of a free constitution and a moderated monarchy to France," and the anger of the French found expression in Isnard's declaration that "if the cabinets of foreign Courts try to stir up a war of Kings against France, we will stir up for them a war of peoples against Kings" (Nov. 1791). This was one of the first expressions of that revolutionary propagandism which the French were to make their main instrument of attack against the existing European system.

For the time, however, the crisis seemed averted; for on September 21st Louis XVI accepted the revised constitution, and Leopold hailed this as an excuse for taking no further steps. But things had really gone too far already. The war-feeling in France was growing daily stronger. The Legislative Assembly, which had on October 1st replaced the Constituent, was dominated by the more extreme party. One section, it is true, desired a war with the Ecclesiastical Electors and with Austria over the question of the *emigrés*, because they hoped it might show up the necessity for a strong executive and thereby force the Assembly to increase the powers and authority of the King. But this "limited liability" war which Narbonne[2] and the "Feuillants" in general desired was not the object of the Girondins. Led by Brissot and Vergniaud they wanted a real war against Austria, a war which would force Louis to choose definitely between acquiescing in the Revolution and declaring himself its enemy. He would either have to place himself at the head of the anti-Austrian feeling which was gaining ground in France, or he would have to show that the accusations of *incivisme*, of disloyalty to France, of preferring the *emigré* and the foreigner to the nation, were really well-grounded.

In November 1791, Louis, at the bidding of the Assembly, formally demanded that Leopold should disperse the *emigré* forces, while the Elector of Treves was given a month in which to comply with a similar request. But instead of taking any steps to meet the wishes of the French, Leopold laid before the Assembly the Resolution (*Reichsschluss*) of the Diet, that the action of France with regard to Alsace had violated the Peace

---

[1] *Dropmore Papers, Hist. MSS. Commission,* vol. ii. p. 159.
[2] Appointed War Minister in December.

of Westphalia (Dec. 3rd). On December 24th he not only refused to disperse the *emigrés*, but complained of the efforts of the French to propagate sedition and discontent within the Empire, and more especially in Belgium. It was hardly likely that the Legislative Assembly would accept such a rebuke quietly, and their announcement that Leopold's failure to give them satisfaction before March 1st would be regarded as a declaration of war might easily have been predicted. With such attitudes on the various sides war was only a question of time. On January 17th, 1792, the Austrian Conference decided to present an ultimatum to the French, demanding that the orders to assemble three armies on the frontiers should be cancelled, and that compensation should be given to the Pope for the loss of Avignon and to the Alsatian Princes. A week later, orders were given to mobilise 40,000 men to reinforce the garrisons in the Netherlands and in Further Austria. Nor did the Emperor neglect the chances of obtaining the assistance of other Powers. On February 7th an offensive and defensive alliance was concluded between Austria and Prussia, pledging both parties to assist each other if attacked, or in case of internal troubles, to guarantee the integrity of Poland and a " free constitution " for that country, and finally to promote a European Concert for the settlement of French affairs. All was thus in train for the formation of a coalition against France, when, on the last day of February, Leopold was suddenly seized with a severe chill, and on March 1st he died. His premature death was a great blow to Austria—indeed to Europe. Had he been at the head of the Coalition, the foolish and offensive proclamation which heralded Brunswick's invasion would probably have never been issued. A statesman of experience and capacity, he would have restrained the *emigrés*, and would have had far more chance of keeping the Coalition together than any other monarch could have had. As it was, the Coalition went to pieces at once for want of a real leader. Francis II, Leopold's heir and successor, did in the end do good service to Austria and to Europe ; but he had not the strength of mind or the experience to prevent Thugut from wrecking the Second Coalition, and still less was he fitted in 1792 to cope with such a problem as that of the French Revolution. So far as the First Coalition had any leader, it was Frederick William II, who was neither a great soldier nor a great statesman, though he fancied himself both, and who, moreover, having always one eye fixed on the chances of aggrandisement in Poland, was unable to devote exclusively to the affairs of France even the very slender capacities as a statesman and a leader with which he was endowed. Meanwhile, Leopold's answer had brought about the overthrow of the Feuillant ministry, and in their place Louis had been forced to accept a ministry drawn from the Girondin party, of which the leading member was Dumouriez (March 1792). The policy on which Dumouriez pinned his faith was that of detaching Prussia from the side of Austria by reviving the old friendly relations between Paris and Berlin. Hoping to isolate Austria, he sent Custine to Berlin and Talleyrand to London, while he spared no effort to keep the minor states of Germany from making common cause with the Emperor.

When, in April 1792, a reply was received from Austria, in which Kaunitz definitely refused to diminish the warlike preparations, and alleged as his reason the menace to Belgium of the Jacobin propagandism, only one course was possible. On April 20th the Assembly declared war on "the King of Hungary and Bohemia,"[1] and Belgium was at once attacked by four converging columns. The invasion proved a complete fiasco, not because the Austrian preparations for defence were specially efficient, but through the disorderliness, insubordination and utter inefficiency of the Volunteers who composed a large part of the invading forces. But the Austrians were in no condition to profit by the disorderly retreat of their adversaries. They had also to wait for their Prussian allies, and the slowness with which the Prussian mobilisation was being carried out was a proof of the decline in the efficiency of the Prussian army.

The failure of the invasion of Belgium had produced wild excitement and much disorder at Paris. Accusations of treachery were brought against the Court and the generals, and it was just this moment that Louis XVI chose for refusing to sign a decree against those priests who had not accepted the Civil Constitution of the Clergy, and to dismiss his Girondin ministry. The result was the riot of June 20th, while three

---

[1] Francis II. was not elected Emperor till July 14th, and the French hoped to keep the Empire out of the war by thus treating Francis merely as the head of the Hapsburgs and make it possible for its members to remain neutral ; which, with the exception of Hesse-Cassel, they all did.

weeks later, on July 11th, the Assembly declared the country in danger.

By this time the Austrians and Prussians were at last ready to take the field. The principal attack was committed to the Duke of Brunswick with 42,000 Prussians, who was to advance into Champagne from Coblence, supported on the left by 14,000 Austrians from the Breisgau and 10,000 *emigrés* and Hessians. On his right another Austrian corps (15,000) was to advance against Thionville, while yet a third under Albert of Saxe-Teschen proceeded to lay siege to Lille. The Allies heralded their advance by publishing in the name of the Duke of Brunswick the famous proclamation of July 27th, which completed the rage and exasperation of the French at this intervention in their affairs. It was really the work of the *emigrés*,[1] approved by Frederick William, accepted by Francis II without enthusiasm and by Brunswick with great misgivings.

It was in the last days of July that the invasion began. On paper the invading armies made a great show, but in the field they were much less formidable. Both Austrians and Prussians suffered from insufficient organisation, bad staff-work and all but non-existent administrative services. The commissariat was especially inefficient, and if the Prussians maintained the rigid regimental discipline of Frederick's days, routine and parade had with them usurped the place of practice. The Austrians, as in 1741, had had more recent experience of war but had not turned its lessons to much profit. Nor did the commander's merits make up for the shortcomings of his army. Brunswick, anxious not to compromise his reputation, was not altogether inclined to an advance on Paris. He would have preferred the systematic reduction of the fortresses on the Meuse ; but Frederick William, relying quite unjustifiably on the assurances of the *emigrés* that France would really welcome the invaders, overruled this cautious plan. The Prussians began well enough. A cavalry skirmish on August 19th saw the advance-guard of the French army of the Centre driven back in confusion. On the 20th, Longwy was summoned ; on the 23rd it surrendered. Verdun capitulated on September 2nd after an equally feeble resistance. This seemed to open the road to Paris, and on September 5th the Prussians crossed the Meuse on their way to Chalons. To

---

[1] Cf. Lord E. Fitzmaurice's *Life of Brunswick.*

oppose them Dumouriez hurried to the front and took command of the troops collected at Sedan. With them he took post in the wooded hills of the Argonne and occupied the passage of Les Islettes by which Brunswick intended to cross. Meanwhile Kellermann was pushing up from Metz with the 22,000 men of the Army of the Centre to join his colleague. Brunswick displayed a great want of energy. Instead of forcing the Les Islettes position and so bringing Dumouriez to battle before Kellermann could join, he tried to turn the position by seizing another of the passes of the Argonnes, and thus let Dumouriez fall back behind the Aisne and take up a position near St. Menehould, threatening the Prussian flank should they continue their advance on Paris. On September 19th Kellermann arrived, and next day occurred the celebrated skirmish which has been dignified by the name of the "battle" of Valmy. The action was confined to a cannonade, in which the excellence of the French artillery and the firm attitude of the old troops of the Line, who formed the bulk of their army,[1] brought Brunswick to a standstill. Finding the French position too strong for a direct attack, he had not enough confidence in himself or his army to continue his advance and risk leaving the French on his line of communications. He came to a halt at La Lune and waited there for a fortnight, the condition of his army becoming daily worse. The administration broke down completely under the strain of war; the troops, excellent as they were on the parade - ground, proved quite unfitted for the practical work of a campaign, sickness decimated their ranks, and Brunswick was in the end lucky to secure an unmolested retreat. This he achieved by means of negotiations with Dumouriez, who, a politician quite as much as a soldier, still clung to his hopes of detaching Prussia from Austria. Thus he was ready to let Brunswick withdraw from a really very perilous position in return for the evacuation of Longwy and Verdun. This arrangement also enabled Dumouriez to transfer himself and his army to the Austrian Netherlands. The Austrians had already raised the siege of Thionville, and on October 7th the Duke of Saxe-Teschen abandoned his futile attack on Lille and fell back to Mons, ready to dispute the invaders' advance along a line from Mons by Charleroi to Namur. On November 6th Dumouriez,

---

[1] Cf. Hauterive, *L'Armée sous la Révolution*, pp. 245–246, and Chuquet, *Les Guerres de la Révolution*, ii. 247 ff.

following him up, attacked and carried his main position at Jemappes, a stubborn fight resulting in the complete defeat of the Austrians. The results of the victory were enormous. Mons (Nov. 7th), Brussels (Nov. 13th), Malines, Liége, Namur, Antwerp capitulated one after another almost without resistance. Saxe-Teschen withdrew the relics of his forces towards Liége. The people welcomed the French as deliverers. On November 16th a decree of the Legislative Assembly declared the Scheldt open to commerce, thus defying the Barrier Treaty and the Treaty of Münster, to say nothing of more recent compacts. On the 19th another decree promised fraternity and assistance to any nation engaged in recovering its liberty; but it throws a rather curious light on these professions that, much to the consternation of its people, on December 13th Belgium was declared part of France, as Savoy and Nice had been a month earlier. Austrian rule was most unpopular in the Netherlands; but the Clericals, who had so vigorously opposed Joseph's reforms, were hardly the people to welcome the Rights of Man and the reign of Reason. Meanwhile, on the Middle Rhine Custine, with the Army of the Vosges, had been carrying all before him, spreading alarm all through the states of Southern Germany. On September 30th he entered Spires. Five days later Worms and Philipsbourg were occupied. Encouraged by the news of the check to Brunswick, Custine resolved to push on into Germany. Mayence surrendered at the first summons (Oct. 21st), and the French crossing the Rhine were received warmly at Frankfort. Only the timely arrival of the contingent of Hesse-Cassel saved Coblence from falling into French hands (Oct. 26th).

It was in this part of Germany that there was most chance for the Revolutionary propaganda to obtain a firm foothold. Custine announced that he was making war on the despots, not on the people; that he had come to make them free, to let them choose their own form of government, and to help them throw off the oppressive yoke under which they were groaning. At first these declarations were believed and the population welcomed the French; for it was only the richer classes, the clergy, the nobles and the big merchants who had to suffer anything at their hands. A Convention was summoned to meet at Mayence to settle the government of the conquered territory, and under the influence of George Förster, one of those Germans in whom the Revolution had awakened sentiments akin to those expressed in England by Charles James Fox, it hastened to vote the union of the country between the Queich and the Nahe with France (March 18th, 1793). The idea of extending France to her " natural frontiers " had by now taken firm hold of the French imagination, and the delegates of the National Convention of Rhenish Germany received a hearty welcome at Paris.

By this time events had moved apace. On the day of the affair of Valmy the National Convention had met at Paris and declared France a Republic. On January 21st the Republican party had burnt its boats by the execution of the King, and on February 1st it had followed this act up by declaring war on England and Holland, which until then had maintained a strict neutrality. It was not merely the execution of the King which alarmed Europe and united practically all the Powers, Denmark, Sweden and Switzerland alone standing aloof, in a Coalition to oppose the Republic. The violent actions and language of the Assembly, its obvious disposition to ignore the received rules of international relations, its interference with the affairs of its neighbours, its open adoption and propagation of revolutionary doctrines, the encouragement given to the discontented and disaffected in every state, the disregard displayed for all treaties and conventions, all these drove the alarmed monarchs of Europe into taking arms in defence of their thrones and their territories.

As might have been expected, the relations between Austria and Prussia had not been improved by the events of 1792. Prussia complained that Austria had failed to fulfil her promises ; Austria that Brunswick had secured an unmolested retreat at the expense of his ally. Moreover, events in Eastern Europe had served to increase their dissatisfaction. The patriotic party in Poland had in May 1791 introduced a new and revised constitution, abolishing the elective monarchy, the *liberum veto*, and the various other anomalies which had contributed so much to the decadence of the nation. This was accepted by the Diet at Warsaw, but not without opposition, and the malcontents, forming themselves into the Confederation of Targovitsa, appealed to Russia as the guarantor of the old constitution (May 1792). Catherine, eagerly grasping at the pretext for intervention, sent Suvorov and a large army to the aid of the Confederates. Austria might have intervened on behalf of the new constitution, which offered a chance of rescuing Poland from the grip of Russia, if she could have got Prussia to join her; but Frederick William would not hear of it, and Austria, paralysed by the death of Leopold and the troubles with France, had no alternative but to conclude a treaty with Russia (July 1792), guaranteeing the old constitution of Poland. Russian troops now poured into Poland and put down the patriotic party, while Catherine concluded a treaty with Prussia (Jan. 23rd, 1793) for the Second Partition of Poland. By a mixture of force and bribery the Diet was forced to give way to the demands of the invading Powers: on July 22nd it signed a treaty with Russia and on September 25th that which allotted to Prussia 2000 square miles of Polish territory, mainly in Posen and Great Poland, but including the much coveted Dantzic and Thorn. It is this which explains the very small part taken by Prussia in the West during 1793. The certainty of territorial aggrandisement in the East was irresistible and drew Frederick William away from a quarter in which his hopes of acquisitions were rapidly growing fainter; but this neglect of the West for the East was in no small measure responsible for the loss of the Prussian territories West of the Rhine a couple of years later.

Dumouriez opened the campaign of 1793 in February by an advance into Holland, moving by Dortrecht upon Leyden and so for Amsterdam. On his right, Miranda laid siege to Maastricht, while Valence took up a position on the Roer to cover these operations against any interference from the Austrians. At first things went well. Breda fell after a somewhat feeble defence. Dumouriez took Gertruydenberg and was on the point of entering Holland when the news reached him (March 3rd) that the Austrians under the Prince of Coburg-Saalfeld had fallen on Valence near Aix-la-Chapelle, beaten him badly and driven him in on Liége in disorder. Miranda, thus exposed, had to raise the siege of Maastricht and to retire by Tongres on Louvain, while a Prussian corps secured Venloo. Dumouriez, his communications thus endangered, fell back behind the line of the Demer with his army in a state of confusion and demoralisation. The practice of the French "liberators" of Belgium had not altogether corresponded to their professions, and their misconduct and exactions had alienated even their own partisans. The discipline of the army was in a deplorable condition, and the general, who had long been at odds with the Convention and with the Ministry of

War, was already contemplating desertion. One last effort he made, attacking the Austrian positions at Neerwinden on March 18th. It was a desperate fight, but the defeat of Miranda on the French left decided the battle against Dumouriez. Beaten again in another action near Louvain three days later, he fell back behind the Scheldt and, failing in his efforts to get his army to declare against the Convention, finally deserted to the Austrians on April 5th. Thus left in the lurch, his army withdrew behind the frontier. Now was the time for a really vigorous effort by the Allies, and Brunswick strongly urged Frederick William to co-operate heartily with the Austrians to secure the Netherlands and break through the French defences. But Frederick William cared far more for Poland than for the French war, and failed to support Austria with all his strength. The declaration of war by the Diet of the Empire (March 22nd) did not add materially to the strength of the Coalition, and neither the operations in the Alps nor in the Pyrenees exercised any real influence on the fate of the campaign. Holland proved an ally of little value, and the unwise economy which had led Pitt to cut down the peace establishment of Great Britain almost to vanishing point prevented England from putting into the field a force adequate to the emergency. It is a platitude to say that had the Coalition displayed in 1793 anything approaching the resolution and vigour the Powers of Europe were to show in 1814 and 1815, the successful march to Paris might have been anticipated by twenty years. For France was in utter confusion. The army seemed to have lost all cohesion ; there was no real executive ; the Royalists had risen at Toulon, at Lyons, and in La Vendée ; the Girondins were taking arms in Normandy and Guienne. Anarchy, administrative chaos and civil strife seemed to leave France helpless at the feet of the Coalition. It was not in the Netherlands only that things had gone badly. Before the end of 1792 Brunswick had recovered Frankfort, and in March Custine, who had taken post on the Nahe between Bingen and Kreuznach, was outflanked and driven from his positions by the Prussians, who had crossed the Rhine (March 27th) lower down at St. Goar. He fell back to Worms and thence to Landau (April 1st), completely abandoning all his conquests save Mayence, which made a desperate resistance. The siege was begun in April, but not till July 23rd did the brave garrison capitulate and evacuate the city, taking with them those of the inhabitants who had espoused their cause. Meanwhile in the Netherlands the Anglo-Austrians had stormed the French camp at Famars (May 25th) and driven them back to Bouchain. This success allowed Coburg to besiege and take Condé (July 12th) and Valenciennes (July 28th).

The Allies had the ball at their feet. Had their statesmen succeeded in subordinating individual ambitions to the common end, had their commanders looked to more than immediate and local advantage, had they displayed any grasp of the general strategic situation, it would have gone hard with France. But it was a war of governments, not of peoples. There was no enthusiasm for the war in Germany. Even the prospect of recovering Alsace and Lorraine from France failed to arouse any keenness or interest. It mattered little to the inhabitants of the left bank of the Rhine what yoke they laboured under. The Southern states supported the war but languidly, and it was being fought too far away from Austria and from Prussia for its importance to be realised in those countries. Even the rulers and their ministers, who might have been expected to understand the issues involved, failed to grasp the importance of cohesion and of loyal and energetic co-operation. Thus the jealousies, the divisions, the delays and the mistaken strategy of the Allies saved France, and gave the Committee of Public Safety time to get firmly seated in power, to provide a really strong executive, to build up and reorganise a most efficient army out of the relics of the really excellent troops of the *ancien régime*, the enthusiastic " Volunteers of '91 and '92," who only needed discipline and experience, and the vast hordes of men placed at their disposal by the *levée en masse*. During this critical time the Allies were engaged in the pleasing but illusory task of dividing between themselves the acquisitions they were to make from France. Thugut, who had replaced Philip Cobenzl as the principal minister of Francis II, when the latter was dismissed on account of the Second Partition of Poland, which he had failed to prevent or to turn to Austria's profit, was keenly set on extending the Netherlands to the Somme, or annexing Bavaria to compensate Austria for Prussia's gains in Poland—the Elector was to receive Alsace-Lorraine, which the Prussians were to conquer. England thought more of securing her commerce by capturing Dunkirk than of the defeat of the main armies of the enemy. Prussia, more concerned for her own acquisitions in Poland than for the success of the common cause, was negotiating with France behind the back of her allies; for the party which favoured the policy of a Franco-Prussian alliance numbered among its adherents Prince Henry, Count Haugwitz, General Mollendorf and the King's favourite Lucchesini, while Brunswick himself so far favoured the idea as to lend but a languid support to the operations of Würmser's Austrians in Alsace.

Thus the critical month of August slipped past. The Anglo-Hanoverians separated from Coburg to lay siege to Dunkirk after clearing the enemy from their path at Lincelles (Aug. 18th), Coburg and the main body, though within 160 miles of Paris, set about besieging the comparatively unimportant Le Quesnoy, while Brunswick remained inactive in the Palatinate, never utilising the chance which the disorganisation of the French Armies of the Rhine and the Moselle offered him. This gave Carnot time to reinforce the armies charged with the defence of the French frontiers and to place more efficient officers at their heads. Between September 6th and 8th Houchard cleared away the Hanoverians and Dutch who at Hondschoote and Menin were covering the Duke of York's operations against Dunkirk, though he failed to prevent the safe retreat of the besiegers to Furnes. A little later the Austrians, who after taking Le Quesnoy (Sept. 11th) had laid siege to Maubeuge, were attacked by Houchard's successor, Jourdan, at Wattignies, and after two days of fierce fighting (Oct. 15th to 16th) were driven from their position, forced to raise the siege and to retire behind the Sambre to join the Duke of York. An advance into West Flanders, however, proved less successful. Nieuport beat off all attacks, and in November the French retired behind their own frontier.

Meanwhile the position on the Middle Rhine had undergone great changes. The necessity of taking Mayence had prevented the Allies from following up Custine's retreat, and when its fall set them free the want of harmony between the Austrians and the Prussians came to the assistance of the French. Würmser, the Austrian commander, was most anxious to advance into Alsace; but Brunswick refused to co-operate, having no intention of conquering Alsace from France to restore it to the rule of the Hapsburgs. At last Würmser advanced alone against the Army of the Rhine, and pushing Southward drove it from the Weissembourg lines (Oct. 13th) and forced it back over the Lauter in confusion. Had Brunswick supported Würmser properly they might have had Strassburg on which the French had retired; but neither Brunswick nor Frederick William would agree to a winter campaign in Alsace, and the favourable moment slipped by. St. Just and Le Bas, the commissioners sent by the Assembly to purge and reform the Army of the Rhine, set about the restoration of discipline with a vigour which soon produced satisfactory results. In Pichégru it received a commander of quite a different stamp from the incompetent officers till then at its head; and with the not less brilliant Hoche sent by Carnot to command the Army of the Moselle a change was not long in coming. The Allied forces, spread out in a long and straggling line from Kaiserslautern to Haguenau, gave Hoche and Pichégru the chance they wanted. Attempting to relieve Landau by a direct attack on the Prussians, Hoche was checked at Kaiserslautern (Nov. 28th to 30th) and forced to change his plan. Pichégru had taken advantage of Hoche's diversion to advance against Würmser, and Hoche, instead of operating by himself, moved Southward to help Pichégru by falling upon Würmser's right. Several days of severe fighting (Dec. 15th to 24th) saw the Austrians driven from Haguenau and Frœschwiller in upon their lines in front of Landau. The culminating battle was on December 26th, when the two French armies, united under the command of Hoche, managed to storm the Geisberg, the key to the Austrian position. Only the arrival of Brunswick, whose inactivity had allowed Hoche to join Pichégru unhindered and was therefore the chief cause of the disaster, enabled the Austrians to avoid a complete rout. As it was, the French relieved Landau and recovered Worms and Spires, the Austrians recrossed the Rhine at Philipsburg (Dec. 30th), the Prussians fell back to Oppenheim to cover Mayence, and the Palatinate West of the Rhine passed again into French hands.

For these reverses the Coalition had chiefly itself to thank. The slackness of the Prussians, Thugut's greed for territorial acquisitions, Coburg's want of energy and strategic insight, the unreadiness of England for war, the feebleness of the efforts made by most of the members of the Empire, were preventable causes, even if the energy of the Committee of Public Safety, the organising powers of Carnot, the enthusiasm of the Revolutionary armies, and the talents of the young generals to whom a great career had been opened were factors outside the control of the Allies. But even now they had not learnt their lessons. Unity of purpose, energy and sincere co-operation were as conspicuous by their absence in 1794 as in 1793. All Pitt's efforts could not induce Prussia to do her duty by her allies. Already Frederick William, tired of the war and anxious to have his hands free to deal with Poland, declared that he would withdraw from the Coalition unless the Empire undertook to support his army. For the Empire to do so was obviously impossible; but England concluded a subsidy-treaty with Prussia in May by which the King promised to put 62,000 men at the disposal of Great Britain, a promise which he did not fulfil in the spirit. With Brunswick and with Hesse-Cassel, Pitt also concluded subsidy-treaties; but he was to have only too clear proof that it is the very falsest economy which so reduces a country's forces in peace that in war-time she must depend on raw recruits and hired foreigners to fight her battles. The Austrian army also was not in as good a condition as it might have been. The Emperor was in nominal command, but he had no military capacity; and though several of the other generals were good divisional leaders, there was no really competent commander-in-chief and bad Staff-work was responsible for an absence of accuracy and precision in carrying out the plans decided upon. In Thugut, Francis possessed a minister who had at least the merits of determination and resolution; but he was most unpopular with the great nobles who held the chief places at the Court of Vienna, and the internal condition of the affairs of Austria[1] was hardly a source of strength to the Coalition.

The plan adopted by the Allies for 1794 was the work of an Austrian officer whose name was to become unpleasantly familiar to British ears before his errors and misfortunes reached their climax at Ulm. General Mack's scheme[2] was that the main body, 85,000 strong, under Saxe-Coburg, should advance between the Sambre and the Scheldt and open a path into Picardy by the capture of Landreçies. It was to be supported

---

[1] Cf. *Dropmore MSS.* ii. pp. 614–636.
[2] *Ibid.* ii. p. 505, cf. p. 525.

on its flanks by smaller corps, that on its right under Clerfayt
stretching from the Scheldt to the sea, that on its left under
Kaunitz and Beaulieu from the Sambre to the Moselle, while
50,000 more troops under Saxe-Teschen were to be collected on
the Moselle in the hopes of the Prussian aid which the Anglo-
Prussian convention seemed to have secured for the Allies.
To oppose them Carnot gave Pichégru command of the Army
of the North, and arranged for the organisation of a new army,
with that of the Ardennes as its nucleus, to co-operate with him.
After some skirmishing the siege of Landreçies was begun on
April 17th; but a simultaneous advance of the French against
both flanks resulted in Pichégru's turning the right of the
Allies, driving in Wallmoden from Courtrai, forcing Clerfayt
back on Tournai, and taking Menin.   Despite this, Landrecies
fell on April 30th; but the efforts of the Allies to catch the
invaders of West Flanders between simultaneous attacks from
the North, to be made by Clerfayt from Tielt, and from the
East, to be made by the main army, miscarried.   After heavy
fighting round Turcoing on May 17th and 18th, of which the
brunt fell on the British columns under Abercromby and the
Duke of York, the Allies fell back behind the Scheldt; and
though Pichégru's counter-attack (May 22nd) was repulsed, he
was able to besiege and take Ypres (June 1st to 17th) and then
to lay siege to Ostend and Nieuport, taking post on the left
of the Scheldt to cover the operation.   But the Allies were in
no condition to interfere.   Clerfayt had fallen back to Ghent,
and the successful advance of Jourdan now compelled Saxe-
Coburg to turn Eastward.   Jourdan had brought up 50,000
men from the Moselle to reinforce the Army of the Ardennes,
till then held in check behind the Sambre and unable to cross,
had forced the passage of the river and laid siege to Charleroi
(June 18th), Beaulieu recoiling on Namur.   Too late to save
Charleroi, which fell on June 25th, Coburg could not withdraw
without a battle, and Jourdan's hard-won victory at Fleurus
(June 26th) decided the fate of the Netherlands.   The Allies
retired, the Duke of York to Malines, the Austrians to Louvain.
Ostend, Mons, Tournay, Ghent and Brussels fell into the hands
of the French.   The Army of the North joined hands with
Jourdan's of the Sambre and Meuse, and before their joint
advance the British, Dutch and Hanoverians fell back to Breda
to cover Holland; the Austrians retired by Tirlemont and

Liége across the Meuse, leaving the remaining fortresses of the Netherlands to make what resistance they could. By September nearly all were in French hands.

The timely reinforcement which Jourdan had brought up from the Moselle to decide the campaign in the Netherlands, had been allowed to leave its original station by the inactivity of the Prussians on the Middle Rhine.[1] Prussia had accepted a heavy subsidy from England, in return for which she had pledged herself to place troops at the disposal of England to aid in the defence of the Netherlands. But far from actively sharing in this task, Prussia failed also to contribute to it by means of a diversion elsewhere. Saxe-Teschen had crossed near Mannheim during May and driven Michaud behind the Queich; but unsupported the Austrian commander could get no farther, and in July the French resumed the offensive, drove Möllendorf's Prussians from Kaiserslautern (July 15th), and forced Saxe-Teschen to recross the Rhine. In September, Jourdan, following up his success at Fleurus, turned Eastward to the Meuse. His right under Scherer secured Namur, and driving Clerfayt's 60,000 men before it, won a great victory near Jülich (Oct. 2nd). Kléber then besieged Maastricht, which fell on November 4th; while Jourdan moving Southward, cleared the left bank of the Rhine of the Austrians, capturing Cologne, Andernach and Coblence. At this point he got into touch with the Army of the Moselle, which had taken Treves on October 8th, and Mayence was again besieged. Meanwhile the Armies of the Alps and of the Pyrenees had been winning successes in their turn. The "natural boundaries" had been reached on all sides; and if the English had defeated the Brest Fleet on June 1st, they had been driven from Toulon and had not done anything for La Vendée.

But the most conspicuous of the successes of the French was yet to come. The position of the English and their auxiliaries on the Waal was seriously threatened by the disaffection of a very large section of the Dutch. There had always been a Francophil party in Holland, and the Committee of Public Safety was counting on this when they rejected all the efforts of the Stadtholder to arrange a peace and sent orders to their generals to push on with the conquest of Holland, even in the depth of a most severe winter. Helped by the memorable

---

[1] Cf. *Dropmore MSS.* ii. p. 577.

frost which had frozen all the wonted water defences of the United Provinces, Pichégru set his forces in motion towards the end of December. The British and Hanoverians fought well, but the numbers of the French and the lukewarmness of the Dutch were too much for them, and the Hanoverian Count Wallmoden, who was in command, after repulsing one French attack on the line of the Lech, had to withdraw his right to Amersfoort, and thus to expose Utrecht and Amsterdam to the French (Jan. 14th). In fearful weather the British retired Eastward upon Bremen, the Hanoverians and Hessians home-ward, while the dramatic capture of the frozen fleet in the Texel by a handful of cavalry under Moreau put the final touch to the conquest of Holland. The foundation of the Batavian Republic and a treaty with France which placed the Dutch navy at the service of its new ally marked the beginning of the end of the Coalition.

For, indeed, the Coalition was fast perishing, not merely by reason of the French successes, but of its own divisions. 1795 saw Spain, Tuscany and other non-German states withdraw from its ranks; and the more important defection, that of Prussia, was no more than might have been expected. Even without Poland to distract the attention of Prussia, the standing jealousy between the Hohenzollern and the Hapsburgs would probably have prevented anything like a sincere co-operation; and all along there had been at the Court of Berlin a party which advocated making friends with the Mammon of militant democracy in the hopes of thereby obtaining advantages greater than those to be gained by opposing it. Once the monarchical crusade against the Revolution and its subversive principles had failed, once it became clear that France must be beaten before she could be partitioned, this party had steadily grown in influence. France, too, was ready for peace. With the repulse of the invasion and the complete success of the French arms the need for an internal government as violent and repressive as that of the Committee of Public Safety had ceased. A reaction against the excesses of the Terror had set in, and the "revolution of Thermidor" had placed in power men of moderate views who had no wish to remain at war with all Europe.[1] Even those among them who, like Rewbell, wished to continue the war against the "hereditary enemies," Austria

[1] Cf. speech of Merlin of Douai to the Convention, Dec. 4th, 1794.

and England, were fully awake to the advantage of detaching Prussia and the rest of the Coalition from the side of their enemies. In January 1795 negotiations were begun at Basel in which Barthélemy represented France, and von Goltz and, after his death (Feb. 6th), Hardenberg acted for Prussia. France demanded the recognition of the Republic and of the Rhine frontier as the boundary of France. This involved the surrender by Prussia of her territory West of the Rhine, Cleves, Upper Guelders and Mors. These, however, Prussia was ready to give up in return for the recognition by France of the neutrality of Germany North of the Main, and the promise that at the conclusion of a general peace Prussia should be compensated for her losses. On these terms a peace was before long arranged, and on April 5th, 1795, it was signed by the plenipotentiaries of the two Powers. The arrangements about compensation were embodied in secret articles, which also translated the promise of the formal treaty that France would accept the good offices of the King of Prussia in favour of those German states which should claim his protection into a definite recognition of their neutrality under a Prussian guarantee. It was further arranged that should Hanover refuse to accept this neutrality, Prussian troops should occupy the Electorate; but Hanover so far disassociated herself from the action of Great Britain as to acquiesce in the arrangement, and not till 1801 did the Prussians take possession of the country.[1]

Few actions have been more criticised than that of Prussia in making peace with France in 1795. In the light of subsequent events it is easy to see that the path on which Prussia thus entered was to lead to Jena and Auerstädt, to the humiliation of Tilsit, and the degradations of 1808–1812. It is easy to see now that England and Austria can plead an ample justification for their refusal to make peace in 1795; that the professions of pacific intentions with which the new system in France was inaugurated were belied by the continued instability of the French Government at home and by the disregard of treaties and of international obligations which the Directory no less than the Convention exhibited in dealing with other nations; that the final outcome of the recurrent constitutional crises in France was the establishment of the

[1] Cf. Chapter XXXV.

most formidable military despotism the world has yet seen.
But it may be urged that the pacific intentions of France were
never given a fair chance; that the continuation of the war
involved financial and domestic troubles which made a military
despotism inevitable; that peace would have freed the Directory
from the difficulties which finally overthrew it; that it was the
Italian campaign of 1796 which gave Bonaparte his first real
start on the road to supreme power; that without the Italian
campaign of 1796 he would never have had a chance, and that
if England and Austria had followed Prussia's example and
made peace in 1795 no campaign would have been fought in
Italy in 1796. Between these two views it is not easy to
adjust the balance of probabilities. For each there is much to
be said. It is clear that Pitt at least was anxious to grasp the
opportunity offered by the establishment of the Directory, and
to test the sincerity of their pacific professions by opening
negotiations.[1] But his overtures fell on unfruitful soil, and
rather encouraged the bellicose element in the Directory. The
fatal thing was Prussia's isolated action. If she was right to
make peace, she was not right to make peace alone. England
and Austria may have let the best chance slip early in 1795
when the tone of the French was fairly moderate, but Prussia's
desertion was an important factor in raising the demands of
the Directory, which, when Pitt made his overtures, had reached
a point far beyond that to which either England or the Emperor
was prepared to go. Perhaps one may say that Prussia's action
was stultified by the line adopted by England and Austria,
but that the course of events fully bore out their expectations.
After all, the question whether, if a general peace had been
made in 1795 the Directory could or could not have provided
France with a stable government capable of living in harmony
with its neighbours, concerns French rather than German
history. It must, moreover, be admitted that Prussia made
the Peace of Basel not so much from a desire to restore peace
to Europe, or even to Germany, as from more selfish motives.
The establishment of a line of demarcation,[2] behind which the
North German states were to enjoy neutrality, was again

---

[1] Cf. "France and the First Coalition before the Campaign of 1796": J. H.
Rose in *E.H.R.*, April 1903.

[2] The line of demarcation ran up the Ems to Münster, thence by Coesfeld and
Borken to the Duchy of Cleves. It then followed the Rhine as far as Duisburg, and

dictated by Hardenberg's wish to revive the Prussian influence over these principalities, rather than by a desire to minimise the area afflicted with war; loyalty to the Empire, into which it introduced a new division, had nothing to do with his action. It was for Prussia's benefit that Brunswick and Waldeck were to enjoy peace, not for their own sake. Austria may have played a feeble part in the war, may have been an inefficient and unsatisfactory ally, Thugut's greed may have contributed largely to the failure of the Coalition, but after all from the point of view of German interests it is impossible not to pronounce Austria's conduct as more praiseworthy than Prussia's. By setting the example of desertion, Prussia shattered the Coalition; by separating the Northern from the Southern members of the Empire she split up what was left of the Holy Roman Empire. After having been foremost in preaching the monarchical crusade against the iniquities of the Revolution, she gave the signal for capitulating when France showed that she would not prove a second Poland.

Austria would, indeed, have been glad to make peace. She does seem to have offered to sacrifice the left bank if France would agree to her annexing Bavaria; but this was after Prussia had already left Germany in the lurch. In July also the Emperor, acting on behalf of the Diet, made overtures through Denmark which were rejected; but Austria would not submit without a further struggle to the terms Prussia had no difficulty in accepting. She did at least continue to resist the annexation by the Republic of the debatable lands between France and Germany, and refused to admit that "the German Rhine" is the natural and proper boundary of France. Prussia had made no effort to hold out for these things. She had tamely acquiesced in the French claims, and proposed to indemnify herself at the expense of weaker Powers who had given her at least no cause for complaint, even if it be admitted that they had practically nothing to plead in defence of the independence they enjoyed. The remaining states of Germany may have condoned and even approved Prussia's action by following her example, but this condemns them rather than excuses

---

went up the Main, crossing to the Neckar, which it followed to Wimpfen. Thence it skirted the frontiers of Bavaria and Bohemia so as to include the Franconian and Upper Saxon Circles. Cf. Haüsser, ii. pp. 6 ff.

Prussia.[1] Austria, no doubt, was fighting for her own hand, but so far as there was a " Germany " in 1795, so far as there was a German national cause or national feeling, Austria rather than Prussia was its champion.

[1] Hesse-Cassel made peace in August 1795, Würtemburg in September. Baden followed suit in July 1796, the Swabian Circle in August, while Bavaria concluded an armistice in September. All these treaties reserved the Diet's ratification, but that was practically assured by the action of the individual voters. Thus Prussia found plenty of imitators whose isolated surrender destroyed all chance of arranging the more satisfactory peace that their joint action might have secured.

CHAPTER XX

FROM BASEL TO CAMPO FORMIO

THE ineffective part played by Prussia in resisting the tide of French conquest can be partially explained, though the explanation is no exculpation, by the fact that her heart was never in the task. As in 1793, so in 1794 the Vistula rather than the Rhine was the point upon which Prussia's hopes and interest were concentrated. The Second Partition had not put an end to the troubles of Poland : it had roused up an intense feeling against Prussia, whose conduct in allying with Poland in 1790 and then not only abandoning her in 1792, but actually joining Russia to despoil her former ally, was looked upon by the Poles as the basest treachery, while even Russia's own partisans seem to have been surprised at the Czarina's cynical rapacity. Some of the authors of the Constitution of 1791 had fled to Saxony, and from that refuge had begun a nationalist agitation. This spread rapidly over Poland and in March 1794 culminated in the outbreak of an insurrection at Cracow. Though disavowed by the King the rebels were at first successful. Their gallant leader Kosciuzsko routed a Russian force at Raclawice (April 4th), and aided by the inhabitants expelled the Russian garrison from Warsaw (April 17th). But his successes were not to be long-lived. Russia put a large force into the field and retook Vilna (Aug. 22nd). Thugut had no intention of letting Austria be again left out of the distribution of spoils which was sure to follow the suppression of the rebellion ; he was, moreover, anxious to renew good relations with Catherine. Austria therefore declared against the Poles and occupied Polish Galicia, and in July 50,000 Russians advanced to Warsaw and laid siege to the town. An insurrection in the provinces acquired by Prussia in 1793 forced Frederick William to raise the siege (Sept. 6th) ; but Suvorov, the best Russian general of the day, advanced steadily West, defeating the Poles in several encounters, of which that at Macejowice (Oct. 10th) was the most important, and stormed the Praga suburb of Warsaw on Nov. 4th. With the fall of Warsaw five days later the independence of Poland passed away. The jealousies and intrigues of the three partners in the overthrow of the Republic protracted the negotiations over the Partition for nearly a year. Russia, which had done the lion's share of the suppression of the rebellion, held the best cards and was disposed to favour Austria rather than Prussia, so as to preserve the balance between them. Once the terms arranged between Catherine and Thugut (Jan. 1795) had been at a favourable moment (Aug. 9th) communicated to Prussia the end was not far off. Unsatisfactory as the division was to him, Frederick William could not oppose Russia's decision, and on October 25th the treaties were signed which divided the unhappy country among its covetous neighbours. Warsaw and the greater part of the Palatinate of Cracow fell to the share of Prussia, Cracow itself, Lublin, Sandomir and part of Masovia to Austria, the remainder to Russia. In extent the territories which Prussia and Austria thus acquired exceeded those they were losing to France beyond the Rhine, and geographically the new provinces were more advantageously situated than were those for which they were in some measure a compensation ; but Prussia had already as large a Slavonic element in her population as she desired, and even the Belgians had more in common with the Austrians than Poles had. Though the anarchy, the selfishness and the want of patriotism which had made the Polish Republic a byword may be said to have to some extent justified the treatment Poland received, it is not unsatisfactory to reflect that the Partition profited its authors very little. The real gainer by the Polish troubles was the French Republic, which owed its great successes on the Meuse and Rhine in no small measure to the preoccupation of Austria and Prussia in playing jackal to Russia's lion in Poland.

Meanwhile hostilities were about to be resumed on the Rhine. Here, as was only natural, Prussia's defection had been the signal for a storm of abuse and bitter recrimination. But it was a little absurd for states, most of which had not made any conspicuous efforts in their own defence or in the defence of their neighbours, to talk of Prussia's " treachery," " breach of oaths and obligation," to make the belated discovery that Germany was one state with one head, not a federation of independent Powers. The hollowness of the outcry was shown by the action of the individual members of the Empire. The states whose territories were covered by the proposed line of demarcation readily grasped the chance of being left undisturbed ; with the fortunes of the rest of the Empire they did not concern themselves. To Prussia's credit it must be admitted that she did not at once give up all hopes of expanding the Peace of Basel into a general peace. To facilitate this she sought to induce France to modify her terms and to give up the demand for the left bank. But of doing this France had not the least intention; all she would concede was that it should be open to any member of the Empire to accede to the Peace of Basel within the next three months.

When the Prussian envoy communicated this offer to the Diet (April), the Emperor replied by an appeal to the states to keep together and not play into the hands of France by acting singly. He proceeded to show the line he intended to adopt by concluding a fresh treaty with England (May 4th), by which he undertook in return for a loan of £4,600,000 to put into the field a force of 200,000 men. At the same time, he was in full agreement with the decree of July 3rd, which announced the anxiety of the Diet to conclude a joint and general peace according to the constitution of the Holy Roman Empire and preserving its full territorial integrity. Indeed, the Emperor went so far as to empower Denmark to make peace proposals to France on behalf of the Empire. These were duly made, but they did not prevent the resumption of hostilities and about the end of October the proposals were definitely rejected by France.

After the conquest of Holland and the expulsion of the Allied field forces from the left bank of the Rhine, military operations had languished, being indeed quite subordinated to diplomatic requirements. Moreover, even the victorious French needed time to reorganise and refit, and so throughout the greater part of 1795 they contented themselves with the sieges of the few places on the left bank, such as Mayence and Luxembourg, which still resisted their attacks.

For the defence of the right bank a considerable army had been got together under the command of Clerfayt;[1] but he made no effort to relieve Luxembourg, as Thugut had come to regard Belgium as definitely lost and hoped to gain more from

---

[1] 250 squadrons and 137 battalions.

the plots for a Royalist counter-revolution in France, which were at this time on foot. In these Pichégru, the commander of the Army of the Rhine and Moselle, was to some extent implicated. His army, some 90,000 strong, lined the Upper Rhine from Huningen to Mayence; and according to Carnot's plan of campaign it was to co-operate with Jourdan and the 85,000 men of the Sambre and Meuse Army, who were on the Middle Rhine, stretching from Coblence to Cleves. Set free to resume the offensive by the fall (June 25th) of Luxembourg, Jourdan put his troops in motion in September, crossed the Rhine at Neuss and Düsseldorf, and by the simple expedient of violating the neutrality of the "line of demarcation," outflanked Clerfayt's right, thus forcing the Austrians to abandon the lines of the Sieg and the Lahn and to retire behind the Main. Meanwhile Mannheim had surrendered to Pichégru at the mere threat of a bombardment (Sept. 20th), and that general's forces were pushing across the Palatinate towards Heidelberg, driving before them Würmser, who commanded the left wing of the Austrian army. The surrender of Mannheim, like that of Düsseldorf a few days earlier, was attributed by the Austrians to treachery on the part of the Elector Palatine. Charles Theodore was on the point of coming to terms with France, and the charge seems to have had some foundation. Indeed, the attitude of Germany as a whole was hardly creditable. The appearance of the French on the right bank and the extension to it of both the official requisitions and the even more exacting unofficial plundering, which had swept the left bank all but bare, were quite enough to check any democratic sympathies. However, instead of uniting in a determined effort to repulse the invader, the Princes of Western Germany sought security in separate understandings with the enemy. Hanover and the North German Princes as a whole gladly availed themselves of the shelter of the "line of demarcation." The Saxon contingent in the Army of the Empire was recalled "to defend Saxony against the dangers which threaten it." Hesse-Cassel had already made peace with France (Aug. 29th); Würtemberg followed suit in September.

But Clerfayt was soon able to put a different complexion upon affairs. Deceiving Jourdan into a belief that he was going to respect the neutral line which Jourdan himself had disregarded, the Austrian commander suddenly crossed the

Main above Frankfurt (Oct. 11th), and moving upon Bergen rolled up the French line from its left. The Army of the Sambre and Meuse went completely to pieces and fell back to the left bank in great confusion, the peasantry whom its ravages and plundering had provoked retaliating in kind on its stragglers and sick. Clerfayt then turned his steps to Mayence, which had been for some time closely beset, and was hemmed into the Westward by strong lines of circumvallation. Against these he delivered, early in the morning of October 29th, a well-planned and well-conducted sortie. Their centre pierced and their left turned, the French had to fall back behind the Pfriem, to cover the line from Worms to Donnersberg. On the same day Würmser, who had checked on September 24th the French advance on Heidelberg at Neuenheim, stormed Pichégru's position on the Galgenberg outside Mannheim. These successes allowed Clerfayt to interpose between the Army of the Rhine and Moselle and that of the Sambre and Meuse. The former was driven back behind the Queich, and then Würmser was left to keep Pichégru in check, while Clerfayt, turning Northward, frustrated Jourdan's efforts to come to his colleague's help, and forced him back to the Moselle. Mannheim was retaken on November 22nd,[1] and on December 21st an armistice was concluded with Pichégru which brought hostilities to a close.

Thus the campaign in Germany ended somewhat more favourably for Austria than had any since the war began. This was mainly due to the failure of Pichégru to co-operate properly with Jourdan; but though Clerfayt's critics declared that a man of more resolution and decision would have achieved even greater victories,[2] his generalship had had a good deal to do with the successful issue of the campaign, and it was a bad thing for Austria that Thugut's omnipotence required the general's dismissal before the next campaign. The all-powerful minister could not brook any independence or any opposition on the part of the generals, much less the outspoken and well-grounded criticism which Clerfayt had bestowed upon the indifferent military administration and on the general

---

[1] Oberndorf, the officer responsible for the capitulation of September 20th, and Salabert, the minister of Zweibrücken, were by Thugut's orders arrested on a charge of treason and kept in prison. This " outrage " on the subjects of a member of the Electoral College was much resented in the Empire, and even the Hapsburg Elector of Cologne joined in the outcry against the action of Austria.

[2] Cf. *Dropmore MSS.* iv. p. 7.

policy of the minister. Moreover, Clerfayt was on bad terms with Würmser, who was in high favour at Court, and despite his victories he was removed from the command.[1] It was an unfortunate step ; for although his successor, the Archduke Charles, was a man of not less capacity, his supersession was a victory for the little " War Office ring," which under the general direction of Thugut endeavoured with the most scanty success to conduct campaigns from Vienna.

During this period negotiations had still been going on, but all efforts to arrange a general peace proved futile. Neither the Emperor nor the Directory would give way, and the negotiations of Russia with France were as far as ever from bringing about any definite result. Hardenberg was already beginning to feel uneasy. He saw the dangers to Prussia involved in continued French successes, and he went as far as to point out to his King that the justification of the Peace of Basel would be removed if it failed to serve as the basis for a general peace ; but it was not to be expected that Prussia would sacrifice the immediate benefits of neutrality for a rather remote general interest, and so, despite the misgivings her line of action excited in the minds of some of her more clear-sighted ministers, Prussia adhered to the path she had chosen at Basel.

For the campaign of 1796 the Directory proposed a three-fold attack upon the hereditary dominions of Austria : Jourdan with the refitted Army of the Sambre and Meuse was to advance by the Main ; Moreau, who had succeeded to Pichégru's command, was to push down the Danube ; while their joint operations were to be assisted by those of the Army of Italy under an officer who had yet to win his spurs in independent command, Napoleon Bonaparte. In the original plan the Italian campaign, though important, was really secondary to the far less famous operations on the Rhine. Only 50,000 men were allotted to it, as against Jourdan's 76,000 and Moreau's 80,000 ; but the genius of the young commander of the Army of Italy altered their relative importance. Massena's victory at Loano in the previous autumn had been too late in the year (Nov. 24th) to be followed up at once, but it had cut off the Austro-Sardinians from the sea, and had opened the way for the brilliant operations by which Bonaparte, breaking through the centre of the Austro-Sardinian positions along the Apennines, thrust Beaulieu's Austrians back upon Milan, and forced the Sardinians, thus separated from their allies, to make peace at Cherasco on the terms he dictated (April 28th). Thus freed from the Sardinians, Bonaparte pushed on Eastward, drove the Austrians out of the Milanese, compelled Beaulieu to take refuge in Tyrol, and laid siege to Mantua, the last bulwark of Austrian rule in Italy. Even before the campaign on the Rhine opened 25,000 men had had to be detached from the Southern wing of the Austrian army in Germany to attempt to check his victorious progress.

This left the Archduke Charles with some 140,000 men to oppose to the combined advance of Jourdan and Moreau. This total included the garrisons of Mayence, Ehrenbreitstein and other fortresses, and the relics of Würmser's wing, now under Latour, an officer hardly fit for an independent command, but more suited to his subordinate position than a self-asserting colleague like Würmser. At the beginning of June, Kléber at the head of Jourdan's left wing pushed across the Rhine at Düsseldorf and, supported by his chief, who crossed at Neuwied, drove the Austrians back towards the Lahn. At Wetzlar the Archduke, who had come up with reinforcements, barred the French advance, and a sharp fight (June 14th) saw the French compelled to retire by the turning of their left. Kray pursued Kléber closely and suffered some loss in an action with his rearguard at Altenkirchen (June 19th); but Jourdan had to recross the Rhine (June 21st), and for the time Franconia was cleared.

But Jourdan had occupied the Archduke's attention, and so allowed Moreau to utilise the chance given him by Würmser's defective dispositions, which the Archduke had had no time to alter. A feint on Mannheim (June 20th) drew Latour off to his right, thereby enabling Moreau to force a passage at Kehl, weakly defended by 7000 Swabians (June 24th). This severed the 10,000 men in the Breisgau from Latour's centre and right, which took post behind the Murg. The news of Moreau's passage of the Rhine brought the Archduke South again. He left Wartensleben with some 40,000 men to "contain" Jourdan, and hurried up to the Murg, only to be attacked by Moreau near Malsch (July 10th) and beaten in a well-contested action. He fell back to Pforzheim and thence behind the Neckar to Cannstadt, thus leaving the road into

Swabia by Stuttgart open to Moreau. On July 22nd the French attacked his positions behind the Neckar, but their assaults were repulsed. However, the news that Wartensleben was retreating before Jourdan and had left Würzburg on the 22nd, decided the Archduke to retire towards the Danube, where he took up a position, its left resting on the river near Gunzburg, while the right extended through Neresheim to Nördlingen. Here he remained halted some days, holding Moreau in check and recovering touch with the division from the Breisgau which was retreating down the right bank of the Danube. His chief concern was to retain touch with Wartensleben and by keeping the interior position between the two French armies to be able at the right moment to concentrate all his forces against whichever of the opposing armies he could attack with most prospect of success.

No better example can be found of the way in which particularism and selfish local feelings dominated Germany, to the exclusion of the national idea and of all sense of community of interest, than the conduct of the minor Powers at this time. The outrages, exactions and excesses of the French armies were enough to have stung the most slack and selfish into activity and to have roused the fiercest opposition; but, as in 1794 and 1795, the states which found themselves threatened by the advance of Jourdan and Moreau hastened to make the best terms they could with the invader, each for itself, without ever realising that the only protection or security worth having was that which was not to be obtained except by showing the enemy that they were capable of defending themselves and each other. Localism was no less strong in Spain, while the excesses of the Armies of the Sambre and Meuse and of the Rhine and Moselle were hardly surpassed by the Napoleonic armies in the Peninsula; but in Spain the separate provinces never attempted to gain their own security by betraying the others, and though, if unaided by regular forces, the guerilla bands would have failed to expel the invaders, the Spanish peasantry did retaliate very effectively upon the plunderers of Cordova and the stormers of Saragossa. But as the French armies approached their territories in 1796 the minor Princes of Germany sought safety in tame surrenders and in the security of a promised "protection." The Swabian Circle set the example of negotiating with Moreau, and withdrew its troops

from the Archduke's army; Würtemberg did the same, concluding an armistice in July and converting it into a definite
peace a month later (Aug. 15th); and Baden concluded a
treaty on practically the same terms (Aug. 22nd). Both
Powers abandoned to France all their possessions on the left
bank;[1] both declared themselves ready to receive ecclesiastical
territory as a "compensation"; both promised not to lend any
help to any Power which was hostile to France. The Saxon
contingent, as in 1795, departed homeward, and the Elector
concluded a convention of neutrality. The three Ecclesiastical
Electors took refuge in the interior of Germany, and many of
the minor Princes followed the example their flight had set.
But while these states were to find the promised protection
a very shadowy affair, they had to pay both in money and
in contributions in kind sums which would have amply sufficed
to defend their territories against the French. The Franconian
Circle had to pay 6 million francs in cash and to provide
goods to the value of 2 millions more; Baden may be held
to have got off lightly with 2 millions; while the Swabian
ecclesiastical territories were heavily taxed with 7 millions.
About the same time the negotiations between Prussia and
France which had been dragging on for some months were
brought to a conclusion, and on August 5th a new treaty was
signed. A new line of demarcation was arranged, while in the
secret articles all pretence about the "integrity of the Empire"
was abandoned, and the principle of compensation at the expense of the ecclesiastical states for territorial losses on the left
bank was accepted. Among other proposed changes the House
of Orange-Nassau was to receive Bamberg and Würzburg as a set-
off against the United Provinces, Prussia thus agreeing that Germany should provide the compensation for a loss of non-German
territory; an arrangement which may be explained by the relation
existing between the families of Orange and Hohenzollern.

Meanwhile the retrograde movements of Wartensleben and
the Archduke had brought them nearer together. With less
than 40,000 men Wartensleben had no chance of arresting
the advance which Jourdan resumed towards the end of June.
He was driven back up the Main, Frankfort, Würzburg and
Bamberg falling one after another into French hands. From

[1] These included Mömpelgard, Hericourt and Ostheim belonging to Würtemberg;
Sponheim, Herspring and Beinheim belonging to Baden.

Bamberg, which he evacuated on August 2nd, Wartensleben fell back Eastward by Nüremberg towards Amberg (Aug. 12th), fearing to expose to Jourdan the magazines collected along the Bohemian frontier should he continue his movement Southward to join the Archduke. This step might have been fatal, as it gave Jourdan a chance of interposing between the Archduke and Wartensleben by a rapid advance to the Danube. But Jourdan was a little slow to grasp his chance. He halted his men at Nüremberg from August 13th to 16th, and at this crisis the Archduke acted with a decision and a calculated daring which entitle him to a high place among commanders. He had by a hard fought action at Neresheim (Aug. 11th) secured an unmolested retreat to Donauwerth, and now, leaving Latour with a comparatively thin screen of troops to hide his movements from Moreau, he crossed to the right bank of the Danube with the bulk of his corps (Aug. 15th), marched down-stream to Ingolstadt and recrossed there (Aug. 16th). Jourdan had resumed his advance on the 17th, had driven Wartensleben back before him to the river Naab, and had thrust a division under Bernadotte out to his right towards Neumarkt. It was on this division, less than 10,000 strong, that the Arch-duke fell with three times as many men on August 22nd. Bernadotte was crushed, and his defeat parried Jourdan's thrust at the Danube and forced him to fall back to Amberg. Here on August 24th the united forces of the Archduke and his lieutenant, over 60,000 in all, attacked Jourdan's 40,000. A fiercely-contested battle ended in the disorderly retreat of the Army of the Sambre and Meuse by Nüremberg to the Main. By a great effort Jourdan so far rallied his men as to stand at Würzburg and offer battle (Sept. 1st) in the hope that Moreau might help him; but Moreau was before the gates of München, and on September 3rd an Austrian attack drove Jourdan from his position. His situation was critical. Pursued by superior forces, with the peasantry turning out to harass his retreat and cut off stragglers, his army was fast degenerating into a rabble, when it was saved from destruction by the interposition of Marceau and a force drawn from the besiegers of Mayence and Ehrenbreitstein. At Altenkirchen (Sept. 20th), Marceau sacrificed his life, but he secured the safe retreat of the relics of Jourdan's broken army behind the shelter of the Rhine.

This set the Archduke free to attend to the Army of the Rhine and Moselle. Moreau had crossed the Danube at Dillingen on August 19th, had forced the passage of the Lech five days later despite Latour's gallant resistance, and had pushed forward into Bavaria, which till then had not been touched by the war. The presence of his plundering hordes completed the distaste which the Bavarians already felt for the war. Distrusting Austria, fearing with only too good reason that she had not relinquished her designs on their country, the Bavarians and their ruler had never been enthusiastic for the war, and now that they found themselves experiencing the horrors of a French invasion they at once began negotiating. Still the Treaty of Pfaffenhofen (Sept. 7th) can only be regarded as the *ne plus ultra* of localism, the carrying to its logical conclusion of that independence of the sovereign Princes of Germany which had been established at Westphalia. Despite the fact that Jourdan was known to have been beaten and to be in full retreat before the Archduke, that Moreau's position was thereby rendered most perilous, Bavaria pledged herself to neutrality, withdrew her contingent from the Archduke's army, paid an indemnity of 10 million livres and a large contribution in kind, and promised to facilitate in every way the retreat of Moreau to the Rhine.

It was largely to this pusillanimous action on the part of Bavaria that Moreau owed his escape from a dangerously exposed position, though his own skilful and well-ordered dispositions contributed to it in no small measure. It must also be allowed that he owed much to the want of harmony among the Austrian forces engaged in harassing the retreat, while the Archduke cannot escape censure for not having hastened sooner to transfer himself, ahead of his forces, from the Main to the Danube in order to give to the pursuit that co-ordination which it lacked from the absence of a single will to direct all the forces engaged in it. Thus when Moreau, who had fallen back to the Iller on hearing of Jourdan's retreat, quitted Ulm (Sept. 27th) and retired upstream to avoid being cut off by the forces moving against his line of communications with the Rhine, divergence of opinion between the Austrian commanders came to his aid. Latour wished to follow him closely, but Nauendorf, who commanded a separate corps at Ulm, was for marching across the chord of the arc by Tübingen to join Petrasch's corps on the Upper Neckar and bar the passage of the Black Forest. Unable to agree, they separated. Latour attacking with only 20,000 men was so badly beaten at Biberach (Oct. 2nd) that he was quite incapable of molesting the retreat further. Thus the French were able to cross the Black Forest by the Höllenthal in safety (Oct. 7th to 15th). Too late the Archduke arrived and took supreme command; he could only check a move downstream on Kehl (Oct. 19th), and was unable to prevent the French recrossing the Rhine at Hüningen unmolested (Oct. 25th).

The popular movement in South Germany which the French invasion had aroused was one of great possibilities had Austria known how to turn it to advantage. The Elector of Bavaria refused to ratify the Treaty of Pfaffenhofen. Other Powers which had made terms for themselves endeavoured to explain their action.[1] But with a man at the head of the Austrian ministry as narrow as Thugut and as incapable of inspiring or feeling confidence, it was not likely that such a chance would be properly used. And peace was as far off as ever. It was useless for England to send Lord Malmesbury to Paris to negotiate in the hope that the expulsion of the French from Germany would have lowered their tone and disposed them to peace, when France could point to victories such as those of Bonaparte in Italy as a set-off against her reverses in Germany, and when the addition of Spain to the allies of France led to the evacuation of the Mediterranean by the British navy.

Since the conquest of the Milanese and Beaulieu's retreat into Tyrol the Italian campaign had centred at Mantua, and had consisted of repeated efforts to relieve that gallantly defended fortress. In July Würmser's advance had forced Bonaparte to raise the siege for a moment; but the victories of Lonato (Aug. 3rd) and Castiglione (Aug. 5th) had sent Würmser back to Tyrol and allowed Bonaparte to resume the blockade, though the fortress had been replenished and the French siege-train destroyed. A second effort in September resulted in Würmser making his way from the Brenta to Mantua and reinforcing the garrison, but at the expense of being cut off from Tyrol and himself besieged. A new army, mainly composed of raw recruits and half-trained Croats, was gathered by Alvinzi, and in November it renewed the attempt. Checked

---

[1] Cf. Haüsser, ii. p. 91.

at Caldiero (Nov. 12th), Bonaparte won a victory at Arcola four days later (Nov. 16th) which threatened Alvinzi's communications and drove him back to the mountains. In January a final attempt was made. The main body came down the Adige from Tyrol only to suffer defeat at Rivoli (Jan. 14th), and a second column under Provera, moving Westward from the Brenta, penetrated to the suburbs of Mantua merely to be crushed in its turn (Jan. 16th). This decided the fate of Mantua. Its fall (Feb. 2nd, 1797) marked the end of Hapsburg predominance in Italy. Though not exactly oppressive, the rule of Austria had been far from popular. The steady drain of money to Vienna from the rich and productive plains of Lombardy had excited resentment. The old traditions of Guelph and Ghibelline had just sufficient existence to make it easy for the enemies of Austria to appeal to time-honoured prejudices. The democratic propaganda of the French Republic had fallen on fruitful soil in the valley of the Po, and the invaders had been welcomed as deliverers from the " German " yoke.

Bonaparte was now free for an advance against the hereditary dominions of Austria. Only some 30,000 dejected and dispirited troops, the survivors of many defeats, were in his way ; and though the Archduke Charles was sent to Illyria in the hope that he might stay Napoleon's advance, the task was beyond his powers. Three divisions under Massena advancing along the foot of the mountains turned the right flank of each line of defence in succession, the Piave, the Tagliamento and the Isonzo, as Napoleon advanced against it in front. Fierce fighting left the all-important Col di Tarvis in French hands, and the Archduke beat a hurried retreat. By the end of March, Bonaparte was in Illyria; on the 25th he occupied Laibach. At Neumarkt and again at Unzmarkt the Archduke was beaten, and by the 5th of April the French headquarters were at Jüdenberg in Styria, their vanguard at Leoben within 80 miles of the Hapsburg capital. Bonaparte's advance produced a panic in Vienna and lent weight to the advice of that party which had for some time past been counselling peace. Thugut, supported by the British Ambassador, Morton Eden, still urged resistance. His hopes of inducing Russia to throw in her lot with the Coalition had been disappointed when on the very verge of success [1] by the sudden death of Catherine (Nov. 17th, 1796), for her successor

[1] Cf. *Dropmore MSS.* iii. pp. 246, 261.

Paul favoured a Prussian rather than an Austrian alliance; but he had still good arguments on his side. Bonaparte's position at Leoben was not without its perils. He was a long way from his base; communication even with Joubert's corps in Tyrol was uncertain, for the peasantry were in insurrection, and neither the Army of the Rhine and Moselle nor that of the Sambre and Meuse could give him any effective assistance.[1] It was at least possible that a last effort might have forced even the victorious Bonaparte to recoil to Italy. But Thugut was too unpopular to rally a nation to an effort of the required description, and too distrustful of popular movements to wish to do so. At the same time, his credit had been somewhat shaken by recent disasters, by Pitt's profession of inability to comply with the rather exorbitant Austrian demands for pecuniary help,[2] and by the failure of the negotiations with Russia. The pacific counsels were therefore well received by the Emperor, and it was decided to accept Bonaparte's offer of terms. On April 13th negotiations were begun, on the 18th they resulted in the Preliminaries of Leoben. It was arranged that a congress should be held to make peace between the French Republic and the Empire on the basis of the "integrity" of the Empire, and Austria ceded Belgium to France on condition of receiving an equitable indemnity elsewhere. This indemnity was defined in secret articles by which the Emperor gave up all his territory West of the Oglio, receiving in return the Venetian territory between the Oglio, the Po and the Adriatic; the Venetian Republic obtaining in exchange Bologna, Ferrara and Romagna. Compensation in Germany was also promised to the Duke of Modena, whom a democratic rising had ousted from his duchy. The conclusion of these preliminaries did not bring negotiations to an end. They dragged on through the summer of 1797, Bonaparte threatening and blustering, Thugut procrastinating in the hope that a revolution in France, which seemed quite within the bounds of possibility, might put the control of affairs into the hands of a more moderate party.[3] During this time both sides went on with their preparations for war as though hostilities

---

[1] Hoche, who had replaced Jourdan, did, it is true, cross the Rhine at Neuwied on April 18th, and he had driven the Austrians back behind the Nidda when the news of the armistice arrived, but he could have done little to help Bonaparte had a determined stand been made and the latter's communications attacked.

[2] Cf. *Dropmore MSS.* iii. pp. 270 ff.

[3] Cf. Haüsser, ii. p. 123.

were quite likely to be resumed, for Austria was most anxious to avoid having to fulfil the obligations of Leoben and hoped to be able to do something for the Empire. However, the tangled skein of diplomacy was rudely broken when the *coup d'état* of "Fructidor" (Sept. 4th) put an end to all chance of a reaction in France. Bonaparte, now feeling that he was treading on firm ground, went to the length of addressing an ultimatum to Thugut; peace must be made by October 1st or hostilities would be resumed. Thugut had no alternative but to send Count Louis Cobenzl—one of the leaders of the pacific party—to Udine to conduct the negotiations. Bonaparte had no wish to press Austria severely, for his aim was to separate Austria from England by making peace acceptable to her, rather than to humiliate her, as the Directory, now in a Jacobinical and ultra-democratic mood, wished to do. The Treaty of Campo Formio, signed on October 17th, was thus by no means unfavourable when looked upon in the light of the dynastic interests of the Hapsburgs, although they had to purchase these advantages by conditions most disadvantageous to the Empire of which Francis II was the nominal head. Austria gave up Lombardy[1] and the Netherlands. In return she was to receive Dalmatia, Istria and the other mainland possessions of Venice, the Adige thus forming the Western boundary of her Italian possessions. The Ionian Islands, which Thugut had sought to obtain for Austria, went to France. The dispossessed Duke of Modena was to receive the Breisgau as a compensation, thus establishing a cadet branch of the Hapsburg family at the head waters of the Danube. The arranging of a peace between the Holy Roman Empire and the French Republic was to be entrusted to a congress which was to meet for the purpose at Rastatt. More important in some ways than these published conditions were the secret articles[2] by which the Emperor promised to secure for France the Rhine as a frontier from Switzerland as far as Andernach, thence the boundary was to ascend the Nette, cross to the Roer, and descend

---

[1] This with Modena, Bologna, Ferrara and Romagna formed the Cisalpine Republic.

[2] These secret articles were subsequently a stumbling-block to a renewal of good relations between Austria and England, as Pitt and Grenville believed that they contained stipulations prejudicial to the interests of Great Britain (cf. *Dropmore MSS.* iv. p. 91) and therefore requested that Thugut would disclose the terms of the agreement. Haüsser, ii. pp. 130-131.

that river to its junction with the Meuse. The object of this was to leave Prussia her old possessions on the left bank, and so deprive her of all claim to compensation on the right bank. Furthermore, as a "compensation" for Belgium, Austria was to receive the Archbishopric of Salzburg and the part of Bavaria between the Inn, the Salza, Tyrol and Salzburg. The Emperor gave up all his own claims upon Italy, and promised that the Empire would do the same. Those Princes who would lose territory through the annexation of the left bank to France, including among others the three ecclesiastical Electors, Bavaria, Zweibrücken, Baden, the two Hesses, Nassau-Saarbrücken and Würtemberg, were to be compensated on the right bank.

Thus Austria, despite her defeats, only lost provinces never very easy to hold or to govern. Belgium was a possession she would have given up gladly any time during the last twenty years, if she could only have obtained a reasonable substitute, and certainly Salzburg and the promised district of Bavaria were in every respect more desirable possessions. Geographically they were adjacent to the hereditary dominions, and therefore their defence fell in with the general scheme of defensive preparations. Their population was closely akin to that of Upper Austria, and would be an addition to the German element among the subjects of the Hapsburgs. Politically there would be no need to set up an entirely separate government for them. In Italy also Venetia with its seaboard was a far more useful possession than the more distant Milanese, and it might be hoped that its acquisition would mark the beginning of a new era in the maritime history of Austria. But these acquisitions did not increase Austria's prestige. The spoliation of Venice was an act of the same class as the seizure of Silesia and the partitions of Poland. Moreover, the adoption of the plan of compensation by secularisation was nothing more or less than making the weakest pay the costs of the settlement, and the concessions included in the secret articles amounted to the abandonment of the rights of that Empire of which Austria posed as the champion. It is true that the suzerainty over Italy still nominally vested in the Holy Roman Empire had for centuries been nothing but a name, but the surrender of this time-honoured form at the bidding of an upstart Republic could not fail to deal a hard blow at an Empire whose very existence was a form. The surrender of the left bank to that same Republic was a not less severe blow to the German Kingdom; but worst of all was the voice which France was to have in the arrangement of the "compensation." One justification and one only Austria can urge for her abandoning the defence of the Empire: the selfishness and utter want of patriotism displayed by every other member of the Empire from Prussia and Bavaria to Lippe-Detmold and Schwarzburg-Sondershausen. She did not abandon the Empire until the example had been set and almost universally followed. Still for the moment Germany was so glad to be rid of the war at any cost that the peace was almost popular.

The Peace of Campo Formio marks the complete failure of the attempt of monarchical Europe to interfere in the affairs of Revolutionary France. By it Austria followed the example of Prussia in making terms with the formidable Power whose hostility their intervention had provoked. England, the only Power which continued the war, had not shared in the intervention on behalf of the Bourbons, and the struggle between her and the French Republic was only another phase of the old maritime struggle she had waged with the French Monarchy. But Austria and Prussia had embarked on the war in a different spirit, and the situation in which they found themselves at the end of it might well have induced their rulers to question the wisdom of the policy they had pursued and to reflect seriously on its lessons for the future.

The ease with which the resources of Austria had stood the strain of the war was no small testimony to the soundness of the work of reform carried on by Maria Theresa and her son, but in many respects Austria was slipping back into old bad grooves of the days before Maria Theresa. She was in sore need of another Haugwitz to guide her internal affairs into more healthy channels, and of another Kaunitz to direct her foreign policy. This was largely due to the fact that Francis II, though careful and observant, anxious to do his duty by his subjects, and anything but a bad man or a bad king, was not strong enough for the task before him. Drastic reforms were urgently needed, but Francis II could neither realise the need nor be persuaded by those who, like the Archduke Charles, were alive to the evils of the situation. Rather narrow-minded, lacking vigour and real statesmanship, his very carefulness degenerated into pedantry and formalism, his painstaking anxiety to do his work left him immersed in unimportant details of routine and unable to take a broad view, his caution made him so over-suspicious that he did not trust his ministers enough. Nor were his ministers the men to compensate for his defects. Kaunitz, old, worn out, and no longer able to exercise his once pre-dominant influence over the affairs of the country, had given up the Chancellorship in August 1792; and with all his faults none of his successors came up to his level as a statesman. Lehrbach was an intriguer, whose only idea was to obtain Bavaria for Austria by fair means or foul; he was a mere instrument in Thugut's hands. Louis Cobenzl, though in-dependent of Thugut, was no statesman. Well versed in intrigue, well acquainted with Court backstairs, he was a man of little capacity. Indeed, Thugut himself was the only man who stood head and shoulders above the mediocrities around him, and his supremacy was hardly to the advantage of his country. Head of the State Chancery since 1793, he had replaced Philip Cobenzl at the Foreign Office in 1794, and he practically ruled the army through his friends and creatures in the War Council. Energetic, resolute, cool and clear-headed, he was utterly unscrupulous, cynical and un-principled. Absolutely without popular sympathies despite his humble origin, he was an ideal minister for a despot, the typical upholder of feudal and religious absolutism against the assaults of Liberalism or democracy. This was best seen in his harsh and severe domestic policy, in the highly-organised and extensive system of espionage which he maintained, in the atmosphere of distrust and suspicion he communicated to all branches of the government, in the rigid centralisation he maintained, in the harsh press censorship, and in the obtrusive police system. In a word, the internal troubles of Austria which culminated in 1848 may be in no small measure attributed to the reactionary and repressive turn which Thugut gave to the Hapsburg government. Nothing could have been further removed from the spirit of Maria Theresa and of Joseph II than the attitude of harshness guided by suspicion which he imparted to the dealings of the rulers of Austria with their subjects.

Under such a man it was not unnatural that Austria fell into a stagnant condition. Routine was everything. All changes were distrusted as such, apart from their merits. Useful developments were prevented or cramped. Reform was looked upon as playing with fire, as likely to lead to revolution, as Jacobinical. Much of Joseph's best work, especially in the religious and educational spheres, was abolished or altered, while his bureaucracy remained and flourished, uninspired by its author's zeal for efficiency, for honesty and for progress. It was to his hold on to the reins of domestic government that Thugut owed his continued tenure of office, for his foreign policy was rather too adventurous for the less enterprising Francis II. In his hatred for Prussia he recalled the days of Maria Theresa; in his adherence to the English alliance and his opposition to France he went back to Leopold I and the Grand Alliance. It was a policy for which there would have been much to be said had it not been marred by a fatal defect. His insatiable desire for territorial gain was published by his designs on Bavaria and Poland, by his readiness to sacrifice the integrity of the Empire for the sake of Venetia. His eagerness to turn to the advantage of Austria the upheaval of Europe caused by the Revolution outweighed his desire to restore the European equilibrium by the reduction of the power of France. Certainly he made it hard for an ally to put much trust in him. And when all this went hand in hand with the methods by which he sought his ends, with his lack of scruple and almost of honesty, it is hardly wonderful if for all his ability his policy went far towards wrecking the Coalition. It may be perhaps an exaggeration to say with von Sybel, "to him France owed her victory in the Revolutionary War," but he must ever be typical of the way in which diplomatic skill may overreach itself, and in which too much cleverness may recoil on itself while simpler methods succeed by reason of their straightforwardness.

Nor was the condition of Austria's great rival any more healthy. Frederick William II had withdrawn from the Coalition partly in the hope that thereby he might allow the finances of Prussia to recuperate, and might be able to cure the abuses which had grown up in the Prussian administration. Moreover, Prussia had a task of no small difficulty to tackle, the assimilation of the million or so of Poles who had just become her unwilling subjects. An even-handed, capable and firm treatment on the lines of Frederick II's administration might have gone far towards reconciling the Polish peasantry to the loss of a national independence which had never meant good government or given them justice or material prosperity, but their discontent was only augmented by an oppressive, exacting and corrupt rule, by lavish and unwise grants of Polish land to Prussian favourites. Nor were the nobles any better pleased with the results of annexation to Prussia. More than any other class they resented the suppression of Poland's national existence, since to them it had meant cherished privileges.

The failure to achieve in the assimilation of the new shares of Poland even as much success as Frederick II had obtained in dealing with the provinces acquired in 1773, is typical of the general decline in the efficiency of the Prussian State. The administration was full of corrupt and indolent officials, zeal and energy were conspicuous by their absence. Here and there individual officials, as, for example, Baron Stein, at this time practically in charge of the administration of the Westphalian provinces of Prussia,[1] were exceptions to an all but universal rule. But patriotism, self-sacrifice, discipline, devotion to the State, seemed all to have disappeared with Frederick II. The nobles were tending to become a more privileged order, the lower classes, groaning under heavy taxation, were indifferent to the welfare of the country, since their lot was in no way improved, however matters might stand.

In the way of Army Reform a certain amount had been accomplished by a War Directory of which Brunswick and Möllendorf were the leading members. It had added to the establishment of officers, had made some amelioration in the conditions of service, and had improved the equipment of the troops. These, however, were but palliatives and could not cure the deep-seated evils which 1792 had displayed.[2] The Army was living in a fool's Paradise on its old reputation, and was doing nothing to keep itself in touch with the changes in tactics and strategy which the Revolution had brought in its train.

The tone of society was not only bad, but, following the example of the Court, it was hypocritical. Frederick William II might try to cloak his immorality behind a show of devotion, his imitators in Prussian society did not trouble themselves with that amount of concession to the proprieties. At the same time

[1] Cf. Seeley, vol. i. bk. i. 2.
[2] Cf. Chuquet's chapter on the Prussian Army, *Les Guerres de la Révolution*, vol. i. ch. iii.

there was much interference with opinion, almost amounting to a religious persecution of a petty and futile description, an attempt to impose on every one a flabby and formal orthodoxy.

In the finances the effects of this decline in efficiency were most marked. Once the bureaucracy lost that automatic precision and punctuality imparted by the iron discipline maintained under Frederick II, the task of making both ends meet proved altogether too much for it. The reserve fund left by Frederick II had been spent; the tobacco monopoly, abolished with so much parade at Frederick William II's accession, had been reimposed in 1797; but the revenue could not nearly balance the expenses.

With the death of Frederick William II in November 1797, certain changes were made, but only in degree, not in kind:[1] Prussia continued to follow the same paths both in domestic and in foreign policy. Free from his father's combination of mysticism, superstition, hypocrisy and immorality, Frederick William III was too narrow-minded and too diffident to pull Prussia out of the mire in which she was becoming involved. By himself he could do little, he needed some really great statesman to help him. Simple, pious and straightforward, but rather stupid, he was lacking in vigour and in decision, and though he did impart to the administration rather more order and economy, he was not the man to carry out wide reforms or to insist upon and obtain administrative efficiency by means of close personal supervision. Nor were his ministers more likely to do this. Haugwitz, in whom love of power was so strong that he was ready to sacrifice any principles or personal convictions which might have proved inconvenient to his master, if only he could thereby indulge his ruling passion, had since 1792 been mainly responsible for the conduct of foreign affairs. Lombard, a clever but untrustworthy man, was all-influential in domestic policy. From them reforms were not to be expected, negligence in discharge of duties went almost unpunished. The selfish and short-sighted policy of peace which Prussia followed to her own undoing was only one manifestation of the thoroughly unsound condition into which the country had fallen. Whatever arguments might have been urged in defence of the Peace of Basel when it was first concluded, the experiences of the years which followed it should have shown a statesman capable of grasping

[1] The "immediate" departments which had hitherto been independent of the General Directory were incorporated with it.

the essential features of the state of Europe how dangerous a policy Prussia was pursuing. Pitt had seized the occasion of the accession of the new King to attempt by the aid of the Duke of Brunswick to oust from office Haugwitz, whom he regarded as mainly responsible for the Peace of Basel and the subsequent inaction of Prussia. But Brunswick, though alive to the dangers of continued neutrality and personally hostile to Haugwitz,[1] was too afraid of the consequences of a breach with the Republic to urge any such departure; and though, as the negotiations of the winter of 1797–1798 showed,[2] it was no longer Haugwitz who was the main obstacle to a change of policy, the advocates of neutrality led by Schulemberg and Prince Henry were still strong enough to carry the day. All that Prussia would offer England was that in return for a considerable subsidy she would mobilise her troops in order to preserve the neutrality of the line of demarcation; and as England was not prepared "to pay an extravagant price for what we think of little value,"[3] Prussia, despite the misgivings which haunted several of her wisest statesmen, adhered to the policy of the Peace of Basel. Between the alternatives of joining the rest of Europe in resisting French aggression and of frankly throwing in her lot with France, she was endeavouring to pursue a middle course which combined some of the disadvantages of both. Mischievous as her conduct was in its influence over Germany, in assisting the spirit of division which it was the aim of France to foster, in offering to the minor Powers "the specious appearance of peace and neutrality,"[4] while Austria was seeking to induce them to join her in a war which concerned them no less than her, Prussia herself was no gainer by her policy. By refusing a definite alliance with France she showed her suspicion and fear of the Republic's successes, and thus failed to obtain any return for the considerable services she was rendering to the Republic by holding aloof from the Coalitions. She earned contempt rather than gratitude; and when she at last realised in 1806 the true tendencies of French policy, France had no reason to spare the country by whose short-sightedness and indecision she had profited so much.

[1] Cf. *Dropmore MSS.* iv. 405.
[2] *Ibid. passim.*
[3] T. Grenville to Lord Grenville, *ibid.* p. 514.
[4] *Ibid.* p. 490.

CHAPTER XXI

RASTATT AND THE SECOND COALITION

IN concluding secret compacts with France in the hope of purchasing her good offices at the coming Congress, Austria and Prussia had not been alone. Indeed, most of the minor Powers had sought to safeguard their interests by this expedient, from which it might have been foreseen that France rather than any German Power would play the chief part at Rastatt, and that her interests would prevail in the resettlement of Germany. Her diplomatists were not slow to grasp the opportunity which the estrangement of Austria and Prussia gave them, and by insinuating to each Power in turn that only the opposition of its rival prevented the realisation of its own desires they managed to still further widen the breach between these two leading German states. At the same time, the French sought to excite the alarms of the minor states, to instil into them distrust of Hapsburg and Hohenzollern alike, and teach them to look across the Rhine for protection. By showing herself well disposed to the Princes and to their claims for compensation, France divided them from the Bishops, at whose cost alone compensation could be provided. Indeed, abortive though the Congress was, the foundations of the Confederation of the Rhine were laid at Rastatt.

The principal questions which occupied the attention of the Congress were those of the Left Bank and of "compensation." On the first point, the French envoys adopted from the outset a most peremptory tone, declaring that the assistance and shelter given to the *emigrés* by the Princes of that district had been one of the chief causes of the war. The Austrians had carried out the Convention of December 1st, and their evacuation of the fortresses as they departed homeward proved conclusively that Austria had made up her mind not to resist, and no other state was likely to oppose the cession. Even the Ecclesiastical Electors were more concerned with the chances of avoiding secularisation than with saving the Left Bank.   There was no one to speak on behalf of the Empire, which would receive no compensation for the 25,000 square miles and the $3\frac{1}{2}$ million inhabitants which it was losing, however skilfully the territorial cards were shuffled.   Dynasties might obtain complete compensation, might even gain, but some one had to bear the loss, and it was upon the helpless and inarticulate corporate body to which they belonged that the dynasties of Germany managed to shift the burden of the loss.   In January 1798 the incorporation of the Left Bank with France, its division into departments, and its complete subjection to French codes and arrangements, took place, though nearly two months more elapsed before the deputation appointed by the Diet formally agreed to the cession (March 11th).

The question of compensation and the closely connected problem of secularisation provided the Congress with ample material for discussion and for intrigues of every kind during the remainder of its existence.   Into these it is unnecessary to go, since the renewal of hostilities brought its deliberations to an abortive close.   The problem was one which if tackled by men who really had the interests of Germany at heart, might perhaps have resulted in a real reform of the Empire, might have given it a new constitution and a new lease of life.   There were not wanting optimists who hoped that the beginning of a new era for Germany might be dated from the Congress of Rastatt.   Such a result, however, difficult to reach under any circumstances, was quite out of the question when the predominant partner in the Congress was the Power to whose interests a real revival of Germany was most inimical.   Even now, if Austria and Prussia could have agreed to sink their differences and to make a stand against the policy of the Directory, it might have been possible to turn the Congress to a useful end.   However, co-operation was as far off as ever. Haugwitz was as much an object of aversion and suspicion at Vienna as was Thugut at Berlin.   The old hostility, the old jealousy and the old suspicions survived in great strength and frustrated the efforts of those who sought to bring the old rivals together; and France spared no efforts to keep the breach between them open.[1]   Both favoured or opposed each proposal, each suggested territorial rearrangement according as it was

[1] Cf. P. Bailleu, *Preussen und Frankreich, 1795–1806.*

more or less disadvantageous to the other. Prussia would give up her claims on compensation if Austria were to receive nothing. Austria was prepared to do without Salzburg if Prussia made no new acquisitions. Moreover, the designs which Thugut entertained on Bavaria were a stumbling-block in the path of any possible understanding.

The Left Bank once lost, the question of secularisation was inevitably brought forward. By secularisation alone could the necessary " compensation " be provided. But it was not without some misgivings that Germany approached the problem. Every one saw that the secularisation of the ecclesiastical states would be the beginning of the end of the old constitution and of the old order of things, but nobody could tell where the process would end, and all felt not a little nervous about the future. Hanover and Saxony, for example, shared Austria's wish to confine any secularising to very limited dimensions. Their rivals would profit more by it than would they themselves, therefore they opposed any wide-sweeping measures. But the smaller states as a whole, those large enough to be sure of getting some morsel of ecclesiastical land, some abbey or priory, clamoured keenly for secularisation as " the only way to restore efficiency to the Empire "[1]— in other words, the only thing likely to benefit them individually.

In May the deliberations of the Congress were rudely enlivened by the production by the French emissaries of an entirely new series of demands. The Rhine was to be free to traffic, all tolls were to be abolished, Kehl and Castel were to be handed over to France, Ehrenbreitstein was to be " slighted," the islands in the river were to be allotted to the Republic. From June onwards the Congress spent its time in making a futile opposition to these and other equally new demands. But it was rapidly becoming more certain that a fresh appeal to the sword was imminent, for the aggressive and disingenuous policy of the Directory allowed little hope of a stable peace ever being reached by negotiation.

In their dealings with Germany the Directors had all along shown themselves tainted with that same disregard for treaties, for the most solemn promises and the most definite agreements, which had characterised the Convention. French emissaries had been sedulously spreading the Revolutionary propaganda

[1] Cf. Haüsser, ii. p. 164.

throughout South Germany, stirring up the peasantry, fomenting social discontent. The Directory did, indeed, disavow these agitators, but their conduct was exactly the same as the line its agents were pursuing in Switzerland and in the Papal States, where democratic discontent was excited, to be used as a pretext for intervention. Similarly, in the matter of Ehrenbreitstein they hardly even pretended to abide by the conditions of the armistice arranged between Hoche and Werneck in April 1797. The fortress was held by an Austrian garrison which was allowed to periodically reprovision itself, though not to increase its supplies beyond the amount in stock when the armistice was concluded. When, in December 1797, the Austrians withdrew, 2500 men in the service of the Elector of Treves replaced them; but the French in deliberate violation of the armistice resumed the close blockade of the fortress. Not content with this, they kept on raiding the Right Bank, levying forced contributions and subjecting the inhabitants to all manner of violence. Such conduct was by itself sufficient indication of the intentions of the French, and an ample justification for breaking off negotiations. Moreover, their behaviour went far to alienate even their strongest supporters in the Rhine lands. The annexation of all ecclesiastical and monastic property, the introduction of the French codes of law, calendar and tables of weights and measures, the appointment of Frenchmen to all the new posts and offices, the abolition of the old German education, briefly, the contrast between the promised liberty and the practical oppression roused a very strong anti-French feeling in the Rhine valley.

In April 1798 relations between France and Austria were still further strained by an incident which took place at Vienna. Bernadotte, the French Ambassador, had been sent there with the definite object of mixing himself up in the internal politics of Austria and endeavouring to overthrow Thugut, or at least to undermine the position of that strenuous opponent of France. On April 13th he provoked a riot by displaying a Tricolour on his house. The mob, enraged by this, stormed the house and tore down the flag. Bernadotte made all the political use he could of this incident. He demanded his passports and even quitted Vienna. This might have been followed by war, but that the provocation came from France before the financial or military situation of Austria had improved sufficiently to enable her to defy the Republic, and the Emperor humbled himself to make a concession to France which for the time averted a rupture : Thugut gave up his post as Foreign Minister (May 1st) and confined himself to domestic affairs, Louis Cobenzl, a strong advocate of peace with France, replacing him. The change was seen in the private negotiations between the Hapsburgs and the French, which now took place at Selz near Rastatt; for Francis was anything but bellicose, and Cobenzl would have been glad to avert a renewal of hostilities by coming to terms with France. But the French were not prepared to bid high enough for Austria's neutrality, and even Cobenzl had to admit that with such a Power it was almost impossible to come to terms. By the middle of July Thugut was back in office, Cobenzl going off on a special embassy to Berlin with the object of inducing Prussia to come into line with Austria and Russia to resist further French aggressions, for events elsewhere were moving rapidly towards the now inevitable war.

The intervention of the Directory in the affairs of Switzerland (April 1798) has already been mentioned (p. 421). The annexation of Biel, Geneva and Mühlhausen to France might be defended on geographical grounds, but it was an arbitrary and rapacious act, extremely disconcerting to the other neighbours of the Republic. The appropriation of the contents of the treasuries of Berne, Lucerne and Zürich—16 million francs in cash besides goods of about equal value—to the purposes of Bonaparte's Egyptian expedition was an utterly unjustifiable example of high-handed violence, and showed that the Helvetic Republic was little more than a vassal of France—in other words, that the strategical situation had been materially altered to Austria's disadvantage, as her armies in Swabia would no longer have their left flank protected by the neutrality of the territory to the South. About the same time (March 1798) the intervention of the Directory in the internal affairs of the Batavian Republic gave an example of the real meaning of the liberty and independence enjoyed by the states under the protection of France. Nor were these outrages confined to the valley of the Rhine. The mixture of treachery and force displayed by Bonaparte's treatment of the Knights of St. John and his seizure of Malta had the important effect of enraging the Czar Paul, already alarmed by the progress of French arms and principles and anxious to test the armies of Holy Russia against the conquerors of the rest of Europe. Austria, finding it likely that she would have the zealous support of Russia if she took up arms, was growing more bellicose, and her warlike dispositions were increased by the action of France in Italy, where the arrangements made at Campo Formio, on the whole not unfavourable to Austria and her friends, were being radically altered. The assassination of the French envoy at Rome, Duphot, served as a pretext for Berthier to attack Rome, drive out Pope Pius VI, and proclaim the Roman Republic (Feb. 1798); and when the King of the Two Sicilies, encouraged by Nelson's victory at the Nile to measure his strength with the Power which was so rapidly subjugating all Italy, rashly attacked this unwelcome new neighbour and occupied Rome (Nov. 29th), Championnet not only promptly expelled the Neapolitans, but followed up his success by invading their territory. The Court took refuge in Sicily, and France added the Parthenopean Republic to the list of her clients (Jan. 1799). Nor was this all. In December 1798, Charles Emmanuel of Savoy was forced to abandon his continental for his insular dominions, and a Prince of the Hapsburg House, Archduke Ferdinand of Tuscany, was forcibly dispossessed of his Duchy.

Such a series of outrages, of violations of treaties, of unprovoked aggressions, could have but one result: indeed, it is only remarkable that the Powers of Europe were so long about uniting to withstand the Directory. It was no fault of England's, for, since the beginning of 1798, Pitt had been seeking to bring together a new coalition. But while acrimonious disputes over the repayment of money lent to the Emperor in the previous war prevented cordial co-operation between Austria and Great Britain, the extravagances and eccentric conduct of Paul of Russia made Francis II more than usually cautious about committing himself to any course of action in which he might find himself left suddenly in the lurch through the vagaries of his unstable Eastern neighbour. The return of Thugut to office (July 1798), the conclusion of a convention with Russia (Aug. 10th) promising military aid to the Emperor, the signature of an Anglo-Russian Treaty (Dec. 29th, 1798), mark stages in the slow progress by which at last Austria came to draw the sword. Her declaration of war (March 12th, 1799) would have been more efficacious had it been launched six months earlier, when France was still staggering under the news of destruction of her Mediterranean fleet at the Nile. The delay is to be attributed to her desire to give her shattered resources time to recuperate, and to the need for more military preparations.

From the Second Coalition, which comprised Austria, England, Naples and Russia, one Power was absent which, both for her own interests and for those of Europe, ought to have been prominent in its ranks. Not the least important causes of the renewal of hostilities was the utterly unreasonable rapacity displayed by the French at Rastatt. Their conduct towards Germany had been too unblushingly aggressive for any German statesman with any claim to foresight or national spirit, or even to a correct appreciation of the interests of his own particular state, to overlook the serious menace to the independence of Germany. Yet Frederick William III clung obstinately to his father's policy of neutrality, which had already been weighed in the balance and found wanting. One may explain, one may to some extent excuse the Peace of Basel; 1806 is the best comment on the inglorious inaction of 1799.

Prussia's continued neutrality was a great disappointment to the Allies. Every effort was made to bring her into line with the other Powers. Her relations with France were not of the most cordial, and Austria and Russia hoped to use this to enlist her on their side. Haugwitz himself had begun to realise how dangerous to Prussia was the supremacy of France, and to see that Prussia had more in common with Austria and Russia than with the Republic; in fact, Prussia had gone so far as to reject the overtures of Siéyès for a definite alliance with France (May 1798). Alvensleben, indeed, foretelling the collapse of the Prussian military system, did argue that the French alliance was the only road to safety, since it would enable Prussia to turn the resettlement of Germany to her own benefit and the disadvantage of Austria;[1] but the King was not well disposed towards such a step. Yet Prussia could not or would not see that for once there was no safety in the middle path. It was in vain that representatives of the four principal Powers of Europe met at Berlin (May 28th) to discuss the formation of an alliance; in vain that England and the Czar sought to induce Prussia to join in a Quadruple Alliance for the reduction of France to her old limits, the restoration of the House of Orange to Holland, and the re-establishment of the integrity of Germany. Beguiled by Talleyrand's assurances that France would respect

[1] Cf. Bailleu, *Preussen und Frankreich*.

the neutrality of North Germany, Frederick William failed to see that the success of France would place Germany at the mercy of the Republic, and that, if the Coalition were victorious, Prussia's voice would not be listened to when the affairs of Europe were resettled unless she had shared in earning the fruits of victory. Hesitation and indecision governed her policy, and there could be no better illustration of her endeavour to run with the hare and hunt with the hounds than the advice she gave to the new Elector of Bavaria, Maximilian Joseph of Zweibrücken. This Prince succeeded to the Wittelsbach inheritance on the death (Feb. 1799) of his cousin Charles Theodore. Bavaria's position was critical. Thugut's designs on the Electorate were an open secret. The events of 1795 [1] had not been forgotten by Austria; it was thought more than probable that Austria's hostility would leave Maximilian no alternative but to rely on French assistance. However, neither the new Elector himself nor his chief minister, the Savoyard Montgelas, regarded the friendship of France with much confidence, and once again, as in 1786, it was to Prussia that Maximilian turned for protection.[2] But Prussia could do no more for Bavaria than advise her most emphatically to do nothing that could give the Coalition reasonable grounds for taking offence. Thus left in the lurch, Maximilian Joseph had only one expedient remaining by which to avert the hostility of the Coalition. He knew that Thugut was doing all he could to incite the Czar against him, for the head of the Holy Roman Empire was so reduced that he dared take no step except with the consent of the monarch who claimed to be the heir of Byzantium, by representing to Paul that Bavaria was a partisan of France and a nursery of Jacobin intrigue. Maximilian therefore threw in his lot with the Coalition, and Bavaria was one of the few minor states of Germany which took an active part in the war. The conduct of the German Princes as a whole was not very creditable either to their patriotism or to their sense. Not even yet awakened to a full understanding of the meaning of French supremacy, they would have much preferred to see the completion of a settlement based on the secularisation of the ecclesiastical states and dictated by France, to the renewal of the attempt to confine the power of France within reasonable bounds.

[1] Cf. p. 399.   [2] Cf. *Der Krieg von 1799*, i. pp. 102 ff.

By the beginning of 1799 it was certain that hostilities would be resumed as soon as the season made operations possible. The gallant defenders of Ehrenbreitstein were compelled to surrender before January was over; for, though Austria was making preparations for war on a considerable scale, the relief of the fortress was out of the question. The Archduke Charles, with a perhaps undue caution, put off the opening of hostilities, although delay was, had he only realised it, even more useful to the French than to their enemies,[1] and in the end it was the French who on March 1st opened the campaign by crossing the Rhine.

The peculiarity of the campaign of 1799 is the prominence of Switzerland as a theatre of operations. Despite the difficulties of moving, feeding and manœuvring armies among its mountains and in its narrow valleys, its position between Italy and Germany made its possession of vital importance to the combatants, since it served as the pivot on which the campaign turned. From it as from a bastion, blows could be struck against the flanks of the forces contending in the valleys of the Po and of the Danube ; it would be exceedingly difficult to defend Swabia against a French advance from Alsace if at any moment the defenders might be taken in flank and rear by forces debouching from Switzerland. Through it also ran the most direct routes by which reinforcements might be detached from one wing to the other. Unless Switzerland were wrested from Masséna's possession Archduke Charles in the valley of the Danube would be unable to communicate with Suvorov in Italy except by most circuitous routes: the French would hold the interior position and be able to direct their blows against either enemy as they would.

Thus while Scherer with 60,000 men took post along the line of the Adige to cover the Cisalpine Republic against the 60,000 Austrians of Kray, and Jourdan with 48,000 advanced across the Black Forest to Rottweil and Tuttlingen to contend with Archduke Charles (70,000) for the upper valley of the Danube, Masséna with 30,000 men pushed forward through Switzerland across the Upper Rhine in the hope of driving the Austrians from the Vorarlberg back into Tyrol, and thereby completely severing their communications and menacing their flanks should their wings be successful.

[1] Cf. Hüffer, *Der Krieg von 1799*, i. pp. 19, 20.

It was about March 6th that Masséna began his advance. The Austrians, some 26,000 men under a general of Swiss birth, the gallant Hotze, extended from Bregenz to Chur. On the left Masséna's vigorous attacks, well conceived and well executed, drove them back into the Engadine. Almost simultaneously Lecourbe forced his way from Bellinzona to Thusis, and pushing on thence by the Julier Pass drove back into Tyrol the detachments of Bellegarde's unduly scattered corps (March 6th to 17th). Dessolles, coming up the Valtelline, forced his way after heavy fighting into the Münsterthal and inflicted on the Austrians a severe reverse at Taufers (March 25th), for which Bellegarde's own carelessness was responsible. Only on their right at Feldkirch did the Austrians manage to maintain their ground; but the end of March saw the French firmly established on the upper waters of the Inn and of the Adige; the Engadine and the Grisons were in their hands; the Austrians, despite considerable numerical superiority, had suffered a loss of 10,000 men, and the communications between Vorarlberg and Southern Tyrol were cut.

On the flanks, however, fortune had been very different. Archduke Charles, whose headquarters were at the moment at Friedberg, was better prepared for attack than was Bellegarde in Tyrol or Auffenberg in the Grisons; and when Jourdan, in obedience to definite orders from Paris but against his own better judgment, advanced again and took post behind the Osterach, the Archduke, though too late to fulfil his intention of forestalling the French at this river, had little difficulty in forcing them to retreat (March 21st). Profiting by the leisurely nature of the Austrian pursuit, Jourdan turned suddenly to bay at Stockach, and as the Austrians reconnoitred his position, delivered a furious counter-attack (March 25th). His principal effort was on his left, where St. Cyr, reinforced by d'Hautpoult and Soult, drove Merveldt's Austrians back in disorder from Liptingen, while the Austrian centre and left had the greatest difficulty in maintaining their position at Stockach. Victory seemed in Jourdan's grasp, and he was aiming a turning movement against the enemy's line of retreat when, just in time, the Archduke brought up reinforcements and quite turned the tables by a successful stroke at the French centre. His success was decisive: the French were driven back and their line cut in half; and though the Archduke failed to make the renewed attack next morning which might have clinched his victory, Jourdan fell back across the Black Forest (March 29th to 30th) without attempting to defend its passes. His army, ill-disciplined and ill-provided, went completely to pieces, and could have been annihilated had the pursuit been hotly pressed. Still even if Jourdan was lucky to escape, the Archduke had achieved no inconsiderable success.

Not only was Jourdan compelled to recross the Rhine in order to cover Alsace against the attack which was expected, but Bernadotte, who had advanced up the Neckar, levying contributions and plundering in the usual style, hastily fell back also ; and, save for the garrisons of Kehl and Mannheim, the Right Bank was free from the French. Moreover, their forces in Italy had also suffered disaster. Schérer, somewhat too old for his work, was less successful in the field than as a Minister of War, and his attempt to defeat Kray before the promised Russian reinforcements could arrive ended in complete disaster. After repulsing the attacks of the French between Legnago and Pastrengo (March 26th), and thwarting an effort they made to cross the Adige near Verona, Kray, a Wallachian of no little talent, popular with his men and trusted by them if not by the little clique which ruled the Austrian War Council, took the counter-offensive with success. Only the energy and skill of Moreau, Schérer's second in command, saved the French army from complete ruin at Magnano, just South of Verona (April 5th). Even so they had to abandon the lines of the Mincio and Oglio, and only about 25,000, not half Schérer's original force, could be rallied behind the Adda. Meanwhile Suvorov had arrived with the first contingent of his Russians (April 15th) and taken command of the Allies.

The veteran Russian general, though nearly seventy, was full of a youthful vigour which was conspicuous by its absence among the slower and more methodical officers of Austria. His enterprise and dash, combined as they were with a power of endurance and a calm resourcefulness not often met with in a nature so impetuous, made him resemble the generals of the Revolutionary school rather than those brought up in the more precise traditions of Frederick II and Marshal Lacy. Keenly alive as he was to the importance of rapidity, of concentrating his troops to strike a decisive blow, he startled the Austrian generals as much by his proposal to push forward, leaving Mantua untaken in his rear, as he annoyed them by compelling their troops to practise the bayonet exercise all day. Nor was it wonderful that he came into collision with the Austrian War Council. Suvorov was not the man to spare criticism where it was as well deserved as it was by the inefficient administration of Thugut and his clique. Moreover, the Council actually went so far as to issue direct orders to the Austrian troops which had been placed under his command, an interference he angrily resented. When it is also added that the policy of Thugut, which included designs on Piedmont and Genoa, differed materially from that of Suvorov and his master and led to violent quarrels, it is not the defeats but the successes of the Allies that excite surprise. Favourable as the opportunity seemed for overthrowing France, with her best general locked up in Egypt, her armies falling back defeated and in confusion towards her frontiers, pursued by the hatred of the populations they had maltreated, her home government discredited and a prey to factions, it was not by a disunited Coalition that her defeat was to be accomplished. When Prussia and most of the other Powers of Germany held aloof, and Austria and Russia entertained antagonistic views as to the policy to be pursued, France had not really much to fear.

Meanwhile the Congress of Rastatt had been continuing its sessions. Long after more than sufficient reasons had been given for the rupture of negotiations, Francis II had clung to the hopes of arranging a satisfactory settlement at Rastatt, and the lesser members of the Empire were too much engrossed in the intrigues and bargains of the Congress to pay any heed to events in Italy or Switzerland. Even after Austria's declaration of war (March 12th), only Lehrbach and Metternich left the Congress. The majority of the minor states eagerly accepted the assurance of the French that they would not be molested unless they supported Austria, for the French never missed a chance of sowing dissension between the Emperor and the Empire. With this object they disclosed the secret arrangements of Campo Formio, and the deliberations of the Congress were only interrupted by the arrival of Austrian troops, who surrounded the town and compelled the plenipotentiaries to disperse, as the Emperor had formally declared the Congress dissolved. The French envoys were given passports ordering them to quit Rastatt within twenty-four hours (April 28th); but delaying their departure until evening, they found the gates closed and did not get out until 10 p.m. They had hardly left the town before they were beset by a party of Austrian hussars, attacked and cut down; two of them, Bonnet and Roberjot, being killed on the spot and the third, de Bry, left for dead. The French version of the affair is that it was intentional, that it was done by Thugut's orders to make the breach with France insuperable, or perhaps to destroy the evidence of Austrian negotiations with France. However, there seems no reason whatever for laying the blame at Thugut's door. He was much too clever a man to have planned an act so brutal, so useless, and so calculated to excite horror and disapproval.[1] It seems rather more probable that the military authorities, well aware that the French had abused their ambassadorial office for purposes of espionage, intended to seize their papers, though no personal injury to the Ambassadors was contemplated,[2] but that the officer entrusted with the affair misinterpreted and exceeded his instructions with disastrous results.[3] It is, of course, possible that the outrage may have been the work of French *emigrés* in the Austrian service;[4] but the evidence is on the whole unfavourable to this theory, though the Austrians endeavoured to get it accepted. Whatever explanation be accepted, the incident was most discreditable to Austria, and Thugut would have done more to clear himself of the suspicion of complicity had more been done to punish the authors of an outrage worthy of the worst days of Revolutionary excess.

One result of the Allied successes in Italy and on the Danube was that the French were unable to retain their advanced position in Tyrol. Lecourbe had to fall back to Chur, and Dessolles to follow suit. Chiavenna was evacuated; Loison failed to maintain his position in the Valtelline and had to retire by the Splügen Pass into the Rhine valley; and Hotze carrying the Luciensteg (May 14th) at a second attempt, the French were expelled from Eastern Switzerland. Greater successes might have been obtained but for the highly culpable slackness of Bellegarde;[5] and, moreover, when the Grisons had been cleared of the French he refused to push on to the St. Gotthard and seize that pass, though this would enable him to cut off the retreat of the French divisions from the Italian

---

[1] Cf. *Der Krieg von 1799*, ch. iii. *passim.*   [2] *Ibid.* i. p. 79.
[3] *Ibid.* i. p. 96.   [4] *Ibid.* i. p. 72.   [5] *Ibid.* i. pp. 57–60.

lakes, but took instead the road to Italy by the Splügen and Como, alleging that his instructions bade him reinforce Suvorov. Even more unfortunate was it that during this period the Archduke should not merely have done nothing to follow up his successes against Jourdan, but made no move against Masséna either. Switzerland after her bitter experiences as one of the daughter Republics with which France had surrounded herself, would have welcomed the once-hated Austrians as deliverers. Masséna with barely 30,000 men in the midst of a hostile population could hardly have hoped to maintain his position against Hotze's 20,000, together with the 40,000 troops of whom the Archduke could have disposed, even if some portions of the Austrian force must have been left to watch Jourdan. To a certain extent this inaction was caused by Bellegarde's defeats, and the Archduke's own health was so bad that for several weeks he was unable to discharge his duties. He himself attributed his inactivity to the insufficiency of his force and to the deficiencies in his equipment and supplies—in other words, to the bad administration of the War Council; but the principal reason[1] was the resolve of the Emperor and Thugut, influenced not a little by political considerations, to wait for the arrival of the large Russian reinforcements which were on their way. The Archduke himself would have resumed operations about the middle of April, but orders from Vienna held him back.[2] The time thus lost by the Allies was of incalculable value to France. Masséna spared no effort to improve his position and to reorganise and refit his troops, and to repress the tentative efforts of the Swiss to rise and free themselves from the yoke of the invaders; while Bernadotte, transferred to the Ministry of War, exhibited wonderful energy and great administrative capacity in getting together a new army 100,000 strong out of the new levies whom the law of the Conscription (Sept. 23rd, 1798) had placed at his disposal.

Not until the end of May were hostilities resumed. Even then the efforts of the Austrian main army were designed mainly to assist Hotze's operations in Eastern Switzerland. The Archduke advanced South against Masséna's positions in the district between the Thur, the Glatt and the Limmat, Hotze moving East from St. Gallen to co-operate with him. Dashing

---

[1] Cf. *Der Krieg von 1799*, i. p. 107.   [2] *Ibid.* p. 109.

at the Archduke, who had crossed the Rhine near Schaffhausen on May 23rd, Masséna was repulsed (May 25th) after heavy fighting, and the Austrians were able to unite and to force the French steadily back on Zürich (May 27th to 29th). To hold this town, important as the point on which many roads converged, Masséna took up a strong position stretching North-Westward from the lake to the Glatt. Here on June 4th he gave battle to the Archduke. On their left the Austrian columns penetrated to the suburbs of Zürich, but were there checked; in the centre neither the column which assailed the Zürich Berg nor that under Hotze which tried to storm the Geisberg was able to gain any decisive advantage; while an equally indecisive result was reached on the right wing in the direction of Afholtern. But Masséna saw that he would not be able to hold his own against the renewed attack which the Archduke was preparing, and accordingly he evacuated Zürich and retired to a strong position behind the Lower Reuss. Meanwhile Lecourbe, who was endeavouring to hold the St. Gotthard against Bellegarde, had been forced back to Altorf at the head of the Lake of Lucerne and the shortest line of communications between the German and Italian theatres of war was once more in Austrian hands. Had the Archduke only pushed forward the Austrians might have gained a real success; they were superior in numbers, and the population of Eastern Switzerland was strongly in their favour. But once again political complications proved fatal to the cause of the Coalition. Thugut was very anxious to get Suvorov out of Italy, lest the Russian general should interfere with his schemes for the disposal of the territory reconquered from the French. While Russia looked upon the restoration to Charles Emmanuel of the mainland possessions of the House of Savoy as one of the principal objects of the Coalition, Thugut had other designs for Piedmont, alleging that only if it were in Austria's hands could it be made a satisfactory bulwark against French aggression, and assuming that Charles Emmanuel had forfeited all claims upon the Allies by deserting them in 1796. Accordingly he readily agreed to a scheme which the English ministry put forward with the Czar's consent, by which Suvorov was to come up from Italy with his Russian corps, unite with the Archduke and with a Russian corps under Korsakov, now on its way to Switzerland, and advance into France. Suvorov was not ill-disposed to this scheme. Considerable as were the successes he had gained in Italy, he found himself continually thwarted by the interference of the Austrian War Council; the Emperor insisted on treating him as though completely at his disposal, and his plans were constantly upset and altered by Thugut. The refusal of the Austrians to co-operate in an invasion of Provence, since they wished to complete the conquest of Italy, increased Suvorov's desire to turn North and join Korsakov in Switzerland.

During the five months which had elapsed since he had taken over the command of the Allied forces in Italy, Suvorov had achieved much. He had begun by capturing Brescia (April 21st) and Cremona, and forcing the passage of the Adda behind which the French, encouraged by the substitution of Moreau for the discredited Schérer, had attempted a stand. But not even Moreau could stem Suvorov's advance. The Austrians of Ott's division forced their way across the river by Cassano (April 27th), and the advantage was pressed home. Moreau, his centre thus pierced, was thrust back Southward, and completely severed from his left under Sérurier higher up the river. The confused retreat of the French resulted in the capture of Sérurier and the bulk of his division, and on April 29th the Russian general entered Milan. Luckily for Moreau, however, Suvorov abandoned his first intention of following hard after the French and cutting them off from Genoa, to turn aside into Piedmont where the population welcomed him as a deliverer. On May 25th he was before Turin, which opened its gates to him two days later. Meanwhile Moreau fell back across the Apennines towards Genoa, not a little fortunate in that he escaped the pursuit which must have ruined the remnants of his army. Arrived at Genoa (June 6th), he covered his communications with France and held out a hand to Macdonald, who after collecting from Tuscany, Rome and Naples the various divisions of the French army in those quarters, some 36,000 in all, had abandoned Southern Italy to its fate and was coming up the Via Æmiliana towards Piacenza, a march which seemed to threaten an attack on the left flank and communications of the Allies.

The situation of the Allies was one of no small peril. They were so much scattered that the main body was little over 20,000 strong; but Suvorov rose to the occasion. Concentrating some 36,000 troops at Alessandria (June 12th), he set off Eastward on the 15th; and so rapid were his movements, that as Macdonald was forcing back Ott's Austrians from the Trebbia to the Tidone (June 17th), Suvorov's vanguard suddenly planted itself across his path and checked the French advance. A fierce struggle was ended about 3 p.m. by the arrival of the Allied main body, headed by the Russian veteran in person. Two more days of desperate and strenuous fighting on the banks of the Trebbia followed. In vain Macdonald sought to cut his way through to Tortona, the place appointed for his junction with Moreau. So stubborn was the resistance of Russians and Austrians alike, that at the end of the third day (June 21st) the French army, broken and demoralised, began a disorderly but unmolested retreat across the Apennines into Tuscany. But that Suvorov had to dash back to Tortona to succour Bellegarde, the lieutenant he had left behind to keep Moreau in check, and was therefore unable to pursue, things might have gone very ill with Macdonald. As it was, he managed to extricate himself from a perilous position by making his way over indifferent roads to the Riviera, thus regaining touch with Moreau, who had fallen back from Tortona (June 25th) the moment Suvorov drew near.

But though the Allies had an excellent chance of expelling the French from Italy, they failed to improve the occasion. As in 1793, the victorious field army was dispersed to besiege Mantua and other fortresses, the direct interference of the Austrian War Council thus wrecking Suvorov's plans when they seemed on the point of success. Clearly as Suvorov realised that if Moreau were once beaten out of Italy the fate of the garrisons he had left behind would be sealed, he could not collect his forces for the pitched battle which alone could give decisive victory till July had been frittered away in sieges of minor importance, and the Directory had been able to send Joubert with large reinforcements to take command of the Army of Italy. Not till August 5th, however, was the new commander free to start to the relief of the beleaguered fortresses, and by that time both Alessandria (July 21st) and Mantua (July 29th) had fallen, and the besieging forces were on their way to rejoin Suvorov. Thus Joubert's advance ended in disaster. Near Novi he found his way barred by Suvorov with superior forces (Aug. 14th), and only after some hesitation did he decide to stand and fight. Next day the battle was begun by an advance of Kray's Austrians on the Allied right, and Joubert hurrying to the spot was hit and killed. Moreau succeeded to the command, and by supreme exertions held his ground against the repeated attacks of Kray of the Russians in the centre. But with the afternoon there arrived on the scene a fresh division of Austrians under Melas, and their intervention—a direct attack on the French right at Novi combined with an outflanking movement more to the Southward—decided the sixteen hours' struggle in favour of the Allies. In complete disorder the French fell back on Genoa. Want of transport prevented an immediate pursuit by the Allies. Tortona was still untaken, and the Austrian corps of Klenau was detached into Tuscany by the War Council instead of supporting Suvorov. Accordingly the Russian general determined to transfer himself to Switzerland, and about the middle of September his columns began to make their way past Bellinzona up the Leventina valley towards the St. Gotthard.

The diversion of Suvorov's corps from Italy to Switzerland was not in itself a mistaken move. Had Archduke Charles remained on the Limmat holding Masséna in check, the appearance of the Russian veteran on the St. Gotthard in the French general's right rear would have seriously endangered his position. But the Archduke with 36,000 of his 60,000 men had moved away down the Rhine long before Suvorov arrived. He was well aware of the danger of leaving Hotze and Korsakov with little over 50,000 men to face the 80,000 men now under Masséna, but he had not the moral courage or the resolution to defy Thugut and refuse to carry out the task allotted to him. There was some idea that by attacking Alsace he would materially assist the efforts of the Anglo-Russian expedition to North Holland, which had just (Aug. 27th) effected a successful landing at the Helder : possibly Thugut was anxious to have Austrian troops in close proximity to the Netherlands in case the efforts of England and Russia should induce Prussia to throw in her lot with the Allies ; always jealous of Prussia, he may have desired to be able to prevent her making acquisitions on the Lower Rhine. Be that as it may, the Archduke's operations had no influence whatever over the fighting along the Zuyder Zee ; and though he managed to relieve Philipsburg, on which the French were pressing closely (Sept. 12th), and stormed their position at Mannheim with complete success, the operations of his 36,000 men had practically no effective influence over the results of the campaign. Though there was a good deal of spasmodic fighting going on along the Rhine, the French making raids, the peasantry supported by small parties of regulars resisting with fair success, it was of quite minor importance. Albini, the chief minister of the Elector of Mayence, had taken advantage of these efforts of the peasantry to organise their resistance, his example had been imitated elsewhere, and fair success had been achieved, so that the Archduke was not wanted on the Neckar and his presence was badly needed on the Limmat.[1]

Masséna was not the man to neglect such a chance as the Archduke's departure gave him. Already, during the middle of August, Lecourbe had resumed the offensive against the Austrian left in the valleys of the Upper Reuss and Upper Rhone. He had managed to regain possession of the Simplon and St. Gotthard passes, and thus, when Suvorov came up from Bellinzona he found the pass in possession of the enemy. Between the 19th and the 26th of September the fate of the campaign was decided. After a series of desperate struggles in which every step of the way was fiercely contested, Suvorov forced his way over the St. Gotthard to the Devil's Bridge and over the Devil's Bridge (Sept. 24th) to Altdorf at the head of the Lake of Lucerne (26th). Thence he turned East, pushed through the Schachenthal (Sept. 27th) and over the Kinzig Kulm into the valley of the Muotta (29th), to find in his front at Schwytz, not Korsakov, whom he hoped to meet, but Masséna. For while Suvorov was struggling over the St. Gotthard, Masséna had concentrated 40,000 men round Zürich, had crossed the Limmat, and hurled Mortier's corps on Korsakov's front while Oudinot outflanked him and threatened his retreat. Two days' hard fighting ended in the complete defeat of the Russian army (Sept. 25th to 26th), the relics

---

[1] The Archduke wanted to use Albini's organisation to found a permanent *Landsturm* in South Germany. The chance was fair ; for, if one may judge its quality by the verbal expressions it found, there was a very violent anti-French feeling in South Germany, and the Franconian and Swabian Circles, Bavaria, Würtemberg and other Powers were raising contingents. However, such a step was entirely opposed to Thugut's policy, and nothing came of the idea.

of which only escaped having to surrender by a prodigious effort which carried them through the encircling French. Simultaneously Soult had forced the passage of the Linth, defeated and killed Hotze, and driven the left wing of the Austro-Russian army back into the Vorarlberg by St. Gall.

Thus Suvorov found that all his efforts had been in vain. His feat in extricating his 16,000 exhausted men from their perilous position and bringing them in safety to the right bank of the Upper Rhine was the supreme achievement of his career; but Switzerland was none the less lost, for the relics of Korsakov's forces had put the Rhine and the Lake of Constance between them and the victorious Masséna.

Thus the campaign of 1799 had ended in defeat and disappointment for the Coalition. In Italy, Liguria alone was left to the French, for Championnet's attempt to profit by Suvorov's departure to recover possession of Piedmont had resulted in the defeat of the Army of Italy by Melas near Genoa (Nov. 4th). Similarly the right bank of the Rhine was clear of all but raiding parties of French; but Switzerland was again in their possession, and the next campaign was to show how great was the strategic advantage they were to derive from this. Moreover, failure had attended the Anglo-Russian campaign in Holland. Not really beaten in the field, the Duke of York had found it impossible to advance in a country so much cut up by canals and marshes with an army largely composed of raw recruits from the Militia, and with Allies as unsatisfactory and untrustworthy as Hermann and his Russians. Moreover, the expedition had been misdirected from the first. When it was first proposed, it had been expected that Prussia would join the Coalition, in which case the true policy would have been to land the troops on the East of the Zuyder Zee, in Gröningen and Friesland, the strongholds of the Orange party, not in North Holland, the most Republican part of the whole country. In Gröningen the Allies would have been in a friendly country and in easy communication with Hanover; and if at the same time a Prussian army had crossed the Rhine to recover Cleves and Guelders, the chances of the Coalition would have been enormously improved. At the root, then, of the failure in North Holland was Prussia's selfish, shortsighted and most reprehensible neutrality. Her refusal to join caused the expedition to be hurried to sea without any definite aim in order to do something, and to this want of definite purpose may be attributed the failure.[1]

With Austria and Russia on decidedly strained terms, and the relations between Russia and England not much better, the fortunes of the Coalition were already on the wane, even before the return of Bonaparte to France (Oct.) and the improvement in her military effectiveness involved in the establishment of the firm and centralised government of the Consulate on the ruins of the Directory (Nov. 1799). Indeed, the Coalition was on the point of dissolving. The exchange of projects for the next campaign only brought Austria and Russia into more violent conflict. On October 22nd, Paul announced his secession from the Coalition; in December the Russian troops started homeward. This destroyed the last chance of inducing Prussia to join the Allies. Earlier in the year, Russia had put strong pressure on her to join. There were not wanting men who proclaimed the unwisdom of the policy of neutrality. Brunswick was among them; and Haugwitz, now realising the dangers of French predominance in Europe, went so far as to explain to Otto, the French Minister at Berlin, that it had not been Prussia's idea, when agreeing to the Peace of Basel, that Holland should remain permanently in the occupation of France. But Frederick William was not to be persuaded to change his policy, and France procrastinated and put off answering until the critical moment was past. Nor did the rest of Germany show much more forwardness in the common cause. When the Diet met, Sweden urged that the Empire should take part in the war; but though the breaking off of the Congress at Rastatt had left the Empire at war with France, there were the usual unending delays about the voting of supplies or contingents, the usual forms and ceremonies, and the vote of 100 Roman months, which the Diet finally passed, was not ratified till October 31st when the campaign was over. Indeed, it is not a little remarkable to find that, despite all Austria's efforts to rouse the German Princes to take part in the struggle against the aggressions of the intrusive foreigner, Bavaria was the only one of the minor states to display any keenness.

[1] Cf. Dunfermline's *Life of Sir Ralph Abercromby*, especially pp. 141–159; Bunbury's *Narrative of the Campaign in North Holland*; and *W. O. Original Correspondence* (Public Record Office), vols. 62–65.

Maximilian Joseph's zeal can hardly have been to the liking of Thugut. The Austrian minister would have rather seen the Elector adopt a line which would have borne out the charges of Francophil tendencies which had been brought against him. He had hoped to be able to denounce Maximilian to the Czar as a traitor to the Empire, and with the Czar's consent to have deposed him and carried out that annexation of the Wittelsbach lands to the Hapsburg dominions after which he so hankered. But this was impossible when Maximilian's ardour disarmed all hostility, and when he concluded a treaty in October 1799 by which he promised in return for a British subsidy to put 20,000 men into the field.

CHAPTER XXII

MARENGO, HOHENLINDEN AND LUNÉVILLE

AFTER the failures in Holland and Switzerland, and the consequent estrangement between Russia and her allies, the prospects of the Coalition for the year 1800 were not of the brightest. Nevertheless, when Bonaparte, with a great parade of his desire for peace, offered Austria the same terms which she had obtained at Campo Formio, she rejected them without much hesitation. When there was hardly a Frenchman on the right of the Rhine, and when the forces of the Republic seemed on the point of being expelled from Italy, it was the height of presumption and arrogance to offer terms Austria had reluctantly accepted when Bonaparte was at Leoben and Hoche at Wetzlar. Her achievements in 1799 might not unreasonably have increased her confidence in her own military prowess, and, moreover, Great Britain had not only arranged subsidy-treaties with Bavaria, Mayence and Würtemberg for 12,000, 3200 and 3200 men respectively, but was proposing to take an active part in the continental war. The expedition to North Holland had at least shown that she was at last coming into possession of a respectable military force, the want of which had hampered her so fatally at the beginning of the war, and the scheme of Sir Charles Stuart for a descent on the Riviera by 15,000 British was one which offered great possibilities.[1] The troops existed, and had the British administration been equal to despatching to the Mediterranean in February 1800 the force which it collected off Cadiz in October, the fall of Genoa might have been hastened by some weeks, and Masséna's gallant resistance might not have given Napoleon the chance he used so well. As it was, the government accepted the plan, but failed to act with the required promptitude: long before the expedition could arrive, the fate of the campaign had been decided.

The Austrian plan comprised a vigorous offensive in Italy as

[1] Cf. Bunbury, *Some Passages in the War with France*, pp. 57–78.

the prelude to an invasion of the South of France, while on
the Rhine Kray was to maintain a defensive attitude. The
fatal defect in this scheme, however, was that the possession of
Switzerland enabled the French to attack either portion of the
Austrian forces in flank, and the concentration of the Army of
Reserve at Dijon put into Bonaparte's hands a formidable weapon,
equally available for employment in Germany or in Italy. His
original idea was to unite with Moreau and strike from Schaffhausen at Kray's left flank and rear, and by placing the French
army on his line of communications, to cut him off from Vienna
and leave him "in the air." But seeing that Moreau was unlikely
to prove a satisfactory colleague, Bonaparte changed his plan ;
he resolved to transfer the Army of Reserve[1] to Italy, where, at
the beginning of April, Masséna (40,000 men) was standing on
the defensive along the Riviera, covering Genoa against Melas.
With his usual keen appreciation of the strategical situation,
Bonaparte saw that a descent from Switzerland upon Turin or
Milan would place him in a commanding position on the
Austrian line of communications with Tyrol, if only Masséna
could hold out long enough and keep Melas occupied while
the Army of Reserve crossed the Alps. Melas meanwhile
had put his 60,000 available men in motion early in April.
By the 19th, Masséna's line had been pierced, his left under
Suchet, 10,000 strong, had been driven back across the Var by
Melas with 28,000 ; he himself with 28,000 men, over half of
them sick and wounded, had been cooped up in Genoa, to
which Ott (24,000) laid siege (April 21st). Early in May the
Army of Reserve started on its way to the Great St. Bernhard.
On May 15th the passage began ; on the 20th Ivrea in the
valley of the Dora Baltea was occupied by the advance-guard
under Lannes. A week later, Bonaparte, while feinting with his
right at Turin, was pushing Eastward over the Sesia, the
Agogna and the Ticino on Milan. This daring stroke had
completely changed the situation. But, while it is unfair to
represent Melas as having been surprised by Bonaparte's
irruption into the valley of the Po,[2] for it is clear that as far
back as May 1st he was expecting such a move, he cannot
escape the responsibility for the negligence which left scattered
and unconcentrated the 30,000 Austrians in Piedmont.[3] Had

[1] Cf. Hermann, *Marengo*, pp. 83 ff. [2] Cf. *ibid.* p. 106.
[3] *Ibid.* p. 110.

they been collected in good time, they might have prevented the French from debouching from the passes; as it was, they were swept away before Bonaparte's advance. On the 1st of June, the French forced the passage of the Ticino at Turbigo and occupied Milan. The next week saw them secure the passages of the Po from Pavia to Piacenza, while 15,000 men under Moncey, detached from the Army of Germany by Bonaparte's orders, came down over the Simplon and the St. Gotthard (May 26th to 27th) to Milan. This reinforcement had been set free by Moreau's successes against Kray in the Danube valley, which had driven the Austrian Army of Germany in behind the Iller.

Meanwhile Melas was at last concentrating his forces at Alessandria. It would have been wiser to have raised the siege of Genoa and hurried North with every available man directly he heard the first news of Bonaparte's movement. But he was expecting to be attacked from the Var, and his forces were so much scattered, and moved so slowly, that he could not even attempt to defend the passage of the Po. His position was perilous, but by no means hopeless; for Bonaparte, departing from the sound strategy of concentration of which he was as a rule the truest prophet, had thrust out divisions far to the East to chase the Austrian garrison of Milan behind the Oglio, and had barely 30,000 men at hand. By this time Melas could dispose of the besiegers of Genoa, for on June 4th Masséna's heroic defence had come to an end, not before it had enabled Bonaparte to carry out his brilliant plan and to place himself in a situation of overwhelming strategic advantage. Ott moved up from Genoa by Novi and Voghera, intending to seize Piacenza and so recover a line of communication with Tyrol; but on June 9th he encountered Lannes and the French advanced guard near Montebello, and was driven back on Alessandria with the loss of 4000 men. Bonaparte, anxious to put the finishing touch to his strategic success by victory in a pitched battle, had crossed the Po on the 8th, intending to bring Melas to action, and now pushed on from Stradella towards Alessandria. On the 13th he drove the Austrian outposts in from Marengo behind the Bormida, and posted Victor with two divisions at Marengo to bar Melas's route to Pavia. At the same time, fearing that the Austrian general might attempt to escape by the Riviera round the French left, he sent off Desaix with a division to Novi to block that route. On the Northern bank of the Po there were two detached divisions on which Bonaparte relied to prevent Melas breaking through the net in which he found himself.

This dispersion of his forces was nearly fatal to Bonaparte. It left him much weaker than Melas; and when on the morning of June 14th the Austrians sallied out across the Bormida and opened the battle by falling on Victor, numbers eventually told. Lannes hurried up to Victor's aid, and prolonged the line on his right in the direction of Castel Ceriolo. The Austrians were checked, but soon came on again. The fight was stubbornly contested, the strength of the French position making up for the Austrian superiority in numbers. The action had already been in progress nearly three hours, when Ott and the left column of the Austrians wheeled to the right after carrying Castel Ceriolo, thereby outflanking Lannes. Almost at the same moment (1.30 p.m.) a renewed attack by the Austrian grenadiers carried Marengo. The French fell back in some confusion. Bonaparte brought up fresh troops under Monnier and St. Cyr, and restored the position for a time. However, Ott drove Monnier back; and as the Austrian main column pressed forward, Victor's two divisions, which had been fighting hard since 9 a.m., fell into disorder. It was in vain that the Consular Guard planted itself in Ott's path; it also was overwhelmed and forced to retreat (3.30 p.m.). The fortunes of the day seemed to have definitely gone in favour of the Austrians, and the French retreat was rapidly degenerating into a rout. Melas, worn out by fatigue, for he was over seventy, and by a slight wound, returned to Alessandria in the full belief that the victory was won. It was an unfortunate step, for if the victory had been won, the situation called imperatively for an energetic and close pursuit. But the failure to follow hard on the heels of the retreating French was typical of the worst vices of the Austrian military system, their slowness, formalism and pedantry.[1] Moreover, the greater part of the cavalry had been wasted during the action, and barely 2000 horse were available. Even so, it was inexcusable that the pursuit should have been so leisurely that touch had been quite lost with the French, when, between 5 and 6 p.m., Desaix suddenly appeared in their front near San Guiliano. He

---

[1] Cf. Hermann, p. 168,

had been delayed in his march on Novi by the flooding of the Scrivia, and so received Bonaparte's orders recalling him before he had gone too far to be able to reach the battlefield in time.[1] He flung his division across the path of the Austrians, advancing somewhat carelessly in the confidence of victory along the high road. Marmont, by a great effort, collected eighteen guns, and his salvoes of case shot and the musketry of Desaix's division checked and staggered the Austrian grenadiers. But it would seem[2] that not even this would have proved decisive by itself. The Austrians rallied, and were coming on again[3] when Kellermann, acting entirely on his own responsibility, delivered the decisive stroke. He hurled his rallied cavalry on the flank of their infantry, unprotected for the dragoons, who should have covered it, had fallen behind. The change of fortune was complete. Surprised by this unexpected resistance, the Austrians fell into disorder. A panic set in, their cavalry disgraced themselves by taking to flight, and in a short time the all but victorious column was being swept back to Marengo in total rout, while Ott and the other flank detachments had some difficulty in recrossing the Bormida in safety. The defeat was too much for Melas. Had he held out in Alessandria, he might have played the part of Masséna in Genoa; for if he had lost 10,000 men, at least 8000 French had fallen.[4] But his nerve was gone, his men were demoralised, and the state of the fortresses was such as to make the success of resistance very doubtful.[5] On June 15th he signed the Convention of Alessandria, by which he undertook to evacuate all Italy West of the Adige and South of the Po, with the exception of Ancona, Borgoforte and Tuscany. Thus at one blow all the conquests of 1799 were lost; Italy passed from Hapsburg under French domination, and Bonaparte, mainly through the lucky accident of Desaix's timely return, obtained as the prize of his Pyrrhic victory results quite out of keeping with the evenly-balanced fighting. That other alternatives were open to Melas seems certain. If he did not fancy the prospects of a move to Genoa, whence by the aid of the English fleet he

[1] Cf. Hermann, p. 136. [2] Cf. *ibid.* ch. vii.
[3] *Ibid.* p. 183. [4] Cf. *ibid.* ch. viii.
[5] For this the blame must be divided between the Austrian War Council and Thugut and his protégé, Zach, the Austrian Chief of the Staff: cf. a narrative of the action (probably written by Radetzky) in Hüffer, pp. 352–367.

might have made his way to Tuscany, there seems good reason to suppose that Bonaparte could not have checked him had he attempted to force his way through the weak and scattered French divisions on the Northern bank of the Po.[1] So tame a surrender was certainly uncalled for, and indicates how unfit Melas was for his command, and how unsound the Austrian military system which could allot such a task to one so unsuited for it, and who, to do him justice, was himself well aware of his incapacity.[2]

Nor had the campaign in Germany redressed the balance in favour of Austria. Whereas in previous years the contending forces of France and Austria had faced each other on either side of the straight course of the Rhine below Basel with the neutral territory of Switzerland covering their Southern flanks, the French occupation of Switzerland and their success in maintaining their grip on it in 1799 had quite altered the situation. Their right wing could be extended from Basel to Schaffhausen so that it outflanked the Austrians along the Black Forest, and could take that defensive position in rear by a descent into the Danube valley by Stockach and Moeskirch. The Austrians had either to expose themselves to an attack on their communications by this route, or if they fell back to the more defensible line of the Iller, to abandon to the enemy Baden, Würtemberg and a large part of the Swabian Circle. Of these alternatives Kray had chosen the former, hoping to cover the large magazines which had been collected at Engen, Stockach and other places, but his 100,000 men were over much extended. His right stretched from the Main to the Rench, and on his left the corps in the Vorarlberg under the Prince of Reuss was dangerously far from the main body at Villingen and Donaueschingen. Moreau, on the other hand, had the 100,000 men of whom he could dispose concentrated in four corps at Strassburg, Breisach, Basel and Schaffhausen. Bonaparte had urged him to concentrate the whole force between Schaffhausen and Lake Constance for a direct blow at Ulm, but Moreau had a plan of his own on which he was so much set that Bonaparte gave way. This was to feint with his left (Ste. Suzanne) and left centre (Gouvion St. Cyr) against the passages over the Black Forest by the valley of the Kinzig and the Hollenthal, while his right centre (his own corps),

---

[1] Cf. Hermann, ch. ix.   [2] Cf. Hüffer, p. 261.

profiting by this diversion, crossed at Basel and united with the right (Lecourbe), which was to cross at Schaffhausen. Ste. Suzanne was to recross the river as soon as he had drawn Kray's attention, to ascend the left bank to Breisach, cross again there and come up by Freibourg on the left of St. Cyr, who was to push forward by St. Blazien to the Wutach, where he would regain touch with the Reserve and Lecourbe. This plan was perhaps better under the circumstances than Bonaparte's more brilliant design, especially as it was to be executed by Moreau and not by Bonaparte. It profited more by the dispersion of the Austrians, since the feint against their right confirmed them in their fears for that wing, and so delayed their concentration ; also it utilised more points of passage over the Rhine. To throw the whole force across between Schaffhausen and the lake would have taken time, possibly so much that Kray would have discovered his danger and concentrated in time. It is true that Moreau risked defeat in detail in case Kray concentrated his forces to fall on St. Cyr or Lecourbe before they had got into touch with the Reserve and with each other ; but this was not likely with so dispersed and slow-moving a force as the Austrians.

In the main the scheme, which was well executed by Moreau and his subordinates, proved successful. On April 25th Ste. Suzanne opened the move; by May 2nd, after much marching and manœuvring and some fighting, Moreau had concentrated three of his corps between the Aach and the Wutach, and Ste. Suzanne had come through the Höllenthal and was at Neustadt on the flank of the Austrians, who were endeavouring to concentrate between Stockach and Geisingen. In this, however, they were unsucessful, for Lecourbe pushing up the Aach fell on their left at Stockach (May 3rd), routed it, and captured the vast magazines there. Meanwhile Kray bringing up his main body from Geisingen came into conflict with St. Cyr at Zollhaus and with Moreau's Reserve at Engen. The battle was stubbornly contested ; Kray on the whole held his own, and only the bad news from Stockach caused him to fall back to Tuttlingen lest Lecourbe's advance on Moeskirch should cut him off from Ulm. Moreau, having let St. Cyr and the Reserve be drawn into battle to his left, could not reinforce Lecourbe and so secure a decisive success, and thus Kray was able to reach

Moeskirch in safety (May 4th). Driven from Moeskirch by the French attack next day, he rallied his men and thrust his right forward to cover the retreat of an isolated division from Tuttlingen; but though successful in this and in checking Lecourbe's advance, he had to fall back to the North of the Danube to avoid being cut off by Ste. Suzanne, who was coming down the Danube from Donaueschingen. By May 12th Kray was back at Ulm, where he rallied some 60,000 men. He had lost nearly 30,000 as well as the magazines for which he had risked so much; but Moreau, having had to detach Moncey's corps to Italy, was in no position to press home his success at once, and was for some time detained by Kray's stand at Ulm. Once he tried to turn the position by thrusting his right across the Iller higher up; but Kray fell on the detached corps left in front of Ulm to cover the French communications with Schaffhausen and brought Moreau back to its succour (May 16th). Undeterred, the French commander renewed the attempt a fortnight later. This time the "containing" corps, left between the Danube and Iller to protect the French communications with the Rhine, held its own against all Kray's attacks, and Moreau's right pushed out to Augsburg. Thence it pressed on to the Danube at Lavingen and Blenheim, the centre preparing to cross at Gunzburg. The French success in securing a passage at Blenheim (June 19th) made Ulm untenable. With his communications imperilled and his retreat along the left bank alone open to him, Kray fell back by Heidenheim to Nördlingen (June 23rd), and passing across the front of the French regained the Danube below them (June 26th), thus placing himself between them and Vienna. Moreau, however, returning South of the Danube overran Bavaria up to the Isar, profiting greatly by the comparatively unexhausted state of the country. On July 15th an armistice put a temporary stop to hostilities, Kray in accordance with its terms retiring behind the Inn.

This want of success in both theatres of war was a powerful argument for those persons at Vienna who desired to accept Bonaparte's renewed proposals for peace. The only real obstacle was that a new subsidy-treaty had just been concluded with England by which Austria received £2,000,000, promising in return not to conclude a separate peace before February 28th, 1801. Thus as Bonaparte declined to admit

England to a peace conference, except on terms England would not contemplate, namely, that he might relieve Malta and Egypt, Austria could only obtain peace by abandoning her obligations to England. The armistice should have expired on September 20th, but it was renewed for another six weeks from that date, a concession which Austria purchased by surrendering Ulm, Ingolstadt and Philipsburg. This had a rather disastrous influence over some of Austria's German allies, who believed that the Emperor was sacrificing the interests of the Empire to the security of his hereditary dominions. The Elector of Cologne, for example, went so far as to obtain passports from the French for the withdrawal of his troops from Ulm to Münster, where they sheltered behind the neutrality of the line of demarcation.[1] Still Austria needed the respite badly. She was making great efforts to resume hostilities if necessary, reinforcing and re-equipping the army, but her preparations were still incomplete. The peace party was, moreover, steadily gaining ground, which was in itself no indistinct indication that Thugut's unpopularity was increasing. He was held responsible for the disasters of the war; and though, indeed, his inefficiency as an administrator was in large measure to blame, it was not on this that public resentment fixed, but on his policy of resistance to France. He was accused, with little reason, of making the interests of Austria subservient to those of England. He was not accused, as he might well have been, of wrecking the campaign of 1799 by his undue haste to reap the fruits of victory without troubling to make success certain by vigorous and whole-hearted co-operation with his allies. It was obvious that his fall was imminent. On October 8th his resignation of the Ministry of Foreign Affairs was announced, and Louis Cobenzl was appointed a member of the Conference and Vice State Chancellor to direct the Court, State and Cabinet Chanceries, Lehrbach taking the Home Office.

Cobenzl's first act was to go in person to Lunéville in Alsace to discuss terms with Joseph Bonaparte. The sole obstacle to peace was Austria's refusal to agree to England's exclusion from the peace congress. Cobenzl would have even been prepared [2] to make a secret treaty with France not

[1] Cf. Hüffer, *Quellen zur Geschichte des Krieges, 1799–1800*, ii. 414.
[2] Cf. Haüsser, ii. 308.

to be divulged until Austria's obligation to England was at an end, but nothing had been settled when on November 26th the armistice came to an end and hostilities were resumed.

Austria had made good use of the armistice. She had brought up her army on the Danube to 130,000, including 12,000 Bavarians in British pay. Of this force 30,000 under Klenau were on the left bank, 20,000 under Hiller in Tyrol, the rest, now under the command of the Emperor's fifth brother, the eighteen year old Archduke John, held the line of the Inn. Similarly in Italy, Bellegarde had replaced Melas and was strongly posted between the Mincio and the Adige, relying on the fortresses of the "Quadrilateral." Opposite them stood Moreau in Bavaria with 100,000 men flanked by 12,000 under Lecourbe in Western Tyrol and 20,000 more under Augereau North of the Danube. In Italy, Brune threatened Bellegarde's front, while a column under Macdonald, crossing the Splügen Pass in the depth of winter, forced its way by the Valtelline into the upper valley of the Adige, and after tremendous perils and sufferings captured Trent (end of December), thus interposing between Hiller and Bellegarde's connecting link, his extreme right under Loudon.

Meanwhile the Austrians in Germany had taken the offensive, had crossed the Inn the day the armistice expired (Nov. 26th), and were moving against Moreau. This action, somewhat rash, since the Austrian troops were not only inferior in numbers to the French veterans, but were mainly composed of raw recruits and were but ill-equipped, is to be explained by the young Archduke's belief that the previous defeats of the Austrians had been due to their excessive caution. This may have been true, but undue temerity was no improvement on undue caution, especially as rain and the bad state of the roads combined with the inefficiency of the Archduke's Staff to so delay the Austrian movements that the original plan of an advance past Moreau's left by Braunau and Landshut on Münich had to be abandoned for a direct blow at the French left.[1] Near Ampfing on December 1st the Archduke fell on Grenier

[1] Nothing stands out more clearly from a study of the documents dealing with the campaign from the Austrian side than the imprudence of the Archduke and his chief advisers, Weyrother and Lauer. The original plan of outflanking the French left might have worked well if executed in good weather and by a well-organised army with an efficient Staff. Under existing circumstances the advance was a piece of almost criminal folly. Cf. Hüffer, *op. cit.* pp. 415-426.

and the three divisions (33,000 men) who formed his corps. Taken by surprise and outnumbered, the French fell back fighting stubbornly on Hohenlinden, being succoured in their retreat by Grouchy's division of the centre; but they left 6 guns and nearly 1000 prisoners behind, and the Austrians were much elated by their success.[1] Hohenlinden lies in a clearing of the Forest of Ebersberg, and though the excellent high-road from Muhldorf to München leads through it, the woods are so close to the road as to convert it into a regular defile, while the side-roads and forest paths on either flank are but ill-fitted for military manœuvres. Yet on December 3rd the Archduke plunged gaily into the defile with 16,000 men, two columns under Latour (11,000) and Keinmayer (16,000) moving parallel with him on his right; while to the Southward Riesch with 13,000 pushed forward on Albaching, intending to outflank the right of Grenier's position at Hohenlinden. The despatch in which Zweibrücken, the commander of the Bavarian contingent,[2] announced to his Electoral master[3] that "your Highness' troops have been sacrificed by ignorance and ineptitude," is a scathing commentary on the Austrian Staff. No proper precautions were taken to secure the simultaneous co-operation of the different columns, the flanks were not protected by patrols, no reserve was told off, and the artillery and baggage were allowed to take the road before it had been properly secured by the capture of Hohenlinden. The culminating complaint was that at the moment the movement began the Archduke and the whole Headquarter Staff were comfortably asleep. Therefore it is hardly surprising that disaster followed.

Utterly uncombined and ill-timed, the Austrian columns came into action one by one. The Archduke, moving faster than his supporters, since his road was the best, engaged Ney and Grouchy around Hohenlinden about 8 a.m. Gradually Latour and Keinmayer came up, but neither could make much impression on Bastoul and Legrand. But it was on the left that matters went most amiss. Riesch, delayed by the bad road and the falling snow, went astray in the woods, and never reached his appointed place. This exposed the left flank of the main column to an attack from the French right at Ebersberg, and Moreau pushed Durutte and Decaen up to

---

[1] Cf. Hüffer, p. 428.
[2] William of Zweibrücken-Birkenfeld, brother-in-law of the Elector.
[3] Cf. Hüffer, p. 452.

St. Christopher to hold Riesch at bay, while under cover of this he hurled Richepanse against the Bavarian division which formed the rear of the Archduke's long column on the high-road. Hampered by the guns and waggons which cumbered the road, the Bavarians could not deploy properly, and simultaneously with Richepanse's onslaught Ney made a counter-attack on the head of the column, outflanking it on both wings. Before this double assult the Archduke's men gave way in disorder. Only the intervention of Lichtenstein's cavalry saved the column from complete destruction. Their defeat was decisive; Riesch had to fall back, and the Austrian right had the mortification of having to do the same just as they were beginning to gain ground.[1]

Leaving 17,000 killed and prisoners behind them, the Austrians recrossed the Inn (Dec. 5th) in a state of demoralisation and exhaustion. Energetically pursued by Moreau, they failed to stand behind either the Salza, the Traun or the Enns, although Archduke Charles, to whom the War Council had turned in its alarm, took over the command and made every effort to rally them. Only when he had outmarched the forces on his flanks did Moreau check his pursuit. North of the Danube, Augereau was pressing Klenau back from Aschaffenburg to Ingolstadt. In Italy, Macdonald's adventurous march had outflanked Bellegarde and enabled Brune to cross the Mincio at Pozzolo and the Adige at Bussolengo, and to take Verona. On neither quarter was there any hope for Austria. Hohenlinden had finally damped the bellicose ardour of the Elector of Bavaria. Defeat had revived his distrust of the Hapsburgs, and had thrown him under the influence of Prussia. So anxious was he for peace that he was prepared to forego the payments due from England, and on December 8th he wrote to recall the relics of the subsidiary corps.[2] So hopeless was the military situation,[3] so broken and dejected the Austrian troops, who had ceased to bear any resemblance to an army and had become a mass of fugitives,[4] that Archduke Charles could only counsel surrender, and on December 25th he had to agree to the Armistice of Speyer, which handed Würzburg and the fortresses of Bavaria over to the French, provided for the evacuation of Tyrol, Carinthia and the Grisons, dismissed the Tyrolese "insurrection" to their homes, and pledged Austria to make peace apart from England.[5] Harsh and exceedingly disgraceful as the terms

[1] Cf. Hüffer, pp. 437–480.   [2] *Ibid.* p. 481.
[3] *Ibid.* pp. 490–492.   [4] *Ibid.* p. 495.   [5] *Ibid.* pp. 508–511.

were, there was no alternative but a defeat which would have left Austria absolutely at the mercy of the enemy.[1] In January an armistice was signed at Treviso for the Italian armies.

Little time was lost in converting these armistices into a definite peace. Bonaparte could name his conditions, and on those conditions he insisted inexorably. Cobenzl made no attempt to obtain the admission of England to the negotiations : his efforts were directed to trying to get Modena and Tuscany restored to their rulers, and to save part of Lombardy for Austria. But the Adige frontier was all that the First Consul would grant; he was prepared to compensate Tuscany with the Legations, but Modena's compensation must be in Germany, and it was imperatively demanded that the Emperor should cede the Left Bank at once in his capacity as head of the Empire. Unpalatable as these demands were, and strenuously as Cobenzl fought point after point, it was not of much use resisting Bonaparte, especially as he had by this time bound the Baltic Powers, including Prussia, to him in the shape of the " Armed Neutrality." Moreover, the spectacle of South Germany, helpless and at the mercy of the French armies, increased the Emperor's readiness for peace. If the discipline and behaviour of the armies of the Consulate was an improvement on that of the troops of the Directory, their presence was sufficiently burdensome and oppressive. There was no appeal against the plunderings of the rank and file when all they did was to follow the example of their generals. With no small part of his own hereditary dominions in French hands, Francis II was most anxious to come to terms. Fear of a Franco-Russian coalition, for Paul was by now as keen an admirer of Napoleon as he had been a bitter opponent of the Republic three years before, made him abandon hope of saving even the ecclesiastical Electorates from being secularised, and on February 9th, 1801, the Peace of Lunéville was signed.

The Peace of Campo Formio was accepted as the basis of the territorial rearrangements, but subject to certain not unimportant modifications. The Emperor signed the peace on behalf of the Empire, openly ceding the Left Bank to France, and no longer attempting to hide this surrender in a secret article.

It was agreed that the rulers thus dispossessed should be "compensated" for their losses by means of secularisation, a provision which practically amounted to the destruction of the existing constitution of the Empire. While France obtained

[1] Archduke Charles to Emperor. Hüffer, p. 513.

MARENGO June 14th 1800

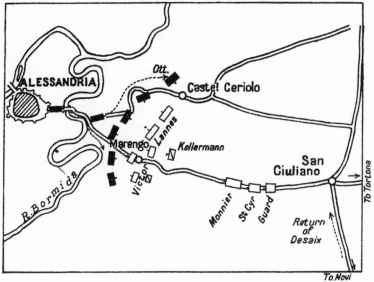

HOHENLINDEN Dec. 3rd 1800.

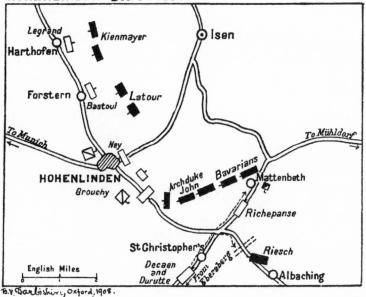

B.V. Darbishire, Oxford, 1908.

recognition from the Emperor of the client Republics with which she was surrounded, the Batavian, the Cisalpine, the Helvetian and the Ligurian, Austria's clients in Italy, her cadet branches at Florence and Modena, lost their lands, and were added to the long list of persons deserving compensation at the expense of the Empire. Tuscany went to the dispossessed Prince of Parma[1] as the kingdom of Etruria, a change of rulers which was not to its advantage; Modena was swallowed up in the Cisalpine, soon (Feb. 1802) to become the Italian Republic. The King of the Two Sicilies was restored to his dominions, but Charles Emmanuel IV did not recover Piedmont. No stipulations were made in the treaty as to its fate, but in April 1801 it was divided into departments; and in September 1802 it was formally annexed to France. Thus with the Adige as Austria's frontier in Italy the peninsula was completely dominated by France.

Still the peace was not altogether disadvantageous to Austria. If it be compared with Campo Formio she really gained in territory, for the secularised bishoprics of Brixen and Trent were a more than ample set-off against the loss of a small strip between the Po and the Adige; and if she gave up the Breisgau, it was to a connection of her own House, the Duke of Modena.[2] Thugut's designs on Bavaria were not realised, but the cession of the Archbishopric of Salzburg to Archduke Ferdinand, the ex-Grand Duke of Tuscany, was most acceptable to the Hapsburgs. To the Empire Lunéville was a severe blow. The definite cession of 25,000 square miles and 3½ millions of people[3] was an absolute loss. The Empire could not comfort itself with the reflection which consoled Austria for the loss of Belgium, that it was losing a source of weakness and gaining a better strategical frontier. The Left Bank territories were an integral and a valuable part of the Empire, and the Rhine had not proved a very strong frontier either in 1796 or in 1800. Moreover, it was only on condition that their fortifications should be "slighted" that the French had evacuated the towns they held on the right of the river.[4]

---

[1] Ferdinand, son of Don Phillip of Spain and Marie Louise, daughter of Louis xv.

[2] (1780–1803), father-in-law of Ferdinand, son of Maria Theresa and Duke of Modena-Breisgau (1803–1806).

[3] Haüsser, ii. 328.

[4] Haüsser, of course, reckons in *German* miles, which are equal to 4·6 or 4·7 English miles: thus the German square mile is, roughly speaking, 22 times as large as the English.

To the inhabitants of the Left Bank the definite separation from Germany came as in some way a relief. In hardly any other part of Germany were the characteristics of German disunion so pronounced. The Left Bank was divided into the most minute parcels; there was not even as large a state as Baden or Oldenburg to give some approach to unity, and the only independent states which exceeded the infinitesimal were precisely those in which there was the least approach to a vigorous localism, ecclesiastical Principalities. The separation from Germany was not likely to be unpopular among people bound to Germany neither by practical nor sentimental considerations. The Empire had been incapable of defending them against the exactions and excesses of the French; as the subjects of the Republic they would at least have a claim to preferential treatment. Nor were German patriotism and national sentiment so strongly rooted among them but that they could be effaced by a few years of careful, honest and appropriate administration. And this they did obtain from the Consulate. Even under the Directory they had been better off than under ecclesiastical or Palatinate rule, and now that, under the direction of Jean Bon St. André, a permanent organisation was substituted for the temporary arrangements of the last ten years, the Left Bank enjoyed a material prosperity which went far to reconcile it to incorporation in France.[1] It was not till France itself began to weary under the burdens which the extension of the Napoleonic supremacy imposed upon her, not till Napoleon's oppression of Germany beyond the Rhine had begun to drive home into Bavarian and Westphalian, into Prussian and Würtemberger, the consciousness that union is strength and that only by a joint effort could Germany free herself of the conscription and the Continental System, that the Left Bank became alive to the fact that the Rhine was a German river, and not the boundary between France and Germany. And not even then was there any strong desire in the Rhineland for separation from France. The return to German rulers was accepted, not welcomed. Had Bonaparte managed to keep the treaties of Lunéville and Amiens, and avoided the continual aggressions which bound Europe together against him, Mayence and Cologne might have become as French as were Metz and Strassburg in 1870.

---

[1] Cf. Fisher's chapter on the Rhine Departments.

CHAPTER XXIII

THE RESETTLEMENT OF 1803

IN the whole history of German disunion [1] and particularism there are few pages more discreditable than that which narrates the protracted negotiations which followed the Peace of Lunéville. The spectacle of the Princes of Germany vying with one another in currying favour with Napoleon, of the bribery, the intrigues, the utter selfishness, the want of any appeal to patriotism or national feeling, is one which has few parallels. It gave Napoleon an idea of the lengths to which it would be possible to carry that principle of *Divide et impera* on which he based his dealings with the Germans. His policy after all was only the policy of Richelieu, Mazarin and Louis XIV attuned to the altered circumstances. Germany must not be allowed to unite. No Power must be allowed to grow strong enough to rally the other states in defence of their common interests. The estrangement between Austria and Prussia must be cultivated and fostered. Austria must be isolated, and at the same time Prussia must not be allowed to make good her pretensions to be the champion of the minor states and their protector against Austria. This was an office to be reserved for France. If the Confederation of the Rhine did not formally take shape till 1806, the bonds which held it together were being forged all through the negotiations of 1801 and 1802.

It might perhaps have been supposed that the territorial resettlement of the Empire was a matter to be left to the Diet to arrange. But the Diet was quite incapable of discharging such a task. The conditions which had contributed to the loss of the Left Bank made it impossible to setttle on the "compensation" for that loss without the intervention of the Power which had carried off the spoils. The first step in the process was, it is true, taken with a celerity altogether foreign to the

---

[1] Cf. Haüsser, ii. pp. 333 ff. ; also Fisher, pp. 38–47.

habits of the Diet. By signing the Peace of Lunéville on behalf of the Empire, Francis II had encroached on the province of the Diet; but that body hastened to condone his action, announced to them on February 25th, 1801, by ratifying the Treaty on March 7th.

The loss of the Left Bank having been thus accepted, together with the principle of compensation by means of secularisation, it remained to arrange a scheme of redistribution, and to settle to whom the drawing up of the scheme should be entrusted. Saxony proposed that the whole Diet should discuss the matter, but the lay states were not inclined to give their ecclesiastical victims a voice in deciding the fate which was to befall them. Bavaria suggested that the Emperor should act as reporter, and should submit a plan to the Diet; a proposal he promptly declined, though he would have been prepared to accept the suggestion of the ecclesiastical states that the entire matter should be entrusted to him without appeal to the Diet. But such a plan was not to the liking of Prussia or Bavaria or any of the other larger lay states who hoped to see as extensive a secularisation as possible. The Emperor would certainly have spared the ecclesiastical Electors, usually his firm adherents, and he would probably have sought to restrict the secularisation even more. Hence a majority in the College of Princes favoured Bavaria's proposal, and the Elector of Mayence, or rather his coadjutor, Charles von Dalberg, a clever but unstable statesman destined to play a leading part in putting Germany at Napoleon's disposal, came round to their side and so carried the proposal through the College of Electors (April 30th). However, the Emperor flatly refused to entertain a proposal which promised him all the invidious work without the satisfaction of the decisive voice. Thus the wearisome discussion and disputes dragged on almost interminably. Not till October 2nd was a Deputation of eight members appointed to arrange a settlement. It was composed of four members from the College of Electors, Bohemia, Brandenburg, Mayence and Saxony, and four from the College of Princes, Baden, Bavaria,[1] Würtemberg and the Grand Master of the Teutonic Order. It was with the aid of France to draw up a scheme to be presented to the Diet for approval. More than ten months, however, elapsed before the Deputation began its labours at Ratisbon

[1] The Elector had a seat in the College of Princes as Duke of Bavaria.

on August 24th, 1802. In the meantime projects without
number had been put forward, only to be found unsatisfactory
and rejected. Every member of the Empire sought to secure
the favour of the all-powerful First Consul for himself or for
his friends. Austria pushed the claims of the Grand Dukes
of Modena and Tuscany; Prussia was urgent for another non-
German claimant, the Prince of Orange, who was connected by
marriage with the Hohenzollern family. Not a scrap of ecclesiastical territory but was claimed by many competitors. Each
state struggled for its own hand, of common action there was
none ; and though a few people, among them Stadion, an
Imperial Knight who was Austrian representative at Berlin, did
try to reconcile Austria and Prussia in the hope of thereby preventing France and Russia from having things their own way,
these efforts proved quite abortive.

At the very outset of the negotiations there had been an
opportunity which the Emperor might have utilised to settle the
matter without the interference of France. Bonaparte was still
at war with England, and the Armed Neutrality of the Baltic
Powers on which he had counted so much had broken down
before the double blow of the murder of the Czar (March 25th,
1801), and of Nelson's victory at Copenhagen. Bonaparte thus
lost the Russian alliance which had allowed him to assume airs
of domination, and he had to somewhat modify his tone. At
this time Bavaria and the other minor states had not been won
over to France by separate treaties, and the relations of Prussia
with France were rather strained. This was due to Prussia's
share in the Armed Neutrality. The Prussian merchant marine
was of sufficiently respectable dimensions to have suffered a
good deal through the rigorous maritime code which the English
applied to all neutrals. Partly for this reason, partly from a wish
not to be left isolated, Prussia had adhered to the Armed
Neutrality in December 1800, and when Denmark occupied
Hamburg and Lübeck on behalf of the Armed Neutrality (March
1801), Prussia did likewise with Bremen, Hanover and Oldenburg. In so doing, Prussia probably only anticipated France ; at
any rate her action was interpreted in this way in Hanover and in
England, and no opposition was offered. She gave out that her
sole object was to preserve the neutrality of North Germany. At
the same time, in the general scramble for territory there was no
harm in having so valuable an asset occupied by her troops.

It was on this that Napoleon worked. He did not wish to see Prussia in possession of the Franconian bishoprics she coveted so much as a foothold in Southern Germany. He therefore urged Prussia to keep Hanover, to which Prussia would not agree unless England's consent could be obtained. Another suggestion, that Prussia should resign Hanover to France, and receive Bamberg and Würzburg, was flatly rejected. Hence there was some coolness between France and Prussia, an opportunity Austria would have done well to seize. Unluckily a quarrel over the sees of Cologne and Münster, left vacant by the death of the Elector Archduke Maximilian (July 27th), created a new breach between the chief Powers of Germany. Prussia proposed that pending the resettlement no election should be made; and when Austria proceeded to use her influence with the Chapters to get Archduke Anthony, the Emperor's youngest brother, elected in his uncle's place (at Münster, Sept. 9th, at Cologne, Oct. 7th), she declined to recognise the election. The Emperor thereupon issued a strongly-worded proclamation condemning Prussia's action.

With Austria and Prussia thus at variance, with all Germany in confusion and disorder, it was not wonderful if the minor Princes appealed to one so firm, so decided and so strong as Bonaparte. Bavaria, after contemplating a scheme put forward by Austria which would have practically allowed her to absorb all the petty states, lay and ecclesiastical alike, of Swabia in return for the cession of most of the Upper Palatinate to Austria, returned to the policy of 1703 and concluded a separate treaty with France as early as August 1801, and confirmed it in the following May. This was indeed the method by which Bonaparte achieved his aims. A series of separate treaties between France and the various Powers of Germany arranged the details of the compensation. These treaties had a double object.¹ On the one hand, they bound the middle states of Germany to Bonaparte, to whom they owed their gains; on the other, by enriching the friends of Russia in Southern Germany, notably Baden, the home of Alexander's wife, and Würtemberg, his mother's country, they conciliated the Czar. Before the Deputation met four of its members had thus pledged themselves, and Dalberg, quick to see that not Austria, nor Prussia, but Bonaparte was the dispenser of patronage and the only Power by whose aid he could hope to save something in the secularisation, was now completely at the First Consul's service.

Thus though the Deputation's deliberations produced no result, the matter was being settled out of court, and all that the Deputation could do was to accept the Franco-Russian proposals. On December 6th the scheme was laid before the Diet without even waiting to obtain the Emperor's assent. Bonaparte might fairly excuse the abruptness of his action by the utter failure of the Empire to arrive at any conclusion as the result of a year's deliberations. If he had not intervened, nothing would ever have been settled. The Diet had no choice but to accept, and Bonaparte, not anxious to drive Austria to extremities when war with England was threatening and when a change of ministry in Russia had substituted the unfriendly Woronzov for Gallophils in Kurakin and Kotschubev, secured the Emperor's assent by concessions. He agreed to let Salzburg go to Archduke Ferdinand, the dispossessed Duke of Tuscany, while the other Hapsburg claimant for compensation, the Duke of Modena, was to receive the Breisgau and Ortenau, Austria obtaining instead the Bishoprics of Brixen and Trent.[1]

Certain slight modifications were made by the Diet in the scheme submitted to it, but on the whole the "Recess" of February 25th, 1803, reproduced the proposals which France and Russia had laid before the Deputation on September 8th, 1802. The final step, the ratification by the Emperor, took place on April 27th, 1803.

The changes thus sanctioned by the Diet really amounted to the destruction of the old order and the dissolution of the Holy Roman Empire. It was veiled under a thin veneer of decency and formality, inasmuch as the execution of the scheme was left to the Diet itself, and a principle was found on which the annexation of the Church lands could be defended. This principle was that of heredity, and as hereditary rulers the Counts and Imperial Knights whose existence contributed so much to the territorial intricacies of South and Western Germany escaped molestation.[2] But with three exceptions the ecclesiastical states disappeared, and the balance of power in the Diet was altogether altered. Moreover, the Imperial villages were mediatised, and their fate was shared by all but six of the Free Cities,

---

[1] Haüsser, ii. 391.   [2] Cf. Seeley's *Stein*, i. 124.

Augsburg, Bremen, Frankfurt, Hamburg, Lübeck and Nüremberg alone retaining their old independence. Their neutrality was indeed guaranteed with full judicial independence and territorial sovereignty, they even obtained slight gains of territory ; but even so they must have felt their position none too secure.

Though so much had been said about compensation, in the actual redistribution there was no attempt to make losses and gains proportionate. Thus while Bavaria, which had lost more territory on the Left Bank than any other Power, including Simmern, Jülich, Zweibrücken and part of the Palatinate, obtained about 6400 square miles in return for the 4800 which she lost; Prussia, whose losses only amounted to a little over 1000 square miles, received nearly 5000 ; Würtemberg was paid fourfold for the 150 square miles of Mompelgard, and Baden's gain of 1300 square miles was out of all due proportion to the 180 she relinquished. Bonaparte used the spoils of the Church not to do justice to the dispossessed, but to buy himself partisans in South Germany.

The net result of the redistribution was to build up a number of medium - sized states with some approach to geographical homogeneity. The separation and division of even the pettiest states, which had been so strong a barrier to administrative unity, to good government, and to the growth of common interests, was to some extent removed. The minor lay states remained but the arguments which had been used to justify the suppression of the abbeys and Free Cities might be urged with equal force against the continued independent existence of the Counts and Knights. The idea of rounding off the dominions of a middle state by the incorporation of the independent parcels which broke up its homogeneity was new, but it was readily accepted. The expediency and propriety of simplifying the political map commended itself strongly to those who survived the process and profited by it. The land-hunger of Bavaria and Würtemberg could be represented as the only chance of political salvation for the scattered districts of Swabia, too small to justify independence, too petty and poor to support the separate court and the complex administration with which every minor potentate surrounded himself. Stein might protest against the incorporation of his hereditary dominions in as small a state as Nassau,[1] but it must be

---

[1] Cf. Seeley's, *Stein*, i. 126.

admitted that in many respects the growth of middle states like Baden and Hesse-Cassel was an advance on the system it replaced. As long as the pettiest Prince claimed an independence which was real enough to prevent the internal union of Germany but a mere farce from an international standpoint, the aggrandisement of the middle states was not without justification. Small as they were, they had possibilities of being healthy and efficient polities which their physical limitations denied to the pettier units. Indeed, if the process had only been carried a little further, it would be easier to justify it. Had all the minor Princes like the Arembergs, the Salms, Thurn und Taxis and the branches of the House of Reuss, been absorbed into larger entities, while only the Electorates and these larger states which like the Hesses or Mecklenburg-Schwerin could pretend to Electoral rank were permitted to maintain their independence, the process might have been represented as an attempt to meet the true needs of Germany. But it was not the interests of Germany, but those of the dynasties which were being consulted, to say nothing of those of the powerful and none too friendly Western neighbour with whom the decision really rested.

Bavaria as the principal loser actually gained most. She received seventeen Imperial cities and villages of which Ulm and Nördlingen were the most important, together with twelve abbeys and priories, mostly in the Franconian and Swabian Circles. There also fell to her lot the Bishoprics of Augsburg, Freisingen, Bamberg and Würzburg—which Prussia especially coveted—and parts of Passau and Eichstadt, which she shared with Salzburg. She lost nearly 800,000 subjects, and a revenue of 5,800,000 gulden, but received 850,000 people producing 6,600,000 gulden of revenue. More than this, her gains lay in the most fertile and cultivated part of South Germany; geographically they were part and parcel of her, and so helped to round her off and to give her a compactness of enormous advantage. Hitherto her rather disconnected condition had given some plausibility to Thugut's schemes for annexing parts of the Electorate to Austria and compensating its ruler elsewhere. Bavaria had now obtained the districts which might naturally have been selected as this compensation, and she had not had to cede anything to Austria. Her aggrandisement was a sufficient answer and barrier to Thugut's designs.

Baden was another state which was treated on the most favoured footing, thanks largely to Charles Frederick's relation to the Czar. The Margrave became an Elector, and his dominions were enlarged by the Bishopric of Constance, by the portions of those of Basel, Strassburg and Spires which lay to the East of the Rhine, and by part of the Palatinate, hitherto Bavarian, including Heidelberg and Mannheim. A population of a quarter of a million and a revenue of 1,250,000 gulden was an ample recompense for the 25,000 people and 250,000 gulden lost with the Left Bank. Würtemberg also owed much to her Russian connection. Nine Imperial cities and about as many abbeys in Swabia fell to the lot of Duke Frederick II, now advanced to the rank of Elector. This increased the number of his subjects by 110,000 and the annual revenue of his state by 700,000 gulden, his losses only amounting to 14,000 people and 350,000 gulden per annum. Würtemberg, moreover, gained greatly in compactness through the disappearance of the petty states which had interrupted her continuity.

Only one other state in South-Western Germany deserves mention. This was the new Duchy erected out of the Austrian possessions on the Rhine for the dispossessed Duke of Modena. In accordance with the treaty between Bonaparte and the Emperor of December 26th, 1802, Duke Ferdinand received the Breisgau and Ortenau, Austria being compensated for her loss by obtaining the secularised Bishoprics of Brixen and Trent, which if somewhat smaller and less populous, were richer, easier to defend, and geographically much more desirable.

Proceeding northward, the next state which deserves mention is the Landgraviate of Hesse-Darmstadt, one of the states which had profited most by the redistribution. In return for certain cessions which only amounted to some 300 square miles inhabited by 40,000 people, the· Landgrave received the old Duchy of Westphalia, hitherto part of the Electorate of Cologne, a few abbeys and villages, the Free City of Friedberg, and portions of the Archbishopric of Mayence, of the Palatinate and of the Bishopric of Worms, a long and narrow strip from the Lippe to the Neckar over 2000 square miles in extent, with 120,000 inhabitants and a revenue of 800,000 gulden.

Hesse-Cassel, on the other hand, received much less territory than she had hoped to get. As the Landgrave had had no possessions at all on the Left Bank, he perhaps obtained all he deserved when he got the Free City of Gelnhausen and the dignity of Elector. But even this hardly consoled him for seeing the ex-Stadtholder of Holland, William v of Orange, of the Nassau-Dillingen line, endowed out of the districts for which he himself had hoped with a Principality composed of the Bishoprics of Fulda and Corvey and the Free City of Dortmund, a scattered holding, but amounting in all to 1000 square miles with a revenue of a million gulden. The other branches of the Nassau line, Weilburg and Usingen, received between them a considerable stretch of territory between the Rhine, the Main and the Lahn, formerly belonging to the ecclesiastical Electors, more than equivalent to their losses on the Left Bank.[1] The cousins, Dukes Frederick Augustus of Usingen (1803–1816), and Frederick William of Weilburg (1788–1816), had agreed to treat their possessions as one Duchy, and ruled it in common.

A little higher up the Main came a new state, the principality created for Dalberg, now as Arch Chancellor of the Empire and Primate of Germany, the only survivor of the ecclesiastical Electors. He obtained Aschaffenburg and district, formerly parts of Mayence and Würzburg, the Cities of Wetzlar and Ratisbon, the secularised Bishopric of Ratisbon, and three abbeys. The revenue of 600,000 gulden which these possessions were calculated to produce was to be supplemented by 400,000 gulden secured on the tolls of the Rhine. Dalberg was now definitely enrolled among the partisans of Bonaparte. Hitherto he had endeavoured to carry on the old traditions of the see of Mayence as the leader among the German Princes, he had wavered between Austria and Prussia: in 1801 he had at first struggled hard to save the Bishoprics, but, realising this was impossible, he devoted himself most zealously to furthering the interests of Bonaparte, as he saw in this the only royal road to security.[2]

In North-Western Germany the principal question of interest was the fate which would befall the rich Westphalian Bishoprics. It was here that Prussia was to find compensation for her loss of Cleves, Guelders and Mors. It was not quite what she had wanted. Hardenberg had been very anxious to see Bamberg and Würzburg in Prussian hands ; Bonaparte was not merely determined to keep Prussia out of Franconia, but he

---

[1] Saarbrücken and Saarwerden.   [2] Cf. Seeley's *Stein*, ii. 365 ff.

would have liked to make her take Mecklenburg as her share, transplanting the Dukes of Schwerin and Strelitz to Westphalia and Franconia. But the refusal of the Dukes to leave their ancestral dominions frustrated this attempt to thrust Prussia back to the East of the Elbe, and Bonaparte was forced to agree to let her take the Bishoprics of Paderborn and Hildesheim, a large part of that of Münster, the town of that name, the Thuringian possessions of Mayence, Erfurt and the Eichsfeld, together with six abbeys and three Cities. These amounted in all to 5000 square miles against a loss of 1050, with a population of 500,000 against a quarter of that number, and a revenue of four millions against one of one and a half. Rich and fertile for the most part, these acquisitions gave Prussia a dominant position in North-Western Germany, since there was only one other state of any importance in that quarter. This was Hanover, which gained but little in the redistribution, having to surrender her rights over Sayn - Altenkirchen to Nassau, over Wildeshausen to Oldenburg, to which there also fell a fragment of the Bishopric of Münster. In return, Hanover obtained Osnabrück permanently.[1] Of other states in this part of Germany, Brunswick-Wolfenbüttel received a couple of abbeys, while various minor dynasties, notably Salm and Aremberg, divided the rest of Münster. Saxony was unconcerned in the redistribution, and the only other features of importance were the survival of the Teutonic Order, of which the Archduke Charles was now Grand Master, and of the Knights of St. John, and the erection of the Archbishopric of Salzburg into an Electorate for the Grand Duke of Tuscany.

Minor potentates like the Princes of Isenburg, Löwenstein, and Thurn und Taxis also survived the storm, and were more or less fairly compensated for their losses. The compensation of the Counts was a more difficult matter, since the estates of the Swabian prelates did not suffice for the purpose,[2] while the promise of compensation with which the Imperial Knights had to content themselves was at the best a dubious guarantee.

Territorial changes so far-reaching naturally involved great political changes. Except that nothing new was substituted, the Recess might be described as the end of the Holy Roman Empire. The Diet and the Imperial Chamber at Wetzlar survived, but their possibility of usefulness was gone. What

<hr>

[1] Cf. p. 46. [2] Cf. Haüsser, ii. 415.

relics of the old federal institutions remained, such as the Circles, were quite incompatible with the new arrangements. Moreover, the disappearance of the ecclesiastical states and the transfer of votes to the lay Princes who had received the secularised prelacies had entirely altered the balance of power in the Diet. The Protestants were now in the majority, for of the 82 voters to which the loss of the Left Bank and the disappearance of the joint votes of the Rhenish and Swabian prelates had reduced the College of Princes, 52 were now Protestant and 30 Catholic.[1] One result of the change was that Austria's influence in the Diet was much decreased. She had usually been able to reckon on the clerical voters, but most of their votes were now in the hands of her enemies.[2]

With the disappearance of the ecclesiastical states the secular element gained the upper hand in Germany completely, even to the extent of the subjection of ecclesiastics to secular jurisdiction. Their disappearance was in so far a benefit that on the whole they had been in a bad condition, and greatly needed the reforms they were more likely to get from their new than from their old rulers. Similarly, not even in their most flourishing days had most of the mediatised towns ever been large enough to justify their territorial independence, and in 1803 they were for the most part much decayed. If the type of administration introduced in the new middle states of Germany under the influence of Napoleonic France tended to be oppressively inelastic and on unduly rigid lines, it was still a great improvement on what it replaced. But what is remarkable about these changes, is the fact that they were effected without apparently exciting any great movement of public opinion. They had been from first to last the work of the dynasties, not of their subjects.

They were accepted with a positive apathy almost everywhere. The inhabitants of the Left Bank, who since 1797 had enjoyed the advantages of being regularly incorporated in France, showed no desire to return to their old allegiance, and accepted readily enough the theory of Görres, that Nature had

---

[1] The vote of the Westphalian Counts alternated ; this reckons it as Catholic.

[2] In the College of Princes, Prussia (formerly 8) had now 11 votes. Bavaria (6) had 9, Hanover (6) 7, Baden (3) 6, the Ernestine Saxons 6, Nassau (2) 4, Mecklenburg-Schwerin 3, Austria 3, Salzburg 3, Oldenburg, Würtemburg and Hesse-Cassel 2 each ; four groups of Counts and 20 single votes made up the total of 82.

created the Rhine to serve as the boundary of France. Material benefits had followed annexation, and the state of these departments was certainly superior to that of their neighbours on the Eastern bank of the river.

The German Revolution, for so it may be described, though in part the effect of the great popular upheaval in France, was not in the least a popular movement. Instead of welding a nation together by destroying barriers between classes and provinces, the German Revolution reinforced and fortified particularism. At the same time, the incorporation of the smallest states in the larger was an example which might be pushed further. The system of rounding off a territorial unit by assimilating the petty states enclosed in it might be greatly extended. The new grouping of Germany paved the way to unification, even while destroying most of the old outward forms of German unity. The greed of the German Princes had destroyed the Holy Roman Empire; the oppression of Napoleon was to build up in its place the German national feeling which the Empire had suggested rather than aroused.[1]

---

[1] Haüsser's chapter (Book III. ch. vii.), *Der Reichsdeputations Hauptschluss*, has been my principal authority for this account of the resettlement of Germany. Compare also Fisher, ch. ii., and Maps xi. and xii. in the *Clarendon Press Atlas*.

CHAPTER XXIV

THE CAUSES OF THE THIRD COALITION

UNSATISFACTORY as the resettlement of 1803 must have been to all patriotic Germans, it was not in itself doomed to inevitable failure. The Recess was not carried out without conflicts between the stronger Powers—Austria and Bavaria, for example, nearly came to blows over Burgau[1]—or protests from the weaker states, who appealed to the protection of the First Consul. But with Austria and Prussia on bad terms, and the middle states bound to Napoleon by gratitude for past favours and the stronger tie of hope of future benefits, an equilibrium seemed to have been established in Germany which was not likely to be disturbed from within if Napoleon only took reasonable precautions to keep on good terms with the Continental Powers. A little moderation, a little regard for the fears and susceptibilities of Austria and Russia, such as true statesmanship would surely have dictated, might have prevented the growth of that Third Coalition, which is rather to be ascribed to Napoleon's aggressions, to his failure to abide by the conditions he had himself laid down, than to the insidious influence of "Pitt's gold."[2] Napoleon was himself Great Britain's best recruiting sergeant and the most influential advocate of the Third Coalition.

The complete decay of the Holy Roman Empire is perhaps best illustrated by the treatment received by the Imperial Knights during the years 1803 and 1804. That their position was anomalous, that their independence was theoretically unjustifiable, cannot be denied. The contention of Prussia, that the privileges of the Knights were usurpations which had grown up under ecclesiastical rule, but which must be restricted now that

---

[1] Cf. Haüsser, ii. 439.

[2] Cf. Rose's *Napoleon*, vol. ii. pp. 5, 6, and also a volume of the Royal Historical Society's Transactions dealing with *The Third Coalition against France: 1804-1805*, edited by Dr. Rose.

secular government had replaced ecclesiastical,[1] had perhaps a little more historical accuracy than characterised the proclamation published by the Elector of Bavaria on October 9th, 1803, which roundly declared that the Knights were mere local landholders who had thrown off the authority of their overlords. Both views, however, were in deliberate violation of the clause in the Peace of Westphalia which recognised the Knights as a component part of the German polity, and guaranteed their enjoyment of their rights and privileges.[2] That their territories were on the whole ill-governed, backward in every way, an incubus on trade and commerce, a menace to public order and security as being the resort of gipsies, vag: ants and criminals, was more or less true ; but their suppression was a matter which should have been effected by legal forms, by the authority of the Diet, and not merely by the right of the stronger.

This, however, was what Bavaria was trying to do. The Elector collected a committee of the Franconian Knights, had himself proclaimed their overlord, ordered the magistrates to join the Electoral courts of justice, and directed that the taxes due to the Knights should be paid into the Electoral coffers. The committee was compelled to admit themselves to be the Elector's subjects, and to pay to him the sums hitherto paid to the Emperor.

His action found many imitators, foremost among them Hesse-Cassel, Hesse-Darmstadt and the Princes of the House of Nassau. Petty Princes like the rulers of Leiningen and Isenburg were not restrained from using violence against their defenceless neighbours by the reflection that their own possessions might with equal justification be subjected to a similar process. Saxony and Baden alone refrained from the game of "grab," which in some places, where more than one claimant attempted to seize the same village, resulted in bloodshed. In vain the Knights appealed to Napoleon. He would not alienate more useful clients for the sake of these helpless applicants for his protection. The Emperor, however, did bestir himself upon their behalf, and an Imperial Commission of the Aulic Council pronounced in favour of the Knights (Jan. 1804), and ordered restoration of the previous state of things. The Emperor, the Arch Chancellor, Baden and Saxony were appointed guardians of the rights of the Knights.

[1] Cf. Haüsser, ii. 485.   [2] Cf. Turner, p. 122.

Bavaria now found herself isolated, for Napoleon was not disposed to intervene on her behalf and to embroil himself with Austria just when the unexpected firmness of the Addington Cabinet had involved him, before he was ready, in a fresh war with England. Accordingly on February 19th the Elector intimated to the Diet his willingness to withdraw. His action had been somewhat over-hasty, but it was typical of the way in which the middle states were seeking to assert their authority over their new acquisitions, and to build up on a small scale autocracies after the Napoleonic model. Bureaucratic centralisation, an extensive and active system of police, complete control over the finances, uniformity in organisation and administration, were the objects aimed at. When the interests of the subject were the chief care of the ruler, as was the case in Baden, where education was fostered by the revival of Heidelberg University, and all possible means were taken to promote good government, this had a good side. In Würtemberg one sees the reverse side of the shield, a caricature of the Napoleonic system, an oppressive rule, sacrificing the interests of the governed to the whim of a selfish ruler, heedless of his subjects. But it is in Bavaria that one has the most typical case of the conflict between the old and the new. In the last days of Elector Charles Theodore, things had not been well with Bavaria. Mistresses, monks and favourites had held sway over an extravagant, corrupt and inefficient government. Taxation had been oppressive, the debt heavy, trade and industry had languished under the blighting influence of monopolies and privilege. Justice was conspicuous by its absence, the administration was at once oppressive and lax. Education was neglected, superstition universal. With Maximilian Joseph a new era had begun. Modern, alert, and if rather lacking in force of character still genuinely anxious to introduce reforms, he found a congenial minister in the gifted Savoyard Montgelas. Together they assailed privilege, priestcraft and feudalism, introduced reforms into the Army, the Church, the administration of justice and of police, into the position of the peasants and the rights of the landowners. It was an assistance to them that Bavaria's acquisitions in 1803 were rich and in many important respects ahead of the rest of Germany. Some indication of the liberal tendencies of the Elector and his minister is given by their grant of toleration to Protestants (Sept. 1800), by their suppression of superfluous monasteries, by their refusal to allow Franciscans and Capuchins to recruit their numbers, by their assuming control of Church property, and placing all schools in the hands of the State.

Meanwhile Napoleon, not content to let well alone, was making peace as impossible for the Continental Powers as he had already made it for Great Britain. His interference in the internal affairs of Holland (Sept. 1801) and of Switzerland (Sept. 1802), his annexations of Piedmont and of the Valais, his election as First Consul of the Italian Republic (Jan. 1802), could not but excite unrest and uneasiness at Vienna and at St. Petersburg, even if they failed to bring home to the dull mind of Frederick William III the dangers of the path he had chosen. And yet he had seen nearer home an act "just such as Prussia might have entreated Napoleon to commit in order to give her an occasion of showing the difference between a policy of non-intervention and a policy of mere passiveness."[1] This was the French occupation of Hanover.

As in 1756 so in 1803 Hanover was the link that bound the maritime and colonial war between England and France to the affairs of the Continent. Through Hanover Napoleon hoped to strike at England, little though either George III or his people concerned themselves with the fate of the monarch's German subjects. But as an inlet by which English commerce might find its way into Europe, Hanover had its importance even to England, and the occupation of Hanover was the first step in that policy of controlling the Continent in order to keep out English trade which led Napoleon on to Moscow.

At the end of May 1803 20,000 French troops under General Mortier crossed the frontier of Hanover. The army of the Electorate was neither very large nor very efficient. Since the Peace of Basel, Hanover had enjoyed the shelter of the "line of demarcation," and the army had been reduced accordingly. Still, if the administration had chosen to make a stand, the Hanoverian troops might have resisted as weak a corps as Mortier's with good prospects of success. But the Electorate was under the lax and placid rule of a bureaucratic aristocracy, too mild to arouse popular discontent and make the invaders welcome, too slack and inert to arouse popular resistance based on patriotic feeling. Thus no preparations for resistance were

[1] Seeley, i. 230.

made till the invaders were on the move.[1] Some trusted to the protection of the Holy Roman Empire, some to the equally futile Prussian guarantee of neutrality.

As early as March 1803 Napoleon had sent Duroc to Berlin to explain that to secure the flank of the Grand Army against an English attack he would have to occupy Hanover. Rather feebly Prussia sought to dissuade Napoleon from a step so inimical to her interests, so derogatory to her prestige, so detrimental to her trade, since it was certain that England would reply to the occupation by a blockade of the Elbe and Weser. But while Prussia hesitated and attempted to mediate between England and France, while the Hanoverian ministry displayed equal hesitation and indecision and only definitely appealed to Prussia when it was too late, Napoleon carried out his plan. It seems probable that had Prussia taken Lord Hawkesbury's hint to Jacobi and, as in 1801, forestalled Napoleon by herself occupying Hanover, England would have taken no official notice of what after all did not concern her, while Napoleon would most likely have acquiesced rather than alienate Prussia. But prompt and decided action of any nature was not to be expected from Prussia. At last (May 25th) a proposal was adopted by which Russia and Prussia were to guarantee the neutrality of Hanover, a payment being made by the Electorate to France, and the Duke of Cambridge acting as Stadtholder; but by this time Mortier's men were on the point of crossing the frontier, and Talleyrand informed Lucchesini that Napoleon intended to occupy "the British possessions on the Continent," though he hinted that his master was well disposed towards a Franco-Prussian alliance which might leave Hanover in Prussian hands.

It was on May 30th that Mortier entered Hanover. He met with no opposition. A *levée en masse* had been ordered but countermanded, and the Hanoverian troops fell back on Suhlingen, while emissaries from the Privy Council attempted to negotiate with Mortier. Neither civil nor military authorities had any idea of resisting, and on June 3rd a Convention was signed at Suhlingen which placed the whole Electorate, with its fortresses and revenues, at the disposal of the French. The Hanoverian army undertook to retire across the Elbe and not to bear arms against France unless exchanged. This, however, did not satisfy Napoleon. He insisted that the army should surrender as prisoners of war, wishing to exchange them against the French sailors on the English prison-hulks whom his fleet so sorely needed. The British ministry not unaturally declined to meet his wishes. Thereupon he refused to ratify the Convention, and bade Mortier disarm the Hanoverian troops. To this Wallmoden, the Hanoverian commander, would not agree, and for a time it seemed as though Hanover would after all resist. But the troops were in bad condition, their discipline was relaxed, they did not understand what was happening, and when the Estates of Calenberg-Celle demanded that the troops should submit, Wallmoden gladly grasped at this excuse for capitulation. Mortier waived the demand that the men should become prisoners of war, and the troops then laid down their arms and dispersed to their homes (July 5th). No small number of them, however, keenly sensitive to the disgrace to the honour of their army, took advantage of the fact that the oath of neutrality had not been administered to them to escape through Holstein to England, there to be formed into that King's German Legion which was to do such good service to the cause of England and of Europe, which was to serve in Denmark and in Portugal, in Sicily and in Spain, and to end a glorious career by playing a prominent part in the "crowning mercy" of Waterloo.[1]

In this way Hanover passed into the power of France: the first district of Germany East of the Rhine to suffer the lot of subjugation to Napoleon, which sooner or later was meted out to the whole country. It exchanged a government which, with all its faults, could not be called exacting or tyrannical, for the heavy burden of a military occupation aimed at draining dry the resources of the country. Not much change was made in the administration, but an Executive Commission was appointed on which fell the task of wringing out of the unfortunate Electorate the sums Napoleon demanded. The normal annual revenue of the country was little over 12,000,000 francs, but nearly 18,000,000 were extorted between July 5th and December 23rd, 1803. Moreover, the French troops had to be supplied and given quarters at the

[1] Beamish's *History of the King's German Legion* contains a full and interesting account of the Legion and its services: for the French occupation of Hanover, see Fisher, ch. iii., and *England and Hanover*, pp. 203 ff.

expense of the inhabitants. In June 1804, when Bernadotte replaced Mortier, matters improved slightly. His yoke was rather milder, his extortions less crushing, the discipline he maintained rather better. Yet even so the Electorate was burdened and taxed unmercifully, while the threat of a like fate wrung from the neighbouring city of Hamburg an unwilling "loan" of three million marks in November 1803.

From the other Powers of Germany no redress was to be looked for by the unfortunate Hanoverians. The Emperor accepted the occupation as a fact: he was as ready to see the French there as the Prussians. Prussia meanwhile put up with the check as best she might. She did, indeed, send Lombard to Brussels (July 1803) to ask Napoleon's intentions and complain about his seizure of Cuxhaven, which belonged to Hamburg. The mission only committed Prussia more and more to France. Lombard returned declaring that Napoleon only meant to respect the rights of neutrals, and that his action had been forced upon him by England's illegalities.[1] A proposal made by Prussia to get Russia to guarantee the neutrality of the Continent so as to secure Napoleon against the foundation of a new coalition by British gold, Napoleon rejected. He had no wish to see Russia and Prussia on good terms, but intended to keep Prussia isolated and so at his mercy. It was a sense of this isolation which caused Prussia in the course of 1804 to make tentative efforts to build up a new League of Princes on the lines of the *Fürstenbund* of 1785. The idea came to nothing; for Duke Charles Augustus of Saxe-Weimar, when sounded by Prince William of Brunswick, did not prove enthusiastic, while Prussia was equally unwilling to let the Duke of Weimar draw her into a league with Austria. The relations of the two leading Powers of Germany were as usual strained, and not even the outrage on the Empire, on treaty rights, international law and public opinion involved in the abduction of the Duc d'Enghien (March 1804) from the shelter of his refuge at Baden, could make them unite to protect the Empire against so flagrant and forcible an outrage. Indeed, it is a striking commentary on the state of Germany that the most strenuous protests should have come not from Austria or Bavaria or Prussia, but from England, Russia

---

[1] She had blockaded the mouths of the Elbe and Weser, and the trade of Hamburg and Bremen was feeling the effects of the blockade.

and Sweden. The conduct of the Elector of Baden was pusillanimous and ignominious in the extreme. Far from bringing the case before the Diet himself, he endeavoured to prevent Russia from moving in the matter at all[1] (July), asking the Diet to let it drop lest a greater evil should follow. Hanover, however, refused to do this, and called on the Emperor to demand satisfaction and redress for the double breach of the rights of the Empire committed by Napoleon in this matter and in the occupation of Hanover. To avoid having to vote on the question, most of the representatives left Ratisbon before the end of July.[2]

Not long after the abduction and murder of the only member of the House of Bourbon on whom he could conveniently lay his hands, Napoleon assumed the Imperial title (May 18th, 1804). This was not quite to the liking of Austria. The new title was felt to reflect in some way on that of Francis. It seemed to hint at a new competitor for the Imperial throne quite capable of ending the Hapsburg monopoly. Moreover, the changes of 1803 had given the Protestants a clear majority in the Electoral College, and it was to make certain that in some form or other the Imperial title should continue in his line that Francis resolved upon the erection of his own immediate dominions into an hereditary Empire.[3] It was on August 14th, 1804, that the decree was published by which this was done: but not before negotiations for the reciprocal recognition of the two titles had for some time been keeping Paris and Vienna in constant correspondence.[4]

[1] Russia at first seems to have contemplated an immediate rupture with France, but decided in favour of the " more circumspect " course of appealing to the members of the Empire to co-operate with the Czar in " restraining the ambition of France " and defending their rights and liberties (*The Third Coalition*, p. 5). However, as Napoleon took offence at Russia's protests against the execution of the Duc d'Enghien, and complained bitterly that Russia was interfering in matters which did not concern her, relations rapidly became strained, and in August 1804 the Russian Minister at Paris, after presenting an ultimatum with the terms of which Napoleon altogether failed to comply, left France altogether. This rupture of diplomatic relations did not, however, immediately lead to war. *Ibid.* pp. 30–32.

[2] Cf. Fisher, pp. 67–75 ; Haüsser, ii. pp. 497 ff.

[3] Some contemporary documents use the title "the Emperor of Germany" in speaking of Francis II (cf. *The Third Coalition*, passim), but it was not, of course, his official title.

[4] Austria's recognition of Napoleon's Imperial title gave much offence to the Czar (*The Third Coalition*, p. 36), and despite the efforts of England to promote a good understanding between Vienna and St. Petersburg, Russia at first actually

Partly with the object of publishing to the world his claim to be regarded as the successor of Charlemagne, partly in order to acquaint himself thoroughly with his new Rhenish provinces, Napoleon undertook in September 1804 a tour through the recent annexations on the left bank of the Rhine. At Aix-la-Chapelle, Charlemagne's old capital, he received the Austrian envoy sent to formally recognise the new Imperial title. Thence he proceeded by Cologne (Sept. 13th) to Mayence, where he was greeted by a large and subservient assembly of German Princes and envoys, including two Electors. The presence of the Elector of Baden was a lurid commentary on that Prince's attitude in the matter of the Duc d'Enghien; the attendance of Dalberg in the city of Mayence was a humiliating proof of the great change in that prelate's policy since the days when he had desired to reconcile the *Fürstenbund* of 1785 to the Hapsburgs, even more since the days when he had urged Archduke Charles to assume the powers of a dictator over Germany. Formerly the stoutest champion of the Empire, Dalberg had at least made a complete change when he turned his coat, and Napoleon had not now a keener supporter. The see of Mayence had always been associated with the Imperial traditions ever since the days of Elector Berthold of Henneberg,[1] and even before his day, and Dalberg was now ready to continue his advocacy of Imperialism, but with Napoleon as his Emperor.

The meeting at Mayence though indicative of future developments, did not see any definite steps towards the organisation of the Confederation of the Rhine. It served to familiarise the minor Princes of Germany with the notion of a German union under the benevolent protection of France, which would secure them against the aggressions of Austria and Prussia. Such a plan had indeed been suggested earlier in the year by Waitz, the principal minister of the Elector of Hesse, but it had been put aside by Napoleon as likely to interfere with the Prussian alliance he was anxious to secure.

refused to recognise the title of "Hereditary Emperor of Austria" (p. 54); this with differences of opinion as to the policy to be pursued towards Turkey (p. 47), and the reluctance of the Austrian ministers, more especially of Cobenzl, the leading man amongst them, to undertake the risks of defying Napoleon, kept the two Courts from forming that alliance by which England hoped to rally Europe against Napoleon until 1805 was far advanced.

[1] Cf. C.M.H. i. pp. 300 ff.

Napoleon was anxious for a Prussian alliance, because he was well aware of the growing hostility of Russia;[1] nor could he overlook the fact that, though men like Cobenzl might be well disposed to him, or at least so much afraid of his displeasure that they would do nothing to provoke it, the old Austrian aristocracy with all its traditions could not so readily accept the mushroom Bonapartist Empire, or forget what Austria had suffered at the Corsican upstart's hands. In view of the hostility of Austria and Russia, it would be most unwise to alienate Prussia. England must not be allowed to unite all the three leading Continental Powers in a great coalition.

But as long as Prussia maintained her policy of neutrality, Napoleon could not feel quite secure of her. Though recent events had rather shaken his belief in passive neutrality, Frederick William III lacked the decision, the courage and the energy for definitely throwing in his lot either with France, as Haugwitz and Lombard on the whole advised, or with her enemies, whose cause was pleaded by the patriotic Queen Louise and by the King's enterprising cousin, Prince Louis Ferdinand. He still clung to his idea of a Russo-Prussian guarantee of the neutrality of the Continent, in return for which Napoleon would evacuate Hanover. He thus quite overlooked the fact that Russia was already more than half-way to an alliance with England, and much more disposed to force Prussia into line with the rest of Europe by threats and menaces than to buy her support with concessions;[2] that it was most unlikely that Napoleon would give up so valuable a pawn in the diplomatic game as Hanover, and that the neutrality Prussia offered was not of the least value to France. What Napoleon wanted was to force Prussia, like the middle states, into an alliance with him which should keep Austria and

---

[1] Russia had begun negotiating with Great Britain as far back as November 1803, when the occupation of Naples by French troops seemed to herald French intervention in the Morea and attempts on the integrity of Turkey (cf. Rose, *Napoleonic Studies*, pp. 364–367); but her anxiety to avoid throwing Austria or Prussia or the minor German states into the arms of France by a too precipitate declaration of policy (*The Third Coalition* (R.H.S.), p. 12), had prevented any immediate action resulting from the negotiations. England and Russia were, however, in substantial accord as to the necessity of putting some check on Napoleon's aggressions.

[2] Cf. *The Third Coalition*, pp. 101 ff. : England seems to have been far keener about securing Prussia's friendship ; Russia, to have thought it would be easier to intimidate than to encourage Frederick William into an alliance.

Russia in check and abate their bellicose tendencies. But he was rather too impatient: by trying to force Frederick William to a decision he alarmed that essentially deliberate monarch, who was endeavouring to play Russia and France off against each other. The Czar, however, losing patience with Prussia's indecision, did not attempt to conceal his opinion of the Prussian King's policy, and Alexander's openly expressed contempt made Frederick William incline towards France. This disposition received something of a check through a fresh outrage on the part of Napoleon, the seizure of Sir George Rumbold, the British agent at Hamburg (Oct. 24th, 1804). This violation of neutral territory was possibly partly intended as a reply to Russia's protests about the abduction of d'Enghien ;[1] anyhow it was an insult to Frederick William, who was Director of the Lower Saxon Circle, and for once he showed some decision. His indignant protests induced Napoleon to release Rumbold as a concession, not to international law, but to the King of Prussia. For the moment Napoleon did not wish to play into the hands of the bellicose party in Prussia, which seemed to have gained ground by recent changes in the ministry. During the summer of 1804 Haugwitz, without actually resigning, handed over the control of the Foreign Office to Hardenberg and retired to his Silesian estates. From time to time, however, he returned to Berlin and took part in ministerial conferences, a most anomalous arrangement which led to great confusion. The expected change in foreign policy did not follow. Hardenberg, much as he distrusted Napoleon, was not prepared to advocate a complete change, and Prussia continued her futile efforts to keep on good terms with both sides.

But by this time war was becoming inevitable. Napoleon's repeated infringements of the Peace of Lunéville had convinced Alexander of the unwisdom of the policy which had assisted Napoleon to rise to so dangerous a strength. The occupation of Naples and Hanover in order to exclude British goods from the Continent, the spectacle of Spain's dependence on the Emperor,— she became involved in Anglo-French war in December 1804,—above all, the murder of the Duc d'Enghien further excited his resentment. In August 1804 the Russian Ambassador at Paris, Count Oubril, had demanded his pass-

[1] Cf. *The Third Coalition*, p. 57.

ports, and though war had not immediately followed it could not be long delayed. Nor was Austria any better pleased with the situation. Only the memories of Marengo and Hohenlinden and the great need for the reorganisation of army administration and finances acted as a check on bellicose leanings.[1] Archduke Charles was too well aware of the deficiencies of the army to desire war, and Cobenzl's knowledge of the internal condition of the realm made him equally pacific. Yet Napoleon's actions in Italy and elsewhere could not fail to arouse resentment and suspicion, and in November 1804 Stadion concluded on behalf of Austria a defensive alliance with Russia, providing for the co-operation of Austria and Russia in case of further outrages by Napoleon. This was followed (April 11th, 1805) by an Anglo-Russian treaty, the objects of which were the expulsion of the French from North Germany, the restoration of the independence of Holland, Switzerland and Italy, and the restoration of the House of Savoy. Sweden had already concluded similar compacts with both Powers, with England in December 1804, with Russia in January 1805; but the rather inconsiderate zeal of Gustavus IV threatened to embroil him with Prussia over Pomerania,[2] and so to impede the attempts of the Coalition to enlist Prussia on their side.

To relate the action and discuss the motives of Frederick William and his advisers is a monotonous task. Hardenberg, Haugwitz and Frederick William were all pessimistic as to the Coalition's chances of overthrowing Napoleon. Russia's ill-timed efforts to force Prussia and Bavaria into an anti-French alliance had only the opposite effect. Prussia hoped to combine the advantages of both policies by adopting neither, and Napoleon's skilful dangling of the bait of Hanover before her kept her undecided. About the end of July 1805 he replied to Lucchesini's complaints about his recent action in Italy by an

---

[1] The despatches of Lord Harrowby, Sir J. B. Warren, and others, printed in Dr. Rose's *Third Coalition* (R.H.S.), contain frequent references to the poverty and financial exhaustion of Austria as the main reason for her reluctance to resume the struggle against Napoleon. It is also clear that Cobenzl's influence was steadily exercised against the "forward party," while the bad relations between Archduke Charles and Thugut forbade the recall to office of that energetic minister, who, with all his faults, at least was the sincere and convinced opponent of Napoleon; *e.g.* p. 69.

[2] Cf. Haüsser, ii. 543.

offer of Hanover,[1] appealing not merely to Frederick William's greed, but to his love of peace also by declaring that Prussia's open adhesion to the side of France would probably keep the Coalition from making war. Even Hardenberg was caught by this prospect of plunder. The Duke of Brunswick,[2] believing that a Franco-Prussian alliance would dissolve the Coalition at once, favoured the annexation of Hanover, and when Duroc came to Berlin at the end of August 1805 all indications pointed to the success of his mission. The dictatorial and minatory tone Russia was assuming had offended Prussia, and seemed likely to drive her into an alliance with Napoleon. But even at this late hour, when the Grand Army was already well on its way from the Channel to the Danube, Frederick William clung to the idea of mediating between the contending forces and so averting war. The natural result of his culpable indecision was that neither side would listen to his proposals, and that both treated Prussia "with a reckless contempt which shows that nothing was hoped, and at the same time nothing was feared from her wooden immobility."[3]

Meanwhile the war had come. The announcement in the *Moniteur* of March 17th, 1805, that the Italian Republic had offered the Iron Crown of Lombardy to Napoleon, was naturally interpreted as a deliberate challenge to the Coalition. The conversion of the Batavian Republic into a kingdom for Louis Bonaparte, the grant of Piombio and Lucca to Elise Bonaparte as a Principality, the annexation of Parma, Piacenza, Guastalla and the Ligurian Republic (June 9th) to France, merely added fuel to the flames. Even Prussia's placid acquiescence in Napoleon's aggressions received a shock which caused the Cabinet of Berlin to recognise the possibility that it might find it necessary to change its policy with regard to France.[4] The Russian envoy who was on his way to lay the last demands of the Allies before Napoleon received orders from the Czar bidding him suspend his journey. Austria's hesitations gave place to a firmer and more resolute tone and to a protest against the last outrage on the liberties of Europe. To

---

[1] Cf. Bailleu, *Preussen und Frankreich*, vol. ii. pp. 354 ff.
[2] Cf. Haüsser, ii. 600 ff.   [3] Seeley, i. 235.
[4] Cf. Novosilzov to Woronzov (quoted in *The Third Coalition*, p. 187). The whole attitude of Germany towards Napoleon is altering; he is "no longer a guardian angel," but a monster who will "swallow up Germany if she persists in a policy of inaction."

this Napoleon answered that he should consider Austria's action as a declaration of war; but the protest was not withdrawn. Hostilities did not at once follow. Indeed, it was not till August 9th that Austria signed the treaty by which she formally adhered to the Russo-British alliance of April 11th.[1] In the interval Napoleon had sent an envoy to warn Austria against the insidious designs of Russia and Britain, to profess his own pacific intentions, and to complain of Austria's unreasonably hostile attitude. At the critical moment of his great design against his arch-enemy England, when he was hoping every day to hear that Villeneuve had released Ganteaume and the Brest fleet from Cornwallis' vigilant blockade, and that the combined squadrons of Brest and Toulon were sweeping up the Channel on their way to Boulogne, Napoleon did not wish to precipitate matters with Austria. If he could put off the breach long enough to allow him to cross the Channel, he expected to be able to dictate terms to a dismayed Europe from the conquered capital of George III.

---

[1] Owing to difficulties raised by Russia with regard to Malta and to the English Maritime Code, it was not till July 28th that this treaty was ratified. The delay thus caused and that due to the reluctance of Austria to commit herself to war as long as any prospect, however faint, of a peaceful settlement still remained, had no slight share in producing the disasters of the campaign.

CHAPTER XXV

ULM AND AUSTERLITZ

AUSTRIA did not embark on a fresh war without serious misgivings. There were not wanting prophets who declared that the time was not ripe, and that neither her political nor her military situation was favourable. Indeed as patriotic a German and as keen an enemy of Napoleon as Gentz despaired of success as long as the administration was in the hands of Cobenzl, Colloredo and their school.[1] The military preparations were in a backward state. In March a complete change had been made in the administration. Archduke Charles, who for some time had been losing his hold on his brother's confidence, had resigned the Presidency of the War Council to Latour, Schwarzenberg becoming Vice-President, and Mack replacing von Duca as Quartermaster-General. This was more than a change of persons, it implied the overthrow of the incompetent gang who had been misusing the Archduke's ill-bestowed favour to let the efficiency of the army decline. Mack, a soldier who had risen from the ranks, was well fitted for his new post. Energetic, painstaking, not without administrative capacity, he was " a good peace general " even if his performances in the field were destined to prove disastrous, and in a short time he did succeed in effecting great reforms. He managed to collect a really considerable force ; but the troops were for the most part raw, their equipment was far from complete, and the men were unknown to their officers. Moreover, the flagrant strategical errors of his plan of campaign more than neutralised his good services as an organiser, and the disturbance caused by his reforms had not had time to settle down. The machinery was put to the severest of tests before it could be properly adjusted to its work.

If there was any step which the Austrians, seeing how unprepared they were, ought to have avoided, it was risking

[1] Cf. Hauser, ii. 556.

a pitched battle with Napoleon before their Russian allies
could join them. Yet this was precisely what Mack did.
Though the first Russian troops did not cross the border of
Galicia till the middle of August, and could not possibly reach
the Inn until nearly the end of October, the Austrians actually
took the offensive, and advanced into Bavaria before the middle
of September. Not only this, but the army which made this
rash move was not the principal Austrian force. Only 90,000
men were allotted to the Danube, while 140,000 were to be
gathered on the Mincio and Adige for a campaign in Italy,
another 30,000 in Tyrol forming a connecting link. Moreover, Austria's foremost soldier, Archduke Charles, who with
all his defects was a man of tried capacity, received the command in Italy, that on the Danube being nominally entrusted
to Archduke Ferdinand, the son of the Grand Duke of
Salzburg, though his appointment left the real direction of
the army completely to Mack. Those who bethought them
of Mack's performances in the field in 1798 can hardly have
been filled with confidence.

It was not merely because the Russians could take no
part in it that the advance into Bavaria was so unwise. The
fate of Mack's army shows clearly how completely the framers
of the plan failed to appreciate either the strategical or the
political situation. By advancing to the Black Forest they
hoped to forestall Napoleon in gaining military possession
of South-Western Germany. But in thinking to surprise
Napoleon they lent themselves to being completely surprised.
They had quite overlooked the strategic possibilities of the
position of the Grand Army along the Channel and
in Hanover. They had not realised that the Grand
Army need not pass through Alsace on its way from
Boulogne to the Danube, that it might just as well direct
its march towards Frankfort and the Main as towards
the Upper Rhine and Strassburg, and that an army which
advanced to meet an anticipated French attack on the line
of the Black Forest would expose its Northern flank to
Bernadotte from Hanover and to Marmont from Holland.
Politically, their calculations were almost as much at fault.
They hoped that their forward movement would cause the
States of South-Western Germany to declare in their favour;
but Napoleon, foreseeing the certainty of war, had been before-

hand in securing the alliance of Bavaria, Würtemberg and Baden. Maximilian Joseph of Bavaria hesitated a little before accepting the proposals laid before him (March 1805), which took the shape of an offensive and defensive alliance between France and Bavaria to be cemented by the marriage of his eldest daughter to Napoleon's stepson Eugene. But jealousy and dread of Austria, and the knowledge that he must choose one side or the other, outweighed his wife's arguments in favour of the Austrian alliance, and caused him to come down on the same side of the fence as the stronger battalions. On August 24th he signed a provisional treaty with France. A fortnight later (Sept. 6th) he received an ultimatum from Austria requiring him to join his forces to hers or be treated as an enemy. Not without hesitation the Elector fled to Würzburg to seek the protection of the advancing French for himself and his army. On October 12th he confirmed the provisional treaty, though the French envoy Otto, in order to give colour to Napoleon's assertion that the Elector had been driven from his territories by a wanton act of aggression, and that the Emperor was merely coming to the assistance of an injured ally, deliberately altered the date of the draft from August 24th to September 23rd. Baden had shown much less hesitation. The Treaty of Ettlingen (Sept. 2nd) bound the Elector to supply a contingent of 3000 men to the French army. Frederick II of Würtemberg made rather more parade of needing compulsion. His connection with Russia and England on the whole inclined him to the Coalition, and the project he laid before Bavaria, Baden, Hesse-Darmstadt and Prussia for an armed neutrality which should exclude both belligerents from the territories of the contracting parties, probably does represent the policy he would have preferred. The failure of this project and the appearance of French troops at the gates of his capital removed his scruples; on October 8th he signed a treaty committing himself to the French alliance and promising the help of 10,000 troops. Of the four Powers whom Napoleon intended to unite in his projected Germanic Confederation, Hesse-Darmstadt alone stood neutral, looking to Berlin for a lead which that hesitating Court failed to give until Austerlitz had left her hardly any choice. The attitude of the Diet was even more pitiable. Occupied with appeals and verdicts arising out of the Recess of February 25th,

1803, with the case of the Knights whom Austria was prepared to abandon if her demand for the admission of enough new Catholic votes into the College of Princes to secure equality between the religions were admitted, the Diet was quite unprepared to cope with such an emergency as this, and when Napoleon claimed that he was acting as its champion and defending the right of the Princes, the Diet's silence could be represented as a tacit admission of his contention.

Thus the Austrian advance into Swabia not merely thrust the head of their army into the lion's jaws, not merely exposed Mack and his men to destruction long before their Russian allies could reach the Inn, also it drove Bavaria over to Napoleon's side. Moreover, Mack capped the original blunder of an advance with the additional error of choosing the line of the Iller rather than that of the Black Forest, the true position for an army seeking to carry out the task on which he believed his to be engaged of repelling an invasion coming from Alsace. So, too, he failed to use his numerous cavalry to gain and keep touch with the enemy. That his forces were unduly dispersed was only in keeping with his other errors. When the storm broke upon him on October 8th, he had men all along the Danube from Neuburg and Ingolstadt to the Iller and even farther Westward.

Meanwhile Napoleon was taking full advantage of the chance Mack's rashness had placed in his hands. Not till August 22nd, when the news reached him that Villeneuve, despairing of his task of raising the blockade of Brest, had turned Southward for Cadiz on August 15th, had the Emperor finally abandoned the idea of invading England and adopted the alternative of a blow at England's continental allies. That for some time past he had been contemplating such a change of plan is practically certain. He saw, none clearer, that the army at Boulogne might easily be diverted to the Danube, and he was ready for either effort. Had the longed-for opportunity of crippling the Coalition by a blow at its heart come to him, he would hardly have been deterred from taking it by the knowledge that 60,000 Austrians were moving slowly up the Danube and that by the end of October 40,000 Russians might be expected on the Inn; but the chance never came, and he turned to a hardly less dramatic if less decisive success. With the beginning of September the Grand Army started on its

famous march to the Danube. Its left, Bernadotte from
Hanover and Marmont from Holland, moved towards the
Main, Davoût's corps was directed on Spires, Soult's on
Mannheim, the Guards, Murat's cavalry, Lannes and Ney
made for Strassburg. Before the end of the month they were
crossing the river, after marches performed with wonderful
celerity and precision. Pushing on through Swabia, their
movements covered from the Austrians by their cavalry, the
French were on the Danube from Donauwörth to Ingolstadt
before Mack had discovered their object. Convinced that
their main attack would be delivered against the line of
the Iller, he had been completely taken in by such feints
as had been made in that direction. Bernadotte's presence
at Würzburg, where he joined the Elector of Bavaria on
September 27th, Mack dismissed as a mere feint to divert
his attention from the true attack; and not even when, on
October 8th, he heard that Murat had seized Donauwörth
and driven Kienmayer's division back upon München did he
realise his danger or take the prompt and decisive steps
which alone might have extricated his army from its imminent
peril.

At the moment when Murat and Soult secured the passage
at Donauwörth (a.m., Oct. 7th), the bulk of the Austrian forces
were on the Iller and at Ulm, only some 20,000 men lining
the Danube from Gunzburg to Ingolstadt. Thus the French
were able to sever Mack from his base with but little trouble.
Pushing out two corps only towards the Isar to thrust
Kienmayer Eastward and to keep the Russians in check should
they arrive in time to attempt a diversion, Napoleon directed
the rest of the Grand Army on Ulm, seeking to close every
possible avenue of escape. Soult after seizing Augsburg
(Oct. 9th) was pushed out to the Southward to secure the
road to Tyrol through Memmingen. Murat and Lannes,
supported by Marmont, took the direct road to Ulm up the
right bank of the Danube, meeting and defeating at Wertingen
an Austrian division which was making Eastward to recover
Donauwörth (Oct. 8th). Ney moved parallel along the left
bank to close the line of retreat which Kray had taken in
June 1800.[1]

Mack was thus in the toils; but had he adopted the

[1] Cf. p. 447.

Archduke Ferdinand's proposal, and at once endeavoured to cut his way out through Nördlingen across the communications of the Grand Army, he might have got away, more especially as, through some misunderstanding, Murat had brought two of Ney's three divisions over to the right bank (Oct. 10th). The third division, that of Dupont, was thus left isolated, and advancing alone on Ulm, was defeated and cut to pieces at Albeck (Oct. 11th). But Mack failed to avail himself of this chance of escape. Beguiled by a false rumour that Napoleon had been recalled to the Rhine by a rising at Paris, he stuck fast to Ulm, and only Werneck's division moved out on the 13th to the comparative safety of Heidenheim. Thus when, on the 14th, Riesch followed, it was too late. Ney by a brilliant stroke secured the bridge of Elchingen, planted his corps in the path of the Austrians, and thrust them back on Ulm. This success allowed the French to close the Northern road again; and with Soult at Memmingen, from which place he had driven Jellachich back into Tyrol (Oct. 13th), the Southern line also was blocked. Archduke Ferdinand with 1500 mounted men did manage to push through by Aalen and Ottingen to Nüremberg and so to Eger, but the rest of Mack's army were less fortunate. Ney's capture of the Michaelsberg, a strong position north of the town, made Ulm almost untenable, and Mack's brave words about dying in the last ditch came down on the 17th to a promise to capitulate if not relieved within a week, and on the 20th to an immediate surrender, which set the whole of the French army except Ney's corps free for further operations. Had he managed to delay Napoleon a week so as to give the Russians time to fall on the screen containing them, he would have done something to mitigate the disaster his rashness, his short-sightedness and his obstinacy had produced. Almost the only Austrian who comes creditably out of the affair is Werneck, who made a gallant but unsuccessful attempt at a diversion by falling on Ney's rear on the 14th, instead of getting away Northward. His mistimed loyalty involved him in the disaster, for Murat overtook him and forced him to surrender at Trochtelfingen (Oct. 16th), so that nothing was left of Mack's whole army but Kienmayer's division and the fugitives who had gained Bohemia with Archduke Ferdinand or Tyrol with Jellachich.

Napoleon was not the man to leave unimproved such a success as Ulm. The line of the Lech was made the French base for the next phase of the campaign, and within four days of the fall of Ulm the French columns were again on the move. Between Napoleon's victorious host and Vienna there were only some 35,000 Russians who had just reached the Inn, and about 20,000 Austrians, Kienmayer's division with various details. Such a force could not hope to stop Napoleon, and orders had to be sent to Archduke Charles to abandon the Italian campaign and return with all speed to save Vienna. Thus Napoleon was able to cross in succession the Southern tributaries of the Danube, beginning with the Inn (Oct. 28th). While his main body moved down the river, Ney's corps and the Bavarians were detached into Tyrol to obtain touch with Masséna's Army of Italy, which, despite a sharp check at Caldiero (Oct. 31st), was following the Austrians as they retreated. Had the Austrians known how to use them, there were in Tyrol the elements for an effective diversion. If the various corps, Hiller in South Tyrol, Jellachich in Vorarlberg, Archduke John in the valley of the Inn, had been properly combined and supported by the Tyrolese "insurrection," which would have given the Austrians 20,000 good shots and hardy mountaineers, an effective blow might have been struck at the French communications. But the opposite was done. There was no cohesion : Jellachich was cut off and taken (Nov. 13th), Archduke John evacuated Tyrol and, moving over the Brenner and down the Pusterthal, joined the Army of Italy in Carinthia, and the French were able to seize the Brenner and to get into touch with Masséna.

Meanwhile Kutusov had retired from one river to another, steadily refusing to fight, a policy much resented by his Austrian colleague Merveldt. The disagreement led to the Austrians taking a Southerly direction after leaving the Inn, with the idea of gaining touch with Archduke Charles. Altering his plan, however, Merveldt moved down the Enns to rejoin Kutusov at St. Pölten, only to encounter, at Steyer, Marmont on his way to Leoben (Nov. 8th), and a sharp fight resulted in the annihilation of the Austrians. This put out of Kutusov's head any idea he may have had of fighting a battle for Vienna. He was already feeling nervous for his communications with the second Russian army now on the frontier of Moravia, for

Napoleon had detached three divisions under Mortier to the left bank, and they were moving down the river. Kutusov therefore evacuated the strong St. Pölten position and fell back across the Danube at Mautern (p.m., Nov. 8th). This allowed Napoleon to push on past St. Pölten to Vienna, where there was only a weak garrison some 13,000 strong; but it gave Kutusov a chance of falling on Mortier's isolated force. As Mortier's divisions moved through the difficult defile of Dürrenstein one Russian division barred their path and another intercepted their retreat (Nov. 11th). Gazan's division was annihilated, and the whole corps nearly destroyed. Still sharp as was the check which Kutusov had the satisfaction of having inflicted on the French, it had little influence on the fortune of the campaign: nothing was done to follow it up, and meanwhile Napoleon had seized Vienna (Nov. 13th) and obtained possession of the great bridge over the Danube.

Kutusov and the garrison of Vienna now fell back Northward, Napoleon's effort to intercept the retreat of the Russians from Krems being foiled by Bagration at Hollabrünn (Nov. 16th), so that they made their way safely through Znaym to Brünn. The Russians were thus able to unite with their second army near Olmütz (Nov. 20th). Napoleon had pushed out as far as Brünn in the hopes of cutting them off; but finding his effort unsuccessful, he came to a halt. The truth of the matter was, that despite his success in seizing his enemy's capital his position was none too secure. The force which he had available—the Guards, Murat's cavalry, and the corps of Soult and Lannes—was not much more than 60,000 men, while the joint armies of Kutusov, Büxhowden and the Austrians were well over 80,000, and a force at least as large was threatening Vienna from the South. This was the united corps of the Archdukes Charles and John, now at Marburg on the Drave. Between these forces Napoleon had indeed the interior position, but his long line of communications had absorbed the greater portion of his force. Two corps (Ney and Augereau) were in Tyrol, one (Marmont) was in Styria, the greater part of another (Davoût) in and round Vienna, Mortier and the contingents of Baden and Würtemberg higher up the Danube, and the only troops within reach were Bernadotte's corps at Znaym on his left and one of Davoût's divisions a little way to the right rear. Had the Allies only refrained from risking all on an immediate action, had they even waited for the reinforcements Archduke Ferdinand was rallying in Bohemia and for those which were still on their way from Russia, the delay would have been all in their favour.

Moreover, there was another and a greater danger threatening Napoleon. On his march through Franconia, Bernadotte's corps had violated the neutrality of the Prussian province of Anspach. The infringement appears to have been deliberate. Had Bernadotte made a detour to avoid Anspach, his arrival on the Danube would have been delayed by at least a day, and Napoleon seems never to have imagined that Prussia's apparently inexhaustible capacity for submitting to insults would not be equal to this additional slight.[1] But it awoke in Frederick William and in Prussia an explosion of furious wrath, which was increased rather than assuaged by the off-hand manner in which Napoleon treated the matter as a mere bagatelle. Prussia began to arm. Hanover, evacuated by Bernadotte, was occupied by Prussian troops, and the resentment which had recently been excited by the Czar's efforts to coerce Prussia into joining the Coalition was now diverted against Napoleon. Alexander hastened to Berlin to arrange in person for the adhesion of Prussia to the Coalition; and though the first news which greeted him there was the tidings of the disaster at Ulm, his influence proved sufficient to keep Frederick William firm in his determination to join the Allies. The opposition of the Francophil party had been revived by the news from the Danube, but Frederick William felt that he had gone too far to recede, and on November 3rd he signed the Convention of Potsdam. By this Prussia was to offer Napoleon certain terms; and if within four weeks he had not accepted them was to join the Allies with 180,000 men.[2] These terms amounted to the independence of all Europe outside the "natural boundaries" of France. The King of Sardinia was to obtain Parma, Piacenza and Genoa in lieu of Piedmont; Austria was to have the Mincio as her boundary in Italy. The question which more than any other had contributed to keep Prussia from joining the Allies, that of Hanover, was relegated to a secret article. Alexander promised to use his good offices with England to obtain not only subsidies on the usual scale, but the cession of Hanover to Prussia. That Pitt should have absolutely refused to con-

[1] Cf. Haüsser, ii. 611.   [2] Cf. *The Third Coalition*, pp. 221 ff.

template the proposal was only natural; it was also one of the causes which made Frederick William finally draw back at the eleventh hour.

It is hardly necessary to suppose that Frederick William was guilty of bad faith in the extraordinary way in which he followed up this treaty. Though there was probably much truth in the Duke of Wellington's opinion, that "the Prussians fancied . . . they could fall upon the rear of Bonaparte in a moment, but I knew that the King of Prussia could not have his troops on the Danube under three months,"[1] this was hardly the King's opinion. Yet he selected Haugwitz as the bearer of this all-important ultimatum to Napoleon, though Haugwitz was the typical representative of the policy whose unwisdom Prussia was now learning. Moreover, Haugwitz delayed his departure till November 14th, and did not arrive at Brünn till November 28th, so that as Napoleon was to be given a month in which to give his answer, Prussia's intervention could not have taken place till practically two months after the Treaty of Potsdam. This need not be ascribed to treachery on Frederick William's part. He could hardly be expected to act with promptitude and decision even when the fate of Europe depended on his action.

Meanwhile the decisive battle had been fought. The heavy responsibility for fighting at Austerlitz must be laid at Alexander's door. The strategic situation made a premature decision the height of folly, for an English force under Lord Cathcart was landing in Hanover and was about to join hands with the Swedes from Pomerania and a Russian corps, another Anglo-Russian expedition was preparing a great diversion in Italy, Bennigsen's Russians were only a few marches away, and Napoleon could hardly have forced on the battle he so sorely needed if the Allies had adopted Fabian tactics. But the Czar was blind to all this. Supremely confident in Russian invincibility, anxious to prove that Napoleon's successes were due to his never having encountered Russia's bayonets, Alexander listened to the advice of his aide-de-camp, Peter Dolgorucki and of a few other hot-headed young men, and rejecting the sounder but less attractive proposals of the cautious Kutusov, determined to fight. He failed to see that any mishap to the Coalition would be sure to exercise an enormous influence over the

---

[1] Cf. Maxwell's *Wellington*, i. 75.

vacillating hesitation and cautious self-seeking of Prussia.
Moreover, Francis II was almost as anxious for battle as Alexander, though Schwarzenberg was against fighting. An effort
was made to induce Napoleon to come to terms, but he asked
too much, and the only result of the negotiations was to inflame
Dolgorucki's zeal for battle by convincing him that Napoleon
desired to avoid it.

On November 27th the Allies began their move on Brünn,
driving in the French outposts from Wischau (28th), and coming
up to Austerlitz by the evening of December 1st. Napoleon
had made great efforts to concentrate all available troops, and
was able to put nearly 70,000 men into the field against 80,000
Allies. His position behind the little Goldbach was at right
angles to the high road from Brünn to Austerlitz on which his
left rested. His right was covered by the marshy lakes of
Mennitz and Satschan, and found a source of strength in the
villages of Sokelnitz and Tellnitz. It was against this flank that
the Allies intended to direct their attack, hoping to drive in
Napoleon's right, and so sever his communications with Vienna.
Kienmayer's Austrians were to lead the way with three Russian
corps in support, some 35,000 men in all being detailed for this
move. In the centre stood the plateau and village of Pratzen.
Here under Kutusov's own direction Kollowrat's Russians and
a few Austrians formed a weak connecting link with Lichtenstein's cavalry, 18 Austrian and 30 Russian squadrons,
Bagration's Russian corps and the Russian Imperial Guard, who
formed the Allied right. Napoleon had realised the Allied
plan when he saw their masses concentrating on their left.
Entrusting to Davoût the task of holding the turning movement
in check, opposing Murat and Lannes to Bagration and Lichtenstein, he launched Soult with Oudinot in support against the
Southern part of the heights of Pratzen, Bernadotte moving
forward on his left against Brasowitz. Just as Kutusov at the
express orders of the Czar was moving to the support of the turning movement, Soult delivered his attack. Kutusov promptly
formed his men to their front to contest the possession of the
Pratzen plateau, and a division of Bernadotte's corps had to
come to the help of Soult. There was heavy fighting for a
couple of hours, a great cavalry contest between the cavalry of
the Russian Guard and those of Napoleon's Guard under Rapp
and Bessières, which ended in the success of the French, frequent

efforts on the part of the Russians to recover the plateau, determined opposition on the part of Soult and Bernadotte. At last success turned definitely to the French, the Russian centre was pierced, and the victorious French, turning to their right, fell in full force on the flank of the Allied left which had been unable to crush Davoût or do more than thrust him back. Caught between Davoût in their front and Soult on their flank, the Russians were driven in upon the Littawa, a stream which runs into the Goldbach below Tellnitz at an acute angle. A few got away across the bridge of Anjesd before it broke, some escaped by the strip of land between the two lakes of Mennitz and Satschan, some over the ice, but the slaughter was tremendous. The ice broke in many places; and though a few battalions sacrificed themselves to save the rest, the columns engaged in the turning movement were practically annihilated.

On the right the fight had been fairly even, inclining in favour of the French, for Lannes' infantry had beaten back the repeated charges of the Russian and Austrian horse; but there the Allies drew off in good order. Their losses had been enormous: 30,000 men and nearly 200 guns is probably no exaggerated figure. Their army, completely disorganised and demoralised by so overwhelming a disaster, withdrew in a South-Easterly direction, as though making for Hungary; but Austerlitz had banished all ideas of further resistance from the mind of Francis II. His willingness to treat for peace was perhaps a little premature. Had Prussia not entrusted her ultimatum to a man to whom the news of Austerlitz cannot have been exactly distasteful, had she intervened even at the eleventh hour, when the army of Archduke Charles was still intact and there was an excellent chance of raising North Germany round the nucleus formed by Cathcart's corps, even Austerlitz need not have been decisive. But Francis had had enough. Resolution was not his most salient characteristic, nor was he the man to make great sacrifices for an idea. He acquiesced in his defeat, and was ready to make peace on bad terms lest a prolongation of the struggle should bring even sterner conditions. On December 6th an armistice was signed between Napoleon and Francis, a contribution of 100,000,000 francs being imposed on the Hapsburg dominions, and the Russian army promptly departing for its own territories.

This meant the collapse of the Coalition. Austria's defection absolved Prussia from the obligations of November 3rd, while Haugwitz hastened to explain away the ultimatum, to congratulate Napoleon on his victory, and to sign, almost at a moment's notice, the Treaty of Schönbrunn, which placed Prussia at Napoleon's disposal (Dec. 15th). This abdication of the mediatory position she had assumed obtained for Prussia the coveted Hanover. In return she ceded Anspach to Bavaria, Neufchatel and Wesel to France, and Cleves to an unnamed Prince of the Empire. If she had made a treaty with France on these terms in July, her policy might have been open to criticism, but there would be less occasion to condemn her conduct. But to receive as a gift from the man against whom she had been fulminating a province belonging to a friendly Power from whom she was actually demanding subsidies that she might avenge—among other things—the wrongs committed by that same man in seizing this very province, such an action could not but destroy any shreds of reputation which yet lingered round the Prussian name. The possession of Hanover gave compactness to her territories in North Germany, it had been one of her principal desires for many years, but it was destined to prove a gain as temporary as it was discreditable. Haugwitz has a heavy burden of responsibility to bear. His slowness in travelling to the Danube, his utter incapacity to deal with Napoleon, his failure to even present his ultimatum, played into Napoleon's hands and contributed very largely to the humiliating situation in which Prussia found herself.

Meanwhile the Treaty of Schönbrunn had deprived the Austrian diplomatists, who were striving hard to obtain good terms from the conqueror, of their last ray of hope. On December 26th, Austria signed the Peace of Pressburg, by which she had to accept and acknowledge the constitutional and territorial changes made by Napoleon since the Peace of Lunéville, and to purchase peace by great cessions of territory. To the Kingdom of Italy she had to cede Venetia, Istria and Dalmatia. Baden and Würtemberg divided between them the Breisgau and the other Austrian possessions in Swabia. Brixen, Trent and the other gains of 1803 went now to Bavaria, and the bitterest blow of all was to be compelled to abandon Tyrol and its gallant mountaineers to the tender mercies of Maximilian Joseph. After this an indemnity of 40 million gulden was a minor aggravation.

Austria did obtain a little territory in return, Berchtesgaden and the Archbishopric of Salzburg, the Elector being compensated with Würzburg, which Bavaria resigned. However, her Imperial position in Germany received a *coup de grâce* in the celebrated fourteenth article of the Peace, which not only mediatised these Imperial Knights whose dominions were situated in the territories of Baden, Bavaria and Würtemberg, but declared that these three Powers should enjoy complete and undivided sovereignty over their states. This formal recognition of their practical independence was completed by the elevation of the Electors of Bavaria and Würtemberg to the rank of Kings, of the Elector of Baden and the Landgrave of Hesse-Darmstadt to that of Grand Dukes. The policy Rewbell had enunciated in 1797, when he declared " il faut reléguer l'Empereur dans ses états héréditaires et la dépouiller de tout la reste,"[1] seemed to have been carried to a successful conclusion. Indeed, Napoleon might justly claim to have realised the object of Richelieu and of Mazarin, to have effected what neither Francis I nor Louis XIV had been able to accomplish, the humiliation of the House of Hapsburg. Whether in imposing such harsh terms .on Austria Napoleon was not a little short-sighted may well be doubted. Austria, annoyed with Russian dilatoriness, angry with England's failure to lend more effective help, furious above all with Prussia's vacillation, might have been won over to Napoleon in 1805, and bound to him by a less galling chain than the alliance of 1811. Talleyrand, indeed, urged upon Napoleon the wisdom of a return to Choiseul's Franco-Austrian alliance, suggesting that by compensating Austria with the Danubian principalities, France might alienate her so completely from Russia that she would be bound to the French alliance.[2] Napoleon's rejection of this suggestion was probably due to his wish to induce Russia and Prussia to accede to the "Continental System," by which he hoped to cripple England completely by excluding her commerce from Europe. If he gave the Danubian principalities to Austria, he would create an insuperable breach between France and Russia. Hence he adopted a policy towards Austria which allowed her in 1809 to identify herself with the cause of German national resistance to his tyranny, which did much to unite the different

[1] Cf. Bailleu, *Preussen und Frankreich*.
[2] Cf. Haüsser, ii. 653, and Rose, ii. 47-48.

races which owned the Hapsburg rule by the bond of common sufferings, which probably went far to decide Austria's course at the crisis of the great struggle in 1813. Had Napoleon wanted to base his power over Europe on a sure foundation, he might have compensated Austria for her loss of influence in South-West Germany by undoing the work of 1741. A Franco-Austrian alliance founded on the restoration of Silesia to Austria need not have alienated Russia, and one may judge by 1806 of the scanty chance of success with which the successors of Frederick II would have resisted a revival of the alliance of fifty years earlier.

CHAPTER XXVI

THE CONFEDERATION OF THE RHINE AND THE OVERTHROW OF PRUSSIA

AUSTERLITZ had in all but in name destroyed the Holy Roman Empire; but as Napoleon had once said, "it was necessary to create something in its place," and it was on this task that he was occupied during the earlier part of the year 1806. That some reconstruction was impending was notorious. It was impossible for a constitution to continue in which the Diet stood mute while some of the Electors made war upon the Emperor. Projects for reform were put forward on all sides, and the wildest rumours were current throughout Germany. That that reconstruction would come from Paris was certain, and all eyes were directed thither. The French troops were still in occupation of Southern Germany; and even if the principal states had not already pledged themselves to Napoleon, his *fiat* could not have been resisted. Moreover, he was beginning that dynastic policy which, on the one hand, erected new principalities for his relations or imposed them on the thrones of older houses, and, on the other, bound the old dynasties to his by marriages. Thus, while a new Duchy was erected on the Rhine for Murat out of Berg (March), which Bavaria gave up, Eugene Beauharnais was married to the daughter of the King of Bavaria, and the Electoral Prince of Baden, to whom she had been betrothed, had to accept in her stead Eugene's cousin Stephanie.

Meanwhile the old game was being played at Paris. Intrigue and bribery were rife once more, only that "mediatisation" had replaced "compensation" as the convenient formula under which the plunder of the weaker by the stronger was being disguised. Scheme after scheme was drafted and placed before Napoleon before he could be satisfied. At last, early in July a plan was adopted, though its publication had to be deferred until the steps necessary to secure the military hold of France on Southern

Germany had been taken. On July 17th the treaty establishing a Confederation of the Rhine was laid before the envoys of the various German states then at Paris. It provided for the union of some sixteen states in a Confederation, under the protection of the Emperor of the French and quite independent of the Holy Roman Empire. The various members were to retain full sovereignty and independence in domestic affairs, while a Diet sitting at Frankfurt was to regulate their foreign affairs, to settle quarrels between members, and discuss matters of common interest. This Diet was to consist of two Colleges, that of Kings, which was to include the Arch Chancellor, the Kings of Bavaria and Würtemberg, and the Grand Dukes of Baden, Berg and Hesse-Darmstadt; and that of Princes, composed of the ten other members of the Confederation, the Princes of Nassau-Usingen, Nassau-Weilburg, Hohenzollern-Hechingen, Hohenzollern-Sigmaringen, Lichtenstein, Salm-Salm, Salm-Kyrburg, Isenburg, the Duke of Aremberg, and the Count de la Leyen. When the two Colleges sat together, the Arch Chancellor, henceforward to be called Prince Primate, was to preside. The dependence of the Confederation on Napoleon was secured by a proviso that the nomination of a successor to the Prince Primate should be entrusted to the Emperor. One article bound the members not to take service except in the Confederation or with its allies, another established a close alliance between the French Empire and the Confederation, which was pledged to take part in every war in which France chose to engage; while yet another fixed the contingents to be supplied by the members.[1] The Confederation was not much more than a military and political union, since the Diet was not empowered to interfere with the domestic affairs of the members, could not legislate, and was not really more than "a political congress in which equals with common interests discuss those interests amicably and agree upon measures for the common utility."[2]

The majority of the articles of the constituting document dealt with a matter of the very greatest interest to the German Princes, the territorial question. Briefly, an enormous simplification was to be effected in the map of Germany by the mediatisation of all the petty states which had the misfortune to find their

---

[1] France was to provide 200,000, Bavaria 30,000, Würtemberg 12,000, Baden 8000, Berg 5000, Darmstadt 4000, the College of Princes 4000.

[2] Cf. Fisher, p. 165.

territories enclosed in the dominions of their larger neighbours. At one stroke the four benches of Counts, the Grand Masters of the Maltese and Teutonic Orders, many princely families which had collective votes, and at least eight which held individual votes, among them Lobkowitz, Thurn und Taxis, Orange-Fulda and Dietrichstein, in all some sixty-seven immediate *Herr-schaften*, were reduced to the rank of subjects. With them the Imperial Knights lost their independent sovereignty, though all the Princes thus mediatised retained their patrimonial property and all non-sovereign rights, while in the matter of taxation they were to be placed on the same footing as members of reigning houses. The magnitude of the change can be best appreciated from the fact that the suppressed states amounted to over 12,000 square miles, and contained 1,200,000 inhabitants. It was a highly necessary change had it only been brought about in a different way. The statelets which thus disappeared were obstacles to good government and to material prosperity. They were the scenes of extravagant efforts to vie with larger Courts; their independent existence had made Germany a complex, involved tangle, in which national life was impossible; and if Napoleon was aiming at his own advantage in thus destroying the forms of a constitution which had kept Germany weak and disunited, if his work of destruction was only unintentionally the necessary preliminary to Bismarck's work of construction, and was only accidentally the means of his own undoing, he had at least cleared away the obsolete débris of the old organisation which had hitherto prevented the growth of a new and vigorous institution.

The members of the new Confederation did not all receive it with enthusiasm; even Dalberg, who had gone further than any man in his desire to see Napoleon's authority over Germany formally established, at first declared that he had not meant to abolish the Germanic Constitution;[1] but his qualms of conscience were shortlived. The ratifications were speedily exchanged, and on August 1st four Electors and twelve Princes announced to the Diet at Ratisbon that they had ceased to belong to the Holy Roman Empire. Had Stadion, now Foreign Minister of Austria in Cobenzl's place, had his way, there would have been no Holy Roman Empire for them to desert. He had urged Francis to abandon the title of his own initiative before he was

---

[1] Cf. Fisher, p. 121.

forced to do so. But Francis had been slow to act, and it was not till August 6th that his proclamation renouncing his title of Holy Roman Emperor elect, and formally declaring the links between himself and the Empire dissolved, brought to an end even the nominal existence of the great institution which Charlemagne had founded.[1]

This action on the part of Francis II amounted to a tacit acknowledgment of Napoleon's new creation. Austria would accept the accomplished fact: after all, her strength had not depended on her connection with the Empire, she was following a policy very much like that Pufendorf had suggested for her.[2] And where Austria acquiesced, it was hardly to be expected that the Power which had concluded the Treaty of Schönbrunn and had accepted its subsequent developments, would do otherwise.

Haugwitz's action in signing the Treaty of Schönbrunn had provoked an indignant outcry at Berlin, especially in the more bellicose circles. The Council of State, however, was not prepared to go to the length of disowning him even though it disliked the terms and wanted to get them modified. The Prussian Ministers wanted to get Hanover, but without committing themselves to hostility to George III. They still clung to the notion that they might mediate a peace between England and Napoleon, and obtain the coveted Electorate as the reward for their good offices. Thus, true to the Prussian tradition of sitting on the fence, they neither accepted nor rejected the treaty. They proposed to take Hanover and hold it on deposit until a general peace should settle all questions at issue in Europe; and accordingly on the departure (Feb.) of Cathcart's expeditionary force, Prussian troops at once reoccupied the Electorate without waiting for Napoleon to signify his assent. But it was a dangerous game to play with Napoleon. His answer was to occupy Anspach and Baireuth, and to point out to the Prussian envoy that as the treaty had not been ratified, Prussia was at war with France. This argument was the more cogent because in a fit of ill-advised economy Prussia had already begun to demobilise her troops. Meanwhile the Emperor, though offering Hanover to Prussia, was also intending to use it

---

[1] For the Confederation of the Rhine, cf. Haüsser, ii. pp. 691 ff. ; Zwiedineck-Südenhorst, *Deutsche Geschichte*, 1806–1871, vol. i. pp. 9–12 ; also Fisher, ch. v.

[2] Cf. p. 8.

in the negotiations with the Whig Ministry which had just come into power in England through Pitt's death (Jan. 23rd, 1806). Prussia thus found herself compelled by a threat of immediate war to sign a treaty pledging her to unqualified hostility against England.[1] This treaty, signed by the unfortunate Haugwitz on February 15th and ratified on March 3rd, gave Prussia Hanover, but at the price of barring the Elbe and Weser to British ships, of giving up Anspach to Bavaria without receiving any compensation and of consenting to the expulsion of the Bourbons from Naples. The extent of Prussia's submissiveness may be judged from the fact that French officers accompanied the Prussians to Hanover to see that the exclusion of the English was complete, that Hardenberg was practically dismissed, under the form of unlimited leave of absence, Haugwitz replacing him in charge of foreign affairs, and that Prussia was promptly involved in war with England, who replied to the exclusion of her goods by blockading the mouths of the Elbe and Weser (April 5th), seizing over 300 Prussian merchantmen, and declaring war on Prussia (April 20th). Napoleon had certainly been successful in sowing dissension between England and Prussia; for, as Fox's letter of April 16th to Talleyrand[2] shows, the action of Prussia in the matter was far more bitterly resented in England than was the part played by France; it was only to be expected that France—an open and avowed enemy—should seek to injure England by all the means in her power. Prussia, on the other hand, was at peace with England, and her conduct was "viewed with pain and disgust."

But if Prussia found herself in the somewhat humiliating position of one of the client states of the French Empire, this was little more than was to be expected from the thoroughly unsatisfactory condition of the country. The King, well-meaning but weak, a mediocrity himself and content with mediocrity in those around him, has been well described as "the most respectable but the most ordinary man that has reigned over Prussia.[3] He was quite incapable of carrying out the reforms that were so urgently needed by Prussia, and Lombard, Haugwitz and even Hardenberg all failed to rouse him to a more vigorous policy. The most capable man among the Prussian ministers

[1] Cf. Seeley, i. 239.
[2] Cf. Coquelle, *England and Napoleon*, p. 89.   [3] Seeley, i. 195.

was undoubtedly the Freiherr von Stein, an Imperial Knight who had entered the Prussian service in 1780, had done well in various administrative posts, notably in charge of the Prussian acquisitions in Westphalia, which had been entrusted to him in September 1802, while in 1804 he had been called to the Ministry of Manufactures and Commerce. Yet not even Stein could do much under the circumstances which prevailed. The chief object of his attacks was the so-called Cabinet, a body composed not of the heads of the various departments, but of the King's personal advisers, who without responsibility or practical connection with the details of administration really decided on the policy of the country.[1] Thus the ministers who carried out the details of the policy had little share in forming it, and the Cabinet intervened between them and the King. The system had grown up under Frederick William II, the Cabinet, originally established by his grandfather as a committee for foreign affairs,[2] superseding the old Ministry of State.

But this was not all. Society was in an unhealthy condition ; it had grown wealthy and luxurious, and with increased luxury it had lost the martial and Spartan tone given it by Frederick II. The Court was frivolous and foolish. An overbearing military set, domineering and bumptious, was living on the reputation of past victories it had not helped to win. It was this party which called insistently for war. Its better elements were summed up in the gallant but erratic Prince Louis Ferdinand, whose lack of self-restraint and steadiness impaired the example of his high courage and enthusiasm. Typical of its baser elements were the arrogant young nobles who boastfully sharpened their swords on the steps of the French Embassy before marching out to Jena.

The Prussian army, in which the whole country reposed a confidence as profound as it was soon to be proved baseless, was still in all essentials the army of Frederick II. It had failed to keep pace with recent changes. A fine army on the parade-ground, in the field it represented an obsolete tradition. When Napoleon's system of requisitions was making war support war, it still depended in a fertile country on magazines at fixed points. It had no co-ordinated divisions of all three arms. Its officers

---

[1] Cf. Seeley, i. pp. 267 ff.

[2] Hence the name " Cabinet Minister " often applied to the Foreign Minister.

were for the most part ignorant of their profession, and the veterans of Frederick's school knew only how to obey. The rank and file were drawn from the lowest classes. Both conscript and long service at once, since the numerous exemptions made twenty years the term of service, the army rested neither on the sound moral basis of universal compulsion nor on the hardly less sound foundation of voluntary patriotic efforts. It was not even national, for its ranks included a very large proportion of foreigners. These and other defects had not escaped the notice of many observers. Gebhard von Scharnhorst, a Saxon by birth who had learnt the military art under the Count of Lippe-Buckeburg,[1] and had served with distinction in the Hanoverian army before joining that of Prussia in 1801, had made some effort to introduce reforms; but the infallibility of the Frederician tradition was still sacrosanct. Nor was it even numerically in a satisfactory state. Nominally nearly 240,000 strong,[2] of whom 186,000 should have formed the field army, it was not able at the critical moment to put more than 120,000 in the field, Silesia and the new acquisitions in Poland and Westphalia absorbing large forces which were not even mobilised. And for economy's sake in each company of infantry some twenty-six men were allowed to be absent on furlough, and their efficiency was more than doubtful. Yet with this army Hohenlohe and Brunswick cheerfully committed themselves to an offensive campaign against Napoleon and the Grand Army.

At the price of a quarrel with England, Prussia had obtained Hanover. She also found herself involved in a conflict with Sweden for Pomerania, which Napoleon was prepared to let her take if she would cede Mark to the new Grand Duchy of Berg. But Prussia was very far from feeling satisfied with her position; she could not but realise that she held these new possessions by the good pleasure of Napoleon. Had he failed to grasp the meaning of her action in 1805? Prussia could not tell whether his professions of friendship were sincere, and she looked with a distrustful and suspicious glance upon the formation of the Confederation of the Rhine. Napoleon cast out suggestions for the foundation of a North German Confederation with Prussia as head; he even hinted at an Imperial crown for the Hohenzollern. But, strangely enough, the other

[1] Cf. p. 371.
[2] 255 squadrons, 546 batteries, 174 field and 58 garrison battalions.

Powers of North Germany did not accept the idea with enthusiasm: it made them eye Prussia rather suspiciously, which was perhaps what Napoleon intended. But the truth would seem to be that the Emperor was not paying much heed to Prussia during the early months of 1806; the organisation of the Confederation of the Rhine and negotiations with England and Russia were more than sufficient to occupy his attention.[1] There are no grounds for supposing that his policy was deliberately designed to drive Prussia into war. For the moment it was the question of Naples and Sicily which was uppermost in his mind.[2] Stuart's brilliant success over Reynier at Maida (July 4th, 1806) had imperilled the stability of Joseph Bonaparte's new kingdom of Naples, and it was in the hopes of inducing the British to evacuate Sicily that Napoleon took the step which finally goaded the supine Frederick William to take up arms. Not the least important effect of the failure of the great expedition to the Weser on which Pitt had founded such high hopes, and which Austria's defeat and Prussia's submission had made vain and hopeless, was that it had served as a final blow to the most persistent of Napoleon's opponents. Pitt's death (Jan. 23rd, 1806) opened the way to office to the Whig politician whose partiality for France had outlived even the establishment of a military despotism on the ruins of Liberty, Fraternity and Equality, and in the negotiations which Fox had promptly (Feb. 20th) set on foot in the hopes of restoring peace, Napoleon found Hanover a very useful asset. On August 6th the King of Prussia received a letter from Lucchesini, his Ambassador at Paris, informing him that Napoleon had offered to restore Hanover to George III if the British would withdraw from Sicily and agree to the compensation of the Neapolitan Bourbons with the Balearic Islands.

Such an insult was more than even Frederick William could endure. Public opinion in Prussia found vent in the most violent expressions of feeling. There was a loud cry for the dismissal of Haugwitz, but Frederick William would not comply with it; and this unfortunate loyalty to the man who was identified with the Treaty of Schönbrunn prevented England and Russia from reposing full confidence in Prussia's desire for war, contributed very largely to keep Austria neutral, and was hardly calculated to inspire in the nation at large a strong belief

[1] Cf. Seeley, i. 244.   [2] Cf. Rose, ii. pp. 79 ff.

in the King's zeal for the cause. The Queen, Prince Louis Ferdinand, Generals Rüchel and Phull, Hardenberg, Stein and other leaders of the patriotic party did what they could to arouse national feeling, and Napoleon materially assisted to fan the flame of hostility to France by his execution of the Nüremberg bookseller Palm (Aug. 25th). A pamphlet, entitled, "Germany in her deep Humiliation," had been published at Vienna. It was a protest against the brutal conduct of the French army of occupation in the "allied" kingdom of Bavaria, where their exactions rivalled the days of the Thirty Years' War. Palm, who was proved to have sold çopies of this publication, was arrested, carried off to Braunau, an Austrian town occupied by French troops, tried by court-martial and shot. This brutal act was intended to terrorise Germany. Its effect was quite the reverse. It excited violent indignation, and made Frederick William for the moment the spokesman of German national feeling, when he demanded that Napoleon should withdraw his armies behind the Rhine.

During this period negotiations had been going on between Napoleon and the Czar. In July, Napoleon had induced the Russian envoy Oubril to sign a treaty, but the Czar's refusal to ratify it had left the two Powers still at war. Hence in challenging Napoleon, Prussia could hope for Russian support; but no steps had been taken to concert a plan of common operations, and the fatuous strategy of the Prussians exposed them to a disaster even more complete than Mack's. Inferior in numbers though they were to the 190,000 men whom Napoleon rapidly concentrated in Northern Bavaria, the Prussians resolved to advance across Thuringia upon Mayence, thinking to fall on Napoleon's communications, and so force him to evacuate Southern Germany to recover the line of the Rhine. It is needless to point out how this exposed their own interior flank to a crushing blow which completely intercepted their retreat to Berlin.

This advance would have been justifiable in one event only, if all North Germany had risen on behalf of the cause. But North Germany did not rise. William VIII of Hesse-Cassel, Elector since 1803, viewed with alarm the aggrandisement of Napoleon, but nevertheless all efforts to induce him to join Prussia failed. However his conduct during the critical period was somewhat ambiguous, and his

failure to demobilise his army or to exclude the Prussians from
his nominally neutral territory brought down on him the wrath
of Napoleon. Brunswick, of course, took part with Prussia,
since its Duke was in command of the Prussian army; but a
more important if less willing ally was found in Saxony. The
Elector Augustus Frederick was a pacific but rather feeble
Prince. Since 1796 he had maintained a consistent neutrality,
fear of Prussia and dislike of France alternately ruling him.
His action in joining Prussia in 1806 was to be ascribed more
to the pressure put on him by the near presence of the Prussian
army than to any keenness in the cause. He had to choose
between joining Prussia and fighting her; and as at the moment
no French were at hand to help him, he had no alternative but
to join Prussia.

With the addition of the 20,000 men of whom the Saxon
army consisted, Brunswick and his colleague Hohenlohe could
dispose of about 140,000 troops. Concentrated behind the
Elbe or even between the Saale and Elster near Jena and Gera,
this force might have effected something; but the impatience
of the army to show the victors of Marengo and Austerlitz that
the successors of Frederick II were prepared to keep up the
traditions of Rossbach had a good deal to do with the decision
to advance beyond this good defensive position. Moreover,
it was hoped by taking the offensive and covering the territories
of Hesse-Cassel to induce the Elector to throw in his lot with
Prussia. But Hohenlohe and Brunswick could not even agree
on a plan. Brunswick, wishing to threaten Mayence, wanted
to feint at Fulda with his extreme right, but to move his main
body forward on Hildburghausen and Meiningen, Hohenlohe
with his corps moving parallel on the left by Saalfeld.
Hohenlohe would have preferred a move against the French
centre and right, but his plan would have equally committed
the Prussians to an advance with the army in two parts,
separated by the Thuringian Forest. The net result was that
October 4th found the Prussians scattered over a front of 85
miles, when news of Napoleon's advance forced them to suspend their westward move. Rüchel with 25 squadrons and 12
battalions was far forward on the way to the Rhine; Brunswick
with the 90 squadrons and 60 battalions of the main army,
70,000 strong, was between Gotha and Erfurt; Hohenlohe's
corps lay in the valley of the Upper Saale, its advance-guard

506 GERMANY IN THE EIGHTEENTH CENTURY [1806

at Saalfeld, the Saxons near Gera, the bulk of the corps on the left of the Ilm, near Hochdorf.

Against a force thus divided and leaders without a real plan, Napoleon was on the point of dealing a tremendous blow. He had his whole army so admirably concentrated on a front of 38 miles that the whole force could be collected at any point under 48 hours. Three roads led Northward from the points at which he had concentrated his army for an advance. Soult (IVth corps) and Ney (VIth), forming the right, took the road by Baireuth on Hof; Bernadotte (Ist), Davoût (IIIrd), the Guards and Murat's cavalry that in the centre on Saalburg by Bamberg and Kronach ; on the left, Lannes (Vth) and Augereau (VIIth) moved through Coburg on Saalfeld. The rapidity and certainty of the French moves contrasted sharply with the somewhat aimless operations of the Prussians. Napoleon had seen the weak spot in their armour, and his blow at their communications brought them hurrying back to avoid being cut off from the Elbe. But Napoleon was much too quick for them. On October 9th, Murat and Bernadotte drove Tauentzien with Hohenlohe's vanguard out of Schleiz, Soult reached Hof, Lannes on the left getting to Grafenthal. On the 10th, Prince Louis Ferdinand, making a stand at Rudolstadt to cover Hohenlohe's return to the Saale, was defeated by Lannes. He himself fell in the action, but Hohenlohe managed to concentrate the Saxons, Tauentzien and his own main body near Jena. The bulk of Napoleon's army was now over the Thuringian Forest, the centre having pushed on as far as Auma, while on the right Soult had reached Plauen. Advancing to Gera next day and meeting with no opposition Napoleon realised that he had got between the Prussians and the Elbe: he therefore thrust his centre forward to Naumburg, which Davoût secured on the morning of the 12th, while he called in the right by the cross-road from Plauen to Gera. On the same day, the 12th, Lannes moved down the left bank of the Saale on Jena, where Hohenlohe was standing inactive and wasting precious time. Had he pushed forward against the French he might have caught them more or less dispersed, but he stood still with the idea of covering the main body under Brunswick, who were moving by Weimar on Auerstadt and Naumburg. This inactivity on his part continued next day. Not an effort did he make to dispute the all-important position of the Landgrafenberg, which Lannes secured and with it the passage of the Saale at Jena. Meanwhile Napoleon was concentrating the corps of Soult, Ney and Augereau at Jena, Davoût was moving forward from Naumburg to seize the defile of Kosen, Bernadotte was making for Dornberg to secure that passage and to connect up Napoleon with Davoût, who from being the centre had become the extreme right of the French. Brunswick also was moving on Kosen; but the division detailed to secure that point failed to achieve its purpose. Rüchel following in rear of Brunswick reached Weimar.

Thus the French on the East of the Saale threatened to interpose between the Prussians and their base, and were prepared to dispute any attempt by Brunswick to recover his line of communications. Had the Prussian commander known their situation, which he does not seem to have done, he might have retreated straight to Magdeburg and there crossed the Elbe; but such a move would have left Berlin and Dresden equally open to Napoleon's attacks.

Of the twin battles of October 14th, that of Jena was no disgrace to the Prussian army, for Hohenlohe's 50,000 men made a very gallant resistance to the 90,000 whom Napoleon brought against them. Their commander was not a little to blame for his failure to drive Lannes off the Landgrafenberg on the previous afternoon; for if, instead of having their leading corps already in position on the Eastern edge of the plateau which commands the passage of the Saale, the French had had to force their way up its steep slopes, the issue of the day might have been very different. But Hohenlohe, intending to retreat as soon as he had covered Brunswick's march from a flank attack, had remained inactive, and the French by great exertions had succeeded in bringing guns and reinforcements up the precipitous path from the valley below. Early on the 14th Lannes opened the battle by falling on Hohenlohe's vanguard at Closwitz. There was sharp fighting in the fog but by 10 a.m. Lannes had secured the line from Lutzeroda to Closwitz, and had gained sufficient room for the other corps to deploy into line as they came up on to the plateau. Soult's leading division had already pushed up the Rauthal, but was closely engaged with a Prussian detachment from Rödingen; while Augereau, taking the line of the Muhlthal and Schneckethal, was in action with the Saxons who formed Hohenlohe's right: Ney, following Lannes, thrust his leading division forward between those of Lannes, and the French front line now advanced against the Vierzehn Heiligen-Isserstadt position just as Hohenlohe delivered a counter-attack. This was about 11 a.m., and for a couple of hours the battle was evenly contested, till two more of Soult's divisions coming up advanced on the right of Gazan's division of Lannes and began to press back the Prussian left. At the same time another of Ney's divisions reinforced the centre, and the Guards moved forward against Vierzehn Heiligen. In vain Hohenlohe hurled his cavalry in fruitless charges against the advancing French; attacking without proper combination, making spasmodic and not united efforts, even their furious on-slaughts could not stem the advance, while the Prussian infantry, already shaken by the fire of the French artillery, gave way as the French advanced. It was at this moment that Rüchel's battalions came up from Weimar. The wisest course would have been to employ them to cover the retreat, but Hohenlohe, not content with this, made a counter-attack on Ney's leading division, a rash and ill-advised stroke which involved Rüchel in the general disaster. Beaten all along the line, Hohenlohe's army fell back in disorder on Weimar, pursued by Murat's cavalry, which had just arrived on the scene. Still though beaten the Prussians had fought well. The precision and accuracy of their manœuvres had excited the admiration of their enemy, even if their lines had smacked too much of the parade-ground and had proved no match for the heavy columns, preceded by dense clouds of skirmishers, in which the French attacked. Hohenlohe rather than his army had been principally at fault; his failure to fall on Lannes on the 13th had allowed the French to gain access to the Landgrafenberg on the 14th, the men had fought well against superior numbers, and but for the tame surrenders and the complete military collapse to which Jena was the prelude, the Prussian army would have no cause to be ashamed of their performance there.

Meanwhile a fight of a very different nature had been raging a few miles to the Northward. About 8 a.m. Brunswick's vanguard under Schmettau came into contact with Davoût's leading division near Hassenhausen. Brunswick hurried to the front to try to secure the hills on his right and to sweep Davoût from his path, while Blücher's cavalry assailed the French on the other wing. But Davoût's infantry stood firm, and beat off

AUSTERLITZ Dec 3rd 1805.

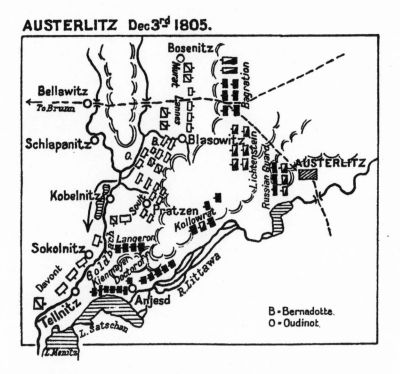

Bosenitz

Bellawitz

← To Brunn

Schlapanitz

Kobelnitz

Sokolnitz

Davout

Tellnitz

L. Satschan

L. Menitz

Murat

Lannes

Blasowitz

Pratzen

Kollowrat

Langeron

Kienmayer

Doctoroff

Anjesd

Soult

Goldbach

Bagration

Lichtenstein

Russian Guard

AUSTERLITZ

R.Littawa

B = Bernadotte.
O = Oudinot.

JENA. Oct. 14th 1806

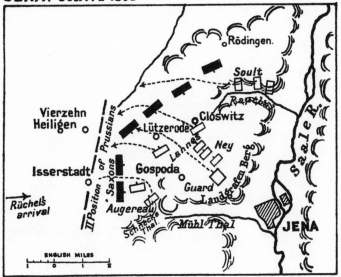

Rödingen.

Soult

Vierzehn
Heiligen

Isserstadt

Rüchel's
arrival

I Position of Prussians

II Position of Saxons

Closwitz

Lützerode

Lannes

Ney

Gospoda

Guard

Augereau

Schlecke
Thal

Mühl-Thal

Landgrafen Berg

Saale R.

JENA

ENGLISH MILES
1   0   1   2

B.V. Darbishire, Oxford, 1906.

all Blücher's attacks. Brunswick brought up reinforcements to renew the effort, but fell mortally wounded; and his fall spread confusion through the Prussian ranks. This gave time for the second division of Davoût's corps, that of Friant, to come up and to take up its position on the right of its hard-pressed comrades of Gudin's division. Again and again the Prussians attacked, but their superior numbers failed to shake Davoût. There was a want of co-ordination about the Prussian efforts, since there was no commander-in-chief; and when about noon, when Morand brought up the third division and began to extend to the Southward of Hassenhausen, Davoût actually ventured a counter-attack, though altogether he had only 27,000 to at least 40,000 Prussians. Outflanked by the cavalry of Vialannes, the Prussian left fell back in confusion; and the right followed its example, though in much better order, both taking the road to Weimar, a direction which before long brought them into contact with the fugitives of Hohenlohe's army fleeing from Murat. On that Brunswick's corps also went to pieces. All cohesion was lost, and the energetic pursuit of the French cavalry completed what the battle had begun. Möllendorf with 10,000 men surrendered at Weimar on the 15th; 16,000 under Kalkreuth laid down their arms at Erfurt next day. Eugene of Würtemberg, standing at bay at Halle to let the rest of the army cross the Elbe, was cut to pieces by Bernadotte (Oct 17th). And while the relics of the Prussian armies were being thrust North and West in utter demoralisation, making for Magdeburg, Napoleon had secured a shorter route to the Prussian capital, and Davoût's corps had secured the passage of the Elbe at Wittenberg and was marching upon Berlin with all speed (Oct. 20th).

But Jena and Auerstadt were as nothing to the disgraces which were in store for the Prussian army. Fortress after fortress, well supplied, strongly garrisoned and capable of a good defence, surrendered tamely on the first summons without firing a shot. Had strong places like Spandau, Cüstrin and Magdeburg made as good a defence as did Blücher at Lübeck, to which distant spot the old veteran managed to draw two French corps in pursuit of the 20,000 men he had rallied, the French might have been detained till the Russians could reach the Oder. Their feeble surrender is almost without a parallel in history.

Hohenlohe had by October 20th collected about 45,000 men

510 GERMANY IN THE EIGHTEENTH CENTURY [1806

at Magdeburg, but they were completely demoralised. The administration had broken down, the men were without pay and without food, their organisation and discipline had gone to pieces. Accordingly the news that Soult, Ney, Bernadotte and Murat were within a day's march of Magdeburg drove Hohenlohe from the town. Leaving over 20,000 men behind him, he started for Stettin through Rathenow and Ruppin; but before he could reach the Oder he was headed off by Murat and Lannes, who on October 28th barred his path at Prenzlau, not 30 miles from Stettin. With 10,000 dispirited and broken men he surrendered. Spandau (Oct 25th) had already opened its gates; Davoût occupied Berlin on the 25th, Napoleon arriving there next day; Stettin surrendered upon a mere summons by Lasalle's light cavalry on the 29th; and though Blücher, who was following Hohenlohe with 20,000 men, managed to make his way to Lübeck, he was forced to lay down his arms to Soult and Bernadotte on November 7th. A day later Magdeburg, a fortress which should have been capable of a longer defence, capitulated to Ney. For once in a way a bulletin of Napoleon's was in prosaic agreement with the facts when on November 12th he announced "the whole of the Prussian monarchy is in my power." But for the garrisons in Silesia, Eastern Pomerania and the Polish provinces, the famous Prussian army had been swept out of existence, while Prussia's one ally in Northern Germany had been detached from her cause by Napoleon's adroit courtesy to his Saxon prisoners. Well aware of the dilemma with which the Prussian ultimatum had confronted Frederick Augustus, Napoleon saw that in the Court of Dresden he might find a useful ally. On October 21st he announced that there would be no more hostilities against the Saxons; and though the Electorate and the Saxon Duchies were taken in charge by French officials and remained in French occupation till the end of the war, being subjected to the payment of an indemnity of 25 million francs and to equally heavy contributions in kind, Napoleon had little difficulty in separating Saxony from Prussia and securing her adherence to the Confederation of the Rhine. This body had already (Sept.) been enlarged by the adhesion of the Elector of Würzburg; it now had not only the Elector of Saxony added to its numbers with the title of King (Dec. 11th), but the five Dukes of the Ernestine line followed his example (Dec. 15th). Contingents amounting in all to over 25,000[1] were thus placed at Napoleon's disposal, while the deposition of the Elector of Hesse (Nov. 4th), of the House of Brunswick—the old Duke died of his wounds shortly after Auerstadt and was succeeded by his son Frederick William, who fell at Quatre Bras nine years later—and of William Frederick of Orange, who thus lost the Principality of Fulda-Corvey he had received in 1803, placed much territory in North-Western Germany at Napoleon's disposal.

From the point of view of German history the subsequent events of the campaign of 1806–1807 are of less importance than the effects of the collapse of Jena, Auerstadt, Prenzlau and Magdeburg on the government of Prussia. A Prussian corps played an honourable part in a campaign fought out in territory German by rule if Polish by geography, but its part was little more than that of the auxiliary of the Russians ; and when the defeat of Friedland decided the Czar to come to terms with Napoleon, Prussia had to acquiesce in the terms which her Eastern neighbour was prepared to accept for her. The first effect of the defeats was a change in the Prussian ministry. Haugwitz retired to ponder at leisure on the fruits of the Treaty of Schönbrunn. His post as Foreign Minister was offered to Stein (Nov. 29th), with which an intricate negotiation began. Stein and his friends sought to use the opportunity to induce the King to abandon his Cabinet[2] in favour of a Council composed of the responsible Ministers. The King went so far in the direction of compliance that he agreed to appoint Rüchel War Minister, von Zastrow Foreign Minister, and Stein Finance Minister ; but he desired to retain Beyme as Secretary of this new Cabinet Council, and on this rock the negotiations foundered. Stein would not tolerate Beyme ; the King refused to dispense with him. Finally, on January 3rd Stein was dismissed. On his refusal to take office, von Zastrow, Voss and Schrötter formed a ministry, Beyme acting as Secretary and Hardenberg attending its meetings. Mainly through the influence of the Czar, who preferred Hardenberg to Zastrow, the former became First Cabinet Minister in April 1807, while in addition to the control over foreign affairs, domestic affairs were also entrusted to his charge, so that he was practically Premier.[3]

---

[1] Würzburg 2000, King of Saxony 20,000, Saxon Dukes 3300.   [2] Cf. p. 501.
[3] Cf. Seeley, i. 291, 339, etc. ; also Zwiedineck-Südenhorst, i. p. 59.

The substitution for Haugwitz of members of the party which favoured opposition to Napoleon had done something to restore public confidence, which was also encouraged by the rejection of Napoleon's offer of an armistice. It would have bound Prussia but not him, and the terms which he offered Prussia were too humiliating. Frederick William, therefore, rather than purchase peace at the price of surrendering his provinces West of the Elbe and joining Napoleon in a close alliance against Russia, resolved to continue the struggle as best he might, with the resources of his Eastern provinces and relying on Russian support.

CHAPTER XXVII

FRIEDLAND, TILSIT AND ERFURT

THE utter failure of the Prussian fortresses to detain the French after Jena made it quite impossible for Frederick William to attempt to maintain the line of the Oder. With barely 20,000 men, all whom Kalckreuth and Lestocq had managed to collect from the Eastern provinces, he fell back across Poland towards his Russian allies; and Napoleon, pushing Eastward with the bulk of the Grand Army, found himself on the Vistula before the end of November. On the 30th, Murat secured Warsaw, the Russians under Bennigsen retiring up the Narew, while Lestocq's Prussians on the right evacuated Thorn, which Ney occupied. The first half of December saw the French establish themselves on the Vistula, one corps under Jerome moving up the Oder into Silesia to reduce that province, another under Mortier remaining in Mecklenburg and Pomerania to secure the coast fortresses. During this period reinforcements joined Bennigsen and emboldened him to advance from Ostrolenka to Pultusk, pushing Lestocq forward to regain Thorn. Napoleon determined to fall upon him, and about December 20th he set his army in motion. On the right Davoût and Lannes advanced against Bennigsen's position at the confluence of the Narew and Bug; in the centre Soult and Augereau, with Bernadotte in support, moved on Buxhowden's corps, which was along the Ukra; on the left Ney tackled Lestocq. Between December 22nd and 26th there was some heavy fighting. Napoleon's effort to surround the enemy resulted in his thrusting out his wings too far apart; and when Lannes tried to intercept at Pultusk the retreat of the Russian centre from Golymin (Dec. 26th), Bennigsen thrust him aside, and Galitzin, though roughly handled by Davoût and Augereau at Golymin, managed to get away. With the retreat of the Russians towards the Niemen, operations came to a standstill. The Grand Army wanted rest, and the state of the country was such as to make operations imprac-.

ticable. The Polish mud had baffled Napoleon's well-laid plans.

About a month later, operations were resumed. Bennigsen made an advance against the corps on the French left which were covering the siege of Dantzic. This was being carried on by Lefebvre with the contingents of the Confederation and the Poles, who had flocked to Napoleon's standard in the hopes that he would undo the work of 1772 and 1795. One of the covering corps, Ney's, had just anticipated the Russian advance by a dash at Königsberg. However, Lestocq had repulsed it at Bartenstein (Jan. 20th to 23rd), and if Bennigsen had moved with greater speed Ney might have been cut off. As it was, the Russian advance miscarried. Bernadotte checked it in front along the Passarge, while Napoleon swung up his centre and right to the help of the left. The French corps were posted from Ostrolenka on the Narew by Neidenberg to Osterode, and their Northward movement threatened Bennigsen's interior flank. Only by a prompt retreat could he save his communications from being severed. Murat, pressing forward, managed to bring the Russian rearguard to action at Hof on February 6th, upon which Bennigsen turned to bay at Eylau. Two days of desperate and even fighting and terrible slaughter ended with the arrival of Lestocq's Prussians just in time to paralyse Davoût's turning movement against the Russian left, whereby the unmolested retreat of the Russians to Königsberg was secured. Napoleon, left in possession of the field, had to content himself with making the most he could on paper out of this Pyrrhic victory. His position was none too satisfactory. The numbers of the Grand Army had been reduced by nearly a half by losses in battle and by disease. Its discipline had become relaxed; the difficulties of making war support war in a country as poor, as thinly peopled, and as roadless as Poland were enormous and taxed to the utmost the powers of the Emperor. He had to put forth all his great powers of organisation to restore the Grand Army to an efficient condition, to collect adequate reserves and make ready for a fresh advance; and meanwhile he had to continue the sieges of Dantzic, of Colberg, so bravely defended by Gneisenau, and of the Silesian fortresses.

This juncture was Austria's opportunity. If Francis II had thrown his sword into the scale in April 1807, his intervention might have been decisive.   But even in 1809 Austria was hardly ready, and in 1807 the reforms of Archduke Charles had had no time to bear fruit, so that his voice was strong for the maintenance of peace, while even Stadion shrank from the prospect of war.   What had alarmed Austria and threatened to rally her to the Allies was Napoleon's encouragement of the aspirations of the Poles ; but Napoleon hastened to assure Francis that he would do nothing to cause trouble in Austrian Poland, and with this assurance Francis was unwisely content.

Thus during the critical spring months of 1807, Austria adhered to the same line of action which had ruined Prussia in 1805.   There was another Power whose conduct was scarcely less short-sighted.   England did indeed join the alliance which Russia and Prussia reaffirmed at Bartenstein (April 26th), but too late (June 27th) to make her share in the league of any practical value.   When 40,000 or even 25,000 men flung ashore in Hanover or Pomerania in rear of the Grand Army might have been of the greatest service, for Hesse and Hanover were ripe for revolt,[1] and Stralsund in Swedish Pomerania would have formed an effective base for an attack on Mortier's corps, the " Ministry of All the Talents " had confined itself to empty promises of aid.   Much might have been done to succour Dantzic and Colberg and enable them to prolong their defence, but no effective steps were taken.   With the advent of the Portland Ministry to power (April), Canning assumed charge of the Foreign Office, Castlereagh of the administration of the Army, and a better era seemed to have dawned ; but before this more vigorous ministry could give effect to its policy of sending active help to our allies, the Third Coalition had received its death-blow.

Bennigsen would have been well advised had he adhered to his original plan of campaign for 1807 and stood on the defensive behind the Pregel until reinforcements could join him from the interior of Russia, until England and Sweden might make an effective diversion in Pomerania, or Austria be induced to join the Allies.   But Bennigsen was a strange mixture of vigour and indecision.   He was tempted by the exposed position of Ney's corps at Gutstadt on the Alle to try again the stroke that had failed in January.   But it was really too late.   Neisse had fallen, and of all the Silesian fortresses only Kosel and Glatz were

---

[1] *Castlereagh Correspondence*, vi. pp. 169, 211, etc.

holding out. Dantzic's brave defence had come to an end on May 26th, which had set the French left free to advance. Nevertheless, Bennigsen took the offensive. Ney retired before him; higher up the Passarge, Soult and Bernadotte held their ground, and the Emperor set all his forces in motion to utilise the chance Bennigsen's rash move had given him, Hastily the Russian general fell back along the right bank of the Alle, the French pushing forward along the opposite bank in hopes of cutting off his retreat to Königsberg. At Heilsberg (June 10th), Soult and Murat brought him to action; but so savage a stand did the Russians make that only the arrival of Lannes prevented the battle from ending in a French defeat. From Heilsberg, Bennigsen continued his march along the right bank of the Alle, which here makes a great bend to the East and North, so that the French, moving across the chord while he followed the arc, were able to outstrip him. On the 13th he crossed to the left bank only to find his way barred by the corps of Lannes. Friedland was a battle Bennigsen should never have fought. It would have been wiser to have fallen back behind the Pregel and united there with Lestocq's corps, which had been moving parallel with the Russians but nearer the sea. Better even to have abandoned Königsberg than to have given Napoleon the opportunity to dictate terms at Tilsit as the result of his victory at Friedland. For Friedland removed from Alexander's mind the last inclination to continue resisting. Dislike for England, which had done so little for her allies and yet enforced against them a most stringent maritime code,[1] admiration for Napoleon, and a real hatred of war, all went for much with him. The party at the Russian Court which had all along favoured peace, Czartoriski, the Grand Duke Constantine, Kurakin and others, was now in the ascendant. A week after the battle the armistice of Tilsit was concluded. Four days later (June 25th), Napoleon and Alexander had their famous interview, and on July 9th the Peace of Tilsit restored peace to the Continent and placed North Germany at the mercy of Napoleon. The Czar did indeed insist on certain concessions in favour of his unfortunate ally, but the peace which Prussia had no option but to accept reduced the kingdom of the Hohenzollerns to half its former dimensions. Not only were the acquisitions of 1803 lost, but also everything else West of the Elbe, including

[1] Cf. Rose, ii. 127.

East Frisia which went to Holland, all that was left of Prussia's share in the Cleves-Jülich inheritance, all the gains made at the Peace of Westphalia and at the Peace of Utrecht. Not even the interposition of Queen Louise could induce the conqueror to leave Magdeburg to his victim. Moreover, the shares of Poland acquired in 1793 and 1795 were transformed into a new state, the Duchy of Warsaw. Dantzic became independent; but as it was occupied by a French garrison, it was really a French city. To sow dissension between Russia and Prussia a so-called " rectification of frontiers " gave the Prussian district of Bialystock to the Czar, while Saxony was also made an accessory to the partition of Prussia by receiving Cottbus. One Power alone Napoleon forgot to conciliate: he consented to restore Silesia to Frederick William when he might have won Austria's gratitude by handing it over to her. Prussia was thus reduced to the lands between the Elbe and the Oder with Eastern Pomerania, East and West Prussia, and Silesia, about 62,000 square miles, with rather under five million inhabitants. Her losses were the more serious because the lands West of the Elbe were richer and more productive than those she retained. It was some advantage that the kingdom in its reduced form was at least geographically united: there were no outlying detached provinces, hard to defend, even harder to unite with the central mass.

But territorial loss was by no means the only humiliation inflicted on Prussia. Napoleon had never imposed a peace on a conquered enemy which did not reimburse him for the expenses of the conquest, and Prussia was not to escape the common lot. Moreover, while the Convention of July 12th made the evacuation of Prussia by the French troops depend on the payment of an indemnity, it somewhat strangely failed to fix the amount to be paid. Of this omission the usual explanation is negligence on the part of Kalckreuth, the Prussian negotiator; but it is at least probable that he was tricked into it by Napoleon's orders, for nothing could have suited the Emperor better. While the debt remained unpaid, Prussia was absolutely at his mercy and could not even enjoy such shreds of independence and initiative as Alexander's good offices had seemed to have secured her. That it was such a hold over Prussia which Napoleon wanted even more than the money, was seen when at last, in September 1808, he finally fixed the indemnity. The sum which he named, 154,000,000 francs, was altogether beyond what Prussia with her diminished resources could hope to pay for a long time, and she seemed to have before her a prospect of many years of dependence. What that would mean might be judged from the dismissal of Hardenberg and Rüchel at the bidding of Napoleon, and by the enforced adhesion of Prussia to Napoleon's great scheme for the ruin of England. In common with the rest of Germany, Prussia had to close her ports to British ships and to fulfil punctually the requirements of the Berlin and Milan Decrees. But there was a touch of irony in the fact that among the men whom Napoleon nominated to fill the vacant offices, Zastrow, Schulenburg and Stein, there should have been one who was destined to prove a far more dangerous foe to the Napoleonic régime than ever Hardenberg had been.

The arrangements made at Tilsit embraced a good deal more than the terms on which Napoleon was prepared to permit Prussia to continue a maimed existence. In the alliance between France and Russia which was there concluded, Napoleon took care that the balance of advantage should be on his side; that while he avoided pledging himself to do anything for the Czar, Russia was committed to the Continental System and to making the rest of Europe fall into line with Napoleon's anti-British crusade. Russia had also to accept the alterations which Napoleon was making in Northern Germany. The principal change which the Emperor proposed was the erection of a new kingdom out of the territory which his despoiling of Prussia and his deposition of the rulers of Brunswick, Hesse-Cassel and Orange-Nassau had placed at his disposal. This Kingdom of Westphalia, the largest and the most important of the new states created by Napoleon in Germany, was formed out of the Prussian provinces West of the Elbe, the Duchy of Brunswick-Wolfenbüttel, the Electorate of Hesse-Cassel together with Corvey and Osnabrück, the Southern portions of Hanover,[1] and smaller districts taken from Saxony. From an area of rather over 15,000 square miles and a population of about a couple of million, it supplied a contingent of 25,000 men to the Confederation of the Rhine. Following the example he had set with the Grand Duchy of Berg, Napoleon bestowed this new creation not on any of the existing dynasties of Germany, but on one of his own relations, his youngest brother, the clever but idle and self-indulgent Jerome.

[1] *i.e.* Grübenhagen and Göttingen.

Next in size and importance to Westphalia came Berg. Originally formed for Murat in March 1806 out of Berg, which Bavaria ceded in exchange for Anspach, and the portions of Cleves on the right bank of the Rhine, Prussia being compensated with Hanover, it was largely increased after Tilsit at the expense of Prussia, receiving Mark, Tecklenberg, Lingen and the Prussian share of Münster, though Murat had to let the important fortress of Wesel be incorporated in the French department on the opposite bank of the Rhine.   At its greatest extent it amounted to nearly 9000 square miles and contained 1,200,000 inhabitants, its contingent to the Confederation's army, originally 5000 men, being increased to 7000 on the addition of Münster and Mark.

These creations disposed of the bulk of the North German lands in the occupation of Napoleon.   They had on coming into his hands been divided into seven military governments (Oct. to Nov. 1806), and Fulda, Erfurt and the coast districts of Hanover remained in this condition for varying periods after the other governments had been incorporated in the more highly organised states of Westphalia and Berg.   In these military governments the old local organisation and customs remained more or less unchanged; but a superstructure of French rule was imposed upon them, the general in command being assisted by an inspector and a receiver to control the finances of the district, and to drain it dry in the attempt to meet Napoleon's insatiable requirements.[1]   Fulda after some two years of French rule was given to Dalberg (Feb. 1810) in exchange for Ratisbon. Hanover itself and the greater part of the Principality of Lüneburg were added to Westphalia in January 1810, but the remaining portions of the Electorate[2] were incorporated in the four new departments which Napoleon added to France in December 1810.   These were formed out of the Duchies of Oldenburg and Aremberg, of the Hanseatic towns, of the Principality of Salm and the Northern portions of Westphalia[3] and of Berg.[4]   His object in making this arrangement was to bring the North Sea coastline under his own immediate rule for the better enforcement of the Continental System, which even his own brothers could not

---

[1] Cf. Fisher, pp. 154 ff.

[2] The old bishoprics of Bremen and Verden, the County of Hoya and Saxe-Lauenberg.

[3] The Department of the Weser.   [4] The Department of the Ems.

be trusted to carry out as he desired. To these districts, whether as military governments or in their later state of French departments, Napoleon gave strong government, a modern code of law, the benefits of the social changes of the Revolution; but the oppression of his tax-gatherers, the hardships entailed by the Continental System, and the demands of the conscription more than sufficed to crush out any gratitude these reforms may have earned him.

Meanwhile a large number of the minor Princes of Germany had averted mediatisation by a timely adhesion to the Confederation of the Rhine. In April 1807 the three branches of the ducal House of Anhalt, the four Princes of Reuss, the two of Schwarzburg, the two of Lippe, and the Prince of Waldeck had become members of Napoleon's new creation. In 1808 it was further increased by Mecklenburg-Strelitz (Feb.), Mecklenburg-Schwerin (March), and Oldenburg (Oct). This completed the reconstitution of Germany. The Imperial cities of Frankfurt and Nüremberg shared the fate of the less distinguished members of their order. They were mediatised, Frankfurt being given to Dalberg, Nüremberg to Bavaria. Thus with the exception of Prussia, Swedish Pomerania [1] and the German dominions of the Hapsburgs, all Germany was either annexed to France or united to her through adhesion to the Confederation of the Rhine. Napoleon, the "protector" of the Confederation, was the real master of Germany. So secure, indeed, did he feel of his position in Central Europe that he turned all his attention to the prosecution of his anti-English designs; to compelling Sweden and Portugal to close their markets to English goods, to which course Austria was forced to pledge herself by the Convention of February 28th, 1808. It was largely with a view to furthering his chances in the great contest with England by strengthening his hold on the Mediterranean, that he embarked on that Spanish venture which was to prove so important a factor in bringing about his overthrow. The events of July and August 1808 did not merely throw into confusion Napoleon's great

---

[1] This province had been invaded by the French in the course of 1807, and by September Gustavus IV had been compelled to evacuate Stralsund and Rügen; but though occupied by the French it was ultimately restored to Sweden in January 1810, when Charles XIII, the successor of Gustavus, came to terms with Napoleon and adhered to the Continental System.

schemes for the partition of Turkey and the subjugation of England by an overland attack on India, they were the first checks which Napoleon's domination over Europe had received, the first intimation to the people who were beginning to feel and to resent the heaviness of his rule, to the nations he had conquered and humiliated, that his power was not invincible. Austria, arming herself for the attempt to undo the work of Austerlitz and Pressburg, was inspired with fresh resolution and hope by the news of Baylen and Vimiero. Germany saw the spectacle of a nation hardly less split up than herself by local and provincial jealousies and differences, animated nevertheless by a common spirit of resistance to the same Power which had dictated terms to the Hapsburg and the Hohenzollern, and which numbered the Wettin and the Wittelsbach among its dependent allies. The example of Spain might prove contagious. Napoleon could not commit himself to the subjugation of the Iberian Peninsula as long as there was a danger that Austria might seize the opportunity of his absence on the Ebro to renew the struggle in the Danube valley. But since the Spaniards had dared to resist his selection of a monarch for their benefit, subdue them Napoleon must, even if he must first secure Germany by a new arrangement with Russia in which the conditions would not be so much in his favour as they had been at Tilsit. Negotiations had been going on all the year between the signatories of the Peace of Tilsit, but no definite settlement had yet been reached. The two sovereigns therefore agreed to meet at Erfurt in September to settle their future relations.

Among other causes of friction between Alexander and Napoleon must be mentioned the treatment Napoleon had meted out to Prussia. Alexander, though beguiled with the prospect of a great expedition to the East, with the idea of acquiring the Danubian Principalities, and by the notion of accomplishing the overthrow of England, was aggrieved by the manner in which Napoleon was grinding down his former ally Prussia, for whom he believed himself to have secured good treatment at Tilsit. He felt his honour to some extent implicated.

Napoleon's treatment of Prussia had been anything but gentle. After naming 112,000,000 francs as the amount of the indemnity (March 1808), he raised it to 154,000,000 on

account of some hostile expressions in an intercepted letter
of Stein's, though even the first sum would have been more
than sufficient to keep Prussia in the position of a debtor for
many years to come, and therefore to postpone indefinitely his
evacuation of the principal Prussian fortresses which he held
as security for payment. All attempts to get him to modify
these terms had failed; Prince William's mission to Paris
(Jan. 1808) was as unsuccessful as Queen Louise's pleading
for Magdeburg. Stein therefore, finding that the indemnity
must be paid, devoted himself to the task of raising the money.
Taxation was greatly increased, notably by introducing an
income-tax after the English model, 70 millions were raised
by mortgages on the Royal domains, over 50 more by bills
which bankers were induced to accept. One proposal which
all Prussians joined in disliking, was that Prussia should
surrender Royal domains to the value of 50 millions; but this
provision Stein had succeeded in evading when he induced
Daru, Napoleon's financial representative at Berlin, to sign
a convention (March 9th, 1808) by which the French agreed
to receive pledges as a guarantee for the payment of some
50 millions.[1] Napoleon, however, gave no orders for the
departure of the French troops until Baylen and Vimiero
created a demand for their presence elsewhere.[2] Negotiations were then begun which resulted in the Convention of
September 8th, 1808, by which the French evacuated all
Prussia except the fortresses of Cüstrin, Glogau and Stettin,
which were to be held as security for the payment of the
arrears of the indemnity. Heavy as this price was, an even
greater humiliation was in store for Prussia. The Convention

[1] Haüsser, ii. 138.

[2] It may be worth mentioning that besides the French troops whom Napoleon
withdrew from Germany to the Peninsula, he called upon his German clients to
provide troops for that service. One division of infantry was required from the
Confederation of the Rhine, Baden, Hesse-Darmstadt and Nassau each supplying
two battalions and Frankfort one. Westphalia was called upon to provide a
separate contingent of an infantry brigade and a regiment of light cavalry. Moreover, there were in the Peninsula several of the German corps already in Napoleon's
service: he had, for example, raised a Hanoverian Legion in 1803 which formed
part of the army which invaded Portugal under Junot: most of the men of this
corps took service with the English after the capitulation of Cintra. Another corps
had been raised out of the Prussian prisoners in 1806, so that with the King's German
Legion in the British service, Germany was well represented in the Peninsula. Cf.
Oman's *History of the Peninsular War*, especially the appendices; Balagny, *Napoléon
en Espagne*, and *Les Allemands sous les Aigles Françaises*.

fixed the establishment of her army at 42,000, and forbade the organisation of a Militia, or of anything in the shape of a *levée en masse*.[1]

At the end of the month which saw these galling restrictions imposed upon Prussia, occurred the famous conference at Erfurt (Sept. 27th to Oct. 13th). It was a brilliant gathering. Most of the Kings and Princes who formed the Confederation of the Rhine were gathered to grace their "protector's" triumph. The presence of Goethe and his interview with Napoleon, from whom he accepted the Cross of the Legion of Honour on the anniversary of the battle of Jena, have added a peculiar interest. Goethe was the literary representative of the cosmopolitanism and lack of patriotism which had enabled Napoleon to attain to his predominant position; the coming literary movement was to be typified by men such as Fichte and Arndt, leaders of one side of that national movement in which the reaction against the triumph of Erfurt culminated.

But the triumph of Erfurt was of a delusive character. Napoleon was not in a position to dictate to Alexander, and he could not succeed in inducing Alexander to assist him in compelling Austria to disarm and to recognise Joseph Bonaparte as King of Spain. Alexander was not prepared to complete the destruction of a Power which he might find useful in the future, though he declared himself ready to assist Napoleon should Austria take the offensive. But this was only purchased by Napoleon's grudging consent to the acquisition by Russia of the Danubian principalities. That Napoleon was not altogether satisfied with his ally was evident from his refusal to make the concessions to Prussia which Alexander asked of him: he absolutely refused to evacuate the fortresses on the Oder, and only consented to reduce the indemnity by 20,000,000 francs. Indeed, in the negotiations of Erfurt more than one hint was given of the coming rupture between France and Russia. The Convention merely reasserted their hostility to England, it accentuated rather than removed the causes of discord. "Napoleon," it has been well said, "used the great pageant of Erfurt to extricate himself from a dangerous position. In the event of a rupture with Austria . . . at least the neutrality of Russia was indispensable." This he had secured,

[1] Cf. Oncken, *Allgemeine Geschichte*, part iv. vol. i. pp. 407–408; also Häusser, ii. pp. 185–190.

at the price of giving Russia a free hand against the Danubian principalities, a concession he made with some reluctance. Moreover, he did not completely relax his hold on Prussia, and to that he owed in no small measure his success in weathering the storms which were to beset him in 1809.

CHAPTER XXVIII

AUSTRIA'S EFFORT TO OVERTHROW NAPOLEON

IF in his dealings with Germany Napoleon reached a pinnacle of power far beyond that to which Louis XIV ever attained, it must nevertheless be admitted that the Bourbon shows to greater advantage in his dealings with Germany than does the Corsican. Bent on a purely personal aggrandisement, consistent with neither the interests, the welfare, nor the ambitions of his French subjects, Napoleon had since 1805 been striving to establish on the twin pillars of military force and centralised autocratic government an entirely new order of things, violating nationality and geography alike. Where Louis XIV had sought to profit by the decay of the old constitution of Germany rather than to destroy it and impose a new one in its stead, where he had aimed at influencing rather than commanding, where he had left the task of keeping Germany disunited to the jealousies of the individual states, Napoleon's reforms had removed many obstacles to the union of Germany, while his oppressions and his aggressions had supplied a motive power to the tendencies towards unity. The example of national resistance given by Spain, the chance afforded to England to intervene on the Continent with effect, the specimen of his conduct presented at Bayonne, were useful lessons to the German Powers. It was obvious that no confidence could be placed upon Napoleon's promises, that no amount of subservience would make a dependent state secure even of its existence if it should suit him to decide otherwise.

But while even the states on which Napoleon had conferred benefits were liable to have their constitutions or territories changed at any moment by the caprice of their "protector," there was one state which had special reason to view with alarm and distrust the spectacle of his aggressions on Spain and Portugal, of his interference in the affairs of the Balkans, of his occupation of the Papal States, and of the harsh measure he meted out to Prussia. Napoleon had beaten Austria in 1805, and he had treated her in a way she could not forgive. Since then he had forced the Continental System on her, and had demanded a recognition of Joseph Bonaparte as King of Spain; but at the same time he had not left her so utterly crushed that she could not hope to rise again. And ever since the Treaty of Pressburg great efforts had been made in Austria to prepare for an appeal against the verdict of 1805 by a renewal of the struggle against Napoleon.[1]

In few countries had a few years produced a greater change than in Austria. Under the vigorous and enlightened leadership of Count Stadion a new spirit was spreading through the Hapsburg dominions. An Imperial Knight by origin, Stadion, after leaving the Austrian diplomatic service in 1793 for a post under the Bishop of Würzburg, had returned to the Austrian service in 1801, had acted as Ambassador at Berlin for two years,[2] at St. Petersburg for two more, and had been called to the Ministry of Foreign Affairs in 1806. Keen and energetic as he was, his want of administrative training and of acquaintance with the internal affairs of Austria to some extent neutralised his good work in arousing a national feeling of hostility to Napoleon. He did indeed succeed in making the war thoroughly popular: the troops fought in 1809 with a keenness and a tenacity which had been lacking in 1805, and the Hungarian Diet of 1808 displayed a rather unexpected bellicose feeling. It voted new levies for the line regiments, agreed to the formation of a Reserve, and placed in the Emperor's hands the right to summon an "insurrection" without the leave of the Diet at any period in the next six years.

Stadion was warmly seconded in his efforts by Archduke Charles. From the misfortunes of 1805 his reputation had emerged unscathed, and his appointment as Commander-in-Chief (Feb. 10th, 1806) gave him, as he was also President of the War Council and Minister of War, a splendid opportunity for carrying out the reforms which he knew to be essential to the efficiency of the Austrian army. Incompetent and indolent officers were dismissed, encouragement was given to those who really desired to study their profession. The treatment and terms of service of the rank and file were improved, the drill was revised, and no effort was spared to make the Austrian troops capable of coping

[1] Cf. Lanfrey's *Napoleon*, iv. pp. 480–482.　　[2] Cf. p. 457.

with the French. Most important was the Imperial Patent of June 9th, 1808, which created a *Landwehr*, composed of all men between nineteen and forty years of age. Still, though much had been effected, much more remained to be done. The Staff was inadequate, the artillery and engineers weak, the transport and commissariat departments deficient, while the higher ranks of the army were to prove singularly barren of men capable of commanding even a corps. The worst deficiencies lay in the finances and civil administration,[1] but the tremendous expenses of an armed peace made either war or disarmament imperative ; and Stadion, though himself free from the bad traditions of the repressive and illiberal system of Thugut and Cobenzl, had not the power or the influence to remodel the old Austrian administration and infuse it with his own patriotic enthusiasm.

The efforts which Austria was making to rebuild her military power had not escaped the notice of Napoleon. As has been already described,[2] one of the objects of the interview of Erfurt had been to induce the Czar to join him in requiring Austria to disarm. But Alexander had been too wary to aid Napoleon by destroying a Power which might some day be a useful ally for Russia, and he had refused to do more than promise his help if Austria should attack Napoleon.[3] Meanwhile Austria had steadily continued her preparations, much hampered and delayed by her financial embarrassments. It was mainly these embarrassments which had made it impossible for Austria to seize what was in some ways a more favourable moment for a rising than that which she actually took, the moment when Baylen, Cintra and the retreat of Joseph to the Ebro made it imperative that Napoleon should forthwith proceed to Spain. At that time North Germany seemed ripe for revolt, and even Napoleon would have found it hard to direct a war on the Danube at the same time that he was conducting his great movements for the re-conquest of Spain. That this occasion could not be used, had been partly due to the action, or rather the inaction, of Prussia, still more to the attitude of Alexander: to lay the blame on Austria [4] is most unfair.

The bellicose party at Vienna had hoped not only for a rising in North-West Germany, for Hessians, Hanoverians and

---

[1] Cf. *Deutsche Geschichte*, 1806–1871, i. p. 137.   [2] Cf. p. 523.
[3] Cf. Rose, ii. 179–182.
[4] Cf. *Deutsche Geschichte*, 1806–1871, i. 135.

Brunswickers were all showing symptoms of restiveness, but also for the assistance of Prussia where a strong party favoured war. About the most anxious to make common cause with Austria against Napoleon's yoke had been Stein: in the autumn of 1808, when a rupture between France and Austria seemed imminent, he had thrown all his influence into the scale on the side of an insurrection. To conciliate the Poles he would even have given up all claim on Prussia's lost Polish provinces. However, Austria had been hardly ready for an immediate breach, and when Hardenberg despaired of the chances of a rising it was hardly wonderful that Frederick William had turned a deaf ear to Stein's advice. The King's own leanings were as usual against desperate measures. As always, he distrusted Austria; and thus, when Alexander on his way to Erfurt had visited Frederick William at Königsberg and sought to dissuade him from joining Austria, the Czar had found his cause half gained already, and Austria, with no hope of Prussia's help and with Russia pledged to keep the peace of Central Europe, had been forced to wait. Thus Napoleon had time to overthrow the Spaniards on the Ebro, to reinstate Joseph at Madrid, and to return to Paris before Austria moved.

In the meantime Stein had fallen. Frederick William's rejection of his proposals made his fall inevitable. Napoleon had already declared against him by publishing in the *Moniteur* of Sept. 8th an intercepted letter in which Stein's hostility to the Emperor was openly expressed, but in deference to Alexander he did not at once press for dismissal. However, Frederick William, having decided against an insurrection, soon made up his mind to part with Stein. On November 24th the Minister was dismissed, Dohna becoming Minister of the Interior, Golz Foreign Minister, von Altenstein Minister of Finance. Almost the only opponent of Napoleon left in office in Prussia at the end of 1808 was Scharnhorst, who was at the head of the War Office.

But though the most favourable moment for a breach with Napoleon had passed, she had gone too far to draw back, and even though Archduke Charles at the Conference of Feb. 8th, 1809, gave his vote against war the majority decided to take the risks. Archduke John was as keen on war as his brother was against it. Stadion urged strongly that the favourable opportunity should not be allowed to slip: he hoped

for much from a rising in North Germany, which could hardly
be expected unless the Austrians took the offensive. Metternich,
too, pointed out that if Austria did not anticipate Napoleon
she would merely be leaving him to choose the favourable
moment for his attack; he had no illusions as to Austria's
attitude and would not fail to attack her when it suited him;
Austria must either strike at once or submit.

For the campaign the Austrian army was organised in eleven
corps in all, amounting to 240,000 men, with the *Landwehr* and
the Hungarian "insurrection," forces which may be estimated
at 100,000 more, behind the first line. Two corps, nearly 50,000
men, were told off as the Army of Inner Austria or of Italy under
Archduke John. Another of 30,000 was allotted to Galicia
to keep the Grand Duchy of Warsaw in check, the rest were
given to Archduke Charles for the campaign on the Danube.

By the spring of 1809 the French troops in Germany
had been considerably reduced, so that Davoût was only able
to concentrate a field force of some 54,000 men at Würzburg.
To reinforce him, four divisions on their way to Spain were
diverted to the Iller; to which river the contingents of Baden
and Hesse were also directed, those of Bavaria and Würtemberg
being ordered to collect on the Danube between Ratisbon and
Ulm. These forces mustered in all some 120,000 men, behind
which large reserves were rapidly prepared. Expecting the
Austrians to take the offensive, Napoleon first ordered Berthier
to concentrate the army behind the Lech, with the right under
Masséna at Augsburg, the centre at Donauwörth, and the left
at Ratisbon, but with detachments stretching as far as Ingolstadt.
Then, as the Austrian advance was somewhat delayed, he altered
his plan. Ratisbon was to be the principal point of concentration, only a small force assembling at Augsburg. Berthier,
however, so far confused the plans that by the 16th of April
Davoût and the left were at or near Ratisbon, seventy-six
miles from Augsburg where the corps of Masséna and Oudinot
were concentrating. Communication between these two
wings depended on the Bavarians under Lefebvre, who had been
thrust back from the Isar by the Austrian advance and were
retiring towards the Danube between Kelheim and Neustadt,
where they expected the support of Vandamme's Würtembergers. The position was one of considerable peril had the
Archduke risen to the opportunity.

The original Austrian plan of campaign had been that the main body should advance from Bohemia to the Main, catching Davoût in flank as it moved, and driving him behind the Rhine, while two corps were to co-operate in Bavaria and South Germany. By operating in force on the Main it was hoped to cover the expected insurrection of North Germany. This plan had its defects; but what was essential was sufficient rapidity in its execution to profit by the dispersion of the French forces. Nothing could have been more fatal than the belated change of plan, which wasted ten invaluable days, threw the commissariat arrangements into disorder, and allowed the French to continue their concentration unimpeded. The new scheme threw the main body of the Army of the Danube upon Bavaria. Six corps were to advance up the right bank, push the Bavarians from the Isar, and then turning North to catch Davoût at Ratisbon between themselves and Bellegarde, who with the two remaining corps was to descend upon the Upper Palatinate from Bohemia. It was in some ways a better plan, as it did not expose the main body to being cut off from Vienna by a rapid advance of Napoleon down the Danube to gain the interior flank of the Austrian army on the Main; but its advantages did not in the least compensate for the invaluable time wasted over the transfer of the Archduke's main body from Pilsen in Bohemia, where it had concentrated, through Linz to the Inn.

Not till April 10th did the Austrians get started on this new advance, and the slowness of their movements wasted even more time. It took them eight days to get from the Inn to the Isar, bad weather, bad roads and bad commissariat arrangements delaying them. After a stout resistance the Bavarians were driven in on Neustadt and Kelheim; but the delays allowed Davoût to concentrate 40,000 men at Ratisbon by April 19th, though, had he made due haste, Bellegarde might have seized that town on the 14th, on which day only one of Davoût's divisions would have been there. Moreover, Napoleon had time to arrive at Dillingen. He promptly remedied Berthier's error by calling Davoût up from Ratisbon to Ingolstadt by Neustadt, and pushing Masséna and Oudinot up from the Lech to Pfaffenhofen. The move was not without danger, for it took Davoût across the front of the enemy, but it restored touch between the dangerously separated French wings.

The Archduke's failure to pierce the enemy's centre by crushing Lefebvre's Bavarians on the Isar had greatly diminished the chances of an Austrian success. His next move was scarcely less unfortunate. Had he even now fallen with his whole force on Lefebvre, he might have cut off Davoût from the Emperor, and been able to concentrate upon the French left when thus isolated. If Lefebvre and Vandamme had been so badly handled as to be even temporarily *hors de combat*, Davoût would have been in great peril, for Masséna and Oudinot were still too far away to help him. But the Archduke moved North with his right and centre upon Ratisbon (April 19th). As this exposed his communications, he had to leave the two corps which formed his left, those of Hiller and Archduke Louis, on the Abens river to cover the operation. Nor was this move well managed. Had his force been properly concentrated he might have checked Davoût's move up stream to join Lefebvre. As it was, Hohenzollern's isolated corps (the left centre) met Davoût near Dinzling, and lost 5000 men in an attempt, unsuccessful because unsupported, to prevent him forcing his way past. Meanwhile by nightfall Masséna had come up to Pfaffenhofen, so that on the morning of the 20th Napoleon was able to hurl Lefebvre, Vandamme and a new corps under Lannes on the Austrian containing force along the Abens, while Davoût stood firm on his left near Dinzling and Masséna and Oudinot pushed forward against Landshut. The result of a day's heavy fighting all along the Abens was that the Austrian left wing, outnumbered and outflanked, had to fall back to the Isar, every step it took removing it farther from the Archduke's main body, which had wasted the day in the comparatively useless capture of Ratisbon. The campaign might yet have been retrieved had the Archduke fallen on Davoût on the 21st while Napoleon was pursuing Hiller and Archduke Louis from Landshut to Neumarkt; but this last chance went the way of the others, and Napoleon did not give him any more. Realising that the Austrian main body was not in front of him, but must be near Ratisbon, Napoleon left the pursuit of Hiller to Bessières, and wheeling 80 battalions and 80 squadrons round to the left moved Northward. The Archduke now moving South with the idea of threatening the French communications, met him next day (April 22nd) just South of Ratisbon along the line Abbach - Eckmühl. The brunt of

Napoleon's attack fell on the corps of Rosenberg, which formed the Austrian left. It held on to Eckmühl most gallantly; but the Archduke failed to support it, though nearer to the Danube his right was hardly engaged at all. After three hours Rosenberg was forced back to Eggloffsheim, and the Austrians were in no small danger of being driven pell-mell into the river. But Napoleon for once paid more attention to the fatigue of his men than to the utilisation of his victory, and his failure to press on allowed the Archduke's army to escape to the North bank (April 23rd), to unite with Bellegarde, and to retire safely along that side of the Danube. Hiller meanwhile had turned on his pursuers at Eggenfelden (April 24th), beaten them and opened himself a road to Dingolfing and Deggendorf; but the Archduke's defeat at Eckmühl made it impossible to reunite so far up the Danube, and Hiller had therefore to make for Linz. Taking the Burghausen road in preference to the better road by Schärding, he could not avoid being overtaken; and though his rearguard did stand at Ebelsberg (May 3rd) and sacrifice itself to let him escape, he only managed to bring 16,000 men across the river at Mautern (May 8th).

Thus the campaign in Bavaria which had promised so well ended in disaster. It was not the rank and file of the Austrian army who had been at fault. They had fought far better than their predecessors in 1805, and had suffered heavier losses before giving way. The failure to obtain that initial success which alone could have roused North Germany and induced Prussia to reconsider her policy was partly due to the shortcomings of the Austrian military administration, but mainly to the errors of Archduke Charles. His initial mistake in changing the whole plan had caused much delay; more time was wasted by the slowness of the move from the Inn to the Isar, which allowed Napoleon to arrive before the errors of his lieutenant had become irreparable; finally, the failure to keep the various Austrian corps concentrated exposed them to defeats in detail. The Archduke's strategy was certainly open to criticism, but it was his execution of his schemes which was so deplorably weak. It certainly contrasts most unfavourably with his 1796 campaign, in which he had shown a far truer appreciation of the importance of keeping his divisions in hand and not exposing them to be defeated one by one. As for lack of mobility, that was a traditional failing of the Austrian army which nothing seemed able to eradicate. And it was not only the Austrian offensive campaign which thus failed. Germany would not rise to aid a defeated Power, Prussia would not risk anything when the venture would only involve her in Austria's overthrow. Thus the attempts at insurrection which had been made during these critical days remained isolated expressions of a general feeling, heroic efforts of desperate individuals to achieve what could only be accomplished by a joint effort.

These attempts, however, have no small importance as indications of the growth of a national feeling in Germany. Though Napoleon's rule had not yet begun to press half as heavily on Germany as it was to do before the Continental System succumbed to its own inherent defects, it had already provoked widespread opposition. He had forcibly interfered in the affairs of every portion of Germany; he had overthrown old established dynasties and replaced them with his own upstart relations; he had torn provinces from their old allegiance to transfer them to foreign rulers. The abortive risings in Westphalia under von Dörnberg, in the Alt Mark of Brandenburg under Katt, at Marburg in Hesse, at Hanover, at Ziegenhayn, effected little but were eloquent of much. Had Archduke Charles adopted the bold policy some suggested after Eckmühl, marched into North-West Germany and raised it to fall on Napoleon's communications, he might have failed, he might not even have checked the Emperor's advance on Vienna, but it would hardly have been because Westphalia and Hesse preferred their new masters to their old. If the hardships which the Napoleonic rule was to inflict upon Germany had not yet begun to bear so heavily on every class of society that the Westphalian burghers and peasants were ready to rise, universal sympathy was felt for the insurgents. No one but officials and soldiers attempted to stop Schill or Brunswick. At the best, the new régime was tolerated on account of the material benefits it had brought: it had not attached any one to it or obtained any popular favour.[1] The exploits of Schill and Brunswick leave little doubt as to the attitude of the country. The Westphalian kingdom, the Confederation of the Rhine itself, rested on one thing only, on the continued military predominance of Napoleon.

Ferdinand von Schill, the colonel of a Prussian Hussar

[1] Cf. Fisher, pp. 249-258.

regiment quartered at Berlin, had been privy to the conspiracy in Westphalia, and expected to be denounced when it failed. Accordingly he decided to call his regiment out on behalf of the insurrection, declaring that he was acting with the King's assent (April 28th). The regiment followed him readily enough, and he was also joined by over 100 men from the Berlin garrison and by many volunteers. At their head he moved by Potsdam and Wittenberg to Dessau. Here on May 4th he learnt not only of Austrian defeats on the Danube, but that Dörnberg's rising had miscarried, and that the King of Prussia, instead of declaring war on Napoleon, had disowned all connection with his own enterprise. He might have moved into Bohemia and taken service with Austria, but he still claimed to be acting as a loyal Prussian, and he set out for the coast, intending to seize some port and hold it till help arrived. Milhaud, the French commander at Magdeburg, sent a column out to intercept him; but Schill brushed it aside (May 5th), and made his way by Domitz on the Elbe to Stralsund (May 25th). Had he at once taken ship he and his men could have escaped, but he decided to stand an attack—a hopeless enterprise, for the townspeople though favourable to him were not prepared to emulate Saragossa, and the fortifications were weak. May 31st saw 6000 Danes, Dutch and Holsteiners gathered before Stralsund. Schill, who had not more than a quarter of the number, was unable to prevent them entering by a weakly held gate which was in bad repair. Street fighting ended in the death of Schill and most of his party. Their effort had been premature, but they had not met a hero's death in vain. They set Germany an example of patriotism and self-sacrifice which the rulers of Prussia might perhaps have done well to follow.

One German ruler, indeed, did profit by the example. Frederick William of Brunswick, third son of the man who had fallen at Auerstadt, had been given the Duchy of Oels in Silesia as compensation for his lost ancestral dominions. In February 1809 he had concluded a treaty with Austria by which he undertook to raise a Free Corps to assist Austria. With this corps, the famous "Black Legion," 1700 men vowed to fight to the death for the liberation of Germany, aided by an Austrian division, he invaded Saxony from Bohemia. At first he was brilliantly successful. The Westphalians and Rivaud's division of Junot's corps who hurried to the help of the King of Saxony proved powerless to prevent the seizure of Leipzig and Dresden. Junot was checked at Bamberg, but King Jerome recovered Dresden (July 1st), and the armistice of Znaym (July 12th) put an end to the operations of the Austrians. But Brunswick preferred emulating Schill to a tame retreat into Bohemia along with the Austrians. The Black Legion was ready to follow him on the daring errand of a raid into Brunswick to raise his father's old subjects. On July 24th he moved from Zwickau by Halle, and after a desperate but victorious encounter with a Westphalian regiment at Halberstadt reached Brunswick on the 31st. He was cordially received, but the prospects of a successful rising were desperate. The Brunswickers had seen previous efforts at insurrection suppressed. French troops were gathering round him. The English army he had hoped to see landed in Hanover had not appeared, and there was nothing to be done but for the Duke and his Black Legion to cut their way through Rewbell's division to the mouths of the Weser, where friends in need in the shape of an English squadron received them. Thus carried to Ireland the Black Legion passed into the pay of Great Britain, its cavalry as the Brunswick Hussars, its infantry as the Brunswick Oels Light Infantry.[1]

Meanwhile on the Danube Napoleon had pressed on to Vienna, Hiller's retreat over the Danube having cleared the path. On May 10th the French were before the walls of the Austrian capital. Archduke Maximilian offered an ineffectual resistance for two days, which resulted in considerable damage to property and the evacuation of the city on the 13th. Napoleon thus for the second time found himself master of Vienna. His success in the principal theatre of operations had already exercised a great influence on the course of events elsewhere. The Army of Inner Austria under Archduke John had crossed the frontier into Italy on April 11th, had turned Eugene's position on the Tagliamento, brought him to action at Sacilio (April 16th), and inflicted a severe defeat on him, a fifth of his 50,000 men being killed or taken. This

---

[1] This battalion was sent to Portugal in October 1810, and after serving for a time in the famous Light Division, from which it unfortunately had to be removed for misconduct and a propensity to desertion, formed part of the Seventh Division from March 1811 till the end of the war, being present at Salamanca, at Vittoria, at the battles of the Pyrenees, and at Orthez. The Brunswick Hussars did good service in the Mediterranean and on the East Coast of Spain, especially distinguishing themselves in Bentinck's affair with Suchet near Villafranca in September 1813.

defeat caused the French to evacuate all Istria; and the Viceroy would have abandoned the Adige and fallen back to Mantua had not Macdonald induced him to stand at Caldiero. Two days' indecisive fighting (April 29th and 30th) saw the French left endangered by the appearance of Chasteler's Austrians at Rovoredo, and the French had no alternative save retreat.

Chasteler's force was part of a corps, the Eighth, which had been detached from Carinthia into Tyrol to aid the peasants to throw off the unpopular Bavarian rule which had been imposed on them at Pressburg. The reforms of Montgelas had irritated all classes by necessitating higher taxes; they had been specially irksome to the clergy on account of their anti-clerical bias. The old hatred of Bavaria, the old local feeling and love of independence thus inflamed, brought the peasants in thousands from their homes and drove the Bavarian garrisons out of the valleys of Tyrol. On April 12th the Tyrolese recovered Innsbrück, on the 14th a Bavarian column under General Brisson pushing through the Wippthal to Innsbrück was hemmed in and forced to capitulate. German Tyrol passed into Austrian hands in a very few days, and Chasteler moving South over the Brenner drove the French division under d'Hilliers out of Italian Tyrol.

This favourable situation was altogether changed by the news from the Danube. Archduke John had to retreat, for Marmont was in Dalmatia and threatening his communications. It was suggested that the Archduke should throw himself into Tyrol and assist the peasants, with whom he was very popular, to defend their fortress-like country; but in the end the Army of Inner Austria retired over the Piave (May 8th) and took post along the frontier of Carinthia to defend the passes over the mountains. Several days' sharp fighting, signalised by some heroic exploits on the part of small bodies of Austrians, saw the Archduke forced back into Styria. He had to retire by Klagenfurt upon Gratz (May 16th to 20th). This left the high road to Vienna down the Mur open to Eugene and cut off the Archduke from Tyrol. There the insurgents had meanwhile been hotly attacked by Lefebvre's Bavarians, whom Napoleon had detached against Tyrol after Eckmühl. They were abandoned by the majority of the Austrian regulars, Chasteler moving down the Drave to Villach to rejoin the Archduke, and Lefebvre retook Innsbrück on May 19th; but the peasantry nevertheless continued with no small success their desperate resistance.

Napoleon's first object on obtaining possession of Vienna was to secure a passage to the North bank of the Danube, if possible, before Archduke Charles could arrive on the Marchfeld. His first effort at Nussdorf and Jedler-Aue (May 16th) was checked by the arrival of Hiller's corps from Korneuburg: on the 16th the Archduke's army began to arrive; by the 19th 146 squadrons and 116 battalions, in all some 105,000 men, were in position on the Marchfeld. For effecting a passage, Napoleon had available part of the Guard, Bessières' cavalry reserve, Oudinot's grenadiers, and the corps of Lannes, Davoût and Masséna, in all 120 squadrons and 149 battalions, some 115,000 men, with 300 to 400 guns. Vandamme's Würtembergers and Bernadotte's corps of Saxons, Nassauers and other Confederates guarded the communications, and had just repulsed an attempt on Linz by Kollowrat's Austrian corps from Bohemia (May 17th).

Resolved to bring the Archduke to action before he could gather reinforcements, Napoleon seized the island of Lobau, which the Austrians had neglected to occupy (May 15th), and threw bridges across from it to the left bank. On May 20th Masséna's corps began the passage, and occupied the villages of Aspern and Essling, which provided an admirable bridge-head for the protection of the passage of the rest of the army. But next morning (May 21st), long before this difficult operation could be completed, the covering divisions were furiously attacked by five converging Austrian columns. The heaviest fighting was on the Austrian right, where Hiller (VIth corps), Bellegarde (Ist) and Hohenzollern (IInd) joined in attacking Aspern. The village was carried by their first attack; but Masséna retook it and by supreme efforts held it against repeated assaults. Similarly on the French right Lannes, who had followed Masséna across, maintained his hold of Essling. When the attention of the French was mainly occupied in the effort to hold these villages at the ends of their line, the Archduke advanced against their centre, depleted to reinforce the wings. To check him, Bessières' cavalry had to be thrown into line to connect the two villages, since the breakdown of the bridges was causing delay in the arrival of reinforcements. Bessières made several dashing charges on the Austrian infantry opposite him, but they stood their ground with un-precedented firmness and repulsed all his charges. Towards evening the Archduke hurled Hiller and Bellegarde in a last attack on Aspern; Molitor's division of Masséna was all but destroyed, and the Austrians managed to obtain possession of half the village before nightfall put an end to the struggle. Next morning (May 22nd) opened with the expulsion of the Austrians from Aspern, Masséna putting Carra St. Cyr's fresh division into the fight. Davoût's corps was now (7 a.m.) coming across the restored bridges into Lobau, and Napoleon prepared to deal a great blow at the enemy's centre with Oudinot's grenadiers, Bessières' cavalry and St. Hilaire's division of Davoût. The Austrians resisted desperately, and were only being forced back towards Breitenlee after very heavy fighting, when the sudden collapse of the great bridge over the main stream of the Danube altered the complexion of affairs. The pressure of the logs and tree trunks brought down by the rising river was too much for the bridge.[1] It gave way, and not only cut off most of Davoût's corps but also the sorely needed reserve of ammunition. Just at this moment (8 a.m.) the Archduke brought up his reserve of grenadiers, and before them the French recoiled to the ridge between Aspern and Essling. Along this and around the two villages the fight was contested with desperate valour on both sides. About 3 p.m., after the sheer exhaustion of the combatants had caused a lull of nearly two hours in the battle, the pressure of the Austrians on the French flanks became so serious that the Emperor had to give orders for a retreat. A Transylvanian regiment finally gained possession of Aspern, and only the Young Guard kept Rosenberg out of Essling, and covered the withdrawal of the exhausted corps of Lannes and Masséna into the island of Lobau. Minimise the defeat as he might, ascribe it if he would to the breaking of the bridges, Aspern was a battle of a very different character from any Napoleon had yet fought. He had not merely, as at Eylau and Heilsberg, failed to defeat his enemy, he had been forced to retreat with a loss of over 30,000 against 24,000 which he had inflicted on the enemy. The Austrians had displayed a remarkable resolution and tenacity. Repulsed from the villages time after time, they had as often returned to the

---

[1] The Austrians seem to have sent heavily-laden barges down the stream to increase the pressure on the bridge.

attack, until at last they had had the satisfaction of seeing the Grand Army retreat before them.

But would Austria be able to utilise the advantage she had won? Much depended on the action of Archduke Charles, even more on the movements of the Army of Inner Austria under Archduke John. If it could prevent the Army of Italy and Marmont from Dalmatia from reinforcing Napoleon, Aspern might prove decisive.

But neither of the Austrian leaders proved equal to the occasion. It would be unreasonable to expect that the exhausted victors of Aspern should have renewed their exertions without some rest,[1] but too many troops had been left to cover Bohemia and menace ineffectually the French communications; and though before Wagram Kollowrat rejoined the main army, the failure to concentrate every available man at the decisive spot was to cost Austria dear. Chasteler's divisions, for instance, which might have kept Bernadotte back from Wagram had they joined the Tyrolese, who fell on the Bavarians with renewed vigour in the week after Essling and drove them in disorder back into their own country, merely wasted their time in futile skirmishes round Klagenfurt with Rusca's Italians, who were keeping open Macdonald's communications with Italy. Archduke Ferdinand in Galicia gained some successes over Poniatowski's Poles, even forcing them to evacuate Warsaw; but the presence of half his 30,000 men on the Marchfeld might have turned the scales on July 6th. Much in the same way the Army of Inner Austria was not turned to proper account. On the day of Aspern Archduke John was at Gratz in Styria, waiting for Jellachich's division to come in from Radstadt on the Upper Salza. Jellachich, however, a thoroughly incompetent officer, moved very slowly and failed to keep a proper lookout, with the result that he could not avoid an action against Eugene at St. Michael on the Mur (May 25th), which resulted in his total defeat, and allowed Eugene to get through to Bruck and so establish communication with Napoleon. This decided Archduke John

---

[1] Thus Oncken (*Allgemeine Geschichte*, part iv. vol. i. p. 426) is perhaps too hard on the Archduke's inaction after May 22nd: his troops had suffered severely and were almost as unfit for action as the French; but still it is undeniable that the failure of the Archduke to follow up his success showed a great want of enterprise and of insight into the situation.

to move into Hungary. On June 1st he reached Körmend, where his troops found reinforcements and supplies. Meanwhile the Hungarian " insurrection " was gathering at Raab, and on June 7th Archduke John, in obedience to orders from his brother, left Körmend to join them. Moving down the Raab by Papocz he reached Raab on June 13th; but he found the "insurrection" had only produced 20,000 raw and untrained recruits instead of the expected 40,000, and detachments for various purposes had so weakened his own force that he found himself much inferior to the four divisions which Napoleon had sent out against him under Eugene, and by which he was attacked on June 14th. The battle of Raab ended in the total defeat of the Army of Inner Austria. The horsemen of the "insurrection" on the Austrian left were thrown into disorder by the French artillery, and gave way before Grouchy's cavalry; their flight uncovered the infantry, who were maintaining a stubborn fight in the centre. With the loss of over 7000 men the Archduke fell back to Komorn. His force was to all intents no longer to be reckoned with : at any rate, he could not hope to bring up to the Marchfeld a reinforcement large enough to turn the scale, which might have been the case had his movements been better arranged and more rapid. He had tried to do too much at once, and had dispersed forces which if properly concentrated might have held Eugene at bay at the Semmering. For the unwise move from Körmend to Raab which brought him within easy reach of Eugene Archduke Charles must be held responsible; had he directed his brother to move by Stuhlweissenberg and Gran, the move would have taken longer, but would have probably meant the arrival of 30,000 men on the Marchfeld, since the corps on the Croatian frontier under Banus Giulay could have joined him. But Archduke John was himself to blame for not falling on the two divisions under Macdonald which had followed him from Carniola and had only regained touch with Eugene on the day of the battle of Raab. Here as at other periods of the campaign it was the want of good leadership which told so heavily against the Austrians. The "insurrectionary" levies had not done much at Raab, but nothing could have been better than the conduct of the disciplined troops of the Line, and even of the *Landwehr*.

The net result of all this was that while Napoleon, who did

realise the importance of concentrating every available man at the critical point, was able to collect nearly 170,000 men in and near Lobau by the end of June, the Austrians had only two men to his three. Napoleon had brought up Bernadotte's Saxons from Linz, replacing them by a Bavarian division recalled from Tyrol; the two corps of Eugene and Macdonald had arrived from Italy, and that of Marmont from Dalmatia, besides minor reinforcements. The corps of Kollowrat was the only real addition to the army of Archduke Charles, though on July 2nd he did send off a despatch to Archduke John bidding him bring up his corps from Pressburg, where it then stood. Received on the evening of July 4th, this order was too late to bring Archduke John up to the Marchfeld before 5 p.m. on the 6th, and by then the decisive action had been fought and lost.

The Austrians since the end of May had retained hold of Aspern and Essling, and so strong was their position that Napoleon realised that the passage to the left bank could not be effected there. Under cover, therefore, of a heavy cannonade and feints against this point, the French made their way over the Lobau branch of the Danube by five bridges flung over it on the Eastern side of the island. Begun about 10 p.m. on July 4th by Oudinot's corps (formerly that of Lannes, who had been mortally wounded on May 22nd), the movement was so far advanced by 6 a.m. on the 5th that the corps of Masséna on the left then moved against Gross Enzersdorf; Davoût on the right attacked Wittau, Oudinot formed the centre. The Austrians made little resistance, evacuating their advanced position (Aspern, Essling, Enzersdorf, Wittau) and falling back to the stronger line of Neusiedel, Baumersdorf, Deutsch - Wagram, Gerasdorf, Stammersdorf. The left of this position was covered by the Russbach, and the right rested on the Danube at Jedlersdorf, to which Klenau's corps (late Hiller's) had retired from Aspern: its chief defect was that its re-entrant angle at Wagram gave the French the interior position, and the total front was so long that orders took nearly four hours to get from flank to flank. It was also exposed on the left, where Archduke John was expected; but he was still many hours away.

The retreat of the Austrians from their advanced position encouraged Napoleon to try a direct attack on the evening of the 5th. He hoped to drive in their left from its position behind the Russbach and so interpose between the main army and the corps of Archduke John : he therefore held the Austrian centre and right in check with his left, Masséna's (IVth) corps, and opposed Bernadotte, Eugene, Oudinot and Davoût to the three corps of Bellegarde, Hohenzollern and Rosenberg, which formed the Austrian left. Bernadotte carried Wagram, only to be driven out again, and as the corps on his right were repulsed from Baumersdorf and Neusiedel the attack proved an expensive failure. Encouraged by this, Archduke Charles decided to take the offensive next morning without waiting for his brother. His plan was for his right, Klenau and Kollowrat, to push forward Eastward, threatening to outflank Napoleon's left and cut him off from Aspern ; but his centre, his Grenadier reserve, and left centre, Bellegarde and Hohenzollern, were also to advance on Aderklaa to keep touch with the right. Napoleon, too, intended his principal effort to be on his right : he meant to storm the heights behind the Russbach and to pierce the Austrian centre by Aderklaa and Wagram ; but he had the great advantage of having his troops concentrated to meet badly timed converging attacks. For the Austrian left moved too soon and had already been repulsed from Glinzendorf by Davoût, when at length Klenau fell on Masséna as the latter came up from Breitenlee to support Bernadotte. The leading division of the IVth Corps, Carra St. Cyr's, was repulsed from Aderklaa, its rear, Boudet, was driven in on Aspern. In vain Masséna tried to make head against the Austrians with Legrand and Molitor : he was pressed back in some disorder, Kollowrat moving forward on Klenau's left caught Bernadotte in flank, while d'Aspre's Grenadier reserve and Bellegarde advancing from Wagram on Aderklaa assailed him in front. By 10 a.m. the French left and left centre were in retreat, and the battle seemed in a fair way to be lost. But Napoleon never rose higher than at so critical a moment. He saw that a successful blow at the Austrian centre would paralyse the advance of their right by cutting it off from their left, and while he checked Klenau and Kollowrat with such cavalry and artillery as he had at hand, he collected a great body of infantry for the deciding stroke. Soon after midday he launched this column against Aderklaa. It was headed by Macdonald's corps and followed by a Bavarian division of Lefebvre's with cavalry on its wings. Simultaneously Eugene renewed the attack on Wagram, Oudinot pushed forward against Hohenzollern's front, Davoût, with Montbrun's cavalry covering his flank, made a turning movement by Neusiedel, driving Rosenberg in before him.

But it was in the centre that the battle was decided. The way had been prepared for Macdonald by the great battery Napoleon had collected, and the Army of Italy, though suffering heavy losses, did pierce the Austrian centre and drive it in on Gerasdorf. The simultaneous success of Eugene against Wagram and of Oudinot and Davoût farther to the right, clinched this advantage. In good order the Austrians drew off all along the line. They maintained a front firm enough to secure them against pursuit; indeed, the French were too exhausted to press on, and the arrival of Archduke John's belated corps at Ober-Siebenbrünn far to the Eastward spread a panic through the French ranks which showed what his appearance earlier might have effected. As far as losses went, the honours of the day were evenly divided. If the Austrians left 8500 prisoners behind them, besides 25,000 killed and wounded, they had inflicted a loss of 30,000 on the French, and could point to 11 guns and 12 eagles as trophies against the 9 guns and 1 colour of which the French could boast. Had their wings only combined their movements better, had Archduke John and his 15,000 men been in time to take up their appointed place and cover the exposed Austrian left, had he played Blücher to his brother's Wellington, Wagram might have been an enlarged edition of Aspern, or might have anticipated Waterloo.

But Napoleon's downfall was not to be achieved by Austria alone. The Archduke who had fallen back on Znaym, where he concentrated 60,000 men by July 10th, was anxious for an armistice. Napoleon had had too strong a taste of the chances of defeat to refuse his overtures. After an indecisive action on the 11th, in which Marmont and Masséna failed to dislodge Bellegarde from his position at Znaym, an armistice was arranged. The military situation hardly made this necessary. Archduke John might have got together 30,000 to 40,000 regulars and as many Hungarian levies for a diversion South of the Danube, and there was still a chance that Prussia might take up arms, or England make an effective if belated diversion in North Germany. However, the opponents of Stadion had gained influence, Wagram had converted the opportunist Metternich into an advocate of peace, and the resignation of Archduke Charles (July 23rd) rather than dismiss his adjutant Count Grünne was a blow to the war party. With him the Archdukes John and Joseph threw up their commands, while Metternich replaced Stadion as Foreign Minister.[1] Count Lichtenstein, who became Commander-in-Chief, was the leader of those who desired peace; and as Russia remained obstinately neutral and Prussia refused to rise unless Austria would denounce the armistice, which Austria declined to do unless Prussia would first take up arms, even the bellicose gradually abandoned hope. England, too, by sending her great expedition not to the Weser but to the Scheldt, destroyed all lingering chance of an insurrection in North Germany. The troops who perished of fever in the Walcheren marshes ought to have been landed in Hanover in June—the Hanoverian population had welcomed Cathcart in 1805[2] and four years of Napoleon's rule had not increased its popularity, — but the quarrel in the ministry between Castlereagh and Canning was largely responsible for the delays through which the splendid opportunity was allowed to slip away; when it finally sailed, there was perhaps as much to be gained by a blow at Antwerp as by landing in North Germany after the best chance was past. The failure of the expedition was due not so much to its destination, as to the feeble execution of the scheme, for which Lord Chatham must be held responsible.

The final blow came when Prussia declined to stir unless she were put on exactly the same footing in Germany as Austria. Rather than this Francis preferred peace with Napoleon, and Lichtenstein was despatched to negotiate a treaty in personal communication with the Emperor. The terms were harsh, but Napoleon was in a position to dictate. Austria ceded to France Trieste, Carniola, Istria, Fiume, Monfalcone, Dalmatia, the circle of Villach in Carinthia, and all her possessions on the right of the Save down to the Bosnian frontier. She abandoned all claims on Salzburg, Berchtesgaben and the Innviertel, which Napoleon handed over to his Bavarian client. Another vassal state, the Grand Duchy of Warsaw, was enlarged by West

---

[1] Stadion offered his resignation July 8th, but Metternich did not finally take over the position from him till October.

[2] *War Office Original Correspondence*, vol. lxviii., Hanover.

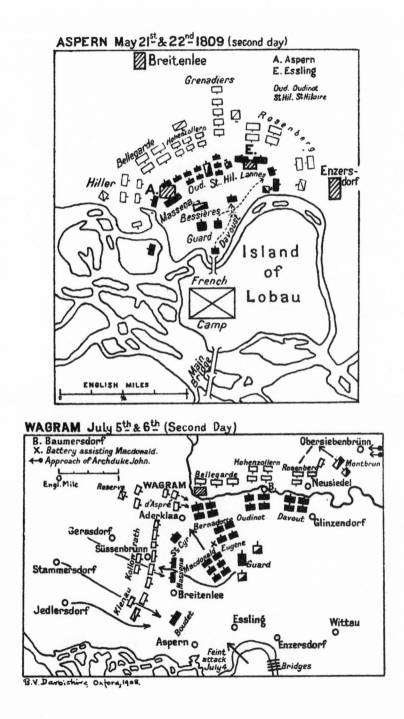

ASPERN May 21ˢᵗ & 22ⁿᵈ 1809 (second day)

🮘 Breitenlee

A. Aspern
E. Essling

Oud. Oudinot
St.Hil. St.Hilaire

Grenadiers

Rosenberg

Bellegarde
Hohenzollern

E.

Hiller

A.

Enzers-dorf

Oud. St..Hil. Lannes

Massena

Bessières

Davoust

Guard

Island
of
Lobau

French

Camp

Main
Bridge

ENGLISH MILES

WAGRAM July 5ᵗʰ & 6ᵗʰ (Second Day)

B. Baumersdorf
X. Battery assisting Macdonald.
←●— Approach of Archduke John.

Obersiebenbrünn

Engl. Mile   Reserve   WAGRAM

Bellegarde
Hohenzollern
Rosenberg

Montbrun

Neusiedel

d'Aspré

B.

Gerasdorf

Aderklaa

Bernadotte Oudinot

Davout

Glinzendorf

Süssenbrunn

St. Cyr

Eugene

Stammersdorf

Kollowrath

Massena Macdonald

Guard

Jedlersdorf

Klenau

Breitenlee

Essling

Wittau

Boudet

Aspern

Enzersdorf

Feint
attack
July 4

Bridges

B. V. Darbishire, Oxford, 1908.

Galicia and Cracow, Austria's share in the 1795 partition, while Russia received the South-Eastern corner of Old Galicia. Austria had, moreover, to acquiesce in the abolition of the Teutonic Order, to accept the Continental System, to limit her army to 150,000 men, and pay an indemnity of 85,000,000 francs. Her loss of inhabitants was 3,500,000, of territory over 40,000 square miles. The Treaty of Schönbrunn (Oct. 14th) thus marked the lowest point to which the power of the Hapsburgs had yet sunk. Cut off from the sea, compelled to submit to Napoleon almost as completely as must Baden or Lippe-Detmold, Austria had the added mortification of having to abandon the gallant Tyrolese. Even after Wagram and Znaym they had continued their heroic but hopeless resistance, and had again repulsed the Bavarians when they for the third time advanced against them (August). The conclusion of peace allowed large forces to be directed against the mountaineers, up the Inn, up the Salza, and from Italy. Still the Tyrolese refused to submit. But this time numbers were too much even for them. By the end of December all was over except the executions. The gallant Hofer met his fate in February 1810, and with him ends one of the most romantic incidents in all German history. South Tyrol now went to the Kingdom of Italy, part of Eastern Tyrol to the Illyrian provinces, the rest to the detested Bavarians.

Moreover, Stadion's resignation marked the abandonment of Austria's effort at a truly patriotic policy. Stadion had made her the champion of German nationality, but the effort had been premature. Her defeat had been in no small measure due to the inaction of some German states and to the active hostility of others, those members of the Confederation of the Rhine whom gratitude to Napoleon or a sense that their gains and new titles would not survive the overthrow of their author made faithful to his cause, since as yet he had not sacrificed their material prosperity to his hatred of England. With Stadion's fall disappeared the popular policy he had advocated. Austria under Metternich was once again subject to the suspicion-ridden system of Thugut and Cobenzl. Had she won in 1809 under the leadership of Stadion and Archduke Charles, Austria could hardly have gone back from the principles they had enunciated, could hardly have abandoned their more Liberal policy to become the chief stronghold of reaction. The failure of 1809 was therefore of momentous importance to her future. But if one of its lessons may have been that Austria should have put all other considerations aside to assist Russia and Prussia in 1807, the conduct of Prussia in 1799 and 1805 was even more responsible for Germany's humiliation and Napoleon's triumph.

CHAPTER XXIX

GERMANY AT NAPOLEON'S MERCY

IT would be one of the gravest errors to regard Austria's failure to overthrow Napoleon as having merely postponed the day of reckoning and involved a change in the conditions under which it was to come about. If one reads the story of 1809 in the light of 1813, if one looks back on Wagram through Waterloo, Leipzig, Vittoria and the Beresina, one is in danger of misreading it. The lesson of 1809 is that Germany had not yet been welded into one by Napoleon's oppression; indeed, Austria owed her defeat in no small measure to the assistance given to Napoleon by his German vassals, and to the apathy or selfishness or timidity of Prussia and the other states to whom she had looked for support. To the South-West of Germany Napoleon was still a benefactor rather than an oppressor, the protector of Bavarian and Franconian against the Hapsburg and the Hohenzollern, the author of manifold ameliorations in the social and material circumstances of the mass of the population; while even in the North-West, in Westphalia and in the Hanoverian districts still under military rule, his yoke was not yet so galling that those who bore it were ready to risk all in the attempt to throw it off. It was in the years between Wagram and the retreat from Moscow that the attitude of the people of Germany towards Napoleon finally crystallised into one of uncompromising hostility, precisely because it was in these years that the pressure of the Continental System on every German household brought home to Hessians, to Brunswickers, to Saxons, to burghers of the Hanseatic towns, of Rhenish cities like Düsseldorf, and of Baltic ports like Dantzic, the fact that the new Charlemagne was prepared to sacrifice their interests and their welfare to his struggle with the Mistress of the Seas. The enforcing of the Continental System, Napoleon's great weapon against Great Britain, was at the root of his aggressions on Germany, of the arbitrary territorial alterations which gave offence to the Princes, of the financial extortions and the interference with trade and industry which inflicted such widespread suffering on the peoples, of the Spanish and Russian campaigns for which the conscription took its toll not from French families only, but from Dutch, German and Italian homes ; finally, his failure to enforce this system on Russia and on Spain brought about that military situation which made the successful rising of 1813 possible.

But in 1809 these things were still in the future. If the modern investigator can see clearly in the Franco-Russian alliance the signs of its coming dissolution, they were not quite so obvious when it had just sufficed to keep Russia's neutrality proof against the temptation of Aspern. With Austria humbled, Prussia's helplessness proclaimed by her inaction, North-West Germany occupied by his troops or carved up into new principalities of his own creation, and the states of South-West Germany his faithful allies, Napoleon might reasonably feel satisfied with the state of affairs in Germany. If he could have induced England to make peace on terms which acknowledged his territorial resettlement of Europe, it is more than possible that his organisation might have endured, at least that it might have lasted his lifetime. But to overcome England he was driven into courses which deprived him of the benefit of much of what he had done for Germany. The destroyer of the *ancien régime*, of social and economic privilege, became lost in the author of the Continental System, and in the master whose servants the conscribing officials were. Gratitude was before long forgotten, and submerged by hatred.

Yet, as 1813 was to prove, the intensity of the hostility to Napoleon varied enormously in different states. It was strongest in Prussia, which had only received insult and injury at his hands, since the remodelling of the institutions of the country on the lines he had laid down elsewhere, the benefits of the abolition of feudalism and privilege, came not from him, but from the Hohenzollern and their ministers. It was weaker in the North-West, which suffered greatly from the Continental System, which had been bandied about from one of his puppets to another, but which had still received from him and his nominees the benefits of an orderly, systematic and modern rule. It was weakest in the South-West, where states like Bavaria and Würtemberg represented the realisation by his help of traditional ideas, were developments, not new creations, and possessed some other justification for their existence than the mere *fiat* of the conqueror. They, too, were sacrificed to the Continental System, their contingents perished for the Emperor in Russia and in Spain; but they owed Napoleon no small debt, and it was only when the Allies guaranteed them the continued enjoyment of the boons he had conferred on them that their German patriotism overpowered Napoleon's hold on their allegiance.

Among these states, Bavaria owed as much to Napoleon as did any other. She had resumed the position she had held in Louis XIV's time of the principal client state of France. This had caused her a great increase of territory, the annexations of 1809 bringing her area up to nearly 40,000 square miles, and her population to over 3,000,000. But her territorial development was of less importance than the work of Maximilian Joseph and Montgelas in building up a well-organised, strongly centralised modern state. More fortunate than his Austrian namesake, Joseph II, the King of Bavaria was able to utilise the ideas and methods of the French Revolution to carry out a revolution from above for which his subjects were by no means prepared. The Liberal principles of the King and his minister were not altogether popular, especially with the Catholic inhabitants of the numerous small towns and with the Tyrolese peasantry, who bitterly resented the interference with their religious rites and customs, the dissolution of their Estates, and the confiscation of Church property. Outside Tyrol, however, a Bavarian nationality was really created. The old constitution was swept away, and a new order established in its place (May 1808). The nobles, while retaining their social privileges, were compelled to pay taxes; personal freedom was guaranteed to all persons and classes. That an army based on conscription was among the innovations, that the *Code Napoléon* was introduced, the administration organised on French lines, and that the country was divided after the French model into fifteen departments [1] named after the rivers, need hardly be mentioned. The government may be best described as a Liberal bureaucratic absolutism, for the representative element in the constitution was so small and unimportant as to be practically negligible. The

[1] Tyrol provided three of these.

chief difficulty was financial: Napoleon's demands on his allies were not easily appeased, nor could a modern administration be provided without considerable outlay: moreover, Maximilian Joseph was not less extravagant than the majority of his family, if he never imitated the wilder performances of some of the later Wittelsbachs.[1]

In Baden a very similar state of things prevailed, though on a somewhat smaller scale. Duke Charles Frederick deserves credit for having endeavoured to spare his subjects as far as possible from the burden of the expense of the increased military establishment. To this end he effected great economies at his Court, while endeavouring to bring the financial system into line with modern requirements. Here also one meets an administration organised on the French pattern: a Council with the five departments of Finance, Justice, the Interior, War, and Foreign Affairs subordinated to it; a Legislative Council of ministers and nominees; an enlightened autocracy governing in the interests of subjects who were hardly allowed any voice in the settlement of their affairs.

Frederick of Würtemberg presents a rather different aspect. If Würtemberg had retained more of its mediæval constitution longer than its neighbours, the change it now underwent was the more complete. An oppressive absolutism was substituted for "*das gute alte Recht*," the nobles found themselves powerless to resist the loss of most of their cherished privileges, and all classes were equally compelled to submit to the interference of the monarch in every sphere of activity. Napoleon secured the allegiance of his German clients by consulting the interests of the sovereigns, not those of the subjects, and the destruction of the old liberties of Würtemberg was typical of the removal of all such obstacles which marred the completeness of his vassal monarchs' control of their principalities, since the more absolute the vassal, the more completely could the overlord dispose of the resources of the subject states. Local liberties were a hindrance, and must therefore be swept away. But with the Napoleonic absolutism Würtemberg received the *Code Napoléon* and the abolition of many of the cramping relics of feudalism which had so much impeded the social and economic development of the country. Frederick has been described as " an inconsiderate despot who oppressed the noble Swabian people

[1] Cf. *Deutsche Geschichte, 1806-1871*, vol. i. pp. 94 ff.

with disgraceful disregard";[1] but for all that he was the real
creator of the Kingdom of Würtemberg; he brought the country
safely through the perils of the Napoleonic era, and out of "a
collection of odds and ends" built up a compact and well-organised monarchy with an efficient army which, if out of all proportion to the size of the kingdom, was yet the best guarantee that
it should be respected by its neighbours. Himself a Protestant,
Frederick was the first sovereign of Würtemberg to secure for
Roman Catholics the toleration hitherto denied to them by the
bigotry of the Lutheran clergy, who had in past time carried
their intolerance to the point of refusing to receive the
Huguenot refugees because they were Calvinists.[2]

Saxony resembled the states of the South-West, inasmuch
as it also had an old dynasty which Napoleon had bound to his
cause by favours and concessions instead of deposing it: it
differed from them, however, in being but little affected by the
reforming movement which was making itself so strongly felt
elsewhere. Very conservative himself, Frederick Augustus was
supported in his opposition to reform by his ministers, Marcolini
and Hopfzarten, who would not hear of any changes in the
internal administration, cumbrous and unworkable though it
was, and did not even attempt to tax the nobles. Not till 1811
did the increased expense of a larger army necessitate some
readjustment of the system of taxation. Saxony thus was less
affected by the changes of the time than any other part of
Germany, though the Grand Duchy of Warsaw which had been
placed under her King by the Peace of Tilsit was organised on
the usual French lines, with six departments, a two-chamber
Assembly whose functions were practically nominal, and a
Council of five to whom the government was entrusted. Baron
Senfft, the Saxon Foreign Minister, would have gladly made
the union between Saxony and Poland closer, hoping to crush
Prussia between them, but this was not what Napoleon· seems
to have intended. The hold of the King of Saxony on the
Grand Duchy was little more than a convenient cloak for
French predominance in its affairs, under which the Poles
might hope for a more complete restoration than it had as
yet been convenient for Napoleon to give them. The connection
with Saxony remained therefore little more than nominal.

[1] *Deutsche Geschichte, 1806–1871,* i. 435.
[2] Cf. A. Pfister, *König Friedrich von Würtemberg und seine Zeit.*

In the North-West of Germany some of the old dynasties remained, in Mecklenburg and in Oldenburg and in Hesse-Darmstadt, where Landgrave Louis X, now Grand Duke, was so wedged in between two of Napoleon's new creations as to be powerless for harm even if he had been hostile to Napoleon, and not, as he was, one of the Emperor's most faithful adherents. Of the new states, the Grand Duchy of Würzburg, given (1806) in exchange for Salzburg to Archduke Ferdinand, who had then for the second time been dispossessed, needs but a brief mention. Admitted to the Confederation of the Rhine in September 1806, he had had to send his contingent of 2000 men to support Napoleon in 1809, but the improved relations between France and Austria inaugurated by Metternich and crowned by the marriage of Marie Louise to Napoleon (April 1810), removed all danger of a collision of interests.

The Grand Duchy of Frankfort, the principality with which the unstable Dalberg was now invested, is a more interesting study. Originally given the Free Cities of Frankfort and Ratisbon with the Principality of Aschaffenburg, Dalberg had had after Wagram to agree (Feb. 16th, 1810) to a modification which gave Ratisbon to Bavaria and compensated him with Hanau and Fulda. His dominions thus formed a curiously shaped strip some 2200 square miles in extent, all but a very small portion being situated on the North bank of the Main. A population of some 300,000, marked by many diversities of race, occupation and religion, was given some measure of unity by having to submit to the same laws and the same administrative system, both borrowed from France, and to provide a contingent of 4200 to the Confederation's army. The abolition of the different local and municipal institutions and the establishment of legal and fiscal unity were but a poor compensation for the heavy taxation, the loss of trade with England, the confiscation and destruction of colonial goods which had been imported through that country. Education was, it is true, encouraged, the administration of justice enormously improved, the position of the Jews in some degree ameliorated, the substitution of the French Penal Code for the *Carolina*, a penal law so barbarous as to be practically obsolete, was a great advantage; but against that the trade of Frankfort was practically ruined, and large numbers of the men of the Duchy met their death in the service of the Emperor for a

cause which could not benefit them or their countrymen.[1]
Had Napoleon maintained his supremacy, the Duchy was to
have passed to Eugene Beauharnais on Dalberg's death; but
its existence was anomalous and unjustifiable, a violation of
history and geography alike, and it did not survive the fall
of its founder.[2]

A rather larger state, the Grand Duchy of Berg,[3] was formed
with part of the much-disputed Cleves-Jülich inheritance as
its nucleus.   Cleves, which had gone to Prussia, and Berg, which
had passed through the Neuburg Wittelsbachs into the hands
of Maximilian Joseph of Zweibrücken and Bavaria, thus came
together again under the rule of Murat.[4]   Murat received a
seat in the College of Kings, and on the formation of the
Confederation of the Rhine the possessions of William Frederick
of Nassau, the ex-Stadtholder of the United Provinces,[5] were
added to the Grand Duchy on the refusal of their ruler to join
the Confederacy; while the overthrow of Prussia led to its being
further increased by receiving Mark, also part of the Cleves-
Jülich inheritance, Tecklenberg, Lingen and the Prussian
portion of Münster—an addition of 3200 square miles and
360,000 people.[6]   The Grand Duchy thus included the valleys
of the Sieg, Ruhr and Lippe, all tributaries of the Rhine,
and the upper waters of the Ems, covering in all some 12,000
square miles, with a population of 1,200,000, and including
some of the chief manufacturing towns of Germany.   "It was
the Birmingham and Sheffield, the Leeds and Manchester
of Germany rolled into one"[7] inasmuch as iron and steel
works, textile manufactures, the cloth, the cotton, the silk and
the wool industries flourished side by side.   But its prosperity
depended on the ready importation of raw material and on
finding a market for its finished products, so the continental
blockade and the rigid protective system of France caught

---

[1] A battalion from Frankfort was in Leval's German division of the Second Corps
which entered Spain in the autumn of 1808; it was badly mauled at Talavera, and
was one of the corps which came over to the British during the fighting round
Bayonne in December 1813.

[2] Fisher, ch. xiv., gives a most interesting account of the Grand Duchy of
Frankfort.

[3] Cf. Fisher, chs. ix. and x.   [4] March 1806.

[5] Cf. p. 372.

[6] At this time the fortress of Wesel, hitherto part of the Grand Duchy, was handed
over to France.

[7] Fisher, p. 206.

the Grand Duchy between the upper and the nether millstones. By 1812 its exports had declined to a fifth of what they had been in 1807, since its markets across the ocean had been lost to it by British commercial and maritime supremacy, and the French Empire was surrounded with an insurmountably high tariff-wall. The Grand Duchy was so far advanced on the road to commercial ruin that in 1811 a deputation was actually sent to Paris to petition for incorporation in the French Empire.

Thus here again the Continental System uprooted any gratitude which the reforms introduced by the French might have earned. But this was not all. Instead of the light taxation which had been the rule before the creation of the Grand Duchy, its inhabitants found themselves borne down by a heavy burden. It was not merely the introduction of the French fiscal system; that might have been expected to increase the revenue somewhat without really increasing its burdensomeness. But instead of the 3,000,000 francs which the Grand Duchy might have provided with ease, in 1813 no less a sum than 10,000,000 was extorted from its taxpayers. And it is easy to appreciate where all the money went and how much benefit its unfortunate inhabitants derived from their exertions, when one sees that between 4 and 5 millions were annually devoted to the army, when one meets with four battalions from Berg fighting Napoleon's battles in Catalonia, and reads of the 6000 men with the Grand Army of 1812 and of the 4000 recruits demanded from her to fill the gaps which the Russian disaster had made.

But in many ways Berg benefited by the French rule. Count Beugnot, the Imperial Commissioner by whom the government of the Grand Duchy was carried on, was one of the best of the officials employed by Napoleon. Honest, painstaking and zealous, under his auspices the French administration was a model of order, method and definition: it was bureaucratic and absolute, it did nothing to teach the people to govern themselves, but it was systematic, diligent, careful, prompt and decided. The French substituted good and simple laws for the chaos of conflicting, obsolete customs and statutes which had hitherto prevailed. They abolished caste privileges, broke down the monopoly of land possessed by the gentry, made all trades and professions free to all to

enter, and enormously improved the social and economic
situation of the peasantry.[1] Public works, education, religious
toleration, the jury system, the French codes, the French
judicial system, were among the benefits of French rule, and
the abuses which they had swept away were exorcised once
and for all. Thus though Murat ceded Berg to Napoleon
in July 1808, and the Grand Duchy remained without a
sovereign till, in March 1809, Napoleon suddenly conferred
it on his five year old nephew, Napoleon Louis, son of the
King of Holland; though in January 1811 the Grand Duchy
was deprived of the portions North of the Lippe, which were
then annexed to the French Empire as the Departments of
Lippe and Ems Supérieur, it needed all the grinding tyranny
of the conscription and the Continental System to provoke
the riots which preceded the arrival of the delivering Cossacks
in November 1813.

The largest and most important of Napoleon's new creations
was that erected for his brother Jerome. Its constitution,
promulgated on November 15th, 1807, was a marked advance
on anything which the Hessians who formed so large a part
of Jerome's new subjects had yet known. Besides the four
ministers to whom the departments of the administration were
entrusted,[2] and a Council of State nominated by the King to
give advice on administrative matters, draft laws and act as
a court of appeal, the kingdom was given elected Estates which
would really seem to have been something more than a mere
form. That the kingdom was divided into departments, of
which there were eight, and subdivided into districts and
cantons, that the Civil Code was introduced, the old seigneurial
jurisdiction swept away to make room for a judicial hierarchy
on the French model, that the Church was subordinated to the
State and no small portion of its revenues diverted to other
purposes, some beneficial others the reverse, that education
was carefully organised, that feudalism was abolished, labour
services done away with or made commutable for money-
payments, all this was the natural result of the application
of French principles of government to Westphalia. Life was
made easier and simpler in many respects, personal freedom

[1] Cf. Fisher, pp. 202–205.
[2] Namely, Justice and the Interior ; War ; Finance, Commerce and the Treasury,
and a Minister of State.

and practical equality before the law were great boons. Commerce was freed from the barriers and restrictions which had hitherto impeded it, and the substitution of one system of finance, and that system thoroughly modern and enlightened, for the complications which had hitherto prevailed in the different provinces from which the kingdom had been made up was a great improvement. Exemptions disappeared, with them went a multitude of minor imposts, difficult and troublesome to collect, and unproductive at the best. Import and export duties were so arranged as to permit the normal development of the resources of the country. If the Kingdom of Westphalia had been in fact what it was in name, a free and independent state, it might have arrived at no small pitch of prosperity. Had the districts which separated it from the sea been added to it, it might have become what the House of Brunswick-Lüneburg might have created but had failed to create, a strong and united state, to be in North-Western Germany what Bavaria was in the South-West. If the Hessians seem to have regretted their old rulers, the Brunswickers were reconciled to the new order by the advantages it brought them, and Prussia had not apparently made herself so dear to her Westphalian provinces that they found the separation hard to bear. But the interests of the Westphalian peoples had not been the object for which the kingdom had been created. Napoleon had only his own benefit in view when he built it up: the selection of Jerome as its king was in itself a sufficient proof of this.

At first energetic and active, Jerome was by nature too indolent, too self-indulgent, too easy-going for the assiduous devotion to his duties which his position demanded. Self-sacrifice and hard work were not to be looked for from him. He had able ministers: von Bülow, a Prussian, looked after the finances with skill and integrity, and when he incurred Napoleon's displeasure and was dismissed (April 1811), Malchus, his successor, proved as able, if harsher and less honest. In the Baron de Wolffradt, Jerome possessed a capable Minister of the Interior, formerly a faithful servant of the Duke of Brunswick, who had taken service with his new master at the request of his old.

Idle, vicious, and devoid of moral strength as Jerome was, ill-suited for the position he occupied, the harm he brought upon

his subjects was a mere trifle compared with the mischief
wrought by the heavy hand of Napoleon.   To one ignorant
of the circumstances under which the kingdom of Westphalia
came into existence, and judging by the treatment it received
from Napoleon, it would hardly seem that the country owed its
creation to the Emperor of the French.   Rather one might
suppose that it was a kingdom on which he desired to avenge
himself for some signal slight or injury.   Westphalia was
compelled to keep up an army of 25,000 men, half of whom
were Frenchmen, an army which fought Napoleon's battles
in Spain[1] at the expense of Westphalia, instead of paying its
way by being hired to foreign Powers, after the manner of that
of Hesse-Cassel in times past.   Moreover, Jerome's kingdom
had to support a permanent charge on the royal domains of
7,000,000 francs in favour of France; and it started its career
with the heavy incubus of a debt of 30,000,000 francs, representing the indebtedness incurred by the Elector of Hesse for
all his rigid parcimony; another of 8,000,000, the cost of the
French occupation during 1807; and worst of all, of a war
indemnity of 26,000,000 more.

To support such a burden was quite beyond the capacities
of the kingdom and even Napoleon had to admit this, and
to consent to modify the terms.   In January 1810 a new treaty
handed over to Westphalia most of the rest of Hanover, and
reduced the indemnity to the more moderate dimensions of
16,000,000 francs, and extended the time within which it had to
be paid from eighteen months to ten years.   Still even this relief
was only partial.   Westphalia had to maintain 18,500 Frenchmen in addition to her own army of 25,000 men, and Napoleon
demanded the annual payment of 4,500,000 francs from the
Hanoverian domains for a term of ten years.   The negotiations
over the cession were still far from complete when, in December
1810, the exigencies of enforcing the Continental System led to
the annexation by Napoleon of the coast districts of Germany
from the Ems to Lübeck.   Napoleon's object in bringing these
lands under his more immediate control was to enforce the
decrees of Fontainebleau (Oct. 1810), which established special

---

[1] There was a Westphalian division with St. Cyr in Catalonia in 1809,
mustering over 5000 men; by June 1st, 1810, it had been reduced to four battalions.
A Westphalian cavalry regiment also formed part of the main invading army
in 1808,

tribunals to try persons suspected of introducing prohibited goods, and to check the extensive system of smuggling by which his attempt to keep out British goods was being circumvented. The districts thus forcibly incorporated in the French Empire included the Hanseatic towns which had been in French occupation since the end of 1806,[1] and their fate was shared by the Duchy of Oldenburg, the Principalities of Aremberg and Salm, and not avoided even by Napoleon's own creations, Berg and Westphalia. The Northern part of Hanover was thus withdrawn from Jerome, and with it went the greater part of the Westphalian department of the Weser.[2] In vain Jerome protested: in the end he was lucky to obtain the reduction of the French troops whom he had to support to their old number of 12,500; in the territorial rearrangement he had to acquiesce with the best grace he could muster.

Where Napoleon treated his own creations with such severity, it was not likely that the lot of Prussia would be particularly happy. Of the means by which Napoleon continued to hold Prussia down, of the great indemnity he had extorted from her, and of his interference with the composition of the Prussian ministry, some account has already been given.[3] That despite all this, and despite the hostility and suspicion with which Napoleon regarded the country he had injured so sorely, Prussia should have carried out in these years of distress social and military reforms of the utmost importance, makes the achievement all the more remarkable. The names which must always be associated with this work are those of Stein and Scharnhorst. The latter's share in the regeneration of Prussia, though of the utmost importance, was of a more restricted character than that of Stein, although when one seeks to estimate their relative work for Prussia it must be remembered that Stein was only in office from the October of 1807 till the following December, that much of the necessary preliminaries to his great measures had been done by others, and that his work was continued by others after he had to fly from the wrath of Napoleon. Still it is Stein who best represents the new Prussia. Himself an Imperial Knight, his position as a Prussian patriot and minister is

[1] Cf. Fisher, ch. xv.
[2] Roughly corresponding to the bishopric of Osnabrück.
[3] Cf. Chapter XXVII.

typical of the way in which the rising tide of German national feeling was to make for the future aggrandisement of Prussia. Indeed, it is a remarkable fact that nearly all the men who played the chief parts in the regeneration of Prussia were not Prussians by birth. Mecklenburg gave her Blücher, to Hanover she owed Hardenberg and Scharnhorst, Gneisenau was a Saxon. But a common hatred of Napoleon seems to have caused them, as it were instinctively, to seek the service of the one German state which owed Napoleon nothing but injuries, and was to that extent marked out as a likely disciple of the gospel of vengeance.

Roughly speaking, the work of Stein was to adapt to the requirements of Prussia the work of the French Revolution. Prussia already possessed highly centralised institutions and all the machinery needed for a benevolent despotism : the Hohenzollern family was identified with the traditions of a vigorous and active personal rule, and Frederick William III, even if deficient in the promptness and decision of Frederick William I, or of Frederick II, did not altogether fail to carry out his task : his share in the reform of his kingdom is more often unduly depreciated than exaggerated. Briefly stated, what Stein did for Prussia and for the Hohenzollern was to inaugurate a series of important social reforms and to identify the dynasty with this work. He did not create the Prussian bureaucracy, but he reformed it, swept away inefficiency and corruption, and infused it with fresh vigour.

It is with the reform of the administration that Stein is most peculiarly connected : that was his special work. When he came into office the General Directory had practically gone to pieces, the King relied on his Cabinet Secretaries, the departments were without proper correlation or supervision. This increased the trouble caused by its want of unity, by the cross division between departments whose clashing produced great confusion.

Stein's plan included the erection of a Council of State to control the administration, audit the accounts of the ministers, decide disputes between the departments, and legislate. It was to include the ministers and ex-ministers, all Princes of the blood over the age of eighteen, and other persons specially appointed. For purposes of administration the Council was to be divided into five departments, those of Foreign Affairs, War, Justice, Finance,[1] and the Interior.[2] This plan was not carried out in its entirety, but the edicts of December 18th reforming the central administration, and of the 26th reforming the provincial government, were almost identical with Stein's unratified edict of November. The Council of State did not come into existence till 1810, and even then it did not control the administration; but on the whole Stein's ideas were accepted.

In local government, Stein abolished the War and Domains Chambers, which, originally merely financial bodies, had become administrative and judicial also. He now divided the provinces into districts (*Bezirke*), in each of which " deputations " corresponded to the departments of the Directory. The old provincial arrangements were so far kept up that Superior Presidents were appointed to exercise a general supervision over groups of districts, and to deal with special emergencies. Justice was separated from administration, rural tribunals being created for minor judicial work.

Stein's aims did not stop at mere reforms in degree. He was anxious to introduce in some form or another representative institutions, possibly a national Parliament. It is as a step in this direction that the Municipal Reform Edict, published in November 1808,[3] is most interesting. The towns of Germany had in the 18th Century fallen into great decay. True municipal life hardly existed. Narrow oligarchies controlled the few towns where the forms of self-government had not given place to the rule of royal officials, appointed quite regardless of their fitness for the posts they held. This edict gave the townsfolk control of their property, the State only interfering to see that its own rights were respected and its laws observed; it placed in their hands local government, justice and police; it freed them from their manorial lords, and placed them all in the same relation to the State, the only distinctions it observed being those of size.[4] This grant of municipal self-government was a free gift, in no sense a concession; indeed it was given to

---

[1] Including the Treasury and the commissions for managing the Taxes and the Domains and Forests.

[2] Under this head were comprised Education, Public Health, Mining, Police and Trade.

[3] Cf. Seeley, ii. 238-243.

[4] Towns with over 10,000 inhabitants were classed as "great," those having from 3500 to 10,000 as "medium," those with from 800 to 3500 as "small."

people not always well prepared or anxious for it. " The people were commanded, not allowed, to govern themselves."[1] With this Municipal Reform must be connected the famous Emancipating Edict of October 9th, 1807.[2] This great measure had been discussed by an Intermediate Commission in July 1807. The Report of August 17th showed how urgent was the necessity for free trade in land ; how the impoverished landowners could not sell part of their estates and so obtain the money they needed, because the middle-class capitalists who had the money to invest were not allowed to purchase noble land/ (*Rittergut*). Hardenberg's Memorandum of September 17th drew an outline of the measures embodied in the edict, and it would seem that the idea of establishing free trade in land originated with Schön, while the work of drafting the edict was performed by Stägemann : still Stein took up the project warmly, supported it with all his might, made it of universal application, and it was he who carried it through.[3]

The edict was fully in accord with his principle of removing all artificial hindrances in the way of the full development of the country. Divided as the population of Prussia was into distinct classes, separated as into water-tight compartments by the strictest lines of caste, nobles, citizens and peasants had hardly anything in common ; for while the peasantry did come into contact with the nobles as landlords and as officers in the army, the citizens were not even brought into line with their fellow-subjects through the army, being non-military in the extreme. What Stein did was that he managed to abolish caste in persons and in land ; for the division extended not merely to the owners but to their estates.[4] Prussia had hitherto been divided into manors, with a primitive and rigid organisation : the peasants were subject to heavy burdens, but they were at least secure against the caprice and arbitrary punishments of their landlords. They had a secure tenure and a definite status. But this was restrictive as well as protective : they could not rise beyond their status. Stein's object was to open all careers to every one, and the Edict of Emancipation made the occupation of the peasants voluntary and no longer obligatory.[5] This celebrated edict[6] abolished personal serfdom,

---

[1] Seeley, ii. 244.
[3] *Ibid.* i. 446.
[5] *Ibid.* ii. 185.
36

[2] *Ibid.* i. 430.
[4] *Ibid.* i. 437.
[6] For the text, cf. Seeley, i. 443 ff.

and especially menial services, together with forced labour ; but it did not free the peasants from the obligations by which they were bound as free persons through the possession of an estate or by special contracts. To these they continued to be liable ; and the opponents of the measure attacked it vehemently, because it put the peasants at the mercy of their creditors, and by encouraging them to sell their land, took away the fixity of tenure their definite status had hitherto secured to them.

What amount of force there was in this charge had more validity against the edicts by which after Stein's dismissal Hardenberg[1] completed his work. These followed on the lines Stein had laid down. That of November 1810 was based on the principle that no one should have the power to close a trade against any man. By this and by the more celebrated Edict of September 1811,[2] which freed leasehold and copyhold alike from all services, and established alienability and free disposition of property, Hardenberg wrought a great change in Prussia, His solution of the land question took the form of a compromise. The peasantry were divided into two classes, leaseholders and those who had hereditary or life claims on their tenements. It was proposed to let the landlords buy out the first class by giving them half their holdings, for compensation in money was altogether out of the question from the want of cash in the country. Finally, copyholders for life were subjected to the same arrangement, hereditary tenants compensating their landlords by surrendering a third of their tenements. This system had been anticipated by Stein when, in July 1808, he had relieved the needs of the peasantry on the royal domains in Prussia, among whom serfdom had been abolished as long ago as the reign of Frederick William I. He had adopted a scheme of Schrotter's,[3] which allowed the peasants to possess their holdings as their own, subject to land-tax and to the resumption by the State of various rights and concessions. At the same time, much was done in the way of abolishing monopolies; for instance, that of making and selling millstones and building mills, hitherto in the hands of the Government, was abolished by Stein for Prussia only in the spring of 1808, for the whole kingdom by Hardenberg in the two following years.

Reforms in the judicial system, aiming at even and speedy

---

[1] Recalled to office as Chancellor in 1810.
[2] Cf. Seeley, ii. 185.   [3] *Ibid.* ii. 192.

justice, with equality before the law, financial measures, including the imposition of an income tax (Sept. 1811), the abolition of that exemption from taxation which the nobles had hitherto enjoyed, the establishment of a State Bank, and the introduction of a paper currency, were among the objects with which Hardenberg was occupied during his tenure of the Chancellorship. In this capacity he did Prussia excellent service, even if he seemed to have abandoned the cause of opposition to Napoleon and dissembled his hatred of the Emperor so well that even Stein distrusted him.[1] But to secure the success and continuity of these reforms something more was wanting. It was useless to introduce reforms unless provision could be made that there should be men to work them, and to work them in the right way. It had not been the machinery but the *morale* of Prussia which had failed her in 1806, and one of the most pressing needs was a thorough reform of the system of education, both primary and secondary. The rising generation must be taught the necessity of patriotism and civic duty, the *gymnasia* must be reformed, and something done to repair the loss inflicted on Prussian education by the cession of Halle and its University to Westphalia. With this branch of the regeneration of Prussia the name of William von Humboldt will always be associated. Appointed Minister of Public Instruction in 1809, he was largely responsible for the foundation in the August of that year of the University of Berlin, supported by the State with a grant which must have been a severe tax on its already burdened exchequer. The share of this University in keeping alive the spirit of opposition to foreign rule and in identifying Prussia with the growing feeling of German nationality was destined to be no small one, and in 1811 a sister University was established at Breslau to help in the work.

Parallel with the civil and social reorganisation of Prussia, went the reform of that army on whose traditions and past glories Prussia had relied with such fatal effect in 1806. Reform was essential, but there was still a school of military thought which adhered to its belief that a dead lion was superior to any number of living animals of other species, and therefore resisted all attempts at departure from the Frederician system. On the Military Reorganisation Commission, of which Scharnhorst had been appointed President, both schools were represented,

[1] Cf. Seeley, ii. 462.

the Frederician being stronger in numbers, the more modern school powerful through the character of its representatives. Scharnhorst himself, Gneisenau the brave defender of Colberg, and von Grolmann, a young major of great zeal and capacity. These three were in full accord as to the essential needs, the formation of a reserve outside the standing army, the nationalisation of the army by uniting all classes in its ranks, and the substitution of a discipline of reason and humanity for the savage rule by terror which was the ideal of the Frederician school.[1] These proposals provoked much opposition, both in the Commission and in the army as a whole; but the King was heartily with the reformers, remodelled the Commission so as to give them the upper hand, and supported them in most of the changes they introduced.

Naturally the first steps taken were in the direction of getting rid of the inefficient and incompetent officers who had been responsible for the shameful surrenders of 1806, of dismissing the foreigners of whom there had always been so large a number in the army since the practice of enlisting them had been introduced by Frederick II, of opening the commissioned ranks to non-nobles, of improving the *morale* of the troops by ameliorating the conditions and the terms of their service. But these were only details compared with the great change Scharnhorst desired to introduce. Frederick William I had established the principle that a subject is by the fact of his allegiance bound to serve his master; but the exemptions so freely granted and the large enlistment of foreigners had made it almost a dead letter. Scharnhorst desired to make national defence the primary duty of every citizen, to cause it to be regarded as a privilege not a burden, and he favoured the establishment of a national militia which would also serve as a bond of political union. This was more than Frederick William was quite prepared for; he rather dreaded the political effects of the arming of the masses, while the Radicals feared that military training would destroy culture. But it was Napoleon who forced a decision by the famous clause in the Convention of September 8th, 1808, which fixed the strength of the Prussian Army at 42,000 and forbade the organisation of a militia. Accordingly, Scharnhorst adopted the plan of passing through the ranks as large a number of men as possible, letting them serve for such a period only as

[1] Cf. *Deutsche Geschichte, 1806–1871*, i. pp. 223 ff.

was necessary to give them an adequate military training, and then dismissing them to their homes. This "furlough system," established by a Cabinet Order of August 6th, 1808, provided for a steady stream of recruits coming forward to replace the men dismissed to their homes; and thus, despite Napoleon's conditions, a reserve of trained men was built up. These men on furlough were maintained in an efficient condition by secret drilling, sergeants being sent round the country for the purpose, by which means Napoleon's refusal to allow the formation of a *Landwehr* was circumvented.

Scharnhorst, however, did not escape Napoleon's notice. When, in 1810, on the fall of Stein's successor, Altenstein, Hardenberg was with Napoleon's consent called to office,[1] the Emperor insisted that Scharnhorst should be dismissed. This, of course, took place; but Scharnhorst did not have to imitate Stein in flying from Prussia: he remained in the kingdom, and took a very large share in the work of military reorganisation nominally carried on by his successor, Hake.

But though in these various ways and at the expense of many of the old traditions of the Frederician system a new Prussia was being built up out of the ruins of the edifice which had collapsed at Jena, Prussia had still to drain the cup of humiliation to the dregs. She had remained inactive in 1809; but when, in 1812, Central Europe was once more plunged into war by Russia's refusal to continue to enforce the Continental System, it was not with inaction that Napoleon was content. Prussia's last humiliation was the Convention of February 24th, 1812, which made her little more than the advanced base of the French invasion of Russia. Not only did she have to send a contingent of 20,000 to Napoleon's army, she had to collect vast magazines of supplies for his use, and to place the country and all its fortresses and resources at his disposal.

For between 1809 and 1812 a great change had come over Napoleon's foreign relations. Russia was no longer the ally, Austria no longer the enemy. With the substitution of the re-actionary and opportunist Metternich for Stadion, Austria had abandoned her championship of German nationalism, and had readily accepted Napoleon's overtures. Metternich was utterly unaffected by sentimental considerations. The traditions of the Holy Roman Empire were nothing to him; he was only

---

[1] *Deutsche Geschichte, 1806–1871*, i. 264.

moved by the new feeling of German nationality inasmuch as it aroused his suspicions and dislike. Anything in the way of a popular movement was sure to arouse the bitterest hostility in him. A reactionary, narrow and suspicious, he hated Napoleon as the man who had humiliated Austria and deprived her of provinces and prestige, not as the representative of military despotism or as the oppressor of Germany. But when Napoleon showed signs of a wish to make friends with Austria, the hope of future favours made Metternich only too ready to overlook past injuries.

The outward sign of these better relations was Napoleon's marriage to Archduchess Marie Louise, celebrated at Vienna not nine months after the battle of Wagram (March 11th, 1810). The haughty Hapsburgs thus descended almost to the level of the Wittelsbachs and the other families with whom the Bonapartes had been pleased to form marriage alliances. Nevertheless, Metternich failed even to secure the concessions he had hoped to obtain; for Napoleon hurried Prince Schwarzenberg, the Austrian Ambassador at Paris, into signing the convention (Feb. 7th), so that he might be able to counter the Czar's rejection of the overtures he had made for the hand of a Russian Princess by the accomplished fact of his Austrian match.

This was one of the causes of disagreement between Napoleon and his ally of Tilsit. More serious was the Continental System. Russia found her interests and her commercial prosperity injured by her faithful fulfilment of Napoleon's demands. Alexander could not help recalling the circumstances of his father's death: why should he sacrifice the trade of Russia to a quarrel which was not his own? Moreover, Napoleon's measures for the enforcement of the Continental System were going beyond Alexander's powers of endurance. The annexation of the German coast-lands from the Ems Eastward (Dec. 13th, 1810) was a high-handed act which would, however, hardly have aroused Alexander's wrath so much had it not involved the suppression of the Grand Duchy of Oldenburg, held by his cousin, Duke Peter. Russia's reply to this was the ukase of December 31st, 1810, imposing heavy taxes on French wines, and permitting the importation of colonial products under a neutral flag. This was practically a defiance of Napoleon; and though the rupture was delayed for more than another year, it was henceforward inevitable.

To come to blows with Russia there was only one road which Napoleon could take, and that lay through Germany, so that the conflict was bound to be of vital importance to Germany even if the question at issue had not really been the continuation of Napoleon's predominance over Europe. But as Germany stood in 1812, the choice of the line to be taken was not hers to make. The states which formed the Confederation of the Rhine were pledged to assist Napoleon, even though the Continental System which Russia was refusing to endure any longer pressed even more heavily on them than on the subjects of the Czar. In Russia there were no interfering French Custom-house officers to make domiciliary visits : no Russian shop-keeper need fear to be dragged off to the galleys for the heinous crime of possessing goods of English origin. Yet to these and similar infringement of their liberty the Germans had been liable ever since the Fontainebleau decrees ; and while the export trade of Germany was practically at a standstill, tobacco, coffee, tea and sugar, luxuries so common as to be practically necessities, could only be obtained with great difficulty and at famine prices. Germany was under a tyrant against whom she could hope for no redress, and her sufferings in this way only emphasised her helplessness. Austria also was about to send a contingent to aid Napoleon. The hope of obtaining some return for her services combined with jealousy of Russia's success in the Balkans to bring about this result. Metternich, indeed, was able to represent this action as unavoidable. To take the side of Russia was out of the question, neutrality without mobilisation would be perilous, armed neutrality too expensive to be considered : Austria must therefore take part in the invasion, but her part in the campaign was typical of her real sentiments. The 30,000 men of whom her contingent consisted took care to do as little as possible for their ally : they formed a separate corps and thus preserved the appearance of inde-pendence ; while the assistance they gave Napoleon was of no serious importance, chiefly consisting of letting Chichagoff's forces slip unmolested past their front on their way from the Lower Danube to the Beresina.

Prussia in like manner had to decide between the desirable and the possible, between defying her oppressor by throwing in her lot with Russia, and submitting to Napoleon's requirements. The question was soon settled. Krusemarck's convention was hailed by the "patriots" as the death-blow to their hopes. "We have signed our own death-warrant," wrote Gneisenau, and he and Boyen and Clausewitz resigned their commissions in disgust and left the country. "All is lost, and honour with it," was Blücher's comment; but the alternative was impossible. If Prussia joined Russia, the Russian forces would have to deprive themselves of an ally far more valuable than even the regenerated Prussian army, the physical difficulties which their country would place in an invader's way. Alone, Prussia could do nothing: for the Russians to advance beyond the Niemen would only invite a repetition of 1807. The Convention of February 24th was a humiliation, but it was the necessary corollary of Prussia's previous policy.

Thus all Germany stood on Napoleon's side as he advanced Eastward. In the army which invaded Russia there were almost as many Germans as Frenchmen.[1] Thus the whole VIth Corps (28,000 men) was composed of Bavarians, the VIIth (19,000) of Saxons, the VIIIth (19,000) of Westphalians. The contingents of Baden, Mecklenburg and Hesse-Darmstadt formed part of Davoût's huge Ist Corps; in the IInd Corps were included the men of the Hanseatic towns; the Würtembergers marched under Ney in the IIIrd Corps, the men of Berg and the minor states came up later with Victor. Macdonald's Xth Corps included the Prussian contingent and a mixed division of Bavarians, Westphalians and Poles. In like manner four of Murat's eleven cavalry divisions were made up of Germans and Poles. In all some 150,000 men from the Confederation of the Rhine formed part of the Grand Army, about a quarter of the total, while among the 200,000 "Frenchmen" in its ranks a small number must have come from the departments on the left bank of the Rhine, formerly part of the Holy Roman Empire. Indeed, if one includes in the reckoning the Austrian and Prussian contingents, the German element in the army of invasion was probably larger than any German army ever collected by the rulers of Germany for an enterprise in which the interests or the aspirations of Germany were concerned. Napoleon had united Germany in a way her own Princes and peoples had never united her before. But the heart of Germany was not in the invasion. It was with the utmost reluctance that the Prussian contingent

[1] Cf. H. B. George, *Napoleon's Invasion of Russia*, which is also very useful for the attitude and policy of Austria and Prussia at this period.

marched against the forces on whom the last hopes of Prussia rested; how little zeal for the cause inspired the Austrians has already been described; and if in the contingents of the Confederation there were many who had good reason to be grateful to Napoleon for the benefits his rule had brought them, there were also many who had been dragged from their homes to serve. Yet there was no approach to disaffection or treachery among the Germans in the Grand Army.[1] The poor success which attended the efforts of Stein and the Duke of Oldenburg to organise a German Legion out of them is a testimony to the hold which Napoleon had over his vassals. Few of the prisoners enlisted, fewer still deserted the Grand Army to join the Legion; and even if the privations they had endured may have accounted for their unwillingness to undergo new hardships under new colours, it also shows that the long-suffering Germans were not yet fully roused against Napoleon, or lacked the courage and the determination to risk anything for Germany. But so far as German nationalism was a real thing and had a real existence, it was all against Napoleon.

And to some degree cosmopolitanism and localism were beginning to give way to a national feeling. The period is one of the utmost importance in German literature; and though for the most part the great writers of the day pursued their own lines of intellectual development, quite regardless of the political situation of their country, some few did turn towards it. The *Tugendbund*, founded at Königsberg in 1808 for the revival of "morality, religion and public spirit," and suppressed at Napoleon's instance in the following year, was in the main the work of these same "intellectuals" who had hitherto held aloof from politics; and even if it and the secret societies to which its suppression gave rise really effected but little, their formation is an indication of the new order of things. The career of the philosopher Johann Gottlieb Fichte is typical of this change from the cosmopolitan to the national ideal. His *Grundzügen des Zeitalters* of 1806 has only to be compared with the *Reden an die Deutschen Krieger*, written two years later. Patriotism and the fate of his country were nothing to him before 1806, but that autumn of misfortune and disgrace changed his attitude. He now urged on his hearers at Berlin the adoption of a national system of education as the only way to cure the evils of localism

[1] Cf. George, pp. 49–50.

and lack of union: he preached a gospel of self-sacrifice for the national welfare, and called on all Germans to sink local differences in striving for a common end.

Another writer who exercised a great influence over his fellow-countrymen, rousing them to a sense of their common interests and common sufferings, was the poet Heinrich von Kleist. Keenly alive to the degradation and humiliating position of Germany, he read the present into the past: his *Hermanns-schlact* is really prophetic, not historic; anti-Gallicanism inspires it; to him the Romans are Frenchmen, and Frenchmen only.

The rise of this feeling was assisted by the great development of universities all over Germany. In Bavaria Maximilian Joseph abolished the Jesuit schools at Bamberg and Dillingen, freed München and Würzburg from clerical control, and called in North German professors of great repute. In Baden von Reizenstein, the enlightened minister of the Grand Duke, did much to revive Heidelberg University, and the Theological Faculty in that body played an important part in rousing national feeling. Of the University of Berlin and von Humboldt, mention has already been made; but great as was the direct service to education which Humboldt thus gave, of even more importance was the indirect result of his work. Till now the great intellects of Germany had been cosmopolitan in their outlook, non-national if not actively anti-national in their ideas. What Humboldt did was to enlist culture on the side of the State, to turn the intellectual movement into a patriotic channel, to reconcile the widely different schools of thought represented by Goethe and Stein.

Thus, despite the great reception which Napoleon held at Dresden on his way to the Niemen, despite the good service done by the German troops in his army—some idea of this may be gathered from the fact that there were no less than 186 Westphalian officers in the casualty list at Borodino,[1] and that one Bavarian light cavalry regiment could only muster 2 officers and 30 men at the close of the day[2]—Germany as a whole waited for the fate of the expedition with feelings in which anxiety for her sons was mixed with hopes for her oppressor's failure.

[1] Cf. Fisher, p. 305.   [2] *Deutsche Geschichte, 1806–1871*, i. 289.

CHAPTER XXX

THE WAR OF LIBERATION, I

COMPLETELY as Napoleon's great invasion of Russia had failed his repulse had by no means settled the question of his supremacy over Central Europe. His yoke was too firmly fixed upon Germany, Italy and the Netherlands to be thrown off in a moment, and after only one defeat; and the completeness of his control of France may be estimated by the prodigious efforts he was able to command from France to retrieve his lost prestige. Though the shattered and demoralised relics of the Grand Army which had straggled back across the Niemen in December 1812 hardly mustered a sixth of the mighty host which had crossed it on the Eastward way, it was far from certain that 1813 might not see the attack renewed by a new Grand Army. Napoleon, who had hurried off to Paris, had thrown himself with characteristic energy into the Herculean task of reorganisation, and never were his great talents as an administrator more conspicuously displayed. Russia, on the other hand, was much exhausted by her exertions; she had worsted Napoleon, but it had been at no light cost that such a victory could be achieved over the master of Western Europe. Many of her generals and statesmen, among them Kutusov himself, were strongly opposed to the idea of risking anything in an attempt to follow up the success of the defensive campaign. They judged, and rightly, that all depended on the action of Austria and Prussia. Unless Russia could rely on the co-operation of those two Powers, to advance across the Niemen would merely court disaster.

And as yet neither Austria nor Prussia saw the way clear before them. Much as Frederick William longed to throw off the yoke of Napoleon, he could not at first nerve himself to the desperate step of defying the Emperor, not even when Metternich opened negotiations and showed himself anxious to turn Napoleon's misfortunes to the advantage of his unwilling allies.[1]

[1] Cf. *Deutsche Geschichte, 1806–1871,* i. 299, also *La Defection de la Prusse.*

And Metternich was only preparing to run with the hare in case hunting with the hounds should prove too dangerous a policy. Jealousy of Russia was with him a far stronger motive than hostility to France: he had no intention of shaking Napoleon's supremacy off Central Europe only to substitute that of the Czar. Public opinion in Austria might be strongly in favour of the bolder policy, but Metternich had no desire for a conflict with Napoleon; all he wanted was an opportunity of establishing an equilibrium in Europe which should secure the independence of Central Europe by balancing West against East; he wanted a peace in which Napoleon would for once not dictate, but accept terms. Schwarzenberg, it is true, went to the length of disobeying Eugene's orders to assist him in holding the line of the Vistula, and withdrew with the Austrian auxiliary corps into Galicia (January); but no immediate breach in the alliance between Austria and Napoleon followed: Metternich was waiting on events. However, while the governments were hesitating, the control of events was taken out of their hands by men who had a more accurate appreciation of the possibilities of the case.

Among these the place of honour must be given to General Yorck, the commander of the Prussian corps which had formed part of Marshal Macdonald's command. With that officer Yorck had soon quarrelled, and as early as October the Russians were making overtures to him in the hope that he would join them and help them to cut off the retreat of the Grand Army. Yorck had acquainted his King with these offers ; but as he had received no new instructions, but only orders to assume the Governorship of East Prussia, he had taken no further step. However, when, in December, Macdonald ordered a retreat, Yorck deliberately allowed [1] Wittgenstein's Russians to interpose between himself and Macdonald, and, under the plea of being isolated, proceeded to enter into negotiations with the Russians. On December 30th, acting entirely on his own responsibility, he took the momentous step of concluding the Convention of Tauroggen. By this the Prussian troops under Yorck were to take post in the territory between Memel, Tilsit and the Haff, which was to be neutralised. Should the convention be repudiated either by the Czar or by the King of Prussia, they were to be free to depart, but were not to serve against Russia before March 1st.

The immediate result of this was that Macdonald found it

---

[1] *La Defection de la Prusse*, pp. 115-118,

impossible to maintain himself at Tilsit, and retired from Königsberg to Dantzic. However, the political importance of Yorck's action in thus disassociating a Prussian force from the alliance with France was far greater than the mere military results of the step. What would the King do? would he ratify his general's bold action by declaring against Napoleon? would he treat Yorck as guilty, as technically he certainly was, of high treason, and disown him? At first the chances seemed to favour this second alternative. To take arms against Napoleon was by no means so simple a matter as it might seem to those who had no thought for anything but the sufferings and the humiliation which Prussia had endured at his hands. The overthrow of Napoleon, even when accomplished, would merely bring up new difficulties. Napoleon had made too many changes in the political complexion of Germany for the removal of his yoke to restore Germany to the condition in which it had been before its subjection to his influence. The fate of the Confederation of the Rhine promised a superfluity of contentious matter, and it was only one among several problems. Thus Frederick William with the idea of appeasing Napoleon did actually disown Yorck and order his arrest; but Wittgenstein prevented the written order reaching Yorck's quarters, Bülow in West Prussia acknowledged him as Governor of East Prussia, and his summons to the *levée en masse* of East Prussia was obeyed with an alacrity and an enthusiasm which left no doubt as to the attitude of the population. In Eastern Germany the peasantry had not received at Napoleon's hands those benefits which his rule had brought to Westphalians and Swabians: to them he was only the enemy and the oppressor, the author not of the Code, but of the Continental System.

It was fortunate for the patriotic party in Germany that at this moment Stein should have been in Alexander's confidence. More accessible to the influence of ideas than was Francis II or Frederick William III, the Czar listened to Stein's advice, and, caught by the notion of associating his name with the liberation of Germany, decided to come forward as the champion of the cause Stein had so much at heart. Thus with insurrection already on foot in East Prussia, the Czar committed to a forward policy, and Austria letting it be known that she would not oppose it since her aim was a peace which could ensure Europe against Napoleon's undue predominance, with Hardenberg supporting

Scharnhorst's pleadings in favour of a bolder policy, Frederick William's doubts were solved for him. But it was only gradually that the decision was reached. The first step was taken when Frederick William retired from Berlin to Breslau, partly in order to be more out of the way, and so better able to avoid a collision with Napoleon, partly because he had some idea of trying to keep Silesia neutral by denying it to both parties. But when, on February 12th, the troops in Pomerania and Silesia were mobilised, and volunteers were called for to bring them up to establishment, recruits flocked in with a zeal and a keenness which went far to decide Frederick William's mind. So insistent was the popular clamour and the demand to be led against the French, that on February 27th a treaty was negotiated at Kalisch which definitely committed Prussia to hostility to Napoleon, and confirmed the decision the King had made four days earlier. This treaty pledged Russia to continue the war until Prussia regained the territories she had possessed before 1806; but it was understood that the restoration should not include Hanover, and that Prussia would give up her claims to the greater part of the acquisitions she had made from Poland in 1793 and 1795. These reservations were most necessary: without the second, Prussia could not hope to secure the indispensable Russian aid, while her claim on Hanover had contributed as much as anything to the ruin of the Third Coalition, and if persisted in now could not fail to lead to trouble with Great Britain, whose help was no less important.

Meanwhile both sides were straining every nerve to get ready for the coming campaign. While the relics of the Grand Army had been thrown into the fortresses of Poland and Prussia and were endeavouring to hold the line of the Vistula, and so keep the Russians at bay, Napoleon was devoting all his marvellous energy and powers of organisation to the creation of an even vaster army with which to wipe out the memories of his defeats. The raw material he had ready to hand.[1] Over 130,000 of the conscripts of 1813 had already been called out, and had been drilling at the depôts since November 1812. A decree of the Senate of January 11th, 1813, placed at his disposal 100,000 men belonging to the classes of past years who had hitherto escaped service, and also anticipated the conscription of 1814 by calling up 150,000 men not due till that year. The

[1] Cf. Friedrich, i. pp. 59-70.

National Guard had already provided 80,000 men, the so-called "Cohorts," who had already been under arms for a year and were now formed into regiments of the Line, another 80,000 of the same force being called upon a little later to fill their places. For a leaven by which these masses of recruits might be turned into efficient soldiers, Napoleon was so fortunate as to have among the survivors of the Grand Army some 20,000 more officers and under-officers than were needed by the units under Eugene and in the fortresses on the Vistula. Without these invaluable veterans the campaign of 1813 would have been impossible. Had the news of the decision to retire from Moscow found Prussia prepared to rise in Napoleon's rear and so to intercept the retreat of the Grand Army, she could have paralysed the military resources of France and averted the awful loss of life in the campaigns of 1813 and 1814. Such a step was, however, impossible. Prussia was too securely held down under Napoleon's heel, and the famished remnant of the Grand Army was on the Niemen before the full extent of the disaster was realised throughout Germany. The Emperor also recalled from every battalion of the army in Spain 150 men to serve as the nucleus of the new units; he summoned from retirement every half-pay officer, every veteran still capable of service; he stripped his useless fleets of marines and of seamen to provide his new army with artillerymen. By these means he succeeded in getting together an enormous force. Nor was it only on France alone that he made these vast demands. His vassal states had to provide their contingents, and no small number of Germans were called upon to do battle to keep Germany in subjection to Napoleon. Thus Westphalia had to put into the field close upon 30,000 men,[1] while from Berg over 4000 were demanded.

Numbers alone do not make an army; and while time was needed to drill, train and equip the new levies, their *morale* and readiness to fight were considerations of even greater importance. On the whole, there was no fault to be found with the spirit shown by the French recruits. Many, of course, deserted; but the great traditions of the French army, the magic of the Emperor's personality, the warlike spirit of the nation, were not slow to assert themselves. With the recruits of the vassal states things were naturally rather different; but it was noticeable that

[1] Cf. Fisher, p. 305.

though the Italian and Illyrian recruits deserted in large numbers and the Bavarians hung back, the contingents of Baden, Würtemberg and other minor states came forward readily enough. A Thuringian battalion raised by the petty Princes of that district who belonged to the Confederation of the Rhine did, it is true, desert as a body to the Prussians just before Lützen, and two battalions were formed by the Prussians from deserters coming from the former provinces of Prussia West of the Elbe;[1] but the South and West of Germany was as a whole still loyal to Napoleon, partly, no doubt, from necessity, but in no small measure from choice.

To meet these vast preparations the Allies had also to make a great effort. The Russians had suffered very heavily indeed in 1812; and though large reserves were on their way Westward, they had far to travel and the force at the front was but weak. Much, therefore, depended on Prussia and in Prussia on the measure of success which should attend Scharnhorst's plans when put to the proof. Thanks to the system of rapidly passing through the ranks a succession of trained men, he had little difficulty in bringing up to their full establishment the 46 battalions and 80 squadrons to which Napoleon had restricted the Prussian army. Indeed, the reservists came forward in such strength that it was possible to organise 42 new battalions.[2] But this was by no means all: volunteers also flocked to the colours in numbers, full of enthusiasm and patriotism, anxious to throw off Napoleon's yoke, many of them belonging to the classes hitherto exempt from military service. These for the most part formed themselves into Free Corps, providing their own uniforms and equipment, doing little drill, and relying mainly on their shooting. Some of them were formed in companies and attached to the regulars for skirmishing work, while others were organised as separate units, of which Lützow's is the best known. In partisan warfare, in raids against French communications, in cutting off messengers and stragglers, these corps did no small service. However, Scharnhorst wisely desiring a more solid reserve for the troops of the Line than these somewhat tumultuary organisations, brought forward a measure based on the *Landwehr* organisation adopted by

[1] Friedrich, i. 41.

[2] These were known as "Reserve Regiments," and must not be confused with the *Landwehr*.

Austria in 1809.[1] A royal proclamation of February 9th declared national defence to be a duty incumbent on the whole
nation, another of March 17th authorised the levy of 120,000 men
by conscription. Lots were to be drawn among the men between
17 and 40 years of age, while the upper classes were brought
into connection with the scheme through the measures adopted
for providing the equipment. Behind this force were to stand
as a last resource the *Landsturm*, armed with such weapons as
they could get, and carrying out somewhat miscellaneous duties.
The poverty of Prussia and the exhausted state of the country
made the equipment of all these recruits a very difficult matter.
Had better weapons been forthcoming much more could have
been done and a larger force placed in the field ; but though a
certain amount of help in money and stores was received from
England, that country, whose action in Germany was, of course,
much influenced by its connection with Hanover, looked rather
towards rousing an insurrection in the old territories of the
Guelphs, and was making the equipment of an Anglo-German
design in that quarter its chief effort.[2] Prussia was thus thrown
mainly on her own resources ; and great as was the readiness of
the whole nation to contribute all it could scrape together, not
even the patriotism and self-sacrifice which all classes displayed
could create resources which did not exist. Thus though troops
of a sort were forthcoming to blockade the French garrisons,
there were not many more than 60,000 Prussians ready for the
field in April, without including Free Corps. The *Landwehr*
for the most part were too ill-supplied to be fit for field service.

It was on March 15th that Frederick William issued simultaneously his declaration of war and his appeal to his subjects
to support him in his struggle for liberty. Four days later,
Nesselrode and Stein acting for Russia, and Hardenberg and
Scharnhorst for Prussia, drew up the Convention of Kalisch. In
this, in the spirit of their denunciation of the Confederation of
the Rhine as the work of the foreign tyrant, they provided that
any German Prince who within a certain prescribed time should
not have joined the Allies, should be liable to be deprived of
his territory.[3] At the same time, arrangements were made for

[1] The *Landwehr* produced some 149 battalions of infantry, averaging nearly 700,
with 116 squadrons of cavalry, rather under 100 strong.
[2] Cf. Friedrich, i. 19.
[3] *Deutsche Geschichte, 1806–1871*, i. pp. 323–324.

the administration of such portions of North Germany as might come into the hands of the Allies.

As yet the actual outbreak against Napoleon in Germany was confined to Prussia, though the feelings which prompted it were no less strong in other quarters. In Austria there was a strong nationalist movement. An influential party, headed by Archduke John and recalling the ideas of Stadion, earnestly desired to join the opponents of Napoleon and to recover Tyrol and the other provinces of which he had despoiled the Hapsburgs. This party aimed at an *Alpenbund*, an alliance between Tyrol, Illyria, Switzerland, Salzburg and the Vorarlberg which would serve as the nucleus for a South German rising against Napoleon.[1] But its views were very far from finding favour in Metternich's eyes. Much as he hated Napoleon's predominance, he hated democracy and Liberalism more, and he was most anxious to prevent anything in the way of a popular movement. If he could manage it, the reduction of the undue greatness of France should be achieved by the governments, not by the peoples.[2] Moreover, he knew that neither the financial nor the military situation of Austria[3] was such as to make war desirable, he distrusted Russia and was determined to thwart her schemes of self-aggrandisement, while he was little better disposed to Prussia. A neutral position was therefore what he desired to adopt, since it offered most prospect of settling the whole matter by diplomacy without an appeal to arms. For it was this which was his chief object. Neither the Austrian minister nor his master seems to have contemplated joining Napoleon, not even when he attempted to bribe them with Silesia and Illyria (March 27th). If they departed from their attitude of neutrality it would be to join Napoleon's opponents; but their hope was to avoid having to take this step. Accordingly, though Metternich went so far in the direction of joining the Allies as to conclude a convention with Russia which suspended hostilities and allowed Schwarzenberg to withdraw unmolested, he announced to Narbonne that his master desired "peace, and nothing but peace," and would

---

[1] *Deutsche Geschichte, 1806–1871*, i. p. 329.   [2] *Ibid.* p. 325.

[3] After the disasters of 1809 the Austrian army had been restricted to a strength of 150,000 men and its regiments were exceedingly weak, so that much time was needed before they could be brought up to war strength by levies of recruits; cf. Friedrich, i. 52–55.

assume a mediatory position, mobilising her forces to procure respect for her mediation. Meanwhile, to prove that Austria had no intention of raising the banner of insurrection in Germany, he induced the Emperor to have Archduke John arrested and sent to his estates, by representing to the jealous Francis that his brother was aiming at erecting for himself an independent kingdom of " Rhaetia."[1]

The attitude of Bavaria was largely influenced by that of Austria, since nothing was more certain than that Austria would seek to recover Tyrol. A premature rising of the Tyrolese would make relations between Austria and Bavaria very awkward. Thus when Prussia sought to induce Bavaria to join the Allies, or at least to send no assistance to Napoleon, offering as an inducement to resign all claims on Anspach and Baireuth, Bavaria was hardly prepared to desert Napoleon. Montgelas was not altogether ill-disposed to the notion, but he disliked the Prussian appeal to the people, fearing that it would lead to anarchy: he was also very much afraid of Napoleon and was alarmed by the rumours of his vast preparations. Thus a Bavarian contingent was in the end to be found under Napoleon's colours, though her zeal for the cause was decidely evanescent.

Somewhat similar was the plight of Saxony. Prussia's hostility to her Southern neighbour was notorious, and directly war was declared by Prussia, Blücher seized Cottbus[2] in the name of his King. Austria, however, was much more kindly disposed: indeed, Metternich was almost ready to promise Saxony compensation for the Duchy of Warsaw, which Alexander was resolved to annex, and in April a convention was concluded between Austria and Saxony, the latter promising to support Austria in her efforts to bring about a peace. The Allies were by this time advancing into Saxony ; and before their approach King Frederick Augustus, uncertain what course to pursue, fled first to Plauen and then to Ratisbon. In his absence the people of Saxony received the Allies with great enthusiasm, though the officials were hostile, and the Saxon army was kept concentrated at Torgau by its commander, Thielmann, well out of the way.

In the meantime the campaign had begun. Eugene's effort to hold the line of the Vistula had been frustrated by Schwarzenberg, who evacuated Warsaw without fighting and withdrew to

---

[1] Cf. Friedrich, i. pp. 20 ff.   [2] Cf. p. 517.

Galicia, which compelled the Viceroy to quit Posen (Feb. 12th) for Frankfort on the Oder, by which Rapp at Dantzic and the other French garrisons on the Vistula were left isolated. But the line of the Oder was in its turn abandoned when raiding parties of Cossacks crossed the river and began to threaten the French communications, one band actually penetrating to Berlin. By the first week in March, Eugene had fallen back to the Elbe, establishing his headquarters at Magdeburg. He had left garrisons in the principal fortresses on the Oder which it would have been better to have kept with the field-army, for the Allies, disregarding these obstacles, pressed on after him, the Russian advanced guard reaching Berlin (March 11th) about a week after he had left it, while on the left the Prussians from Silesia under Blücher moved on Dresden; and farther North, Tettenborn's Russian light troops occupied Hamburg (March 18th), which Carra St. Cyr had evacuated.

As Wittgenstein continued his advance on Magdeburg (April 2nd), he fell in a little to the East of that town with Eugene, who had taken the offensive in the hope of catching the Allies unconcentrated. The effort proved a failure, for a sharp action between Nedlitz and Möckern (April 5th) ended in the retreat of the French, who fell back across the Elbe to the Saale, which allowed the Russians to move up the Elbe to Dessau, cross there (April 9th), and gain touch with Blücher who, after occupying Dresden, from which the French had withdrawn, had pushed on to the Mulde.

It was a critical situation for Napoleon, for had the Allies pressed on resolutely they might have fallen upon the troops he was concentrating to support Eugene—and organising and training, too, simultaneously with their concentration—before they could be ready to go into action. Scharnhorst pleaded urgently for such a move, but the Allies were not prepared to run the risk until Miloradovitch's Russian corps could come up; and this was not three days behind, as it should have been, but fourteen. Thus the critical moments slipped by, and on April 24th Napoleon arrived at Erfurt and was within supporting distance of the Viceroy's troops on the Saale. The Emperor had with him about 80,000 men, comprising the Guard and the corps of Ney (III.), Bertrand (IV.), Marmont (VI.), and Oudinot (XII.), all of which were mainly composed of raw recruits, hastily formed into battalions and imperfectly trained and equipped. He was very weak in cavalry, having barely 8000 horsemen, for it was in this arm that it was most difficult to fill the gaps which 1812 had made; and though well supplied with artillery, his army was one with which only a most daring general would have ventured to undertake a bold offensive movement.

Yet such was Napoleon's design. Dresden was the point on which he was moving, though Leipzig was his immediate objective. He aimed at executing the converse movement to that which had led to the brilliant success of Oct. 1806, that is, he wished to fall on the right flank of his enemy, crush it, and so push through to the Elbe and place himself between them and Prussia.[1] Wittgenstein also meant to take the offensive. He had concentrated the field army of the Allies, including the Prussians of Blücher[2] and Yorck[3] and some 40,000 Russians, partly under his own command, partly under Winzingerode, in all about 90,000 men, to the South of Leipzig. Despite his inferior numbers, he resolved on a daring stroke, a flank attack on the French as they moved forward on Leipzig.

Napoleon had reached Weimar on the 28th of April, and next day an advance to Weissenfels brought his columns into touch with Eugene's men, who came up to Merseburg.[4] From the Saale Napoleon pushed forward towards Leipzig by Markranstädt and Lindenau. Meanwhile Wittgenstein moved from behind the Elster by Pegau on Lützen, hoping to fall on Napoleon's right flank and rear, and by surprising the young French troops to throw them into confusion.

It was about midday on May 2nd, while Napoleon was watching his advanced guard, Lauriston's corps, drive Kleist's Prussians in upon Leipzig, that Wittgenstein delivered his attack. To cover the movements of the rest of the army against any interruption from the Southward, Napoleon had left Ney's corps on his right flank, and it was on this corps, posted between the villages of Gross Görschen and Starsiedel, that Wittgenstein's blow fell. Though outnumbered, Ney offered an obstinate resistance, clinging resolutely to the villages, and only being

---

[1] Cf. Yorck von Wartenburg, ii. 247.

[2] 52 squadrons and 38 battalions.

[3] 16 squadrons and 19 battalions.

[4] Eugene's force comprised the corps of Lauriston (V.), composed of the regiments formed out of the "cohorts" of the National Guards, Reynier (VII.) and Macdonald (XI.), these last two representing the reserves of the Grand Army which had escaped the disaster of 1812: he had in all some 70,000 men.

forced back from the Görschens and Rahna to Kaja after very heavy fighting. This gave Napoleon time to alter his dispositions, to divert to their right Macdonald and the Guard, who had been following Lauriston, and to hasten back to Ney's succour. Had Ney been unsupported he must have been overpowered, but Marmont's corps came up on his right and relieved the pressure on him by occupying Starsiedel; and of this village the French retained possession all day, Bertrand arriving about 4 p.m. and supporting Marmont. Wittgenstein had to devote all his Russians to the contest in this quarter, and thus he had no troops left to support Blücher, whose success in driving in Ney from the villages to which he clung so tenaciously could not be followed up. Indeed, he was unable to maintain the ground he had won; for Napoleon, judging the situation critical, sent the Young Guard and one of Marmont's divisions forward against Kaja, retook it and the other villages, and hurled the Prussians back. The arrival of some Russian reinforcements was more than neutralised by that of Macdonald, who pushed forward over the Flossgraben against the Allied right and decided the day. Had Napoleon had any cavalry available for the pursuit, he might have done much; as it was, the Allies were strong enough in this arm to secure an unmolested retreat. They had lost no guns and very few prisoners, and the 15,000 casualties they had suffered were exceeded by the losses they had inflicted on the French, which probably amounted to 25,000.[1] Still the battle was a great triumph for the young soldiers of France, more especially for their officers, who had in so short a time made their raw conscripts capable of facing the Allies in a pitched battle. Discipline they had not yet acquired, and it was largely because his army was neither physically nor morally capable of great exertions immediately after a battle that Napoleon was unable to follow up the battle of Gross Görschen as he had followed up Jena. He did, it is true, push on in the wake of the retreating Allies to Dresden, which he occupied on the 8th, the Allies retiring behind the Elbe; but his want of cavalry prevented his pursuit from doing them any serious damage.

Having reoccupied the Saxon capital, Napoleon's next step was to send an ultimatum to the King of Saxony demanding that he should do his duty as a Prince of the Confederation of

[1] Rousset, *La Grande Armée de 1813*, p. 90.

the Rhine. Frederick Augustus, impressed by the spectacle of Napoleon again victorious, obeyed, and his troops took the position assigned to them as the 24th and 25th Divisions in Reynier's (VII.) corps. Meanwhile Vandamme moved North against the Allied force which, after occupying Hamburg, had crossed the Elbe into Hanover and inflicted a defeat on Morand's division at Lüneburg (April 2nd). The nucleus of the Allied force in this quarter consisted of some Russian troops under Tettenborn; but Swedish help was expected, and it was to this district that the Russo-German Legion, organised out of the German prisoners taken in 1812, was sent. But in addition to these forces, much was done in the way of raising battalions among the inhabitants of North-Western Germany who had suffered so much from Napoleon's Customs officials. In this work England played a prominent part, providing arms and equipment and sending over to Germany some 500 men of the King's German Legion to stiffen the new levies, while the 3rd Hussars and two artillery batteries of that force together with an English rocket battery of the Royal Artillery were also added to this very miscellaneous corps, which was placed under the command of a Hanoverian general, Count Wallmoden. The arrival of the French reinforcements quite changed the situation on the Lower Elbe. After some sharp fighting the Allies had to retire to the right bank of the river, and Hamburg was re-occupied by the French (May 30th). Bülow also, who had come up to Magdeburg and Wittenberg, fell back to Berlin, and the whole line of the Elbe from the Bohemian frontier to the sea was again in French hands.

Napoleon did not spend more time than he could help at Dresden. The victory of May 2nd had been far from decisive, and he was most anxious to bring the Allies to battle again. They made no attempt to dispute the line of the Elbe, and on the 12th Napoleon began to transfer his army to the right bank. He believed that the Russians had separated from the Prussians, and that the latter were retreating on Berlin, their allies up the Oder to Breslau. Accordingly he divided his own forces, directing Ney with the IIIrd, Vth and VIIth Corps against Berlin, advancing himself with the Guards, the IVth, VIth, XIth and XIIth Corps into Lusatia.

But his idea that the Allies had adopted divergent lines of retreat was quite erroneous. On the contrary, they had received considerable reinforcements, including 14,000 Russians under Barclay de Tolly and some Prussian reserves, and had taken up a strong position behind the Spree at Bautzen, and were quite prepared for battle. Here it was that Napoleon found them when he pushed forward into Lusatia, expecting to drive the Russians before him. As soon as he discovered that they meant to give battle, he sent orders to Ney to change his route and to come back to the aid of the main body, directing him to move on Drehsa in the right rear of the Allies' position in order to outflank them, cut them off from Silesia, and compel them to retreat, not on Breslau but against the Bohemian frontier. Ney received these orders at Hoyerswerda on the 19th of May, on which day the rest of the army was assembled to the West of Bautzen.

The position of the Allies was one of some strength : they were drawn up on the heights behind the Spree, their right— Barclay's Russians—thrown back from Plieskowitz to Gleina, where it rested on the Blösa, an affluent of the Spree. Blücher's corps formed the right centre, Yorck being on his left, the main body of the Russians beyond that. Somewhat in front of the main line were Kleist's Prussians at Burk, and Miloradovitch's Russians in and to the left of Bautzen itself. This was a strong position, but it had the grave defects of being intersected by the narrow valley of the Blösa and of being rather too long for the numbers available. Moreover, the Allies were seriously handicapped by the want of a proper commander-in-chief; Wittgenstein's control over their operations was little more than nominal, for Alexander had practically taken the direction of affairs out of his hands, and the Czar had no pretensions to match himself against Napoleon.

Wishing to deceive the Allies into the belief that he was aiming rather at turning their left flank than their right, and at cutting them off not from Silesia but from Bohemia, Napoleon began his attack on the 20th with Oudinot's corps, which formed his extreme right. Oudinot crossed the Spree at Grubschütz and forced the Russians back with some success, while Macdonald and Marmont advanced against Bautzen and the IVth Corps assailed Kleist's position. The fighting was well contested, but at length a division of Marmont's corps (VI.) carried Bautzen, and by outflanking Kleist forced him also to retire from the heights of Burk to the second line. Oudinot on the right had been checked, but the result of the day's fighting was on the whole favourable to the French. Ney had hardly been engaged: he had had some sharp fighting on the 19th at Königswartha against Barclay who had been pushed out thither to check him; but though the Allies gained some successes at first, Ney had in the end forced them back behind the Spree. On the evening of the 20th his leading brigade reached the left bank of the Spree at Klix.

Next morning (May 21st) the Emperor decided to defer the serious frontal attack until Ney's turning movement had developed sufficiently to really threaten the Allied retreat; but that Marshal, after forcing Barclay back from Malschwitz to Preititz by 10 a.m., forbore to push forward, partly because he misinterpreted Napoleon's order to be in Preititz by 11 o'clock into a command not to be beyond Preititz at that hour, partly because he thought he had the Russian Guards in front of him, though they were in reality already engaged with the French centre round Baschütz. As soon as the sound of Ney's guns had told the Emperor that the turning movement had really begun he had committed his troops to the frontal attack. On the Allied left St. Priest's Russians had some success against Oudinot, but the advance of the IVth Corps by Nieder Gurick and of the VIth on Basankwitz compelled Blücher and Yorck, who came to his help, to fall back from Kreckwitz behind the Blösa. Had Ney been as far forward as Napoleon hoped he would be, the Prussians would probably have found it impossible to extricate themselves; but Kleist had managed to regain Preititz, and though thrust from it when Reynier's Saxons and Lauriston reinforced Ney, he so far delayed the turning movement that the Allies were able to escape from the net Napoleon had cast for them. But with their right driven in, their retreat endangered, and Macdonald and Oudinot pressing hard upon St. Priest and the Russian Guards, they had no alternative but to go back all along their line. By abandoning the contest before they had really been defeated, and by using their numerous cavalry to protect their retirement, they got away in good order, leaving but few prisoners and hardly any guns behind. It was then that Napoleon felt most bitterly the want of the squadrons he found it so hard to create out of his new conscripts and his untrained horses. If he could have overwhelmed the Allied cavalry, their retreat might have been changed into a disastrous rout, and Bautzen might have ranked with Austerlitz and Marengo. As it was, the Allies retired in good order by Bunzlau to Liegnitz and by Löwenberg on Goldberg, thence turning Southward to Schweidnitz.

The reason of the Allies for turning away from the Oder and placing themselves in the triangle formed by Glatz, Neisse and Schweidnitz, were, in the first place, that they wished to keep touch with Austria in case that Power should, as they fervently desired, throw in her lot with them ; secondly, that a retreat behind the Oder, the only other alternative, would have been an enormous incentive to Napoleon. Had the Allies given so clear a proof of their discouragement, he would hardly have made the fatal blunder of an armistice. But the decision was taken in opposition to the wishes of the Russian generals, especially of Barclay, who had succeeded to the command which Wittgenstein laid down in disgust.

The Allied army, indeed, was in no condition for another action. Their losses at Bautzen had been lower than those of the French, who must have had at least 18,000 casualties,[1] but still the two defeats had shaken their *morale* considerably, especially that of the Russians, and had produced a good deal of friction between the Allies. Directly after Bautzen Barclay declared that the condition of his army was such that it was imperative for him to retire behind the Oder to recruit and refresh his men ; and indeed their numbers, equipment, discipline and general tone did leave a good deal to be desired.[2] But the Prussians were aghast at so fatal a proposal. To abandon to Napoleon so fertile and productive a district as Silesia would be most harmful. Their troops were in rather better condition than were the Russians : recruits were coming in freely, and they felt, not without good reason, that so retrograde a movement would be the beginning of the end. It would perhaps bring Barclay's weakened forces nearer the reinforcements they so badly needed, but it would deliver the greater part of Prussia over to Napoleon, would as much discourage the national movement in the parts of Germany still under his rule as it would encourage his troops and confirm in their allegiance to his cause those who were wavering. Moreover, it would greatly increase the difficulties of co-operating with Austria if Francis II. should be induced to declare against Napoleon.[3]

---

[1] Cf. Rousset, p. 96.   [2] Cf. Friedrich, i. 3.   [3] *Ibid.* i. 2.

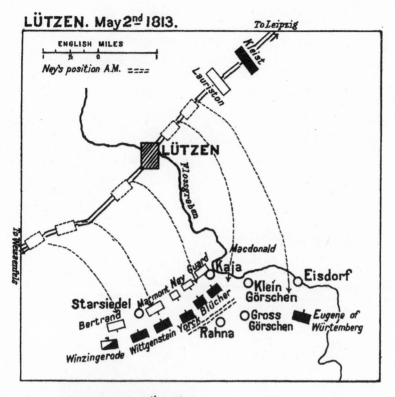

LÜTZEN. May 2nd 1813.

ENGLISH MILES

Ney's position A.M. ====

To Leipzig

Lauriston

Kleist

LÜTZEN

Flossgraben

To Weissenfels

Macdonald

Starsiedel

Bertrand

Winzingerode

Marmont Ney Guard Kaja

Wittgenstein Yorck Blücher

Rahna

Klein Görschen

Gross Görschen

Eisdorf

Eugene of Würtemberg

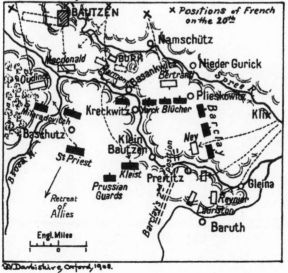

BAUTZEN May 20th & 21st 1813.

BAUTZEN

× Positions of French on the 20th

Namschütz

Macdonald

Oudinot

BURK

Basankwitz

Nieder Gurick

Bertrand

Spree R.

Plieskowitz

Miloradovitch

Basthutz

Kreckwitz

Yorck Blücher

Barclay

Klik

St Priest

Klein Bautzen

Ney

Black R.

Kleist

Prussian Guards

Preititz

Barclay

Gleina

Reynier

Lauriston

Retreat of Allies

Baruth

Engl. Miles

B.V.Darbishire, Oxford, 1908.

The divergence between the views of the Allies might have had serious consequences, indeed the Russians were within measurable distance of separating from the Prussians when the intervention of Austria resulted in the Armistice of Poischwitz.[1] Austria's action at this critical moment was of the utmost importance. Metternich may not have been a man of high principle, his policy and aims may have been reactionary, illiberal and opportunist, but he handled the diplomatic situation with great acuteness and skill. He saw that were Austria now to assist Napoleon to make good his threatened predominance in Europe, she would merely rivet the chains more firmly on her own neck ; but he was determined to avoid encouraging the popular movement in Germany, and he desired as little change in the existing territorial arrangements as might prove compatible with the secure independence of Austria and the restoration to the Hapsburgs of at any rate the provinces they had lost in 1809. Further, knowing as he did the state of the Austrian finances and of the Austrian army, he was anxious to avoid having recourse to arms if he could possibly gain his ends by any other means. He was therefore well pleased when the mission of Stadion to the headquarters of the Allies and of Bubna to Napoleon's camp resulted, despite all Napoleon's bluster and threats, in the conclusion of an armistice (June 4th). At the moment Napoleon's headquarters were at Neumarkt, his left wing was nearing Breslau, his right close to Schweidnitz, the Allies being concentrated between Strehlen and Nimptsch. Oudinot, after one success against the Prussian force covering Berlin at Hoyerswerda (May 28th), had been repulsed when he again attacked Bülow at Lückau (June 4th), and had fallen back to the Black Elster. Victor had relieved Glogau, and Davoût had reoccupied Hamburg and got into touch with the Danes. The line of demarcation, therefore, which was now arranged had to correspond to this situation. Leaving Hamburg and Lübeck in French hands, it ran up the Elbe to Magdeburg, thence followed the frontier between Saxony and Prussia to the Oder, which it reached at Müllrose. From there it ascended the Oder to the Katzbach, where it divided, the French having to keep behind the Katzbach, the Allies behind the Striegau Wasser, the intervening space being declared neutral. During the suspension of hostilities, beleaguered fortresses might be supplied

---

[1] Cf. *Deutsche Geschichte, 1806–1871*, i. 348.

from outside but must not increase their stock of provisions, and no troops were to cross the lines of demarcation. This last provision was none too well observed by some of the irregulars attached to the Prussian army, notably the well-known Free Corps under Lützow, which after raiding Erfurt and the Saxon Duchies was brought to action by Arrighi's cavalry at Kitzen near Leipzig and destroyed (June 17th).

In agreeing to this armistice, Napoleon played into the hands of his enemies. Military and political considerations alike should have induced him to reject the proposals. Lützen and Bautzen had cost him dear, and the exertions his young soldiers had made had nearly exhausted them ; but for all that the campaign had so far gone in his favour, the Allies could hardly have hoped to avert defeat in another battle, and it was at least doubtful whether the Russo-Prussian alliance would survive another defeat. Even if the Allies remained true to their alliance, great military advantages might have been gained by pushing forward to the Lower and Middle Oder ; beleaguered fortresses might have been relieved, and the veterans who formed their garrisons would have been a welcome stiffening to Napoleon's young conscripts. Moreover, to accept an armistice would publish to the world the fact that all was not well with the Emperor's position ; why otherwise should he halt in a career of victory? Austria and other waverers were more likely to rally to his cause if he showed himself confident of victory, than if he confessed himself unable to follow up the advantages he had secured.

But the campaign in Saxony had shown Napoleon some weak points in his armour, above all his want of cavalry, and he was in sore need of time in which to supply his deficiencies in that arm. Moreover, his raw troops were hardly fit for another desperate struggle like that of Bautzen. Munitions and supplies were nearly exhausted, his communications with the Rhine and with France were being harassed by the Free Corps, which were playing the part which Spanish guerillas and Portuguese militia had played in the Peninsula, his men were worn out and in bad need of rest. But the Emperor failed to see that useful as delay would be to him, the respite which the armistice would give might be turned to even better use by the Allies, that their need of a breathing space in which to refresh and reorganise their forces was even greater than his; that their resources if more distant were larger. Yet, though it was largely because he wanted time in which to refit and increase his forces that he concluded the armistice, there can be little doubt that the fear of Austrian invention was also most influential with him. The retreat of the Allies towards the Austrian frontier seemed to point to an understanding between them and the government at Vienna, and at the moment the Emperor was not inclined to face the Austrians as well as the Russians and Prussians. It was mainly the great strategic advantage of their position in Bohemia which made the Austrians so formidable : posted across his flank, they could sever his communications with France by a move down the Elbe. To neutralise this Napoleon was relying on the demonstration which the Army of Italy was to make against Carniola, and at the end of May the Army of Italy was only just beginning to take shape under Eugene.

In his appreciation of the political situation, Napoleon was even more at fault; if it was a serious blunder to have accepted the armistice, it was an even graver error not to have accepted the very favourable terms Austria suggested. But just as he could not believe that he could fail to overthrow the Allies, even if Austria threw in her lot with Russia and Prussia, so, too, he seems to have failed to grasp the policy of Metternich, and to have relied too much on the influence of his marriage to Marie Louise,[1] almost expecting it to blind Austria to her own interests : he never imagined that a judicious mixture of threats and bribes would fail to bring Austria to heel.

But Metternich gauged the situation too acutely to be caught by the bait of Illyria and Silesia and the redistribution of Germany to the disadvantage of Prussia. Napoleon's word was but a poor security for the punctual performance of the promises made to Austria in his hour of need : once he had overthrown the renascent power of Prussia and hurled Russia back behind the Niemen by Austrian aid, the Hapsburgs might wait in vain for their wages. Much as Metternich disliked Prussia, he was not prepared to indulge his hatred of the Hohenzollern at the heavy price of re-establishing Napoleon's supremacy over Europe : he preferred maintaining a balance of power by helping Prussia to regain her old position to receiving even Silesia as the vassal of Napoleon. The only effect of Napoleon's victories was, therefore, to convince Metternich that Austria must draw nearer the Allies lest Alexander should lose

[1] Cf. *EHR, 1887*, p. 391.

heart and accept the overtures which Napoleon was making to him through Caulaincourt. By the time the Congress of Prague was arranged Metternich had come to the conclusion that the only course open to Austria was to take arms against Napoleon ; and he seems to have welcomed the Congress, because he expected that it would convince Francis II that no other solution was possible. Francis was more inclined to cling to peace, more anxious to build a golden bridge across which Napoleon could retire without any humiliation to his pride ; but Metternich was able to bring the Emperor round to his own views, and to induce him to agree to the convention which was the result of the negotiations with the Czar on which Metternich now embarked. This convention, signed at Reichenbach on June 27th, laid down certain indispensable conditions upon which Austria would insist as the basis of her mediation. They were the abolition of the Grand Duchy of Warsaw and its partition between its three former owners, the liberation of the Hanseatic towns and of the rest of the German coast-lands seized in 1810, the restoration of Illyria to Austria, and the evacuation by the French of the Polish and Prussian fortresses still in their hands. If by July 21st Napoleon should not have accepted these terms, Austria pledged herself to join the Allies and declare war against the Emperor of the French.[1]

The first result of Austria's interposition was that Napoleon, after vainly attempting to bully Metternich into submission, agreed (June 30th) to accept her mediation and that a Peace Congress should forthwith be held at Prague. To allow time for the deliberations of this Congress, it was agreed that the armistice should be extended to August 10th.

The negotiations of the Peace Congress, which duly met at Prague on July 10th, were felt from the first to be a mere form : Napoleon showed no indication of intending to treat them seriously, and, indeed, he was far more occupied with preparing his forces for the great campaign which was to humble Austria as well as Russia and Prussia. Similarly, on the side of the Allies it is the discussion of the plans for the coming operations which are of real interest and importance.

In these discussions a prominent part was played by Bernadotte. Greatly to Napoleon's disgust his former Marshal, who had been chosen as Crown Prince of Sweden in 1810 and

[1] Cf. Friedrich, i. 30.

had at first applied the Continental System most rigorously, had not remained true to the French alliance. By no means a devoted adherent of Napoleon, and anxious above all things to identify himself with his adopted country, Bernadotte had not hesitated to relax the Continental System when he found what disastrous effects it was having on Sweden. Infuriated by this, Napoleon had (Feb. 1812) reoccupied Swedish Pomerania, which had only been restored to Sweden in 1810. Thereupon Bernadotte concluded the Peace of Abo with Russia (April 1812) and bestirred himself to reconcile the Czar with Great Britain. He had followed up his success in this diplomatic endeavour by concluding treaties with England (March 3rd, 1813) and Prussia (April 22nd), pledging him to hostility to Napoleon; but his demand that Sweden should be indemnified with Norway for the loss of Finland to Russia had caused a hitch in his negotiations with that Power and with Prussia. His proposal to compensate Denmark with the Hanseatic towns and other parts of North Germany had not unnaturally been disliked by Prussia, and Frederick William had at first refused to ratify the treaty of April 22nd. However, Lützen and Bautzen forced the Czar and Frederick William to change their tone and to fall in with Bernadotte's proposals. It was agreed that 35,000 Russians and 27,000 Prussians should be put under his orders and should join the 18,000 Swedes with whom he landed at Stralsund on May 24th. This, of course, decided the action of Denmark, which promptly threw in her lot with Napoleon's, concluding a treaty (July 10th) of no small influence on the fortunes of Germany, as it removed all possibility of the creation of a strong Danish state on the Lower Elbe.[1] The assistance of some 12,000 Danes, who joined Davoût at Hamburg, went far to secure that important position, the extreme left of the line Napoleon was now taking up on the Elbe.

Meanwhile the utmost efforts were being made on all sides to put into the field every available man. Napoleon's officers had to teach their recruits the elements of drill and discipline as they marched across Germany to the Elbe. From the interior of Russia large reinforcements were slowly pushing Westward. In June England concluded subsidy treaties with Russia and Prussia, agreeing to pay them respectively over a million and half a million sterling. Munitions, too, were

[1] Cf. Friedrich, i. pp. 11-18.

shipped in considerable quantities to Stralsund and Colberg, and, thanks largely to this source of supply, it was found possible to equip the *Landwehr* for field service. Muskets were served out to them instead of the pikes with which so many of them had till then been armed; they were formed into battalions and squadrons, and were now brigaded with the older troops, whose depleted ranks had again been brought up to full strength by vigorous recruiting.

At the same time the arrangement of a plan of campaign was being steadily pushed forward. Long before the Peace Congress had begun to display its futility by meeting, Austrian generals had been framing schemes in consultation with the Allies. The eagerness with which this was being done was itself a proof that no one regarded the chances of a pacific settlement as worth considering. Still none of the plans gave universal satisfaction, and the want of a Commander-in-Chief was badly felt. Scharnhorst had been badly wounded at Lützen, but despite his wound he had gone to Prague to consult with the Austrians. However, he became suddenly worse, and died on June 28th, not having lived to see Prussia reap the harvest of vengeance on Napoleon which his hard work had sowed. His death left von Knesebeck as Prussia's principal representative in the councils of the Allies, Toll and Barclay being Russia's spokesmen, Schwarzenberg and his able Chief of Staff, Joseph Radetzky, Austria's. Into the details of the various schemes it is impossible to go;[1] they illustrate the divergent interests and points of view inevitable in a coalition, but at length the Russian and Prussian headquarters decided on a plan by which three armies were to be formed, one in the Mark of Brandenburg under Bernadotte to cover Berlin, one in Silesia under a Prussian commander, which would serve to maintain the communications of the main army in Bohemia with Russia by way of Poland. This main army was to be formed by the union of the greater part of the Russo-Prussian forces near Schweidnitz with the Austrians. Submitted to the Austrians, the idea met on the whole with their approval; but they proposed that the main army should adopt a defensive attitude, leaving the initiative to Napoleon, and that the Swedo-Russian Army of the North, with the aid of Bülow's corps, should alone on the Allied side take the offensive.[2]

---

[1] Cf. Friedrich, i. 71–86.   [2] *Ibid.* i. 87–88.

However, Bernadotte's assent had to be obtained, and he had some time before this been pressing for a personal interview with the Allied monarchs as the only possible means of reaching any satisfactory decision : this meeting now took place, the Czar, Frederick William and the Crown Prince of Sweden coming together at the Castle of Trachenberg near Breslau (July 9th). A conference of some three days resulted in the adoption of the plan of campaign generally known as the Compact of Trachenberg, a plan which on the whole followed the lines laid down by the Crown Prince, and which, having been submitted to the Austrians, was by them adopted with some modifications [1] which Radetzky suggested.[2]

The keynote of the scheme of operations finally accepted by the Allies was the employment of a policy of attrition. Instead of the combined offensive operations suggested by Toll the Allies were to adopt a defensive strategy, to refuse Napoleon the chance of fighting a pitched battle until marches and counter-marches against one point after another in the surrounding semicircle of hostile armies, which always retired as he approached, should have so diminished his numbers and worn out his men as to let the Allies attack them with every prospect of victory. But while a pitched battle with the main army of the enemy was to be avoided, any isolated or detached corps was to be brought to action and destroyed. The three armies which were to be formed—Bernadotte's in the North; Blucher's in Silesia, consisting of his own Prussian corps with that of Yorck and the Russians of Langeron and Sacken ; the main army in Bohemia, which was to be reinforced by the greater part of the Russo-Prussians from Schweidnitz—were all to adopt the same strategy : each was to retire before Napoleon if he advanced against it, to advance and threaten the French flanks and communications should Napoleon move against either of the others. Thus, should the Emperor, as was expected, invade Bohemia, the main army would draw back up the Elbe ; Bernadotte, leaving 20,000 men to contain the Danes and Hamburg, would move against the Middle Elbe, aiming at Leipzig ; Blücher and the Army of Silesia was to push forward to the Elbe, cross the river between Dresden and Torgau, and obtain touch with the Army of the North.[3]

This strategy is one which has been criticised as a reversion

[1] Cf. Friedrich, i. 89–92.   [2] *Ibid.* i. 94–96.   [3] *Ibid.* i. 96–99.

to the dilatory and over-methodical operations of the 18th Century; as a failure to appreciate or to practise the cardinal principle of strategy of which Napoleon had been so brilliant an exponent, the principle of concentrating all available forces against the enemy's main force to decide the issue once and for all by a pitched battle.[1] Pertinent as this criticism is, it is nevertheless one-sided: the strategy of the Allies had as its ultimate objective a pitched battle; they wanted to make Napoleon do their work for them by wearing out his young troops through constant but fruitless exertions, to refuse him the chance of a general action would exasperate and annoy him, and in the end, when the work of attrition had been done, the offensive would be taken.

Meanwhile about the time of the conference at Trachenberg good news had reached the Allied Headquarters. Napoleon's efforts to conceal or minimise the tidings from Spain had been unsuccessful, and the letter of Francis II to Bernadotte of July 9th [2] is only one of many instances of the encouraging effect of the news of Vittoria. Wellington's great victory (June 21st) was a battle of far more than local importance; it was not merely that the French had been driven headlong out of the Peninsula, and that the "intrusive King" had looked for the last time on his Spanish dominions. Any lingering doubts in Austria's mind were now dispelled. The Allies already seemed to see Germany delivered from Napoleon's rule as Spain had been. The Czar ordered the performance of the first *Te Deum* that the Russian Court had sung for a victory gained by other than Russian troops.[3] Moreover, now that France was threatened with invasion not another man could be withdrawn from the Bidassoa to the Elbe, and Napoleon had to send Soult, the Marshal most capable of exercising an independent command, to try to restore affairs in the Peninsula: not many days were to pass before he would feel his absence from Saxony.

By this time the end of the armistice was close at hand, and the deliberations at Prague had produced no tangible result. Austria asked more than Napoleon would give, and neither side would give way, for each expected success as the result of an appeal to the sword. Thus the time limit was reached and passed. On August 11th the Prussians from Silesia set foot as allies on Bohemian soil, and next day Austria published her declaration of war.

---

[1] Cf. Friedrich, i. 99.　　　[2] Cf. Rose, ii. 321.　　　[3] *Ibid.*

CHAPTER XXXI

THE WAR OF LIBERATION—TO THE BATTLE
OF KULM

THE good use which Napoleon had made of the armistice may best be estimated from the fact that at its conclusion the forces under his command on German soil alone amounted to nearly 600,000 men, a total hardly inferior to that of the great host collected sixteen months before for the invasion of Russia. Not that all these were available for active operations in the field. The fortresses to the Eastward still holding out for the Emperor absorbed 50,000 men, survivors for the most part of the Grand Army of 1812; another 25,000 garrisoned the fortresses along the Elbe, and about the same number maintained the line of communications with France through Erfurt and Würzburg. Far away on the Emperor's left Davoût at Hamburg had some 40,000, 12,000 of whom were Danes, ready for field operations. In like manner on the extreme right Wrede's Bavarian corps, 25,000 strong, watched the Austrians under Count Reuss on the Danube. Two incomplete corps, one of cavalry under Milhaud, one of infantry under Augereau, which were being formed at Mayence and Würzburg, amounted to 15,000 more. But when all these deductions had been made there remained 400,000 available for the main operations which the Emperor intended to conduct himself. He was well provided with artillery, having over 12,000 guns, and on paper he had made good his dangerous weakness in cavalry, having brought together 380 squadrons or, about 70,000 sabres. Even so, however, he was much outnumbered in this arm by the Allies, and the difficulty of improving cavalry was to be emphasised on many occasions by the indifferent work and conduct of these hastily raised squadrons. This main body of the Emperor's forces comprised the Guard, the kernel of the whole army, 60,000 strong, five corps of cavalry and eleven of infantry together with independent divisions at Magdeburg, to keep open the communications with Davoût, and at Leipzig.

But this great force was by no means entirely composed of Frenchmen. One corps, the VIIIth, was exclusively composed of Poles; five infantry divisions and some odd battalions were provided by the Confederation of the Rhine, the Kingdom of Italy supplied one whole division and parts of others. Naples was represented by a brigade, while among the troops nominally French were Dutch, Belgians, Swiss, Germans from the Rhinelands and the shores of the North Sea, and many Italians.[1] Thus, as in 1809, it was with an army which included no small number of Germans that Napoleon prepared to reassert his claims to dominate Germany: much would depend on the loyalty of his German vassals to him and of their subjects to them. Would the sentiment of German unity and nationality be strong enough to overpower the bonds of military discipline and local patriotism, if Napoleon were successful? would military discipline and localism be strong enough to resist the seductions of German sentiment, if fortune inclined to the side of the Allies?[2]

But enormous as were the French forces, the efforts of the Allies had produced an even larger total. Apart from their

---

[1] No less than three whole infantry divisions usually described as French came from the North Italian departments of the Empire.

[2] My principal authority for the composition of Napoleon's Army of 1813 is Major Friedrich's valuable work on *The Autumn Campaign of 1813*, to which I shall have constant occasion to refer throughout this chapter. His appendices (III. V. VI. and VII.) give the details as to the contingents provided by the Confederation of the Rhine. Out of the 502 battalions of the field army, 65 came from the Confederation, Saxony supplying 19, Bavaria 15, Würtemberg 11, Westphalia and Hesse 6 apiece, Baden 4, Würzburg and the Saxon Duchies 2 each. In the cavalry the proportion was rather larger, a sixth, 63 squadrons out of 372, being German. Here again Saxony had the largest contingent, 17 squadrons, Westphalia sending 10, Würtemberg 8, Bavaria and Berg 6 apiece, Baden 5, Hesse and Mecklenburg 4 each, Anhalt 2, and Würzburg 1. Sixteen batteries of artillery were also provided by the Confederation, and it must be remembered that among the garrisons of the fortresses there was a considerable proportion of German troops. For example, Dresden was held by 5 Westphalian battalions and some Saxon garrison artillery (p. 450). Unfortunately, Major Friedrich does not give the composition of the garrisons, nor is this to be found in M. Camille Rousset's *La Grande Armée de 1813* (Paris), to which I have referred for the statistics about the corps of Augereau (IX.) and Davoût (XIII.). The former's 23 battalions included 4 belonging to the 113th of the Line, a regiment raised at Genoa ; the rest of the corps and all Davoût's 28 battalions were Frenchmen. As a rough estimate, a seventh of Napoleon's army may be said to have been Germans.

three main armies, those of Bohemia, Silesia, and the North, there
were the miscellaneous levies which Wallmoden was opposing
to Davoût;[1] there were the troops, mainly *Landwehr*, occupied
in blockading the fortresses in French hands; there were the
Free Corps and other irregular forces, detachments which would
probably not be overestimated at 100,000.[2] Of the three main
armies that of Bohemia was the largest. In addition to the
Austrians, some 117 squadrons and 107 battalions, not less than
125,000 in all, it included 109 squadrons and 92 battalions of
Russians under Barclay de Tolly, rather over 80,000 men; the
second Prussian Army Corps under Kleist, 44 squadrons and 41
battalions amounting to 37,000; and the 7000 men, 8 squadrons
and 6 battalions, of the Prussian Guards. In accordance with
the scheme arranged at Reichenbach, these forces had moved
from Silesia into Bohemia by way of Glatz and Schweidnitz,
had crossed to the left of the Elbe and joined the Austrians
on the Eger (August 16th) the day before the six days' grace
over and above the armistice expired.

Next in size was Bernadotte's Army of the North in which
the Prussians, 72,000 strong, outnumbered the combined Russians
(30,000) and Swedes (23,000). One of the two Prussians corps,
Tauentzien's, 29 squadrons and 48 battalions, was almost
entirely composed of *Landwehr*; the other, Bülow's, 42 squadrons
and 40 battalions, was the most efficient portion of the whole
army, as the Swedes had had little experience of warfare, and
over a quarter of Winzingerode's Russians were Cossacks, who
were of little value in battle. Really the Army of Silesia, though
weaker by nearly 20,000 men, was a much more efficient force;
it included Yorck's Prussian corps, 48 squadrons and 43
battalions, 38,000 strong, and the two Russian corps of Sacken
and Langeron, which between them amounted to 67 squadrons
and 74 battalions, or nearly 70,000 men.

All told, the three armies mustered about 480,000, roughly
speaking a fifth again as large as Napoleon's main body. But
against that the Emperor could set the advantages of a central
position and of unity of command, considerations which went
far to neutralise his numerical inferiority.

---

[1] Friedrich, i. 58.

[2] Major Friedrich (i. 59) puts the forces of the Allies not in the first line at the
gigantic total of 350,000; but this includes not only reserves, depôts and garrisons,
but the Austrian corps facing Eugene in Italy and Wrede in Bavaria.

The choice of a Commander-in-Chief had been a matter of great difficulty to the Allies. Alexander would readily have taken the post himself, but his military capacities were altogether inadequate and Metternich would have opposed the suggestion. Bernadotte had yet to earn the full confidence of his new allies, and Moreau, who hurried over from America to place his services at their disposal, had not the necessary position or authority. The Allies had indeed at their disposal a general whose reputation stands at the present day far higher than that of any other possible candidate, but at that time Archduke Charles was still under the clouds of Wagram, and, moreover, he was on very bad terms with his brother and with Metternich. Accordingly, Austria put forward as her candidate for the command of the army of Bohemia, Prince Schwarzenberg, who had commanded the Austrian auxiliary corps in the invasion of Russia. He was a man of considerable military experience and of respectable capacities, though of altogether insufficient calibre to be matched against Napoleon. He was too cautious, too anxious, too wanting in self-confidence, decision and energy to be a great general, but the unfavourable verdicts so often passed upon him fail to do justice to what he did accomplish. He had not merely to direct the movements of an enormous army and to combine his operations with those of two other armies which were practically independent, but he was the general of a coalition, and he had at his headquarters the three Allied monarchs whose presence could not fail to be a serious handicap. Add to this his many vigorous and opinionated colleagues and the multitude of counsellors of great experience, including besides Barclay de Tolly and Moreau, Radetzky, Toll and Jomini, always ready with the best conflicting advice, and Schwarzenberg's achievements seem not so very poor after all. No one would pretend that it was Schwarzenberg's strategy which was the chief cause of Napoleon's overthrow. Bernadotte rather than the Austrian general was the author of the plan Schwarzenberg had to carry out, and all that there is to be urged on his behalf is the rather negative praise that no great strategical blunder is to be laid to his door ; his errors were errors of omission not of commission, he did not do anything much and therefore did little wrong. Still in keeping the Allies together, and preserving good relations between them, his tact and diplomacy were of the utmost value ;

it may certainly be questioned whether the Allies could have improved upon the choice.

Still the operations of the Allies lacked the accurate co-ordination which could only be given by a Commander-in-Chief of really great capacity and authority, whose office was a good deal more than a name, and who could plan a campaign and rely on having his plan put into execution in the manner he intended. On the whole the scheme arranged at Trachenberg was faithfully adhered to, but it cannot be maintained that it was by superior strategy that the Allies succeeded in ousting the French from Germany. They owed their victory largely to the comparatively indifferent quality of the French army, especially of the cavalry, to whose inefficiency may be attributed the failure to obtain accurate information which did so much to ruin Napoleon's plans, largely to the errors and misfortunes of Napoleon's subordinates, partly it must be admitted to Napoleon's own errors,[1] but in great measure to the waning fidelity of his long-suffering allies and vassals. Austria had given the example of rejecting the Emperor's specious offers, it remained to be seen whether Bavaria and Saxony and Würtemberg would do the same. It was the uncertainty of the political situation which did so much to paralyse the Emperor's movements. In 1812 he had had little reason to fear for his communications with France, even when he had won the Pyrrhic victory of Borodino in the heart of Russia. After Bautzen and after Dresden he could not feel sure of the far shorter line from the Elbe to the Rhine. Germany was seething with disloyalty in his rear ; and though as yet the states of the Confederation were bound to his cause by their uncertainty as to the Allies' intentions towards them, individuals began to desert even before the tide of success turned against the Emperor. As early as August 22nd the two Westphalian Hussar regiments which formed the cavalry brigade of the IInd Corps, Victor's, came over to the Allies,[2] and at the critical moment in the battle of Leipzig it was the defection of a Saxon division which secured the French defeat.

---

[1] Count Yorck von Wartenburg in his *Napoleon as a General* is very, but not perhaps unduly, severe in his criticisms on the Emperor's strategy in this campaign, especially on his failure to concentrate his forces at the decisive point, and his neglect to strike at the enemy's main army.

[2] Friedrich, i. 173.

The end of the armistice found the greater part of the French army on the right bank of the Elbe, in a position, therefore, which gave them the advantage of being able to operate on interior lines against the converging forces of their enemies. Yet despite this it did not see Napoleon putting his whole force in motion for one of the bold offensive movements usually so characteristic of his strategy. Such a stroke, whether directed against the Army of Silesia or against the Austrians in Bohemia, could only prove successful if it resulted at once in a decisive battle. Should the force assailed evade an action by retreat, the Emperor would only expose his flanks and rear to the other Allied forces if he allowed himself to be drawn into a pursuit, while he could not call on troops so young and raw as the majority of his were for the great efforts in marching by which alone a reluctant enemy might be compelled to stand and fight. The adoption of the defensive was therefore the policy which his circumstances made advisable. To await in his central position in Lusatia the advance of his enemies, until one or the other came near enough to let him dash at it, bring it to battle, crush it, and turn against the other, was the strategy which promised the best results. But Napoleon was impatient; he longed to reassert his supremacy and encourage his young troops by a speedy victory; he could not reconcile himself to the mere defensive, to accommodating his movements to those of the enemy. And with good reason he feared the bad effects on the fidelity of his allies and the *morale* of his troops which were bound to result from the spectacle of his inactivity. Accordingly, while he took post on the Elbe and in Lusatia with the greater part of his army, ready to parry any advance of the Allies from Silesia or Bohemia,[1] he decided to take the offensive against Bernadotte's Army of the North, whose fighting capacities he somewhat underestimated.

His scheme was that three corps of infantry, those of Bertrand (IV.), Reynier (VII.) and Oudinot (XII.), with Arrighi's cavalry, should advance Northward on Berlin, Davoût co-operating by a move Eastward from Hamburg against Bernadotte's communications with Stralsund. The defeat of Bernadotte would, so Napoleon calculated, secure his threatened hold on North Germany, especially Westphalia, and would also allow him to relieve the beleaguered garrisons of Cüstrin, Stettin and even

[1] Cf. Friedrich, i. 116.

Dantzic. By obtaining command of the Lower Oder the French would outflank the Army of Silesia and threaten its communications with Russia. However, by detaching 70,000 men against Berlin, Napoleon seriously diminished the forces he had available to meet the combined advance of the Allies from Bohemia and Silesia, the foes from whom he had most to fear, and over whom alone a decisive victory could be won.[1] It might have been wiser, as St. Cyr and Marmont advised,[2] to be content with holding Bernadotte in check, and to concentrate as large a force as possible against the main armies of the Allies. At the same time, in the hands of Soult or Davoût with 100,000 of the better troops at Napoleon's disposal, the move might have proved a success; but it would have necessitated the adoption of the strictest defensive in Silesia, and as it was the Emperor did not choose the right general or detach a force sufficient either in numbers or in quality to secure success. Oudinot, though a brave soldier and a capable subordinate, was hardly fitted for so important an independent command, and his troops, even if Girard's divisions at Magdeburg and Wittenberg be included in the total, only mustered 84,000, while the Army of the North came to half as many again. Moreover, they were of rather indifferent quality, a mixture of nationalities, with hardly any good French troops among them. A third of his infantry (35 battalions out of 106) and over half his cavalry (35 squadrons out of 67) were Germans from the Confederation of the Rhine, troops whose loyalty to the Emperor would be subjected to a severe strain; another division (14 battalions) was drawn from the kingdom of Italy; and three of the four " French" divisions were French in name only, being recruited from the Italian provinces of the Empire; while the remaining one, Durutte's, was mainly composed of " disciplinary" regiments.[3] Arrighi's cavalry were mostly French, but even they were of little value, a collection of single squadrons of different regiments, raw recruits indifferently mounted, hardly able to perform the simplest manœuvres, and quite incompetent to conceal the movements of their own army or discover those of their enemy.[4] Moreover, to add to Oudinot's difficulties, Davoût had his hands too full with Wallmoden to be able to carry out his proposed diversion against Bernadotte's communications with Stralsund.

[1] Cf. Friedrich, i. 128–130.   [2] Ibid. i. 133–135.
[3] Ibid. i. 367.   [4] Ibid. i. 367 ff.

While Oudinot was collecting his forces for the attack on Berlin, Napoleon was by no means inactive. Acting upon the mistaken impression that the force which had moved from Silesia to join the Austrians in Bohemia only consisted of Wittgenstein's Russians, and was 40,000 not, as was really the case, 125,000 strong, the Emperor directed his attention to the Army of Silesia, imagining that Blücher rather than Schwarzenberg was at the head of the principal army of the Allies. The troops upon whom he was relying to keep the Army of Silesia in check were Sebastiani's cavalry and the infantry of Ney (IIIrd Corps), Lauriston (Vth) and Macdonald (XIth). These were posted along a line which rested its right on the Riesengebirge near Friedeberg, and its left on the Oder near Parchwitz. Similarly Kellermann's cavalry and Poniatowski's Poles (the VIIIth Corps) faced Southwards towards Bohemia on the right bank of the Elbe, and in conjunction with St. Cyr's infantry (XIVth Corps) and L'Heritier's cavalry on the left bank covered Saxony and Lusatia against the Army of Bohemia. The Guard in and around Görlitz, Vandamme's corps (Ist) at Bautzen, Victor's infantry (IInd) and Latour-Maubourg's cavalry between Görlitz and Zittau with Marmont's corps (VIth) at Bunzlau formed the central reserve, available for service on either front.

The Emperor's original idea seems to have been to push forward into Bohemia up the right bank of the Elbe; possibly he hoped so to catch Wittgenstein in flank before he could execute his bold march across the French front. However, it was soon discovered that the Austrians and their allies were all on the left bank,[1] and Napoleon, still under the impression that the Army of Silesia, which had just (August 17th) begun to press in upon the French corps in its front, was the principal force of the Allies, decided to turn against it and to defer the invasion of Bohemia until after the destruction of the Army of Silesia, when he would be able to use the Lusatian passes for an advance against Schwarzenberg. He saw that an advance even to Prague would be a blow wasted on the air unless it brought on a decisive action, and that even a victory over Schwarzenberg would leave him in a difficult position if in the meantime his communications with Lusatia through Zittau and Görlitz were to be severed by Blücher driving Ney's containing

[1] Cf. Friedrich, i. 189.

force in upon Dresden. Accordingly the Emperor left Victor and Vandamme to support Poniatowski and Kellermann and to keep touch with St. Cyr at Dresden by means of the bridges at Pirna and Königstein ; and having thus, as he thought, provided against any move Schwarzenberg was likely to make, he hastened (Aug. 20th) with the rest of the reserve to the assistance of Ney's "Army of the Bober," against which the Army of Silesia was beginning to push forward. Blücher's advance had forced Ney to fall back rather rapidly from the Katzbach to the Bober (Aug. 17th to 20th), and the Army of Silesia was about to follow up its success by an attack on the French positions between Bunzlau and Löwenberg when the arrival of Napoleon and his reserves was announced to the Prussian commander (Aug. 20th). For an action against one of Napoleon's lieutenants the Army of Silesia was ready and even anxious, but to fight the Emperor himself was a very different matter, and in accordance with the fixed principle which governed the Allies' operations, Blücher decamped hastily Eastward rather than give Napoleon the chance of a pitched battle, a decision for which Lützen, Bautzen and Dresden afford ample justification. Napoleon pursued vigorously, and there was some sharp rearguard fighting in which the Allies suffered severely; but they made good their escape behind the Katzbach, and Napoleon had to admit that they had evaded him. He could press the pursuit no further, for urgent messages reached him from St. Cyr that the Army of Bohemia had crossed the Erzgebirge and was threatening Dresden. Accordingly Napoleon had to turn back towards the Elbe to St. Cyr's assistance, taking with him the Guards, Marmont and Latour - Maubourg, and leaving Macdonald with his own corps and those of Ney (now under Souham), Lauriston, and Sebastiani to contain Blücher (Aug. 23rd).

Thus the French army, instead of being concentrated in superior force against one of its three opponents, had become separated into three or rather four portions, one opposing each of the Allied armies, and Napoleon with the central reserve hurrying back across Lusatia to save Dresden from Schwarzenberg. The position was critical, but Napoleon hoped for the best. If only his lieutenants proved equal to the tasks allotted to them, if, for example, St. Cyr could keep the Allies at bay until Napoleon could cross the Elbe at Pirna and fall in force on the communications of the Army of Bohemia, the most brilliant success might be looked for.

But Napoleon's lieutenants were destined to disappoint their master's expectations grievously. Oudinot had concentrated his army round Baruth by August 18th, and next day began his advance on Berlin. His road lay through the belts of wooded and swampy country which lie to the South of the Prussian capital, and which offer many good positions to a defending force, besides making very difficult lateral communications between columns moving forward parallel along the main roads. Still at first he made good progress. On the 21st he came into touch with the Army of the North between Trebbin and Zossen, and drove in its outposts after some sharp fighting, so that by the evening of the 22nd, despite the difficulties of the country, he had won his way through the worst part, and all that remained was to attack the main position of the Army of the North. This force was standing at bay with its right at Gütergotz and its left—Tauentzien's *Landwehr*—at Blankenfelde. Bernadotte, indeed, being for political reasons very anxious to avoid all risks of a defeat, would have preferred not to give battle South of the Spree at all, but to have retired across that river so as to make use of the defensive capacities of the country to the North of it, which was admirably adapted for the policy he wished to adopt of keeping the enemy at bay without allowing him to force on a battle. However, the protection of Berlin had been one of the tasks assigned to his army at Trachenberg, and Bülow was urgent in his demands that a battle should be risked for the Prussian capital. For this purpose the position Bernadotte selected was well adapted; it was fairly strong, and it covered the three main roads which converge on Berlin from the Southward. The French, having still some woods to pass through, were moving in three columns quite independently and not expecting a battle. This, with the indifferent scouting of their cavalry, was the main cause of the disaster which befell them. Their attacks were not delivered simultaneously, and their left column, Oudinot's own corps and Arrighi's cavalry, was so much behind that it practically took no part in the action. Thus though Reynier, moving by the central road, carried Gross Beeren at the first attack, and maintained himself there from 3 p.m. till after 7, he received no assistance from his colleagues, and could only oppose 18,000

men to Bülow, who had double that number.[1] Even so the
VIIth Corps did very well, and Sahr's Saxon division, though
exposed to a heavy cannonade, held on most tenaciously to
Gross Beeren until simultaneously taken in flank by Borstell's
Pomeranians and assailed in front by the three other Prussian
divisions. Gross Beeren was lost, and Durutte's French division became involved in Sahr's overthrow. Lecoq's Saxons
then intervened and endeavoured to retrieve the day by an
advance against Bülow's right; but they were checked by
some Swedish light infantry, and Reynier's whole corps went to
its rear in confusion, leaving over 3000 men behind. Too late
Oudinot's own vanguard reached the field : the rout of the
centre compelled it to retreat. Bertrand meanwhile had
opened the action with some success against Tauentzien, who
was barring the Eastern road at Blankenfelde ; but he had failed
to push his advantage home and now had to conform to the
retrograde movement. By September 2nd Oudinot was back
at Wittenberg, the *morale* and the physical condition of his
troops badly shaken. His defeat had led to a further disaster,
for Girard, moving up from Magdeburg to cover Oudinot's left,
had found himself dangerously exposed by the Marshal's retreat,
and in endeavouring to regain touch with his colleagues he
was brought to action by Hirschfeld's *Landwehr* at Hagelberg,
and totally defeated after an action of very varying fortune
(Aug. 27th).

Nor was this the only bad result of Gross Beeren. Wallmoden, whose operations have a special interest for English
readers, inasmuch as his force included the only British troops
which played an active part in this momentous campaign,[2] had
some 25,000 to 30,000 men at his disposal. However, Davoût,
despite a check at Kammin (Aug. 21st) was forcing him to
retire Eastward, had himself advanced to Schwerin and had
pushed Loison's division as far as Wismar, forcing Vegesack's
Swedes back to Rostock, when the news of Gross Beeren compelled him to retire to the Stecknitz and adopt a defensive
attitude.

In like manner Macdonald had come to grief. As already

---

[1] Friedrich, App. IV. and V.

[2] He had the 2nd battalion of the 73rd Regiment, one of six sent out to garrison
Stralsund in July 1813, a Rocket Troop and two batteries of the Royal Horse
Artillery, and the 3rd Hussars of the King's German Legion.

mentioned, Blücher had fallen back from the Bober just in time to avoid an action with Napoleon and had retreated by forced marches to Jauer (Aug. 22nd to 24th), thus returning to the positions from which he had advanced at the end of the armistice. The weather had been very bad, the roads difficult and supplies often short, so that what with the long marches, many of them at night, the want of rest, the hardships and privations they had undergone, the constant rearguard actions and the apparent uselessness of all their exertions, the Army of Silesia was rapidly being reduced to a wreck. Yorck protested violently against operations which had brought his *Landwehr* battalions almost to the point of disbanding,[1] and had cost his corps not only 4000 men in action, but many more through the toils of the march.[2] The state of the Russians was little better, and Blücher, realising that to continue to carry out his orders to keep close touch with his opponents and yet avoid a battle would mean the ruin of his army, at length decided to fight. He was moving back from Jauer to the Katzbach when he met the French advancing to meet him (Aug. 26th).

Macdonald had received orders from Napoleon to drive the Army of Silesia back beyond Jauer, and then take up a position behind the Bober to cover the principal operations against Bohemia from interruption by Blücher.[3] The order was unwise, for Macdonald was hardly strong enough to put out of action an enemy as numerous as was the Army of Silesia, and Napoleon's rear might have been as efficiently protected against Blücher without the advance to Jauer. But the Marshal had learnt that the enemy were somewhat disorganised by their sufferings, and he seems to have been to some extent counting on this. It was rather to his surprise, therefore, that he found Blücher moving towards him. His dispositions had been made for a fight at Jauer, and were none too well adapted for immediate action. Souham's corps on the left had started late and was some distance behind, and two divisions, one of Lauriston's and one of Macdonald's own, had been detached to the right to contain St. Priest's Russians near Hirschberg who were keeping touch between the Army of Silesia and Bohemia. Thus Macdonald had under 50,000 men at hand with whom to engage the 80,000 Allies in front of him.

The position of the Allies was divided in two by the Roaring

---

[1] Friedrich, i. 41.   [2] *Ibid.* i. 286–289.   [3] *Ibid.* i. 202, cf. 295.

(*Wüthende*) Neisse, on the left of which stood Langeron's Russians, their right touching the river at Schlaupe, their left resting on the high hill of the Monchswald. On the other bank Yorck's Prussians with Sacken's Russians beyond them were drawn up between the villages of Bellwitzhof, Eichholtz and Ober Hochkirch, some way back from the edge of the plateau which rises abruptly Eastward from the Neisse. Macdonald pushed Lauriston forward on his right through Seichau against Langeron and sent his own corps and Sebastiani's horsemen over the Katzbach at Kroitsch, over the Neisse at Nieder Crayn and Weinberg and up the slopes beyond. It was raining and the rivers were rising rapidly; but Macdonald attacked nevertheless in this somewhat precipitate manner, when he would have done better to wait for the arrival of Souham, or until the enemy should attack.

On the French right things went well enough. Lauriston not only drove in the Russian front, crossing the two small streams which protected it, and carrying the village of Hennersdorf, but pushed some battalions in between Langeron's flank and the Monchswald, and by thus turning his left drove him back on Peterwitz. But in the centre Macdonald's infantry and Sebastiani's cavalry had become much mixed; they got in each other's way, and their attacks, delivered in disorder and without cohesion, soon came to a standstill. Yorck's corps then advanced to deliver a counter-attack, and for some time the struggle was evenly contested until a flank attack by Sacken's Russians on the French left sent cavalry, infantry and artillery in headlong confusion down the steep slopes and into the swollen and rising rivers. This quite decided the day; for Souham's own division, which had just arrived and was endeavouring to assist its comrades, became involved in the general rout, and Blücher was enabled to send his reserves to the assistance of Langeron and so to bring Lauriston to a standstill. Too late to do any good, two more of Souham's divisions appeared on the extreme left, and engaged Sacken; but the battle was lost, and though Lauriston held on to Hennersdorf till nightfall and beat back Langeron's repeated attacks, he could do no more than retire in fair order. The retreat was a terrible experience: Macdonald's corps went completely to pieces and became a huddled mass of fugitives; Lauriston and Souham managed to preserve some measure of order, but the weather was most inclement, and Gneisenau pressed the pursuit with relentless energy, though hampered by the continual rains and the swollen mountain torrents in his way. By the 1st of September the relics of the Army of the Bober were behind the Queiss, a rabble rather than an army; discipline had lost its hold over the men, whole divisions had been cut to pieces, over 100 guns and 18,000 prisoners had fallen into the hands of the Allies, while as many more had perished. But for the moment the condition of their pursuers was little better: Yorck's ill-equipped *Landwehr* regiments had dwindled in some cases to a tenth of their establishment, and the exertions and hardships of the pursuit had been so great that it could not be pressed any further.[1] Moreover, news had come from Dresden which made Blücher pause.

If the advance of the Army of Bohemia had been conducted with rather more energy and definiteness of purpose a great deal more success might have been obtained. But the roads over the mountains were in a very bad condition, and the Staff of the army was hardly equal to moving so large a force. Nor was the object of the advance very clear. Schwarzenberg was somewhat loath to embark upon it, he would have preferred to leave to the enemy the difficulties of crossing the mountains in order to bring on a battle. However, Napoleon showed no disposition to fall in with this desire, and the main army could not afford to remain idle while Blücher and Bernadotte might be being beaten in detail. Accordingly on August 19th the Allies set out Northward with the idea of striking a blow at Napoleon's communications by seizing Leipzig. Moving in four columns they crossed the watershed on August 22nd, and made for Chemnitz; but finding that only on the right (Wittgenstein's Russians) was any resistance offered, and that an advance to Leipzig would not bring them into contact with any of their enemies, they had to alter their plans. At a council of war held at Zöplitz on the 22nd, it was decided to turn North-Eastward against Dresden, which was known to be but weakly held. It was this advance of which the news reached Napoleon at Görlitz on the evening of the 23rd, and brought him back in haste to the Elbe.[2]

On the afternoon of August 25th the vanguard of the Allies appeared before Dresden. Marshal St. Cyr had fallen back before them with three of his four infantry divisions, a force which even when the 5000 troops of the garrison be added to it cannot have much exceeded 25,000. His remaining division was

---

[1] Cf. Friedrich, i. 327.   [2] *Ibid*. i. 209.

at Königstein seeking to keep open that line for Napoleon's projected advance.   Marshal Vandamme, whose corps was the
nearest to Dresden, and might have been in that city by the
evening of the 24th,[1] had not moved from Rumburg and New-
stadt, and Victor was still farther away.   Thus, if the Allies had
attacked at once, it is probable that they would have captured
the town.   It is true that less than half of their total force had
arrived, but the 80,000 on the spot ought to have been more than
sufficient for the task : the garrison was less than a third of their
strength, and the extensive fortifications, too large for so small a
force, were hastily constructed and weak.   But the Allies hesitated,
and let the opportunity escape.   The responsibility for this
grievous oversight has been repudiated on behalf of all the
principal persons on the Allied side.   Jomini and others have
blamed Schwarzenberg for the delay, whereas that general's bio-
grapher, Prokesch, claims that he was anxious to attack ; and it
would seem that really it was the Czar who was responsible
for the inaction of the Allies, and that Schwarzenberg allowed
Alexander to overrule his own better judgment.[2]

Be this as it may, the delay saved Dresden.   That evening
the garrison were able to see on the Eastern horizon the distant
bivouac fires of the returning Guards ; and when, about six o'clock
next morning (Aug. 26th), the Allies did at last attack, the
assault was not directed with much vigour.   On the Allied right,
Wittgenstein's Russians made some headway along the low
ridge running along the Elbe from the Blasowitz woods to the
city.   Next to them Kleist's Prussians effected a lodgment in
the Grosse Garten, the public park on the South-East of the
town, while the Austrians on the left centre carried the village
of Plauen only to be repulsed from the Wildsruffer suburb.
Beyond the little river Weisseritz also the Austrians made much
headway, carrying Lobtau and driving the French back into the
Friedrichstadt ; but in no one ·quarter was the attack pressed
home, and every minute brought the reinforcements from Lusatia
nearer.   It was between one and two in the afternoon that the
leading regiments of the Young Guard hurled themselves into
the fight on the extreme French left, dislodging the Russians
who had begun to make their way into the Pirna suburb.   From
that moment a continuous stream of troops came pouring across
the great bridges over the Elbe, and Dresden was safe.

[1] Cf. Friedrich, i. 208.   [2] *Ibid.* i. 179-181.

It was when all real chance of success was gone and they would really have done better to be preparing to retreat, that the Allies suddenly launched their belated attack in force against the town. It was everywhere repulsed. Mortier on the left drove Wittgenstein back beyond Striesen. Pirch and Ziethen by a great effort carried the Grosse Garten, and reached the suburb behind, only to be hurled back by another division of the Young Guard. On their left another Prussian brigade went reeling back in disorder to Strehla, and even Colloredo's Austrians, who had made a lodgment in one of the French batteries and were pressing on, were driven from the ground they had so hardly won by the bayonets of the Old Guard. All along the line the Allies had to go back. West of the Weisseritz their attacks had made little further advance, and about 6 p.m. Murat headed a sortie which drove them back to Lobtau and the adjacent villages. By nightfall the French had not only recovered all the ground they had lost, but were well posted for following up their success by a counter-attack next day. The Allies would have been well advised if they had retired: there was nothing to be gained by retaining their positions, especially as their supplies were beginning to run short. But Frederick William felt that it would be too much of a confession of weakness to retire, and it was largely due to him that they remained to tempt their fate.

The principal effort of the French on the next morning was directed against the Allied right. Here Mortier with two divisions of the Young Guard and Nansouty's cavalry outflanked the Russians, and pushing them back towards the South and West gained possession of Seidnitz and Gross Dobritz, thus driving them off from the Pirna road. St. Cyr advancing from the Grosse Garten deprived the Prussians of Strehla, while Marmont, who continued the line to the Westward, kept the Austrians opposite him in play. Beyond the Weisseritz, Victor attacked and carried the heights between Dolzschen and Wolff-nitz, while under cover of his operations Murat was directing Latour-Maubourg's cavalry and an odd brigade of Vandamme's corps in a sweeping movement round by Burgstadtel which was to roll up the Austrian left. About midday the battle rather languished. Mortier carried Reick, but could get no farther, for the Russian reserve cavalry outnumbered Nansouty by three to one and menaced his flank. Similarly, St. Cyr could not obtain secure possession of Leubnitz. It was on the left of the Weisseritz that the decisive stroke was dealt. Soon after Victor had carried Ober Gorbitz, thereby cutting off part of Alois Lichtenstein's division and forcing that of Weissenwolff to retire, Teste's infantry and Chastel's cavalry appeared in rear of the Austrian left at Pennrich. The rest of Murat's horsemen were quickly thrown into the fight. Ten Austrian battalions were cut off and taken to a man, the rest of their left wing fell back in complete confusion along the Kesselsdorf road with Murat's troopers at their heels.

After this there could be no question as to the retreat of the Allies: to stay on would play into Napoleon's hands, and, moreover, Vandamme, though stoutly opposed by the Russian corps under Eugene of Würtemberg, which had been left at Pirna to keep open the road to Töplitz, was beginning to make his presence felt. Luckily for the Allies, Napoleon did not press home his attacks on the afternoon of the 27th; his men had had a full share of marching and fighting, and were tired out, and he was also waiting to let Vandamme's operations develope. Thus the Allies maintained their positions till the evening and withdrew under cover of night, Barclay with the Russians and Kleist being given the road by Peterswalde to Töplitz, the Austrians of the centre that by Dippoldiswalde to Brux, Klenau's unengaged reserve and the relics of the left wing taking the road through Tharandt to Freiberg. Thus the 28th found the Army of Bohemia in full retreat across the Erzgebirge. Worn out by their exertions and hardships, ill-clad, short of food, ill-equipped, their columns, even though but leisurely pursued, left numbers of stragglers and prisoners behind as they toiled in inclement weather along the indifferent mountain roads. The Poles in the Austrian ranks deserted freely, and some of the Prussian *Landwehr* battalions lost all cohesion. A more vigorous pursuit might have turned the retreat into a rout, and if Vandamme had been able to forestall the Allies in reaching Töplitz their plight would have been perilous. But Vandamme, partly owing to the gallant resistance of Eugene of Würtemberg, partly owing to the mistakes made by the other pursuing columns, partly to the accident that Barclay's disobedience of his orders brought Kleist's corps unexpectedly to Fürstenwalde on the evening of the 29th, failed to accomplish his task. He had with him nearly 40,000 men, all his own corps save a few battalions, a division of St. Cyr's (Mouton's), a brigade of Victor's and a light cavalry division (Corbineau's) of Latour-Maubourg's corps. He had crossed at Königstein on the 26th, had been sharply engaged with Eugene most of that day, finally gaining possession of the Pirna plateau, and by the 28th he had obtained a position which flanked the great road to Töplitz and threatened to prevent Eugene retiring by that way.

Eugene, however, was fully alive to the importance of not letting Vandamme secure undisputed possession of this all-important road, so on the 28th instead of falling back to Maxen in obedience to Barclay's orders, which would have left the road to Töplitz open to Vandamme, he determined to push past the Ist Corps and get between it and Töplitz. To do this he made an attack on Vandamme's lines with his own corps, under cover of which Ostermann's division of the Russian Guards got across the front of the French. He achieved his purpose but at a heavy cost, for his corps was dispersed, and Vandamme came pressing hard on his heels. At Priesten, in front of the last pass over the mountains, Eugene stood at bay next day, and after a fierce and stubbornly-contested action, which brought his losses up to 6000 out of his 15,000 men, he had the satisfaction of keeping off Vandamme until the simultaneous arrival of reinforcements and nightfall stopped the fight. By the next morning (Aug. 30th), when Vandamme renewed his attempts, such large reinforcements had arrived that Eugene was not only able to maintain his hold upon Priesten and so keep the French right and centre in check, but three Austrian divisions pushed forward through Karbitz against Vandamme's left. They were gradually gaining ground; and as none of his efforts could shake the Russian hold on Priesten, the prospects of success for Vandamme were becoming very faint, when his failure was suddenly converted into disaster by the arrival of Kleist's Prussians in his rear. This corps, delayed by Barclay's action in taking the Dippoldiswalde road in preference to that by Peterswalde, in consequence of which the road became overcrowded, had reached Fürstenwalde on the evening of the 29th and had there received an urgent summons to the help of Eugene. Moving in answer to this appeal, Kleist did not make straight for Priesten, but took a South-Easterly direction across the hills to Nollendorf. Much to his surprise and relief he found no French troops on the road; for Napoleon, hearing that the Allies were retiring South-West, had diverted the XIVth Corps, which was to have followed Vandamme, towards Maxen, and Pajol, who commanded St. Cyr's cavalry, had formed an erroneous impression as to Kleist's route, and had gone astray to the Westward.

When he perceived his peril, Vandamme made a most vigorous attempt to extricate himself. His artillery sacrificed themselves in an endeavour to keep the Russians at bay, while a strong column of infantry backed by Corbineau's cavalry hurled themselves on the Prussians. At the same time eight infantry battalions took post at Arbesau, and their stubborn resistance prevented the Austrians from completing their outflanking movement and joining the Prussians. In and around Vorder Tellnitz there was a tremendous struggle. The desperate energy of Vandamme's attack was more than the Prussians could stand. The *Landwehr* gave way by battalions, and the whole corps was shattered and rent asunder. But the French had spent themselves in the effort, and on finding their path barred at Jungferndorf, a few miles farther North, by a brigade which Kleist had pushed out thither to secure his rear, many of those who had made their way through Tellnitz laid down their arms in sheer exhaustion. Still a good many escaped, including most of the cavalry; while Mouton, whose division formed the extreme right of the French line, seeing that retreat through Kulm along the high road was out of the question for him, took at once to the hills and so got away to Ebersdorf and Fürstenwalde. Still the Ist Corps as a fighting force had ceased to exist, 10,000 men were killed and wounded, as many more were taken together with their commander and 82 guns. It was a disaster of enormous importance. Not merely had Napoleon's plan for reaping the fruits of Dresden miscarried entirely, but the Army of Bohemia, which on the 28th had been retiring in the deepest dejection and depression, could now claim a victory won almost under the eyes of Napoleon. Not much had been wanted to convert the failure of the blow at Dresden into a disaster, now the tables were turned and the fears that the Emperor might reply to that stroke by a victorious march on Prague need no longer be entertained. Indeed, even before the news of Kulm, Napoleon had been forced to abandon all idea of an immediate invasion of Bohemia by hearing of the defeats of Oudinot and Macdonald, and to some extent the successes of Blücher and Bernadotte contributed to that of August 30th by calling off the Emperor's attention from the pursuit. Had he been giving his undivided mind to its direction, it is hard to believe that he would have lost touch with Kleist or left Vandamme altogether unsupported. One reason no doubt for his failure to utilise his victory at Dresden was that he overestimated it, believing it another Jena and not understanding the great difference in the *morale* of his opponents since 1806. Thus, Dresden notwithstanding, these critical last ten days of August had gone emphatically in favour of the Allies. Gross Beeren, the Katzbach and Kulm were an ample set-off against their one repulse, and in mere numbers the French losses exceeded those of the Allies. But the moral advantages of their success outweighed its material result. If Napoleon himself had not yet been beaten, it had been conclusively proved that his lieutenants were not invincible, and that even he could not altogether disregard the loss of half a million of soldiers. He had not managed to secure even the partial success of the spring campaign; his hold on Germany had been challenged and the challengers had survived the conflict. A decisive success for Napoleon at Dresden might have confirmed the Confederation of the Rhine in its adherence to his cause, the partial success of the Allies went far to shake the allegiance of his German vassals and to encourage those who yearned to be free from his heavy yoke.

CHAPTER XXXII

THE WAR OF LIBERATION—LEIPZIG AND HANAU

EVEN after the disaster of Kulm, Napoleon could not bring himself to a mere defensive. To adopt a passive attitude would be a confession of failure, an admission that the initiative had passed from his hands, an invitation to his wavering vassals to desert the cause of one whose own actions proclaimed him no longer master of the situation. But notwithstanding the object-lesson he had received of the inherent viciousness of the plan of operating offensively against superior numbers in several quarters simultaneously, Napoleon failed to return to the sounder strategy of concentrating all available forces against the enemy's main army. Adhering to his error, he sent Ney to take command of Oudinot's force and resume the attack on Berlin, at the same time that he himself moved Eastward to the succour of Macdonald and to force an action on Blücher, taking with him the Guard, Latour-Maubourg's cavalry and Marmont's infantry. But as before, Blücher's hasty retreat prevented the Emperor from winning the much desired victory over the Silesian Army; and as the Army of Bohemia, which he believed to be quite out of action for the time being, was, on the contrary, actually threatening Dresden, he had once more to return to the Saxon capital (Sept. 3rd).

Meanwhile Ney had taken command of the Army of Berlin at Wittenberg (Sept. 3rd) and was advancing Northward. At Zahna he was stoutly opposed by Tauentzien's *Landwehr* (Sept. 5th), and not until Bertrand came to the assistance of the XIIth Corps were the Prussians forced back to Juterbogk. Tauentzien's corps had fought very well, and it left 3000 dead behind it and Ney under the impression that he had had the whole Army of the North in action against him. He therefore took no precautions to discover where Bülow and Bernadotte might be, and moved forward next morning, believing the enemy to be in full retreat. But when Bertrand neared Dennewitz he came into contact with Tauentzien, who was moving Westward to regain touch with Bülow. The French at once attacked. An even and well-contested struggle had just been decided in favour of the French by the arrival of Reynier, when Bülow came up to Tauentzien's help. His fresh divisions, moving up by Niedergorsdorf on the right of the hard-pressed *Landwehr*, fell upon an Italian division of the IVth Corps and routed it. Reynier intervened and stayed the Prussian advance, but reinforcements joined Bülow and he succeeded in driving the French out of Golsdorf. Next Oudinot appeared on the scene from Ohna, and engaged and drove back Bülow. However, Tauentzien was pressing so hard on Bertrand's right, a division of Würtembergers, at Rohrbeck, that Ney, instead of pushing home the advantage he had gained against Bülow, disengaged Oudinot and transferred him to the right to reinforce Bertrand. This left Reynier alone to face Bülow ; and before the renewed attacks of the Prussians his Saxons and disciplinary battalions, outflanked and outnumbered, had to give back. Just as they were driven from Golsdorf, Bertrand's corps gave away also, and in its disorderly retreat from Rohrbeck Oudinot became involved. In hopeless confusion the French fell back on Torgau; and had the pursuit been pressed with real energy, Ney's whole army might have been annihilated. As it was, the remnants of it which rallied behind the Elbe were in the most deplorable state. Its losses amounted to 29,000, of whom 15,000 were prisoners, and the discipline, equipment, and moral and physical condition of those who remained with the colours left much to be desired. The Germans now began to desert in numbers : it was not only defeat which was too much for their loyalty to Napoleon, the even stronger incentive of hunger bade them depart. The country had been eaten bare of food, and with partisan bands growing increasingly active on the French communications rations began to be scanty and irregular.

After Dennewitz there was somewhat of a lull in the operations. After his return to Dresden from Silesia (Sept. 6th) the Emperor moved South again, hoping to engage Schwarzenberg; but once more he was baulked of his desire, not indeed because Schwarzenberg retired, for after the outposts had fallen back to the main position the Austrian commander stood his ground, but because of the impassable state of the roads over the

KATZBACH Aug.26ᵗʰ 1813

Oberhochkirch

Sacken

Eichholtz

English Miles

Katzbach

Souham

Flank attack

Sebastiani

Bellwitzhof

Yorck

Wütende Neisse

Peterwitz

Macdonald

Neisse

Weinberg

Schlaupe

Langeron

Russians
driven back

Kroitsch

Nieder
Crain

Lauriston

Hennersdorf

Seichau

Mönchswald

DENNEWITZ, Sept. 6ᵗʰ 1813 (On Oudinot's Arrival)

English Miles

The numbers denote divisions
"Arr = Part of Arrighi's Cavalry Corps

JÜTERBOGK

TAUENTZIEN

(Wurtembergers)

BERTRAND

38

Rohrbeck

Swedes

Thümen

W

15

Arr.

Saxons

Nieder-
Görsdorf

12

Dennewitz

Krafft

Ü

32

Arrighi

Borstell

B

Hesse

Homburg

REYNIER

24

(Saxons)

25

14

OUDINOT

Arr.

13

Ohna

Gohlsdorf

29

(Bavarians)

B.V. Darbishire, Oxford, 1908.

Erzgebirge.[1] Napoleon therefore had again to return to Dresden (Sept. 12th). Another advance towards Nollendorf and Kulm had the same result (Sept. 17th to 19th), it prevented Schwarzenberg from carrying out a stroke he was aiming at Napoleon's communications in the direction of Leipzig; but though there was some sharp fighting round Kulm, no general action followed, and the only result was that Blücher was able to press Macdonald in on Dresden.

Once again, therefore, Napoleon dashed at Blücher (Sept. 22nd to 24th), but as before without result. His weakness in cavalry made it difficult for him to keep touch with his enemies; an even heavier handicap was the want of stamina of his troops, which diminished their mobility and to that extent detracted from the advantages of the central position, while the growing difficulty of obtaining supplies in a country so exhausted and impoverished as Saxony seriously increased his troubles. Indeed the Emperor's position was growing most unsafe, and common prudence would have dictated a retreat behind the Saale, for the position of the Austrians in Bohemia outflanked the line of the Elbe and made it strategically most unsafe. But a retreat behind the Saale would have abandoned Saxony, and the evacuation of that kingdom would have been the beginning of the end for the Confederation of the Rhine. To keep up his waning prestige, political and military, Napoleon must show a bold front; but as days slipped past and the great victory he so much needed still remained to be won, his hold on his half-willing allies grew weaker. His movements during this critical period display hesitation and indecision most unusual in him: plan after plan was formed, begun and abandoned incomplete. One great reason was the insecurity of his communications. Turn whichever way he would, he must expose his flanks and rear; and, above all, warnings were not wanting that he could not rely on the fidelity of the states which lay between him and France.

Indecisive as were the military operations upon which the month of September 1813 was spent, that month saw an event of the very greatest diplomatic importance, the negotiation of the Treaty of Töplitz (Sept. 9th). Hitherto Southern and Western Germany had remained faithful to Napoleon; but not so much from love of him as from fear of the Allies, and from a belief that the triumph of Austria and Prussia would be the

[1] Yorck von Wartenburg, ii. 315.

death-knell of the independence of the minor states. This fear was now removed, and a door was opened by which Napoleon's vassals might desert him. The Treaty of Töplitz provided, it is true, for the restoration to Austria and Prussia of the dominions they had held in 1805, the friendly co-operation of the Allies in deciding the fate of the Grand Duchy of Warsaw, the re-establishment of the House of Brunswick-Lüneburg in its old territories, and, above all, for the dissolution of the Confederation of the Rhine; but it guaranteed the independence of the members of that body.

This treaty was a great triumph for Metternich over the party which desired a complete reconstruction of Germany, and therefore urged that the partisans of Napoleon ought to be involved in their master's overthrow. Metternich's success undoubtedly contributed to the speedy expulsion of the French from Germany; for had Bavaria and Würtemberg felt that their independent existence was bound up with the cause of Napoleon, they would have made strenuous efforts on his behalf instead of deserting his standard. Where Stein's uncompromising policy would have driven the clients of France to desperation, Metternich's opportunism cut the ground from under Napoleon's feet. That this at the same time greatly delayed anything in the way of the unification of Germany cannot be denied; but seeing what the relations and aims of Austria and Prussia were, a thorough reconstruction would hardly have been possible without an appeal to the sword, for which neither Hapsburg nor Hohenzollen was prepared.

The first result of the Treaty of Töplitz was the defection of Bavaria from the side of Napoleon. Bavaria was not prepared to continue the struggle on the Emperor's behalf and to risk the hostility of Austria when such a way of escape lay open to her. And though the withdrawal of Augereau's corps, which had been called off to Saxony, had left the Wittelsbach kingdom with barely 40,000 men to meet an Austrian attack, Austria was ready to forego the chance of profiting by the exposed condition of Bavaria if she could thereby secure her Western neighbour for the side of the Allies. In Bavaria, Montgelas favoured neutrality but General Wrede and the Crown Prince saw that the surest way to avoid being involved in the overthrow of Napoleon was to associate Bavaria as closely as possible with the work of bringing about the tyrant's downfall. They therefore pleaded for joining the alliance, and carried their point. By the Treaty of Ried (Oct. 8th), Bavaria committed herself to the side of the Allies : she promised to restore to Austria such territory as might be needed for the rounding off of Austria's dominions, including, of course, Tyrol, but she was promised an adequate compensation. Reuss's Austrians, who had been opposing Wrede, now joined him, and the joint force prepared to intercept Napoleon's communications with the Rhine.[1]

Meanwhile the decisive movements of the campaign in Saxony had begun. By the end of September, Napoleon had come to the conclusion that he must abandon the right bank of the Elbe, and he had drawn in the greater part of his army to Dresden and its neighbourhood, though he had had to send Marmont and Latour-Maubourg back to the Mülde to support Ney. That general was occupied in reorganising the army beaten at Dennewitz in order to dispute the passage of the Elbe should Bernadotte, now on the right bank between Zerbst and Wittenberg, attempt to cross. Further afield an action of some importance had been fought by Wallmoden, which began the isolation of Davoût's corps. That Marshal had detached a division towards Magdeburg to clear the intervening district of the Allies and secure his communications with the main army of the French. Thereupon Wallmoden, having collected some 5 regiments of cavalry and 15 battalions of infantry, crossed the Elbe at Dömitz (Sept. 15th) and, pushing forward to Dannenberg, brought the French to action near the Göhrde Forest (Sept. 19th). A smart contest ended in the defeat and retreat of the French, the one British infantry battalion present, the 2nd battalion of the 73rd Foot, distinguishing itself by the capture of a battery from which a German corps had been repulsed.[2] Thus Wallmoden not only checked Davoût's move on Magdeburg, but established himself on the left bank of the Elbe, thereby encouraging the inhabitants of Hanover and Brunswick to take arms, Davoût the while remaining inactive, and eventually (end of October) retiring into Hamburg.

Thus the line of the Elbe which Napoleon was endeavouring to maintain could no longer be said to be in his hands, and his delay in the dangerously advanced position of Dresden became

---

[1] The Bavarian contingent with Napoleon's field-army, already much reduced by its losses in action and by desertion, now withdrew from his ranks, returning homeward.

[2] Cf. Beamish's *King's German Legion*.

daily more inexpedient. His repeated failures to bring one or other of the Allied armies to battle had only served to exhaust his troops and reduce their numbers. Every day that passed without the decisive success in a pitched battle which alone could have saved Napoleon made that decisive success more unlikely, for the ranks of the Austrians and Prussians were being replenished with recruits, and the Russian Army of Reserve under Bennigsen, 60,000 strong, was daily drawing nearer. Napoleon, on the contrary, had but few reinforcements to expect. Augereau was bringing up the newly organised IXth Corps to Leipzig, though his march was harassed by partisan corps, by Platof's Cossacks, and by an Austrian light division under Maurice Lichtenstein which had pushed forward from the extreme left of the Army of Bohemia ; but even this corps and the cavalry of Milhaud who accompanied it, some good regiments from the Army of Spain, did not between them amount to more than 20,000. Yet the Emperor would not fall back behind the Saale although the danger to his communications kept on compelling him to detach portions of his army farther and farther West to keep the line open.

September 27th saw the decisive movements begin. On that day Blücher, leaving 20,000 men to threaten Dresden from Bautzen, started North-Westward to join Bernadotte, and simultaneously the Army of Bohemia began a movement to its left, under cover of the divisions which were observing Dresden from the Southward. The object of these joint movements was that the Allies should concentrate behind the Saale and so interpose between Napoleon and France, and force on the battle it was no longer their object to avoid. One thing only could have saved Napoleon, a rapid concentration behind the Saale, followed by prompt blows against the converging forces of the Allies before they could unite. But such a course was unlikely, partly because the quality of the French troops was such that their mobility was low, partly because Napoleon was badly served by his cavalry and seems to have been ill supplied with news of his enemies' movements, but also because when he moved from Dresden he failed to first concentrate his army before trying to bring his enemies to action.

Blücher took with him some 65,000 men, Yorck's Prussians and the Russians of Langeron and Sacken. By October 3rd he was at the confluence of the Elbe and Black Elster, where he set about attempting a passage. Simultaneously Bernadotte advanced against the bridges of Acklow and Rosslau lower down the river, in order to occupy the left wing of the French Army of the North and prevent Reynier, whose corps had charge of those passages, coming to the aid of Bertrand who was opposing Blücher's crossing.[1]

Bertrand made an obstinate resistance and inflicted no small loss on Yorck, but the latter's numbers were too much for him, and enabled Blücher to force his way across at Bleddin on Bertrand's right. Accordingly the IVth Corps fell back towards Düben and Bitterfeld, on which places Reynier also retired, having failed to prevent Bernadotte from forcing the passages at Acklow and Rosslau. Thus October 4th saw both the Army of the North and that of Silesia established on the left bank of the Elbe, and three days later their forces came into touch between the Mülde and the Saale, threatening Leipzig from the North, while from the South Schwarzenburg was moving upon that city, having put his troops in motion on September 26th. Meanwhile Napoleon had at last left Dresden. On October 7th he had announced his intention of evacuating Dresden and falling back to the Mülde, where he meant to adopt a central position at Würzen, from which he could assist either the corps holding the passages of the Middle Elbe or those covering Leipzig against Schwarzenberg. These had been placed under Murat, and included Victor, Lauriston, Poniatowski and L'Heritier's cavalry, in all about 40,000. By the evening of the 8th the move had been carried out and the Guard, Sebastiani and Macdonald were at Würzen, giving a central force of 64,000 men, Marmont and Latour-Maubourg with 25,000 more being in easy reach at Taucha. But this force should have been nearly 30,000 stronger had not Napoleon, with an unwisdom almost incredible in one who had written,[2] "Whenever one wishes to fight a battle, one should not divide but concentrate all one's forces," left St. Cyr with his own corps and the remnants of the Ist, now under Lobau, to hold on to Dresden, a position which had ceased to have any great strategical value the moment the line of the Elbe was abandoned.

[1] After Dennewitz, Oudinot's corps (XIIth) was so much reduced that the remnants of it were incorporated in the IVth and VIIth Corps, which mustered between them about 20 to 25,000 men, instead of the 65,000 these three had totalled before Gross Beeren. The two Saxon divisions of Reynier were amalgamated at the same time.
[2] Napoleon to Berthier, Dec. 6th, 1811.

The Emperor's next move was to the Northward, yet another attempt to catch the wary foe who had so frequently escaped, but once again Blücher evaded the action which Napoleon sought to force on him. To do this he had indeed to sacrifice his communications, but he was successful in slipping away Westward across Napoleon's front and placing himself behind the Saale in touch with Bernadotte. That commander, nervously apprehensive of the political consequences of a defeat, would have been glad to withdraw from such dangerous proximity to the Emperor, but the representations of Charles Stewart, the English representative with the Army of the North, induced him to abandon his intention of retiring to the comparative safety of the right bank of the Elbe, and thus the joint armies of Silesia and the North took post on the left of the Saale, menacing Leipzig from the North-West, and ready to move in upon it as soon as Schwarzenberg's cautious advance from the South-East should make co-operation possible.

The result of Blücher's Westward move, a step probably taken by the advice of his Chief of Staff, Gneisenau, was that Napoleon on pushing forward to the Elbe found no one but Tauentzien's *Landwehr* in his front (Oct. 9th to 11th). Thus the Emperor's scheme for driving Blücher and Bernadotte out of reach of their allies miscarried completely. In vain he secured the passages over the Elbe and drove Tauentzien back with some loss; the news of Schwarzenberg's advance on Leipzig stayed his advance further. The Austrian commander was pushing steadily forward, forcing Murat back before him; and even Napoleon could not venture to attempt any of the hazardous projects of a dash on Berlin, or of a move up the right bank of the Elbe to Torgau to recross there and strike at Schwarzenberg's rear, which he contemplated only to lay aside.

Accordingly, on October 12th the Emperor gave orders for the troops under his immediate command to return to Leipzig. This decision was undoubtedly correct. Now that Schwarzenberg was really placing the Army of Bohemia within the Emperor's reach, the only chance of victory lay in Napoleon's being able to defeat him before Blücher or Bernadotte could intervene. Every available man should have been set on the road to Leipzig; and it was a grievous error to have let Reynier, who had crossed to the right bank of the Elbe on the 11th, push his pursuit of Tauentzien further on the 12th. Leipzig was the critical spot, and

Map to illustrate Movements between DRESDEN & LEIPZIG

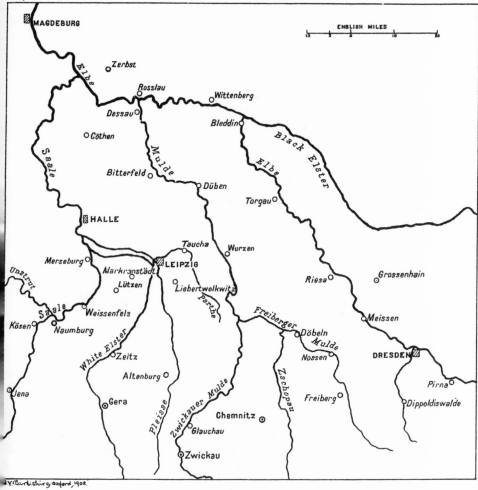

Leipzig was in some peril, for Schwarzenberg had driven Murat right in on the town; and though a sharp action around Wachau and Liebertwolkwitz on the 14th had resulted in the repulse of the Allies, the French counter-attack had failed.

By the evening of the 15th Napoleon had concentrated round Leipzig between 170,000 and 180,000 men, though several divisions, including one of the IIIrd Corps (Ney's) and all Reynier's (VII.), were still absent. Schwarzenberg, though actually superior in numbers, had not so large a proportion of his army with him, and unless the Army of Bohemia were supported by its allies from beyond the Saale there seemed a chance that Napoleon might snatch a victory at this eleventh hour. But nothing short of complete victory would suffice. Failure to defeat Schwarzenberg would mean that the ultimate victory was only a question of when the Allies' reinforcements would be up.

Napoleon's main body lay to the South of Leipzig: its right, Poniatowski's Poles (VIII.), on the Pleisse between Connewitz and Mark Kleeberg. Next them stood Victor (II.) at Wachau, and Lauriston (V.) at Liebertwolkwitz, with Augereau's IXth Corps, recently arrived from Bavaria, flung back so as to cover the left flank of the line and holding Zuckelhausen and Holzhausen. In support of these infantry were the cavalry corps of Kellermann at Dösen, of Latour - Maubourg at Zweinaundorf, and of Sebastiani in support of Augereau. When the battle began Macdonald (XI.) was at Taucha moving up towards Holzhausen, and Souham with two of Ney's divisions (III.) had reached Mockau. To the North of the town Marmont (VI.) was between Breitenfeld and Möckern, Bertrand (IV.) at Eutritzsch, Arrighi's cavalry in support. The Guards were at Reudnitz and Crottendorf as a general reserve, and Reynier (VII.) was on his way from Düben. Had the Emperor decided there and then to engage Schwarzenberg, the chances would have been in favour of the French; for Blücher, who was on the road from Halle, had not got beyond Gross Kugel, and Bernadotte at Zölbig and Oppen was still farther away. However, the Emperor, never believing that Blücher or Bernadotte would be able to interfere in the least with his operations next day, let the valuable hours slip by unused, making all preparations to concentrate every man South of Leipzig next morning to fall on Schwarzenberg.

But next morning (Oct. 16th), when Marmont prepared to move from the North of the Parthe to Liebertwolkwitz to support the great attack on the Austrians which the Emperor had planned, he found Blücher pressing in so close upon him that he had to face about, taking post from Möckern on his left to Widderitsch on his right, where Ney's divisions were beginning to arrive. Meanwhile to the South the main action had begun. Here the Army of Bohemia was moving forward on both sides of the Elster and of the Pleisse. Schwarzenberg's plan was that Giulai's Austrians should push down the left bank of the Elster from Markranstadt on Lindenau, with the twofold object of getting into touch with the Army of Silesia, and securing the great road from Leipzig by Lützen and Erfurt to Mayence, the road along which the French must retire if defeated. On Giulai's right the Austrians of Merveldt and Alois Lichtenstein were to push forward between the Elster and the Pleisse, to cross the latter river at Connewitz and turn the French right flank, some 38,000 men being in all allotted to these tasks. The rest of the Army of Bohemia stretched from the Pleisse to the Kolmberg, Kleist's Prussians (30,000) being next the river and opposite Mark Kleeberg, Eugene of Würtemberg at Gossa opposite Wachau, Gortschakoff beyond him opposing Lauriston, the Austrians of Klenau (25,000) on the right again. In reserve were the Russian and Prussian Guards, the whole force being over 130,000. The first stages of the day's fighting went somewhat in favour of the Allies, who forced the French to give ground, though they failed to carry the villages, to which Victor, Poniatowski and Lauriston clung with stubborn determination. About midday the Emperor had all ready for a counter-attack. Macdonald replaced Augereau on the left, and the IXth Corps pushed across to the Pleisse to fall into line between the Poles and Victor; the Young Guard supported Lauriston, Drouet massed a great battery near Wachau, and Murat collected all the available cavalry in order to hurl them on the Allied centre.

For a time all went well. Macdonald with Mortier and some of the Young Guard supporting him stormed the Kolmberg and drove Klenau back by threatening his right flank: on the other wing Augereau pushed forward to Crostewitz and wrested it from Kleist, Victor aided by two divisions of the Young Guard under Oudinot stormed Auenhayn; only at Güldengossa did the Allies manage to hold the French at bay, and there Gortschakoff had the greatest difficulty in repulsing Lauriston. About three o'clock Murat delivered his great charge, launching some 12,000 horsemen on the Allied batteries near Güldengossa, where there was a gap between Eugene of Würtemberg's right and Gortschakoff's left only filled by a few Russian cavalry. The French squadrons reached and captured the guns, but the timely arrival of the Allied reserves saved the day. The Austrian Reserve came up from Zobigker, assisted Kleist to make head against Augereau and even to regain lost ground. Latour-Maubourg was wounded, and the French cavalry, their horses spent by their charge, failed to press the advantage they had gained, wavered and finally gave way before the attacks of the cavalry of the Russian and Prussian Guards. A Russian Grenadier division came to Eugene's aid and, after a stubborn contest, retook Auenhayn and forced Victor to retreat, while Klenau, rallying his corps, managed to hold Macdonald in check and prevent him executing the flanking movement in which he had not received the expected assistance of Ney's corps.

Thus all along the line the French had to recoil, and evening found them in the positions they had occupied in the morning, reduced in numbers and much exhausted. The timely intervention of the Austrian Reserve had been the decisive point in the engagement, and had prevented Napoleon from gaining the victory which had seemed in his grasp. But the Army of Silesia also had had an important influence over the action to the South of Leipzig, for it was its pressure on the French to the North of the city which had prevented the expected supports from that quarter from joining in Macdonald's turning movement by Seiffertshayn.

The command of the French forces in this quarter had been entrusted to Marshal Ney, who had under him Bertrand, Marmont, Arrighi's cavalry, and, when they should arrive, his own corps, now under Souham, and that of Reynier. But the Emperor was so far from anticipating any attack by the Army of Silesia that he had ordered Marmont to move to the assistance of Lauriston, an order Marmont was unable to fulfil because he found himself attacked by the Army of Silesia, and spent the rest of the day in a desperate struggle for the villages of Möckern and Widderitsch. In like manner Bertrand's corps, which Ney despatched to Liebertwolkwitz in place of Marmont's, had to be diverted elsewhere before it could reach the Southern scene of action, for Giulai was pressing in on Lindenau, and threatened to close the French line of retreat. Souham also started to support Macdonald but never got into action, being recalled to the North of the city to succour the hard-pressed Marmont, so that he spent the day in fruitless countermarches between one battlefield and the other, as d'Erlon was to do on the day of Ligny.

Meanwhile Marmont was very hard pressed. His left rested on Möckern and the Elster, in front of his centre he held Lindenthal, his right was at Widderitsch. With some 20,000 men available he had to face treble his numbers, for the whole Army of Silesia attacked him: but his troops were of better quality than most of the French, 17 of his 42 battalions being Marines. Yorck assailed Möckern; Sacken carried Lindenthal and came up in support of Yorck; Langeron attacked Widderitsch and carried it, only to lose it again when the belated third division of the IIIrd Corps arrived from Düben and succoured Marmont's right. The fighting on this side was about the most obstinate of the day. Möckern and Widderitsch were taken and retaken repeatedly. Nightfall found Marmont actually in possession of Möckern; but his corps had suffered so heavily and been so much reduced, that under cover of darkness he fell back over the Parthe, having lost 8000 men and 53 guns which he could not remove.

Indeed it was only to the South-West that the French had gained any real advantage. Hampered by the difficulties of the ground in which they were operating, Merveldt and Lichtenstein had achieved nothing and had failed to cross the Pleisse; while Bertrand not only recovered Lindenau, to which Giulai had penetrated, but by driving the Austrians back as far as Klein Zschocher kept open the line of retreat.

October 17th saw but little fighting. Both sides were spent by their exertions; the French had lost over 25,000 men, the Allies at least half as many again, so that they had good reason to wait, for every hour brought their reinforcements nearer. Colloredo's Austrians reached Cröbern that evening, Bennigsen and the Russian Army of Reserve were not far behind, and the 60,000 men of the Army of the North came up to Breitenau in the course of the day. This force, indeed, might have taken part in the fighting of the 16th had Bernadotte displayed rather more eagerness for battle;[1] but Sir Charles Stewart's entreaties had not availed to move the Crown Prince forward from Halle.

[1] Cf. Cathcart, *War of 1812–1813*, pp. 314–318.

The inaction of the Allies was not turned to good account by Napoleon. There can be little doubt that after the drawn battle of the 16th, he should have endeavoured to extricate himself from his dangerous position before the net closed in completely on him. He does seem to have contemplated a retreat, but did nothing to prepare for it, an omission which was to cost his army dear two days later. All that the Emperor did was to draw the army in nearer to Leipzig, so that on the morning of the 18th their positions formed a semicircle from the Elster at Dölitz, where Poniatowski and Augereau stood, through Probstheida, held by Victor, Stötteritz and Mölkau, defended by Macdonald, Paunsdorf where Reynier took post on arriving from Düben, to the Parthe at Schönfeld which Souham held. Marmont covered the left flank by taking post behind the Parthe, Lauriston was in second line behind Victor and Macdonald, the cavalry and the Guards formed a general reserve, while Bertrand was thrust out along the road to Weissenfels to secure the defile of Kösen.

Meanwhile the Allies had made their dispositions for the attack. Schwarzenberg is at least open to criticism for not having done more to intercept the Emperor's line of retreat Westward; what he seems to have feared most was that Napoleon would make a desperate attempt to break out through the circle which was closing in on him in the direction of the Elbe, through the gap in the Allied line which Bernadotte was to close with the Army of the North. The main attack thus took the shape of an advance of the Army of Bohemia and Bennigsen's reserves in three columns against the French right wing. Giulai so far from being strongly reinforced, was actually called upon to send back one of his divisions from the West of the Elster to reinforce the attack on Lossnig.

It was about 7 a.m. that the attack was begun. Hesse-Homburg's Austrians, pressing forward along the right bank of the Pleisse, carried Dölitz and Dosen after heavy fighting but could not wrest Connewitz from the Poles. On their right Kleist and Wittgenstein assailed Probstheida; but Victor would not be dislodged and repulsed repeated attacks. The third column under Klenau, which attempted to wrest Holzhausen from Macdonald, had at first little success; but about 2 p.m. Bennigsen came up to his help and Holzhausen was carried, though even then their efforts to take Stötteritz were less fortunate, and

Bennigsen, swerving more to his right in order to get into touch with the Army of the North, could not get beyond Engelsdorf for Reynier's Saxons, who formed the right of the force with which Ney was prepared to oppose Bernadotte, held on firmly to Mölkau and Paunsdorf. Thus the attack of the Army of Bohemia came to more or less of a standstill, the strong and stoutly defended position of Stötteritz-Probstheida, with Lauriston and much reserve artillery supporting its defenders, defying their assaults. Both these villages remained in French hands till nightfall, Kleist and Wittgenstein suffering heavily in their unsuccessful attempts on Probstheida, while Klenau and Ziethen's Prussians, less closely engaged, lost fewer men but achieved no more against Macdonald.

But meanwhile the battle was being decided elsewhere. Not, indeed, by Blücher, who had detached Langeron to co-operate with Bernadotte, and thus had only Yorck and Sacken with whom to engage Marmont. He was successful in driving in the French outposts from Gohlis and Pfaffendorf, but their main position behind the Parthe proved too much for him: at one time he managed to force a passage, and even to gain possession of Reudnitz, but the Emperor sent up reinforcements and recovered the lost ground. It was the arrival of the Army of the North which really decided the battle. About midday Bernadotte's vanguard reached Taucha and got into touch with Langeron, who had crossed the Parthe at Mockau to assist the Crown Prince's operations. Langeron then advanced against Ney's left at Schönfeld, while Winzingerode pushed across to Paunsdorf to establish communications with Bennigsen, thus closing the gap between the left of the Army of Silesia and the right of that of Bohemia.

Encouraged by the prospect of the arrival of the Army of the North, Bennigsen's troops resumed their attacks on Reynier's position at Mölkau and Paunsdorf. As Bubna's Austrians also pressed forward, the troops opposed to them, instead of resisting their advance, came over in a body and threw in their lot with the Allies. These deserters were the Saxons, who formed so large a part of Reynier's corps, and their defection was followed by that of a Würtemberg cavalry brigade nearly 1500 strong. Even apart from the moral effect on the Allies and on the French alike of so striking an incident, so public a proclamation of Napoleon's failure to retain the fidelity of his allies, the desertion of the Saxons was of great immediate and practical importance, for Reynier's remaining division gave way before Bubna's attack, and the Austrians occupied Paunsdorf. To the success of this attack the presence with Winzingerode's cavalry of the one unit which represented England in this great "battle of the nations" contributed appreciably. Captain Bogue's rocket-troop of the Royal Artillery played a most effective part in aiding Bubna's advance, its novel missiles doing much execution and creating quite a sensation.

Ney hastened to Reynier's assistance with such reserves as he had at hand and temporarily recovered Paunsdorf; but before the steady pressure of the advance of the Army of the North even Ney had to recoil and to content himself with extricating Reynier's remnant. In vain Nansouty brought the cavalry of the Guard to Ney's help. Bülow's arrival forced Ney back on Reudnitz, and Langeron returning to the attack after several repulses at last wrested Schönfeld from its defenders. Thus all round the line the French were being pressed back into Leipzig; and even Napoleon could no longer conceal from himself the fact that retreat was inevitable. Fortunately for him the road to the West still presented a way of escape; for Giulai, his force reduced to one division by the recall of the second to succour Hesse-Homburg, had been unable to hold his own against Mortier and two divisions of the Young Guard, who had thrust him aside and cleared the road to France.

But hardly any preparations had been made for a retreat. No extra bridges had been laid over the Elster and Pleisse, the troops were in great disorder and disorganisation, and the utmost confusion prevailed. Had Schwarzenberg made better arrangements for hindering the retreat, the entire French army might have been cut off. As it was, the orders intended for Bianchi, who had replaced Hesse-Homburg, never reached him, and his column instead of crossing the Elster and supporting Giulai remained near Leipzig on the 19th. Blücher had started Yorck, whose men had been in reserve all the 18th, off towards the Unstrutt on the evening of that day; but he had to make a detour by Halle, and only came up with the rear of the French as they were crossing at Freiburg on the 22nd, while Bertrand was able to keep Maurice Lichtenstein and Giulai at bay near Kösen. A very large number of prisoners were certainly taken by the Allies, but this was due to Napoleon's neglect to make proper arrangements for the retreat and to the premature destruction of the bridges over the Elster, rather than to the efforts of the Allies. They devoted themselves on the morning of the 19th to assaulting the various gates of the city, which were stoutly defended by the contingents of the vassal states, the Poles, the Italians, the handful of Spaniards, the Illyrians, the Dutch-Belgians, the Swiss, and such Germans as had not yet deserted, while the French were filing out of the city Westward. In all about 80,000 troops managed to make their way to Markran-städt by the evening of the 19th; but the Allies secured with the city of Leipzig not less than 250 guns and 50,000 prisoners, of whom over 20,000 were wounded. In killed and wounded they had themselves probably lost almost as heavily as the French;[1] but the capture of so large a number of prisoners made all the difference, reducing the Grand Army to less than half of its strength before the battle.

There was no thought now among the French of a stand East of the Rhine. The Grand Army had one object only, to place that river between themselves and their enemies: only behind its shelter could they feel safe, there only could they find reinforcements and succour. Germany was lost irrevocably; for great as the military success of the Allies had been, that was nothing when compared with the political results of Leipzig. It completed the collapse of the tottering Confederation of the Rhine. The minor states hastened to follow the lead of Bavaria. French rule disappeared from Berg and from Westphalia amid an outburst of popular enthusiasm. Benefits were forgotten in the general hurry to be rid of Napoleon's yoke. The general joy at the overthrow of the Emperor found expression in patriotic poems and songs, notably in Arndt's demand that the Rhine should once again become a German river. Popular feeling ran high, nationalist sentiments were openly expressed, other Liberal ideas not less distasteful to Metternich were current everywhere. He saw with alarm Germany on the verge of being thrown into the melting-pot of "reconstruction": he had good reason to dread the turn which events might take unless something were speedily done to check the flow of the tide. There were two things he detested with about equal fervour: Liberalism and Nationalism. By admitting Napoleon's vassals to terms he

---

[1] *Deutsche Geschichte, 1806–1871*, i., gives their losses as: Austrians, 15,000; Prussians, 16,000; Russians, 22,000.

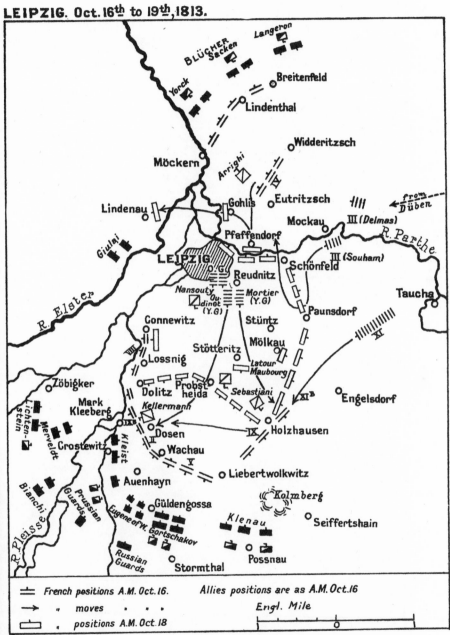

LEIPZIG. Oct. 16ᵗʰ to 19ᵗʰ, 1813.

Langeron

BLÜCHER Sacken

Yorck

Breitenfeld

Lindenthal

Widderitzsch

Möckern

Arrighi

from Düben

Gohlis

Eutritzsch

Mockau

III (Delmas)

Lindenau

Giulai

Pfaffendorf

R. Parthe

LEIPZIG

Reudnitz

III (Souham)

Schönfeld

Taucha

Nansouty

Ou-dinot (Y.G)

Mortier (Y.G)

Paunsdorf

R. Elster

Connewitz

Stüntz

Mölkau

VI

Stötteritz

Lossnig

Latour Maubourg

Zöbigker

Dolitz

Probst heida

Sebastiani

XI ᴮ

Engelsdorf

Mark Kleeberg

Kellermann

IX

Holzhausen

Lichten-stein

Merveldt

Crostewitz

Kleist

Dosen

Wachau

Bianchi

Prussian Guards

Auenhayn

Liebertwolkwitz

R. Pleisse

Güldengossa

Kolmberg

Eugene of W. Gortschakov

Klenau

Seiffertshain

Russian Guards

Stormthal

Possnau

⊥ French positions A.M. Oct. 16.   Allies positions are as A.M. Oct. 16

→   "   moves   "   "   Engl. Mile

▭   "   positions A.M. Oct. 18

B.V. Darbishure, Oxford, 1908.

hoped to checkmate both, to prevent the reconstruction on Liberal lines which he was determined to avoid. His hatred of reconstruction was in large measure inspired by his dislike of Prussia. Reconstruction must involve a definite settlement of the relation between Austria and Prussia, and Metternich did not intend to allow this to come to pass. Hence he seized the earliest possible opportunity of coming to terms with the South German Princes: Frederick I of Würtemberg was no less anxious to be admitted to terms, hoping thus to secure the gains he had made by Napoleon's help by bringing them under the shelter of an Austrian recognition. A champion of particularism and a bitter enemy of German nationalism, he desired to escape the fate which had befallen Saxony and which was threatening his dominions, of being seized and administered by the Allies as a "common possession." The Treaty of Fulda (Nov. 2nd) saved Würtemberg from being treated in this way, from being taxed and requisitioned to the limits of its capacity to defray the expenses of the Allies. Würtemberg, like Bavaria, not only received official sanction for her existence, but promised to send a contingent of 12,000 men to assist Austria. Her action was imitated by Baden, by Nassau, by the Saxon Duchies and by Hesse-Darmstadt. The last-named concluded a military convention with Austria (Nov. 2nd) which three weeks later was expanded into a definite treaty of alliance. Even more effective as a check on the popular movement and the nationalist spirit than the recognition of these states which owed so much to Napoleon and had been his vassals so long, was the recall of the old rulers, whose dominions had gone to make up those creations of Napoleon's which were bound to fall with him. To Brunswick, Electoral Hesse, Hanover and Oldenburg their dispossessed sovereigns came back in the spirit of the most uncompromising *emigré*, determined to restore the old *régime* and as far as possible to obliterate the immediate past, to slur over the reforms effected in their absence and which were in so strong a contrast to their own negligent rule.

But the immediate task of the Allies was not to reconstitute Germany, but to complete the work of Leipzig. There were two things to be done: Napoleon must be pursued, cut off if possible, driven over the Rhine if he should escape capture; secondly, the fortresses still held by his troops must be blockaded or taken. Klenau's Austrians and Bennigsen's Russians had therefore to be left on the Elbe to attend to the French strongholds on that river, Dresden, Torgau, Magdeburg and Wittenberg; Kleist's Prussians with the assistance of Winzingerode's Russians took charge of Erfurt; Bernadotte moved North to assist Wallmoden against Davoût and the Danes. Wallmoden, encouraged by his success at the Göhrde, had begun to pass his troops over to the left bank of the Elbe soon after that action, and had pushed them forward to Bremen and Hanover, stirring up insurrections in those districts, with the result that Davoût had been quite cut off from his master. Bernadotte's arrival compelled the Marshal to retire into Hamburg, where he maintained himself for the rest of the war, while the Danes, driven back into Holstein and pursued by Wallmoden, were forced to conclude the Treaty of Kiel in January 1814. By that time several of the fortresses had fallen, Dresden and Torgau having succumbed early in November, Stettin, Wittenberg and Dantzic before the end of the year, and the garrisons of the remainder, closely beset by the Army of the North, now broken up, and by the *Landwehr*, who came forward in great numbers, were condemned to a useless inactivity.

In the other part of their task, the interception and capture of the retreating Grand Army, the Allies were less successful. Napoleon had reached Weissenfels on the evening of October 20th and had hastened to cross to the left bank of the Saale, thus leaving the main road up the right bank by Naumburg for fear that the difficulties of getting through the narrow defile of Kösen would afford opportunities to his enemy. The change of road took the French through hilly country, and so far delayed them that Yorck caught up their rearguard just as the main body had got across the Unstrutt, and inflicted some loss on it. However, even so the Prussians failed to check the retreat; and as Bertrand kept Lichtenstein and Giulai at bay at Kösen, the relics of the Grand Army regained the high road at Buttelstadt and arrived at Erfurt in safety on October 23rd. Here a short stay was made, and Napoleon was able to do something to refit and reorganise his shattered army. But advantageous as the position of Erfurt would have been for a stand had Napoleon adopted it earlier when his army was still intact, the time for a stand was past: not even with the Harz Mountains to cover his left and the Thuringian Forest to protect his right,[1] did he contemplate another action. With Southern Germany rising

[1] Cf. Cathcart, pp. 274-276.

against him in his rear, with the North-West seething with hostility, with the structure he had raised collapsing around him, and the main body of the Allies in pursuit, he had no option but to fall back, and on October 25th he resumed his retreat towards Frankfort.

The Allies were moving in two main bodies, Schwarzenberg taking the road by Jena on Weimar, Blücher with Langeron and Yorck moving by Merseburg and Freiburg on Langensalza. But for the intercepting of Napoleon they relied mainly on Wrede, who with his own Bavarian corps and the Austrians of Prince Reuss had come up from Anspach by Würzburg to Hanau (Oct. 28th) and was blocking the high road to France. Expecting that Wrede's intervention would force the French to turn aside and seek to regain the left bank of the Rhine at Coblence, Blücher changed his course and made for Giessen and Wetzlar, thus losing touch with the French. His move enabled Napoleon to win a last victory on German soil. On October 30th the French vanguard found Wrede's 40,000 men drawn up on the North bank of the Kinzig, in front of Hanau, barring their road to France. There was some sharp and even fighting, but finally a great attack by all the cavalry that Nansouty and Sebastiani could collect was directed against Wrede's left, the way having been paved for it by Drouet, who massed a great battery against that point. The Allied flank was beaten in and the road cleared, Wrede's men retiring across the Kinzig. Next day Napoleon attacked them in their new position, employing the corps of Bertrand and Marmont, which fought uncommonly well considering all they had recently been through. By this means he occupied Wrede's attention and gained time for his rearguard, the Young Guard under Oudinot, to get past Hanau, whereupon the rest of the French retired also. On November 2nd the columns of the Grand Army were trailing safely over the Rhine at Mayence. It was not Wrede's fault that the Emperor had got away. The pursuit after Leipzig was none too well managed, though a little more energy might have saved the losses of the next year's campaign. It would have been far better to send every available sabre and bayonet straight after the Grand Army rather than to pay so much attention to reducing fortresses, whose fate was but a secondary affair. But here, as always, the lack of an effective Commander-in-Chief hampered the operations of the Allies.

CHAPTER XXXIII

1814 AND THE TREATY OF PARIS

THUS at last was Germany freed from Napoleon's rule; but, successful as the efforts of the Allies had been, 1813 had no more ended the struggle than had 1812. Just as the advance into Germany had been needed to reap the fruits of the repulse of the invasion of Russia, so the liberation of Germany could only be made secure by following up the expulsion of Napoleon from German soil. For the man whose rule was founded on victory could not afford to acquiesce in defeat, not even a Leipzig would induce him to accept the highly favourable terms on which the Allies would gladly have given him peace. He at least had not had enough of fighting, though France, exhausted by the prodigious efforts she had made in response to his demands, had neither the capacity nor the inclination to repeat her useless sacrifices. Napoleon hoped that the prospect of invasion would produce a reaction in his favour, would provoke a popular movement against the foreigner similar to that of 1792; but although twelve days before Napoleon left Leipzig a victorious enemy had already crossed the frontier of France, Wellington's men when they crossed the Bidassoa (Oct. 6th and 7th, 1813) found themselves among a population who displayed nothing like the hostility which the French peasantry had shown to the Austrians and Prussians twenty years before. France had begun to realise that Napoleon was making her fight his battles and not hers, and her response to his appeal was but half-hearted.

The campaign of 1814 was one which ought never to have been fought. Politically, France had nothing to gain; from the military point of view Napoleon had nothing to hope for. With barely 80,000 men to oppose to the overwhelming forces of the Allies even he could not expect to win: the weight of numbers was bound to crush him; despite the marvellous exhibition of skill and resource which he gave, despite the repeated blunders of his enemies, he was in the end overpowered by numbers. That he persisted in fighting was largely because pride and obstinacy would not let him admit defeat, because self-confidence bade him expect victory, but mainly because, not without good reason, he trusted to the dissensions of his enemies.

That there was no small divergence between the views of Austria and of Prussia Napoleon was well aware. He knew that Metternich's hostility to him had its limits, and that rather than favour anything likely to provoke a Jacobinical reaction, as, for example, the restoration of the Bourbons, the Austrian minister would be prepared to let him retain the throne of France. Indeed, the excellent terms offered to Napoleon in November 1813, the so-called "Proposals of Frankfort," may be taken as embodying the views of Austria rather than of her allies. To give France the Rhine, the Alps and the Pyrenees as her boundaries would have been distasteful to England, which much disliked leaving Antwerp and all Belgium in her hands; the mere restoration of the former rulers in Italy, Holland and Germany, and the recognition by Napoleon of the unconditional independence of Germany and Italy would have been far from satisfying the desire for revenge which animated Prussia and Russia; but the Allies agreed to the offer, and it was from Napoleon that the rejection came. He demanded instead the fortresses of Wesel, Kehl and Cassel, a kingdom for Jerome in Germany, and compensation in Italy for Eugene, who would be deprived of his reversion of the Grand Duchy of Frankfort. If Napoleon had wished to make peace impossible he could hardly have adopted more successful means. His obstinacy compelled the Allies to subordinate their discords to the one thing they had in common, their desire to compass his overthrow.

But though resolved not to let the fruits of their victory escape them, the Allies found some difficulty about settling on a plan of campaign. Radetzky and Gneisenau advocated an immediate invasion, judging that it would be better to undergo the hardships of a winter campaign than to give Napoleon time to build up a new army. This was opposed by von Knesebeck, who was in great favour with the King of Prussia, and who with the support of his master and of the Austrian von Duka declared that the fortresses on the Rhine must be taken before an invasion could be attempted. Schwarzenberg, however, so far departed from his usual policy as to reject this cautious plan and to declare for an advance. He did not, however, adopt Gneisenau's suggestion that the Army of Silesia with part of that of the North should invade France through Belgium, while the Army of Bohemia moved on Paris by Mayence and Metz. The plan which Schwarzenberg and Radetzky preferred was that the Army of Bohemia should move through Switzerland, thereby turning the lines of the Rhine and Vosges, and descend on Paris from the plateau of Langres, a country which had long been spared the horrors of war and was therefore well adapted to support and supply an advancing army. Blücher with the Army of Silesia and part of that of the North was to move due West from the Middle Rhine, crossing the river between Mannheim and Coblence. The rest of the Army of the North was either operating against Davoût under Bernadotte or blockading the fortresses the Allies were leaving untaken in their rear, or assisting Sir Thomas Graham and an English corps of some 8000 men to expel the French from Holland.[1]

The Allies had not less than 300,000 men available for the invasion. Their main army amounted to 90,000 Austrians,[2] 50,000 Russians,[3] 29,000 Bavarians under Wrede, a corps from Würtemberg 14,000 strong, and the 6000 men of the Prussian Guards, in all not far short of over 200,000 men. Blücher had Yorck's Prussian corps and the Russians of Sacken and Langeron, in all about 80,000, while a reserve army was being collected in South Germany from the states whose contingents only a year before had been flocking to Napoleon's banner: it included 19,000 Hessians from Cassel, the so-called IVth "German League Corps," 9000 from Nassau, Berg, Waldeck and other minor states (Vth Corps), a Hesse-Darmstadt corps (the VIth) brought up to 10,000 by contingents from Würzburg, Reuss and Frankfort, and one from Baden (the VIIIth) of 10,000 men. When one adds to these numbers the forces in the Netherlands, those left behind in Germany, the Austrian Army of Italy which was steadily wresting that peninsula from its Viceroy, Eugene, not forgetting the 90,000 British and Portuguese at whose head Wellington was pushing forward irresistibly through the South-West of France, one has some conception of the mighty effort needed to free Europe from Napoleon's

---

[1] Cf. *Der Feldzug 1814 in Frankreich*, by Lieutenant-General von Janson.
[2] 4 corps and 2 light divisions.
[3] Their Guards and 2 corps under Wittgenstein and Barclay de Tolly.

dominion. The forces the Grand Alliance had put into the field a century earlier to repel the aggressions of Louis XIV seem insignificant in comparison.

To oppose them Napoleon had a field-force of little more than a quarter of the total available for the invasion. His Guard, reorganised in three corps under Ney, Oudinot and Mortier, mustered 35,000; the relics of the Grand Army provided some 12,000 cavalry and four skeleton corps of infantry amounting to 23,000. Behind these were forming new battalions of conscripts, National Guards and others, most of which were drawn into the fighting line as the campaign proceeded, but which were not available when the invasion began.

The main interest of the campaign of 1814 lies in a subject which does not call for very detailed treatment here, the marvellous skill with which Napoleon kept the overwhelming forces of his enemies at bay. The proceedings of the Allies, their quarrels, mistakes and failures, need rather more attention, and to them must partly be attributed Napoleon's success in maintaining the unequal struggle so long. As the armies of the Allies neared the frontier of France their fear of Napoleon, the common interest which had hitherto held them together, began to give place to hopes of individual advantages to be gained by his overthrow; the cohesion of the Coalition began to show signs of weakening, differences of aim to exercise their influence over the actions of the Allies.

It was at the end of December that the Austrians began their march through Switzerland; by January 18th the Allied Headquarters reached Langres and began descending the valleys of the Seine, Aube and Marne: Wrede had turned aside to Alsace to secure that province with the assistance of the VIth and VIIIth German League Corps. Blücher meanwhile having detached part of Yorck's corps to seize Luxembourg, Metz and Thionville, and left Langeron to besiege Mayence, had found himself too weak to do much independently, and was moving Southward to gain touch with the main army. This exposed him to Napoleon, and on January 29th the Emperor, who had concentrated 33,000 men at Vitry on the 25th, fell on the Prussian commander at Brienne sur Aube and drove him back up the river. Following in pursuit, Napoleon again engaged the Prussians at La Rothière (Feb. 1st). The battle might have gone against them had not an Austrian

division despatched by Schwarzenberg to Blücher's help succoured
the Prussian left, while at the critical moment Wrede brought up
his Bavarians from Joinville, a movement undertaken entirely
on his own initiative. This gave the Allies so great a numerical
superiority that Napoleon had to fall back to Arcis sur Aube.
Meanwhile Yorck had been in action with Macdonald near
Chalons (Feb. 2nd to 3rd) and had forced him back down the
Marne. In the hope of profiting by this success to separate
Macdonald and Napoleon, Blücher now moved to join Yorck,
taking with him also Kleist and Langeron, who had come up from
the rear. On February 8th he began a march down the Marne
on Paris, relying on the Army of Bohemia to move down the
Seine, and so contain Napoleon who had fallen back to Nogent.

Blücher's move was so conducted as to afford Napoleon
a splendid opportunity. In the attempt to get between
Macdonald and the Emperor the Prussian commander allowed
his divisions to become widely separated, with the result that
Napoleon fell with 30,000 men on Olsuviev's Russians at
Champaubert (Feb. 10th) and cut the Army of Silesia in two,
Yorck at Chateau-Thierry and Sacken at Montmirail being
thus separated from the headquarters near Vertus. But instead
of retreating promptly to the right of the Marne, Blücher made
a desperate effort to concentrate on the left bank. The result
was that while Marmont kept Blücher in check at Vauchamps,
Sacken (on the 11th) was defeated at Montmirail and driven
back on Yorck, and the two corps were bundled across the
Marne in a shattered condition. Blücher, who had wasted two
days in inaction at Vertus (Feb. 11th and 12th), expecting
Yorck and Sacken to join him, was then in turn assailed by
Napoleon and badly beaten (Feb. 13th). By February 16th
the Army of Silesia, weaker by 16,000 men than it had been
six days earlier and not a little demoralised and shaken, was
at Chalons, and Napoleon dashed off Southward, fell on the
Würtembergers at Montereau (Feb. 18th) and thus paralysed
Schwarzenberg's tardy advance. The Austrian commander's
delay may be explained, though not excused, by the fact that
he had been expecting the negotiations then in progress at
Chatillon to result in the conclusion of peace. The Allies
indeed had, after much debate, agreed to accept Caulaincourt's
suggestion of an armistice, and the Army of Bohemia had
made but little progress, and so was quite unable to assist

Blücher in any way. The 21st saw it back at Troyes, and when
Blücher moved across to Méry on the Seine to communicate
with his ally, all Schwarzenberg could suggest was a retreat
to Langres, since Augereau from Lyons was threatening his
communications, and he had had to make large detachments for
their protection. Napoleon, meanwhile, believing that victory
had returned to him, was now forming the wildest schemes and
forbidding Caulaincourt to accept anything short of the proposals of Frankfort.

Fortunately for the Allies, the troops of Bülow and Winzingerode, which belonged to the army under Bernadotte, were
at this moment within easy reach, and, mainly at the instigation
of Lord Castlereagh, it was decided to risk offending Bernadotte
by disregarding the orders he had given to his subordinates,
and summoning them to march at once to the assistance of
the main body. To co-operate with Bülow, Blücher was to
move North, the Army of Bohemia standing on the defensive
and "containing" Napoleon while Blücher and Bülow took the
offensive. The move was risky; once again the Allies failed to
concentrate and force on a battle under conditions which would
allow them to utilise their numerical superiority, once again
they gave Napoleon the chance of defeating them in detail.
Marching by La Ferté and Meaux Blücher exposed himself
to Napoleon: an attempt on Meaux (Feb. 28th) saw Sacken
and Kleist repulsed by Mortier, while Napoleon, leaving
Macdonald and Oudinot to keep Schwarzenberg occupied,
hastened after Blücher. On hearing of this Blücher had to
make for the Aisne in the hopes of joining Bülow before
Napoleon could overtake him. All turned on Soissons. It
had been taken by the Russian Winzingerode, but Mortier had
recovered it and placed a garrison in it. If this garrison could
have held out it would have kept Bülow and Blücher from
uniting, and so have allowed Napoleon to catch Blücher's corps,
exhausted by constant marching and frequent fighting, with
the Aisne at their backs.[1] Soissons, however, capitulated
tamely on March 3rd, and Blücher was able to reach the
comparative safety of the North bank of the Aisne. Without
attempting to dispute the passages of the Aisne, the Allies

---

[1] Cf. Wolseley, *Decline and Fall of Napoleon*, pp. 100–103. *Deutsche Geschichte,
1806–1871* (i. 478), denies that Blücher was in danger, alleging that he could have
bridged the Aisne.

retired to Craonne. Driven thence by Napoleon's attacks (March 7th), they fell back to Laon, where Napoleon again assailed them two days later. This time he was less successful. On the left, where he himself opposed Bülow and Winzingerode, the French carried the village of Ardon but could get little farther. Marmont on the right drove Yorck and Kleist back some way, but was checked by Langeron and Sacken, who reinforced the Prussians. The day thus ended indecisively; but in the night Ziethen's cavalry surprised Marmont's bivouacs, and thus threatened Napoleon's retreat to Craonne. But the advantage was not followed up. Blücher was incapacitated by illness, and Gneisenau, who succeeded to the command, seems to have lost his head. He displayed an extraordinary vacillation and confusion, and with the Prussian army thus relapsing into inaction Napoleon was able to slip away unpursued under cover of an attack on Bülow's corps, and to hurry back to the Seine to meet Schwarzenberg's renewed advance. Unimpeded by the Army of the North, which remained stationary on the Aisne for over a week, with Blücher ill and Yorck and Gneisenau at furious feud, Napoleon moved by Rheims, where he surprised and routed St. Priest's Russians (March 13th), and La Fere Champenoise (March 18th) to the Aube, joined Macdonald, who was withstanding Schwarzenberg's renewed advance with barely 30,000 men (March 20th), and on the 21st delivered an attack on the Allies at Arcis sur Aube. Including the troops he had brought from Rheims, a corps of 10,000 which had joined him from Paris and Macdonald's command, the Emperor had little more than 50,000 men, the Allies being enormously superior, as Schwarzenberg was concentrating all his outlying divisions. This superiority in numbers gave the Allies the victory in what was in some ways the decisive battle of the campaign. Had Schwarzenberg been beaten there can be little doubt but that he would have fallen right back to Langres, leaving Blücher and Bülow in the lurch. But in the end the French were badly beaten. Even the interior position could not compensate for the odds against them. Wrede's Bavarians thrust Ney back from Torcy. Giulai's Austrians at the other end of the line drove the French right from Vilette, the Russians in the centre gained ground steadily, and by the end of the day the French had had to retire over the Aube, and were in full retreat Northward towards Sézanne.

The reason for Schwarzenberg's concentration is to be found in the determination of the Allies to put an end to the struggle. Though after La Rothière Napoleon had agreed to a conference at Chatillon, his object had not been to conclude peace but to separate Austria from her Allies—a possibility always present to his mind. He played the game of procrastination with some temporary success, but with the final result of convincing the Allies that his overthrow was indispensable if peace were to be secured.[1] Alexander was now keen upon his deposition, and the Allies were in accord on that point, if there seemed little prospect that, when they had got rid of him, they would be able to agree as to his successor. The Treaty of Chaumont, concluded mainly through Castlereagh's influence (March 1st), brought them a stage nearer unity. France was to be restored to her ancient limits, her vassals were to be set completely free, and Germany was to be reconstructed as a Federal Union.

After Napoleon's repulse at Arcis sur Aube the Allies held a council of war, which came, not without misgivings, to the all-important decision to press on straight to Paris and so force a conclusion of the whole matter. They had just had the good fortune to intercept a despatch from Napoleon to Marie Louise in which the Emperor announced his resolve to try the effect of a blow at the communications of the Allies, a desperate move by which he hoped to paralyse the advance on Paris which he found himself unable to stem ; he still hoped to cajole or intimidate Austria into deserting the Coalition, and the move would also allow him to gather reinforcements from the fortresses of the Eastern frontier. Accordingly he moved from Sézanne on Vitry and St. Dizier, defeated a Russian corps at the latter place on the 28th, and then learnt that the main army of the Allies, instead of being, as he hoped, in full retreat for the Rhine, was moving on Paris. He hastened Westward, but it was already too late; he had only reached Fontainebleau when the news came that Paris was already in the hands of the Allies.

The idea of disregarding communications and pushing on to Paris originated with the Russian Toll. Alexander took it up

---

[1] M. Fournier (*Der Congress von Chatillon : die Politik im Kriege von 1814*) shows that it was the capture by the Allies of the letter to Caulaincourt, written by Napoleon on March 19th, which finally persuaded Francis II that Napoleon was playing fast and loose with him, and could not be trusted to abide by any concessions which might be extorted from him. Thus Napoleon's efforts to work on Austria's jealousy of Russia and Prussia, which had at one time seemed to be bearing fruit, came to nothing.

at once with great warmth, and Schwarzenberg and Frederick William acquiescing, the Army of Bohemia had started for Paris as Napoleon moved East (March 20th). The Army of Silesia had resumed its march on the 18th, pushing the corps of Marmont and Mortier back before it. These detachments had fallen back to Vertus when Napoleon summoned them Eastward to join him. In obeying his orders they met the Army of Bohemia at La Fère Champenoise (March 25th), were beaten and driven in on Paris. By the 29th the Army of Bohemia, which had moved by Melun and Corbeil, was at Charenton, Blücher had come up by Meaux to St. Denis. On March 30th there was sharp fighting outside Paris. Only at a heavy cost did the Allies wrest Montmartre, Montreuil and Vincennes from Marmont's corps; but the positions were gained, and Paris, exposed without appeal to a bombardment, could only avert that disaster by opening its gates. March 31st saw the Allies enter Paris in triumph, and even Napoleon had to confess himself beaten, for his army would not follow him to a campaign behind the Loire. On April 6th he agreed to abdicate, and on the 11th a provisional treaty was signed between him and the Allies. Napoleon renounced the throne of France and retired to Elba, and with the conclusion of the definite Treaty of Paris (May 30th), by which France was left with the frontier she had possessed in 1792, his overthrow seemed accomplished ; and the problem before Europe, and especially before Germany, was no longer to destroy the structure he had reared, but to rebuild something stable out of its ruins.

The Treaty of Paris was a sad disappointment to those who had hoped to have their revenge upon France for the injuries inflicted upon Germany under Napoleon's auspices. The Allies by adopting the principle that Napoleon alone was responsible and that France must not be punished, had refused to satisfy those—and there were many of them in Germany—who had desired an eye for an eye and a tooth for a tooth, who clamoured for a war indemnity, territorial cessions, safeguards against future aggression. Had the leaders of the great popular movement in Germany had their way, had the views expressed by Arndt been shared by those in authority, France would not have got off lightly. But in the conclusion of the Treaty of Paris the preponderating influence was that of the Czar : it was he rather than Frederick William or Francis II who had the last word, and his zeal for the emancipation of Germany was already dying down and being replaced by a generous wish to spare the defeated French. Stein was losing his influence over him, and Talleyrand, adroitly utilising the Czar's weakness for a principle, had enlisted him on behalf of the Legitimism in which the astute Frenchman had divined the best defence that France could oppose to those who wished to despoil her. The Allies, while professing to restore the state of things which had existed before the Revolution, could hardly deprive France of Alsace and Lorraine. England was not less warm in supporting the Legitimist principle, and Castlereagh defended the restoration to France of most of her colonies as being likely to incline her to peace by giving her no cause for dissatisfaction. Austria, despite Metternich's quarrel with the Czar over the violation of Swiss neutrality, was not disposed to press France hard. She wanted to avoid change as much as possible, to limit the area affected by the inevitable but distasteful reconstruction, and she had no reason to fear a restoration of the Bourbon monarchy to the full extent of its old dominions. There remained only Prussia; but neither Frederick William nor Hardenberg had fully identified themselves with the aspirations of the national party in Germany, nor were they likely to oppose the unanimous voice of their allies. German nationalism might desire that not only the annexations which Napoleon had made on the left bank of the Rhine should be taken from France, but that the opportunity should be taken to recover the provinces lost to Louis XV and Louis XIV; but the Irridentist spirit found opponents rather than champions in the men who would speak for Germany at the coming congress. Dynastic not national considerations were to regulate the settlement. The thorny problem of building up a really united Germany was avoided by statesmen who saw that the autocracy of the Princes, their masters, was absolutely incompatible with union on nationalist and popular lines. It would be impossible to adopt the principle of nationalism and at the same time to stifle the dreaded voices of Liberalism and democracy.

CHAPTER XXXIV

THE CONGRESS OF VIENNA

EVEN before the meeting of Congress which was to recast the political map of Europe, enough had happened to make it abundantly clear that the reconstruction would be the work of the princes, not of the peoples, and that the main object of the negotiations would be to confine the necessary changes within the narrowest possible limits. Thus the projects for the reconstruction of Germany, with which every publicist was busy from Cologne to Königsberg and from Münich to Hamburg, hardly received even a nominal consideration from Metternich and his fellows. Stein alone among the plenipotentiaries present at Vienna was in sympathy with the aspirations of the nationalist party in Germany; and Stein was present, not as the representative of any German state, but among the Russian deputation; and even in that capacity he was far less influential than he had been twelve months earlier, when he had enjoyed a greater share of the Czar's confidence.

But not even Stein himself seems to have contemplated anything like the German Empire of the present day; he had no idea of excluding Austria from Germany, but apparently wished to see a federation under the leadership of Austria, in which Prussia and Austria were to co-operate on terms of practical equality. Now as always, he was the bitter opponent of the middle-sized states, in which he saw the main obstacles to the unification of Germany. The Bavaria or the Baden of 1814 could make out a far better case for its independent sovereignty than had been possible to the Bavaria or Baden of 1794. To obtain some degree of unification and of subjection of the middle states to the central organisation, Stein at one time proposed the resuscitation of the Holy Roman Empire. This was only what had been proposed by the Treaty of Kalisch when Prussia and Russia had announced their intention of

" re-establishing the venerable Empire" to afford "effective protection and defence" to the people of Germany. But since March 1813 things had changed. The popular movement to which the sovereigns had then appealed was now the force they were endeavouring to curb and control, and the Kalisch appeal, which had contemplated a reconstruction effected by the joint action of princes and peoples, had become one of the things best forgotten. But the idea of a revived Empire was by no means without support: in advocating it Stein did but agree with one of the many projects which were being put forward in unofficial circles. This was the scheme of the Professor of Civil Law in the University of Halle, Christian Daniel Voss. He declared that legally the Holy Roman Empire still existed, since it had never been dissolved; but he differed greatly from Stein in going on to propose that, in order to maintain a due equality between Austria and Prussia, the head of the House of Nassau should be chosen Emperor with Frankfort as his capital. But this proposal, like that which would have given Bavaria the headship of the revived Empire, and another which would have made the Imperial dignity rotate between half a dozen of the leading Houses, was altogether out of the range of practical politics, and Austria's absolute refusal to have the Empire restored, except on terms which none of the other Powers would ever have contemplated, proved decisive. It was hardly wonderful that Austria should have taken this line. The nominal headship over states which did all they could to make that headship still less effective, which took every chance of hampering and obstructing the authority of the head, had no attractions for the Hapsburgs. It would be not unfair to say of Metternich what has been said with far less truth of Joseph II, that he neglected the German for the dynastic interests of the Hapsburgs. He saw a chance of establishing Austrian supremacy over Italy, and to secure that he made no attempt to recover the ground Austria had lost in Germany. Thus although Austria's intervention may be said to have decided against Napoleon the struggle for the liberation of Germany, Austria made no attempt to profit by it to reassert her claims or strengthen her influence over Germany. Stadion and the Archdukes Charles and John might have managed to identify Austria with the national revolt against French domination, but unfortunately for Austria it was by the spiritual heir of Thugut that her policy was guided at the critical moment.

Thus though unofficial writers like Grüner of Coburg might point out that what Germany needed was the "union of its forces to preserve freedom and independence, homogeneity of administration through the subjection of individual states to a common system of law," the realisation of this desired unity was bound to be prevented by the fact that a centralised organisation, if it were to be effective, must involve the partial suppression of the internal independence which the middle-sized states had secured under Napoleon's rule. The Princes would not surrender sovereign rights on which they set as much store as they did on that of making treaties with other Powers, still less would they agree to submit their domestic affairs to the supervision of the officials of the Confederacy, and yet unless some means were provided by which the Confederacy could secure the due performance of their duties by its members, its existence would soon be as much of a fiction as that of the Empire had ever been.

But the constitutional reconstruction of Germany was not the only task which awaited the Congress when it assembled at Vienna on October 1st, 1814. An even harder task was that of territorial redistribution. Differences of opinion over the constitution had the effect of making it more negative, since the less definite the constitution the less acute the differences: hence they were somewhat of the nature of an academic discussion, and not likely to lead to a serious conflict. Quarrels over the constitution could always be averted by adopting a solution so indefinite as to really amount to the shelving of the disputed point; quarrels over territory were far more important: there was something tangible at stake, and but for the return of Napoleon from Elba it is possible that the map of Europe would not have been settled without an actual collision between the former allies.

The plenipotentiaries assembled at Vienna had not an absolutely free hand. Their deliberations were bound to take account of the arrangements already made by the four Treaties of Kalisch, Töplitz, Chaumont and Paris, which have been well described as "the preamble to the Congress of Vienna."[1] These had removed from the path two of the old obstacles on which European coalitions had come to grief. At Töplitz, Prussia had renounced all claims on Hanover, the stone on which the Third

[1] Rose, p. 325.

Coalition had stumbled, while a corollary of the same agreement, the Treaty of Ried, had seen Austria renounce her more extensive designs on Bavaria in the hope of compensation in Italy, though she recovered Tyrol, Salzburg and the other acquisitions which Bavaria had made from her by Napoleon's aid. Two very important questions remained: the fate of Poland and—closely connected with the Polish question—the treatment of Saxony. There was no idea of undoing the work of secularisation effected in 1803 and the subsequent "mediatisation" which had between them reduced the "sovereign" states of Germany from the 300 of 1786 to the 39 of 1815; but even so in the three states more particularly identified with Napoleon which had shared his overthrow, Westphalia and the Grand Duchies of Berg and Frankfort, and in the recovered districts West of the Rhine, there was ample store of plunder out of which every German dynasty hoped to make acquisitions to be veiled under the blessed name of "compensation."

But these four treaties had settled certain other things which marked out the lines along which the discussions were to run. At Kalisch, Prussia had been promised an Eastern frontier connecting Silesia with West Prussia, and compensation in Northern and Western Germany for her surrender of the rest of her Polish possessions to Russia. At Töplitz the German Princes between the Elbe and the Rhine had been promised "full and unconditional independence." At Chaumont a federal alliance had been selected as the most satisfactory form for the reconstituted Germany. Finally, by the Treaty of Paris, Italy was to be divided between Austria and the various Houses which Napoleon had dispossessed, the House of Orange was to receive an accession of territory, and the ex-departments of Mont Tonnerre, Sarre, Rhin et Moselle and Roer were to be divided between Prussia and the minor states of Germany.

October 1st found the plenipotentiaries assembled at the Austrian capital, but it was decided to postpone the opening of the actual negotiations for a month to allow the preparation of *agenda*. All the principal statesmen of Europe were present. Austria had as her principal representative Metternich, whose voice carried as much if not more weight in the deliberations than that of any other negotiator, and whose position was appropriately recognised by his election as President of the Congress; he was assisted by the able and energetic von Wessemberg-

Amfingen, and by von Gentz who acted as Secretary to the Congress. From England came Lords Cathcart and Castlereagh,[1] with Count Münster as the envoy of Hanover. France sent Talleyrand, who was to display his diplomatic prowess to the greatest advantage. Prussia entrusted her interests to Hardenberg and von Humboldt. Most of the minor sovereigns of Germany were present in person, and all were represented, even down to the various "benches" of Counts suppressed at the time of the great mediatisation. Russia characteristically sent two foreigners, the German Stein and the Italian Capo d'Istria, among the colleagues of her Foreign Minister, Nesselrode, while the Czar was also present. It was generally felt that Alexander's share in the Congress would be no small one; but those who feared or distrusted Russia might take comfort in the evident signs of antagonism between him and Metternich. This opposition, partly personal, accentuated by the action of Austria in 1814 and over the violation of Swiss neutrality, had had its origin in Metternich's successful opposition to the Czar's wish to assume the command of the Allied forces in 1813. The Polish question, if no other, seemed bound to provoke a conflict between them.

The question of German reconstruction, the least contentious of the problems before the Congress, but still bound to be a lengthy affair, had begun to be discussed by a committee a fortnight before the Congress opened.[2] Stein and Hardenberg had come forward with a project, based on the Treaty of Chaumont, for the management of German affairs by a Directory composed of Austria, Bavaria, Hanover and Prussia. This was to include commercial union, with no internal tariffs against other German states, an Assembly which should include representatives of local Estates, and a federal revenue to be derived from Customs and from an *octroi* on the Rhine. An alternative suggestion of Hardenberg's was that the new federation should exclude all Prussian territory East of the Elbe, and

---

[1] In January the latter had to return home for the opening of Parliament, and the Duke of Wellington took his place.

[2] The work of the Congress was mainly conducted by separate committees appointed to consider each individual question (*e.g.* the reorganisation of the Swiss Confederation), while the envoys of the Powers which had assisted to conclude the Peace of Paris, Austria, France, Great Britain, Portugal, Prussia, Russia, Spain and Sweden, formed a "Committee of Eight," which for all practical purposes was the effective part of the Congress.

all that of Austria save Berchtesgaden, Salzburg, Tyrol and the Vorarlberg. For the rest of their territory, Austria and Prussia would stand outside the federation, merely concluding close alliances with it and guaranteeing its integrity and independence.

But neither of these schemes found much favour with the Congress, and in the end Hardenberg acquiesced in the Twelve Articles which Metternich put forward,[1] and which were submitted to the consideration of a special committee (Oct. 16th). On this committee Austria, Bavaria, Hanover, Prussia and Würtemberg were represented, but it soon became evident that its deliberations were not likely to produce any satisfactory result. The scheme drawn up under Metternich's direction would have divided Germany into Circles, two to be directed by Austria, two by Prussia and one each by Bavaria, Hanover and Würtemberg; it would also have established two Councils, one composed of the Heads of the Circles, and another of the other members. The Council of Heads was to represent Germany in foreign affairs, decide on peace and war, and to act as a legislative chamber in conjunction with the Council of Members. The Heads were also to be charged with the execution of the decisions of the Confederation and with the conduct of military affairs. The right of secession was secured to the individual states, and they were to enjoy full sovereignty except where expressly limited. There was to be no formal head of the Confederation, but Austria was to preside in both Chambers.[2]

But this scheme did not commend itself to Bavaria and Würtemberg. They protested vigorously against the loss of the right to conclude alliances and to make war on their own account. Moreover, a clause which pledged the individual states to govern constitutionally and to give constitutional rights to their subjects, excited their most strenuous opposition. They argued with no small force that to apply to the minor states of Germany institutions which larger states had gained as the result of long struggles, would be altogether premature and out of keeping with the state of political development at which Germany had arrived.

The clause was certainly one which it is surprising to find in any scheme drawn up under the auspices of Metternich. It was not exactly in accord with his professions or his practice, and

[1] Cf. *Deutsche Geschichte, 1806–1871*, i. 527 ff.   [2] *Ibid.* i. 527–529.

might be thought to have been inserted to produce dissension. Anyhow, the committee's labours proved fruitless: Würtemberg declared (Nov. 16th) that it would be impossible to arrange the affairs of the Confederation until the boundaries had been settled, and therefore withdrew from the committee, which in consequence suspended its sittings, although Metternich, Hardenberg and some of the other plenipotentiaries continued, more or less informally, to draft and discuss schemes of reorganisation. Meanwhile the representatives of the minor states had been meeting and discussing the situation. They talked vaguely of reviving the Empire, but showed no inclination to do anything to make a revived Empire an effective institution, or to give the Emperor the powers without which his position could be nothing but a farce. Stein, who had not yet abandoned all hope of seeing a constitution adopted which would permit the development of that national feeling on which almost every other German statesmen looked with so much distrust, did what he could to encourage the idea, but it was out of the question. A Brunswick Privy Councillor, von Schmidt, went so far as to submit to Count Münster, the chief Hanoverian representative, a memorandum which laid down four functions as the proper sphere for the Emperor's authority ; but these involved concessions Austria could never have obtained from the Princes, and without the power to superintend the execution of the decisions of the Confederation, without the control of the administration of justice and of the defensive system of the Empire, the right of presiding over the meeting of the Confederation would have been worthless. Münster, indeed, could only reply to von Schmidt that he had himself urged Austria to revive the Empire, but that he found her determined to stand by the clause in the Treaty of Chaumont, which prescribed a federative alliance as the new constitution for Germany. Thus it was in the end as a federative alliance, not as a united nation, that Germany emerged from the Congress, when in March the sudden escape of Napoleon from Elba and his return to France precipitated a settlement. This took the shape suggested by Metternich, who resolutely refused any revival of the old Empire. He saw that Austria's own dominions were enough in themselves to form an Empire, and that the loose and indefinite relations which would prevail under a Confederation would be better adapted for maintaining Austrian influence over the South

German states than any accurately defined constitution. Nor was there any Power in Germany which felt disposed to champion the cause of that national sentiment which the struggle of 1813 had aroused, but which, now that it had served its purpose, was muzzled and impotent. Nothing could have been further from the minds of Prussia's representatives in 1814 than the idea of trying to oust Austria from Germany in order to identify Prussia with this national sentiment of which fifty-six years later the Hohenzollern were to make such excellent use.

Thus the Germanic Confederation, to the formation of which the representatives of the states of Germany formally agreed on June 15th, 1815, was little more than the Confederation of the Rhine, with the addition of Austria and Prussia, and without Napoleon as "Protector." Five Kingdoms, Bavaria, Hanover, Prussia, Saxony and Würtemberg ; eight Grand Duchies, Baden, Hesse-Cassel, Hesse-Darmstadt, Luxemburg (which belonged to the King of the Netherlands), Oldenburg, Mecklenburg-Schwerin, Mecklenburg - Strelitz and Saxe - Weimar ; eight Duchies, Anhalt - Bernburg, Anhalt - Dessau, Anhalt - Köthen, Brunswick, Holstein and Lauenburg (which belonged to the King of Denmark), Nassau, Saxe-Gotha and Saxe-Hildburghausen ; twelve Principalities, Hesse-Homburg, Hohenzollern-Hechingen, Hohenzollern-Sigmaringen, Liechtenstein, Lippe-Detmold, Saxe-Coburg, Saxe-Meiningen, Schaumburg-Lippe, Schwarzburg-Rudolstadt, Schwarzburg-Sondershausen, Reuss and Waldeck ; and four Free Cities, Bremen, Frankfort, Hamburg and Lübeck, were included in the Confederation, whose affairs were entrusted to the control of a Diet under the presidency of Austria. To this body were delegated the tasks of providing the Confederation with the fundamental laws the Congress had not the time to lay down, and also that of arranging the details of the military and other organisations which had to be erected. It was to have two Chambers, an ordinary Assembly sitting permanently at Frankfort and consisting of 17 members, and a General Assembly of 69 members, summoned intermittently when more important matters called for discussion. But the control of the Diet over the members of the Confederation was neither very complete nor very effective ; private war between members was forbidden, but in domestic affairs each might go his own way. One of the clauses of the Act of Federation did indeed declare that a constitution should be established in each state, but nothing was done to enforce this provision, and in the absence of a "sanction" it was in most cases a dead letter from the very first. This was in no small measure due to Metternich: he desired to allow the minor states to enjoy the utmost possible independence, and therefore made Austria the champion of localism. Prussia had shown herself less unfavourable to the proposals for the unification of Germany, and Bavarian and Saxon particularists were beginning to look on her as the chief danger to their independence. Hence Austria's rôle was now to be that of the guarantor of the rights of the minor states; Metternich was to make her the supporter of the very principles which had brought about the failure of her efforts to unite Germany. It was a strange inversion of parts, but the work of disintegration had been completely done, too thoroughly to allow any prospect that it could be undone, and Metternich thought that more might be gained by keeping on good terms with the South German states and devoting the efforts of Austria to securing control over Italy. Thus it was Metternich who succeeded in so amending Humboldt's "Fourteen Articles" that the Council of the Confederation, instead of being an efficient and vigorous executive, found its sphere of activity so much curtailed and its initiative so much cramped that it was all but powerless.

Lengthy as the negotiations over the constitution had been, those over the territorial redistribution excited far more interest and feeling. Of all the members of the Confederation of the Rhine the King of Saxony had adhered with most fidelity to Napoleon in 1813. Taken prisoner after Leipzig, he had not been able to secure himself or his dominions by such a compact as those made by Würtemberg at Fulda and by Hesse-Darmstadt, so Prussia proceeded to claim the kingdom as hers by right of conquest and in compensation for the losses she was prepared to suffer farther East. Alexander for his part was firmly resolved to have Poland, not merely the Russian shares of the three partitions, but if possible the whole country. He desired to rebuild Poland as a kingdom to be united to Russia by a personal tie such as that between Great Britain and Hanover. Influenced by Czartoriski, he hoped to rally Polish national feeling to him by this means. If he could gain this end he was prepared to see Saxony pass to Prussia, while Austria was to be left to recoup herself as best she could in Italy. This would have involved a division by no means acceptable to the other members of the Congress, and least of all to Castlereagh, whose policy, following in the lines laid down by Pitt, was to restore as far as possible that distribution of territory which had the authority of tradition. That Russia's efforts in the cause of Europe entitled her to the lion's share of the Grand Duchy of Warsaw was generally admitted, but there was not the same disposition to include as a corollary Prussia's preposterous claim to the whole of Saxony. At first, however, England contemplated letting Prussia have Saxony : not free from suspicions of Russia, she had no wish to see her unduly strong, and hoped by reconciling Austria and Prussia to make the Germanic Confederation a powerful factor in European politics. Were they united the rest of Germany must follow them, and Russia would find herself balanced by her neighbour on the West. To this end Castlereagh would have reluctantly sacrificed Saxony ; but Metternich, though he had no desire to press Austria's claims on Poland, was full of distrust of Alexander, even if he had not been bitterly opposed to the extension of Prussian influence. However, it was in Talleyrand that Saxony found her most effective ally. That astute diplomatist had no intention of letting France be kept out of her share in the councils of Europe: he argued that it was Napoleon, not France, that had been the universal enemy ; it was therefore unfair to punish the Bourbon for the wrong-doings from which he also had suffered ; France ought not to be treated as a pariah, but as a friend. The claim was one the Powers could not but admit. At the same time, Talleyrand had been doing all he could to establish good relations between France and the smaller states. A better opportunity of acting as their champion than that afforded by the case of Saxony he could not have desired. The project was exceedingly unpopular in Saxony, where no element of the population was prepared to be handed over from its old rulers to the detested Hohenzollern, nor was it much better liked in other parts of Germany. Bavaria and the other Princes, vigorously supported by Talleyrand, protested that without a free and independent Saxony there could be no stable federal Germany, and the French minister had little difficulty in persuading England and Austria to adopt this view.

Alexander and Frederick William were furious. They were in military possession of Saxony, and declared that they would not give it up. For a time it seemed as if it might come to a question of force, and Austria, England and France went to the length of concluding a defensive alliance (Jan. 3rd, 1815) with a view to this possibility. With all the rest of Germany on its side, for outside Prussia public opinion as expressed by the journalists and writers was strongly in favour of Saxony, this coalition was a strong incentive to a more reasonable attitude on the part of Russia and Prussia, and after a period of considerable tension Metternich managed to arrange a compromise which was accepted. Saxony escaped wholesale annexation at the price of a partition (Feb. 11th) which left the greater part of the country to its King, and handed over to Prussia Lower Lusatia, including Cottbus, the greater part of Upper Lusatia, and the North-Western portion of the Electorate, including Wittenberg, Torgau and Merseburg. All the efforts of Hardenberg, however, failed to obtain for Prussia the much-coveted Leipzig, and the portions which the House of Wettin retained, though only little more than half the area of the kingdom as it had been in 1812, contained 1,200,000 inhabitants out of 2,000,000 and included the richer as well as the more populous districts. At this heavy price Saxony was saved. A reluctant consent was extracted from Frederick Augustus (April 6th), on which the Prussians proceeded to evacuate the territory they had hoped to make their own. It is, however, open to question whether from the French point of view it might not in the long-run have been better to let Prussia take Saxony and to compensate the dispossessed monarch with a kingdom on the Rhine made up out of the old ecclesiastical Electorates with Cleves-Jülich and Zweibrücken. The majority of the subjects of such a kingdom would have shared their ruler's religion, whereas on the Elbe the Catholic Wettins ruled a Protestant population. There would also have been no slight advantage to France in keeping Prussia well to the Eastward, and in giving her Saxony with its traditional connection with Poland, thereby making it more likely that she would be brought into conflict with Russia than with France. By being established on the Rhine, Prussia became ultimately identified with the ideas embodied in the popular poem *Die Wacht am Rhein*: should a new Napoleon arise in France it would be Prussia which would bar his path into Germany. Moreover, the elements which the Rhenish provinces brought into the Prussian polity gave her more in common with the Catholics of the South than she had hitherto possessed, and made her leadership less unpalatable to the rest of Germany than it would have been had she been concentrated to the Eastward, apart from and outside the districts in which the ideas of the revolutionary epoch had taken root and on which the Napoleonic administration had left its mark. The more scattered the territories of Prussia, the more diverse the racial and social elements included within her dominions, the easier it would be for her to identify herself with Germany. The acquisition of the Rhenish provinces was a great step on the way to a distant but wider concentration, the annexation of Saxony would have given an immediate concentration at the probable sacrifice of the future. In the hands of the Hohenzollern Cologne, though separated from Berlin by a wide extent of non-Prussian territory, was an outpost which when the time should come would serve to make easy the absorption of the intervening independent states. But in 1815 not even Talleyrand's astuteness could have been expected to see so far into the future.

This solution of the question of Saxony removed the principal difficulty : it allowed that of Poland to be settled also. The lion's share, 37,000 square miles, with 2,500,000 people, fell to Russia, Austria contenting herself with recovering Galicia,[1] and letting Cracow become an independent Republic. Prussia kept her share of the original partition, West Prussia, Ermeland and the Netze District, and also Dantzic, Thorn and Posen out of the territories she had annexed in 1793, but she gave up the greater part of that share and all the gains of 1795. It was therefore out of the kingdom of Westphalia and the Rhenish provinces that she received the bulk of her " compensation." Of her old possessions she relinquished East Friesland, Goslar, Lingen, Osnabrück and part of Münster to Hanover, while Anspach and Baireuth remained in Bavarian hands ; but the rest of her lost territories were restored to her, including the Altmark, Cleves, Halberstadt, Guelders, Mark and Ravensberg, Magdeburg, Minden, Paderborn and most of Münster. Not less important were the new acquisitions, the greater part of the three ecclesiastical Electorates, the long-coveted Berg and Jülich, to which the Electors of Brandenburg had first laid claim more than two hundred years earlier, some portions of Nassau, Thuringia and Westphalia, and, last but not least, Swedish Pomerania, with Rügen and the much-desired Stralsund. These acquisitions enormously improved and strengthened

---

[1] The frontier was not quite identical with that of 1773, but what she now held corresponded approximately to her share of the First Partition.

Prussia's position. In actual extent she covered less territory than in 1806; but for what she lost in the way of Polish wastes and swamps the rich, fertile and thickly-populated Rhenish and Westphalian districts were a more than ample compensation. As in 1806, her territories were scattered and disconnected, though less so than before, and the dispersion was not an unmixed evil.

Of the territory remaining disposable, after Hanover had been reinstated in its old possessions with some additions, the bulk went to Bavaria in return for the provinces she had restored to Austria. Aschaffenburg and part of Fulda from the suppressed Grand Duchy of Frankfort, the Grand Duchy of Würzburg, given up by Archduke Ferdinand who returned to Tuscany, together with Anspach and Baireuth, were her principal acquisitions East of the Rhine, while it was only appropriate that a considerable share of the former Rhenish departments should go to the head of the Wittelsbach family under the name of the Bavarian Palatinate. Hesse-Darmstadt obtained the left bank lands between Bingen and Worms as a compensation for losses in Westphalia; Oldenburg received Birkenfeld, and Saxe-Coburg the little district of Lichtenberg; Mecklenburg-Strelitz, which had some claims on the left bank of the Rhine, was brought out and became a Grand Duchy, as did Oldenburg, Saxe-Weimar and Mecklenburg-Schwerin. William IX of Hesse-Cassel obtained part of Fulda and the now meaningless title of " Elector." Minor rectifications of frontier were too numerous to merit separate mention. Mayence became a Federal fortress with a mixed garrison of Austrians and Prussians, while some of the territory of the old Electorate went to the Duchy of Nassau, at this time held jointly by Frederick Augustus of Nassau-Usingen and Frederick William of Nassau-Weilburg. This Duchy also received part [1] of the territories of Orange-Nassau, the rest of which [2] went to Prussia in return for some portions of Guelders which were incorporated in the new kingdom of the United Netherlands. This new state, to which geographical unity was to prove unable to give permanence in face of racial, political and religious differences, although ruled over by a German prince, and composed of states once part of the Holy Roman Empire, was quite unconnected with Germany except through Luxemburg, which at the same time sent

[1] *Deutsche Landes und Provinzial Geschichte*, p. 176.
[2] Siegen and the district on the right bank opposite Bonn and Coblence.

deputies to the Estates General of the Netherlands and representatives to the Diet, since it formed part of the new Germanic Confederation by whose troops its fortresses were garrisoned. The cession of Swedish Pomerania to Prussia in return for a sum of 2,000,000 dollars severed the connection between one Scandinavian kingdom and Germany, a connection which had brought no good either to Sweden or to Germany since the fall of Gustavus at Lützen. The other Scandinavian kingdom, however, did remain bound to Germany by its complicated relations with Schleswig-Holstein, to which was now added the little Duchy of Lauenburg. Frederick of Denmark had hoped for better terms when he consented to cede Norway to Sweden; he had expected to receive Swedish Pomerania, but he had to pay the penalty for his loyalty to Napoleon.

The only other territorial readjustments which deserve mention were the acquisitions in Italy with which Austria sought to recompense herself for her neglect of Germany. Not only did she recover Istria and Dalmatia,[1] for which geography provides some justification, but Venetia and the Milanese, in which now were included Napoleon's annexations of Bormio, Chiavenna and the Valtelline, were formed into a kingdom, while Austrian bayonets were the true foundation of the power of the Hapsburg or kindred dynasties now restored in Modena, Tuscany and Parma.[2] Why Austrian rule over Italy, accepted placidly enough in the 18th Century, should have been so unendurable to the 19th Century Italians, is a problem which belongs to the history of Italy rather than to that of Germany; but that Austria should have sought her gains here rather than lower down the Danube valley does not give Metternich much claim to foresight or to appreciation of the situation in the Italian peninsula and of the changes which twenty years of Napoleon's rule had wrought in the sentiments of the Italians.

Throughout these arrangements nothing had been heard of the wishes of the populations thus bandied about from one dynasty to another. Racial divisions, traditions, sentiment, even geographical considerations, had to give way to the selfishness of

---

[1] She also, besides recovering from Bavaria Tyrol, Salzburg, Vorarlberg and parts of Upper Austria, regained possession of Carinthia, Carniola and the other districts which France had ruled directly under the name of the Illyrian Provinces, including the territories of the Republic of Ragusa. This gave her a much larger seaboard than she had hitherto possessed.

[2] Given to Marie Louise, Napoleon's wife.

the princes. The territorial rearrangement was a fitting counterpart to the constitutional settlement. Both served rather to postpone than to forward the realisation of that German unity of which so much had been heard in the opening months of 1813. The peoples of Germany might have then discovered that they were one and the same nation, poets and orators might have applauded unity, the rulers of Germany collected at Vienna were determined that the outcome of the " War of Liberation " should be a very different thing from that which the popular leaders had sought. Repression, not emancipation, was the watchword of the governments in 1815. And this could the more easily be accomplished since the nationalist and Liberal forces, practically without leaders or organisation, were powerless. To a certain extent they had wrought their own undoing by reinforcing the hands of their rulers in the struggle against Napoleon. To throw off the French yoke popular enthusiasm had had to ally itself with the governments. Patriotic fervour had played no small part in the successes of 1813, but it had been compelled to flow along the official channels. By submitting to military discipline the popular movement had given up the control over itself to the princes and their ministers and generals. It was thus powerless to defend itself against the measures now taken to retain it under control. Its ally had become its master. At the same time the general weariness of war and strife made people ready to acquiesce in the decisions of the Congress, and there was no small truth in the argument of the Bavarian delegates [1] that Germany was not yet qualified to receive representative institutions and constitutional government. Before unity could be achieved there was much still to be done. The middle states, Bavaria, Würtemberg, Saxony and the rest, had to continue by themselves the work of consolidation begun under Napoleon's influence. Prussia had to reorganise the provinces she had recovered from France and her vassals, and to assimilate her new acquisitions. Above all, there was yet another round to be fought out in the great struggle between Austria and Prussia. Germany could not be united until the question had been settled under whose hegemony the union was to take place. While that remained undecided no rearrangement of Germany, territorial or constitutional, could be other than temporary and a makeshift. Indeed, when the Act of Federation was signed (June 18th), it

[1] Cf. p. 649.

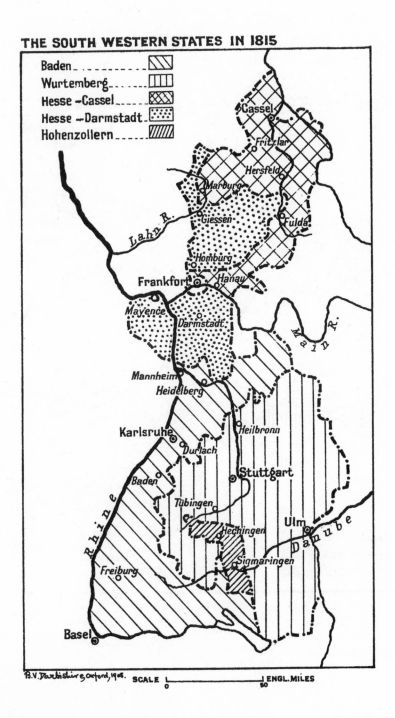

THE SOUTH WESTERN STATES IN 1815

Baden .... (hatched)
Wurtemberg .... (vertical lines)
Hesse –Cassel ...... (cross-hatched)
Hesse –Darmstadt ... (dotted)
Hohenzollern ...... (diagonal lines)

Cassel
Fritzlar
Hersfeld
Marburg
Fulda
Giessen
Lahn R.
Homburg
Frankfort
Hanau
Mayence
Darmstadt
Main R.
Mannheim
Heidelberg
Karlsruhe
Heilbronn
Durlach
Stuttgart
Baden
Tübingen
Ulm
Hechingen
Danube
Sigmaringen
Rhine
Freiburg
Basel

B.V. Darbishire, Oxford, 1905.   SCALE |_____| ENGL. MILES
0   50

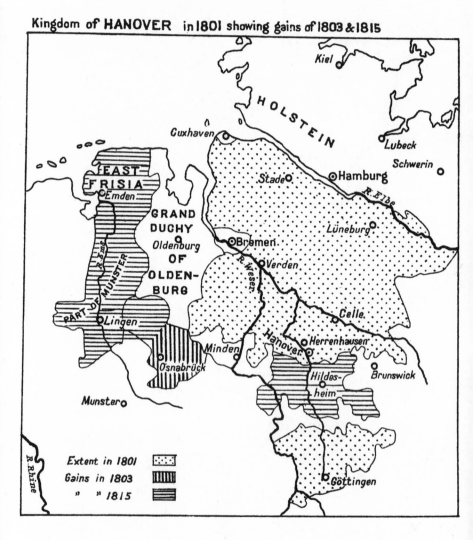

Kingdom of HANOVER in 1801 showing gains of 1803 & 1815

HOLSTEIN

Kiel

Cuxhaven

Lubeck

Schwerin

EAST
FRISIA

Emden

Stade

Hamburg

R. Elbe

GRAND
DUCHY

Oldenburg

OF
OLDEN-
BURG

Bremen

R. Weser

Verden

Lüneburg

PART OF MUNSTER

R. Ems

Lingen

Minden

Osnabrück

Hanover

Celle

Herrenhausen

Hildes-
heim

Brunswick

Munster

R. Rhine

Extent in 1801
Gains in 1803
"   " 1815

Göttingen

was still uncertain whether its provisions would not be subjected to a complete revision at the hands of the founder of the Confederation of the Rhine. Had Napoleon been victorious at Waterloo the work of the Congress of Vienna would hardly have escaped radical modification.

CHAPTER XXXV

THE HUNDRED DAYS

NAPOLEON may have been quite sincere in the desire for peace with the rest of Europe which he professed on his return from Elba, but it was hardly to be expected that the Allies would take him at his word. They could not afford to overlook the promises he had made and broken in the past, they could not trust him even if he were speaking the truth, for circumstances he could not control must have driven him into an attempt to retrieve the defeats of 1813 and 1814. His Empire was founded on victory and military prestige, and the reputation of the French arms required that Leipzig and Vittoria should be wiped out; moreover, once his expulsion of the Bourbons had challenged the settlement of 1814, it was inevitable that, sooner or later, he would have to tear up the Treaty of Paris and seek to recover at the least the "natural boundaries" of France. Indeed, the Allies had no alternative but to take up their arms again and endeavour to repeat the work of 1814. Less than a week after the news of the Emperor's escape reached Vienna (March 7th), the representatives of the eight Powers which had signed the Treaty of Paris issued a declaration that Napoleon had forfeited all rights by his breach of the arrangements made with him and was consequently delivered over to public justice (March 13th). A fortnight later (March 27th), Austria, England, Prussia and Russia renewed the Treaty of Chaumont, the minor states adhering to the anti-Napoleonic alliance, though without much enthusiasm. Even Napoleon's faithful partisan Denmark did not stir on his behalf; and though the King of Saxony procrastinated, hoping to obtain some modification of the harsh treatment which was being meted out to his kingdom, in the end he, too, joined the Coalition (May 27th). Naples was the only exception, and Murat took up arms not so much with the idea of assisting his old master, as in the hope of rousing a national insurrection in Italy against Austria and Sardinia, and of driving those Powers out of the peninsula as the champion of Italian nationalism and unity.[1]

The attitude of Germany towards Napoleon in 1815 was rather different from what it had been two years earlier. Then he had been the foreign tyrant, the oppressor whose alien yoke the nations of Europe were yearning to throw off. The opposition he encountered in 1815 was one of governments, not of peoples. Conservatism took arms to repel the attacks of militant Revolution. It was the "crowned Jacobin" whom Metternich dreaded: when everything seemed satisfactorily settled the return of Napoleon threatened to throw reconstructed Germany back into the melting-pot and to provoke an explosion of the forces Metternich thought he had managed to stifle and keep down. Prussia's point of view was different. Prussia was the only German state in which there was real enthusiasm for the war. To Prussia more than to any other of his enemies Napoleon had been the oppressor; in Prussia the hatred of him was deepest and bitterest and the cry for revenge strongest and most insistent. Moreover, his return threatened Prussia's recent acquisitions on the Rhine, and the nation was unanimous in its determination to retain them. The King appealed to the nation, and volunteers flocked forward in reply. But if in the other states which formed the alliance there was less keenness against Napoleon, one and all prepared to take their part in the task of carrying out the sentence pronounced against him.

For the moment, however, it was impossible to undertake active operations. The only troops immediately available were some 30,000 Prussians who formed the army in occupation of the new territories allotted to Prussia on the Rhine, 10,000 British, the troops who had made the campaign of 1814 in the Netherlands under Sir Thomas Graham and still remained in that country,[2] 14,000 Hanoverians belonging like the British to the army which was occupying the Netherlands pending the conclusion of the Congress of Vienna, and the greater part of the King's German Legion, which had been collected in Brabant on its way from the South of France to Hanover, where it was to be disbanded. It supplied about 3200 cavalry, 600 artillery and 4000 infantry, while another 8000 men must

---

[1] Cf. R. M. Johnston, *Napoleonic Empire in Southern Italy*.

[2] Some 15 battalions of infantry, for the most part very weak, and, as they were second battalions, mainly composed of raw recruits.

be added for the available forces of the Kingdom of the Netherlands. The total of these forces amounted even on paper to only about 70,000, and they were so heterogeneous and so utterly unprepared for a campaign that an immediate move was out of the question. Thus it was impossible to crush Napoleon there and then; and while the Allies were gradually collecting their forces from all quarters, the Austrians from the Theiss and Danube, the Russians from the distant Don and Dnieper, the British from as far West as North America, to which quarter the flower of the Peninsular army had been sent, Napoleon had time to organise an effective army out of the veterans whom the peace had released from their confinement in Germany, England and Russia.

Wellington was at once nominated to the command of the Allied army in the Netherlands, which was reinforced by all the available troops from Great Britain and Hanover, by a Brunswick contingent rather over 6000 strong, by a brigade of 2800 men from Nassau, and by considerable forces of Dutch-Belgians. At the same time the Prussian army was rapidly augmented to a strength of over 100,000; but it included a strong contingent of Saxons who were anything but well affected to the Allied cause, and whose disaffection resulted before the campaign opened in open mutiny, while the population of the Rhenish districts recently annexed to Prussia contained a considerable Francophil faction.[1] Behind this army, which was placed under the command of Blücher, was being collected a Prussian army of reserve, which would eventually provide about 70,000 men, but would not be ready to take the field for some time. Two other armies were also to be put into the field, one of Russians, which was making its way across Germany in three columns, amounting in all to 160,000 men; another under Schwarzenberg, composed of a nucleus of Austrians together with the contingents of Bavaria, Würtemberg and the other South German states, was gathering on the Upper Rhine.[2]

[1] Cf. Houssaye, *Waterloo*, p. 85.

[2] Lord Cathcart, the English representative at Vienna, made great endeavours to have the contingents of Hesse-Cassel, Hesse-Darmstadt and several other states placed under Wellington's command; but this was resolutely opposed by von Knesebeck, who for political reasons wished them to serve with the Prussians. In the end the Hesse-Darmstadt contingent, 8000 strong, was attached to Schwarzenberg's Army of the Upper Rhine, most of that of Hesse-Cassel was allotted to the garrison of Mayence, while Baden (16,000), Bavaria (60,000) and Würtemberg (25,000)

But these two last-mentioned armies could not possibly be ready to begin operations till the end of June, and therefore the Allies had to choose between giving Napoleon all that time in which to organise the resources of France and, if they preferred to attack him while his preparations were far from complete, doing so with only a small part of the great force they would eventually have at their disposal. Wellington at first favoured a prompt attack, and suggested May 1st for beginning operations, a proposal which the enterprising Blücher cordially supported. Austria and Russia, however, refused to entertain the idea, and it was therefore abandoned.[1] Gneisenau then put forward a plan closely resembling that which the Allies had adopted in 1813. By it three armies should assemble on the Upper Rhine, the Lower Rhine and in the Netherlands, with a central reserve behind them, and should move concurrently but independently on Paris. If Napoleon fell on one of these three it was to retire on the reserve and the other two were to press forward, so that Napoleon would have to give up the pursuit of the one he was attacking and turn aside to protect his flanks and communications.[2] Weighty objections were urged against this scheme; but as it was never put into force they need not be discussed, for it was decided to wait until the Russians and Schwarzenberg were ready to co-operate with Wellington and Blücher, a choice which let the initiative pass from the Allies to Napoleon.

To have adopted a defensive attitude would have fitted in best with the peaceful professions Napoleon had made on his return from Elba: had he waited for the Allies to assume the offensive, he could have represented that the Powers were assailing the liberties and independence of France, and could have appealed to the sentiments of 1792. But he did not quite trust the French democracy, and he preferred to make his appeal to the military spirit and to the national love of glory and conquest with which he had identified his Empire, rather than to Republican traditions. Moreover, the initiative was more in keeping with his active and enterprising genius than was the

supplied about half Schwarzenberg's army. Thus the German element in Wellington's army was smaller than it should have been. Cf. Wellington's *Supplementary Dispatches*, vol. x. pp. 11–14 and 117–120.

[1] Cf. *Deutsche Geschichte, 1806–1871*, i. 567; and Houssaye, pp. 90–92.

[2] Cf. *Supplementary Dispatches*, x. 172.

tamer defensive; he hoped by a speedy success over the English and their allies in the Netherlands to rally Belgium to his standard, and to meet the main armies of the Coalition with all the prestige of restored victory. Who could say what influence the defeat of Wellington and Blücher might exercise on the old members of the Confederation of the Rhine, or even on Austria? Accordingly, Napoleon decided to take the offensive before the middle of June, and to throw the 125,000 men who formed his available field-army on the point where the left of Wellington's cantonments touched the right of Blücher's.

This critical point was, roughly speaking, defined by the great road from Charleroi to Brussels, and it was between Avesnes and Philippeville to the South of Charleroi that the French were concentrated by the evening of June 14th. Napoleon's design was to attack the two armies of Blücher and Wellington separately before they could unite, and by interposing between them and thrusting forward on Brussels, to push them apart as he had the Austro-Sardinians in 1796. He calculated that Blücher, if beaten, would retire Eastward, towards the Meuse, and that Wellington's only way of escape from disaster would be a rapid retreat to his base, Ostend.

The Waterloo campaign is a subject so thorny and so bristling with difficulties that one naturally shrinks from the attempt to tell again the story of the eventful four days (June 15th to 18th) which saw Napoleon, despite his initial success over the Prussians at Ligny, utterly and completely beaten when those same Prussians, whom he believed that he had put out of action, came back to the aid of the English and their allies. Still the campaign was of vital importance to Germany; and even if it is to be told mainly from the point of view of the Prussian army and its share in the campaign, it is impossible to attempt even that without relating the doings of Wellington's army, more especially of the Germans under his command, or without discussing to some extent the plans and the actions of Napoleon.

In the first place, it must be pointed out that the success of Napoleon's plan depended mainly on the promptitude and precision with which it was put into force, that the attack on the Allied centre placed Napoleon at the point at which it was easiest for both Allied armies to come into action, that there is a good deal to be said for Wellington's view that the Emperor would have done better to make that attack on the English communications, which the Duke so much feared. Had he done so, Wellington must either have retreated Northward, abandoning his direct communications with Ostend,[1] or have given battle on the 16th, probably somewhere between Ath and Hal, without any chance of Blücher coming to his aid in force.[2] By attacking at the point of contact, Napoleon made it essential that he should destroy and not merely defeat the army on which his first attack fell, and that he should lose no time about following up the advantages he might gain.

At the moment Napoleon delivered his attack, the Allied armies were certainly dangerously extended. Both Wellington and Blücher were misled by receiving intelligence from France that Napoleon would adopt the defensive, and the French concentration was certainly admirably conducted, inasmuch as hardly any accurate information about it seems to have leaked across the frontier. Thus June 15th found Wellington's headquarters and his reserve (25,000 men) at or near Brussels; his cavalry corps (10,000) between Ninove and Grammont; Hill's corps (27,000) distributed between Ghent, Ath, Oudenarde and Alost; that of the Prince of Orange (30 000) between Mons, Seneffe, Braine le Comte, Nivelles and Genappe.[3]

[1] It should be remembered that at the moment the campaign opened Wellington was receiving continual reinforcements from England by way of Ostend. Thus Sir John Lambert's brigade, two old Peninsula battalions, 1/4th and 1/40th, and one which had seen service on the East coast of Spain, 1/27th, only reached the field of Waterloo during the action, having come up from Ghent by forced marches; the 7th, 29th and 43rd, three strong battalions which had been among the best of the whole Peninsula army, landed at Ostend on June 18th, June 13th and June 16th respectively, indeed the 29th actually got near enough to hear the guns of Waterloo.

[2] A containing force of the strength of that detached under Grouchy after Ligny would have sufficed to keep at bay the corps of Ziethen, which would have been all the Prussian commander could have brought up on the 16th. Pirch and Thielmann, who only reached Sombreffe about 11 a.m. and 1 p.m. respectively on the 16th, could not have exercised much influence over a battle Westward of Nivelles on that day.

[3] Of this force about 69,000 were infantry, the British providing 29 battalions with a total of 20,310, the King's German Legion 8 battalions (3285 men), the Hanoverians 23 battalions (13,788 men), the Brunswickers 8 battalions (5376 men), the contingents of Nassau and Orange-Nassau 8 battalions (7100), 5 of which were included in a Dutch-Belgian division, the Dutch-Belgian contingent of 33 battalions being 19,674 strong. The cavalry came to 14,500, 5913 of whom (16 regiments) were British, 5 regiments mustering in all 2560 belonged to the King's German Legion, 3 were Hanoverians, one and a squadron of Uhlans came from Brunswick, 7 were Dutch-Belgians. The army included 32 batteries of

Blücher had his headquarters at Namur, his army being divided into four corps, of which that of Ziethen was nearest to the threatened point, being distributed between Thuin, Charleroi, Marchienne, Moustiers and Fleurus. The next corps, that of Pirch, was at Namur, with portions at Heron, Huy and Hannut. Thielmann's corps, distributed between Ciney, Dinant and Huy, was a good deal farther from the critical spot; and Bülow's, at and around Liége, was not less than 45 miles from the place appointed for the concentration. This was Sombreffe, about 14 miles from Namur and the same distance from Charleroi, to which place it must be pronounced to have been dangerously near, seeing how widely the Prussian cantonments were scattered. If Wellington's cantonments also were too far apart, he did not commit the mistake of selecting as the point of concentration a position so far advanced as Sombreffe: Blücher must be accounted lucky in that Napoleon did not, by attacking a little earlier on the 16th, overthrow Ziethen's corps before those of Pirch and Thielmann could arrive.

The Prusssian army was rather larger than that underWellington. Three of its four corps averaged about 31,000, the fourth, that of Thielmann, being only 24,000 strong. This was due to the mutiny of the Saxon troops originally belonging to it. These troops, when it had been proposed to allot the soldiers individually to the Prussian or to the Saxon service in conformity with the distribution of the districts they came from between Prussia and Saxony, had broken out into open revolt, "declaring that

artillery, 18 British, 3 K. G. L., 2 Hanoverian, 2 Brunswick and 7 Dutch-Belgian : these varied from 4 to 8 guns, and in all provided 204 pieces. This did not complete Wellington's force, as he had under his command, though not in the fighting line, von der Decken's Hanoverian Reserve Corps, 13 battalions or 9000 men, while 6 British battalions on garrison duty amounted to 3200 more. Of these troops the British and King's German Legion were by far the best, 18 battalions and 12 cavalry regiments of the British having served in the Peninsula, as had also 5 battalions and all the cavalry of the German Legion, though even these corps had a good many recruits in their ranks. The Hanoverians were nearly all young troops, and most of them *Landwehr*; and much the same was the state of the Brunswickers. Three of the Nassau battalions had served in Spain, but on Napoleon's side, they being the troops which had come over to Wellington before Bayonne in December 1813. The Dutch-Belgians were the least efficient part of the army : many of them, including practically all the officers, had been in the French service, and their zeal for the Allied cause was worse than doubtful. Their conduct during the campaign was such as to make them an element of weakness rather than of strength to their commander, and Wellington would have gained could he have exchanged them for a much smaller number of British troops or even of Hanoverian *Landwehr*.

they were the soldiers of the King of Saxony, and would serve no other cause."[1] The mutiny was repressed, the Saxon Guards and the two Grenadier battalions implicated were disbanded, several of the ringleaders were shot; and as the whole body of the Saxon troops, 15,000 men in all, continued unanimous in their opposition to the transfer, it was finally decided to send them all back to Westphalia.[2] Thus Thielmann's corps was short of the 4500 to which the brigade it had been proposed to form out of the transferred Saxons should have amounted. In support of the Prussian army a corps of some 20,000 men was being collected at Treves, composed of the contingents of Mecklenburg, Anhalt, Reuss, Lippe and other minor states of North Germany; but it was not called upon to take any active part in the campaign.

The concentration of the French had not been effected without some indication of it reaching the Allies, but the information which Wellington received on June 14th from the Belgian van der Merlen at Binche, and from Major-General von Dörnberg who commanded the British cavalry brigade in front of Mons, was not sufficiently definite to do more than put him on the alert. The news that French columns were massing in the direction of Avesnes, and that they seemed to be withdrawing from opposite Wellington's right, might only be an elaborate blind to conceal the stroke against his communications which the British commander feared. Meanwhile Blücher hearing from Ziethen late on the 14th that the French were gathering in his front, sent orders to Pirch to move to Sombreffe, to Thielmann to come up to Namur, and to Bülow to concentrate at Hannut.

Next morning (June 15th) the French advance began. Napoleon had collected a force superior in average quality to either of the armies opposed to him, but one which, as M. Houssaye shows,[3] was as little to be relied upon in some ways as it was formidable in others. In numbers it was superior to either of its enemies, inferior to the two combined in the proportion of 3 to 5.[4] It included the Guard, over 20,000 strong, four corps of cavalry amounting to 13,000 men, and five of infantry varying from the 25,000 of Reille's corps to the 11,000

---

[1] *Supplementary Dispatches*, x. p. 220.
[2] *Ibid.* x. pp. 238–240, 245, and 266.   [3] P. 83.
[4] Wellington's army may be put at about 90,000 effectives, Blücher's at 115,000, Napoleon's at 125,000.

of Lobau's. It was much better supplied with artillery than was Wellington, and somewhat better than were the Prussians.

On June 15th the French got on the move about daybreak, marching in three columns on Marchienne au Pont, on Charleroi, and on Châtelet. Very early they came into contact with Ziethen's outposts, which gave way before them not without some brisk skirmishing. Between 9 and 10 a.m. the French columns reached the Sambre, Reille's vanguard under Bachelu at Marchienne, Pajol, who led the centre column, at Charleroi. Here they were checked for a time; but about midday both passages were secured, and Steinmetz from Thuin and Pirch II from Charleroi were retiring by Gosselies and Fleurus on Ligny, where the other two divisions of Ziethen's corps were concentrating.[1] The French plans had been somewhat upset by Vandamme's lateness in starting, a delay due to his orders not having reached him, and similarly d'Erlon and Gérard failed to carry out punctually the movements prescribed to them. Thus Steinmetz was able to make good his retreat to Fleurus, despite Reille's efforts to intercept him. To this success Pirch II's stubborn stand at Gilly from about 2 to 6 p.m. contributed materially, as he prevented Pajol's cavalry from pushing forward along the direct road to Fleurus. However, when Vandamme at last delivered his attack, the division had some difficulty in extricating itself and retiring to Fleurus. As the Prussians started to go to the rear they were assailed by the French cavalry; one battalion was ridden over and cut to pieces, another escaped only by forming square and cutting its way through its assailants into the shelter of the woods. Yet, badly as the division was mauled, Ziethen's corps had certainly done well in withdrawing from its extended positions and concentrating between Ligny and St. Amand with the loss of only 1200 men killed, wounded and prisoners. It had performed its task of delaying the French advance with very fair success, the time gained was of great value, but it was unfortunate that Ziethen should have neglected the principal duty of the commander of an outpost screen such as that formed by his corps, namely, that of forwarding complete and prompt information of what is going on at the front to the commanders of the main forces whose

---

[1] Each Prussian corps was made up of four so-called "brigades," corresponding in strength rather to the divisions of the Anglo-Dutch army, so that it is less misleading to describe them as "divisions."

concentration he was covering. He had, it is true, sent off a messenger to Blücher directly the first shots were heard in his front (5 a.m.), and a message seems to have been sent to Wellington about 8 a.m.;[1] but to Ziethen's neglect to send any further news must be mainly attributed the slowness of the British concentration. Wellington, hearing no more of the attack on Ziethen, had no reason to suppose that it was more than a feint, and still believed that the real attack would come on his right. The Prince of Orange arrived about 3 p.m. with news that the Prussian outposts were falling back, but he had left the front about 10 a.m. before the French attack had thoroughly developed, and his information was hardly conclusive; thus orders for the concentration of the army at Nivelles were not given till after 7 p.m., when at last a despatch saying that all was quiet on the side of Mons arrived from Dörnberg. The latter's share of the responsibility for the delay in the concentration is no small one, for his failure to send earlier information in conjunction with Ziethen's neglect left the Duke uncertain as to the true line of the advance. Certainly some valuable hours might have been saved had Ziethen done his duty in sending full and constant information so as to show Wellington that the attack near Charleroi was the real thing.

Meanwhile the IInd Prussian Corps had by the evening of the 15th come up almost to Sombreffe and was at hand to support Ziethen ; while Thielmann, who had reached Namur, was only about 15 miles away. Bülow, however, largely through Gneisenau's fault,[2] had failed to do more than make arrangements to concentrate at Hannut on the morning of the 16th, which had made it certain that the IVth Corps would take no part in any action that might be fought on the 16th.

Thus at nightfall on June 15th the position of the Allies was none too satisfactory. Wellington's concentration had not begun; Blücher had only two of his corps together, and they were in dangerous proximity to the French. Luckily for the Allies, however, the French movements had not been all that the Emperor desired. Bad Staff work had been the cause of several delays; Vandamme, d'Erlon and Reille had all started behind time, and thus Napoleon's intention of occupying Quatre

---

[1] *Dispatches*, xii. 473.

[2] Cf. J. von Pflugk - Harttung, *Vorgeschichte der Schlacht der Belle - Alliance*, pp. 252 ff.

Bras and Fleurus had not been accomplished. On the right, where Grouchy was in command, the vanguard of cavalry was just short of Fleurus, with Vandamme a little way behind. Gérard's corps was not yet over the Sambre. In the centre, Lobau had still to cross the river, the Old Guard was between Charleroi and Gilly, the Young Guard had reached Gilly. On the left the cavalry had not got beyond Frasnes; Reille's infantry were between Mellet, Wangenies and Gosselies; d'Erlon had two divisions nearly up to Gosselies, but two still on the Sambre. What had happened in this quarter was that after Steinmetz had cleared his way past Gosselies to Heppignies and Fleurus by a bold counter-attack on the advance-guard of Reille's corps,[1] Ney, who commanded the left wing of the French, had not pushed on in force towards Quatre Bras, judging reasonably enough that it would be inexpedient to thrust forward too far in front of the rest of the army. Thus only some cavalry had got as far as Frasnes which they found occupied by a battalion of the 2nd Regiment of Nassau. This battalion stood firm, and the French had to send back for infantry support. The delay allowed Prince Bernhard of Saxe-Weimar to bring the regiment of Orange-Nassau up from Genappe,[2] and so bold was the front he showed that, after some skirmishing, Ney decided not to attempt to capture Quatre Bras that evening.[3] Thus though the day had on the whole favoured the French, though they had established themselves in close proximity to the line on which the Allies proposed to carry out their still incomplete concentration, they had not made all the progress needed to assure success. The morning of the 16th found them anything but ready for an immediate attack either on the Prussians or on Wellington, and the six hours' delay which followed was all-important in deciding the fortunes of the campaign.

Indeed it was not till June 16th was well advanced that further fighting took place. Vandamme did not bring his corps up into position opposite the Prussians till after 10 a.m., and

---

[1] *Circa* 3 p.m.   [2] About 6.30 p.m.

[3] Prince Bernhard, who had acted on his own responsibility, had only anticipated the orders of General Perponcher, the divisional commander ; and it would seem that Quatre Bras had been named as the point for the brigade to concentrate, for another battalion of the 2nd Nassau came up independently from Bezy (Siborne, p. 117) ; but nevertheless the Prince's action and that of Major Normann and his battalion of the 2nd Nassau deserve much credit. Though officially part of the Dutch-Belgian army, these troops should rather be regarded as Germans.

Gérard was three hours behind him. About 11 a.m. Napoleon arrived on the scene from Charleroi. The scheme which he had formed overnight was based on the assumption that the retreat of the Prussian outposts to the North-East pointed to an intention to retire towards their base, Liége and Maastricht, and to abandon the attempt to combine with Wellington, who the Emperor concluded must be in full retreat on Antwerp or Ostend. Thus he did not expect any serious fighting on the 16th; he meant to push his right forward as far as Gembloux, driving in any rearguard the Prussians might leave at Sombreffe and then to transfer his central reserve to the left wing and reinforce Ney, who was meanwhile to have adopted a waiting attitude at Quatre Bras. This done, Napoleon meant to advance straight on Brussels, which he expected to reach in the morning of the 17th. This plan was completely upset by Blücher's resolve to stand at Ligny, a resolve to which the Prussian commander clung even when he discovered that Bülow's disobedience would deprive him of over a quarter of his force. Nor does the decision appear to have been prompted by any hope, much less by any definite promise, of help from Wellington.[1] Blücher certainly hoped Wellington would arrive, but his mind had been made up long before his interview about noon with the Duke, whose promise of help was purely conditional on his not being attacked himself.

The Emperor thus found that instead of a rearguard action with a force trying to cover the Prussian retreat, he would have to fight a battle on a considerable scale, for which he was not yet ready. Though Ziethen's corps alone was actually in position between Ligny and St. Amand, Pirch's was just arriving; and Thielmann, who had left Namur at 7 a.m., came up shortly after midday, though it was not till between two and three that his whole force arrived. Still, even with only Ziethen in his front, the Emperor was not prepared to attack without a rather larger force than the 24,000 to which Vandamme and the cavalry of Pajol and Excelmans amounted. Accordingly the

---

[1] The attempt of Herr Delbrück in his Life of Gneisenau to prove that Blücher was relying on Wellington's assistance, and would not otherwise have fought at Ligny, is quite unsuccessful. Cf. Houssaye, p. 142; also *Vorgeschichte der Schlacht der Belle-Alliance*, by J. von Pflugk-Harttung, quite the most judicial and unbiassed German account of these events; the instalment of the *Geschichte der Befreiungs Krieg*, which deals with 1815, Herr von Lettow-Vorbeck's *Napoleons Untergang*, unfortunately reproduces the Prussian "legend of Waterloo" in its most extreme form.

attack had to be put off till Gérard's corps had deployed into line, and its leading columns did not appear till after one. The delay was of the utmost value to the Prussians, for long before the attack was delivered Pirch had taken up his position in support of Ziethen, and most of Thielmann's men had arrived, and thus Blücher's uncovered left had been secured.

The Prussian position was not one of any great strength. It consisted of the heights of Bry, Sombreffe and Tongrines, which lie along the Northern bank of the Ligny brook; on its right it was bounded by a ravine down which a smaller rivulet flows into the stream, and a similar ravine flowing from the village of Botey into the Ligny brook marked the natural limit of the position on the left. The Ligny brook, however, does not flow in a straight line, but, after running to the North-East through St. Amand and Ligny, bends due East at the hamlet of Mont Potriaux just South of Sombreffe, and then curving round to the South past Tongrines at one time actually flows South-Westward. Near the village of Boignée, however, it bends again to the East, to end by joining the Ormeau near Mazy, the spot where the Namur-Nivelles road crosses that tributary of the Sambre. The centre, therefore, of an army taking post on the Northern bank of this stream is much "refused," the wings being thrust forward, especially the right wing at the Western end of the position. Dotted all over these heights and along the course of the Ligny brook and its affluents are various villages and hamlets, some, like Ligny and St. Amand, of fair size, others, as, for example, Balâtre and Tongrenelles, quite small. These provided much cover for a defending force, and were the pivots on which the action was bound to turn.

Part of Ziethen's corps, which formed the Prussian right, was flung back *en potence* along the line of the rivulet which joins the larger brook at St. Amand, so as to face South-West and protect St. Amand and Ligny against a flank attack. This face of the position, with the villages of Hameau St. Amand, Wagnelée and St. Amand la Haye, was entrusted to Steinmetz's division. St. Amand itself was held by 3 battalions of Jägow's, the other 6 of which were being in reserve; in Ligny were 4 battalions of Henckel, whose other 2 were on the slopes behind the village, Pirch II's division being in reserve near Bry and the mill of Bussy. The cavalry on being driven in from the front took post between Jägow and Pirch.

The importance which Blücher attached to his right may be judged from the fact that the entire IInd Corps, Pirch I's, was drawn up in support of Ziethen along the Namur-Nivelles road just west of Sombreffe. The centre was formed by Börcke's division of Thielmann, posted near Sombreffe with a battalion at Mont Potriaux, the rest of the IIIrd Corps being more to the left, with battalions in Tongrines, Tongrenelles, Boignée and Balâtre, and the cavalry under von Hobe covering the extreme left of the position.

Unfortunately for Blücher the slopes south of the Ligny brook were slightly higher than those on which his army was posted, so that it was very difficult to conceal his movements from the enemy, and his reserves were throughout exposed to a cannonade: to get cover he must have posted them so far back that they would have found it almost impossible to lend timely support to the fighting line along the brook. The ground certainly was most unfavourable from a tactical point of view, it provided practically no cover; and the defects in the posting of the Prussian army did not escape the notice of Wellington, who about noon came over from Quatre Bras to consult with Blücher. In vain he urged his colleague to alter his dispositions; Blücher would not hear of it, with the result that Wellington's curt comment to Hardinge, "If they fight here they will be damnably mauled," was proved only too true a prophecy before the day was out. Besides this, the position was too long for the numbers available to defend it, and being without any definite boundary to its right rear was liable to be turned from the direction of Frasnes.

About 2.30 p.m. the attack was begun. Vandamme assailed St. Amand, Gérard hurled Pecheux's division upon Ligny, Grouchy's cavalry supported by another of Gérard's divisions engaged the Prussian left and by demonstrations against Balâtre and Tongrines kept a large part of Thielmann's corps occupied. The struggle for the villages was long, desperate and even. Time after time the French were forced back only to return to the assault. At the fourth attack on Ligny, Pecheux, supported by a brigade of the remaining division of the IVth Corps, obtained possession of the portion of the village which lies on the upper or South bank of the stream. In vain Henckel's reserve battalions joined in the fight, the French pressed on and effected a lodgment on the farther bank, only to be driven back across the stream when Jägow brought up the greater part of the Third Division. More and more reinforcements were thrown into the fight on both sides: Krafft of the IInd Corps replaced Henckel's broken battalions, Gérard hurled Vichery's remaining brigade at Lower Ligny and gradually gained ground. In despair Krafft appealed for reinforcements, but for the moment Blücher had none to send (*circa* 5 p.m.).

Meanwhile Vandamme had begun by ousting the three battalions of Jägow's division from St. Amand. Succoured by Steinmetz they returned to the charge, and Vandamme had to deploy Berthézéne's division on the left of Lefol's and to send Girard's of the IInd Corps, which had come up from Ransart to join in the attack, against the villages which lie to the North-West of St. Amand. These villages, La Haye, Hameau St. Amand and Wagnelée, Girard carried at the first rush; a success which filled Blücher with anxiety, for he attached the utmost importance to preventing the French from turning his right and so severing his communications with Wellington. He therefore hurled the last unengaged division of Ziethen's corps, that of Pirch II, directly against Girard, and prepared to turn his flank by sending against Wagnelée, Tippelskirch's division of the IInd Corps supported by Jürgass with Pirch I's cavalry.

Pirch II had some success. He shook Girard's hold on La Haye, and only by a prodigious effort did the French general rally his troops and recover the village, perishing himself just as the Prussians gave way. The flanking movement was less successful. Surprised in column of march before they could deploy, Tippelskirch's infantry were thrown back in disorder, and Jürgass was unable to effect anything in face of Domon and the light cavalry of Vandamme's corps.

Now it was (about 5 o'clock) that Blücher himself hurried to his right, rallied Pirch II, supported him with battalions from the IInd Corps, and sent him forward again against La Haye, at the same time relieving Steinmetz, whose efforts to recover St. Amand had resulted in the complete exhaustion of his division, and rallying Tippelskirch. These efforts were rewarded by the recapture of La Haye, from which the relics of Girard's division were again driven; but at Hameau St. Amand they rallied and made a stand. More reinforcements were needed, and Blücher had to fetch up the last reserves of the IInd Corps, several battalions of which had become involved in the carnage in Ligny. The repeated calls on his reserve had reduced it to vanishing point, and to fill the position in front of Sombreffe, left vacant by Langen's division (of the IInd Corps) moving to the right to join in the struggle for St. Amand, part of Thielmann's corps had to move up from the left. It would certainly seem that the Prussian commander was overhasty in throwing in his reserves and in withdrawing battalions to the rear before their condition became absolutely desperate, unless, indeed, he had not the same confidence in his men's endurance that Wellington had in the staying powers of his British and Legionaries. Certainly the last Prussian reserves were utilised at a far earlier period in the battle of Ligny than was to be the case with the Anglo-Allied army at Waterloo two days later. Wellington no doubt posted his men better, and thereby exposed them less and demanded rather less from them; but Blücher was certainly rather precipitate in utilising his reserves. Nor has the Prussian general's use of his reserves escaped well-merited censure.[1] Situated as he was, offensive tactics were hardly suitable until Bülow or some portion of Wellington's army came to his succour. Yet instead of confining himself to the defensive and beating off the attacks of the French, Blücher had resolved to take the offensive with his right. Accordingly, just before 6 o'clock, Tippelskirch and Jürgass advanced again by Wagnelée against the French flank, and Pirch II supported by Brause and some of Krafft's battalions assailed St. Amand and the other villages. Girard's division, reduced to less than half its original strength, fell back from Hameau St. Amand. Lefol and Berthézéne were unable to maintain their hold on St. Amand itself, for the sudden appearance of strange columns in the direction of Mellet had caused a panic among their men.

It was the approach of this unknown quantity and the consequent retreat of Vandamme before the attacks of Brause and Pirch which compelled Napoleon to suspend the decisive blow he had been on the point of delivering. He had not failed to notice that Blücher had diverted every available bayonet to the Prussian right, and that the Prussian reserves were practically all engaged, and he was preparing to launch the Guard and Milhaud's cuirassiers against Blücher's weakened centre, when

[1] Cf. Siborne, p. 257.

the news from his left forced him to desist, and to send Duhesme with the Young Guard and three regiments of the Middle Guard to the help of Vandamme.

But the strangers were not, as had at first been imagined, Wellington's men coming to complete a victory over Ney by playing a decisive part in the contest at Ligny. It was the corps of d'Erlon whose unexpected appearance in that quarter had so disconcerted its comrades. The Ist Corps had been late starting from its bivouacs South of Gosselies, and its leading columns had not yet reached Frasnes when, about 4.15 p.m., Colonel Forbin-Janson handed to d'Erlon the Emperor's order, sent off at 3.30 p.m., directing him to move towards St. Amand. Had d'Erlon been as far forward as the Emperor supposed him to be, a move on St. Amand would have brought him up in rear of the Prussian right; as it was, his direct route to St. Amand involved his appearing in Vandamme's rear. But the misfortunes of the Ist Corps were not yet at an end. Forbin-Janson had failed to proceed to Ney's headquarters and to acquaint the Marshal with the change in d'Erlon's orders, and Ney only heard of the movement from one of d'Erlon's Staff officers without receiving any explanation of it from the Emperor. Accordingly he hastened to recall d'Erlon towards Quatre Bras; and his messenger overtaking d'Erlon about 6.30, caused the Ist Corps to retrace its steps, Napoleon making no effort to retain it within his sphere of operations.[1]

Thus the Ist Corps disappeared from the field of Ligny without taking any part in the action except on the extreme left; there Jacquinot's light cavalry engaged some Prussian cavalry who were threatening to outflank Girard's much-harassed division. The chief effect of d'Erlon's appearance was to delay by over an hour Napoleon's intended attack on the Prussian centre, and that delay was to prove a factor of the utmost importance. Meanwhile the movements and counter-movements of the Guard seem to have made Blücher believe the French were on the point of retiring, and that victory was in his grasp. Rallying his right therefore, which had given back before the Young Guard, he prepared for a final stroke. He gathered together the relics of Tippelskirch, whom Duhesme

---

[1] Even if, as Houssaye (p. 177) argues, it was too late for a wide turning movement on Bry, d'Erlon might have been directed towards Wagnelée in support of Vandamme's left.

had sent back behind Wagnelée, of Brause, whom Girard's much-enduring men had driven again out of Hameau St. Amand and La Haye, and of Pirch II, from whom Lefol and Berthézéne had recovered St. Amand: to these he added a few battalions of Langen's, the division of Steinmetz which had been out of action since 5 o'clock, and finally Stulpnägel from near Sombreffe. But even this last effort failed. Duhesme's battalions were too much for it, and at the same moment Napoleon launched the Old Guard at the Prussian centre. This stroke was a brilliant success. As the Guard advanced Gérard's men made a final and successful effort, driving the defenders of Ligny out of the shattered village and up the slopes in rear. In vain Langen and Krafft sought to rally their men: Milhaud's cuirassiers following close in the wake of the Guard were upon them. In vain Blücher hurled the Prussian cavalry at the advancing French: the infantry of the Guard beat off every charge of Röder's squadrons. Now was the time when a reserve would have been invaluable, but even Thielmann was too hotly engaged on the left to have a man to spare. Only the darkness and the exhaustion of the French troops on whom the brunt of the action had fallen, prevented Ligny from being a victory such as Napoleon needed to ensure the success of his plan of campaign. He had a considerable intact reserve in the shape of Lobau's corps, and with another hour of daylight much might have been done. As it was, the piercing of the Prussian centre ended the active part of the day's operations. The bulk of the defenders of Ligny got away through the darkness to Bry, where Pirch II and his division made a stand which enabled them to rally. Some other battalions halted nearer Sombreffe, into which village Stulpnägel's division threw itself. Farther to the Prussian right Jürgass covered the withdrawal of Ziethen and Pirch I towards Tilly, a movement conducted with remarkably little difficulty. On the other wing Thielmann's men held on unmolested to Tongrines and Mont Potriaux until 3 o'clock next morning. The French spent the night on the slopes to the north of Ligny and St. Amand, which had formed the position of the Prussian main body during the day. With the field of battle they found themselves also in possession of 21 guns which the Prussians had failed to carry off; but their victory lacked completeness, and the fact that the Prussians contrived to retire unmolested after so close and fierce an engagement is the best testimony to the impression, physical and moral, their stubborn defence, their repeated rallies, their constant efforts to recover the lost villages, had made on their victors.

It would be no exaggeration to say that it was in the twelve hours which followed the close of the battle of Ligny that the Waterloo campaign was decided. The French had lost some chances through delays; but had they promptly followed up the success of Ligny as they had followed up that of Jena, the campaign would have probably been a triumphant success. But Napoleon let his prey slip through his grasp, and with the unmolested and unobserved retreat of the Prussians the best chance of a French victory slipped away. Badly though it had been mauled, the Prussian army was still "in being," and quite capable of playing its part in the further developments of the campaign. Directly the troops had been got into order again, Gneisenau gave directions for a further retreat, though not to-wards Liége and Namur, the bases on which it would have been natural for the beaten Prussians to retire. The direction given was Northward towards Wavre,[1] so that they might not lose touch with Wellington's army, which the Prussian retreat would force to withdraw from its position at Quatre Bras, a position it had been fortunate enough to maintain against all Ney's attacks throughout the 16th, but which became dangerously exposed by Blücher's retreat from Ligny. Only the leading incidents of the battle of Quatre Bras need mention here. Ney's orders from the Emperor[2] contemplated the Marshal remaining more or less inactive about Quatre Bras till Napoleon, having settled with the Prussians opposing Grouchy and the right, should transfer himself with his reserve to the left and begin the advance on Brussels. Partly therefore, lest a premature advance on his part should dislocate Napoleon's plans, and partly because the brave show made by Perponcher with his Nassauers and Dutch-Belgians imposed upon him, Ney did not attack the force in front of him till nearly 2 p.m. The French had then just driven Perponcher's men back into the wood of Bossu, and were on the point of seizing Quatre Bras when the arrival of Picton with the British brigades of Kempt and Pack, and the Hanoverians of Best saved the situation (2.40 p.m.). Next, part of the

---

[1] The part Gneisenau played on the morning of the 18th must not be allowed to diminish the credit due to him for this courageous and important resolve.

[2] Cf. Siborne, pp. 136–13S.

Brunswick corps arrived and took up their ground between Picton's right, East of the Charleroi-Nivelles road, and the wood of Bossu. Seeing the French infantry advancing in column, Wellington met them in the old Peninsula style with an advance of Picton's division in line, with the result that the French columns were driven back in much confusion. However, the French cavalry now advanced to the attack, and though their charge failed to shake the Peninsula veterans of Picton's division, it broke through the raw Brunswick levies, who fled headlong to the rear, cavalry and infantry involved in the same confusion. In the effort to rally his men Duke Frederick William was mortally wounded, and only the stubborn defence of Picton's squares repelled the French attack. It was renewed almost at once by Kellermann, who had just arrived with a division of cuirassiers. Again the British infantry beat off the charges; and though one of Best's Hanoverian *Landwehr* battalions was caught by a body of lancers and ridden down before it could form square, the rest of the brigade stood their ground. About five o'clock Alten's division came up to the assistance of Picton, the Brunswickers rallied on the arrival of two belated battalions of their corps, and after another onset by the French cavalry had been beaten back, Kielmansegge's Hanoverians of Alten's division behaving no less steadily than did Picton's veterans, the British Guards came up and secured Wellington's right by recovering the wood of Bossu, from which the Dutch-Belgians had been driven. This enabled Wellington to order a general advance before which Ney gave way, retiring to the heights in front of Frasnes where d'Erlon joined him about 9 o'clock.

The nature of the struggle at Quatre Bras may be best understood from the respective losses of the units engaged on the Allied side. The British had some 2300 casualties out of rather over 11,000 engaged, Picton's two brigades losing between them 30 per cent. of their numbers. The Brunswick corps also lost heavily, its 800 casualties representing about a seventh of its strength, and the Hanoverians with under 400 casualties among the 5700 present got off comparatively lightly. In Perponcher's division there were some 1000 killed, wounded and missing out of 7500, but the comparatively high proportion of the latter diminishes the merits of their performance. The French, whose numbers at the end of the fight were considerably inferior to those opposed to them, confessed to over 4000 casualties among

21,000 engaged : at the same time it should be remembered that the Allied force did not outnumber Ney's until Alten arrived, and that even then about a third of Wellington's 26,000 consisted of Dutch-Belgians on whom but little reliance could be placed. Foy's admission that " conceal it as we may, Quatre Bras was a defeat for us," is no more than the truth. Ney's attacks had been repulsed with loss, and as the arrival during the night of the greater part of the British cavalry supplied the deficiency in that arm which had so hampered Wellington during the day, there is no reason to suppose that if the Marshal had done what some of his critics would have had him do and renewed his attack early on the 17th, he would have been much more fortunate than on the 16th. But for the delay in attacking on the 17th it is hardly Ney who should be held responsible.

Knowing what force he had before him, and anxious to do nothing which should in any way compromise the Emperor's movements, Ney forbore from any movement on his own initiative, waiting for orders. Not till midday did Napoleon send off a messenger to Ney, bidding him attack the English at once and adding that he was himself on his way to Quatre Bras to assist him. But by this time even the English cavalry who formed the rearguard were quitting the position.

Wellington had been left without any news from his Prussian allies, as the only messenger Gneisenau sent him was intercepted by the French. Hence the delay of the Allied forces in their somewhat exposed position. However, the inaction of Napoleon averted the peril thus risked. The Emperor's conduct on the morning of June 17th has been criticised and explained times without number. His neglect to move at once to Quatre Bras directly he received, at 7.30 a.m., Ney's account of the previous day's operations was an error far less serious than the failure to keep touch with the Prussians, or to discover the true direction of their retreat. Very early on the 17th Wellington had patrols out, and was thoroughly on the alert. From one of these patrols, which had pushed as far as Tilly and communicated with Ziethen's rearguard, he heard about 7.30 that the Prussians were retiring on Wavre, so that directly the French showed signs of being about to attack he could have set his troops in motion rearward. As it was, the infantry moved off about 10 a.m. and reached the position of Mont St. Jean, where Wellington had decided to make his stand if only one corps of

LIGNY June 16th 1815

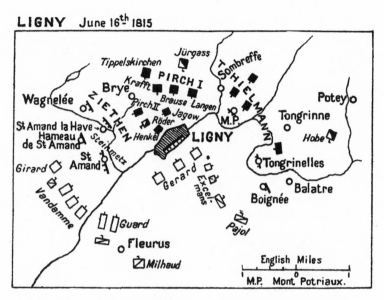

Jürgass

Tippelskirchen

Sombreffe

PIRCH I

Krafft

Brye

Pirch II

Brause Langen

Wagnelée

Jagow

Potey

ZIETHEN

Röder

Tongrinne

St Amand la Have

Henkel

LIGNY

Hobe

Hameau
de St Amand

Steinmetz

M.P.

TIELMANN

St
Amand

Tongrinelles

Girard

Gerard

Excel-
mans

Balatre

Vandamme

Boignée

Guard

Pajol

Fleurus

Milhaud

English Miles

M.P. Mont Potriaux.

PRUSSIAN GAINS WEST OF THE ELBE IN 1815

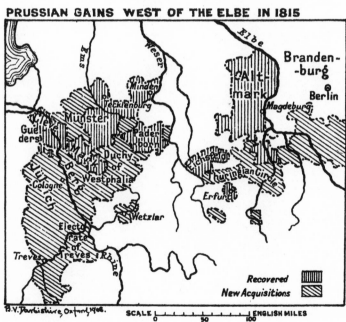

Ems

Weser

Elbe

Brandenburg

Alt-mark

Minden

Recklenburg

Berlin

Munster

Magdeburg

Guelders

Paderborn

Cleve

March

Berg

Duchy
of
Westphalia

Eichsfeld

Thuringian Circle

Cologne

Erfurt

Wetzlar

Juliers

Electorate
of
Treves

Treves

Rhine

Recovered

New Acquisitions

B.V. Darbishire, Oxford 1906.

SCALE 0 50 100 ENGLISH MILES

the Prussian army would join him, without being in the least pressed. Similarly Lord Uxbridge and the cavalry who covered the retreat, though closely pursued by Napoleon, had little difficulty in performing their task without much loss, a sharp skirmish at Genappe, in which the French lancers repulsed the 7th Hussars but were routed by the much heavier Life Guards, being the only important incident of the retreat.

Thus the evening of the 17th found Wellington with the bulk of his forces, 67,600 men with 150 guns,[1] along the ridge which runs from the château of Hougoumont past the farm of La Haye Sainte towards Ohain; one Anglo-Hanoverian division [2] and some 10,000 Dutch-Belgians being posted at Hal to protect the Duke's communications with the sea and, in case of need, assist to cover a retreat to the North-Westward. Napoleon with the Guard and the cavalry of Milhaud, Kellermann, Domon and Subervie, and the corps of d'Erlon, Reille and Lobau, in all some 74,000 men with 240 guns, lay opposite to him. At the same time Grouchy with the 33,000 men entrusted to him for the purpose of pursuing the Prussians and completing their defeat [3] had not got beyond Gembloux. This is not the place for an adequate discussion of Grouchy's proceedings and of his share of the responsibility for the results of the campaign. That he showed a lack of energy and initiative is not to be denied, even by those who regard the master rather than the subordinate as mainly to blame for the disaster which befell the French. Grouchy's orders certainly contemplated a pursuit of the Prussians away from the English, though they admitted the possibility that the Allies might seek to reunite to cover Brussels. There was nothing in his instructions about rejoining the Emperor to fight a battle against Wellington; and even the orders sent off by Napoleon at 10 a.m. on the 18th, which speak of co-ordinating the movements of the detached force with those of the main body, direct the Marshal to continue his move on Wavre. Such information as Napoleon had at 11 p.m. on the 17th coincided with his own belief, a belief to which perhaps the wish was father, that the Prussians were retiring towards the Meuse. Pajol

---

[1] Of these 24,000 were British, 15,000 being infantry, 6000 cavalry and 3000 artillery; the King's German Legion had 2000 cavalry, 500 gunners and 3300 infantry: of Hanoverians there were about 11,000, 1000 being cavalry and artillery, the Brunswick contingent was a little under 6000, the Nassauers of Kruse and Prince Bernhard were somewhat stronger, and the rest, nearly 14,000, were Dutch-Belgians.

[2] Colville's.   [3] Cf. Houssaye, p. 225.

had sent in word that his light cavalry had found guns, waggons and stragglers on the road to Namur, and the French vedettes near Tilly and Gentinnes had failed to notice or to announce the retreat of the Prussians from those villages or the direction which it had taken. The true causes of Grouchy's failure to prevent the Prussians from coming to the aid of their allies at Waterloo were firstly, Napoleon's assumption, warranted perhaps by the general principles of strategy but partially based on a false estimate of the success he had gained on the previous day,[1] that Namur or Maastricht would prove to be the point on which the beaten Prussians had fallen back, and secondly, the Emperor's extraordinary inactivity on the morning of the 17th. The touch which was then lost with Blücher's retreating forces, the hours that were then wasted, contributed far more to bring about the defeat of Waterloo than Grouchy's resolve to continue his march from Sart a Walhain to Wavre instead of striking to his left across the Dyle towards Planchenoit and the sound of the guns. And even had Grouchy resolved to depart from his orders and make a move for which he had no authority, it is still most unlikely that any appreciable fraction of his corps could have arrived on the battlefield in time. The physical difficulties which retarded Bülow and Ziethen would have been no less potent to delay the French. The passage of the Dyle would have been no simple or rapid operation when 33,000 men with 116 guns had only a wooden bridge at Moustier and a stone bridge at Ottignies by which to cross. In short, as Mr. Hereford George has remarked in his just and trenchant criticism of Judge O'Connor Morris' *Campaign of 1815*,[2] " it is only upon the map, not on the real ground, that Grouchy could have saved Napoleon from defeat."

Meanwhile the Prussian army had managed to get away unhindered and almost unobserved from the dangerous position in which the timely advent of night had found it on June 16th. Under cover of the friendly darkness the Prussians had rallied in a manner which speaks volumes for their discipline and for the spirit by which they were animated. Despite the fact that their losses in killed, wounded and prisoners amounted to nearly 12,000,[3] and that many members of the contingents drawn from the Rhenish and Westphalian provinces lately annexed to Prussia had hastened to disassociate themselves from a cause

[1] Cf. Houssaye, p. 315.   [2] Cf. *E.H.R. 1900*, p. 816.   [3] Houssaye, p. 184.

for which they had no zeal by a headlong flight towards Aix-la-Chapelle and Liége, the bulk of the army rallied directly the action ceased. There seems to have been great disorder in the centre and considerable confusion on the left, but the troops of Ziethen and Pirch I withdrew in very fair order[1] and a rearguard of the Ist Corps held Bry till daybreak, Sombreffe being in like manner occupied by a portion of Thielmann's corps, the bulk of which remained almost in their battle positions till 3 a.m. on the 17th, when they withdrew to Gembloux.

For the decision to retire by Tilly and Mont St. Guibert on Wavre, Gneisenau was responsible. Blücher had been unhorsed and badly injured in the closing stages of the battle, and did not resume control of the army's operations until 11 a.m. on the 18th. In thus retiring Northward Gneisenau did not absolutely sacrifice his communications. If he abandoned the lines of retreat by Namur and Liége, those by Tirlemont or Louvain on Maastricht or Wesel were still open to him, and his action on the 18th makes it clear that he had by no means subordinated everything to the chance of joining Wellington.

The retreat was effected with very little difficulty. Ziethen moving from Tilly by Mont St. Guibert established his troops on the left bank of the Dyle soon after midday. Pirch I from Gentinnes after halting at Mont St. Guibert to cover Ziethen's passage of that defile, followed through it in his turn and bivouacked between St. Anne and Aisemont on the right bank of the river. Thielmann after remaining stationary at Gembloux from 6 a.m. to 2 p.m., a piece of most culpable imprudence, which only escaped the severest punishment through Napoleon's equally extraordinary laxity in pursuing the defeated Prussians, arrived at Wavre late in the evening. Most of his corps crossed the Dyle and encamped at La Bavette, but his rearguard remained on the right bank. Finally, Bülow, whose troops had advanced no farther than Baudeset on the evening of the 16th, where his orders found him about 9.30 a.m. next day, arrived at Dion le Mont after a somewhat leisurely march by Walhain and Corroy. Detachments under Colonels Lebedur and Sohr were left to cover the main army and to keep a lookout for the advance of the French, and patrols were thrust out on the left bank of the Dyle to collect intelligence of Wellington's army and their opponents.

[1] Houssaye, p. 181.

It was not long after his arrival at Wavre that Blücher received Wellington's message, sent off at 9.30 a.m., in which the Duke announced that if he could be secure of the assistance of, at any rate, one Prussian corps he would give battle in front of Waterloo on the following morning. This assurance Blücher was in a position to send him ; for, very fortunately, the Prussian reserve ammunition park had arrived safely at Wavre in the course of the afternoon, and the corps of Pirch and Ziethen were thus able to replenish their exhausted pouches and limbers, and so to put themselves in a fit condition for another action.

The facility with which the retreat of the Prussians had been accomplished had been partly due to the negligence of the French outposts near Tilly and Gentinnes; partly to the fact that Pajol's cavalry, thrust out to their right to seek for the retreating enemy, had found enough traces of fugitives to make them believe the line chosen was that towards Namur and Liége ; partly to Berton's cavalry failing to send full information back to headquarters, when, pushing out to Gembloux about 9 a.m. they found that village still occupied in force by Thielmann, and again neglecting to observe the Prussians closely when they did retire. Nightfall found Grouchy at Gembloux under the impression that though a portion of the Prussians might be making for Wavre with the idea of joining Wellington, part were certainly retiring Eastward to Namur while the bulk of their army was on its way to Liége through Perwez.

It was not, however, by this impression that his proceedings on the next morning were governed. His letter to Napoleon, written at 6 a.m., regards the Prussians as concentrating at Wavre in order to fall back on Brussels ; but he omitted to consider that they might as easily move to their flank towards Ohain as to their rear towards Brussels. The only way to make certain of their movements was to close with them as early as possible, and Grouchy's delay on the morning of the 18th was a most serious error for which he cannot evade the responsibility. Not till after 7 a.m. did Vandamme's corps set out, and Gérard was two hours later in starting. Thus Grouchy had not got beyond Walhain when, a little before midday, the distant sound of cannon became audible. A sharp discussion between Grouchy and Gérard resulted in the Marshal deciding to continue his move on Wavre and rejecting his lieutenant's appeal to him to march towards the sound of the guns. He had just heard from his cavalry that they had fallen in with the Prussian rearguard near Wavre, and before he left Walhain he received the despatch sent off by Napoleon at 10 o'clock bidding him move on Wavre.

Between 9 and 10 a.m. (June 18th) Excelmans' cavalry had reached the wood of La Huzelle and sighted Prussian troops on the heights between them and Wavre. However, Excelmans made no effort to engage, but withdrew his main body to Corbais. This allowed Ledebur and the detachment left at Mont St. Guibert, whose retreat was in danger of being cut off, to force their way through the French outposts and take up a position at the Southern end of the defile made by the road from Gembloux to Wavre in passing the wood of La Huzelle. To force this defile the French had to wait for Vandamme's infantry. These did not appear till after 3 p.m., and it was already near 4 o'clock when the French having pushed through the wood, from which Ledebur had withdrawn, prepared to attack Wavre. By this time the rearguard of the IInd Corps had already crossed the Dyle by the bridge of Bierge, which they destroyed behind them. Indeed, the whole Prussian army was in motion towards Waterloo, a few detachments excepted. The appearance of the French forced Thielmann to retrace his steps, and in obedience to Blücher's orders the IIIrd Corps took up a position on the left bank of the Dyle to dispute the passage of the river and thereby cover the movement of the rest of the army towards Waterloo from any interruption—a task which it performed with complete success despite the superior numbers Grouchy was able to bring against it.

The movement which it was Thielmann's task to cover was that to which Blücher had pledged himself on the previous evening, and on which Wellington was relying, when, with an army somewhat inferior in numbers and certainly very inferior in average quality, he faced Napoleon at Waterloo. It cannot be said that the move was executed with as much promptitude or skilful management as is usually represented. As it was all-important that the Prussian reinforcements should be at Wellington's disposal as early in the day as possible, one would naturally have expected that the corps detailed to lead the way would have been one of the two which had bivouacked on the nearer side of the Dyle. But instead of choosing Thielmann, who at La Bavette was only six miles from St. Lambert, the point on which Bülow was in the first instance directed, or

Ziethen, who at Bierge was about half a mile nearer, the Prussian commander—or more probably his Chief of Staff, Gneisenau—selected Bülow's corps, which not only had nearly nine miles to cover, but had to pass through Wavre on the way, in doing which it was considerably delayed by a fire in the main street. Bülow's corps had, of course, not been engaged on the 16th, and it was natural to select it rather than the shaken corps of Ziethen and Pirch; but Thielmann had not suffered at all heavily at Ligny, and it is difficult to understand why his corps should not have headed the movement. From La Bavette to Ohain is barely seven miles, and if Thielmann had set out at 8 o'clock his corps ought to have been at Ohain well before midday. Bülow and Pirch could have covered the move of Thielmann and Ziethen quite as effectively as the Ist and IIIrd Corps covered the advance of the IInd and IVth; while if Pirch, who was ordered to follow Bülow, had only been allowed to precede him, the IInd Corps, having more than two miles less to cover, might have been at St. Lambert soon after 10 o'clock. As things were managed, Bülow's vanguard was at St. Lambert about 11; but the bulk of the corps was much later, and the rearguard did not arrive there till nearly 3 p.m. Pirch's men were under arms from 7 a.m. until midday, when at last they left their bivouacs at Aisemont; at 2 o'clock half the corps had not yet crossed the Dyle. Similarly, Ziethen's men only began their march towards Ohain about midday; and the fact that the arrangements which directed Ziethen on Smohain and Pirch on St. Lambert involved additional delay through these corps crossing each other's path, has been justly but severely criticised by Clausewitz.[1] More than this, Bülow's advance-guard halted directly it had crossed the defile of the Lasne, and remained inactive in the Wood of Paris for some hours. And yet there are those who represent the late arrival of the Prussians at Waterloo as due merely to the bad roads over which they had to move. Undoubtedly the roads were bad, and the passage of the defile of the Lasne was a matter of great difficulty, especially for the guns, and was partly responsible for the delay, but the physical difficulties do not adequately explain the fact that it was after 4 o'clock before a shot was fired by any of the Prussian army, when at daybreak the most distant portion of it, Bülow's corps at Dion le Mont, was less than thirteen miles from Mont St. Jean.

[1] *Der Feldzug von 1815*, p. 110.

Gneisenau's notorious distrust of Wellington must be taken into account in dealing with the Prussian movements on June 18th. He seems to have feared that the British general would retire without fighting, and thereby expose to the joint attacks of Napoleon and Grouchy the Prussian detachments which were on their way towards Waterloo. Moreover, injured and shaken as Blücher was, it seems only reasonable to ascribe to Gneisenau more responsibility for the arrangements of the Prussian movement than would otherwise have been the case. The intervention of the Prussians was, of course, the decisive factor in the day's fighting; but it was in no sense an accident due merely to Grouchy's negligence: their co-operation was an essential feature in the scheme on which the battle was fought; it was as much part of Wellington's calculations as were the movements of his own divisions; the Prussians were behind their time and so endangered his left, which was his weak spot.[1] Indeed it seems certain that the Duke looked for the arrival of the Prussians at quite an early hour; that he must have almost expected the corps for which he had asked to be up in its place on the left of his line before the French attack began. It is not too much to say that if Wellington had not received a definite promise of assistance he would never have given battle at Waterloo. The delay, of course, added to the dramatic effect of the intervention. Wellington's coolness, steadfastness and tactical skill, and the courage and endurance of his troops had been taxed to a very high degree before at last the pressure of Bülow upon the French right and the arrival of Ziethen at Ohain afforded the long-desired succour; but had the Prussian Staff work in managing their movement been better done, or had Gneisenau had a little more of that confidence in his colleague which induced Wellington to risk being defeated by Napoleon before his tardy allies appeared, the resisting powers of the Allied army would never have been exposed to so great a strain.

Numerous as are the criticisms which have been urged against the strategy of Wellington in the Waterloo campaign, little fault has been found with his tactics in the great contest which raged between Hougoumont and Papelotte on that momentous Sunday from before midday till after 8 o'clock. The failure to adequately support Major Baring and the 2nd Light Battalion of the German Legion, who maintained so splendid a

[1] Cf. Sir Harry Smith's *Memoirs*, p. 276.

defence of La Haye Sainte till after 6 o'clock, is the only serious blot in the Duke's management of the battle. His admirable dispositions enabled him to utilise to the full the advantages of the ground to cover his men from the French cannonade, his employment of his reserves was judicious and timely. He was nobly seconded by his subordinates and by the troops under his command. It may perhaps not be out of place to say something of the individual parts played in the battle by the various German contingents. First and foremost among them the King's German Legion deserves mention. Waterloo is perhaps the brightest page in its history. The five cavalry regiments charged again and again, and the two infantry brigades behaved with a steadiness none could surpass. Of these two Ompteda's brigade was posted on the right of the high road from Charleroi to Nivelles, having Kielmansegge's Hanoverians on their right and Picton's division on their left on the other side of the road. It was to this brigade that Baring's battalion belonged, as did also the two unfortunate battalions, the 5th and 8th Line, which having at separate times been rashly deployed by the express orders of the Prince of Orange to drive off the French skirmishers, were caught by the French cavalry and practically destroyed.[1] The other brigade, Duplat's, which belonged to Clinton's division, was in reserve behind the right wing at the beginning of the action, but was moved up into the front line about 5 o'clock during the attacks of the French cavalry, and took post to the East of Hougoumont. Portions of it also shared in the defence of Hougoumont. Of the four Hanoverian brigades present in the action, those of Vincke and Best were posted on the extreme left of the line, beyond Picton's British brigades, that of Kielmansegge was in the right centre between Ompteda and Colin Halkett's British brigade, that of William Halkett was in reserve till nearly 6 o'clock, when it moved forward on the right, two battalions supporting Duplat, the other two taking post on the Nivelles road to prevent any turning movement by Piré's light cavalry. Of these brigades that of Kielmansegge unquestionably underwent the severest ordeal; its heavy losses, over 33 per cent. of its strength, testify to the strain put upon it. The solitary Hanoverian cavalry regiment present, the Cumberland Hussars, hardly came out of the battle as creditably as did its comrades of the infantry. On being

[1] Cf. Siborne, pp. 460 and 480.

brought forward by Lord Uxbridge to support the infantry of the centre, the entire corps abandoned the not very exposed position in which the Earl had placed them, and, disregarding alike his orders and expostulations, went solidly to the rear to spread panic and false rumours of defeat through Brussels.

The Brunswickers behaved upon the whole in a most creditable fashion: one battalion took part in the great struggle for Hougoumont, and the greater part of the division was employed on the right to fill the gap caused by Byng's Guards reinforcing the defenders of Hougoumont, in which position they resisted with great steadiness the charges of the French cavalry. About 7.30, at the time of the last great French attack, Wellington moved five battalions of the Brunswickers more to the centre, placing them in the front line between Kruse's Nassauers and Colin Halkett. On coming under a very heavy fire from the advancing French the young Brunswick battalions gave way and fell back in disorder, in which the brigades of Kruse, Kielmansegge and Ompteda became involved. This was the most critical moment in the battle, for the Guard was then ascending the slopes just to the East of Hougoumont, and d'Erlon's men were making their final effort. By great efforts Wellington rallied the Brunswickers, who re-formed and checked the French just in time; then, when Vivian brought up his Hussars in their support, they moved forward again, the Germans of Kielmansegge and Ompteda also rallying and advancing, so that the Third Division once again resumed its ground, sending the French back down the hill. Kruse's brigade, whose loyalty to the Allied cause was by no means above suspicion, since the battalions had served in Spain under the French colours, came out of the ordeal well. When the Brunswickers gave way Kruse's men did the same, and were only prevented from breaking by the 10th Hussars, who blocked their way to the rear; but the Nassauers rallied like the rest of the right centre. Prince Bernhard's brigade defended Papelotte with great steadiness, and the detachments of the 2nd Nassau in Hougoumont took their full share in the defence of the post. As to the Dutch-Belgians, Bylandt's brigade had some excuse for breaking when d'Erlon charged, as they had been much exposed to the French artillery; but Chassé's division could plead no such extenuation for the high percentage of "missing" among their casualties.[1] Trip's cavalry declined to face the French, and the small losses suffered by Ghigny and van Merlen show how insignificant was their part in the fight.

The services of the Prussians can hardly be explained without some narrative of the leading features of the action. It may be divided into six stages. The first of these is from the opening of the cannonade between 11.30 and 12 to the advance of d'Erlon just before 2 p.m. Of this stage Reille's attack on Hougoumont and the cannonade which paved the way for d'Erlon's assaults were the principal features. The second stage is that of the great attack of d'Erlon's corps on the Allied left centre. This was checked by Picton's infantry and converted into a disastrous repulse by the charge of the Household and "Union" cavalry brigades. Meanwhile most of Reille's corps had become absorbed in the desperate struggle for Hougoumont. The third stage, beginning about 3 o'clock and lasting till nearly 6, is that of the repeated attacks of the French cavalry against the British and German squares to the West of the high road. These charges were varied by a heavy cannonade, and by the attacks of the numerous skirmishers whom the French thrust forward. However, neither artillery nor cavalry nor skirmishers succeeded in breaking a single square, for the 8th Line Battalion of the German Legion, which was caught in open order by French cavalry and cut to pieces, had been foolishly deployed by the Prince of Orange. During this period d'Erlon more than once renewed his attacks on the British and Hanoverians to the East of the high road, but with no better success than before, while the struggles for Hougoumont and La Haye Sainte continued to rage with unabated fury. However, all Reille's attacks were repulsed, and Baring maintained his hold on La Haye Sainte. The fourth stage was marked by the advance of Bachelu's division of Reille's corps with a brigade of Foy's of the same corps between Hougoumont and the high road. It seems to have been then, about 6 o'clock, that Wellington brought up the brigades of Duplat and Adam to aid his hard-pressed right, and apparently it was largely by them that Bachelu and Foy were repulsed.[2] However, at this

---

[1] The claim of Dittmer's brigade to have repulsed the Imperial Guard is one which, despite M. Houssaye's support, I cannot admit to be borne out by the evidence ; cf. *Quarterly Review*, June 1900, for a criticism of M. Houssaye's account.

[2] Cf. *Waterloo Letters*, accounts of Adam's brigade.

moment success finally rewarded the assaults of the French on La Haye Sainte, and the importance of the capture of the post was at once seen from the vigour and success with which the French skirmishers pressed forward against Alten's division in the right centre and against Lambert and Kempt to the East of the road. To drive off the skirmishers, the Prince of Orange ordered Ompteda to deploy the 5th Line Battalion of the Legion into line ; Ompteda, obeying against his better judgment, for he knew that French cavalry were close at hand, led the battalion forward only to have his forebodings verified: a regiment of cuirassiers charged in upon its right flank and cut the unfortunate battalion to pieces, Ompteda himself being among those who perished. However, though La Haye Sainte was lost Hougoumont was still untaken, and the steadfast squares of infantry, reduced though some were to mere handfuls, kept their ground unflinchingly. A fresh effort was needed if the French were to win. Their cavalry had spent themselves in their repeated charges, all the attacks of d'Erlon and Reille had been repulsed. But there remained the Guard, and the fifth stage of the great battle came when, about 7.30, this last reserve was thrown into the scale.[1] As the Guard advanced the persevering infantry of d'Erlon came on again—Allix and Marcognet on the East of the high road, Donzelot to the West of it pushing forward against Alten's shattered division. This Wellington had just reinforced with five battalions of Brunswickers from the right. It was at this moment that the Brunswickers on coming under the heavy fire of Donzelot's infantry were seized by the temporary panic

[1] According to M. Houssaye only five battalions of the Guard took part in this attack, though it seems most doubtful whether, as he alleges (p. 369), the 4th Chasseurs had lost so heavily at Ligny as to have been reduced to one battalion (cf. Professor Oman's article in *E.H.R. 1904*, p. 689), and one may fairly put the force engaged in this attack at six battalions at least. All eight battalions of the Young Guard and two of the Old had been diverted to Planchenoit : one was at Caillou guarding the military chest, two halted at Rossomme as a reserve, while four were not sent forward to the attack, but held in reserve to be pushed forward "if all went well"—Houssaye, p. 402. If this was actually the case, it is difficult to understand what the Emperor can have expected to achieve by sending only 3000 men against a position from which nearly double that number (*i.e.* Foy and Bachelu) had just been repulsed. If the Guard were to be put in at all, every available battalion should surely have been utilised. It is, of course, possible that the old version of the attack of the Guard in two columns is after all not so inaccurate as has been represented, and that two or three of these apparently unemployed battalions did actually move forward in support of their comrades only to be caught in flank and destroyed by the 52nd.

which threatened to produce a disaster;[1] but they rallied, and aided by the rest of the division recovered the position they had so nearly lost. To the East of the road Pack brought his battalions back into the front line on the left of Kempt and Lambert,[2] and between them they sent Allix and Marcognet back in disorder down the slopes. It was at this moment— 7.45 p.m.—that the cry went up from the French ranks, "The Guard recoils"; for, confronted by the brigades of Maitland and Colin Halkett, caught in flank by Colborne, who wheeled the 52nd up into line, a masterly stroke in which he was copied by the rest of Adam's brigade, and with Duplat's Legionaries and William Halkett's Hanoverians pressing forward more to the right, the forlorn hope of the French gave way and fell back in disorder. And as Adam's men with the light cavalry of Vivian and Vandeleur pressed forward on the heels of the defeated Guard, the battle passed into its sixth and final stage, that of the counter-attack.

Long before this, of course, the approach of the Prussians had begun to make itself felt.[3] Indeed, even before d'Erlon's first and most formidable attack, while the cannonade was still paving the way for that effort, Napoleon's attention had been called to the presence of troops far out on his right flank in the direction of St. Lambert. It was at first supposed that these might be Grouchy's men, but the capture of a prisoner belonging to the Silesian Hussars proved them to be Bülow's vanguard. However, they did not advance, and Napoleon contented himself with pushing out the cavalry of Domon and Subervie to observe their movements, at the same time instructing Lobau to support this cavalry screen. But for this it is possible that the VIth Corps would have been used to renew the attack on the left and left centre which d'Erlon had made with such little success. It is not to be denied that this second attack, which d'Erlon made about 3 or 3.30 p.m.[4] with his own men only, would have had far more chance of success if the 8000

---

[1] *v.s.* p. 689; cf. Siborne, pp. 515–517.

[2] After the repulse of d'Erlon's first attack, when Lambert's 2000 fresh bayonets arrived, Pack's brigade had been withdrawn to the second line; cf. *Waterloo Letters.*

[3] Unquestionably the best summary of the questions as to the Prussian co-operation at Waterloo is the chapter on the subject in Dr. J. H. Rose's *Napoleonic Studies*, which was published after the first draft of this chapter was written, but which I have consulted when revising my account of the campaign.

[4] Cf. *Waterloo Letters*, pp. 354 and 404.

bayonets of the VIth Corps had at the same time pushed forward by Papelotte and turned the left flank of the Allied line. The Prussians remained inactive, but the menace of their presence at Chapelle St. Lambert was enough to "contain" Lobau, and d'Erlon's attack failed completely, being beaten back by the British infantry without much difficulty or the intervention of the cavalry. This was the first point at which the Prussians in the least influenced the battle. It is also possible that their presence at St. Lambert may have induced Napoleon to support instead of suspending the cavalry charges which Ney began somewhat prematurely about 4 p.m.[1]

Blücher, who had left Wavre about 11 o'clock, seems to have caught up the bulk of Bülow's corps about two hours later. It was then still on the Eastern side of the miry valley of the Lasne, the two battalions and the cavalry regiment which formed the advance-guard having alone crossed and taken position in the Wood of Paris.[2] However, far from at once pushing forward to Wellington's assistance, it was not till he learnt from his scouts that there was no prospect of any French troops interfering with his passage of the defile that Blücher set his men in motion towards Planchenoit. By that time it was nearly 2 o'clock.[3] Such were the difficulties of the passage, particularly for the artillery, that the two miles between Chapelle St. Lambert and the Wood of Paris took fully two hours to cover, and only by the greatest exertions were the guns brought across the stream. Thus it was not till half-past four that Bülow's two leading divisions at last debouched from the Wood of Paris and advanced along the road to Planchenoit, driving before them Domon and Subervie. To meet them Napoleon moved Lobau's corps to the right, and the 8000 infantry of the divisions of Jannin and Simmer advanced against the oncoming Prussians and drove them, superior in numbers though they were, back upon the Wood of Paris. But Blücher had reserves at hand and about 5.30 p.m. the two remaining divisions of Bülow advanced from the Wood of Paris and joined in. Lobau had to recoil towards Planchenoit, against which Blücher thrust forward Hiller's division with Ryssel and the cavalry of the corps under Prince Augustus William of

---

[1] Cf. Houssaye's note, p. 357.
[2] It was these troops whom Napoleon first perceived about 1 or 1.15.
[3] Houssaye, p. 366.

Prussia in support, while with Losthin and Hacke he assailed Lobau in front.   Only one brigade of the VIth Corps could be spared for the defence of Planchenoit, and outnumbered and assailed in front and flank, it was ousted from the village after a severe struggle (6 p.m.).   The other three brigades, posted to the North of the Planchenoit-St. Lambert road, kept the Prussians at bay, but the capture of the village at once threatened Lobau's flank and the line of retreat of the whole French army. The recovery of Planchenoit was therefore imperative, and Napoleon directed Duhesme thither with the eight battalions of the Young Guard.   Attacking with great dash they thrust Hiller's division out of Planchenoit.   However, the Prussians were at once reinforced and returned to the attack, and Duhesme's men, though fighting most obstinately, had to give way before the superior numbers of their assailants.

It was then about 7 o'clock.   Though sorely tried and much reduced in numbers Wellington's line was still unbroken, and Napoleon, having used up all the rest of his army in his fruitless efforts to drive the Allies from their positions, found himself forced to play his last card and send forward the veterans of the Old and Middle Guard to see if they would succeed where their comrades of the Line had failed.   But at the moment that he was preparing to launch this magnificent reserve against Wellington's line, the pressure of the Prussians on his right compelled him to detach two battalions to Planchenoit which Bülow's renewed assault had just succeeded in wresting from Duhesme.

The intervention of the Old Guard, however, was more than Bülow's men could stand.   They gave way before the veterans, who, pushing forward, retook the village.   Encouraged by their assistance the troops of Duhesme and Lobau rallied, and once more Bülow was thrust back all along the line.   However, the corps of Pirch I was now beginning to arrive in Bülow's rear, and behind the Allied left Ziethen was at last putting in a belated appearance.   His advance-guard, indeed, consisting of three regiments of cavalry and four battalions of infantry, had arrived at Ohain over an hour before, but harassed by conflicting orders,[1] had not pushed on until sent forward by Ziethen himself, a delay which, seeing how valuable every man was to Wellington at that moment—he had even called up Chassé's Dutch-Belgians from Braine l'Alleud—might have

[1] Rose, *Napoleonic Studies*, p. 297 ; but cf. Houssaye, p. 387.

proved most disastrous. However, the fact that Ziethen was at hand allowed Wellington to withdraw from his extreme left the light cavalry of Vandeleur and Vivian and part of Vincke's Hanoverians, thus stiffening his shattered right centre at a most critical juncture.[1]

The final attack of the Guard, if incomparably the most dramatic moment in the battle of Waterloo, was hardly the decisive point. Once Bülow had begun to seriously menace the French retreat, and once Ziethen had come within reach, the French had lost any real chance of victory. It is possible that if all the Old Guard had been put in when Bachelu and Foy advanced on the West of the high road just after 6 p.m., about which time Duhesme was driving Bülow from Planchenoit, Napoleon might have utilised the chance given him by the tardiness of the Prussians, and broken the English line before their allies could arrive. At 7 o'clock it would probably have been wiser to use the Guard to cover a retreat.[2] The Guard, whatever the number of battalions that took part in the attack, could hardly have hoped to succeed. Maitland, Adam, and Colin Halkett between them must have had 3000 bayonets remaining, not to mention Duplat's Legionaries and William Halkett's *Landwehr*. But at the time (7.30–8 p.m.) that Napoleon put into the fray his last reserves, Ziethen's columns were debouching by Smohain and Papelotte against Durutte on d'Erlon's extreme flank, and his men had got into touch with the flanking parties Bülow had thrown out towards Frischermont. Simultaneously Bülow moved forward again, with Pirch's leading brigades to help him. Tippelskirch led the attack on Planchenoit supported by Hiller and Ryssel : Bülow's right wing, connected with his left by the cavalry of the IInd and IVth Corps, moved forward against Lobau. Thus the advance of the Guard coincided with the final and most formidable attack of the Prussians on the forces covering the right flank of the French array. Even had the veterans broken Wellington's line the success could hardly have been followed up with three Prussian corps at last at hand. However, despite the vigour of the Prussian attack, Lobau and Duhesme stood their ground with splendid tenacity. The struggle for Planchenoit was especially desperate, the two battalions of the Old Guard which had flung themselves into that village held on to the churchyard with the greatest determination, repelling

[1] Cf. p. 689, and Siborne, p. 515.   [2] Cf., however, Houssaye, p. 388.

every frontal attack until at length the Prussians succeeded in outflanking the village. By this time (8.30 p.m.) all was over. The Guard had been repulsed. With Ziethen's corps close at hand Wellington had been able to take the risk of a check since reinforcement was certain; and seeing the whole French army staggering under the blow of the failure of the Guard, he had at once followed up his advantage by pushing forward against its retreating masses Adam's infantry and the all but intact cavalry brigades of Vivian and Vandeleur. These troops had made a vigorous counter-attack, forcing their way into the French centre, compelling the reserves of the Guard to retire, and thus threatening Reille's right and d'Erlon's left. But these divisions also were retiring; and as the relics of the Allied army advanced all along the line, the French fell into great disorder. The bonds of discipline seemed to become unloosed. The army degenerated into a rabble. Ziethen's leading brigade began to press heavily on Durutte and to drive his division back. Its retreat uncovered the left flank and rear of Lobau's corps which had till then held its ground against Bülow. As Ziethen's men fell on its flank the VIth Corps gave way and became involved in the universal confusion, in which even the last reserves of the Old Guard were swallowed up. Pelet's men, recoiling from Planchenoit, with difficulty beat off the attacks of the Prussian cavalry who were now crowding forward to take up the pursuit. On the ridge which had formed the main position of the French, Wellington halted his exhausted men (8.30 or 8.45 p.m.). To pursue was beyond their power, but the Prussians of Pirch and Ziethen were comparatively fresh, and Gneisenau's chase of the beaten army was as vigorous and relentless as Napoleon's pursuit of the fugitives from Jena and Auerstadt. Not till he reached the heights of Frasnes did he desist from the chase, and not till they had put the Sambre between them and the Prussians did the beaten troops of France rally to any appreciable extent.

The completeness of the overthrow of the French at Waterloo is to be in part ascribed to the very lateness of the Prussians in arriving, which has given rise to the impression, in Germany and elsewhere, that their arrival "saved the English army from destruction." In a sense, of course, this statement is true, but it is so partial and one-sided a version of the truth as to be relatively false. If Wellington's command was in danger of destruc-

Map to illustrate THE CAMPAIGN OF WATERLOO June 15th–18th 1815

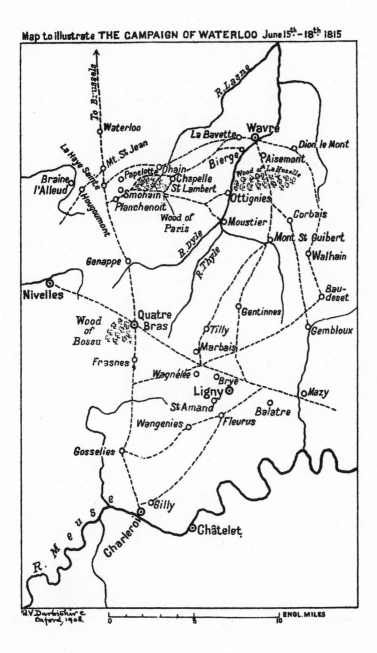

R. Lasne

To Brussels

Waterloo

La Bavette

Wavre

Dion le Mont

La Haye Sainte

Mt. St Jean

Dhain

Bierge

Aisemont

Papelotte

Chapelle St Lambert

Wood of La Hazelle

Braine l'Alleud

Hougoumont

Smohain

Ottignies

Corbais

Planchenoit

Wood of Paris

Moustier

Mont St Guibert

R. Dyle

Walhain

R. Thyle

Genappe

Baudeset

Nivelles

Quatre Bras

Gentinnes

Wood of Bossu

Tilly

Gembloux

Frasnes

Marbais

Wagnélée

Brye

Mazy

Ligny

St Amand

Balatre

Wangenies

Fleurus

Gosselies

R. Meuse

Gilly

Châtelet

Charleroi

B.V. Darbishire Oxford, 1908.

0   5   10   ENGL. MILES

tion, that was mainly due to the lateness of the Prussians in appearing, a lateness which has already been shown to have been anything but unavoidable. That Wellington would have been defeated had he given battle to Napoleon and his 74,000 men with only his own motley host and altogether unaided by the Prussians, is no more to be denied than it is to be supposed that Wellington would ever have given battle at Waterloo if he had not expected Prussian co-operation, and that at an earlier hour than it actually arrived. If when the Prussians intervened their allies were nearly at the end of their tether, the fact is hardly as creditable to the late-comers as it is to the troops whose endurance had been so sorely tried and had stood the test so well. No doubt the delay of the Prussians encouraged Napoleon to go on attempting to defeat Wellington before his allies could arrive, when the more prudent course would have been to have disengaged his army and withdrawn. Had a Prussian corps arrived at Ohain between 12 and 1, when Wellington seems to have expected them to appear,[1] it would have been fairly easy for Napoleon to draw off with his forces practically intact, and the indifferent manœuvring capacities of the Allied army would have made a counter-attack on intact troops very risky. By 7 o'clock both French and Allies had got very near the limits of their powers of endurance, and consequently the intervention of the Prussians was proportionately more decisive.

The losses of the combatants are most instructive. The British had over 7000 casualties, roughly 30 per cent. of their total strength. The King's German Legion suffered almost as heavily, having 1600 casualties among under 6000 men. The Brunswickers, Hanoverians and Kruse's Nassauers lost respectively 11, 14, and 22 per cent. The Dutch-Belgians had 4000 casualties among about 18,000 men,[2] but of these 4000 nearly a third were "missing." The Prussian losses were very heavy in proportion to the time during which they were actively engaged. In about four hours Bülow had nearly 6000 casualties out of 30,000 men. This figure includes about 1200 "missing," probably stragglers who had failed to keep up with the long marches the corps had

---

[1] M. Houssaye (p. 351) seems to follow Muffling in putting the hour at which Wellington expected the Prussians as between 2 and 3; but, amongst other things, it seems probable from the Duke's dispositions that he was counting on the Prussian corps, whose succour Blücher had promised, to take post on his left, and so secure that somewhat weak wing, at quite an early hour. But it was after noon when Ziethen started.

[2] If Prince Bernhard's brigade be included among them.

made since leaving Hannut; but even when these men are deducted the Prussian losses bear eloquent testimony to the stubbornness of the resistance offered by the 15,000 Frenchmen who withstood their attacks, and also to the superiority of the line over the column : the Prussians drawn up in the solid columns common to the Continental armies suffered losses out of all proportion to those of the British, who when opposed to the hostile infantry fought in line. Ziethen and Pirch had between them 600 casualties, a third of whom were "missing."[1]

The rest of the campaign is soon told. Grouchy had begun attacking Thielmann's position about the time that Bülow first advanced on Planchenoit. A sharp action saw the Prussian rearguard driven over the Dyle, but the French failed to force the passage at Bierges or to make their way across from the suburb on the right bank into the town on the left. However, Pajol and Teste carried the bridge of Limale, more than a mile higher up, and supported by two divisions of Gérard's corps established themselves on Thielmann's right flank before night put an end to the conflict. Next morning the battle was resumed, and was going in favour of Grouchy, who had forced Thielmann to abandon Wavre and fall back towards Louvain, when, about 10.30, an officer brought him news of the total defeat of the Emperor. A hasty retreat on Namur was the only course open to him; and this he successfully accomplished, though Pirch I was pushed out to intercept him, and was actually at Mellery, six miles nearer to Gembloux than Grouchy was, when the Marshal began his retreat. Pirch did not advance beyond Mellery on the 19th; and though next day he overtook Grouchy as the latter was about to cross the Sambre at Namur, his efforts to intercept the retreat were beaten off, and he and Thielmann's cavalry, who had also come up, suffered a loss of 1500 men in trying to storm Namur, which Teste and Grouchy's rearguard defended with great success.

But Grouchy's escape could not alter the fortunes of the campaign. The main army made some efforts to rally, but it could not face the Allies again or arrest their steady advance on Paris. On June 24th Colville's division stormed Cambray; three days later Ziethen's advance-guard secured the bridge of Compiègne, and on the 29th Blücher reached St. Denis. To intervene between Paris and the arrival of any assistance from the

[1] Siborne, pp. 587–592.

South (July 2nd), he next crossed the Seine and established himself at Meudon and Chatillon, Wellington's army taking post at
St. Denis. This move of Blücher's would have been most risky
and dangerous if Paris had meant to fight, but Napoleon's
efforts to get France to rally to his side had proved unsuccessful; Fouché and Talleyrand were in the ascendant, and France
would not stir. July 4th saw a convention signed at St. Cloud
which placed Paris in the hands of the Allies, the French troops
retiring behind the Loire. Napoleon had already fled, after
abdicating in favour of his son, and on July 8th, the day that
the Emperor embarked at Rochefort, hoping to get away to
America, Louis XVIII re-entered Paris.

But before peace could be finally restored or the affairs of
Europe definitely settled, much remained to be done. A provisional Government had established itself at Paris with Fouché
at its head, while on July 10th the Allied monarchs arrived at
the French capital. A certain number of the fortresses on the
North-Eastern and Eastern frontiers had refused to surrender or
to accept the suspension of hostilities, and operations thus went
on in some places for a couple of months and more after the fall
of Napoleon. The Prussians, whose political views caused them
to impart more vigour to their operations than was displayed by
the other Allies, managed to possess themselves of about a
dozen French fortresses; but the main army of the Allies under
Schwarzenberg[1] after some sharp fighting with Rapp and the
corps detailed for the defence of Alsace, concluded a suspension
of hostilities on July 24th.

The activity of the Prussians in besieging and reducing the
French fortresses is to be attributed to the bitter feelings by
which Blücher and his compatriots were animated: it was their
ardent desire to make France drink to the dregs the cup of
humiliation which she had compelled Prussia to drain after Jena
and Friedland. But in this animosity to the vanquished Prussia
stood alone among the Allies. Wellington's conduct in his
march on Paris had been very different from that of his
colleague. His troops had paid their way, pillaging and plunder
had been strictly prevented, and the fortresses which surrendered
to him were occupied in the name of Louis XVIII, since it was
not against France but against Napoleon that England was

---

[1] This included besides Austrians the contingents of Bavaria, Saxony, Hesse-
Darmstadt, Würtemberg and several minor states.

fighting. Similarly when the Allies reached Paris, Blücher was only prevented from blowing up the Pont du Jéna by Wellington placing an English picquet on guard over that bridge. Blücher, however, carried his point when he demanded that the trophies and spoils taken from Berlin to adorn the French capital should be handed over to their original owners, and in this the other nations whose treasures Napoleon had annexed imitated him.

When it came to settling the terms of peace the same discrepancy was evident. Prussia clamoured for extensive cessions of territory and a heavy war indemnity: England declared she had taken part in the war as an ally of the King of France, and that she would never agree to such treatment of her ally. Prussia's proposals voiced the opinion of Germany, which favoured the severest measures; France must be treated as a conquered state, the annexations of Louis XV and Louis XIV must be taken from her, at least she must make good the damage she had inflicted on Germany under Napoleon's rule. The Crown Prince of Würtemberg urged that for the protection of South Germany France should be deprived of Alsace. When Capodistria suggested that a pecuniary indemnity would be sufficient, Hardenberg declared that at least the frontier fortresses must be handed over, and von Knesebeck, the mouth-piece of the King of Prussia, took the same line. But the deciding voice in the affairs of Europe and among them of Germany was to be that of the Czar.

Alexander had not been altogether pleased with the fact that the great victory had been won and Napoleon overthrown without his presence: he was equally annoyed by Blücher's action in concluding the Convention of July 4th, considering that the matter should have been referred to him. Hence there was a coolness between Prussia and Russia which Metternich, always on the lookout for a chance to isolate Prussia, assiduously fomented. Alexander had long ago thrown over his ideas of freeing Germany, and much influenced by his semi-mystical religious views he had come to look on Napoleon as the embodiment of irreligion and sin, and to desire to make his overthrow the basis for the resettlement of Europe on Christian lines. Universal peace, the union of Christian nations in one family, the overthrow of heathendom by the expulsion of the Turks from Europe, these were among his projects, and in accomplishing these he thought the re-establishment of France would be more useful to him than the aggrandisement of Prussia, either at the expense of France or by any rearrangement of Germany on lines calculated to increase her influence. Moreover, he had no intention of doing anything to strengthen a Power which might be troublesome to him, as Prussia might, in Poland. Austria was as little disposed to do anything to assist Prussia or to humiliate France. All she desired was a satisfactory settlement of the affairs of Italy, for Frimont's victory over Murat at Tolentino (May 2nd) had laid the peninsula at her feet, and marked the beginning of Austrian predominance in Italy. Accordingly Prussia, finding herself unsupported by any of the other Great Powers, and by no means unanimously supported by the minor German states, several of whom had good reasons of their own for preferring the restoration of France to her pre-Revolution position to the predominance of Prussia, had to give way.

The Second Treaty of Paris (Nov. 20th), with its exaction of an indemnity of 700,000,000 francs, its arrangements for the division of that indemnity and for the occupation of the principal fortresses of France by an Allied army of 150,000 men in order to provide security against such another disturbance of the peace of Europe, touches on German history mainly through the rectification of frontier, which was the principal penalty inflicted on France for her share in the Hundred Days. Bouillon, Marienburg and Philippeville on the North-East, Landau and Saarbrück on the East, were taken from her, the frontier of Rhenish Bavaria was moved up to the Lauter, and the little county of Gex was given to Geneva. The fortifications of Hüningen were to be destroyed, and no new fortress erected within a radius of three leagues. At the same time, some changes were made in the redistribution of Germany, Bavaria giving up the Innviertel to Austria and obtaining Landau instead.

With the Second Treaty of Paris the end of one great epoch in the history of Germany is reached, though the treaty marks only the end of the first act of the great drama which had begun with the dissolution of the Holy Roman Empire and was to end at Versailles in 1871. Indeed, in some ways 1806 is a better dividing line than 1815. In the history of Prussia this is certainly the case, but up till 1815 the history of Prussia is only a part of the history of Germany. What happened in 1815 was that in the resettlement following the final overthrow of Napoleon, and with him of the structure he had raised in Germany, Austria made no effort to resume the nominal headship which she had laid down in 1806. She now definitely adopted a line of policy which drew her away from Germany and from the German traditions of the Holy Roman Empire. Yet she did not so completely withdraw herself from Germany as to allow of the establishment of a new organisation which could hope to be permanent.

Thus it is that while the liberation of Germany from the yoke of Napoleon may be regarded as the final act of the drama which was begun in 1792 by the intervention of Austria and Prussia in the internal affairs of France, yet it also belongs to the history of nineteenth-century Germany. The forces which Napoleon called into being, both by his reforms and by his oppression, were to be the influences which actuated and agitated Germany until unity, though a not quite complete unity even then, was at last achieved under the leadership of Prussia, until a "German Empire" was created which is neither the Holy Roman Empire nor the mediæval Kingdom of Germany. But in 1815 those forces, let loose though they had been when Germany rose to shake off the yoke of Napoleon, had for the time been put under restraint. With Metternich at the helm and the "Holy Alliance" an accomplished fact, Europe and with it Germany had slipped for a time into a backwater of reaction.

I. THE HOUSE OF HAPSBURG

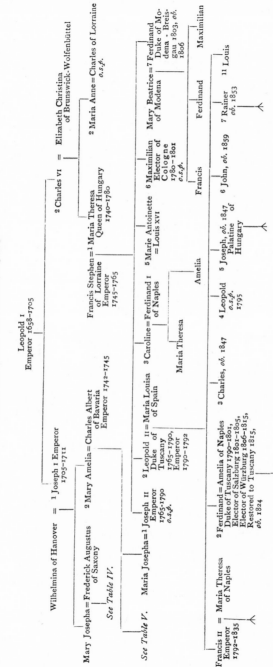

II. THE HOUSE OF BRUNSWICK

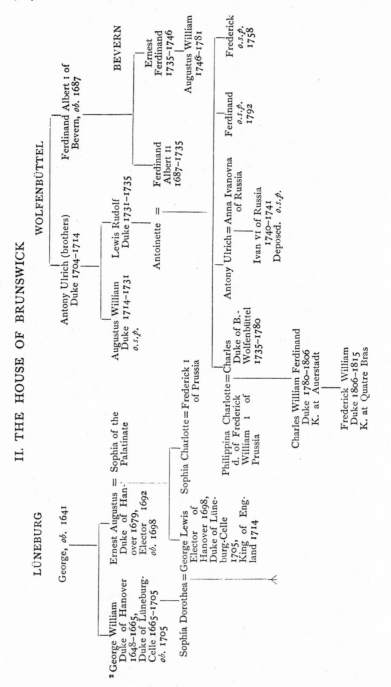

III. HOUSE OF HOHENZOLLERN

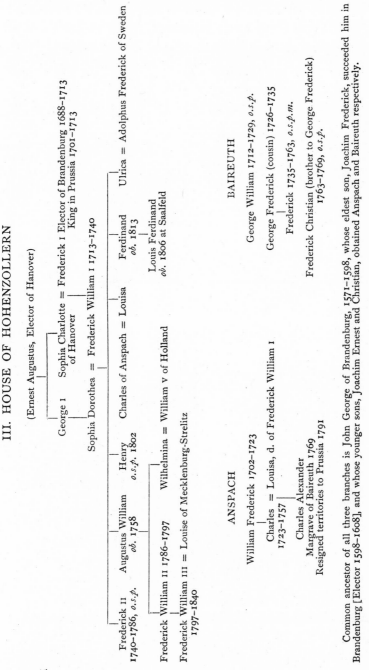

(Ernest Augustus, Elector of Hanover)

George I | Sophia Charlotte = Frederick I Elector of Brandenburg 1688–1713 / King in Prussia 1701–1713

Sophia Dorothea = Frederick William I 1713–1740 | Charles of Anspach = Louisa | Ferdinand *ob.* 1813 | Ulrica = Adolphus Frederick of Sweden

Louis Ferdinand *ob.* 1806 at Saalfeld

Frederick II 1740–1786, *o.s.p.* | Augustus William *ob.* 1758 | Henry *o.s.p.* 1802 | Wilhelmina = William V of Holland

Frederick William II 1786–1797
Frederick William III = Louise of Mecklenburg-Strelitz 1797–1840

ANSPACH

William Frederick 1702–1723

Charles = Louisa, d. of Frederick William I 1723–1757

Charles Alexander
Margrave of Baireuth 1769
Resigned territories to Prussia 1791

BAIREUTH

George William 1712–1729, *o.s.p.*

George Frederick (cousin) 1726–1735

Frederick 1735–1763, *o.s.p.m.*

Frederick Christian (brother to George Frederick) 1763–1769, *o.s.p.*

Common ancestor of all three branches is John George of Brandenburg, 1571–1598, whose eldest son, Joachim Frederick, succeeded him in Brandenburg [Elector 1598–1608], and whose younger sons, Joachim Ernest and Christian, obtained Anspach and Baireuth respectively.

IV. HOUSE OF WETTIN (ELECTORAL BRANCH ONLY)

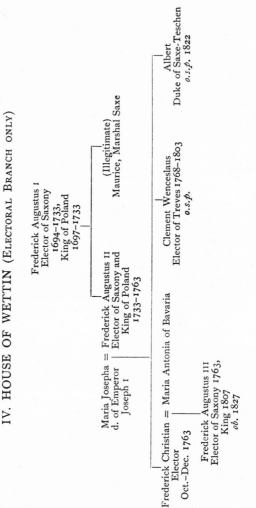

Frederick Augustus I
Elector of Saxony
1694–1733,
King of Poland
1697–1733

Maria Josepha = Frederick Augustus II   (Illegitimate)
d. of Emperor   Elector of Saxony and   Maurice, Marshal Saxe
Joseph I   King of Poland
                   1733–1763

Frederick Christian = Maria Antonia of Bavaria   Clement Wenceslaus   Albert
Elector   Elector of Treves 1768–1803   Duke of Saxe-Teschen
Oct.–Dec. 1763   *o.s.p.*   *o.s.p.* 1822

Frederick Augustus III
Elector of Saxony 1763,
King 1807
ob. 1827

V. HOUSE OF WITTELSBACH

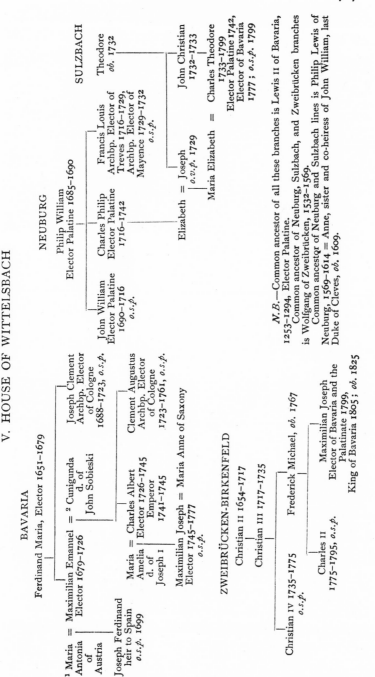

BAVARIA

Ferdinand Maria, Elector 1651–1679

¹ Maria Antonia of Austria = Maximilian Emanuel Elector 1679–1726

= ² Cunigunda d. of John Sobieski

Joseph Clement Archbp. Elector of Cologne 1688–1723, *o.s.p.*

Joseph Ferdinand heir to Spain *o.s.p.* 1699

Maria Amelia d. of Joseph I = Charles Albert Elector 1726–1745 Emperor 1741–1745

Clement Augustus Archbp. Elector of Cologne 1723–1761, *o.s.p.*

Maximilian Joseph Elector 1745–1777 *o.s.p.* = Maria Anne of Saxony

NEUBURG

Philip William Elector Palatine 1685–1690

John William Elector Palatine 1690–1716 *o.s.p.*

Charles Philip Elector Palatine 1716–1742

Francis Louis Archbp. Elector of Treves 1716–1729, Archbp. Elector of Mayence 1729–1732 *o.s.p.*

Elizabeth = Joseph *o.v.p.* 1729

Maria Elizabeth = Charles Theodore Elector Palatine 1742, Elector of Bavaria 1777; *o.s.p.* 1799

SULZBACH

Theodore *ob.* 1732

John Christian 1732–1733

Charles Theodore 1733–1799

ZWEIBRÜCKEN-BIRKENFELD

Christian II 1654–1717

Christian III 1717–1735

Frederick Michael, *ob.* 1767

Christian IV 1735–1775 *o.s.p.*

Charles II 1775–1795, *o.s.p.*

Maximilian Joseph Elector of Bavaria and the Palatinate 1799, King of Bavaria 1805; *ob.* 1825

N.B.—Common ancestor of all these branches is Lewis II of Bavaria, 1253–1294, Elector Palatine.
Common ancestor of Neuburg, Sulzbach, and Zweibrücken branches is Wolfgang of Zweibrücken, 1532–1569.
Common ancestor of Neuburg and Sulzbach lines is Philip Lewis of Neuburg, 1569–1614 = Anne, sister and co-heiress of John William, last Duke of Cleves, *ob.* 1609.

INDEX